W9-DEP-890

The Papers of
Henry Laurens

SPONSORS

SOUTH CAROLINA HISTORICAL SOCIETY

John E. Huguley, President

Mrs. Granville T. Prior, Director

NATIONAL HISTORICAL PUBLICATIONS COMMISSION

James B. Rhoads, Chairman

E. Berkeley Tompkins, Executive Director

———◆———

ADVISORY COMMITTEE

Charles E. Lee, Chairman	*Richard B. Morris*
John R. Alden	*Robert D. Ochs*
Julian P. Boyd	*Joseph I. Waring*
Lyman H. Butterfield	*Walter Muir Whitehill*
Elizabeth Hamer Kegan	*Louis B. Wright*

Martha Laurens (1759–1811) who married David Ramsay in 1787.
Portrait by John Wollaston painted in Charleston about 1767.

The Papers of
Henry Laurens

Volume Four: Sept. 1, 1763 — Aug. 31, 1765

George C. Rogers, Jr., *Editor*
David R. Chesnutt, *Assistant Editor*
Peggy J. Clark, *Editorial Assistant*
Walter B. Edgar, *Editorial Assistant*

Published for the South Carolina Historical Society by the

UNIVERSITY OF SOUTH CAROLINA PRESS
COLUMBIA, S.C.

0767478

FIRST EDITION

Copyright © 1974 by the South Carolina Historical Society

Published in Columbia, S. C., by the
University of South Carolina Press, 1974

International Standard Book Number: 0-87249-308-3

Library of Congress Catalog Card Number: 67-29381

Manufactured in the United States of America

CONTENTS

0767478 82036

CONTENTS

xii   CONTENTS

Introduction

"*Money is not so very plenty nor ready with me as you seem to imagine, but if I had as many pounds as there are bean Leaves before me I would not depart from an established maxim for the rule of my conduct as a Citizen & member of community 'To do my Duty rather than pay to buy it off with a fine.'* "—Henry Laurens to James Cordes, Jr., 31st August 1765.

INTRODUCTION TO VOLUME FOUR

The fourth volume of *The Papers of Henry Laurens* covers a period of exactly two years, from September 1, 1763 to August 31, 1765. The partnership of Austin, Laurens, & Appleby had expired on August 1, 1762. Since that date HL had been engaged in winding up the affairs of the firm. By September 1, 1763 George Austin had retired to England. George Appleby was still in the province but making plans to sail for England which he did on May 9, 1764. Their Carolina fortunes enabled both Austin and Appleby to establish themselves as country gentlemen in their native Shropshire.

The Treaty of Paris which had ended the Great War for Empire was proclaimed in Charleston on August 25, 1763. New enterprises headed by younger men soon sprang up to exploit the fruits of victory. Although Laurens was curtailing his role as merchant and becoming more of a planter, he did not divorce himself completely from commerce. English friends still urged him to accept consignments of slaves. Although he turned some of these over to Brewton & Smith, he gave most of his patronage to the new firm of Price, Hest, & Head which was composed of his former clerks— William Price, William Hest, and Edmund Head.

A greater degree of specialization was now apparent in the economy of South Carolina. The country factor, who operated on a somewhat smaller scale than did the great overseas merchant, emerged as a key figure. His interests were more in tune with the planter in the country than with the merchant in London. He marshaled the country produce at his stores on his wharf in Charleston and sold this produce to the exporting merchant. William Gibbes, Alexander Chovin, Thomas Lind, John Champneys, and Maurice Simons, whose names appear often in this volume, were good examples of men performing this role.

By 1763 HL had already purchased Wambaw and Mepkin plantations, both of which his brother-in-law John Coming Ball was managing. When Ball died in October 1764, Laurens was forced to take up the role of planter more seriously. These letters, therefore, give a detailed picture of life in two lowcountry parishes—St. James, Santee and Lower St. John. Slaves were bought, overseers secured, and roads rebuilt. The land between the Cooper and Wando rivers sustained a growing and improving society.

HL was equally busy in Charleston where he was having a house built on his new land in Ansonborough. He also had a wharf constructed so that his schooners could easily ply between his town house and his country estates. Bricks were brought from Zachariah Villepontoux's works on Back River and slaves were sent down from the plantations to build a great wall to enclose the garden upon which Mrs. Laurens lavished so much care. HL also played his part in civic improvements, particularly in laying out streets to join the new suburb of Ansonborough with the older parts of the city. John Bartram who visited HL during the summer of 1765 admired all of this enterprise.

Although Mepkin was his home estate, HL was adding out-lying interests in Florida, Georgia, and the backcountry. James Grant, who had been commander of the Cherokee expedition of 1761, came out to East Florida in the fall of 1764 as the new governor. He relied upon Laurens for tools, slaves, overseers, even a pilot boat, for the development of the new English colony. In turn Laurens expected Grant to help him secure good Florida lands.

In Georgia, Lachlan McIntosh not only assisted HL in secur-ing his Altamaha grants, but also sold him Broughton Island. HL was eager to visit his Georgia properties, but family deaths and births and then the Stamp Act crisis forced him to postpone again and again his intended journey. It was only after the Stamp Act crisis had passed that he was able to make the trip.

HL was drawn into a backcountry settlement with the arrival in the summer of 1764 of two young protégés of Richard Oswald. James Theodore Rossel and John Lewis Gervais, both of French Huguenot descent from Hanover in Germany, were eager to make their fortunes. HL introduced them to Andrew Williamson and others who had supplied the 1761 Cherokee expedition with cattle and horses. Gervais was to settle an estate at Ninety Six; Rossel to manage HL's Broughton Island plantation.

Laurens was almost everywhere successful, adding greatly to his fortune. With success went a sense of duty which he expressed so well in a letter, almost the last in this volume, which he wrote to James Cordes, Jr., explaining that although it would be a great inconvenience to call out his slaves for work on the parish roads he would do his "Duty rather than pay to buy it off with a fine." This sense of duty strengthened by success would be challenged in the Stamp Act crisis, the period with which the next volume will open.

The letters in this volume are drawn from two principal sources. One was a "foreign letterbook" found among the Laurens Papers in the South Carolina Historical Society; the other was a "domestic letterbook" in the collections of the Historical Society of Pennsylvania. There are a few scattered letters from other sources. There are documents from the South Carolina, Georgia, and English archives such as deeds, advertisements, court cases, letters of attorney, bills of sale, appointment as a commissioner of the pilotage, payment for an executed slave, appointment to the royal council, contract for a pilot boat, ship registrations, and diary entries.

Chronology is the principal guide to the placement of the documents in the volume. When several letters or documents fall on the same date, they are placed in the following order: outgoing letters (first from the domestic letterbook, then from the foreign letterbook, and finally from other collections), incoming letters, land records, court cases, advertisements, etc.

Editorial procedures are the same as those followed in earlier volumes. Those letters or portions of letters such as postscripts which were copied by HL himself have been identified in the source notes.

The editors have tried to give a citation for each fact used in the footnotes so that the reader will know immediately where the information has been obtained. This rule has been departed from only with reference to packers and woodmeasurers which were offices filled by annual elections held in Charleston on Easter Monday. The editors have compiled lists of these local officeholders which are in their possession. When this information has been used, no citation has been given.

As set forth in the previous volumes, many persons and organizations have contributed to *The Papers of Henry Laurens*. There is no need to repeat their names here. Those who have given particular help for this volume are William Avery Baker, Peter Becker, C. W. Black, Pat Bryant, Esse Cohen, Kenneth Coleman, E. G. Earle, Jeffery Ede, Julian Gwyn, Lilla M. Hawes, W. Robert Higgins,

Sara Jackson, John D. Kilbourne, Herr Koster, Dr. Loose, Helen G. McCormack, Richard D. Mahone, E. F. J. Mathews, Matthew Neil, K. C. Newton, Jaime de Olazabal, Barbara Oliver, Mary B. Prior, M. M. Schofield, George W. Williams, M. E. Williams, and B. Woelderink.

Permission to publish documents from their collections has been given by the Archives of the Moravian Church, Bethlehem, Pennsylvania; Georgia Historical Society; Haverford College Library, Haverford, Pennsylvania; Historical Society of Pennsylvania; Hunt, Roope & Co., Ltd., Oporto, Portugal; Moravian Archives, Winston-Salem, North Carolina; Public Record Office, London; and South Carolina Department of Archives and History.

The editors would like to thank the members of the National Historical Publications Commission for assigning Walter B. Edgar as Editorial Fellow to *The Papers of Henry Laurens* during the year 1971–1972. He has made an important contribution to the editing of this volume.

The editors would also like to thank President Thomas F. Jones and the University of South Carolina for their continuing support of this enterprise.

LIST OF ABBREVIATIONS

Abstracts of Wills, 1740–1760 for *Abstracts of the Wills of the State of South Carolina, 1740–1760,* ed. Caroline T. Moore (Columbia, S. C., 1964).

Abstracts of Wills, 1760–1784 for *Abstracts of the Wills of the State of South Carolina, 1760–1784,* ed. Caroline T. Moore (Columbia, S. C., 1969).

Acts of Privy Council, Colonial for *Acts of the Privy Council, Colonial Series* (6 vols.: London, 1908–1912).

Appendix to the Extracts for *An Appendix to the Extracts from the Proceedings of the High Court of Vice-Admiralty in Charlestown, South-Carolina, &c. containing strictures upon, and proper answers to, a Pamphlet entitled The Man Unmask'd, Published by Egerton Leigh. Together with A full Refutation of Mr. Leigh's Attempts to vindicate his Judicial Proceedings* (Charleston, S. C., 1769).

A Representation of Facts for *A Representation of Facts, Relative to the Conduct of Daniel Moore, Esquire; Collector of His Majesty's Customs at Charles-Town, In South Carolina, From the Time of his Arrival in March, 1767, to the Time of his Departure in September following. Transmitted By the Merchants of Charles-Town, To Charles Garth, Esquire, in London, Agent for the Province of South-Carolina; and Recommended in a Letter from the Honourable The Committee of Correspondence* (Charleston, S. C., 1767).

Bartram, *Diary of a Journey* for John Bartram, *Diary of a Journey through the Carolinas, Georgia, and Florida from July 1, 1765, to April 10, 1766,* in *Transactions of the American Philosophical Society,* New Series, XXXIII, Part 1 (Philadelphia, Penn., 1942).

Boddie, *History of Williamsburg County* for William Willis Boddie, *History of Williamsburg, Something About the People of Williamsburg County, South Carolina, from the First Settlement by Europeans About 1705 until 1923* (Columbia, S. C., 1923).

BPRO for Sainsbury Transcripts of Records in the British Public Record Office deposited in the South Carolina Department of Archives and History.

British Statutes for *The Statutes at Large, from Magna Charta to the end of the Eleventh Parliament of Great Britain, Anno 1761. Continued,* ed. Danby Pickering (33 vols.: Cambridge, Eng., 1762–1780).

xxi

Cole, *Wholesale Commodity Prices* for Arthur H. Cole, *Wholesale Commodity Prices in the United States, 1700–1861, Statistical Supplement* (Cambridge, Mass., 1938).

Colonial Records of Georgia for *The Colonial Records of the State of Georgia,* ed. Allen D. Candler and Lucian L. Knight (26 vols.: Atlanta, Ga., 1904–1916).

Colonial Records of North Carolina for *The Colonial Records of North Carolina,* ed. William L. Saunders (10 vols.: Raleigh, N. C., 1886–1890).

Corkran, *Creek Frontier* for David H. Corkran, *The Creek Frontier, 1540–1783* (Norman, Okla., 1967).

Country Journal for *South Carolina Gazette & Country Journal.*

DAB for *Dictionary of American Biography.*

Deas, *Ball Family* for Anne Simons Deas, *Recollections of the Ball Family of South Carolina and the Comingtee Plantation* ([Summerville, S. C.] 1909).

DNB for *Dictionary of National Biography.*

Donnan, *Documents Illustrative of the Slave Trade* for *Documents Illustrative of the History of the Slave Trade to America,* ed. Elizabeth Donnan (4 vols.: Washington, D. C., 1935).

Ga. Archives for Georgia Department of Archives and History, Atlanta, Ga.

Gazette for *South-Carolina Gazette.*

General Gazette for *South Carolina and American General Gazette.*

Georgia Wills for *Abstracts of Colonial Wills of the State of Georgia, 1733–1777* (Atlanta, Ga., 1962).

Gipson, *The Triumphant Empire* for Lawrence Henry Gipson, *The British Empire before the American Revolution,* Vol. IX: *The Triumphant Empire: New Responsibilities Within the Enlarged Empire, 1763–1766* (New York, 1956).

HL Papers for *The Papers of Henry Laurens.*

Irving, *A Day on Cooper River* for John B. Irving, *A Day on Cooper River* (3rd edition, Columbia, S. C., 1969).

Journal of a Lady of Quality for *Journal of a Lady of Quality; Being the Narrative of a Journey from Scotland to the West Indies, North Carolina, and Portugal, in the years 1774 to 1776,* ed. Evangeline Walker Andrews, in collaboration with Charles McLean Andrews (New Haven, Conn. and London, 1939).

"Journal of Lord Adam Gordon," for "Journal of an Officer who Travelled in America and the West Indies in 1764 and 1765," in *Travels in the American Colonies,* ed. Newton D. Mereness (New York, 1916), pp. 367–453.

"Journal of Pelatiah Webster" for "Journal of a Voyage to Charleston in So. Carolina by Pelatiah Webster in 1765," ed. T. P. Harrison, *Publications of the South Carolina Historical Society* (Charleston, S. C., 1898).

Letterbook of Robert Pringle, 1737–1745 for *The Letterbook of Robert Pringle, April 2, 1737–April 29, 1745,* ed. Walter B. Edgar (2 vols.: Columbia, S. C., 1972).

London Directories for the directories of London from 1736 to 1770, which were consulted in the Guildhall Library, London.

Loyalist Transcripts for Transcripts of the Manuscript Books and Papers of the Commission of Enquiry into Losses and Services of the American Loyalists held under Acts of Parliament of 23, 25, 26, 28, and 29 of George III preserved amongst the Audit Office Records in the Public Record Office of England, 1783–1790, made for the New York Public Library, microfilm, S. C. Archives.

McDowell, *Documents relating to Indian Affairs* for *Documents relating to Indian Affairs, 1754–1765,* ed. William L. McDowell, Jr. (Columbia, S. C., 1970).

Mowat, *East Florida* for Charles Loch Mowat, *East Florida as a British Province, 1763–1784* (Gainesville, Florida, 1964).

Namier and Brooke, *The House of Commons, 1754–1790* for Sir Lewis Namier and John Brooke, *The History of Parliament: The House of Commons, 1754–1790* (3 vols.: New York, 1964).

Naval Office Lists, 1757–1764 for Naval Office, Port Charles Town, South Carolina, 1757–1764, CO 5/510, Public Record Office, London.

Naval Office Lists, 1764–1767 for Naval Office, Port Charles Town, South Carolina, 1764–1767, CO 5/511, Public Record Office, London.

Oliver, *History of Antigua* for Vere L. Oliver, *The History of the Island of Antigua, One of the Leeward Caribbees in the West Indies, From the first settlement in 1635 to the present time* (3 vols.: London, 1894, 1896, 1899).

OED for *Oxford English Dictionary.*

Papers of Henry Bouquet for *The Papers of Henry Bouquet,* Volume I (December 11, 1755–May 31, 1758), ed. S. K. Stevens, Donald H. Kent, and Autumn L. Leonard (Harrisburg, Penn., 1972).

Pares, *War and Trade in the West Indies* for Richard Pares, *War and Trade in the West Indies, 1739–1763* (London, 1963).

Penn. Hist. Soc. for Historical Society of Pennsylvania.

Records of the Moravians in North Carolina for *Records of the Moravians in North Carolina,* ed. Adelaide E. Fries (11 vols.: Raleigh, N. C., 1922–1969).

Register Book for the Parish Prince Frederick Winyaw for *The Register Book for the Parish Prince Frederick Winyaw,* ed. Elizabeth W. Allston Pringle (Baltimore, Md., 1916).

Register of St. Philip's Parish, 1720–1758 for *Register of St. Philip's Parish, Charles Town, South Carolina, 1720–1758,* ed. A. S. Salley, Jr. (reprint, Columbia, S. C., 1971).

Register of St. Philip's Parish, 1754–1810 for *Register of St. Philip's Parish, Charles Town, or Charleston, S. C., 1754–1810,* ed. D. E. Huger Smith and A. S. Salley, Jr. (reprint, Columbia, S. C., 1971).

Rogers, *Evolution of a Federalist* for George C. Rogers, Jr., *Evolution of a Federalist: William Loughton Smith of Charleston, 1759–1812* (Columbia, S. C., 1962).

Rogers, *History of Georgetown County* for George C. Rogers, Jr., *The History of Georgetown County, South Carolina* (Columbia, S. C., 1970).

Salley, *History of Orangeburg County* for A. S. Salley, Jr., *The History of Orangeburg County South Carolina From its First Settlement to the Close of the Revolutionary War* (Orangeburg, S. C., 1898).

S. C. Hist. Soc. for South Carolina Historical Society, Charleston, S. C.

SCL for South Caroliniana Library, University of South Carolina, Columbia, S. C.

SCHM for *South Carolina Historical Magazine.*

S. C. Archives for South Carolina Department of Archives and History, Columbia, S. C.

S. C. Statutes for *The Statutes at Large of South Carolina,* ed. Thomas Cooper and David J. McCord (10 vols.: Columbia, S. C., 1837–1841).

SHC for Southern Historical Collection, University of North Carolina, Chapel Hill, North Carolina.

Wallace, *Life of Henry Laurens* for David D. Wallace, *The Life of Henry Laurens* (reprint, New York, 1967).

Weir, "South Carolina and the Stamp Act Crisis," for Robert M. Weir, "Liberty and Property and No Stamps; South Carolina During the Stamp Act Crisis" (unpub. PhD diss., Western Reserve University, 1966).

WLCL for William L. Clements Library, University of Michigan, Ann Arbor, Michigan.

PRINCIPAL DATES OF LAURENS' LIFE

1724	*Feb. 24.* Born in Charleston, S. C.
1744–1747	Received business training with James Crokatt.
1747	*June 3.* Arrived in Charleston from London; began mercantile career.
1750	*June 25.* Married Eleanor Ball, daughter of Elias Ball.
1756	*May 11.* Purchased Wambaw plantation.
1757	*Sept.* Elected to S. C. Commons House of Assembly.
1760	*Sept. 16.* Commissioned lieutenant colonel of the S. C. regiment.
1761	*April 2–Nov. 14.* Engaged in Cherokee campaign.
1762	*June 5.* Purchased Mepkin plantation.
	Aug. 1. End of A., L., & A. partnership.
1763	*May 18.* Received grant south of the Altamaha River.
	July 23. George Austin sailed for England.
	Aug. 25. His son Henry Laurens born.
1764	*April 18.* His daughter Eleanor Laurens died.
	May 9. George Appleby sailed for England.
	July 10. Recommended for appointment to the royal council of S. C.
	Oct. 20. Death of John Coming Ball.
1765	*Oct.* Crisis in Charleston over Stamp Act.
	Nov. 26. His son James Laurens born.
1766	*June–July.* Journey to the southward.
1767–1769	Vigorously protested against actions of Egerton Leigh as judge of the vice admiralty court in Charleston.
1770	*May 22.* Eleanor Laurens, his wife, died in Charleston.
1771–1774	In Europe, chiefly England, for the education of his three sons.
1775–1777	Leader of the revolutionary movement in S. C.; served as president of the general committee and of the council of safety, and as vice president of the new state.
1777	*July 22.* Seated as delegate of S. C. in the Continental Congress at Philadelphia.
	Nov. 1. Elected president of the Continental Congress.
1778	*Dec. 9.* Resigned as president of the congress.
1780	*Sept. 3.* Captured by the British while on his way to Holland as commissioner to negotiate treaties of amity and commerce.
	Oct. 6. Prisoner in the Tower of London until Dec. 31, 1781.
1782	*Nov. 30.* Signed, with other commissioners, preliminary treaty of peace between the United States and Great Britain.
1792	*Dec. 8.* Died at Mepkin.

TO JOHN COMING BALL[1]

[Charles Town] 1 September 1763

Mr. Creamer[2] is in Town & I shall send Nails & wo'd have done so before if I could have been informed within some Thousands.

Muscovado & Spanish Sugars will make handsome abatement by the quantity.

I did not know when the *Wambaw*[3] went last. Shall send the Clo. to your Ho. She is to go soon to Santé for Turpentine.

I have good Shoes at 16/ per pair. If you think proper, I shall send as many as are wanted.

As soon as possible shall make out the Accounts of the Wambaw plantation[4] & Schooner. Rice in Jamaica not sold.[5] You shall have half the Turpentine that I get at Cooper River & Freight for it if I can. That Freight per Green[6] about 33/ per Ton.

Assist Creamer if you can in the Bill[7] for a Schooner to be built at James Island[8] for Mepkin.[9]

SOURCE: Letterbook copy, Letter Book of Henry Laurens, Oct. 30, 1762–Sept. 10, 1766, Penn. Hist. Soc. This letter was copied by HL.

---

[1] John Coming Ball (1714–1764) was HL's brother-in-law. *HL Papers*, II, 72n.

[2] Timothy Creamer was HL's overseer at Mepkin. See HL to Timothy Creamer, Jan. 26, 1764. Creamer owned two male slaves, between the ages of 16 and 60, whom he was ordered on Aug. 6, 1764, to make available for work on the parish roads. Minute Book of Commissioners of Roads, St. John Berkeley, 1 (1760–1798), S. C. Hist. Soc.

[3] The schooner *Wambaw* was owned by HL, John Coming Ball, and Benjamin Perdriau. See Registration of the Schooner *Wambaw*, Sept. 15, 1764.

[4] HL and John Coming Ball had been planting Wambaw plantation jointly. *HL Papers*, II, 180; III, *passim*.

[5] HL had shipped rice from Wambaw plantation to Jamaica in January 1763. *HL Papers*, III, 218–219.

[6] The snow *Susannah*, Young Green, arrived from Bristol on July 31 and sailed for Bristol on Sept. 21. *Gazette*, Aug. 6, Sept. 24, 1763.

[7] The bill of scantling set forth the dimensions and quantity of lumber needed for building the schooner.

[8] There were shipyards on James Island across the Ashley River from Charleston. *HL Papers*, II, 15n, 19n.

[9] HL had purchased Mepkin plantation on the Cooper River on June 5, 1762. *HL Papers*, III, 100.

1

TO COWLES & HARFORD[1]

[Charles Town] 1st September 1763

Gentlemen,

This Vessel[2] being detain'd by contrary Wind gives me an opportunity of adding to what I have already wrote by her under the 29th Ulto.—that I have agreed to load the *Susanna* Snow, Capt. Young Green, with Pitch, Tar, & Turpentine on my own account on or before the 20th Inst. & tis probable that she will sail about that day for Bristol, Poole, or Portsmouth which I shall not determine till she is Loaden. My Interest in her will be about Four Hundred & fifty pounds Sterling. Be pleas'd to Insure the Sum of Three hundred pounds provided you can at a premium not exceeding 45/ per Cent,[3] otherwise only Two hundred & fifty pounds & I will risque the remainder. She is a Stout strong Vessel & the Goods not Liable to damage by a little Water. As I am to have the Freight pretty cheap, say about 32/6 per Ton, if you perceive that the goods will very well bear it you may in such case Insure Four hundred pounds at 45/ per Cent. I am—

SOURCE: Letterbook copy, HL Papers, S. C. Hist. Soc.; addressed "Bristol"; "per Capt. Ker. [*Copy*] per Johnston."

TO MARTIN & STEVENS[4]

[Charles Town] 1st September 1763

Gentlemen,

Since my last to you of the 3d May[5] per Capt. Martin[6] with Account Sale of your Rum per the Sloop *Sally*[7] I have not receiv'd any

---

[1] James Cowles and John Harford. *HL Papers*, III, 72n. For the dissolution of this partnership see HL to William Fisher, Feb. 27, 1766, Penn. Hist. Soc.

[2] The brigantine *Minerva*, Alexander Ker, cleared for Bristol on Aug. 27. Naval Office Lists, 1757–1764, p. 134.

[3] This premium would be at the rate of £2.5/ per £100, which would make the rate 2.25%. HL wrote Lachlan McIntosh, Sept. 27, 1763, that he would insure McIntosh's interest in a sloop if the premium did not exceed "two per Cent."

[4] Thomas Martin was senior partner in the firm of Martin & Stevens of Antigua. *HL Papers*, III, 190n.

[5] *HL Papers*, III, 432.

[6] The sloop *Wolfe*, Daniel Martin, arrived from Antigua on March 27 and was ready to sail for Antigua on May 4. *Gazette*, April 2, May 6, 1763.

[7] The sloop *Sally*, John Henderson, was entered inwards from Antigua on Feb. 24, 1763, with a cargo of 19 hogsheads of rum and 26 barrels of limes. Naval Office Lists, 1757–1764, p. 117.

of your favours. I am this day disposing of the squar'd Timber which
had been provided on your Account for that Sloop & hope to get rid
of it without any loss to you except from porterage which will be a
good thing considering the extravagant prices at which Lumber was
rated when that was bespoke, & then I shall make out & transmit your
Account Current.

I have lately receiv'd a protested Bill the draught of Mr.
George Leonard, Junior, for £150 Sterling with a Letter of attorney
from Mr. Thomas Willing[8] of Philadelphia empowering me to recover
the Amount of said Bill & charges with orders at the same time to
transmit the said Bill, &ca., to you in case that Mr. George Leonard
should not make his appearance in this place before the 6th Inst.
Hitherto I can learn nothing of him & I give you this previous notice
that you may be aware of the matter & you may expect the necessary
papers by the first opportunity after the limitted time expires unless the
party in the mean while should give me occasion to make use of them
here.

Our Crops of all kinds will be plenty & early at Market provided we have no hurricane to injure the Rice which is still expos'd.
The rest are pretty well secur'd. Rum is low. It sells every Vendue day
at 14/ to 15/ per Gallon for Leward Island & very often good Jamaica
at 19 to 21/ which will not pay cost & charges. I am with great
respect—

Exchange 721.

SOURCE: Letterbook copy, HL Papers, S. C. Hist. Soc.; addressed "Antigua"; "per Capt. Wood."

TO SMITH & BAILLIES[9]
[Charles Town] 2d September 1763
Gentlemen,
Please to be refer'd to what I wrote you under the 25th Ulto.
& 1st Inst.[1] per Capt. Conyers & Capt. Wood[2] & now to receive In-

[8] *HL Papers,* I, 249n.
[9] James Smith, Alexander Baillie, and James Baillie. *HL Papers,* III, 537n.
[1] There is no letter copied for Sept. 1.
[2] The sloop *Carolina,* Clement Conyers, cleared for St. Kitts on Aug. 27, and the
sloop *Charming Ann,* Horace Wood, cleared for Antigua on Aug. 29. Naval Office
Lists, 1757–1764, p. 134.

voice & Bill of Loading here inclos'd for 133 Barrels & 50 half Barrels of Rice ship'd on your Account per this Bearer the Sloop *Ann & Elizabeth,* Capt. Stovell,[3] the amount being £2,370.14.10 is pass'd to your debit & if Free from error will be noted by you in conformity.

The quality of this rice is much better than I did expect to have got & I believe you will find it to be equal to any that goes from hence at this Season except some of the half Barrels a little dusty. I have Ship'd 15 Barrels & 1 half barrel more on your Account per the *Relief,* Capt. Williams,[4] & may if there is room Ship a few more. The Vessel is chiefly Loaden with Lumber & will have no other Rice but yours on board, but she will sail in a day or two & I shall then have occasion to trouble you again. Mean time I remain with great regard, &ca.—

SOURCE: Letterbook copy, HL Papers, S. C. Hist. Soc.; addressed "St. Christopher"; "per Capt. Stovell. Copy per Williams."

TO SMITH & BAILLIES

[Charles Town] 3d September 1763

Gentlemen,

You have herewith a duplicate of what I wrote you per the *Ann & Elizabeth,* Capt. Stovel, with duplicate Bill of Loading & abstract Invoice to which please to be refer'd. This covers Invoice & Bill of Loading for 15 & ½ Barrels of very good Rice on board this Bearer the *Relief,* Capt. Williams, which is all that he could take on board of the quantity that I had provided for you. The remainder I shall dispose of without any loss or charge. The Amount being £216.9.8 is also pass'd to your debit & with the former parcel will at the Exchange that I have agreed for, Vizt. 721 per Cent[5] make up £358 Sterling for which Sum or thereabout I shall in 10 or 12 days pass my Bills on Augustus & John Boyd, Esquires[6] at 60 days sight or longer, if I can obtain it, but if you will be pleas'd to

---

[3] The sloop *Ann & Elizabeth,* Samuel Stovell, cleared for St. Kitts on Sept. 1 with 217 barrels and 50 half barrels of rice. Naval Office Lists, 1757–1764, p. 134.

[4] The sloop *Relief,* Benjamin Young, which was owned by William and Cornelius Williams of Bermuda, cleared for Bermuda on Sept. 2 with a cargo which included 15 barrels and 1 half barrel of rice. Naval Office Lists, 1757–1764, p. 134.

[5] At this rate of exchange £721 South Carolina currency equaled £100 sterling.

[6] Merchants of London. *HL Papers,* 1, 329n.

inquire you will find these the very highest terms on which Bills are sold. I remain with great respect—

SOURCE: Letterbook copy, HL Papers, S. C. Hist. Soc.; addressed "St. Christophers"; "per Capt. Williams. Copy per Basset."

TO JOHN NUTT[7]

[Charles Town] 6th September 1763

Dear Sir,

In December 1759 the House of Austin, Laurens, & Appleby wrote a Letter to you in favour of Messrs. Liston & Benfield two Young Gentlemen who were then setting out upon an equal footing in trade.[8] They afterward extended their firm by taking Mr. Jones into partnership, & I am now inform'd that Mr. Liston having offers made to him which appear more advantagious has withdrawn himself from the House & left Messrs. Benfield & Jones to carry on that Business in which they had all been engaged; this circumstance if I am truly inform'd will not impair their capital except by one third part of their profits when all accounts are settled.[9] Nevertheless these Gentlemen diffident of their Interest & still inclin'd to correspond with you have applyed to me requesting another Letter recommending them as far as I can upon this occasion. You must by this time be better acquainted than I can pretend to be with the Value of their correspondence in every respect & therefore most capable of judging for yourself; for my own part as things appear I think them carefull Active Men who seem to be striving by every Laudable measure in their power to get a livelihood & make some figure in

---

[7] *HL Papers,* I, 192n.

[8] This letter of Dec. 1759 has not been found.

[9] Thomas Liston and John Benfield had taken Maurice Jones into their partnership, which expired on Sept. 30, 1763. *Gazette,* Oct. 1, 1763. Liston, Benfield, & Jones filed a number of suits to recover debts owed to the partnership. Judgment Rolls, 1764, Nos. 45A, 196A, 197A, 198A; 1765, No. 348A, S. C. Archives. Benfield & Jones announced a new partnership with Stephen Drayton in the *Gazette,* Dec. 24, 1763. Maurice Jones died on Oct. 9, 1770, "esteemed by all who knew him." *SCHM,* XVI (1915), 132. Thomas Liston joined Thomas Middleton and William Hope in the new firm of Middleton, Liston, & Hope. The partnership of William Hope & Co. of Beaufort had recently been concluded. *Gazette,* Oct. 8, 1763. Pelatiah Webster recorded on June 3, 1765, in his journal: "Dined this day with Mr. Thomas Liston, a reputable mercht born here: is a man of great openess & politeness, of generous sentiments & very genteel behaviour." "Journal of Pelatiah Webster," p. 10.

business. Their Sales have hitherto been as considerable as they could reasonably expect & after proper allowance for outstanding debts, &ca., will probably leave them a handsome Balance of gain. These particulars I thought it my duty to enquire into before I would write to you & altho the information comes from themselves, I have not the least doubt of the truth of it. I wish you a long & beneficial connexion with them & remain with great regard, &ca.—

SOURCE: Letterbook copy, HL Papers, S. C. Hist. Soc.; addressed "London"; "per Capt. Pamour. Original & Copy delivered to Messrs. Benfield & Jones."

TO THOMAS COOPER[1]

[Charles Town] 8th September 1763

Sir,

When your first parcel of Turpentine came to Town I went to receive; but the Negro patroon of Watboo Boat,[2] told me that you had directed it to Mr. Edwards[3] he believ'd; & shew'd me a Letter for that Gentleman, & I thought that it might be so; because he had no Letter for me, so the Turpentine lay upon the Wharf for three or four days & then seeing it going to destruction I enquir'd of Mr. Edwards & Capt. Hutchens[4] who both said they had receiv'd no directions about it. Therefore I concluded that you must have intended it for me & that your Letter was left behind, & as the Barrels were in exceeding bad condition I judged it for your Interest to take immediate care of it. Many heads & some both heads of Barrels were out, the hoops & Staves rotten. A Cooper with three hands have been about it six days at least & now I declare to you that it is still in such bad order that I would much rather pay twenty pounds than Ship it for I am afraid that I shall receive a very bad account from the other side of the Water. The last 99 Barrels are come in

---

[1] A planter of St. Stephen parish. *HL Papers,* III, 534n.

[2] This was a schooner that plied regularly between Charleston and Wadboo Barony at the head of the Western Branch of the Cooper River. *Wadboo Barony, Its Fate as Told in Colleton Family Papers, 1773–1793,* ed. J. H. Easterby (Columbia, S. C., 1952). Watboo Johnny was the patroon. HL to John Coming Ball, March 2, 1764.

[3] John Edwards, Charleston merchant. *HL Papers,* II, 213n.

[4] Capt. Joseph Hutchins. *HL Papers,* III, 145n. Hutchins advertised in the *Gazette,* Jan. 14, 1764, that all debts due him "as a factor" should be paid.

much the same bad order that the first were in & besides that are come too late for me. Nevertheless as you are so kind as to give me the preference of it I will take it & do everything that I can to make the charges light & when this parcel is Cooper'd I shall send you an Account of the whole. Your loss will be very considerable but that must always be expected when Barrels have laid so long expos'd to weather as yours have. This you may depend upon that I shall act for you as if the Turpentine belonged wholly to myself.

I am much obliged to you for the Offer of purchasing 4 or 5 hundred Barrels of Turpentine for me at 15/ per Ct. but the day is past, & I cannot afford to give above 11/ or 12/ for the very best because Freight is not to be had now as it was some Weeks ago.

I have been offered some at 12/6 per Ct. which came down two days before your last by Mr. George Livingston a Factor[5] from whence you may be assur'd that I have paid proper regard to the confidence you were pleas'd to repose in me, by allowing you 15/ & making no difference between the first & the last parcel. I remain, &ca.—

P.S. When you have occasion of Money from me, be so good as to give a little Notice & you will not be disappointed.

SOURCE: Letterbook copy, Letter Book of Henry Laurens, Oct. 30, 1762–Sept. 10, 1766, Penn. Hist. Soc.; addressed "Fair Forest."

TO COWLES & HARFORD

[Charles Town] 12th September 1763
Gentlemen,

You have herewith Copies of my Letters 1st & 29th Ulto. & 1st Inst. to which please to be refer'd. The *Susannah*, Capt. Green, is now nearly loaded & I hope she will depart in 8 or ten days. I

---

[5] George Livingston was called "an eminent Factor" at the time of his death on Dec. 26, 1769. *SCHM*, XXXIV (1933), 61. He was granted a lot in Beaufort on Dec. 21, 1743, was of St. Helena parish in 1755, and at the time he wrote his will had two sons who were "store keeping on the Indian Lands." *SCHM*, IX (1908), 158; XXIII (1922), 129; "Will of George Livingston," dated Sept. 14, 1768, proved Jan. 6, 1769, Charleston County Wills, XII, Book B (1767–1771), 468–470, S. C. Archives. His daughter Anne married John Champneys, his partner in the firm of Champneys, Livingston & Co. *Gazette*, Oct. 22, Nov. 5, 1763.

shall have on board her 3 or perhaps four Hogsheads of untrimmed Deer Skins.[6] They are really not quite so fine as I could wish them & yet I have culled them pretty well too, but they may or may not be as you please on our joint Account. The cost is 12/6 per lb. If wholly on mine please to add £100 Sterling to my Insurance; if half add £50 Sterling.

I have taken the liberty on the 10th Inst. to pass two Bills on you at fifty days sight for Eleven hundred & thirty eight pounds Sterling, Vizt.

to Robert Philp's order[7] £638
Robert Raper's order[8] 500

I hope that I have or shall soon have sufficient fund in your hands to pay these but I cannot certainly know before you furnish me with our old Accounts. 'Tis a disagreeable circumstance to me to draw Bills just now but I am forced to do it to raise Cash for in these troublous times tho I have large Sums due to me by many safe & I may say best hands yet I cannot collect enough to carry on, as I chuse to do, even the little business that I transact. I am, &Ca.—

SOURCE: Letterbook copy, HL Papers, S. C. Hist. Soc.; addressed "Bristol"; "per Capt. Johnstoun for Cowes. Copy per Green."

TO LACHLAN McINTOSH[9]

[Charles Town] 13 September 1763

I have receiv'd by the hands of your Brother George McIntosh[1] your favour of the 26 Ulto. & he has paid to me on your account £255 Current Money which I have placed to your Credit & shall lay out the whole Sum in my hands in goods to the best advantage agreeable to your order & send them by a Schooner of

---

[6] HL paid £32.14 export duties on deerskins shipped by Green for Bristol. Public Treasurer, Journal B: Duties, 1748–1765, p. 357, S. C. Archives.

[7] HL Papers, III, 30n.

[8] HL Papers, I, 38n. HL was helping Philp and Raper to secure funds for their trip to England. Robert Philp and Robert Raper returned from London in November 1764. Gazette, Nov. 12, 1764.

[9] HL Papers, III, 278n.

[1] HL Papers, III, 361n.

Mr. Forbes's[2] that your Brother points out to me to Sail in a few days.

An alteration in Mr. Deas's family affairs by the sudden death of Mrs. Seamans and a smart visit of the Fall Fever to himself & Mrs. Deas will probably hinder him from going to Altamaha in October.[3]

Mr. Hopton is now very Sick & so is his Son & Mrs. Hopton continues since her late illness very full of complaints & besides he has lately lost a Man who used to conduct the business of his Tan Yard which adds much to his own Labour & care. These are circumstances that I do suppose will hinder him.[4]

And for my own part I go or not go as I find a possibility about the time appointed or a Little later; at present I can perceive two or three obstacles to my going early—two Vessels to load— removal to Ansonburgh in which I am thrown a Month or two behind by Mr. Dean's delay.[5] Mr. Perdriau's invalidity is worse than all.[6] Therefore upon the whole I can fix no time, tho I wish to go & will endeavour to go as soon as I can with convenience.[7]

---

[2] John Forbes, formerly of Georgetown, was by this time a merchant of Charleston. *HL Papers*, II, 133n. George Cox was master of Forbes' schooner *Elizabeth*. See HL to Lachlan McIntosh, Sept. 20, 1763; *Gazette*, Oct. 1, 1763.

[3] Mrs. George Seaman died on Sept. 2, 1763. *SCHM*, x (1909), 161. Mrs. Mary Seaman's first husband had been William Allen. John Deas had married their only child Elizabeth Allen in 1759. Alston Deas to the editor, Jan. 12, 1966. John and David Deas had just concluded their partnership. *Gazette*, Sept. 10, 1763.

[4] John Hopton, the son of William and Sarah Hopton, who had been born Nov. 6, 1748, would serve as a clerk in HL's counting house. *HL Papers*, I, 102n. William Hopton owned a plantation "Starve gut Hall" on the Wando River. Bartram, *Diary of a Journey*, p. 14. He was contemplating selling his plantation on the Wando before going to Europe. *Gazette*, Feb. 4, 1764.

[5] Robert Deans, a joiner from Scotland, known in Charleston as carpenter and architect, was building HL's house in Ansonborough. E. Milby Burton, *Charleston Furniture, 1700–1825* (Columbia, S. C., 1970), pp. 80–81. At this time Deans was also surveyor of the Orange Garden and a commissioner of the market. *Gazette*, Sept. 24, Oct. 22, 1763. HL would take chambers in Robert Deans' home during his London visit, 1771–1774. HL to William Cowles, April 20, 1772, HL Papers, S. C. Hist. Soc. Deans' estate in S. C. was confiscated in 1782. *SCHM*, xxxiv (1933), 14.

[6] HL's aunt Jane Laurens had married John Perdriau on Feb. 21, 1721. *Register of St. Philip's Parish, 1720–1758*, p. 151. John and Jane Perdriau had two sons, John and Benjamin. John, the son who married Esther Guerry on May 21, 1744, had two sons, John and Samuel. Benjamin, the second son, who married Mary Barton in 1747, had several sons of whom Benjamin, Jr. was the eldest. HL did employ Benjamin, Jr., as a clerk, and he is most certainly the Mr. Perdriau mentioned here. See HL to John Knight, Dec. 22, 1763.

[7] HL did not go to Georgia at this time.

I have the pleasure to inform him that his journey to Sessions may be laid aside. Mr. Egan frankly forgives him & will not carry on the prosecution. Mr. Leigh will do the needful to render his Nonattendance wholly inoffensive, &ca.[8]

Shall write again with the goods & am, &ca., &ca.—

SOURCE: Letterbook copy, HL Papers, S. C. Hist. Soc.; addressed "at Darien, Georgia." This letter was copied by HL.

TO JOHN RUTHERFORD [9]

[Charles Town, 19th September 1763]

The 19th September 1763—put under a blank Cover one small packet & one Letter lately receiv'd for him from London which with a small square Box also lately Receiv'd by Capt. Ball[1] is delivered

---

[8] Edmund Egan as surveyor had laid out HL's lands south of the Altamaha. Lachlan McIntosh had then succeeded Egan as surveyor for HL and his friends who were securing Georgia lands. There is evidence that Egan was peeved by this change. *HL Papers*, III, 405n, 433, 436–438, 455. The friction between Egan and McIntosh was on the verge of erupting into charges to be made by Egan against McIntosh in the next court of general sessions in Charleston. Egan had been at some expense for he owed constable fees. After HL had paid Egan a sum which covered his expenses, Egan told his lawyer Egerton Leigh to drop the proceedings. See HL to Lachlan McIntosh, Sept. 27, 1763. Early in 1764 Egan took the place of James Lingard in the partnership of Nathaniel Greene, James Lingard, and William Coats who were woodsellers, carters, and watermen. On Oct. 29, 1765 he entered a bill of complaint against the three former partners on the plea that he had been induced by fraud to take Lingard's place in the partnership when the company was in debt. Egan claimed that Greene had taken all the profits for himself, and he was asking for a return of the money that he had invested in the firm. *Gazette*, Sept. 17, 1763; typescript index to Equity Records and Equity Bundle, 1763–1786, S. C. Archives. In 1766 Egan with John Calvert established a brewery which soon brought him the fortune that he had been seeking. Walter Richard Walsh, "Edmund Egan: Charleston's Rebel Brewer," *SCHM*, LVI (1955), 200–204.

[9] John Rutherford (Rutherfurd) (1722–1782) was receiver-general of quit rents in North Carolina, 1750–1757, 1761–1775. Rutherford had obtained a royal warrant, dated Feb. 5, 1761, ordering the receiver-general of quit rents in S. C. to pay Mrs. Rutherford, the widow of Governor Gabriel Johnston of N. C., a large sum of money due to Johnston for back salary. *HL Papers*, III, 168n; *Journal of a Lady of Quality*, pp. 291–299.

[1] The ship *Friendship*, Thomas Ball, was entered inwards on Sept. 19 from Havana with goods originally shipped from London. Naval Office Lists, 1757–1764, p. 122.

at Mrs. Woods[2] to Mr. Clayton[3] who promises to convey them safely as directed.

SOURCE: Letterbook copy, HL Papers, S. C. Hist. Soc.; addressed "Esquire. North Carolina." This letter was copied by HL.

TO AUGUSTUS & JOHN BOYD

[Charles Town] 19 September 1763

Gentlemen,

Above you have a Copy of my last under the 30th Ulto. to which please to be refer'd.

The Brigantine *Portland*[4] is now far advanced in her Loading & all her Cargo lies ready. Wherefore I hope that she will proceed to Sea very early in October. Some little diveation from or rather addition must be made to Your order of a few pieces of small scantlin to stow up the Hold where otherwise Room would be lost or wholly fill'd with Shingles which would not be so well.

I have hired a faithful Man to attend constantly to see that no bad Stuff creeps into the Cargo; as well as to mark the several pieces AB and to exact good Stowage, & I have reason to expect that the whole will be well performed.

I lately loaded on Account of Messrs. Smith & Baillies, Merchants in St. Christophers, per the Sloop *Ann & Elizabeth*, Captain Stoval, for that Island 133 Barrels & 50 half Barrels Rice Amount £2,370.14.10 & per the Sloop *Relief*, William Williams, Master for the same place 15 Barrels & 1 half Barrel of Rice Amount

---

[2] When the justices of the peace met on Easter Monday in 1763 at Robert Dillon's tavern in Broad St., Elizabeth Wood was given a license to sell spirituous liquors at her store in Tradd St. *Gazette*, April 9, 1763. She was the wife of John Wood, shopkeeper. "Will of John Wood," dated Oct. 1, 1771, proved Oct. 25, 1771, Charleston County Wills, XIV, Book A (1771–1774), 93–94, S. C. Archives.

[3] Francis Clayton and Robert Hogg had recently commenced a partnership in Charleston. *Gazette*, Feb. 19, 1763. Hogg & Clayton sold off their stock at 8 for 1 and put up their store for rent in March 1766. *Country Journal*, March 18, 1766. The Invoice Book for this firm, 1762–1766, is among the Robert Hogg Account Books, 1762–1775, #343, SHC. Robert Hogg was a prominent figure in the commercial life of Wilmington, N. C. from his arrival from Scotland about 1756 until his departure for England in 1775. Hogg was a loyalist. *Journal of a Lady of Quality*, pp. 323–324.

[4] The brigantine *Portland*, George Higgins, was cleared outwards on Oct. 11 for St. Christophers with 10 barrels of rice, 45,000 feet of lumber, and 46,000 shingles. Naval Office Lists, 1757–1764, p. 135.

£216.9.8 as per abstract Invoices here inclosed in which I am so minute because they direct me, & agreeable to their orders I have in part of said Amounts This day Valued on You for Three hundred & forty pounds Sterling at 721 per Cent Exchange in two Bills at 60 days sight, Vizt.

> To the order of Mr. Richard Milford[5] £240
> The order of Richard Millish, Esquire or of the
> Receiver general of His Majesty's Customs for
> the time being[6] --- 100
>   ——

£340 Sterling at 721 per Cent Exchange is to their Credit—£2,451.8—for which Sum I make no doubt of their having made provisions given timely advice but in case of unforeseen accidents & to guard against such be pleased if needfull to recommend my draughts to Mrs. Sarah Nicholson & Company[7] in London or to Messrs. Cowles & Harford in Bristol. I remain with great regard, &ca.—

SOURCE: Letterbook copy, HL Papers, S. C. Hist. Soc.; addressed "Esquires. London"; "per Watts. Copy per Green with Invoices."

TO THOMAS COURTIN[8]

[Charles Town] 19 September 1763

Sir,

I do not at present recollect any thing of consequence to add to what I have already wrote to you (a Copy of my last under the 29th Ulto. you have above) save only that I would not desire you to come to Sea with barely one suit of Sails. Therefore be looking about betimes to get something of spare Canvas good & cheap that

---

[5] Richard Milford had a store on the Bay in Charleston. *Gazette*, Oct. 1, 1763. He intended to leave the province in the fall of 1764. *General Gazette*, April 18, 1764.

[6] William (not Richard) Mellish (1710–1791) was receiver-general of customs from 1760 to Jan. 1763 when he was turned out of office in the proscription of Newcastle's friends. He was reappointed to the office of receiver-general in 1765. Romney Sedgwick, *The House of Commons, 1715–1754* (2 vols.: New York, 1970), II, 252–253.

[7] *HL Papers*, I, 9n.

[8] Thomas Courtin was supervising the building of the *Flora* for HL in Poole. *HL Papers*, III, passim.

we may not loose a good Ship *"because our Anchor and Cable are at home."*

A good Mate is another very essential article. A Man to please you, to be a good Ship keeper, & in other respects to do his duty shall not always remain a Mate if I have ability to serve him, and I shall likewise be glad if you get two or three hardy Lads of honest sober parents, to be bound to the Owners of the Ship, which I think will be attended with no great difficulty when their Parents are assured that I do always delight in promoting Young Men that behave well of which you can give some examples.

I have been thinking much about an outward freight but am come to no conclusion. If Salt can be purchased at Lymington[9] as cheap as at Liverpoole I should be glad that you took in 2,500 to 3,000 Bushels of that article. It will do the Ship no harm & may pay for taking in. If a Corn freight to Spain or Portugal can be procured so as not to detain you from this place longer than the Month of March at latest that may be accepted but I would by all means have the Ship here in March & as much sooner as possible.

If neither of these nor any thing better can be engaged & that she must come out in Ballast let that Ballast be partly of flat paving Stones & the remainder in broken pieces & Stones for filling up a Wharf[1] & pray be so kind to bring for my Garden about the Quantity of 15 or 20 Hogsheads of Gravel & small Stone Ballast.[2]

---

[9] Lymington was an English port at the mouth of the Lymington River which flows through the New Forest into the Solent.

[1] HL was building a wharf on his property in Ansonborough. William Gerard De Brahm advised Thomas Eaton in 1759 that if he wished to build a wharf in Savannah he should: "drive two Rows of Piles as far assunder as he desired his Wharf to be wide, and as far towards the River as low Water Mark; secure their Tops with plates and to trunnel Planks within on the Piles; this done, then to brace the Insides with dry Walls of Stones, intermixed with willow Twigs, and in the same Manner to shut up the Ends of the two Rows with alike Front along the Stream, to build inside what Cellars he had Occasion for, then to fill up the Remainder with the Sand nearest at hand out of the Bluff, or high Shore of the Stream, under the Bay, this Plan has been followed ever since to this day." *De Brahm's Report of the General Survey in the Southern District of North America,* ed. Louis De Vorsey, Jr. (Columbia, S. C., 1971), pp. 158–159. The Charleston wharves were built in a similar fashion. HL later stated that a boat could come in and go out the same tide at his wharf "if she does not draw above five feet Water." HL to Zachariah Villepontoux, May 11, 1764.

[2] Robert Pringle had ordered 20 or 30 tons of gravel to be sent over as ballast in 1740—"it being for the Walks of my Garden & very proper for this Climate." Robert Pringle to Andrew Pringle, June 14, 1740, *Letter Book of Robert Pringle, 1737–1745,* I, 224.

Please to observe that if You strike out any thing for the benefit of the Ship I shall be satisfied with the event, prove as it may, and if any thing further occurs to me I shall communicate it to you in time.

I hope you will not think that I sail too fast in my expectation of having the *Flora* here in all March. If she is not, I am afraid that she will make a ragged Year of it.[3]

SOURCE: Letterbook copy, HL Papers, S. C. Hist. Soc.; addressed "Captain. Poole"; "per Watts. Duplicate per Green."

TO COWLES & HARFORD

[Charles Town] 19th September 1763

Gentlemen,

In my last of the 12th Inst. as per Annexed Copy I advised you among other matters that I had on the 10th made two draughts on you to Robert Philps order £638 & to the order of Robert Raper £500, in the whole £1,138 Sterling, repeated here to guard by the Copy against extraordinary accidents.

This is intended to wait on you by the Snow *Susannah*, Capt. Young Green, by whom I have ship'd to your address 676 Barrels Turpentine, 166 Barrels of Pitch, & 55 Barrels of Green Tar, also on your Account & mine in Moiety or wholly on my own as you please three Hogsheads of Deer Skins as per Invoices, Bill Loading, & two Bounty Certificates[4] herewith inclosed. If the Skins are on our joint Account you will be pleased to give me Credit for the Freight at 25/ per Hogshead.

You will perceive that I have engaged to pay Freight to Capt. Green by the Lump for the whole Cargo relying upon his assurances that the Snow would carry upwards of 145 Tons of goods & having

---

[3] There is the following entry in the Poole Custom House Letter Books for March 16, 1765: "Inclos'd we transmit your Honours a Rice Licence for the *Flora* of Poole, Thomas Courtin, Master, dated 11 February 1764 and as we apprehend the Requisites of Law are duly comply'd with, we beg your Honours Directions for Cancelling the Bond when the half subsidy is paid which we believe will be very soon." The editor is indebted to E. F. J. Mathews of Poole for this information. This entry indicates that the *Flora* secured a license to carry rice south of Cape Finisterre before departing England. The *Flora* did not arrive until Aug. 10, 1764. See HL to Cowles & Harford, Aug. 10, 1764.

[4] Certificates were sent to England where the importer collected the bounty on colonial naval stores.

an intention at first to Ship a large quantity of Mahogany The Freight of which could not be so well ascertain'd by the Ton, which Turns out to me much worse than I expected & I have but too much reason to think that there is too great a quantity of his own Staves or other goods on board or that the Vessel is very badly stowed of which I intreat you to take proper & timely notice. I am also a little dissatisfied with the Stowing of the Skins & am afraid they will receive much damage which I have signified to the Captain. I wish that my apprehensions may be groundless but otherwise he certainly should make good all the losses.

I say nothing more about the sale of my goods leaving that wholly to your own discretion, only that I would not have them lay long upon hand if You can avoid it.

We have fine Harvest weather which puts it almost beyond a doubt that the Crop of Rice will be large but Ships are daily dropping in to wait for its coming to Market.

SOURCE: Letterbook copy, HL Papers, S. C. Hist. Soc.; addressed "Bristol"; "per Green. Copy per Watts with B. Loading & Abstract Invoice."

TO ISAAC KING[5]

[Charles Town] 20th September 1763

Sir,

I have not had occasion to trouble you with a letter since mine of the 21st July per Cutter & Michie.[6] In the mean time your acceptable favours of 2d April & 3d June are come to hand & I duly note their several contents.

Governor Debatt[7] in a former letter to A., L., & A. intimates that he is intitled to a return of premium on that Insurance made by you & I am of your opinion that he has no intention to defraud the Underwriters. However he is at hand & can best explain his

---

[5] Isaac King was a partner in the firm of Mrs. Sarah Nickleson & Co., Carolina merchants, Bush Lane, Cannon Street. This firm was not listed after 1769. In 1770 Isaac King was a merchant at No. 27 Nicholas Lane, Lombard Street. *London Directories.*

[6] The ship *Russia Merchant,* William Cutter, cleared for Cowes on July 19. The ship *British King,* James Michie, cleared for Cowes on July 20. Naval Office Lists, 1757–1764, p. 133.

[7] Joseph Debat was governor of Gambia. *HL Papers,* III, 257n.

claim & no doubt support it by vouchers that will admit of no controversy. Therefore if You will be so good as to write to him on this subject My late partners as well as myself will be further obliged to you.

I take notice that you have declined the Purchase of a small Vessel for the Winyaw Trade,[8] which to me is not at all disagreeable because I had no desire to enter into a connexion of that sort & had consented to hold a Share of a proper Bark merely because I would not put a Negative upon a request made by Mr. Brown.[9]

As Mr. William Hodshon[1] was introduced thro' your kind intentions to a correspondence with our late House, which I was (at the close of their affairs) induced to take up in order to serve him as well as I could in a business that was not very clearly explained on his part & where I then thought & have more reason now to think delay would have been attended with danger, & as he has also hinted to me that you would write to me again upon the same subject, I have taken the liberty under this cover to inclose a letter to him[2] & some other papers which I request you to peruse & then Seal & deliver it to Mr. Hodshon. I have certainly done every thing that was in my power to serve his Interest & some folks do say that I have done more than could be expected under such circumstances & in return he has sent me two of the most unthankful boorish letters that ever were pened by a Merchant; He might have cavilled & grumbled & yet have preserved some decency until he had heard my defence but now whether my conduct be right or wrong, he has censured me unheard & his manners are unjustifiable. I shall be much obliged to you as the source of this correspondence to interpose at this time & to do me justice. Let it fall on which side it may whether for or against me, and I shall take it very kind of you to give me your sentiments by the first opportunity after you have considered what I have now offered upon this disagreeable Incident, which from a consciousness of my endeavours to serve as well as of my success in serving Mr. Hodshon I had not the least suspicion of, but I shall not further intrude upon your time at present save only to repeat that I am with great respect—

---

[8] The trade between London and Georgetown, S. C.

[9] Joseph Brown of Georgetown. *HL Papers*, III, 106n, 389.

[1] *HL Papers*, III, 136n.

[2] The letter that HL wrote to William Hodshon, Aug. 26, 1763, was sent as an enclosure in this letter to King. *HL Papers*, III, 542–546.

P.S. We have fine Harvest Weather as ever was known which will be a means of securing a large Crop.

SOURCE: Letterbook copy, HL Papers, S. C. Hist. Soc.; addressed "for Mrs. Sarah Nickelson & Company, London"; "per Watts. Copy per Green."

TO EDMOND GOMOND[3]

[Charles Town] 20 September 1763

Sir,

In a seperate packet you will receive all the Books & papers belonging or relative to the Estate of the late Capt. John Whitborn[4] which packet Capt. Green the bearer hereof promises to deliver with his own hand to you.

The Account Current Capt. John Whitborn with Austin & Laurens on which is a smal Ballance (not enough to pay the expence we have been at), Vizt. £24.16/ Current Money is all that I properly knew anything of. The other Account which Mr. Appleby[5] was so kind as to transact in my absence from home has always remain'd till this day in his hands—he has now put the Ballance, Vizt. £344.9.3 into mine—& I shall endeavour as Bills of Exchange are very scarce to pick up as much silver & Gold as both will Amount to & Ship per the next Vessel for Bristol. Otherwise I shall desire Messrs. Cowles & Harford to pay the same at the Current course of Exchange on my Account when I shall request the favour of you to give them an indemnification on my behalf.

Nothing astonished me more than to find poor Whitborn's Little Books & Memorandums so extremely crude & imperfect as you will see they are, of which I have too much reason to believe some people have made an advantage.

There are two Bundles of Gold or Tinsel Lace now laying in my Counting House said to be the property of Messrs. Devonsheir,

---

[3] Edmond Gomond, who was listed as merchant and sailmaker at 37 Princes St. in *Sketchley's Bristol Directory* for 1775, died Feb. 29, 1784. *Bristol Lists: Municipal and Miscellaneous*, compiled by Alfred B. Beaven (Bristol, Eng., 1899), p. 351.

[4] John Whitborn, captain of the *Brislington*, had made many voyages to Charleston before his death in 1758. He was buried in Charleston on Aug. 10, 1758. *HL Papers*, I, 62; II, passim; *Register of St. Philip's Parish, 1754–1810*, p. 289.

[5] George Appleby.

Reeve, & Lloyd[6] & lodged in our House by Mr. John McQueen[7] into whose hands Capt. Whitborne had put them for Sale. This is all that I know of them.

If you think that I can be further serviceable in these affairs you may freely lay your commands upon me, who am—

SOURCE: Letterbook copy, HL Papers, S. C. Hist. Soc.; addressed "Bristol"; "per Green."

TO LACHLAN McINTOSH

[Charles Town] 20th September 1763

Dear Sir,

I applyed to Mr. Forbes for Leave to Ship your goods in this (his) Schooner which at first he receiv'd with some coolness, as that he did not chuse the same kind of goods that he was sending on his Account should be Shiped by other hands, but since that he has frankly offer'd me Freight & I was about to Ship them, when another objection was started, Vizt. that the Schooner was not clear'd out at the Custom House, &ca., that the expence of clearing would be more than the Freight that you ought to pay would Amount to, & that to Ship only upon permit as he has done will not give me a proof of exportation sufficient to recover the drawback upon Rum & Sugar which will be considerable.[8] Therefore upon the whole I am

---

[6] *HL Papers,* I, 224n, 251n.

[7] *HL Papers,* II, 110n; III, 17n. John McQueen had died on Nov. 9, 1762. *SCHM,* x (1909), 161. He had recently been a partner of John Gordon in the firm of McQueen & Gordon. He had instructed the executors of his estate to see that his sons, John, Alexander, and George, were brought up to the law or physic or to be a merchant. Although HL had been named as an executor, there is no record of his qualifying to serve. John Gordon and James Parsons did qualify as executors. "Will of John McQueen," dated Nov. 28, 1760, proved Feb. 4, 1763, Charleston County Wills, IX, Book A (1760–1767), 339–344, S. C. Archives.

[8] The problems stated here were those which would involve HL with the customs officials in 1767. The cost of clearing vessels differed according to the destination of the vessel—to England, to south of Cape Finisterre, to other British dominions in America. Coasting vessels sailing from one destination to another within the same province did not clear, although Parliament would soon act to close this loophole. See *British Statutes,* XXVI, 33–52. Ordinarily a vessel sailing from S. C. to Georgia would clear and pay fees. However, to post a bond it was necessary to return a certificate to cancel the bond. If a schooner was going to Darien on the Altamaha, there were no customs officials there to return a certificate. Sunbury, on the Midway River to the north, however, was a port of entry. One alternative to obtaining a clearance each time was to obtain a "permit" which could be used

forced to seek for another opportunity & have heard of a Sloop belonging to Messrs. Dunbar & Young[9] of whom I shall enquire & hope there will be no obstacles in my way, in which case you may depend upon having your goods in that Vessel. I remain with great regard, &ca.—

SOURCE: Letterbook copy, HL Papers, S. C. Hist. Soc.; addressed "Georgia"; "per Capt. Cox."

TO MARTIN & STEVENS

[Charles Town] 22d September 1763

I beg leave to refer you to what I wrote the 1st Inst. per Capt. Wood & now inclose the following papers by directions & on account of Mr. Thomas Willing of Philadelphia, Vizt.

George Leonard Bill of Bassnett & Hardgraves,[1] London, for Sterling £150.

The Act of protesting the said Bill.

Mr. Willing Account of the Amount of the Bill & charges— £180.5.9 Sterling.

Besides Blanks to be fill'd up.

Sickness in my family & a fair wind for this Vessel sooner than I expected occasions my being more abrupt than I had Intended to be in my present address which I beg you will excuse. I am, &ca.—

over a period of six months. "Permits" were also called "Half yearly Certificates" or "a Sufereance for Six Months." Actually a merchant like HL in this instance faced a situation not fully covered by the navigation acts. A customs collector such as Beaufain had always made the rules sit easily upon the shoulders of the Charleston merchants. This would change after Beaufain's death and bring on a major crisis in Anglo-South Carolina affairs. Beaufain had charged on an average £6.12.7 currency to clear schooners for Georgia. Daniel Moore, Beaufain's successor, would charge HL £14 currency. A "permit" had cost as little as 30 shillings. For a full discussion of these matters see HL's *A Representation of Facts* to be printed in Volume V of *HL Papers*.

[9] John Dunbar and Thomas Young with William Lyford, John Simpson, and Tunis Tebout owned the 20-ton schooner *Georgia Packett,* William Lyford, which was registered in Charleston on May 12, 1763 as having been built that year in S. C. Ship Register, 1734–1765, p. 215, S. C. Archives. Dunbar, Young, and Simpson had a store at Sunbury in Georgia. *Georgia Gazette,* March 29, 1764.

[1] Bassnett & Hargraves were West India merchants of Fenchurch St. Nathaniel Bassnett was one of the two partners. *London Directories.* Nathaniel Bassnett had traded with Robert Pringle of Charleston as early as 1739. *Letterbook of Robert Pringle, 1737–1745,* I, 124, 181, 257, 262, 362.

SOURCE: Letterbook copy, HL Papers, S. C. Hist. Soc.; addressed "Antigua"; "per Capt. Bassett."

TO THOMAS BOWREY [2]

[Charles Town] 22d September 1763

Advised him that the Brigantine *Portland* was pretty well advanced in her Loading & the remainder all ready & that I hoped she would Sail early in October. Sent Copy of my last.

SOURCE: Letterbook copy, HL Papers, S. C. Hist. Soc.; addressed "In his absence to Mr. Nicholas Dromgoole at St. Christophers"; "per Capt. Basset Via Antigua." This letter was copied by HL.

PURCHASE OF TWO HUNDRED ACRES OF MARSHLAND

September 23, 1763

[On this date Thomas Savage,[3] Charleston merchant, deeded to HL for the consideration of £5 currency "All that Tract of Two hundred Acres of Marsh Land including several small Islands adjacent to the same situate in Berkley County between Town Creek and Hobcaw Ferry, bounded to the west, on the said Creek to the East, on that part of the Cooper River that's opposite to Hobcaw, being surrounded by the waters of the said River. . . ."[4] The deed was witnessed by Mark Morris[5] and Charles Minors,[6] attested by Jacob Motte as

---

[2] Thomas Bowrey managed Augustus Boyd's Fountain Estate near Basseterre on the island of St. Christophers. *HL Papers,* II, 384; III, 42, 63, 518, 521.

[3] *HL Papers,* III, 147n.

[4] This was apparently the island which is now called Drum Island and upon which the spans of the modern Cooper River Bridge rest. HL may have been helping Mark Morris and Charles Minors, shipwrights who witnessed this deed, to establish a shipyard on this island.

[5] Mark Morris was the nephew of William Dandridge. He witnessed the wills of a number of Charleston tradesmen. *Abstracts of Wills, 1760–1784,* pp. 101, 122, 189, 222, 229. He married Margaret Tew of James Island on June 14, 1770. *SCHM,* XI (1910), 93.

[6] Charles Minors, shipwright, may have come to Carolina from Bermuda. Henry C. Wilkinson, *Bermuda in the Old Empire* (London, 1950), p. 42n. He had been the master and owner of the schooner *Susannah,* which was built at Little River in 1751 and registered on Sept. 19, 1753. Ship Register, 1734–1765, pp. 120–121, S. C. Archives. In 1763 when Jane Laurens Perdriau Savineau wrote her will, she mentioned "the heirs of the body of Susannah Minors," her daughter who by that

justice of the peace on September 29, and recorded by William Hopton, public register, on November 23, 1763.]

SOURCE: Deeds, AAA, pp. 297–299, S. C. Archives.

ADVERTISEMENT

September 24, 1763

ALL persons having any demands on the late Co-partnership of AUSTIN, LAURENS, & APPLEBY, or against GEORGE AUSTIN, Esq. are requested to call immediately for payment, of

GEORGE APPLEBY

September 22, 1763

SOURCE: Printed in *Gazette,* Sept. 24, 1763.

TO LACHLAN McINTOSH

[Charles Town] 27th September 1763

Dear Sir,

My last was on the 20th Inst. per Mr. Forbes's Schooner. This waits on you according to promise by the Sloop *Pandora,* Capt. Dickinson,[7] & incloses an Invoice for sundry goods Shiped on her on your Account Amounting to £2,250.5.10 which I have charged to your debit & shall bring opposite hereto the Drawback on Rum & Sugar as soon as the same is Receiv'd by me.

I have kept as close to your order as I could & hope that all the articles will prove profitable to you & give satisfaction. You see the Amount goes far beyond the Money that you had lodged in my

---

date was probably dead. "Will of Jane Savineau of Georgetown," dated 1763, proved May 19, 1764, Charleston County Wills, x, Book B (1760–1767), 509, S. C. Archives. On Feb. 14, 1765, John Perdriau was cited to administer the estate of Robert Minors, ship carpenter. *SCHM,* XXII (1921), 97. On March 31, 1770, Sarah Minors was cited to administer the estate of Charles Minors, late of Charleston. *SCHM,* XLIII (1942), 62. From the above information it would seem that Charles Minors had been married to HL's first cousin and that HL was now trying to help a poor relation.

[7] The sloop *Pandora,* Jeremiah Dickinson, arrived from Georgia on Sept. 15 and sailed for Georgia on Oct. 12. *Gazette,* Sept. 17, Oct. 15, 1763. This sloop was not cleared outwards according to Naval Office Lists, 1757–1764.

hands. However I would not cramp your order as I hope & heartily wish that this attempt may lead you into some further branches of commerce wherein in my humble opinion you will be more likely to succeed in laying up something for the bairns (if I spell it right if not you know my meaning) than by planting only & this perhaps may be carried on too at the same time. If the Strouds[8] do not please you, you may return them.

I believe that it will be prudent at this Season of the Year to make an Insurance on at least a part of your Interest in this Sloop & therefore will do so if the premium does not exceed two per Cent, & tho I have not your orders for so doing, yet I am persuaded you will not be angry with me for guarding your Interest as I would my own in a like case.

By one of the Ships lately arrived from London we are advis'd that the Lands granted on the South side of the Altamaha will remain the property of the present Grantees, altho the whole is to be annex'd to the province of Georgia. This I am heartily glad of because I shall probably be enabled to compell my 3,000 Acres to make an acknowledgement that remains justly due from it.[9] 'Tis said Colonel Grant will soon make his appearance in a New Character in one of the new provinces in or near Florida.[1]

I hear nothing more from Mr. Hopton about our Voyage to your River but that tis his fix'd resolution to prosecute it as soon as he can & I have not seen poor Mr. Deas for a long time past.

28th. I am in treaty with Mr. Pendergrass for your favourite triangular piece of Swamp & will if possible secure it for you.[2]

---

[8] Strouds, from Stroud in Gloucestershire, were a coarse, heavy woolen cloth, usually in plain weave, used in the Indian trade of North America. *OED*.

[9] This news was probably brought by the ship *Union*, James Smith, owned by John Beswicke of London, which was entered inwards on Sept. 26. Naval Office Lists, 1757–1764, p. 122.

[1] On Oct. 8 four Scotsmen were appointed governors of the newly acquired territories: James Murray of Quebec, James Grant of East Florida, George Johnstone of West Florida, and Robert Melville of the Grenadas. *Gentleman's Magazine*, XXXIII (1763), 518.

[2] HL purchased 1,200 acres of land from Darby Pendergrass on Nov. 28, 1764, which he sold on Oct. 9, 1765, to Lachlan McIntosh. He obviously made the purchase out of consideration for McIntosh's desire to secure this particular tract. See Purchase of Land south of the Altamaha River, Nov. 28, 1764 and Sale of Land south of the Altamaha River, Oct. 9, 1765. Darby Pendergrass had been one of those obtaining lands south of the Altamaha. *HL Papers*, III, 370, 433n, 438, 455. In 1764 he had a store in Elliott St. at the corner of Gadsden's Alley. *Gazette*, Feb. 4, 1764.

Mr. Egan has given me a Receipt at the foot of an Account for charges to Constable, &ca., £10 or £9.7, in full on Account of your controversy & so that affair is over & upon my word, think what you will of him he has behaved genteely & generously in this affair at least. I tempted him with a large Bill put into his hand urging that he must have been at more expence besides a good deal of trouble, but he turned it away with disdain declaring in the most solemn manner that he would not touch one penny more than the very amount paid out of his Pocket & tis beyond doubt that he might have squeezed & plagued you a good deal if he was disposed to make an advantage of you. There is something in this conduct that looks well & I am really inclin'd to attribute his faults or foibles rather to the Head than to the Heart. I am, &ca.—

SOURCE: Letterbook copy, HL Papers, S. C. Hist. Soc.; addressed "Darien in Georgia"; "per Capt. Dickinson with Invoices, &ca., inclosed." The continuation written on the 28th was copied by HL.

TO JOHN KNIGHT[3]

[Charles Town] 30 September 1763

Wrote at the foot of an Invoice that My Clerk being Sick abed & myself very unwell I had defered writing till I had only time to cover said Invoice & B. Loading for some Ship Timber (Vide Invoice) which I desired him to order to be sold on my Account & to add that I am, &ca., &ca.—[4]

SOURCE: Letterbook copy, HL Papers, S. C. Hist. Soc.; addressed "Leverpoole"; "per *Upton,* Capt. Maxwell." This letter was copied by HL.

TO RICHARD HEATLY[5]

[Charles Town] 4th October 1763

Sir,

Your favour of the 13th July to the late House of Austin, Laurens, & Appleby is in my hands & I have receiv'd the Wine therein

---

[3] *HL Papers,* I, 204n.
[4] The clerk was Benjamin Perdriau, Jr.
[5] A London wine merchant with Oporto connections.

mention'd per the *Prince of Wales,* Capt. Brown.[6] You could scarcely have fallen upon a more unlucky article for the Carolina Market than Wine. This is almost always the case as many Gentlemen on your side the Water can witness, but it is rather worse now than I have known it (I mean the Market) to be for 15 or 20 Years past. We have lately had no less than 1,250 pipes of Madera & Canary Wines fairly imported besides no small quantity from Lisbon, &Ca., which supplies the demand of purchasers tho it makes no appearance at the Custom House.[7] Some hundred pipes of Madera, Vidonia, & low Clarret have been from day to day selling at public Auction where the former went from £110 to £135, the Vidonia from £75 to £90 per Pipe at which rates I am sure no gain can result to the Owners. This Account will give you no room to hope for a profit upon your own adventure, nor indeed can I flatter you with a tolerable prospect, but this you may depend on, that I shall do all in my power to make the best of a bad Market & that as soon as possible I will convert the produce of your goods into a firm Bill of Exchange as you direct & remit it to you.

I am glad to find that the House at Oporto[8] have made some payment to Mr. Cowles on Account of my late partner Austin & myself. The uncommon delay of that remittance has given me much concern & I believe hinder'd a correspondence, as I hate to keep one alive merely with dunning Letters.

We have a very large Crop of Rice now pretty well secur'd & out of danger. It must be carried off but where shall We find Markets for it? Our Crops of Indigo are also very good & I am of opinion that we shall export the ensuing Year near twice as much as we did the last.[9] We generally account the Era of our Crops in this country from November to November. Please to return my respects to Mr. Croft[1]

---

[6] The ship *Prince of Wales,* John Brown, arrived from London on Sept. 23 and sailed for London on Jan. 25. *Gazette,* Sept. 24, 1763, Jan. 28, 1764.

[7] This is an admission that some wines were smuggled into Charleston.

[8] Thompson, Croft, & Mitchell of Oporto. *HL Papers,* II, 23n, 86n.

[9] 103,671 barrels of rice were exported from Charleston in the period from Jan. 5, 1763 to Jan. 5, 1764; 110,216 barrels of rice in the period from Jan. 5, 1764 to Jan. 5, 1765. The respective figures for indigo during these two periods were 438,908 pounds and 529,079 pounds. Lewis C. Gray, *History of Agriculture in the Southern United States to 1860* (2 vols.: Gloucester, Mass., 1958), II, 1022, 1024.

[1] Thomas Croft, one of the partners in the firm of Thompson, Croft, & Mitchell of Oporto. *HL Papers,* II, 86n, 135.

& be assur'd that I shall always be glad to serve him & yourself, who am with great respect—

SOURCE: Letterbook copy, HL Papers, S. C. Hist. Soc.; addressed "at Thomas Croft, Esquire, London"; "per *Adventure,* Capt. Headlam."

TO THOMAS BOWREY

[Charles Town] 15 October 1763

Sir,

Agreeable to the advices that I have transmitted to you under the 5 August & 22d Ulto. I have Loaden the Brigantine *Portland,* Capt. Higgins, for Basseterre in St. Christophers with Lumber & ten Barrels of Rice on Account of Augustus & John Boyd, Esquires, consigned to you as per Bill of Loading inclosed & the annexed Invoice.

I was ordered to cause a certain number of pieces of Timber to be marked AB & gave directions to have the same carefully perform'd by a Carpenter whom I employed to attend particularly to the quality of the Pine as well as to the Stowage made in the Vessel but by some means or other that part is very ill done. I am told by him that there is a much greater quantity marked than was ordered & that he can't tell exactly which they are, the mistake arising first from the officiousness of the person that supplied this Lumber who without being desired marked a great many pieces before the Carpenter discovered it & those were stowed away so there could be no reform without unloading the whole. I here inclose an Account of what should have been marked. If you find so many pieces in the Cargo marked all will be well & the purpose answered. The rest may go into the common heap. I have never known a Cargo of Lumber to conform precisely to order. There are necessarily so many ignorant or careless hands employed that it is next to impossible to succeed therein. But in the present case my disappointment is the greater because I had taken uncommon pains. However I hope you will find enough to answer the uses intended for Mr. A. B.[2] & then the blunders which have been made will be insignificant.

P.S. As the Freight is to be paid here you will attend to the delivery of the whole quantity inserted in the Bill of Loading.

---

[2] Augustus Boyd of London.

SOURCE: Letterbook copy, HL Papers, S. C. Hist. Soc.; addressed "at Basseterre in St. Christophers & in his absence to Mr. Nicholas Dromgole"; "per Capt. Higgins." This letter was copied by HL.

TO COWLES & HARFORD

[Charles Town] 15th October 1763

My last to you was 19th Ulto. per the *Susanna*, Green, & a Copy thereof went per Capt. Watts[3] since which I have not been able to write many Letters to Europe, prevented by attention to business out of doors & to some of a more serious nature within, to wit, much sickness in my family. I have had of my Children & Servants from four to seven down for some Weeks past & particularly my Clerk which obliges me to go through almost every thing with my own hands, but thank God I have lost only one (a fine Young Man bought of Capt. Condon)[4] & circumstances begin to mend a little under my own roof. The Town & Country has been & is still very sickly & many have died of various disorders which pass here under the common term of Fall Fevers. I say so much because I am conscious of delinquency on my part toward some of my Friends & as sure that you will excuse me to them if occasions offer.

Your Brigantine *Favourite,* Capt. Brownett, arriv'd this evening & brought me your esteemed favour of the 25 July continued to the 2d August.[5] I shall pay due regard to your orders respecting the dispatch & return of that Vessel & my endeavour for your Interest therein shall not be wanting.

The Captain according to custom has Entered minutes of a protest[6] apprehensive of or to guard against damage in his Cargo by a leak which opened after he got to Sea but from his own Account I hope his caution will prove to have been unnecessary.

We have now a very large Crop of Rice secured but there will be rather too many Vessels waiting for it & the Planters talk of opening

---

[3] The ship *Active,* Richard Watts, owned by Peter Jolliffe of Poole, cleared outwards for Poole on Sept. 12. Naval Office Lists, 1757–1764, p. 134.

[4] Capt. Richard Condon of the *Gloucestershire* had sold HL "two black boys John & Bristol." *HL Papers,* III, 496, 498.

[5] The brigantine *Favourite,* Edward Brownett, owned by Cowles & Harford of Bristol, was entered inwards on Oct. 18 from Bristol with "Sundry Brittish Goods per 6 Cocketts." Naval Office Lists, 1757–1764, p. 123. See also Advertisement, Oct. 22, 1763.

[6] This instrument of protest has not been found.

the New as they have most surprisingly wound up the old Market at 50/ per Ct., but surely this cannot be.[7]

Many of my Friends about Winyaw are employed in making Pitch & I shall have the first offer of all from them & will be looking out in other quarters too.

The Crop of Indigo I am told is in general good both as to quantity & quality.

Deer Skins have lately sold at 13 to 14/ per lb. but the usual quantities have not been brought to Charles Town. I have refused some parcels on Account of the price & others because of their foulness.

I shall do every thing that you would desire me to do in order to keep your old Friends steady, but some will fall off & may be, return again. The Carolina business is of such a nature that I presume to think it is not in every Man's power to transact it in Bristol upon as good terms as you can, taking one time with another.

I thank you for the honour you have done me in holding a part of the Ship *Flora*. I hope this connexion will give mutual satisfaction. Capt. Courtin will of course communicate to you all that I have wrote to him which indeed is not very important & you will be pleased to make any alterations that shall appear to be necessary. I had deposited more than a sufficient fund in London for the whole of that Ship which made me take the Liberty that I lately did of drawing upon you.

As tis now late & I must Copy this twice over to night permit me to conclude with assurances that I remain with true respect, Gentlemen, &ca., &ca.—

---

[7] The price of rice at Charleston fluctuated between 40 and 60 shillings per hundred weight between Sept. 1763 and June 1766.

	1763	1764	1765	1766
Jan.	37.5	45.0	40.0	50.0
Feb.	37.5	45.0	40.0	50.0
Mar.	40.0	40.0	40.0	55.0
Apr.	40.0	41.7	40.0	57.5
May	40.0	43.3	40.0	60.0
June	40.0	45.0	47.5	60.0
July	57.5	43.8	45.0	60.0
Aug.	50.0	42.5	47.5	60.0
Sept.	50.0	41.2	50.0	65.0
Oct.	50.0	40.0	50.0	62.5
Nov.	50.0	50.0	50.0	60.0
Dec.	50.0	40.0	50.0	50.0

Cole, *Wholesale Commodity Prices*, pp. 49, 51, 53, 54.

37674 78

SOURCE: Letterbook copy, HL Papers, S. C. Hist. Soc.; addressed "Bristol"; "per the *Adventure.* Copy per the *Benjamin's Conclusion.*" This letter was copied by HL.

T O B E N J A M I N J O H N S O N[8]

[Charles Town] 19th October 1763

Sir,

On the 8th Inst. I was favour'd with yours of the 17th Ulto. per the Brigantine *Good Intent,* Thomas Hardy, Master[9] inclosing Invoice & Bill of loading for Twenty Hogsheads Rum & seventeen Hogsheads of Melasses, & I am sorry to inform you that the whole is come to hand in exceeding bad order. The Hogsheads are the worst I have seen particularly those with Melasses are so bad that they can hardly be made to bear their own weight & to add to this bad circumstance you have sent that article to the worst market on the Continent. We have no distillers in this Country & the Little demand for Treacle in private families is chiefly supplied by our Sugar Bakers.[1] I have endeavour'd to sell it to some of the Rhode Island Shippers but they wont give above 5/ per Gallon. Some few Hogsheads I have sold at 6/1 to 6/3 & the rest must go to Vendue where I sent two Hogsheads yesterday which were return'd because nobody would give my Limit of 6/ but it will be for your Interest to let it go even at 5/. The Quality of the Rum is good & I am concern'd to see every one of the Hogsheads in such bad order as this will compel me to precipitate the Sale or to put you to a great deal more expence to shift the whole, but you may depend upon it I shall do the most in my power to serve your Interest therein.

Now for the Vessel, Gentlemen, she is such a very crazy worn out Bark, that your Master Hardy expresses his amazement at his safe arrival at this port, & every Body that has loo'd at her are equally surpriz'd. I have endeavour'd however to comply with your orders & to get her repair'd & to that end got a Carpenter to examine her &

---

[8] Benjamin Johnson of Tortola was a Quaker and a merchant. Charles F. Jenkins, *Tortola, A Quaker Experiment of Long Ago in the Tropics* (London, 1923), p. 77.

[9] The brigantine *Good Intent,* Thomas Hardy, owned by Benjamin Johnson and Absalom Zeagers of Tortola, was entered inwards from Tortola on Oct. 10 with a cargo of 20 hogsheads of rum and 17 hogsheads of molasses. Naval Office Lists, 1757–1764, p. 123.

[1] A sugar baker was a sugar refiner. *OED.*

make an estimate of the Cost to make her Seaworthy. His report to me was that he would not undertake her for that she was absolutely good for nothing. I then caused a Survey to be made by two Workmen & two Ship-Masters & their report in writing is that she is utterly unfit for Sea & the Carpenters add that to repair her would cost Three Thousand pounds a price which she will not be half worth when finish'd. I have since that had two other Carpenters to search her over again & they declare to the same effect. Therefore I must give up all thoughts of repairing her since it is evident that it would run you to a vast unnecessary expence. If it should be sloven'd over no body would venture in her nor would any body Insure upon her. If the work is done effectually the delay & expence will be more than equal to building a New Vessel & you will have but a piece of botch'd work at last. To lay her by for your further orders would be attended with some expence & lessen the Value of the hulk & endanger the Sails to damage by Rats, &ca. Upon the whole therefore by the advice of Capt. Hardy, Mr. Clarkson[2] who is well known to Mr. Zeagers,[3] & of several Gentlemen here of good judgement & undoubted integrity as well as from a full conviction in my own mind that it will be for your Interest & advantage I have determin'd to sell the whole. I wish you may approve of this resolution & in my next you shall be inform'd of what I shall do in consequence thereof. Meantime I am with great regard, &ca.—

SOURCE: Letterbook copy, HL Papers, S. C. Hist. Soc.; addressed "Tortola. Directed to Messrs. B. J. & Co., Owners of the Brigantine *Good Intent*"; "to the care of Smith & Baillie per Barker."

TO SMITH & BAILLIES

[Charles Town] 19th October 1763

Gentlemen,

My last trouble was under the 2d Ulto. per Capt. Stovell & Capt. Williams to which please to be refer'd. I Charter'd this Bearer the Brigantine *Nicholas & Mary*, Thomas Barker, Master with intent to Load her on our joint Account agreeable to the plan you propos'd

---

[2] Anthony Clarkson, *HL Papers*, III, 32n.

[3] Absalom Zeagers had two daughters. Rebecca in 1748 became the second wife of John Pickering, lieutenant governor of Tortola. Dorcas in 1757 married William Thornton. Charles F. Jenkins, *Tortola, A Quaker Experiment of Long Ago in the Tropics* (London, 1923), pp. 42–44, 75–76.

& the Freight that I was to pay including 2/3ds port Charges Amounting to about £312 your Currency for the whole I thought was cheap & low enough but finding it utterly impracticable to get good Pork in time & also very difficult to obtain a sufficient quantity of New best or very good old Rice I have been induced to Let out a part of the said Vessel & to load on her 95 Barrels & 4 half Barrels Rice, 104 Barrels of Corn & pease, 15,600 Cypress Shingles, & 328 Inch pine Boards as per Invoice & Bill of Loading here inclosed Amounting to £2,184.5.6 one half of which I charge to your Account & shall in Twenty or thirty days time reimburse myself for the same by a draught on Messrs. Augustus & John Boyd as you direct.[4] One quarter of the Net proceeds you will pass to the Credit of Mr. Robert Smyth of this place, Merchant[5] who hired me the Vessel & insisted upon being so much Interested in whatever I should load in her & the remaining Quarter to my Credit which you will be pleas'd to remit to me in Rum when you are in Cash. You will find every article good in its kind & I have purchas'd the whole payable on demand & for Cash without which the best goods cannot be procured.

Now, Gentlemen, as this Cargo does not exactly conform to your order in the respective articles (Pork being omitted) nor come near to it in point of time you have a right, unless in the mean while you have given me discretionary orders in answer to mine of the 25th August, to reject the concern & sell 3/4ths on my Account to which I shall chearfully acquiesce altho I have been wholly induced to embark under your orders & hoping that the adventure will prove beneficial to you, & I was encouraged to it too by meeting with a parcel of exceeding good old Corn which must be a good deal ahead of the New & appear better at your Market than any that will be there at

---

[4] The brigantine *Nicholas & Mary*, Thomas Barker, was cleared outwards on Oct. 17 for St. Christophers with 233 barrels of rice, 35 half barrels of rice, 800 bushels of corn and peas, 5,700 feet of lumber, 34 hogsheads and barrels of lime, 15,000 shingles, and 328 pine boards. Naval Office Lists, 1757–1764, p. 135.

[5] Robert Smyth had been the partner of Edward Newman who was buried Oct. 7, 1761. Judgment Rolls, 1763, No. 162A, S. C. Archives; *Register of St. Philip's Parish, 1754–1810,* p. 299. Robert Smyth and Thomas Shirley were executors of Edward Newman's will. "Will of Edward Newman," dated Oct. 6, 1761, proved Oct. 16, 1761, Charleston County Wills, IX, Book A (1760–1767), 168, S. C. Archives. Robert Smyth and Thomas Farr, Jr., announced a new partnership in the *Gazette,* Nov. 5, 1763. Smith & Farr imported 5 cargoes of slaves, 1764–1765. *SCHM,* LXV (1964), 208. The partnership was dissolved in June 1765. *General Gazette,* July 3, 1765. In 1775 Smyth was involved in one of the famous episodes of the Revolution in S. C. David H. Villers, "The Smyth Horses Affair and the Association," *SCHM,* LXX (1969), 137–148.

its arrival & in such case if I have pass'd Bills on your Account for your now one Moiety I shall order Mrs. Sarah Nickleson & Company my friends to repay the same to Messrs. Boyd together with Interest thereon.

I wish I could have persuaded Capt. Barker to have made a Corn room it would have been a means of saving us some Freight but he made many objections & upon the whole did not care to do it. If I meet with an hundred Barrels of good Pork by & by I shall probably Ship them to you & maybe make up a small Cargo on our joint Account in a Month or six weeks.

Our Crop of Rice is now secur'd & will be the largest ever made here & come early to Market.[6] I expect some in a fortnight but the old being clean carried off the price will break high perhaps 50/ but I think tis impossible to hold it there for we have dismal advices of the Sale in all the European Markets. Rum & Sugar are too plenty & very low with us. The Sale of Negroes has been beyond all former Years. A fine Cargo of Gambia but chiefly Men lately averaged £36 Sterling & the remittances at 3, 6, & 9 Months all in the Bottom.[7] This cannot be expected every day but I do believe that great prices will continue to be given even all the ensuing Winter & until the importation shall become excessive, which may probably be the case early in Next Summer from this great encouragement. I remain, &ca.—

Exchange 714 to 721 per Cent.

P.S. If tis in your power to assist Capt. Barker with any Freight upon his return to this Port & for such other favours as you shall be pleas'd to shew to him I shall be obliged to you. I have found him to be a very honest & good natured Man during his abode here.

SOURCE: Letterbook copy, HL Papers, S. C. Hist. Soc.; addressed "St. Christophers"; "per Barker."

---

[6] This was the largest crop produced in South Carolina up to this date. Lewis C. Gray, *History of Agriculture in the Southern United States to 1860* (2 vols.: Gloucester, Mass., 1958), II, 1021–1022.
[7] Middleton, Liston, & Hope sold 200 slaves from Gambia on Sept. 27. *Gazette,* Sept. 24, 1763. This was the seventh and last cargo of slaves sold during 1763. Donnan, *Documents Illustrative of the Slave Trade,* IV, 381.

TO COWLES & HARFORD

[Charles Town] 20th October 1763

Gentlemen,

I advis'd you the 15th Inst. of the arrival of your Brigantine *Favorite* & as the Vessel by which I wrote is still detain'd by cross Winds I cannot help adding two circumstances which I know must give you pleasure. First the Leak sprung at Sea which Capt. Brownet was afraid would occasion the trouble & expence of heaving down is happily discovered & in all probability will be effectually stoped without any other than the expence of a Little Caulking or perhaps a trenail[8] may do the business, & the second is that the Cargo is now almost all deliver'd & what remains on board is in sight & will be out tomorrow. The whole is free from damage except one Bale to Messrs. Downes & Jones.[9]

I have purchased some Turpentine & some Tar & shall endeavour to procure Pitch as speedily as possible. There is not the least prospect of obtaining Freight at near your Limit & therefore I must go on to Load on the best terms I can upon your own Account but I shall get as much Indigo & Skins as possible on Freight. I remain—

SOURCE: Letterbook copy, HL Papers, S. C. Hist. Soc.; addressed "Bristol"; "per the *Adventure*."

ADVERTISEMENT

October 22, 1763

Just arrived in exceeding good order, and landed from on board the Brigantine Favorite, *Capt.* Brownett, *from* BRISTOL, *and to be sold at any time, before I remove from the house in which I now dwell, upon as good terms as such goods can in general be imported.* ABOUT fourteen bales of white NEGRO CLOTH, some of which is the best kind; the prices taking a whole bale are, 6s.9d., 7s., 8s.9d., 9s.6d., 9s.9d. per yard.—The whole or part of the said house, with convenient

---

[8] A treenail was "a cylindrical pin of hard wood used in fastening timbers together, especially in ship building and other work where the materials are exposed to the action of water." *OED.*

[9] Richard Downes and Evan Jones. *HL Papers,* III, 33n.

back stores, to be lett, and may be enter'd upon, before the first of *December* next.

Enquire of

HENRY LAURENS

ALSO a few bales of DUFFIL blanketing, to be sold very cheap.

SOURCE: Printed in *Gazette,* Oct. 22, 1763.

TO MEYLER & HALL[1]

[Charles Town] 29th October 1763

Gentlemen,

Your favour of the 13th August is just come to hand, & at present Mr. Laurens is out of Town[2] but on his return which will be in a few days, your orders & directions will be Strictly observed and Comply'd with. I am for that Gentleman—

SOURCE: Letterbook copy, HL Papers, S. C. Hist. Soc.; addressed "Jamaica"; "per the Sloop *Pandora,* Capt. Hague." This letter was written by HL's clerk.

ADVERTISEMENT

October 29, 1763

TO BE SOLD at public vendue, the 28th of November 1763. ALL the effects of MR. JOHN ASLINE Merchant, deceased,[3] amongst

---

[1] Jeremiah Meyler and Charles Hall. *HL Papers,* II, 4n.

[2] HL may have been at Mepkin supervising the final stages of the harvest.

[3] When John Asline wrote his will in 1759 in Lincoln, Eng., he was about "to Depart on a Voyage to the Island of Jamaica." In Sept. 1763 he was importing goods to sell at Richard Baker's shop in Bedon's Alley in Charleston. *Gazette,* Sept. 10, 1763. Before his death, Asline had requested HL and Thomas Legare to manage his property in South Carolina. As Asline's will was not discovered at the time of his death, Laurens and Legare were appointed on Oct. 22, 1763, administrators of his estate. Asline's will was found in England and under its terms John Davies the elder of Lincoln and Thomas Marshall of Netherhall near Dorchester in England were qualified as executors. The elder Davies and Marshall sent John Davies the younger as their attorney to Charleston where Asline's will was recorded on June 28, 1765. On July 5, 1765, HL and Thomas Legare transferred to the younger Davies £11,643.12.9 currency, the balance of the estate, and obtained a release. On the same date John Davies

which, are many good and useful articles; the goods are fresh, he being but two years in trade in this province, from the arrival of his first cargo. All to whom the said JOHN ASLINE was any ways indebted, are desired to send in their demands properly attested, to

HENRY LAURENS ⎤
THOMAS LEGARE[4] ⎦ Administrators

SOURCE: Printed in *Gazette*, Oct. 29, 1763.

TO JOSEPH BROWN

[Charles Town] 5th November 1763

Dear Sir,

This Accompanies a packet that Came in Capt. Barnes[5] from London which I just open'd at one end to slip out your Bill of Loading for goods on board the *Minerva*. From that I made out an Account of Packages & gave it to Capt. Cogdell[6] who has on board his Schooner all the said goods & would have sail'd some days ago if the Wind had permitted him.

the younger signed a bond of £23,287.5.6 currency to Laurens and Legare, which bond was considered to be satisfied as long as no claims were made against Laurens and/or Legare in their former capacities as administrators of the estate of John Asline. Both the release and the bond were witnessed by William Burrows and William Roper, Jr. William Roper, Jr. swore to the signatures on July 9 before George Johnston, justice of the peace and public register who recorded both documents that date. "Will of John Asline," dated June 18, 1759, proved at Lincoln Dec. 22, 1763, recorded at Charleston June 28, 1765, Charleston County Wills, IX, Book A (1760–1767), 384–386, S. C. Archives; Miscellaneous Records, MM, Part I (1763–1767), pp. 293–299, S. C. Archives.

⁴ Thomas Legare (1732–1801), the son of Solomon Legare (1703–1774), the tanner, married Elizabeth Bassnett in 1753. "Early Generations of the Legare Family in South Carolina," *Transactions of the Huguenot Society of South Carolina*, XLVI (1941), 72–81. Thomas Legare was a Charleston factor. *A Representation of Facts*, p. 15; *Gazette*, Oct. 26, 1769. At his death in 1801 he was a planter on Johns Island. "Will of Thomas Legare," dated Sept. 9, 1789, proved March 3, 1801, Charleston County Wills, XXVIII, Book A (1800–1807), 97–103, S. C. Archives.

⁵ The ship *Minerva*, John Barnes, arrived from London on Oct. 25 and sailed for London on Feb. 5. *Gazette*, Oct. 29, 1763, Feb. 11, 1764. The *Minerva* was owned by Isaac King and Sarah Nickleson of London. Naval Office Lists, 1757–1764, p. 123.

⁶ John Cogdell was master of the schooner *Good Intent* of Georgetown. *HL Papers*, III, 531n.

I likewise send you with this another packet containing £1,500 Currency by the hands of Mr. Joseph Allston[7] which you will be so good to apply to my Credit toward purchasing Indigo on our joint Account. I observe the progress you have made by yours of the 26th & 29th Ulto. As you are a good judge of the article I have no doubt about the quality & for the prices that you have given you are upon as good terms as other folks for I find that Mr. Allston has Actually sold his at 30/ per lb.[8] Nevertheless I advise you not to be too eager for by the last Account & I have seen some from the most judicious Men Indigo was much more likely to fall than to rise & there was certainly a large quantity unsold in the first hands. Therefore I would not go beyond 25/ to 26/ for the best Copper.[9] Something exceeding

---

[7] A planter on the Waccamaw River. *HL Papers*, III, 231n.

[8] The price of indigo at Charleston varied between twenty-one shillings two pence and twenty-six shillings one pence currency per pound between Sept. 1763 and June 1766.

	1763	1764	1765	1766
Jan.	40.0	25.0	23.8	22.1
Feb.	40.0	25.2	23.8	21.9
Mar.	27.8	25.2	23.8	21.7
Apr.	27.8	25.1	23.8	21.5
May	27.8	24.9	23.8	21.2
June	27.8	24.8	23.5	21.5
July	27.2	24.6	23.3	21.8
Aug.	26.6	24.4	23.1	22.0
Sept.	26.1	24.2	22.9	22.2
Oct.	25.6	24.1	22.7	22.5
Nov.	25.0	23.9	22.5	22.5
Dec.	25.0	23.8	22.3	22.5

Exceptional indigo might command higher prices. Cole, *Wholesale Commodity Prices*, pp. 50–55.

[9] James Crokatt had described the three kinds of indigo in 1747:

"There is three different kinds of Indigo, and applied to different Uses, *viz.* that called Copper Indigo, which when broke, shines something like Copper, without being rubbed, is most in Demand in *England,* and used by all Dyers of Woollens. The Consumption of it is more than of both the other kinds; it is esteemed better or worse, the more or less it appears to shine when broke, for such as shines only when rubbed is much worse, and even of that Kind it is esteemed the more or less it shines when rubbed; and what will not shine when rubbed is of the worse kind, and inferior to the best by 1s. or 1s. 6d. the Pound.

That called Purple Indigo, looks more of a Purple Colour when broke, than the Copper-kind; but does not shine unless rubbed; it is used mostly by Foreigners, and here to mix with Starch, &c. by our Blue-makers for Sale to Families, and others who wash or whiten Linen; it is in most Demand in all Countries where Linen is made; but not in such Demand, as the Blue or Copper.

The Blue Indigo looks of a fine strong Blue Colour when broke, and if rubbed looks like polished Copper, it is always very light, and when broke seems to have a Body like Chalk; it is used mostly by Dyers of Silk, Linen, and Thread,

fine might tempt one to run a little higher in which there can be no direction given at this distance. Your judgement must have its scope & be exercised according to the subjects that lay before you.

Money is an article that grows scarcer with me than I could have expected from the large Sums that are due to me, but instead of payments I every day receive appoligies. Therefore let me intreat you to be as gentle in your demands as may be consistent with our Interest for I would rather forego a profit than be distress'd which I should certainly be if people were to call upon me twice for Money, but having engaged I shall take care that you shall suffer no distress if even borrowing can avert it.

I find several folks here are very shy & will not touch Indigo at more than 25/, & express much surprize that any body has given more, but I do not believe implicitly all that is said or pretended upon such occasions.

My plan is to Ship as much Indigo as I can on board a Vessel[1] that I have bound to Bristol by which I think there's a reasonable prospect of advantage. If that market should not be quite so good as that of London we may have it for a very triffling charge of 4/6 per Ct. transported[2] or it may be exported to a Foreign Market & the difference of charges together with the difference of Waste & pilferage between London & Bristol I believe will pay the charges of carriage or exportation. If you concur with me in opinion you will be so good as to send down all that you have on hand when the next Schooner comes this way, but indeed at all events it will be best to have it here ready for shipping, when good opportunities offer. I am in great want of Pitch & beg you to recommend all that you can to me.

Mrs. Laurens joins with me in affectionate Salutes.

SOURCE: Letterbook copy, Letter Book of Henry Laurens, Oct. 30, 1762–Sept. 10, 1766, Penn. Hist. Soc.; addressed "Geo.-Town."

Callico-Printers, and all fine Goods, and much in Use, both here, in *Germany,* and in *Holland,* and indeed will serve for all Uses in the Dying way."
[James Crokatt] *Further Observations Intended for Improving the Culture and Curing of Indigo, &c. in South-Carolina* (London, 1747), pp. 2–3.

[1] The brigantine *Favourite,* Edward Brownett.

[2] This is most probably 4/6 sterling for transporting 100 pounds of indigo from Bristol to London.

TO WILLIAM THOMPSON[3]

[Charles Town] 5th November 1763

Dear Sir,

It was not my fault that you had not a piece of Negro Cloth by Mr. Dick[4] the Last Trip for I never heard of it before your Letter of the 19th October came to hand.

I have sent you a piece of Negro Cloth & a Box of Sugar as per Bill of parcels inclosed. The Negro Cloth is the Cheapest that ever you bought & you must not be angry if the Sugar is too much for you. It is so good that I am in hopes your Neighbours will be very glad to help you off with all that you do not want. I am now in much want of good Pitch & Green Tar & I am a purchaser of good Indigo.

Please to pay my respects to Mrs. Thomson & all your good family, who am, D. Sir, &ca.—

SOURCE: Letterbook copy, Letter Book of Henry Laurens, Oct. 30, 1762–Sept. 10, 1766, Penn. Hist. Soc.; addressed "Black Mingo."

ADVERTISEMENT

November 5, 1763

For BRISTOL directly, *(And will be loaden within the month of November)* The Brigantine FAVOURITE, EDWARD BROWN-ETT, Master, LAYING at Mr. Raven's wharf.[5] For freight of Deer Skins, Indico, and other light goods, or for passage, apply to the said Master on board, or to

HENRY LAURENS.

SOURCE: Printed in *Gazette*, Nov. 5, 1763.

---

[3] Written "Thomson" in the letterbook. *HL Papers*, II, 138n.
[4] George Dick. *HL Papers*, III, 124n.
[5] This wharf may have belonged to William Raven who died in October 1765. "Will of William Raven," dated Oct. 14, 1765, proved Oct. 22, 1765, *Abstracts of Wills, 1760–1784*, p. 60.

TO ALEXANDER DAVIDSON[6]

[Charles Town] 7th November 1763

Dear Sir,

I believe you[r] Nephew[7] will tell you that I have been very ready to serve him. I have done all that he desired of me & have offered to do more if he stood in need. I think if he is as you say in your favour of the 21st Ulto. a compleat Joyner & Cabinet Maker you are going to bury him by keeping him at Black Mingo,[8] but you know best & I hope will excuse this freedom.

I was out of Town when your Cask came on shoar. Mr. Dick was very hasty in getting it filled with Rum. I hope it is very good but if the quality does not quite please you George must be responsible for his quickness when there was no necessity for so much hurry. Underneath is an Account of it.

I am in much want of Pitch such as you some times used to make. I am, &ca.—

SOURCE: Letterbook copy, Letter Book of Henry Laurens, Oct. 30, 1762–Sept. 10, 1766, Penn. Hist. Soc.; addressed "Black Mingo."

TO JOHN TARLETON[9]

[Charles Town] 9th November 1763

Sir,

The last trouble I gave you was on the 18th August per the *Lever*, Capt. Briggs,[1] duplicate per Capt. Maxwell[2] to which please

---

[6] *HL Papers*, III, 143n.

[7] Alexander Davidson, planter of Craven County, named his nephew Robert Davidson as an executor of his estate. "Will of Alexander Davidson," dated Nov. 15, 1763, proved July 14, 1766, Charleston County Wills, x, Book B (1760–1767), 778–780, S. C. Archives. Alexander Davidson had been a carpenter in the 1740's and 1750's; Robert Davidson later followed his trade as carpenter in the parish, 1769–1775. *Register Book for the Parish Prince Frederick Winyaw*, pp. 88, 110, 196, 199, 214, 225.

[8] Black Mingo Creek flowed into Black River which flowed into Winyah Bay at Georgetown. During the Revolution Francis Marion drew many of his soldiers from among the producers of indigo and naval stores along Black Mingo Creek. Rogers, *History of Georgetown County*, pp. 134, 145, 150, 170.

[9] *HL Papers*, III, 26n.

[1] The ship *Liver*, William Briggs, owned by Joseph and Jonathan Brooks of Liverpool, was cleared outwards for Liverpool on Aug. 13. Naval Office Lists, 1757–1764, p. 134.

[2] The ship *Upton*, Hugh Maxwell, was cleared outwards for Liverpool on Sept. 26. Naval Office Lists, 1757–1764, p. 134. The *Upton* had brought 370 slaves from Angola who were advertised for sale on Aug. 11 by Brailsford & Chapman. *Gazette*, Aug. 6, 1763.

to be refer'd. I am now to advise you of the arrival of your Brigantine *Elizabeth*, Capt. Thornton,[3] in Ballast & that I have this day receiv'd your favour of the 18th April with an order to load the said Brigantine for the West Indies which order I shall comply with as nearly as possible & hope to give the Vessel good dispatch so as to get her away in about a Month. The Cargo shall be of the best in Quality & I shall acquaint you with my proceedings as I go forward.

Rice begins to come to Market. The first parcel of 31 Barrels sold so high as 50/ per Ct. but as the Crop is undoubtedly a large one I think that this price cannot be supported. However I shall not keep your Brigantine (as you require dispatch) for trifling considerations.

I have engaged 1,000 Bushels of Corn at 12/6 & have the promise of a sufficient quantity of Pease & Pork but the latter is an article in which I must be most careful & most likely to suffer disappoint. I am in treaty for Scantling, Staves, & Shingles. Nothing shall be Wanting on my part to promote your Interest in the present concern & on all occasions to testify that I am with great regard, &ca.—

SOURCE: Letterbook copy, HL Papers, S. C. Hist. Soc.; addressed "Liverpoole"; "per *Adventure* or the *Benjamin's Conclusion,* Transport. Copy per the *Success,* Man of War."

TO JOHN ETTWEIN[4]

Charles Town, 10 November 1763

Reverend Sir,

I find my self indebted for your favours of the 6th August & 26th ult. which came as very acceptable presents to me because your correspondence is truly agreeable & I must beg your pardon for delaying so long to acknowledge the first.

I remark that you have advised your Brethren in Germany if any of them intend to join you at Wachovia to make their route thro Charles Town & also that you have mentioned my name to them. Your advice is certainly very good. They will make the easiest & least expensive passage by the way that you have marked out and should

---

[3] The brigantine *Elizabeth*, Richard Thornton, owned by John Tarleton and James Brown of Liverpool, was entered inwards on Nov. 9 from Grenada. *Naval Office Lists,* 1757–1764, p. 123.

[4] Spelled "Edwin" in the letterbook. John Ettwein was the leader of the Moravians in N. C. *HL Papers,* III, 56n.

any of them arrive here and apply to me you may be assured that I shall render them all the good offices in my power & likewise use my best endeavours to facilitate their journey to Bethabara. That place Bethabara I often think of with great affection and as often wish for the prosperity of those who dwell in it.[5]

You talk of the peace in Europe as a subject that afforded you great satisfaction, but that your Joy had felt some alloy by the new defection of our Savage Neighbours upon this Continent.[6] The general Peace was an event most desirable to every good Man & for my own part I have all along thought that the terms upon which it is established are honourable & advantageous to Great Britain, but some people in that Kingdom affect to be highly offended by it & these Men thro their incessant Labours have embroiled the whole Nation in domestic quarrels, which are more pernicious to the state & therefore to be dreaded more than any dispute with a Foreign power. You will see too much of these Home contentions in the English prints[7] of which Mr. Gammeron[8] carries a good many.

As to the present Indian War to the Northward, I do believe

---

[5] Laurens had visited Bethabara in January 1761 on his recruiting expedition to North Carolina. *HL Papers,* III, 56. The Bethabara Diary had the following entry for Dec. 8, 1763: "We were made happy by the unexpected arrival of letters from Germany, together with the Text Book for 1764. The package was started by Br. Broderson on Sept. 9th of this year; was forwarded four weeks later from London on the *Hope* to Mr. Nicholson in Charlestown; he sent it to Mr. Kirshaw at Pinetree; he to Mr. Mitchell at Salisbury and he sent it on by our neighbor, Mr. Phelps. We are delighted that this first package direct from Germany by way of Charlestown has come safely, and hope hereafter we may hear more quickly this way than through Bethlehem." *Records of the Moravians in North Carolina,* I, 277.

[6] Pontiac's Rebellion began May 1763 with the siege of Detroit. By June 21 every post in the Great Lakes region to the west of Niagara had fallen except Fort Detroit. Fort Pitt had also been besieged, and the frontier settlements of Pennsylvania plundered. Gipson, *The Triumphant Empire,* pp. 94–110.

[7] HL probably agreed with the London merchants who commended the King on May 18, 1763 for securing "a treaty of peace, every where marked with moderation and equity." In spite of the peace there had been a savage attack upon the Earl of Bute led by the *North Briton* and taken up by newspapers and pamphleteers for obtaining Canada and Florida while giving back Guadeloupe and Cuba to the French and Spaniards. Bute had resigned on April 8, 1763. Gipson, *The Triumphant Empire,* pp. 22–25.

[8] Abraham von Gammern. *HL Papers,* III, 374n. The Bethabara Diary had the following entry for Nov. 21, 1763: "Last night Br. Gammern returned from Charlestown. He had acquainted himself with the circumstances of our trade there, and had met the merchants." *Records of the Moravians in North Carolina,* I, 277. Among the items carried to Bethabara were ten kegs of red lead which HL sold to Abraham von Gammern on Nov. 9, 1763. HL to Devonsheir & Reeve, Sept. 12, 1764.

it springs from our own avarice & misconduct but tho we (Christians) shall be pretty well scourged, yet in the end the Natives must submit & become less formidable than they have heretofore been, since it is certain that they must suffer most by a contest with an Enemy who have continual resources while they themselves have none. Thank God the flame hath not reached these Southern borders & altho the Creek Indians have been intolerably insolent, I hope the measures to be pursued at the present Congress will be productive of at least this happy effect to keep them quiet till the Northern Tribes are reduced to a necessity of begging for Peace.[9] Mean time the poor back settlers of Virginia, &ca., are in the most piteous circumstances & I frequently reflect upon Mr. Lash's long journey & wish to hear of his safe arrival in Pensilvania.[1]

Those Lands which were lately run out on the South side of Altamaha by the people of this Colony may be still subjected to new Grants for it seems the measures of the Ministry were not a Little disconcerted by those that were taken in our Council & it is even said that an act of Parliament will be passed to vacate all the grants made by Governor Boone, but this appears to me to be a whisper from Interested persons & at the same time so futile that I give no Ear to it; and with respect to our new acquisitions more remote I can learn very little of them save only that some private Juntos have here & there made large purchases from the late French & Spanish proprietors in which it is to be feared many frauds will be attempted & much confusion ensue.[2]

---

[9] Governors Francis Fauquier of Virginia, Arthur Dobbs of North Carolina, Thomas Boone of S. C., and James Wright of Georgia, with John Stuart, the Superintendent of Indian Affairs for the Southern District, met the chiefs of the Chickasaw, Choctaw, Creek, Cherokee, and Catawba Indians at Augusta, Georgia, early in November and signed a treaty on Nov. 10. "Journal of the Proceedings of the Southern Congress from the Arrival of the several Governors at Charles Town, South Carolina, on 1st October to their Return to the same Place &ca. the 21st November 1763," BPRO, xxx (1764–1765), 16–123, S. C. Archives; John Richard Alden, *John Stuart and the Southern Colonial Frontier* (Ann Arbor, Mich., 1944), pp. 176–191. The Upper Creeks were nervous, and the Lower Creeks had to be inveigled to attend the conference at Augusta. Corkran, *Creek Frontier*, pp. 237–241. The *Gazette*, Nov. 12, 1763, reported that the Creeks were delaying the conference; the *Gazette*, Nov. 19, 1763, stated that the Creeks were the "least friendly" at Augusta.

[1] Jacob Lash (Loesch) was making a trip to Pennsylvania. *HL Papers*, iii, 76n. He returned safely to Bethabara on Dec. 23. *Records of the Moravians in North Carolina*, i, 278.

[2] John Gordon, the former partner of John McQueen and also of Grey Elliott, was the principal local speculator. He with Jesse Fish and others pur-

I heartily thank you for your tender expressions of good will towards my family. Methinks our religious sentiments are so little different & I believe our endeavours are so much the same that I am full of an humble confidence that after we have passed thro this Vale of Sin & misery we shall enjoy everlasting communion in the presence of the one ever blessed & adorable God, Father, Son, & Spirit. These are my most comfortable thoughts. Amen!

I have benefited from this short acquaintance with your Mr. Vangammeron & wish he had enabled me to have been more serviceable to him in his affairs, but I have told him frankly that he may at all times lay his commands upon me & I shall strive by some means or other to answer his expectations. I perceive that he is very shrewd & understanding in the business of Merchandize. He was wise to come to town himself & I am persuaded he will always give a good account of his Stewardship. Your family I see have not escaped those Fevers which have been more general in Carolina than I have ever known in former Years; scarcely an House here has been exempted from this late visitation & many people especially young Folks have been carried to the Grave.[3] I have had from five to seven persons sick under my own roof for near two Months but now as the Cold weather sets in all are grown well again except one Young Negro Man that died. Let me now conclude, my Dear Sir, with the most respectful salutes to you & yours assuring you that I remain with true Love and esteem, your most Obedient Servant—   Henry Laurens

---

chased during September and October "several hundred thousand acres" for £10,000 sterling from the departing Spaniards. The most extensive tract was purchased on Oct. 20, 1763, from Juan Chrystomo for £770 sterling. The deeds were proved in St. Augustine before Maj. Francis Ogilvie, the commanding officer, for want of a proper civil official. Gov. James Grant, who would never recognize and record the grants, told Gordon that he must apply to His Majesty for relief. *The Case of Mr. John Gordon with respect to the Title to certain Lands in East Florida, purchased of His Catholick Majesty's subjects by him and Mr. Jesse Fish, for themselves and others His Brittanic Majesty's subjects; in conformity to the twentieth article of the last definitive treaty of peace* (London, 1772). When John Gordon wrote his will on July 28, 1774, he stated that he was then "entitled to certain lands in the province of East Florida in North America by virtue of divers conveyances made to me and Jesse Fish of St. Augustine by the several Spanish owners of whom we purchased the same under the sanction of the treaty of peace of 1763." *SCHM,* IV (1903), 286–287. Gipson, who believed that Gordon had a good case under article twenty of the Peace of Paris, stated that the Board of Trade did recommend reimbursement in 1775. Gipson, *The Triumphant Empire,* pp. 183–189.

[3] Five children were buried in September and seven in October by St. Philip's Church alone. *Register of St. Philip's Parish, 1754–1810,* pp. 304–305.

SOURCE: ALS, Moravian Archives, Winston-Salem, N. C.; addressed "To the Reverend Mr. John Edwin." Letterbook copy, Letter Book of Henry Laurens, Oct. 30, 1762–Sept. 10, 1766, Penn. Hist. Soc.; addressed "Bethabara, North Carolina."

TO JOSEPH BROWN

[Charles Town] 12th November 1763

Dear Sir,

You have here inclos'd a Letter per Harbison.[4] Muir[5] is just by. If you have any Letters in him & they come to hand before Mr. Dubourdieu[6] departs they shall be put under this cover.

Buy not a pound of Indigo more at a higher price than 22/ for the very best Copper until you hear more from me. Some Accounts by Passengers[7] from on board Muir announce distruction to the Shippers of last Years Growth whose Indigo remain'd unsold of which they say there was a Great very Great quantity. Slow sale or rather no demand at 3/3 per best.[8]

Remember pitch for my Vessel now Idle. I am, &ca.—

[*P.S.*] Here's one Letter per Capt. Muir.

SOURCE: Letterbook copy, Letter Book of Henry Laurens, Oct. 30, 1762–Sept. 10, 1766, Penn. Hist. Soc.; addressed "Geo. Town."

TO WILLING, MORRIS & CO.[9]

[Charles Town] 12 November 1763

Put under a blank cover Account Sale of 10 Casks Linseed Oil, & put into the hands of Capt. Thomas Hardy for the delivery.

SOURCE: Letterbook copy, HL Papers, S. C. Hist. Soc.; addressed "Philadelphia"; "per Capt. Mason."

---

[4] The snow *True Britton,* Thomas Harbison, arrived from Bristol on Nov. 10. *Gazette,* Nov. 12, 1763.

[5] The ship *Little-Carpenter,* William Muir, arrived from London on Nov. 10. *Gazette,* Nov. 12, 1763.

[6] Joseph Dubourdieu was clerk of the Winyah Indigo Society. Rogers, *History of Georgetown County,* pp. 37, 88, 92.

[7] Sampson Neyle, Isaac Holmes, Arthur Peronneau, and James Gordon were among the merchants returning. *Gazette,* Nov. 12, 1763.

[8] This was the price in sterling for the best indigo sold in England.

[9] *HL Papers, 1,* 249n.

TO HENRY BRIGHT[1]

[Charles Town] 12th November 1763

Sir,

Your esteemed favour of the 6th March never reached me until the 15th of the past Month by Capt. Brownett which I am sorry for as the want of earlier permission from you after the repeated offers of my service had prevented my waiting on you so often as I should have done with advices of this Market.

Our Crop of Rice is now secured, is certainly very large, & begins to come to Town but the price demanded & at which the first hundred Barrels sold, Vizt. 50/ per Ct., is exhorbitant & must distress the waiting Ships of which there are too many for the times. No Freight for Europe yet engaged but I do believe that Ships may be had at 50/ for Holland. This is too low but as the Alarm is given so early in the Season a remedy may be found by people whose Vessels are not already on their passage. Naval Stores are at present very scarce but many hands are employ'd upon Kilns & we shall soon have both pitch & Tar tho at high prices. The article of Indigo will make a considerable figure in our exports the ensuing Year. Such parcels as are already sold have brought 27/6 to 30/ per lb., I mean for the best. These prices I also think too high & from the advices we have now receiv'd from London am of opinion that people will be more wary in their purchases hence forward.

The Season for Negro Sales is over in the present Year. The last Sales were beyond any former, Vizt. Angola & Windward Coasts averaged from £32.10/ to £34, & one Cargo of Gambia did really sell so high as £36.9/ round, but they were chiefly grown, & the prosperity of our planters will in all probability open the next season as well as the late one has been concluded.[2] I shall obey your orders in Shipping the old Guns when an opportunity offers & upon all occasions testify that I am with great regard, &ca.—

Exchange 721 per Cent.

SOURCE: Letterbook copy, HL Papers, S. C. Hist. Soc.; addressed "Esquire. Bristol"; "per Capt. Seagers."

---

[1] *HL Papers*, I, 350n.

[2] Brailsford & Chapman had sold 200 slaves from the Windward Coast on June 10 and 370 slaves from Angola on Aug. 11. Middleton, Liston, & Hope had sold 200 slaves from Gambia on Sept. 27. These were the largest of the seven cargoes sold during the year. Donnan, *Documents Illustrative of the Slave Trade*, IV, 381.

TO COWLES & HARFORD

[Charles Town] 12th November 1763

Gentlemen,

Since the arrival of your Brigantine *Favourite* I wrote to you the 15th Ulto. per the *Adventure & Benjamin's Conclusion*[3] & again on the 20th per the former to which please to be refer'd. That Brigantine has now on board near 200 Barrels of Pitch & Tar but at the exhorbitant rates of 75/ per barrel for the former & 50/ for Tar. I do assure you that £4 was bid for the Pitch after I had bought by the Gentlemen who load this Billander.[4] I found it necessary to secure something for a begining to keep the Vessel on her legs & also to maintain that preference which has been given to me for Naval Stores & in order to shun a pernicious clashing with those Gentlemen I have spared them upward of 160 Barrels of Turpentine & some Pitch & Tar to complete their Cargo which hath been a very long time collecting. Now I must unavoidably remain Idle for sometime 'till more Naval Stores come down & perhaps the prices may be more moderate especially as Rice begins to appear at Market. The first 100 Barrels of this article came into my hands & was catch'd up in an instant at 50/ per Ct. but this is a price that cannot be afforded for the European Trade & therefore I think cannot be supported after the demand for a few Northward & West India Barks is supplied.

I am using my utmost endeavours to secure some Skins & Indigo upon Freight & hope to obtain a little. As to the other goods no body will come near to your limits. One Vessel here of 1,100 Barrels Rice burthen will sail in two or three days with a load of Pine & other Lumber at a Freight of only £400 Sterling for the whole & I do believe that Vessel might be had this day at 50/ for Holland. I have been offer'd one at that rate for Portugal. These are very unpleasing

---

[3] The ship *Adventure*, Thomas Headlam, was "near loaden" for London in the middle of October. *Gazette*, Oct. 15, 1763. The ship *Benjamin's Conclusion*, Richard Ware, arrived from St. Augustine on Sept. 16 and sailed for London on Oct. 25. *Gazette*, Sept. 17, Oct. 29, 1763. These two ships were neither entered nor cleared as they were transports. When the *Albemarle* had been directed to Pensacola as a transport in August 1763, the naval officer made the following notation in place of the usual information for a clearance: "This ship was taken up in the Transport Service." Naval Office Lists, 1757–1764, p. 122.

[4] The bilander *Joseph*, James Seager, was cleared outwards on Nov. 10 for Bristol with a cargo of 98 barrels of rice, 50 barrels of pitch, 493 barrels of tar, 205 barrels of turpentine, 6 hogsheads of deerskins, 5,139 pounds of indigo, and 5,300 feet of lumber. Naval Office Lists, 1757–1764, p. 135.

advices to Gentlemen on your side of the Waters but as they go out so early in the Crop it will give a timely alarm. I shall do every thing in my power to dispatch your Vessel & tho I am sure that I shall not do so well for you as I wish to do, yet when you compare notes with other people I hope you will find that I have not been remiss. There was a Sale of Cherokee Skins this Week. The Skins were really good but for want of advices since your last discouraging Accounts I let them slip by me at about 13/10 per lb.[5] Some new Indigo goes home in this Billander, the *Joseph,* which cost 30/ per lb. I have made some purchases of the very best sort at 27/6 to 28/ & am afraid that is rather too high. Part of mine shall go on board of your Brigantine *Favourite.* Please to Insure thereon Three hundred Guineas. I shall probably have more than double that Value on board. The Duffils that you Ship'd to me per *Indian King*[6] prove to be poor stuff not worth the price you paid for them. The Plains per *Favourite* arrived too late & I am endeavouring to run them off [at] a low price just to save my own Money. Those four pieces which you say are of a new manufacture seem to be very good at the price 13d but are too narrow & being a little harsh leaves some doubt about the wear. If a bargain of 100 or 200 pieces of Irish Oznabrug should fall in your way be pleas'd to purchase & ship them on my Account. I mean something good in quality & under the common trading price. Otherwise omit it until I add some other articles which I shall have occasion to do a few days hence. I remain with true respect, &ca.—

Exchange 721 per Cent.

SOURCE: Letterbook copy, HL Papers, S. C. Hist. Soc.; addressed "Bristol"; "per the *Joseph,* Capt. Seagers. Copy per *Success,* Man of War."

---

[5] The sale had taken place on Nov. 11 "at the W[h]arf of Mr. Thomas Lamboll near the Vendue House on Charles Town Bay" with Thomas Lamboll, Thomas Shubrick, Gabriel Manigault, John Savage, and Thomas Smith, "the Directors of carrying on the Publick Indian Trade," in attendance. They had advertised on Oct. 28 "a considerable Parcel of heavy drest Deer Skins, some light Ditto and a few Beaver" for sale to the highest bidder. McDowell, *Documents relating to Indian Affairs,* pp. 533–534.

[6] The ship *Indian King,* Richard Baker, had arrived from Bristol on June 6 *Gazette,* June 11, 1763.

TO ELIAS B. DELAFONTAINE[7]

[Charles Town] 12th November 1763

Sir,

Since mine of the 19th April I have only your favour of 28th of the Same Month & that did not reach me sooner than the 4th of the last. You sent it by the Packet[8] & it lay by somewhere on the Road between New York & this place.

As the payment for the Lawns is now become due I have pressed the purchasers Messrs. Ogilvie & Forbes[9] & Messrs. Ward & Leger[1] to a speedy payment urging the great loss that you sustain by Mr. Miller[2] as a spur to me to remit what is saved without delay; people in this Country in general do not like to be dunn'd so precisely therefore some argument by way of appology was necessary & I have gone so far as to offer my help (& even to join with them if it is needful) to borrow the Amount. They have promis'd to do all in their power to comply & by some means or other I hope soon to remit you the whole or very near it, & if I fail you may be assur'd it shall not be owing to inattention. As to the poor lost Young Man, Mr. Miller, he absconded from this province some time ago leaving a Little Current

---

[7] Elias Benjamin DelaFontaine (spelled "DeLaFontain" here), general merchant of Leadenhall St., was listed as a bankrupt in September 1763. *London Directories; Gentleman's Magazine*, xxxiii (1763), 467.

[8] The packet from England to New York.

[9] Charles Ogilvie and John Forbes. Judgment Rolls, 1763, No. 94A, S. C. Archives; *HL Papers*, ii, 133n. Peter Horry (1747–1815) was placed with John Forbes "to be taught Merchandize" while Forbes was still in Georgetown. Horry viewed Forbes as a man "Solely Involved in making money, it was all in all with him." Horry moved with Forbes from Georgetown to Charleston. "My Master F. Entered into Copartner with Mr. Ogilvie of Charles Town, a Merchant of Emenence. They Carried on business very Extensively, with the Spaniards of St. Augustine, they buying at Charles Town & my Masters Adventuring to that Garrison. Mr. Ogilvie was much of a Gentleman, was Generous, Just & humain. I could have lived with him forever. I knew of but one failing he was adicted to. He was as many others were too fond of the fair Sex. His Adventures in this way were Sometimes unfortunate & his Constitution as well as Purse Suffered more than Usual. Forbes here [*in Charleston*] continuing his Injustice to me & as well his Ill Temper toward me I could brook it no Longer. Ogilvie would not Enterfere & Said I was Forbes young man—not his. I was now Several years Living with these Masters." Since Ogilvie returned to England in 1761, these comments must refer to the period just prior to that date. Journal of Peter Horry, Books 1 & 2, pp. 16, 22, 29, SCL; *SCHM*, xxxviii (1937), 49. These episodes may explain how one leading patriot, Gen. Peter Horry, acquired anti-Scottish feelings.

[1] John Ward and Peter Leger. Judgment Rolls, 1767, No. 631A, S. C. Archives; *HL Papers*, ii, 133n.

[2] John Ferdinand Miller. *HL Papers*, iii, 32.

Money & a few Bonds with a Letter of Attorney in the hands of Mr. Waldron,[3] a Young Gentleman almost a stranger in this province. Mr. Waldron after being talked to, behaved very well upon this occasion. He brought to me the ready Money, Vizt. £87.14/ Currency & the Bonds, & consented that your Servant Mr. Gray[4] should deliver me two Chests of rusty Guns & a few other trifling articles left by Mr. Miller only insisting that he should have the bringing up the Books in which he has made no progress yet; I believe he has full employment in that way from other people. Both that gentleman & Mr. Gray promis'd from time to time to call upon me to make the best Schedule & Account that might be of the effects & Books but have omitted to do so & I should have been more urgent with them if an attatchment of Mr. Millers effects in my hands had not been serv'd upon me by one of his Creditors. This circumstance I am advis'd will be rather advantageous to you than otherwise as it will afford an opportunity of proving myself a Creditor in possession & then I shall be enabled by the Court to demand & recover debts due to John Ferdinand Miller which at present I have no power to do.[5] I wish this advice may be well founded for I find his debtors have no inclination to be Volunteers in payments. Permit me to say once more, Sir, that I shall do all that I can to serve you in this unlucky circumstance & tho I do not love to complain yet I cannot help saying that it is an exceeding troublesome affair to me & therefore I hope you will accept of my best endeavours altho I should not compass all that you have a right to & that I really wish to obtain for you.

Mr. Miller left a short Letter to be deliver'd to me after his departure in which he still pretended great gratitude to you & that he would one day or other convince us both that he had no intention to defraud you; God knows only what are his designs & intentions, but I am afraid you will never get any more from him than what is now in my hands, & yet tis evident that if he had been quite a Knave he might have put you upon a worse footing than he left you.

---

[3] Patrick Waldron. See Austin, Laurens, & Appleby versus Miller, Nov. 29, 1763. In 1764 Patrick Waldron married Mary Porter, daughter of a Colleton County planter. In 1767 Waldron was a tavern keeper at Dorchester. Miscellaneous Records, MM, Part 2 (1763–1767), pp. 651, 695–697, S. C. Archives.

[4] Mr. Gray has not been identified.

[5] A writ of attachment had been issued directing HL to place the property of Miller in his possession under the control of the courts of law. See Austin, Laurens, & Appleby versus Miller, Nov. 29, 1763. In order to clear up matters HL himself asked for a writ attaching all of Miller's property.

The Accounts of Sale that are sent to you contains the several specific articles of Merchandize that came to the hands of A., L., & A., & these I hope will enable you to adjust an Account so far with Mr. Heathcote[6] & I shall as soon as possible send an Account of all the rest but I believe the Candlesticks, Lead vices, &ca., will remain for ever unsold in this Country. Before I conclude I will observe the Gentlemen who purchased your Lawns barely saved themselves & therefore the Sale here upon the whole was best for you in which I followed the advice of those to whome I consign'd the first 50 pieces. I remain with great respect, &ca.—

SOURCE: Letterbook copy, HL Papers, S. C. Hist. Soc.; addressed "London"; "per Capt. Seager. Copy per *Success,* Man of War."

BENJAMIN STILES, HENRY LAURENS, & WILLIAM BANBURY, EXECUTORS OF SAMUEL WINBORN, VERSUS JOSIAH DUPREE[7]

November 12, 1763

[On this date during the November term of the court of common pleas a jury awarded the plaintiffs £81.9.4 currency plus costs.]

SOURCE: Journal, Court of Common Pleas, 1763–1769, p. 35, S. C. Archives.

TO JOSEPH STOKES[8]

[Charles Town] 13 November 1763

Sir,

Only yesterday yours of the 29th July came to my hand & I sit down quickly to reply to it & chiefly with a view to prevent your

---

[6] Gilbert Heathcote. *HL Papers,* III, 230n.

[7] For this and earlier judgments obtained by the executors of Samuel Winborn, see *HL Papers,* III, 218n. The executors had obtained a judgment against James Dubois on Aug. 9; a jury found for the defendant in the case against Edward Fisher on Nov. 17; and on Feb. 23, 1764 a jury awarded Beswicke & Co. £16,528.15.7 currency plus costs in that company's suit against the executors. Journal, Court of Common Pleas, 1763–1769, pp. 14, 40, 54, S. C. Archives.

[8] Father of the Rev. Joseph Stokes who had died in Charleston on Nov. 22, 1762. *HL Papers,* III, 138n.

taking any more such *"Freedoms"* & to recommend that in case you make a future correspondence with me you will be pleas'd to express yourself in more decent terms, which I think should always be done every where people have a right to make demands. If you do not, I shall lay your Letters aside without any further notice of them.

You might have answer'd your own enquiry without sending so far, *"whats the reason that I've not the Account of the Sales of the Adventure of the Bottled & Cask Liquor, &ca., sent per Baker*[9] *& Doran"?*[1] Why, because I never receiv'd any consignments of adventures from you by those or any other persons nor indeed ever had a Letter from you; how, therefore, could you be so rude as to call me to Account & more so by the manner in which you have attempted it? I should be very justifiable if I was abruptly to drop you here & lead you no nearer to information but, Sir, as all my design in my past transactions relative to your Son the Reverend Mr. Stokes & his Widow[2] was to serve people who stood in need of my assistance I shall from the same motives acquaint you that your Son did put a parcel of Bottled Beer & Barrel'd Beer on his Account into my hands. These were landed from on board the *Indian King*, & afterward his Widow & Administratrix Mrs. Mary Stokes did put other such like goods into my hands. Both parcels were sold & I have long since render'd Accounts of Sale being first very largely in advance for the Nt. proceed for which I am not to this hour reimburs'd. This advance (as I made a present to the Widow of my Commission & other charges) is all that I have gain'd by the consignment save only the trouble of writing this long Letter in answer to your very polite enquiry of the 29th July.

These things are out of my way, Mr. Stokes, & I would not have undertaken the Sale but merely to save your Son (who was recommended to me by a friend in London[3]) the Commission & otherwise to serve him. That Barrel'd Beer which he lodged in my Cellar was certainly very good, or I thought it so, but being landed in the very heat of Summer it sower'd before the Season for Sale came on. You will see by the above that you have no right to call for Accounts

---

[9] Capt. Richard Baker of the *Indian King.*

[1] The snow *Success,* James Doran, arrived from Bristol on Jan. 8. *Gazette,* Jan. 8, 1763.

[2] Mrs. Mary Stokes. *HL Papers,* III, 138n, 416n.

[3] Monkhouse Davison. *HL Papers,* III, 138.

& returns from me, as well as that I have already made both to the only person authoriz'd to demand them & if you will take the trouble to enquire among the Merchants in Bristol I believe you will be inform'd that I have never given occasion to any body to make such calls upon me. I am, &ca.—

SOURCE: Letterbook copy, HL Papers, S. C. Hist. Soc.; addressed "Bristol"; "per Capt. Seager."

TO BENJAMIN GARDEN [4]

[Charles Town] 16th November 1763

Dear Sir,

Your favour of the 1st Inst. reach'd me only to day. It is so long a time since Mr. John Neyle[5] first spoke to me about your Rough Rice & indeed since he last spoke to me & expressed some doubt & uncertainty about it, that I have sold the very Schooner[6] which I told him should go to fetch it from your landing & the subject was gone from my attention.

My motive, (as I told Mr. Neyle when he applyed to me) for offering to purchase it was merely to serve you, which I shall still be glad to do as far as 'tis in my power, for I neither wanted the Rice then, nor do I want it now, for any purpose of my own; but as I had been inform'd that it would be a convenience to you to sell your Crop in the Shell I meant to lend you a helping hand therein first by sending my own Schooner for it & afterward selling it for you free from charges & with as little delay & waste as possible or which would have been much the same thing by taking it without further trouble to you at Market price tho I might have been obliged to sell it afterward at the same rate into different hands & waited for a return of my Money.

---

[4] Benjamin Garden (1736–1789), the son of the Rev. Alexander Garden, was born on Dec. 23, 1736. *Register of St. Philip's Parish, 1720–1758*, p. 77. He married HL's niece Elizabeth Bremar, daughter of Francis Bremar, on Sept. 16, 1759. She was buried on Nov. 18, 1761. *Register of St. Philip's Parish, 1754–1810*, pp. 157, 300. He had been an executor, along with HL, of Francis Bremar's will. *HL Papers*, III, 68. At the time of his second marriage, to Amelia Godin on Jan. 17, 1765, he was a planter in Prince William parish. *SCHM*, XI (1910), 28.

[5] A merchant. *HL Papers*, III, 436n.

[6] HL must have just sold the schooner *Live Oak* which was reregistered on May 29, 1764. *HL Papers*, III, 127n.

'Tis not now in my power to send a Schooner for it but if you can procure one & shall think proper to send your rough Rice down to my care you may depend upon it I shall do my best to serve you in the Sale of it but I cannot flatter you with hopes of the price that you ask, Vizt. 10/ per bushel at the landing. I have enquired & find the price is only 10/ delivered here & perhaps a large quantity may cause some abatement, which you will think of & lay your commands as you shall determine upon, Dear Sir, &ca.—

SOURCE: Letterbook copy, Letter Book of Henry Laurens, Oct. 30, 1762–Sept. 10, 1766, Penn. Hist. Soc.; addressed "the Parish of Prince William."

TO JOSEPH BROWN

[Charles Town] 24 November 1763

Dear Sir,

I reciev'd the 8 Casks of Indigo per Capt. Blythe[7] & had ship'd them on board the ship *Heron,* Capt. Chisman,[8] apprehending that she was bound to London & had consign'd it as you wish'd to Mrs. Sara Nickleson & Company on our joint account but just upon signing the Bills of Loading I was inform'd that the ship was bound to Portsmouth which surpriz'd me greatly & gives me the trouble to reship it on board the brigantine *Favourite,* Capt. Brownett, for Bristol where I shall consign it to Mess. Cowls & Harford to be sold by them or sent forward to our London friends as between them shall appear most for our Interest. The Charges of transporting it to London in case of need will not be near so much as the advantages or chances of gain that we have, besides time that we shall save, as none of the London Vessels will go for many Days after this Brigantine & probably the first ship will carry a considerable quantity & stagger the market for I do believe that the price must go down very quick in London.

I hope that you are not distress'd for want of Money from me. If you are signify it & I must & will borrow for I can no longer rely

---

[7] William Blythe was master of the schooner *Winyaw of Charles Town,* 20 tons, owned by John Mayrant, built in 1763, and registered on Feb. 3, 1763. Ship Register, 1734–1765, p. 211, S. C. Archives.

[8] The ship *Heron,* Thomas Chisman, arrived from Poole on Aug. 21 and sailed for Portsmouth on Nov. 27. *Gazette,* Aug. 27, Dec. 3, 1763.

upon fair promises which are daily made to me without effect but I must repeat my request to buy no more Indigo unless you can get the best Copper at about 22/6. I fancy we shall find that as high as can be afforded. If you can help Dickinson[9] to a frieght you will oblige me. Pitch above all other articles, next turpentine or Tar, but anything rather than nothing & I suppose that freight will begin to move by the time he gets up with you.

SOURCE: Letterbook copy, Letter Book of Henry Laurens, Oct. 30, 1762–Sept. 10, 1766, Penn. Hist. Soc.

TO CHRISTOPHER ROWE[1]

Charles Town, 24 November 1763

Sir,

I have receiv'd your favour of the 19th Instant inclosing fifty Pounds which is pass'd to the Credit of your account & agreeable to your order I now send to you one Bale of white negro Cloth, quantity & amount as per Bill below. You will please to observe that at this price I should loose by the Cloth unless I am paid in ready money or in a short time. The longest Credit that I have given to the merchants here who have bought of me to sell again is to the 1st January next & I shall charge this payable on that day which I beg you will confirm in your next letter because as I sell these goods upon such very low terms I should be too great a sufferer if I was not either soon put in Cash or receiv'd some equivalent for the advance of my money.

I have no white linnen to sell & as you do not mention the sort that you want I shall defer buying a piece until I hear from you again. Mean time I am, Sir, Yours, &c.—

---

[9] Capt. David Dickinson of the *Wambaw*. *HL Papers*, III, 144, 425, 426, 484, 507, 531, 532, 535. Joseph Dickinson, the son of David and Avis Dickinson, was baptized on July 4, 1765. *Register of St. Philip's Parish, 1754–1810*, p. 62.

[1] Christopher Rowe was a prominent figure in Orangeburg District. *HL Papers*, II, 225n. In 1757 he was lieutenant of the Orangeburg Company of Col. John Chevillette's Berkeley County Regiment. Council Journal, XXVI (Jan. 3, 1757–June 6, 1758), p. 87, S. C. Archives. In 1765 when he was captain of his militia company he was appointed a commissioner to supervise the building of a chapel in Orangeburg Township of the newly created St. Matthew parish. *S. C. Statutes*, IV, 230–232. In 1769 he was appointed a commissioner to supervise the building of a jail and courthouse for Orangeburg District. Richard M. Brown, *The South Carolina Regulators* (Cambridge, Mass., 1963), p. 154. By the time of the Revolution Rowe was lieutenant colonel of his militia regiment. Salley, *History of Orangeburg County*, passim.

P.S. Bill payable 1st January 1764.

SOURCE: Letterbook copy, Letter Book of Henry Laurens, Oct. 30, 1762–
Sept. 10, 1766, Penn. Hist. Soc.; addressed "Charles Town." The postscript was copied by HL.

TO JERMYN WRIGHT[2]

[Charles Town] 24th November 1763

Sir,

  I beg leave to refer you to your Brother Charles Wright, Esquire for what has passed between him & me relative to your Lands
or Marsh & Lands at the North end of Charles Town & also to the

---

[2] Charles and Jermyn Wright were older brothers of James Wright, governor
of Georgia. They were sons of Robert Wright who had been chief justice of
S. C., 1731–1739. All three brothers had been born at Russell St., Bloomsbury,
London. One sister had married James Graeme, chief justice of S. C., 1749–
1752; another John Hume with whom Charles and Jermyn Wright had been
engaged in trade in the early 1750's. Another became the second wife of
Richard Lambton, who was attorney for Lord Anson in S. C. Kenneth Coleman
to editor, April 12, 1971; *HL Papers*, I, 149n, 343. Charles and Jermyn
Wright's particular interests were concentrated in Granville County on the
north side of the Savannah River. Jermyn had obtained a grant of 500 acres
on the Savannah River on Feb. 17, 1736 and 1,000 on May 11, 1739. Charles
had obtained a grant of 3,450 acres in Granville County on March 14, 1757;
Jermyn 800 on Jan. 16, 1758 and Charles 691 on Oct. 5, 1763. Index to
Grants, S. C. Archives. They were both justices of the peace for Granville
County in the lists of 1756 and 1765. *SCHM*, xx (1919), 74; *Gazette*, Oct.
31, 1765. In 1759 Charles Wright lived "at or near Purrysburgh." Judgment
Rolls, 1759, No. 179A, S. C. Archives. They were both listed as grand jurors
of the parish of St. Peter in the list of 1767. Manuscript Act No. 958, S. C.
Archives.
  The property HL had purchased in Ansonborough on Sept. 7, 1762, had
once belonged to Jermyn Wright. When HL made his purchase, a wharf
and some marshland had been reserved to Lord Anson. The rights to the wharf
and marshland had since then come again into Jermyn Wright's possession.
HL was therefore now trying to purchase the wharf and marshland in order
to round out his Ansonborough properties. *HL Papers*, III, 116–117, 419n,
531n. Presumably Jermyn Wright's title was not clear so the heirs of Lord
Anson might have a claim. In order to remove this flaw in the title, HL was
consulting Richard Lambton. HL did not know at this time that Anson had
signed a release in fee simple to Jermyn Wright on Dec. 9, 1761. Deeds, BBB,
pp. 69–71, S. C. Archives. HL finally purchased the wharf and marshland on
March 24, 1764. See Purchase of Land in Ansonborough, March 24, 1764.
  In May 1768 HL purchased the Wrights' Savannah plantation from the
provost marshal. Deeds, LLL, pp. 448–460, S. C. Archives. The estates of
Charles and Jermyn Wright were confiscated in 1782. *SCHM*, xxxiv (1933),
195.

enclosed opinion[3] (which I have procured at the expence of £20) upon the Case stated by you.

You see the probability there is of further expence by a Suite in Chancery before you can be established in your property especialy as Mr. Lambton[4] declares that the conditions upon which the Surplussage of your Land or of Money arising from the Sale thereof after paying your Bond to Lord Anson was to revert to you have not been comply'd with, to wit, the payment of his Commission, &ca., which is Stipulated and insisted upon in Mr. Briggs Letter.[5]

Upon the whole, Sir, if I make a purchase of you I must expect to encounter some dificulties with the Heirs of his Lordship a Combat that may be render'd less doubtful on my side if I satisfy Mr. Lambton which I shall indevour to do by the easiest compromise that may be obtain'd & when that is as it must be effected the Heirs I shou'd think can have no such grounded scruples against executing a reconveyance to you or to your assigns. Viewing things in this light I beg to be inform'd of your lowest price for the Wharf reserv'd in my Title deeds to Lord Anson & the Marsh & high Land to the Southward of my Marsh of which there is about one Acre & an half Marsh & a piece of 104 feet or thereabout front of high Land & 30 to 40 feet deep or in short your whole claim, pretention, or property there which price I intreat you to set forth at one word taking upon yourself or leaving upon me the adjustment necessary to be made with Mr. Lambton, & according to your proposals which I beg to have as clearly & as expeditiously as possible I shall proceed to improve my Marsh or determine to let the whole lay dormant.

If I accept of your price it will be essential on your part to execute such a Bond as my Council hath advised & therefore you will add an appointment of the time & place for that purpose. I have not at present time to make a duplicate of the Case & opinion be so kind therefore to return that paper to me when you have perused it. I remain—

SOURCE: Letterbook copy, Letter Book of Henry Laurens, Oct. 30, 1762–Sept. 10, 1766, Penn. Hist. Soc. This letter was copied into the letterbook after that of Dec. 29.

---

[3] The enclosure has not been located.

[4] Richard Lambton was also deputy auditor of the province. *HL Papers*, III, 169, 419n. Anne Wright Lambton died in Charleston in October 1770 at the age of 66. *SCHM*, x (1909), 159.

[5] Mr. Briggs must have been attorney for the heirs of Lord Anson.

TO ELIAS B. DELAFONTAINE

[Charles Town] 26th November 1763

Sir,

The annex'd is a duplicate of what I wrote you the 12th Inst. per Capt. Seagers Via Bristol to which I will beg leave to refer & proceed to acquaint you that upon the fair promisses made to me by the two Houses therein mentioned of helping me to Cash I have made a purchase, five Bills of Exchange as underneath Amounting to Nine hundred & Eighty five pounds eighteen shillings & two pence Sterling & charged to your Account Current at the rate of 707 per Cent Exchange Six Thousand Nine hundred & seventy pounds seven shillings & two pence Current Money. The 1st Bill of each sett you will find here inclosed & will be pleas'd to note to my Credit conformable to the above. These Bills I have procur'd at an easy Exchange, Bills being extremely scarce & of late 721 per Cent has been given for most of the few that have been drawn, & I am well assured by a Gentleman who recommended them & who I know would not deceive me nor even mislead me that I may rely on their goodness & I know that a cautious careful Man to whome the Seller & one of the endorsers was recommended did offer what is called the par of Exchange, Vizt. 700 per Cent for them. Therefore upon the whole I have good reason to hope that you will suffer no disappointment. I have said so much upon this subject because I have known too many Bills of the West India draughts to have been returned & tho in the end they were paid yet the delay was very inconvenient to those who expected & depended on punctuality.

I am now in hopes of obtaining an easy riddance from the attachment of Mr. Millers effects, at least my Lawyer[6] flatters me with *hopes* of it, & also that Mr. Waldron will do every thing in his power to enable me to recover the debts (that are recoverable) due to Mr. Miller. He has promis'd for this purpose to sign an Act of substitution[7] upon Mr. Millers Letter of Attorney to him or to consent that suits

---

[6] William Burrows was HL's lawyer in this case. Burrows had arrived in Charleston in 1741 at the age of 13 or 14, married Mary, the daughter of John Ward in 1749, become one of Charleston's leading lawyers, and died in 1783. Harriet P. and Albert Simons, "The William Burrows House of Charleston," *SCHM*, LXX (1969), 155–176.

[7] Waldron had received a power of attorney from Miller. Waldron was offering to have HL's name substituted for his own. Apparently this was not done inasmuch as Miller made out a power of attorney to HL on Dec. 17, 1763. See Letter of Attorney, Dec. 17, 1763.

where needful be carried on in his name & the Moneys receiv'd to be paid to me for your use.

I most heartily wish that a more able hand was employ'd to wind up these affairs but whilst they remain in mine, every thing that I can do shall be done to serve you. I remain, &c.—

The above Letter directed to Mr. Elias Benjamin Dela Fontain on his own account & on Account of Mr. Gilbert Heathcote.

Account of 5 Bills of Exchange remitted in the preceeding Letter on Account of Mr. Elias Benjamin Dela Fontaine & Gilbert Heathcote, Esq. & endors'd payable to the order of either of them.

Jno. Hurst[8] on Richard Adny[9] 7 October 1763 at 60 days £100.
William Stanley[1] on Hillary & Scott[2] 13th September
  1763 ditto   185.
William Livingston[3] on Sir Geo. Colebrook[4] 13 October
  1763 ditto   250.
     ”   ”   3 ditto   200.18.2
     ”   ”   14 ditto   250.
                                                            ————
                                                            £985.18.2

£985.18.2 Sterling for which I have paid Capt.
Thomas Seymour[5] at 707 per Cent Exchange ....£6,970.7.2.

Rice 50/ ⎫
Indigo 26/ to 28/ ⎪
Pitch 75/ ⎪
Tar 50/ ⎬ all too high for your Markets
Turpentine 15/ ⎪
Deer Skins 13/ to 14/ ⎪
Exchange 721 per Cent ⎭

---

[8] Dr. John Hurst married Margaret Nanton on Aug. 17, 1749 in the parish of St. John, Antigua. Oliver, *History of Antigua,* II, 92–93.

[9] Richard Adney was a merchant at Mr. Bond's in Bond's Court, Walbrook. *London Directories.*

[1] William Stanley was presumably a West India merchant.

[2] Richard Hillary and John Scott of Liverpool. *HL Papers,* III, 229n.

[3] William Livingston, merchant, married Christian Doig on July 26, 1759 in the parish of St. John, Antigua. He owned lots, tenements, and wharves in the town of St. John's. In 1763 he purchased Andrew Lessly's plantation for £24,000 sterling. He was buried on April 14, 1774. Oliver, *History of Antigua,* II, 190–193.

[4] Sir George Colebrooke (1729–1809), the son of a London banker, married Mary, the daughter and heiress of Peter Gayner of Antigua, in 1754. He sat for Arundel, 1754–1744. He was contractor for victualling the forces in America. He succeeded his brother James on May 10, 1761, as second baronet. Namier and Brooke, *The House of Commons, 1754–1790,* II, 235-237.

[5] Capt. Thomas Seymour of New York was the owner of the brigantine *Fanny* which was entered inwards on Nov. 15 from Antigua in ballast. *Naval Office Lists, 1757–1764,* p. 124.

SOURCE: Letterbook copy, HL Papers, S. C. Hist. Soc.; addressed "London"; "per the *Success,* Man of War."

TO JOHN COMING BALL
[Charles Town] 29th November 1763
Dear Sir,

I duly receiv'd your favour of the 23d & have been considering your proposition to give five thousand Pounds for my part of Wambaw Lands or to accept of that Sum for your part; to which you desire my answer "that you may direct your business accordingly."

I must not therefore keep you *longer in suspence* & tho I am but a poor judge of the Value of lands myself & have not met with one proper person to consult upon this subject; I shall *not hesitate to declare* that *I accept* the purchase & will be ready to make good the consideration money whensoever the Deed of conveyance from you to me are duly executed. This I think is my Duty & do in justice to my Children; & my way of calculating is simply this. That the Land was thought to be very cheap when I bought one half of it, & if so, it must be worth a great deal more now according to the common rise of Land throughout the province, exclusive of the great & expensive improvements that have been made upon it.

You have now *my answer & I am bound*; but at the same time I do not insist upon binding you unless your next Letter confirms your last, for I have also *a great regard for your Children* & should be sorry to enter into any bargain that might prejudice their Interest. I would therefore recommend to you to deliberate again upon this point & if you do not insist upon my performance I would rather continue to plant the Land as heretofore under some new regulations than that you should part with it for £5,000—which in my opinion you cannot replace any where with so much convenience to yourself & *advantage to your family,* & both these considerations have great weight with me. But it is nevertheless true that I am not a competent judge of Planting Interest & therefore I submit the matter *(bound at the same time myself)* to your further & final resolution.

Meantime rather than under value our Land might we not shun the inconveniences that I apprehended in case of the death of either party by entering into mutual obligations upon the Heirs, Executors, &ca. to submit to a public Sale within 6 or 9 Months after such decease, the number of our Negroes to be some what reduced or more plantations establish'd to employ the whole, every expence & even every Loss to be borne by the general Interest. The Overseer if he employs any Negroes of his own to draw a share of the Crop of Rice in proportion to the number of such his Negroes & no more. With other notes that may occur to your mind. What I have said proceeds purely from friendship & a disinterested regard for you & yours. But I should not have been tedious if you had fixed a price that would have made it indifferent to me—give or take—but now I feel myself somewhat embarass'd on either hand.[6]

Your reply will relieve me & set all things to right. Our Wambaw Schooner has on board a good back Freight for George Town & is detain'd by these Cross Winds; as soon as she returns you may depend on her attendance at the Wambaw Landing.[7]

I understood you that 1 piece of the 2 Duffils lately sent was for Wambaw but I shall send two pieces more by the Schooner & Mr. Brenard[8] may return what is not wanted. I am sorry your Brother's people[9] can't assist me. I think you said that Cain could. My Love attends you all & I remain, &ca.—

SOURCE: Letterbook copy, Letter Book of Henry Laurens, Oct. 30, 1762–Sept. 10, 1766, Penn. Hist. Soc.

---

[6] HL had bought 1,250 acres for £2,749 currency on May 12, 1756. This was one-half of Wambaw plantation. *HL Papers*, II, 180. On Feb. 13, 1759, HL and John Coming Ball had bought 500 acres of Wambaw Swamp for £1,500. *HL Papers*, III, 2. HL's investment was therefore £3,499 currency for 1,500 acres. As HL was being offered £5,000 in 1763 for this property, land values had risen about 50%. Since this sale did not take place before John Coming Ball's death, a division of these 3,000 acres had to be made later. Writs of Partition, 1754–1777, pp. 161–164, S. C. Archives.

[7] Wambaw landing was on the Santee. Wambaw Creek, now the boundary between Charleston and Berkeley Counties, flows into the Santee from the south side of the river. Georgetown was on Winyaw Bay, the next inlet on the coast north of the Santee River.

[8] James Brenard was the overseer at Wambaw. *HL Papers*, III, 425, 481, 525. On May 25, 1764, James Brenard requested that the assembly pay him £18.15 in constable's fees for calling a court of justices and freeholders to try a slave. The assembly stated that he had overcharged 15/ but granted him only £8.12.9. House Journal, XXXVI (Jan. 24, 1763–Oct. 6, 1764), 25, 78, 212, S. C. Archives. James Brenard may have planted in the parish of Prince Frederick after he left the employ of Laurens at the end of 1764. "Will of James Brenard," dated Feb. 11, 1775, proved ———, *Abstracts of Wills, 1760–1784*, pp. 234–235.

[9] Elias Ball (1709–1786) had 43 male slaves (from 16 to 60) at Kensington plantation. Entry for Sept. 27, 1762, Minute Book of Commissioners of Roads, St. John Berkeley, I (1760–1798), S. C. Hist. Soc.

TO GILBERT HEATHCOTE

[Charles Town] 29th November 1763

Sir,

Last Saturday Morning I had wrote the inclosed Letter to Mr. Elias Benjamin Dela Fontain to which I beg leave to refer requesting that after you have perus'd it you will be pleas'd to make a proper delivery which I trust will give no offence to our unfortunate friend.[1] In the Evening of the same day your favour of 10th September came to hand by Capt. Coombes informing me that some "undeserv'd & unexpected misfortunes["] had obliged that Gentleman to stop payment & directing me to remit one moiety of moneys recover'd on your joint Account from Mr. John F. Miller, to yourself.[2]

You will see what I had done previous to the receipt of your said favour & what is added since, Vizt. to make the Bills payable to his or your order which in all right & justice ought to be, because they arise from the Sale of goods expressly belonging to you both which goods were obtain'd from your Factor by virtue of your joint Letter of Attorney & my correspondence hitherto with Mr. Dela Fontain alone, was in consequence of & conformity to the Letters receiv'd always under his Sole Firm[3] but were meant & are expressive enough on both parts to be on your joint Account. The precaution which I have now taken will I hope guard you against the danger of an unjust appropriation of your Money & my Books will appear at all times clear & unperplexed.

I am really in advance for the purchase of these Bills & did hope that my alledging *that*; would have prov'd a further spur to the Gentlemen who are your Debtors but hitherto it has produc'd no effect. Indeed Money is at present very scarce in almost every House here for altho I had heard nothing (except a distant hint the day before yours arriv'd) of Mr. Dela Fontaines circumstances & had no cause to doubt that he was upon a Firm basis yet for some time past it run in my mind that the want of so much Money as I knew had been unjustly detained from him by Mr. Miller might be of some

---

[1] HL to Elias Benjamin DelaFontaine, Nov. 26, 1763.

[2] The ship *America,* William Coombes, owned by John Beswicke, William Greenwood, and William Higginson of London, arrived from London on Nov. 26 and was entered inwards on Nov. 28. *Gazette,* Nov. 26, 1763; Naval Office Lists, 1757–1764, p. 124. This vessel had brought the news of DelaFontaine's bankruptcy.

[3] DelaFontaine's signature.

prejudice to him & the more if he happen'd to have other unlucky connexions in America.

You must not flatter yourself with great expectations from any Book debts due to Mr. Miller. I am afraid there are not many good ones but his Books are in a Shameful state, they have not been posted for several Years past & the Labour that is apprehended will attend the putting of them into tolerable order is what I suppose deters that Young Man whom he recommended from attempting it. I spoke to him within these two days & have receiv'd a fresh promise that he will make a beginning before Christmas. If he fails I shall apply again or endeavour to get some other person to do it.[4] Upon the whole it is a most troublesome affair to me & I wish I could get rid of it in any manner consistent with your own & the Interest of poor Mr. Dela Fontain with whom I most heartily sympathize & wish it was in my power to hold out relief or assistance to him. I am with great respect, &ca.—

SOURCE: Letterbook copy, HL Papers, S. C. Hist. Soc.; addressed "London"; "per *Success,* Man of War. Copy per *Bonnetta,* Man of War."

GEORGE AUSTIN, HENRY LAURENS, & GEORGE APPLEBY VERSUS JOHN FERDINAND MILLER

November 29, 1763

[In an action to attach the property of John Ferdinand Miller begun by John Ward a writ of attachment had been served on HL. HL came into the court on November 29 and swore to a schedule of Miller's property which was in his hands. HL's affidavit along with the list of debts is printed below. On motion of William Burrows, HL's attorney, the court ordered that Austin, Laurens, & Appleby have leave to proceed as creditors in possession of the effects of John Ferdinand Miller. Burrows thereupon entered an action on behalf of Austin, Laurens, & Appleby to attach Miller's property. The court ordered an appraisement and then a sale of the goods by the provost marshal.[5]

---

[4] Miller had failed to transfer items from his cash book to the permanent ledgers of accounts.

[5] The *Gazette* has been searched, but no evidence of the sale of Miller's property has been found.

To support his allegation that he was a creditor HL had produced a copy of the bond that Miller had executed on December 30, 1762, to Austin, Laurens, & Appleby. Under the terms of this bond Miller had promised to pay £2,525 sterling to Austin, Laurens, & Appleby for the use of Elias Benjamin DelaFontaine and Gilbert Heathcote of London on or before February 1, 1763.]

LIST OF DEBTS

Account of Sundry Debts & Books of Account, Goods & Chattles Lodged in my hands by Mr. Patrick Waldron being left by Mr. John Ferdinand Miller late of Charles Town, Merchant, on Account of a Bond for Two Thousand & five hundred pounds Sterling given by him to the late House of Austin, Laurens, & Appleby for the proper use & Account of Mr. Elias Benjamin DeLafontaine & Mr. Gilbert Hethcote of London, Merchants.

the 9th June 1763

Cash Eighty seven pounds 14/ Current Money			£ 87.14
Bonds & Notes			
Isaac Godin[6]	Bond	£479.14.2	
Mary Greenland[7]	Bond	581.10	
Farquar McGillivray[8]	Bond	191. 8.1	
	Note	100	
John Hawes[9]	Bond	101. 3.9	
Alexander McGillivray[1]	Bond	460. 4.5	
John Tuke[2]	Bond	484.15	
John Denton[3]	Note	41. 6	
John Hume	Note	593.19.3	£3,037. 0.8

---

[6] Isaac Godin, son of Benjamin Godin, lived at Fontainbleu plantation on Goose Creek. In 1759 he married Martha Mathews. He died on Sept. 23, 1777. *SCHM*, x (1909), 225; xxix (1928), 71–76; "Will of Isaac Godin," dated Aug. 22, 1777, proved ———, Charleston County Wills, xvii, Book B (1774–1779), 700–703, S. C. Archives.

[7] Mary Greenland may have been a widow, daughter-in-law of Catherine Greenland, who died in 1761. *Abstracts of Wills, 1760–1784*, p. 18.

[8] Farquar McGillivray, Charleston cabinetmaker, died Aug. 20, 1770. *SCHM*, x (1909), 159; xvi (1915), 131; E. Milby Burton, *Charleston Furniture, 1700–1825* (Columbia, S. C., 1970), p. 106.

[9] John Hawes might have been the husband of Ann Hawes, who kept a tavern "up the Path." *Gazette,* April 6, 1769.

[1] Alexander McGillivray, mariner, died before Jan. 6, 1764. *HL Papers,* ii, 24n.

[2] John Tuke, who had been a schoolmaster, bought James Marshall's tavern on the Bay in the fall of 1764. *Gazette,* Dec. 3, 1764. In 1765 he was sued by William Bampfield for 18¾ dozen bottles of Bell's Ale at 70/ per dozen— £65.12.6. Judgment Rolls, 1765, No. 256A, S. C. Archives. His wife Hannah Tuke was listed as tavern keeper in the *Gazette,* April 6, 1769. She died on

a parcel said to be about 26 Groce Shirt Buttons, 18 Vol: of printed old books, 8 vo. & smaller size, 1 Box Card, 2 Tea pots, 1 Shovel & Tongs, 19 Empty dirty bottles, 1 Earthen dish & China Mug, 1 Glass Tumbler, 1 Seymaker, 1 Cartouch Box empty, 1 Tin Cannister with some Loaf Sugar in it & one ditto with some spoil'd Tea, 1 Sand Box, 1 Marking Iron, 2 ordinary black Trunks without Keys, & 1 good Deal painted Chest or Box, 19 Books of Accounts &ca. from the Leidger down to blotters, including one Receipt Book. Sundry old Papers in bundles & upon Files.

Charles Town, South Carolina, 29th November 1763
Errors Excepted
Henry Laurens

AFFIDAVIT

Henry Laurens upon whom a Copy of the Writ of Attachment issued in this Cause was served being duly Sworn maketh Oath That the Articles mentioned on the other side of this Paper is a just & true Account of all the Moneys, Goods, Chattells, Debts, & Books of Account now in his hands, Custody, or possession of which at the time of serving the said Write of Attachment he had belonging to the said John Ferdinand Miller, and that the same were obtained loyally & Bona fide without any tortious Act And this Deponent further saith That he is a Creditor in possession to the amount of Two thousand five hundred pounds Sterling money of Great Britain by Bond payable to this Deponent, George Austin, & George Appleby, and this deponent further saith that no part of the above sum hath been paid to his knowledge, and that he doth not in any wise or upon any Account whatsoever stand indebted to the Defendant John Ferdinand Miller And he verily believes that neither the said George Austin or George Appleby are in any wise indebted to the said Defendant And further this Deponent saith not—

Henry Laurens

Sworn to in Open Court this 29th November 1763
D. Campbell, C. C. Pleas[4]

Dec. 1, 1806 at the age of seventy-three after upwards of fifty years in the city. *SCHM,* xxx (1929), 188.

[3] John Denton, searcher of the customs, died on Sept. 14, 1766. *SCHM,* xvi (1915), 34; "Will of John Denton," dated March 13, 1764, proved October 1766, Charleston County Wills, x, Book B (1760–1767), 795, S. C. Archives.

[4] Dougal Campbell was appointed clerk of the common pleas on Nov. 6, 1754. Miscellaneous Records, KK (1754–1758), p. 113, S. C. Archives. On July 11, 1759, Governor Lyttelton appointed him clerk of the crown and peace in place

SOURCE: Judgment Rolls, 1763, No. 112A, S. C. Archives; Journal, Court of Common Pleas, 1763–1769, pp. 45–46, S. C. Archives.

TO JONAS MAYNARD[5]

[Charles Town] 30th November 1763

Sir,

I have also receiv'd yours; & the contents of it has caused a surprize here at least equal to your own. I have endeavour'd to serve you & should have been glad to have gone on to the end without any covetous eye to your Commission, an article that has never appeared valuable to me but where I was sure that I had earned it & if you will please to enquire you will find that I have truly earn'd the whole arising from your business tho shared with Mr. Austin.

I do not know of any claim you have upon me as an individual & as you give me no cause to flatter myself with that my further officious services will be acceptable to you I shall stop where I am, holding myself always ready to render a just & fair Account as one partner (or rather Pack Horse) in the late House, of any effects of yours in my custody. At the same time I determine to suffer myself to be no longer made The Butt—& therefore request the favour of you to empower some person here to settle your Account & relieve, Sir, &ca.—

SOURCE: Letterbook copy, HL Papers, S. C. Hist. Soc.; addressed "Esquire. Barbadoes"; "per Gilcrist."

---

of William Simpson who had resigned. Miscellaneous Records, LL, Part 1 (1758–1763), p. 198, S. C. Archives. On March 24, 1761, he received at the Court of St. James a crown patent to the office of clerk of common pleas which was recorded in Charleston on Nov. 21, 1763. Miscellaneous Records, MM, Part 1 (1763–1767), p. 2, S. C. Archives. He was granted a leave of absence for six months beginning July 1, 1769. Miscellaneous Records, OO, Part 1 (1767–1771), pp. 126–127, S. C. Archives. At the beginning of the August term of the Court of Common Pleas on Aug. 8, 1769, James Johnston presented his commission as deputy clerk of the crown and peace and also of the court of common pleas. Journal, Court of Common Pleas, 1763–1769, p. 413, S. C. Archives. As Campbell was about to leave the province he drew up a will in which he made Dr. Alexander Garden, Robert Wells, and James Johnston (who had served him for five years as a clerk) his executors. "Will of Dougal Campbell," dated ———, proved Dec. 28, 1770, Charleston County Wills, XIII, Book C (1767–1771), 960–961, S. C. Archives.

[5] *HL Papers*, III, 213.

TO ROBERT DEANS

Charles Town, 2d December 1763

Sir,

I am very sorry that I happen'd to be from home when you call'd upon me because I realy did want to see you and wonder'd much at your keeping away so that I cou'd not help taking notice of it & asking Mr. Legitt[6] if you were dead or alive.

SOURCE: Letterbook copy, Letter Book of Henry Laurens, Oct. 30, 1762–Sept. 10, 1766, Penn. Hist. Soc.

TO JOHN TARLETON

[Charles Town] 3d December 1763

Sir,

The annex'd is duplicate of what I wrote to you the 9th Ulto. to which I beg leave to refer. As I had been lucky in meeting with a wraft of exceeding good Scantlin which was left behind by a former Vessel & saved much time I was in great hopes that your *Elizabeth* would have been at Sea two days ago but the people on board seem to be small folks to which Capt. Thornton ascribes the tediousness in taking the Lumber on board. It is now in & a Corn Room is building. Therefore I hope in Six or Seven days more to clear her out, as every article except the Pork & Pitch are ready & I shall not think it for your Interest to detain her for either in case they do not come to Market in the mean time.[7] Rice sells as briskly as ever I knew it at 50/ Cash down & there seems to be Vessels enough in Port to carry off 20 to 30 Thousand Barrels. I remain with great respect, &ca.—

SOURCE: Letterbook copy, HL Papers, S. C. Hist. Soc.; addressed "Liverpoole"; "per his Majesty's Ship *Success*. Copy per *Bonnetta*, Man of War."

---

[6] Mr. Legitt must have been one of Robert Deans' workmen. HL was anxiously awaiting the completion of his house.

[7] The brigantine *Elizabeth,* Richard Thornton, was cleared outwards for Grenada on Dec. 21 with a cargo of 108 barrels and 119 half barrels of rice, 10 barrels of pitch, 10 barrels of tar, 15 barrels of turpentine, 60 barrels of pork, 1,260 bushels of corn, 6,000 feet of lumber, and 30,000 shingles. Naval Office Lists, 1757–1764, p. 136.

TO RICHARD OSWALD & CO.[8]

[Charles Town] 3d December 1763

Gentlemen,

Since my last of the 19th June per Gunn[9] & Curlet[1] I am honour'd with your favour of the 3d October by the hands of Lieutenant Thomas Aubery[2] who I hope will experience the great regard that I pay upon every occasion to your orders & recommendations.

Mr. Rutherford's Warrant hath hitherto produced him no more than to serve for running Cash. Whither the Receiver General here is in fault or not I do not determine but our friend in North Carolina is in daily expectation of some powers whereby he shall enable me to quicken that Gentleman's pace toward the pay-Table. Mean time he is extremely desirous & anxious to discharge his obligation to you & to oblige him I will by some means or other put Cash or effects in your hands before the 1st February (I mean the remittance from hence) to the Amount of One Thousand pounds Sterling altho I should advance the whole upon the security of the said Warrant which is at present in my Desk.[3]

Rice sells as briskly as ever I knew it at 50/ per Ct. Cash down & there seems to be Tonnage enough in port to take off 20 or 30 Thousand Barrels; the whole Crop will be very large & I think that admitting a considerable abatement before the Year comes round, yet the average added to a Large produce of fine Indigo will make our annual export far beyond that of any preceeding Year. The planters must therefore have ability (& they have always inclination) to make large purchases of Negroes, & to give as good prices as were given this last Summer which were very great, not Less than £33.10/ round per head on the several Cargoes that were imported.

The late meeting at Augusta of the Governors of North & South Carolina, Virginia, & Georgia with the principal Men of the

---

[8] *HL Papers*, II, 169n; III, 35n, 43n.

[9] The ship *Heart of Oak*, Henry Gunn, sailed for Cowes on June 22. *Gazette*, June 25, 1763.

[1] The ship *Maria*, Patrick Curlett, was cleared outwards for Cowes on June 28. Naval Office Lists, 1757–1764, p. 133.

[2] Lt. Thomas Aubrey, who was on his way to St. Augustine, must have sailed in the schooner *Harlequin*, Abiel Camp, owned by Thomas Buckle of Charleston, which was cleared outwards for St. Augustine on Dec. 3. Naval Office Lists, 1757–1764, p. 136; HL to Thomas Aubrey, Jan. 9, 1764.

[3] The receiver-general of quit rents for S. C. paid HL £300 sterling in 1763 on John Rutherford's warrant and £700 sterling in 1764. Quit Rents, 1760–1768, Receipts & Disbursements, pp. 112, 142, S. C. Archives.

Cherokee, Creek, Chickesaw, Choctaw, & Catabaw Indians, has ended pretty well & we have some prospect of being at Peace with those very troublesome Neighbours for some Years to come in which time I hope we shall gain such an establishment as will make Peace most desirable to them.

Waiting your further commands I remain with great regard, &ca.—

SOURCE: Letterbook copy, HL Papers, S. C. Hist. Soc.; addressed "London"; "per his Majestys Ship *Success*. Copy per *Bonnetta*, Man of War."

TO COWLES & HARFORD

[Charles Town] 3d December 1763

Gentlemen,

You have in the above a Copy of what I last wrote to you under the 12th Ulto., since which I have receiv'd yours of the 23d September & duly regard the contents thereof. Mr. Appleby has something to observe upon the Accounts of A., L., A., but as he is now sick abed I shall defer the information until he is up again which I hope will be in a few days.

Your Brigantine *Favourite* has on board about 550 Barrels of Pitch & Tar on your Account & I think it more for your Interest to dispatch her with Rice than to wait another return of the Schooners from George Town in hopes of Pitch. They came in a few days ago & brought none, in short not a Barrel has escaped me as Capt. Brownett will inform you, but there hath been very little made & what is now preparing I cannot expect in less than 14 or 20 days perhaps Longer & tis not worth while considering the high price to detain the Vessel for it. If I had been so fully appriz'd of this before; she should have been at Sea by this day but I was kept in hopes of what has not come to pass. I should have fill'd her with Rice this week but have not met with a quality to please me tho I have sold at least 700 Barrels. She has on Freight a few Casks of Indigo & 11 Hogsheads of Skins & Pink Root & I do not expect much more.[4] I think it probable that I shall

---

[4] The *Favourite* was cleared outwards for Bristol on Dec. 20 with a cargo of 138 barrels and 13 half barrels of rice, 228 barrels of pitch, 311 barrels of tar, 14 hogsheads of deerskins, 12,312 pounds of indigo, 2,600 feet of lumber, and 4 hogsheads of pink root. Naval Office Lists, 1757–1764, p. 136. The root of

Interest you four or five hundred pounds Sterling in Indigo & my self double that Value per the *Favourite* which I hint because there may want other opportunities to advise. As to my own except the Three Hundred Guineas which I have already desired you to Insure I shall risque it or make Insurance here & keep & transmit Accounts of the Interest quite distinct.

Rice sells very briskly at 50/ per Ct. & there seems to be Vessels enough in port to take off ¼th of our large Crop. This added to the article of Indigo will make our Export 1763 to 1764 Amount to a very considerable Sum.

I pray you to forward those other Accounts for which I have so often troubled you & you will further oblige, &ca.—

SOURCE: Letterbook copy, HL Papers, S. C. Hist. Soc.; addressed "Bristol"; "per *Success,* Man of War. Copy per *Bonnetta,* Man War."

TO AUGUSTUS & JOHN BOYD

[Charles Town] 3d December 1763

Gentlemen,

I have not troubled you with a Letter since the 19th September per Capt. Watts & Capt. Green altho the *Portland* Brigantine Loaded on your Account for St. Kitts sail'd above six weeks ago, but I defer'd writing on Account of some apparent errors in the delivery of the Lumber on board her, in order to have those remov'd & a clear Account establish'd; for notwithstanding the great caution us'd on my part of hiring a Man on purpose to receive no other than such Timber, Boards, &ca., as were contained in your order, & to mark so many pieces as were there directed; yet I found upon the whole that there was great confusion between him & the Planter who provided the Cargo; & the former declares that he was very exact & marked all the pieces agreeable to order & no other; but that Mr. Miller (the Plant-

---

spigelia marilandica, called Carolina pink, was used as a vermifuge and purgative. *OED.* Catesby described "the Indian Pink" and stated that "a decoction made of this Plant is good against Worms." Mark Catesby, *The Natural History of Carolina, Florida, and the Bahama Islands* (2 vols.: London, 1771), II, 78. John Lining gave the medicinal properties of the "Indian Pink" in *Edinburgh Essays and Observations, Physical and Literary,* I (1754), 386–389. Also see Alexander Garden, "An Account of the Indian Pink," *Edinburgh Essays and Observations, Physical and Literary,* III (1771), 145–153.

er)[5] had a Little wantonly & without any order, also marked a great many pieces which he did not discover before it was stowed away. They differ Likewise in their Accounts of the quantity nor is there half as many Inch Boards as I had order'd. My agreement however was to pay for no more than Receipts from the Captain or Mate should be produced for. Upon this foundation I have made my Accounts & hitherto regulated my payments also; & I think there is no room for a dispute on Mr. Miller side; tho he expresses some dissatisfaction & insinuates that there are mistakes to his prejudice. I explained in the best manner I could to Mr. Bowrey the case of the Timber Mark'd AB. If I am not deceiv'd he will find pieces enough to tally with your order & the rest may go in the common heap.

Please now to receive inclos'd an Invoice & Bill of Loading for said Cargo including the Freight paid here Amount to your debit £3,337.11.7 for which I shall take the Liberty in a day or two to pass Bills on you at the rate of 721 per Cent which is the very highest Exchange. I trust you will find my Accounts free from error but if you discover any to your prejudice I shall on the first information make amends.

The Crop of Rice which is certainly as large as ever was made is beginning to sell at 50/ per Ct. The demand is brisk on Account of many Vessels in port enough in my judgement to carry off 20 or 30 Thousand Barrels. Some Freight is taken on a Vessel or two for London at 50/ per Ton but this cannot be afforded & therefore must fall if the price of Rice holds up. Our Crop of Indigo is likewise very considerable & the price high enough; good Copper sells at 25/ to 27/6 per lb. & Flora 30/ to 40/. These articles will make a Large export & enrich our Planters. Negroes sold very high all the past Summer. The general Average was upward of £33 Sterling per head & early Cargoes the ensuing Year will meet with as good a reception. I remain with great regard, &ca.—

SOURCE: Letterbook copy, HL Papers, S. C. Hist. Soc.; addressed "Esquires. London"; "per the *Success,* Man of War. Copy per *Bonnetta,* Man of War, with 2d Bill loading & abstract Invoice."

---

[5] Stephen Miller supplied lumber for HL's West Indian vessels. *HL Papers,* III, 261n. He was, in spite of his English name, of the Huguenot group that dominated the parish of St. Thomas. His father Etienne Mounier was a Charleston merchant turned planter. The family changed the spelling of Mounier to Miller between the signing and the proving of the father's will. "Will of Etienne Mounier," dated Nov. 2, 1747, proved Jan. 19, 1749, Charleston County Wills, VI (1747–1752), 266–269, S. C. Archives.

TO JOHN RUTHERFORD

[Charles Town] 3d December 1763

I have but just time by this opportunity to acknowledge the receipt of a Letter from you without date which reached me the 5th Ulto. & to say a word or two more.

Mr. Saxby seems to regard the talks of suing him only as mere threats & no more. A possitive order from you for such an attack would probably produce some effect. It might produce at least an Account from him & give you the satisfaction of being inform'd. He has made no payment since the last trifle noted to you but promises me another trifle soon.

I lately received a Letter from Messrs. Oswald & Co. They were well. Your name was mention'd & a hint of the expected remittance from you through my hands. My inclination is to serve & oblige you both but I can't effect it without means. However I shall now strain a point & remit on your Account above One Thousand pounds Sterling before the 1st February & told them so last night.

I am sure you will take measures to save me from Loss by the advance of my Money. I am, Sir, &ca.—

SOURCE: Letterbook copy, HL Papers, S. C. Hist. Soc.; addressed "Esquire. North Carolina"; "delivered the 4th to Mr. Stone." This letter was copied by HL.

TO ANDREW WILLIAMSON [6]

[Charles Town] 5th December 1763

Sir,

I receiv'd your favour of the 27th Ulto. & with it one of the

---

[6] Andrew Williamson (1730?–1786) first appeared in the backcountry in 1758 driving cattle and hogs. On March 5, 1758, Lt. Col. Henry Bouquet wrote from Charleston to Ensign Lachlan McIntosh at Fort Prince George: "The Bearer Williamson has been pay'd for the driving of his Steers & Porks, & shall be employ'd for the future as long as he behaves well & punctually." *Papers of Henry Bouquet,* I, 321. In the years immediately following he supplied horses, steers, pork, and other provisions for the frontier forts and army expeditions. House Journal, XXXIV (March 26, 1761–Dec. 26, 1761), 130, 138, 141, S. C. Archives. He had been appointed a lieutenant in the provincial regiment on Sept. 22, 1760, and had therefore been one of HL's officers. During the Revolution he never seemed to be quite patriot or quite tory. Anne King Gregorie, "Andrew Williamson," *DAB.*

Horses that Mr. Terry[7] made me pay for, for which I am very much obliged to you & shall always be mindful of this & many other kind acts of yours toward me.

If Colonel Grant calls here in his way to St. Augustine (you may depend upon it) I will not forget to give him a hint of your request & if I have any influence with him my endeavours shall not be wanting to facilitate your business of supplying Beef for his Garrison which I may presume you can & will do upon at least as good terms as any body else & that you only require that preference that is usually & very justly given to old Correspondents.[8]

My Compliments to Capt. Bell[9] & hearty wishes to you & yours are now offer'd again by, Sir, &ca.—

SOURCE: Letterbook copy, Letter Book of Henry Laurens, Oct. 30, 1762–Sept. 10, 1766, Penn. Hist. Soc.; addressed "Hard Labour, Ninety Six"; "per Mr. Bole."

TO THOMAS GODFREY[1]

[Charles Town] 6th December 1763

Mr. Thomas Gadsden[2] was so good as [to] leave your favour of the 30th Ulto. at my house. It cover'd as you say Two hundred & forty seven Pounds 14/6 & 6d more which is with my thanks duly passed to your Credit & I remain, Sir, your humble—

SOURCE: Letterbook copy, Letter Book of Henry Laurens, Oct. 30, 1762–Sept. 10, 1766, Penn. Hist. Soc.

---

[7] Champness Terry of Ninety Six District. "Will of Champness Terry," dated Sept. 14, 1775, proved ————, Charleston County Wills, XVII, Book B (1774–1779), 502-503, S. C. Archives.

[8] The *Gazette*, Nov. 26, 1763, contained an announcement of the appointments of James Grant and George Johnstone to the governorships of East and West Florida.

[9] Thomas Bell was granted 200 acres on Wilson's Creek near Ninety Six on March 17, 1760. Index to Grants, S. C. Archives. He was the commander of the garrison in Fort Ninety Six to April 1761. *Gazette*, April 11, 1761. He was a justice of the peace for both Granville and Colleton counties in 1765. *Gazette*, Oct. 31, 1765. In 1767 he was appointed lieutenant colonel of a new regiment on the southwest frontier of Carolina. *Country Journal*, Oct. 20, 1767. In May 1770 Major Andrew Williamson was cited as principal creditor to administer the estate of Thomas Bell lately deceased. *SCHM*, XLIII (1942), 119.

[1] *HL Papers*, III, 145n.

[2] *HL Papers*, III, 145n. Godfrey and Gadsden had a store in Georgetown where they sold "A large and complete assortment of European and East-India Goods." *Gazette*, Dec. 31, 1763.

TO BENJAMIN GARDEN

Charles Town, 6 December 1763

Dear Sir,

Mr. John Neyle's information to you with respect to your rough Rice as you represent it is as well as I can remember very just. The distance of time between his first speaking to me and some doubts that he express'd the second time had both lost the Subject in my Mind & made some difference as to my sending a Boat of my own but as you have removed that obstacle & my intentions were purely to serve you be pleased to send down the Rice & your expectations shall not be disappointed from any default in me who am, Dear Sir, yours, &ca.—

SOURCE: Letterbook copy, Letter Book of Henry Laurens, Oct. 30, 1762– Sept. 10, 1766, Penn. Hist. Soc.

TO WILLIAM FISHER

Charles Town, So. Carolina, 6th December 1763

[The copy of this letter which is in the Haverford College collection was misdated. The date should have been written as Dec. 6, 1762. The text of this letter was printed under the correct date in HL Papers, III, *186–187, from the letterbook copy in the* HL Papers, S. C. Hist. Soc.*]*

SOURCE: Copy, Charles Roberts Autograph Collection, Haverford College; addressed "2 Copy. Copy per Williams. Original per Kelly." Endorsed: "H. Laurens letter dated 6 December 1763."

TO JAMES HOUSTOUN [3]

[Charles Town] 7th December 1763

Sir,

Upon Receipt of your favour of the 10th Ulto. I apply'd to

---

[3] James Houstoun (spelled "Houston" here) was the younger brother of Sir Patrick Houstoun, both of whom came from Glasgow. He petitioned for 500 acres on the neck between Vernon and Little Ogeechee rivers on Nov. 7, 1755. He represented Vernonburgh in the Georgia assembly in 1755 and 1756. *Colonial Records of Georgia,* XIII, 7, 81, 293; Edith Duncan Johnston, *The Houstouns of Georgia* (Athens, Ga., 1950), pp. 22, 73.

Mr. Appleby, one of my late partners, in whose hands Hugh Roses[4] Bond & Mortgage had fallen & shew'd him what you had wrote to me upon the subject of that debt & he has since inform'd me that he has surrender'd both to Mr. Robert Brisbane[5] on your Account. I am, &ca.—

SOURCE: Letterbook copy, HL Papers, S. C. Hist. Soc.; addressed "Esquire. Savanna in Georgia"; "per Mr. Lloyd."

TO GRAHAM, READ, & MOSSMAN[6]

[Charles Town] 7th December 1763

Gentlemen,

Some Night about a Week since, a Lad belonging to a Pilot Boat with a bundle of loose papers was brought up into my dining room. He said he was advis'd to bring those papers to me. I ask'd him what they were & when he had got them? The Evening before replied he I found them in the Bay & there are papers & Letters of consequence here. Why did you bring them to me in particular of all the people in Town? Because you will find a Letter directed to you amongst the papers.

---

[4] Hugh Rose of St. Peter parish, Granville County, died on Sept. 26, 1761. James Houstoun of Savannah was an executor of his will. *Georgia Wills*, p. 119; "Will of Hugh Rose," dated Sept. 26, 1761, proved Nov. 24, 1761, Charleston County Wills, IX, Book A (1760–1767), 311–312, S. C. Archives.

[5] Robert Brisbane (1707–1781), a graduate of the University of Glasgow in 1723, came to Carolina in 1733. His brother William (1710–1771), who was trained as a surgeon and apothecary, was also a merchant. *SCHM*, XIV (1913), 123–127; "Will of William Brisbane," dated May 11, 1771, proved Nov. 1, 1771; "Will of Robert Brisbane," dated Aug. 26, 1774, proved Dec. 28, 1781, *Abstracts of Wills, 1760–1784*, pp. 162, 329. Robert and William Brisbane, Charleston merchants, bought land in Granville County on June 19, 1764. Deeds, DDD, pp. 735–749, S. C. Archives.

[6] James Graham, James Read, & James Mossman. John and James Graham had a store at Yamacraw; James Mossman "on the Bay" in Savannah. *Georgia Gazette*, July 7, 1763. When James Box advertised in the *Georgia Gazette*, July 21, 1763, that the debts due to Grahams & Mossman be paid, the partnership had already long expired. John Graham had sailed for Cowes on July 9. *Georgia Gazette*, July 14, 1763. When John Graham returned in July 1764, he was a member of the royal council. *Georgia Gazette*, July 5, 1764. James Read who had moved his interest from S. C. to Georgia in the mid-1750's had joined with James Graham and James Mossman in the new partnership. *HL Papers*, II, 213n; III, 136n. James Read and James Graham were commissioners of the pilotage for Savannah. *Georgia Gazette*, Jan. 19, 1764.

This Led me, in presence of my Clerk & a Gentleman who was at my house, to look so far into them as to come at my own Letter (which I knew by the handwriting on the outside was from Messrs. Meyler & Hall) & to discover that your Names were on all the other papers or so far at least as to satisfy my self that all the rest belonged to you & then I caused my Clerk in presence of the pretended finder to Seal up the whole in a packet as I now transmit them by the hands of Mr. Lloyd.[7]

I know not how to Account for this odd circumstance but in this one way. That some curious friend of mine has taken up a packet directed to me from Jamaica with one inclosed for you, have satisfied their itch by perusing the contents, & then not quite so diabolical as to throw it into the fire have given it the chance of a foundling. I have heard many people complain of injuries of this nature in our Town. I am, &ca.—

SOURCE: Letterbook copy, HL Papers, S. C. Hist. Soc.; addressed "Savanna"; "per Thomas Lloyd, Esq."

TO AUGUSTUS & JOHN BOYD

[Charles Town] 7 December 1763

The foregoing is duplicate of what I wrote to you the 3d Inst. per *Success,* Man of War.[8] Please now to receive a second Bill of Loading & abstract Invoice for the Cargo per *Portland* Brigantine & to be informed that I have of this date passed two Bills on you at 40 days sight payable to the order of Benjamin Stead,[9] Vizt. One Bill for £462.18.3 Sterling on your Account & passed to your Credit at 721 per Cent Exchange £3,337.11.7. The other for One hundred & fifty pounds Sterling on Account of Messrs. Smith & Baillies of St. Kitts in part of their Balance with me for one half Amount of a Cargo

[7] Thomas Lloyd was a Savannah factor and merchant who sold rum, wine, sugar, and slaves on his wharf. *Georgia Gazette,* Jan. 24, Aug. 15, 1765. He died in Charleston on Aug. 31, 1766. HL to John Lewis Gervais, Sept. 1, 1766, Letter Book of Henry Laurens, Oct. 30, 1762–Sept. 10, 1766, Penn. Hist. Soc.

[8] HMS *Success,* John Botterell, sailed over Charleston bar with HMS *Bonetta,* Lancelot Holmes, on Dec. 10 bound for Sheerness. Ship's log, HMS *Success,* Adm. 51/940, Public Record Office, London.

[9] Benjamin Stead, formerly a Charleston merchant, had returned to England in 1759. Rogers, *Evolution of a Federalist,* pp. 15, 16, 22, 60, 80, 82, 115n, 128; *HL Papers,* II, 22n.

Shiped on their Account per Brigantine *Nicholas & Mary,* Capt. Barker, for that Island & a Shipment formerly mentioned to you. I made Insurance on the whole Cargo in this place which renders it unnecessary to transmit you the Bill Loading, &ca., as they had order'd me to do in other cases.

Those Gentlemen lately desired me, if possible, to avoid drawing on you & to wait until they should remit me from their Island, which method I am morally sure would prove very injurious to both parties. To me first because so long waiting I should sink my Commission & probably more money; & to them because there is no commodity can be sent from thence (unless an accidental purchase of Slaves should favour them) that will yield within 10 per cent of cost & charges. I know this by experience being daily selling Rum & Sugar to my own & the Loss of other people, which hath been the case for some Months past & from the large importations lately made of Rum there is not the least prospect of amendment for many Months to come. Nevertheless for this one time I would without regard to my own Interest have indulged them but I had engaged my Bill, was complimented with the highest Exchange, & could not conveniently substitute another in its place. I trust that they have a sufficient fund with you for the present purpose. If not be so good as to recommend the draught to my friends formerly Noted in London or Bristol who will pay it on my Account, & I must submit to the disappointment.

SOURCE: Letterbook copy, HL Papers, S. C. Hist. Soc.; addressed "London"; "per *Bonetta,* Man of War. Copy per *Success.*" This letter was copied by HL.

PURCHASE OF BROUGHTON ISLAND PLANTATION

December 8, 1763

[*HL bought Broughton Island plantation of 900 acres from Lachlan McIntosh for £4,500 currency.*[1]]

SOURCE: Lease and release, Dec. 7, 8, 1763, Conveyances, Book CC, pp. 990–992, Ga. Archives.

[1] Lachlan McIntosh had traded two 500 acre tracts on the Newport River for Broughton Island and a 100 acre tract on the north side of the Altamaha River which were owned by Jonathan Bryan. Conveyances, Book CC, pp. 989–990,

TO RICHARD HEATLY

[Charles Town] 9th December 1763

Sir,

After referring you to the foregoing duplicate of what I wrote to you the 4th October I have to inform you that some Casks of your Wine are sold at low prices, Vizt. £4 per doz. for that in Bottles & £30 per Cask for that in quarter pipes. This is poor doing but tis the best our glutted Market affords. I have try'd it upon several different days at Vendue but without success. I have lately seen large quantities of Wine in bottles which appears to be of the same quality as your White sold at 50/ per doz. I shall do all in my power to make the best end of both Sale & remittance & remain, &ca.—

SOURCE: Letterbook copy, HL Papers, S. C. Hist. Soc.; addressed "London"; "per the *Bonetta,* Man of War."

TO LUKE KIERSTED [2]

[Charles Town] 10th December 1763

Sir,

As I have not had the pleasure of hearing from you since you left Carolina I take the liberty of requesting that you wou'd be pleas'd to transmitt me an Account of my Rice & of what remittances you may have made To Mr. William Hodgson of London because without such an Account I cannot Settle with that Gentleman & he begins to be very Anxious to have an end put to his concerns in this part of the World & as I do not love to be troubled with dunns I beg you will do that part which you have undertaken in this affair & advise me by the first opportunity. I am, &ca.—

Ga. Archives. Bryan had been granted Broughton Island which consisted of 900 acres in 1758. Royal Grants, Book A, p. 652, Ga. Archives. Bryan was originally from Granville County in S. C. He established a plantation on the Savannah River just east of Savannah Township between 1750 and 1752. He was the first Carolinian to be appointed to the royal council of Georgia on Oct. 30, 1754 in which he served until the end of 1769 when he was expelled for his opposition to the Townshend Acts. *Colonial Records of Georgia,* VI, 333, 369; VII, 9; W. W. Abbot, *The Royal Governors of Georgia, 1754-1775* (Chapel Hill, N. C., 1959), p. 151.

[2] The sloop *William & Anne,* Luke Kiersted, who was also one of the owners, cleared outwards on April 20, 1763, for New York with 195 barrels of rice. Naval Office Lists, 1757-1764, p. 130.

SOURCE: Letterbook copy, HL Papers, S. C. Hist. Soc.; addressed "Captain. New York"; "per the Sloop [Industry] Capt. Rose per New York."

TO GRUBB & WATSON[3]

[Charles Town] 12 December 1763

Gentlemen,

I have before me your many favours contain'd under the 15th June, 12th July, 6th, 17th August, 19th September, 4 & 6th October, & thank you for these regular advices of your markets, for the acceptance of my Bills, for the compliment that you are pleased to make to me on our connexion in the Ship *Heart of Oak*,[4] & particularly for your attention to my friend Mr. Henderson.[5]

I thank you too for not adding to my Loss by the rice in the *Two Brothers*, Capt. Denning,[6] which you might have done.

You think that the particular manner in which my Bill of Loading for the Cargo of Rice per the *Hope*[7] was fill'd up gave me a real advantage in the Sale of it; but have left me uninform'd what that advantage is; for hitherto I can only discover that I have paid an extrordinary Freight & premium of Insurance in order to obtain some advantage by having every Market open to me & that my Rice sold exactly at the same price of other Cargos many weeks after & restricted to a particular Market; free too from the above mention'd additional charges; this I suppose you must know to be fact. There

---

[3] Richard Grubb and Alexander Watson. *HL Papers,* III, 41n.

[4] The ship *Heart of Oak* had been built in South Carolina by John Rose who was the owner at the time that it was registered in Charleston on April 27, 1763. *HL Papers,* III, 478n. The vessel was cleared outwards with Henry Gunn as master on June 14 for Cowes. Naval Office Lists, 1757–1764, p. 132. When the ship *Heart of Oak,* Henry Gunn, was entered inwards on Feb. 14, 1764, from London, it was listed as having been registered in London on Nov. 11, 1763, with the owners as Henry Laurens, James Laurens, John Edwards, John Savage, and John Rose of Charleston and Grubb & Watson of London. Naval Office Lists, 1764–1767, p. 70.

[5] HL had written a letter of introduction for William Henderson, former master of the Charleston Free School, to Grubb & Watson, April 23, 1763. *HL Papers,* III, 416n, 417.

[6] The ship *Two Brothers,* Timothy Denning, had sailed for London on July 9, 1762. *HL Papers,* III, 131n. The *Two Brothers* carried 655 barrels and 82 half barrels of rice. Naval Office Lists, 1757–1764, p. 101.

[7] The brigantine *Hope,* Anthony Marshall, was cleared outwards on March 29, 1763, with 753 barrels and 103 half barrels of rice for Cowes. Naval Office Lists, 1757–1764, p. 130; *HL Papers,* III, 379.

are many proofs of it & I have one within my own concerns. I know that you do not Love to be Chid, & I declare to you that nothing is more painfull to me than to be pointing out faults which I also Know often appear in the consequence of a well design'd & promising act but in this case you have said too much & I am obliged either to pass over the Subject with a contemptuous silence or just to hint to you that I do take some notice of what is going forward in the commercial World. My Love & regard for you will not Suffer the former & I hope on the other hand that you will not be offended at my remarks which are not intended to do you any prejudice.

I find that my part of the Freight home per *Heart of Oak* was paid into your hands. This has emboldened me to pass a Bill on you to the order of Mr. George Appleby for £159 & two others to the order of Mr. William Hopton for £50 each, all at 40 days sight, which I recommend to your accustom'd punctuality.

When that Ship arrives I shall do all in my power to promote the General Interest but at present our prospect is rather unfavourable. Rice has broke too high this Year to hope for any advantage from it in the Europian Markets & Indico goes of[f] far beyond those prices which you were so kind as to hint to me, & yet methinks I never saw more eager purchasers of both articles which must arise from the benefit of better inteligence or from a greater necessity of Sterling Money than I have at present. I wish for the sake of the concern'd that it may be from the first. If you will be pleas'd to continue your advices I shall chearfully throw a Commission in your way provided I can barely have a return of my own money & upon such terms wou'd Ship with Spirit. I am with true respect, &ca.—

SOURCE: Letterbook copy, HL Papers, S. C. Hist. Soc.; addressed "London"; "per Capt. Ball. Copy per White."

TO RICHARD OSWALD & CO.

[Charles Town] 12 December 1763

Gentlemen,

I wrote you the 3d Inst. per the *Success* & *Bonetta,* Man of War, & according to my promise have begun to put Money into your hands by a Shipment now per the *Friendship,* Capt. Ball,[8] of 2,463¼ or it may be 2,464 Dollars (there being some difference as to the Number of pieces) Weight if the first 2,144 Ounces as per Bill Loading inclosed & proportionably more if the Latter Number. This Silver you will be pleas'd to dispose of to the Credit of my Account & transfer the same again to the Credit of John Rutherford, Esq. on his Bond & to advise me thereof as soon as you can.

If Silver shou'd be low upon the arival of this & you think the price will soon change for the better you will be so good as to defer the Sale to a proper time. I remain, Yours, &ca., &ca.—

SOURCE: Letterbook copy, HL Papers, S. C. Hist. Soc.; addressed "London"; "per Capt. Ball. Copy per Brownett."

TO WILLIAM HODSHON

[Charles Town] 12 December 1763

Sir,

My last trouble was under the 26th August per Capt. Watts to which please to be referr'd. I have not fail'd in due & constant application to your Debtors in Georgia but hitherto without further success than thru a payment of £421.2.6 Current Money for amount of Timberlakes protested Bill on Boulk[9] for £50 Sterling Re Exchange, Intrest, & Charges thereon which Sum is passed to your Credit & I now remitt you by the *Friendship,* Capt. Ball, as per Bill Loading inclos'd 250 Spanish Dollars at 31/6 per the price at which I rece'd them (tho' they are now sold as high as 31/9½ per piece.)[1] I have Charged the same to your Debit £393.15.0. The Gentlemen in Georgia affect to be very anxious to pay off their whole Balance & have lately tender'd more Bills upon New York which I have refused & hope they will soon fall upon some other better method

---

[8] The ship *Friendship,* Thomas Ball, cleared outwards on Dec. 20 for London. Naval Office Lists, 1757–1764, p. 136. The silver was not recorded as a part of the cargo.

[9] Richard Timberlake's bill, dated Sept. 4, 1762, drawn on John Bourke, merchant of London. *HL Papers,* III, 233, 535, 542. "Boulk" should have been copied as Bourke.

[1] The dollar was valued in Charleston at 31 shillings currency in June 1757. *Papers of Henry Bouquet,* I, 117. For a quotation of the value of silver in London see *HL Papers,* III, 528.

or that you will have appointed a more capable person to close this troublesome affair. I remain your, &ca.—

P.S. You see that every Bill from Jamaica is not absolutely good for nothing.

P.S. 22d December. I have good reasons to expect a further sum of £270 Sterling or thereabout in currency for New York Bills which come offer'd to me & since Sold payable the Middle January which shall be sent forward as soon as Gold, Silver, or Bills can be procured.

SOURCE: Letterbook copy, HL Papers, S. C. Hist. Soc.; addressed "London"; "per Capt. Ball. Copy per White with 2d Bill Loading."

TO MONKHOUSE DAVISON[2]
[Charles Town] December 12, 1763

Having too long put of[f] to write to you by this Conveyance both on Mrs. Stokes' & my own Account, I have barely time while the Ship is getting under Sale[3] to enclose a Certificate for the two Cases of Hyson Tea which you sent me by her, Vizt. The *Friendship,* Capt. Ball, the Amount of said Tea being Eighty Eight pounds Ten Shillings & five pence Sterling [*which*] I hope you have rec'd as I desir'd of Mrs. Sarah Nicholson & Co. If not, be pleas'd to call for it by this Letter & my next to them which will be tomorrow shall take further Notice of it. I am glad you ship'd me no more Tea. I imported it to serve a poor friend & Relation[4] who can make no hand of commerce & I shall probably loose twenty per Cent by it. I am, &ca.—

SOURCE: Letterbook copy, HL Papers, S. C. Hist. Soc.; addressed "London"; "per Capt. Ball."

---

[2] *HL Papers,* III, 138n.
[3] Sail.
[4] HL did have many cousins who were the children and grandchildren of his aunt Jane Laurens Perdriau Savineau and of his uncle Augustus Laurens. A number of these were of the tradesman class.

TO LLOYD & JAMES [5]

[Charles Town] 13 December 1763

Gentlemen,

I thank you for your favour of 26 July which came duly to hand informing me of your junction in trade in which I heartily wish you success & that it may be at any time in my power to contribute thereto, consistant with those Natural engagements which I have frankly confess'd myself to be under with some other worthy Gentlemen in your City. In such cases you shall find that my offers of service are not merely the effects of formality. Our friend Joseph Brown of Winyaw sent me today a small hogshead Indico to be ship'd to your address & I have already put it on board the Brigantine *Favourite,* Capt. Brownett. You will be pleas'd to insure on said Indico on Mr. Brown Account Ninety Pounds Sterling. The Vessel I hope to clear out on the 17 Inst. Rice Sells currently at 50/ per Ct. & Indico from 27 to 28/, Good Copper. I never saw the town so Eager in purchasing both & yet methinks there is but little encouragement given in our late advices from your Side. Naval Stores are excessively scarce & Dear. Pitch 80/, Tar 50/, Turpentine 15/, Deer Skins 13 to 14/, Exchange 721 per Cent. I am—

SOURCE: Letterbook copy, HL Papers, S. C. Hist. Soc.; addressed "Bristol"; "per Ball. Copy per White."

TO JOHN KNIGHT & THOMAS MEARS [6]

[Charles Town] 14 December 1763

I hope this will reach a Ship now getting under Sail to advise you of the *Austin's* arrival here last night from Barbadoes.[7] Every

---

[5] Lloyd is written "Loyd" in the letterbook. Edward Lloyd was a partner in Devonsheir, Reeve, & Lloyd by May 22, 1755, but no longer a partner on Sept. 15, 1762. *HL Papers,* I, 251n. Edward Lloyd was seeking business on his own at the end of 1762. HL to Edward Lloyd, Nov. 25, 1762, *HL Papers,* III, 170. As this letter indicates, he had very recently joined a partnership with William James. Lloyd was dead by July 16, 1765. Judgment Rolls, 1767, No. 414A, S. C. Archives.

[6] *HL Papers,* I, 245n.

[7] The snow *Austin,* Matthias Holme, was entered inwards on Dec. 14 from Liverpool and Barbados with a cargo of 1,880 bushels of salt and sundry British goods. Naval Office Lists, 1757–1764, p. 125. HL had complained in February 1763 that the time consumed in unloading salt from the *Austin* would delay her departure. *HL Papers,* III, 252, 256.

thing shall be done for her Interest that my abilities can effect, but your Salt! your Salt! is again in the way of her being a first Ship[8] which I would have her but for that, altho some people have much the start of me which could neither be foreseen nor avoided, but I shall have the honour of writing more before tomorrow Morning. Mean time, &ca.—

SOURCE: Letterbook copy, HL Papers, S. C. Hist. Soc.; addressed "Owners of the *Austin,* Leverpoole"; "per Ball. Copy per (destroy'd)." This letter was copied by HL.

TO JONAS MAYNARD

[Charles Town] 14 December 1763

Sir,

I wrote you the 30th Ulto. per Capt. Gilchrist[9] to which please to be refer'd. Yesterday your favour of 14th Ulto. came to hand inclosing John Lindsays protested Bill for £111.1.2 Sterling Endors'd by Edward Blake[1] who has settled an Account of said Bill & Charges already & has given me satisfactory Security to pay in Seven days, & within two or three days after such payment if I cannot meet with a better Bill shall remitt one of my own for One hundred & twenty three Pounds 12/6 Sterling being the Balance of Bill, re-exchange, &ca., after deducting my commission. This goes by way of Antigua. Therefore do not inclose your Account Current but I hope you will very soon empower some person here to settle it with me according to my late request. Such person will be impartial & therefore less lyable to Err than the parties concern'd. I remain—

SOURCE: Letterbook copy, HL Papers, S. C. Hist. Soc.; addressed "Esquire. Barbados"; "per Capt. Seymour."

---

[8] With rice for Portugal.
[9] The sloop *Elizabeth,* James Gilcrist, was cleared outwards on Nov. 29 for Barbados. Naval Office Lists, 1757–1764, p. 136.
[1] Edward Blake, a sea captain familiar with the West Indies, would establish himself in Charleston as a factor late in 1764. See HL to Meyler & Hall, Nov. 10, 1764.

TO BENJAMIN ROBERTS[2]

[Charles Town] 15th December 1763

Sir,

I have consider'd the offers made by Mr. Wigfall[3] & find that his prices are too high for boards & planks. If the following rates are acceptable, he may go on cutting as soon as he pleases—

10,000 ft. ¾ Inch 30 ft. long at 40/		
5,000 — 1¼ Inch .... at 50/		
5,000 — 1½ Inch .... at £3		all to be
10,000 — 2 Inch		good lengths
5,000 — 2½ Inch	.... at £5	
5,000 — 3		

The plank to be of the full thickness equal or pretty near equal breadth at each end & free from exceptions. These are prices that I shou'd think worth any Mans notice & I cannot afford to go beyond them. To be deliver'd not later than the 15th March. I am—

SOURCE: Letterbook copy, Letter Book of Henry Laurens, Oct. 30, 1762–Sept. 10, 1766, Penn. Hist. Soc.

TO JOHN HASLIN

[Charles] Town 15th December 1763

Sir,

In Consequence of your Acceptable favour of the 20th Ulto. I have already wrote into the Country an order for a Cargo of Lumber agreable to your abstract for Loading our Mutual Good friend Mr. Manesty Ship *Barter*[4] & hope to have provision for her in time. It is difficult to guess at near or exact quantity of Lumber for a Ships Loading by her computed Tonnage but I have been

---

[2] Benjamin Roberts, planter of the parish of St. John Berkeley, died on May 30, 1772. *SCHM*, x (1909), 168; "Will of Benjamin Roberts," dated March 15, 1763, proved July 3, 1772, Charleston County Wills, xiv, Book A (1771–1774), 282–284, S. C. Archives.

[3] John Wigfall lived in the neighboring parish of St. Thomas. *HL Papers*, iii, 466n.

[4] The ship *Barter*, James Gough, owned by Joseph Wharton of Philadelphia and Joseph Manesty of Liverpool, was entered inwards on Jan. 18, 1764, from Barbados with a cargo of rum. Naval Office Lists, 1764–1767, p. 69. Joseph Manesty, a Liverpool slave merchant, went bankrupt late in 1764. *HL Papers*, ii, 441n; London *Daily Advertiser*, Oct. 31, 1764.

often puzzled in this business and am ariv'd at some degree of judgment in it which I shall exercise in the present case for the Ships benefitt as far as may be. You judg'd very well in giving me this previous Notice by which the intrest will be better serv'd & the Vessell suffer less detention. One thing you have omitted & that is to inform me in what manner I am to be reimburs'd for the amount of the Cargo which will probably occur to you before the Sailing of the Vessell herself. Give me leave to tender you my best services in this place & am your, &ca.—

Rice 50/ per Ct.
Freight to Holland 55/ per Tonn.

SOURCE: Letterbook copy, HL Papers, S. C. Hist. Soc.; addressed "at Barbados"; "per Seymour."

TO JOHN & THOMAS TIPPING

[Charles Town] 15th December 1763

Gentlemen,

Two Nights Ago Capt. Holmes in the Snow *Austin* arived here & deliv'd me your esteem'd favour of the 20th Ulto. with Invoices & Bill Loading for Sundry goods on account of our Mutual good friends Messrs. Knight & Mears of Liverpool. The dry goods are come to hand in good order but the rum not yet Landed. The Salt I have Sold at 5/ per Bushell a wretched [*price*] but I obtain'd even that only by means of giving Credit. There are three or four Cargos now on Sale retailing at the 100 Bushells at 4/ per Bushell. The difference is 25 per Cent. Rum is very Low here. Sold daily at Vendue from 14/ to 15/ per Gallon for the best Leward Island produce.

If Mr. Knights Ship *Hope*[5] brings any prime Slaves in her I expect to make a very great Sale of them. I do think that a fine

---

[5] Donnan thought that the brigantine *Hope,* William Royall, whose cargo of 170 Angola slaves was advertised in the *Gazette,* Feb. 18, 1764, for sale on Feb. 21, might have been Knight's cargo. Donnan did note, however, that George Smith advertised that cargo and not HL. Donnan, *Documents Illustrative of the Slave Trade,* IV, 386. The brigantine *Hope,* William Royall, which was entered inwards on Feb. 16 with "117" slaves was owned by Antigua merchants. Naval Office Lists, 1764–1767, p. 70. John Knight's ship *Hope,* Thomas Dennison, was entered inwards on Jan. 9 from Barbados with a cargo of rum and wine, but with no slaves. Naval Office Lists, 1764–1767, p. 69.

Cargo to arrive early in February or March will average above £36 Sterling but the Coast[6] is dangerous to encounter at that Season with a Live Cargo & I speak only of what may be done if every [*thing*] conspir'd in ones favour at the same time. It is my opinion that Negroes will Sell very well here all the Next Summer. I am with great regard, Your, &ca.—

Rice 50/ per Ct.
Freight to Holland 55/ per Tonn.

SOURCE: Letterbook copy, HL Papers, S. C. Hist. Soc.; addressed "in Barbados"; "per Seymour."

TO MARTIN & STEVENS

[Charles Town] 16 December 1763
Gentlemen,

I Lately rece'd your favour of the 20 October & am extreemly sorry to hear complaints of that Lumber ship'd on Hendersons Sloop.[7] At that time necessity obliged us to send Vessels up the river becase the Country people wou'd not venture near to Town on account of the Small Pox. As I told you before I had confidence in a Man with whome I had long delt & who never before deceiv'd me. He made strong promises to give me none but good pine which in conscence he ought to have done for the horrible price which he made me pay & Mr. Henderson promis'd too that he wou'd take none on board his Vessell but what was good. Yet I have some reason to think from a late information upon enquiry that Mr. Miller was not so careful as he ought to have been. Indeed I told him of my suspitions some time ago & that if you were not satisfyed I shou'd insist upon some return from him. I have now an Account to Settle with him & shall strive hard to obtain a proper abatement of him on your Account.

---

[6] HL is probably referring to the change of climate and its effect upon the slaves rather than the dangers of the seas at this time of the year.
[7] The sloop *Sally*, John Henderson, had sailed for Antigua on April 9, 1763. *Gazette*, April 9, 1763. The *Sally* was cleared outwards on March 28 with 14,330 feet of lumber and 17,600 shingles. Naval Office Lists, 1757–1764, p. 129. The cargo can be compared with HL's order sent to Stephen Miller. *HL Papers*, III, 268.

When that is over I shall send your Account Current & remit the Ballance which will be in a few days. Capt. Henderson was mistaken about giving me notice of any Plank left behind. I heard of it from Mr. Miller some time after he was gone & then between Mr. Millers Negroes & as they say the neglect of a Clerk of mine who is gone to England[8] a great part of them was stolen of[f] the Wharf. As soon as I Knew they were there I secured the remainder & shall be accountable for them either to you or to the Captain. Indeed I think it hard that he shou'd suffer at all by it. Mr. Miller had such a run of business upon him for Lumber about that time & a Show of a great Many Vessells at his own Landing his mind agitated between the hopes of gain which he did not care to forego & the dread of death with the Small Pox which he did not care to submitt to accounts in some measure for these Errors. His Neighbours which used to Supply Pine Timber wou'd rather loose the Sale for a while than put themselves in the way of danger & so he became almost an ingrosser. I shall expostulate with him upon this head & hope to prevail on him to do what I think is but right & just. If you'll please to look back to my Letters of the 7th February to your Mr. T. M.[9] per Outerbridge[1] & Lightburn[2] you will find that Hambleton's[3] bill for one hundred & fifty pounds Sterling was accounted for. Mrs. Sarah Nicholson & Co. have actualy paid so much Money on your Account to Messrs. Trecothick & Co.[4] whose receipt I have for the same. I shou'd be extreemly sorry to break our correspondence by declining a concern in a Cargo with you upon

---

[8] William Price, who had been clerk to A. & L. and to A., L., and A. for five years, went to England in the spring of 1763 to arrange for the establishing of a new commercial house in Charleston. *HL Papers*, iii, 463. When he returned, he took over HL's old counting house. HL to Isaac King, March 15, 1764. In Dec. 1764 he formed the house of Price, Hest, & Head. HL to John Knight and John Blackburne, Jr., Dec. 21, 1764. In May 1772 he married Ann Nicolls. *SCHM*, xi (1910), 97. In 1782 his estate was amerced 12% by the patriots. *SCHM*, xxxiv (1933), 199. He was a planter when he died in 1788. "Will of William Price," dated March 8, 1788, proved July 12, 1788, Charleston County Wills, xxii, Book A (1786–1793), 300–301, S. C. Archives.

[9] Thomas Martin.

[1] The sloop *Ranger*, Joseph Outerbridge, sailed for St. Christophers on Feb. 13. *Gazette*, Feb. 19, 1763.

[2] The ship *America*, Samuel Lightburn, cleared outwards on Feb. 26 for St. Christophers. Naval Office Lists, 1757–1764, p. 128.

[3] John Edward Hamilton's bill on Augustus and John Boyd. *HL Papers*, iii, 199.

[4] Trecothick, Apthorp, & Thomlinson. *HL Papers*, iii, 238.

the conditions you propose if it cou'd be conducted barely without Loss to you or me but I think in the present State of the Rum Trade in this place it is impossible to effect even that. When there is an opening of better times, I shall be glad to receive your commands & hope to convince you that I am very truly, Gentlemen, your, &ca.—

Rice 50/ per Ct.
Corn 12/6
Pork £14
Rum 14 to 16/
Freight 55/ to Holland
Exchange 700 to £721 per Cent as the draughts are Not'd.

SOURCE: Letterbook copy, HL Papers, S. C. Hist. Soc.; addressed "Antigua"; "per Seymour. Copy per [blank] not sent. Vesey arrived."

LETTER OF ATTORNEY FROM JOHN FERDINAND MILLER

December 17, 1763

[On Dec. 17, 1763, John Ferdinand Miller, formerly a merchant at Charleston, issued on the Island of Santa Cruz a letter of attorney to Henry Laurens. The letter was couched in unusually broad terms, and empowered HL to act completely in Miller's stead. The letter was witnessed by William Miller and Nicholas Neilson. Nicholas Neilson swore to the signature before William Burrows, Esquire, on Feb. 18, 1764.]

SOURCE: Miscellaneous Records, MM, Part 1 (1763–1767), pp. 63–64, S. C. Archives.

ADVERTISEMENT

December 17, 1763

Imported in the snow AUSTIN, Mathias Holme, master, from Liverpoole and Barbados, IRISH linen, Manchester checks, bed ticks, flowered Mecklenburgh, scarlet and black silk everlasting, a large quantity of sail cloth, from No. 1 to No. 8, and about forty hogsheads of exceeding fine BARBADOS RUM, to be sold, by

HENRY LAURENS

SOURCE: Printed in Gazette, Dec. 17, 1763.

TO COWLES & HARFORD

[Charles Town] 19th December 1763

Gentlemen,

Besides the Pitch & Tar mention'd in my Last of 3d Inst. per the *Success* & *Bonnetta,* Men of War, to have been on board your Brigantine *Favourite* I have shipt on your Account about One hundred & forty five Barrels of Rice. On our joint Account as much Indigo as will amount to Eleven hundred pounds Sterling & on Account of Mr. Joseph Brown & myself about five hundred pounds Sterling Value. Be pleas'd to insure this latter sum on account of said Brown & myself & let the former Sum which I desir'd to be done stand on that part of my intrest join'd with yours in the said Sum of Eleven hundred Pounds & I will risque the remainder. I hope Capt. Brownett will Sail tomorrow or next day at furthest by whom I shall further trouble you. Mean time I am, Your, &ca.—

SOURCE: Letterbook copy, HL Papers, S. C. Hist. Soc.; addressed "Bristol"; "per Alenby."

TO LLOYD & JAMES

[Charles Town] 20 December 1763

Gentlemen,

I troubled you with a Letter the 13th Inst. per Capt. Ball & Capt. White[5] & therein requested you to insure £90 Sterling on a Cask of Indigo on Account of Mr. Joseph Brown to be shipp'd per this bearer the *Favourite,* Capt. Brownett, for Bristol. Be pleas'd now to receive inclos'd a Bill of Loading & Bounty Certificate for the same & following his directions which I presume are given in a packet that I forward herewith. Rice holds its own at 50/. Indigo sells very readily at 27/6 per lb. for good Copper. These are fine prices for our planters. Mean time Exchange is £721 per Cent. I am with true respect, Your—

SOURCE: Letterbook copy, HL Papers, S. C. Hist. Soc.; addressed "Bristol"; "per Capt. Brownett."

---

[5] The ship *Carolina Packett,* William White, cleared outwards for London on Dec. 20. Naval Office Lists, 1757–1764, p. 136.

T O   S H E P H E R D ,   L A N G T O N ,   &   B I R L E Y [6]

[Charles Town] 20th December 1763

Gentlemen,

Your favour of 19 August to the late house of Austin, Laurens, & Appleby I have rece'd being the only one remaining in business. Mr. Austin arriv'd in England about the date of your Letter. Mr. Appleby is winding up his affairs in order to embark in May next & will not further entangle himself with new accounts.[7] I have likewise receiv'd your Seven Bales of Sail Cloth therein mention'd, in pretty good order save two or three peices drubed in the Vessell's Hold with Tar but not of much consequence. The Cloth seems to be good but rather too narrow which will be a detriment to the Sale. You have sent too much of it at one time. The consumpt is very little except in cases of accident which cannot be depended upon & the few Vessells that are built here have all their matterials for rigging & Sails Imported.

Sail Cloth of the Worcester Manufacture from Bristol comes charg'd at the same rates as yours but hath these advantages of being a full Inch Wider & the Bounty of 2 pence per Ell which makes a considerable difference. However I am to suppose that you have avail'd yourselves of the bounty & shall view the peices accordingly.[8] I have advertiz'd your Cloth in both Gazetts, at most of our publick places, & Spoken to some of our principle sail makers.[9] My acquaintance with Masters of Ships is not small & I have always some Vessell in hand so that I think you have as good a chance for a Sale as this place can afford. Nevertheless I must tell you candidly that I fear it

---

[6] William Shepherd, Thomas Langton, and John Birley of Kirkham. *HL Papers,* II, 290n.

[7] George Appleby advertised March 21, 1764, that he was leaving for England about May 1 and was ready to answer to the terms of the Attachment Act. *General Gazette,* April 18, 1764. George Appleby sailed May 9, 1764 for London in the snow *Portland,* George Higgins, which had been cleared outwards on May 5. HL to Willing & Morris, May 29, 1764; Naval Office Lists, 1764–1767, p. 80. The *Portland* arrived at Deal off the coast of Kent on June 14. London *Daily Advertiser,* June 18, 1764.

[8] The invoice, dated Oct. 16, 1765, made out by Richard Grubb for goods shipped on the *Little Carpenter,* John Muir, to Hogg & Clayton in Charleston listed the bounties received upon exportation. In the list there was a sum of £8.19.4 for 1,076 ells of sail cloth at a bounty of 2 pence per ell. Invoice No. 42, Invoice Book Inward, Robert Hogg Account Books, 1762–1775, #343, SHC.

[9] The advertisement in Peter Timothy's *South-Carolina Gazette* is printed in this volume under date of Dec. 17. There is no issue extant of Robert Wells' *South Carolina Weekly Gazette* for this period.

will be very slow, but you may rely on my endevours to quicken it & remitt the produce thereof. If I was to offer it at 7 for 1[1] it wou'd not help it much for 'tis an article bought only as people want it but I shall try every means for your Intrest. Oznabrug the other article mention'd by you is of great consumpt in this Country but then every Shop here imports its own goods from Oznaburg to Lawn from an Anchor to a Minikin Pin[2] & so in every other Branch; therefore I think there is no encouragement for your attempts unless you can afford to sell so low as to make it more for their intrest to purchase from your Factor than to import which can hardly be expected. I say this in refference to any large quantitys of your Goods. As for two or three hundred peices in a Year as you have formerly experienc'd by our Accounts if those were satisfactory I think you may depend on having as good ones now & better if I can make them for you, but if you do any thing further in this way permitt me to recommend to you to inform me of the lowest genuine prices with or without the Bounty the want of which often stagnates the Sale & gives purchasers a handle to disrepute goods by saying they are Dear Bought. Upon the whole if you can find a tolerable vend for your manufactures at home I am of opinion you had better make sure of that then plague yourselves with this distant & precarious Market.

Our Crops of Rice & Indigo are the greatest ever was made & what is wonderful they sell beyond all expectation, Rice Current at 50/ & Indigo from 25/ to 35/. Shipping is hereby a little distress'd. Freight to Holland only 55/ per Ct. but many more Vessels than we now have will be wanted to carry of[f] the whole & how the Year will end is uncertain. Exchange 721 per Cent. Whenever you think that I can serve you be pleas'd to command me, who am with great respect, Gentlemen—

SOURCE: Letterbook copy, HL Papers, S. C. Hist. Soc.; addressed "Kirkham"; "per Brownett for Bristol. Copy per Brunett for Cowes."

TO COWLES & HARFORD

[Charles Town] 21st December 1763

On the other side is duplicate of what I wrote you the 19th

---

[1] That is at cost. *HL Papers*, III, 401, 464, 494, 527.
[2] The smallest kind of pin. *OED*.

since which having met with a quantity of about 1,500 lb. Weight of Flora Indigo at 35/ per lb. I have purchased & determine by a port Entry to Ship it on board the *Favorite,* as Capt. Brownett says he can make room for it. The Amount will be near £400 Sterling on our joint Account. Be pleas'd therefore to Insure further on my Account per said Vessel for my Moiety of that Indigo & a parcel of Silver taken in payment at 36/6 per Oz. which I can't readily pass again at the same rate Four hundred & eighty pounds Sterling at 2½ per Cent as under. Otherwise leave the odd £80 open to me. Tis probable the *Favorite* will Sail with this Vessel. She will be quite ready when this Indigo is on board. I am, &ca.—

SOURCE: Letterbook copy, HL Papers, S. C. Hist. Soc.; addressed "Bristol"; "per White. Copy per Brownett." This letter was copied by HL.

TO JOSEPH BAIRD[3]

[Charles Town] 22d December 1763

Sir,

I have just now rec'd your favour of the 17 Current & had also in due time the former one that you referr to. In answer to both you may depend upon having Bills for £200 Sterling more & more still if I can possibly spare them to you but I dare not promise absolutely.

I have been in hopes that one or both of your debtors whose Bonds are here wou'd have brought in some Cash but neither of them have nor will I am affraid without your asking again. I am—

SOURCE: Letterbook copy, Letter Book of Henry Laurens, Oct. 30, 1762– Sept. 10, 1766, Penn. Hist. Soc.; addressed "St. Stephens."

---

[3] Joseph Baird was the brother of Jeremiah Baird, a planter of St. Stephen parish. HL to Jeremiah Baird, Jan. 22, 1765. In 1756 and 1757 Joseph Baird sent thousands of feet of timber from Wadboo for the construction of St. Michael's Church in Charleston. George W. Williams, *St. Michael's, Charleston, 1751–1951* (Columbia, S. C., 1951), pp. 135, 145.

TO JOHN KNIGHT & THOMAS MEARS

[Charles Town] 22d December 1763

Gentlemen,

I wrote you a few Lines under the 14th Inst. per Capt. Ball & promis'd to write again the next day but I deferr'd it a Little in hopes of giving you some Account of the Sale of the *Austins* Salt as well as of other goods on board her & in the mean time one Vessell unexpectedly Slip'd away.

The Salt I have sold at 5/ per Bushell giving three Months Credit which generly prooves to be Six and often longer in this Country but I must comply with it or you must suffer, for that article has been Selling here some time past at 3/9 to 4/ per Bushel measured out in small Quantitys. Capt. Holmes is now pretty forward in delivering & I hope will be clear in this week after which depend upon it not a moment shall be lost in filling the Snow up with a fine Cargo of Rice but before I can do nothing but Urge the buyer of the Salt to take it away which I constantly do & offer any assistance in my power. You observe that she was three weeks too late for Port Market[4] last Year but if my good friends will remember she laid no more than twenty four or rather twenty three days in this place to deliver her Cargo of Salt & Load full with Rice. The Loss then arrose from her long Voyage or too late setting out & to the same causes must be ascrib'd her not being a first Ship at Market this Year which she most certainly must have been if her presence had render'd it practicable because I had the command & Sale of the first 200 Barrels Rice that came to Market & receiv'd 700 in a Very few days after so that it was clearly in my power if the *Austin* had been in the way to have sent her far enough ahead of any other. I often thought of & wished for her on your Account but that was all I cou'd do. I am sure you do not wish her intrest more nor take more pleasure in promoting it than I do. Last winter I said often to Capt. Holmes it wou'd have been advantagious to you if the Salt had been thrown into the Sea & you wou'd have saved the time of taking in & unloading it. This Year the Case varies a Little. You cannot without some fatal accident to others be first at Market. One

---

[4] The *Austin* had been cleared outwards for Oporto on Feb. 28, 1763. Naval Office Lists, 1757–1764, p. 128.

Vessel is already Sail'd & another that has been waiting several Months past is near Loaded but she shall not be long after them.[5]

Messrs. Tipping of Barbadoes have sent me on your Account by the *Austin* sundry peices of Irish Linnens, Checks, &ca., which including the Salt Amounts per Invoice to £219.1.1 Sterling & also forty Hogsheads of exceeding good Barbadoes Rum all which I have rece'd in good order except the Rum Hogsheads which are in a bad way & will cost much Cooperage & perhaps Shifting to save some of it, & further that part of one Hogshead leak'd out before it was landed. I shall dispose of these goods in the best manner our place will admitt of which at present as usual is full of all sorts of Goods especialy Rum which is carried to Vendue & then sold about 11/6 for New England, 14/ to 15/3 for Antigua, &ca., & 18/ to 20/ for Jamaica, by which great hopes must follow. I have sold one hogshead of yours long Credit at 17/6 per Gallon & having advertiz'd it with its proper caracter shall wait some weeks rather than abate of that price by the Single hogshead. Upon the whole permitt me to repeat that I shall pay the uttmost attention to your Intrest. I shall if possible make up the Sales of the *Austins* former Cargo this Evening but if not you may depend upon having it very soon after this reaches you. There is still an article unsold of Holy Water potts, & some of the hogsheads of earthen ware turn'd out so broken that they were return'd on my hands & I was forced to open & Retail them at Vendue in order to make the most I cou'd for you.

I shall for the present take leave with assuring you that I remain with the most sincere Love and respect—

SOURCE: Letterbook copy, HL Papers, S. C. Hist. Soc.; addressed "Liverpool"; "per Brownett. Copy per White."

TO JOHN KNIGHT

[Charles Town] 22d December 1763

Dear Sir,

On the 30th September last I enclos'd an invoice & Bill Loading to you for 41 pieces of Oak Timber & 39 pine planks per

[5] The snow *Douro,* Richard Shepheard, was cleared outwards on Dec. 5 for Figueira, the port of Coimbra, with 297,123 pounds of rice. The ship *Caroline,* Andrew Candee, was cleared outwards on Dec. 23 for Oporto with 340,588

the Ship *Upton,* Capt. Maxwell, & wrote a few lines at the foot of the Invoice requesting you to sell those articles for me.

I had a most severe spell of autumnal fevers in my family about that time & for five or six Weeks never left them, four sometimes Seven Blacks & Whites down. Thank God I escaped with the Loss only of two Negros but what affected my Accounting house most was the Sickness of a very deserving young Man[6] that succeeded my Late Clerk Mr. Price to whome I had been pretty indulgent in letting him go to London before he properly finished his business here. This obliged me to act both within and out of doors. At the same time the situation of my family & some unavoidable attention to old affairs of A. & L. & A., L., & A. render'd it impracticable for me to keep up my Books or to write so frequently to my friends as I ought to have done. I have now more assistance[7] & shall soon recover what I am behind hand. Meantime let me assure you, Sir, that tho' you have not heard from me so often, your concerns in my hands have not suffer'd save some little damage which has been done by Moth to your narrow Cloths & Shalloons while my Young Man was Sick for otherwise it was almost his daily work thro' the Summer to air, brush, & beat them. Most of those Cloths, Shaloons, Trimmings still lay on hand as do some of the Hatts notwithstanding I have offer'd them at prime Cost & to give 12 Months Credit. Nay I had lodged peices in the hands of the Vendue Master with orders to sell them at 5 for 1, but he has return'd them assuring me his hands are full of such & better & that with great difficulty he cou'd raise 30/ for Cloths of 4/ & 4/6 Sterling per Yard.[8] One wou'd imagine that such a loosing Trade cou'd not allways hold & yet by some means or other it seems to be allways kept up here; & as now even our Taylors import Cloths, &ca., there is not the least prospect of amendment. There is not one of them but what I have apply'd

---

pounds of rice. Naval Office Lists, 1757–1764, p. 136. HL was under the impression that the *Douro* had sailed for Oporto. HL to Thomas Mears, Feb. 24, 1764. The *Austin* would be cleared outwards on Jan. 11 for Oporto with 303,442 pounds of rice. Naval Office Lists, 1764–1767, p. 73.

[6] Benjamin Perdriau, Jr.

[7] William Hest was also now serving HL as a clerk.

[8] If HL sold the cloths at prime cost and the exchange was 7 to 1, and if he then tried to sell them at 5 to 1, he would be selling them below prime cost. The vendue master was apparently barely able to get 7 for 1 for the most expensive cloths. He was selling for 30/ currency cloth that had cost 4/ and 4/6 sterling per yard in England.

to, wrote into the Country, & tryed the Vendue so often that nothing remains but to send them to Philadelphia where they will probably Sell for something but here after the tryals that Have been made I may be alow'd to say would yield nothing. I shall therefore pack them up & consign them to Mr. William Fisher with orders to remitt the nett proceeds to you. What other little articles will then remain I shall send to our Vendue & soon transmitt you a Sale; however except for the Brandy & some few other articles I have not rece'd one penny for what is sold tho principle part of which is to two Country Shopkeepers[9] payable in Last Month but no notice yet taken of it. When the *Hope* comes which by your account will be very soon I shall make a close of the whole & in the mean time shall send an abstract of the accounts as they stand.

I am now to acknowledge your very kind & very obliging favours of the 25th September & 4th November, the former per *Austin,* the latter per Capt. Minshall.[1] That of the 6th August which you refer to never came to hand. First let me say that I pay'd due attention to your hint about the distinct interests of the Snow *Austin* & Ship *Hope* last Voyage & so shall in case they fall in together this. I shou'd do the same were they both wholy your own for Rule & orders sake, so as not to injure one by the other. My Letters to the owners of the Snow is very full & leaves only to add that Mr. Mears's observation upon detaining that Vessell in order to keep down the price of Rice must be made upon such conduct anterior to the last Voyage.

Now, Sir, for the Ship *Hope.* I shall do all that I can to promote your intrest in the Sales of what Cargo she may bring & Loading her again having due regard to your orders & shall not presume to exercise my own judgment but when you will in all probability benefitt greatly by it. At present appearances are against the Shipping. Our Rice is high & advices from foreign Markets very discouraging but the Crop is very large & perhaps the bad accounts lately gone abroad of Freight may stop some Ships & work a change

---

[9] Christopher Rowe of Orangeburg was one of the country shopkeepers. HL to Christopher Rowe, Nov. 24, 1763. Thomas Godfrey of Georgetown may have been the other. HL to Thomas Godfrey, Dec. 6, 1763.

[1] The ship *Fair American,* John Minshall, arrived from Liverpool on Dec. 20 and sailed for Lisbon on Feb. 5. *Gazette,* Dec. 24, 1763, Feb. 11, 1764. This vessel had been built in S. C. in 1762 and was owned by John Edwards of Charleston and Charles Goodwin and Walter Thomas of Chester, England. Ship Register, 1734–1765, p. 198, S. C. Archives.

in our favour. If she comes soon 'tis likely that Oporto which you seem inclin'd to will be her destiny. I have a high opinion of Mr. Byrne[2] & wou'd embark again in one or two small Cargos if determin'd for Port[o] in order to keep the bulk of the Rice in his hands. One Snow I was offer'd at 40/ per Ton to Load half of her which I agree'd to upon condition of consigning the whole to him but the Gentleman who directs her was afterwards inclin'd to alter the Voyage which I rather encouraged than objected to.

The last subject I have to trouble you upon at present is your very affectionate manner of throwing further gain into my Lap in that advantagious branch the Guinea trade. I had well consider'd what you said under the 25 September about the *Pocock*[3] which I know wou'd be only a Leading String to other Vessells & after observing to a friend that you were resolved to make a Negro Merchant of me again I had come to this resolution to accept your kind offers provided you wou'd gratify me so far as to be my Partner which of all right I thought you ought to be so far as concern'd the Commissions arrising from my Sales & agreable hereto had notified to some of my old acquaintance in the Country (who have been often teezing me to import more Negroes) that I shou'd have a Cargo of Slaves ready for them early in the Spring & perhaps a Second which I did purpose to ask you for. When just at the time your next favour of the 4 November reach'd me, & directed me in case of adhering to my former plan of Shunning the African Trade to signify the same [to] Messrs. Shirley & Martin[4] to whome in such case you had order'd

---

[2] Henry Byrne of Oporto. *HL Papers*, II, 113n.

[3] Donnan listed the *Pocock*'s cargo as having been sold in Charleston on June 27, 1764. Donnan, *Documents Illustrative of the Slave Trade*, IV, 386. But Donnan was wrong in assuming that the *Pocock* had arrived in Charleston. The London *Daily Advertiser*, July 31, 1764, under a dateline of Liverpool, July 27, stated: "The Brig *Pocock*, Capt. Miller, from hence, is cut off by the Negroes, as she was coming out of the River Cutcheo, near Gambia, with 190 Slaves on board."

[4] Thomas Shirley and Edward Martin. Judgment Rolls, 1765, No. 247A, S. C. Archives; *HL Papers*, III, 33n. Thomas Shirley imported two cargoes of slaves in 1759–1760; Shirley & Martin two in 1763–1765. *SCHM*, LXV (1964), 209, 210. Pelatiah Webster recorded on May 27, 1765, in his journal: "Dined this day with Mr. Thomas Shirley, a very polite English Gent. residing here in very genteel fashion: is an ingenuous ready man: was bread a mercht, has traveld much, understands several modern languages: passd the afternoon agreably with him." "Journal of Pelatiah Webster," p. 7. The partnership was dissolved June 15, 1765. *General Gazette*, July 3, 1765. Edward Martin later married Elizabeth Trapier, daughter of the Georgetown merchant Paul Trapier, and ended his days as a planter on the Waccamaw River. Rogers, *History of Georgetown County*, p. 284n.

Captain Miller[5] to deliver his Cargo. Upon my own Account I must chearfully Acquiesce in this alteration & have declared myself to that House accordingly & this you may depend upon, Sir, that whenever your Interest is concern'd my good wishes will be there & my attention and assistance too as far as I dare with decency & good Manner extend them. Your remark upon Mr. Shirley's praises of me (which indeed he had better Spared) do quite overwhelm me. I can only say again what I have wrote & Said a thousand times that I shall as long as I Live bear the most grateful remembrance of you & be ready upon every occasion to testify that I am with uttmost regard—

P.S. In my declaration to Messrs. Shirley & Martin I did on your Account take the Liberty to reserve to myself a right to interfere in the *Pocock*'s Cargo in case that by death or other accident in their House it should become necessary.

SOURCE: Letterbook copy, HL Papers, S. C. Hist. Soc.; addressed "Leverpoole"; "per Capt. Brownett. Copy per White."

TO THOMAS MEARS

[Charles Town] 22d December 1763

Sir,

My last trouble to you was under the 13th August per Capt. Briggs who I see was arriv'd & therefore I hope you have rece'd the Cedar posts sent in his Ship. I am now to acknowledge the favour of your kind Letter by the *Austin* under the 22d September & Shall as you desire follow strictly the Letter from her Owner to whome I have wrote so largely that I think it needless to trouble you with a repetition. Sorry indeed I am that it is not possible to make her a first Ship this Year as she was the Last but it cannot be helped. I have been wishing & looking for her & as Capt. Holmes talk'd of being here early in November when he was last in Charles Town tho' he doubted of comming himself I began to dispair of her arival at all thinking she might be on some new track.

We have no Wood in this Country that is easily got if it be for the purposes you mention except Cypress & that is paltry unless

---

[5] Capt. Miller of the *Pocock*.

'tis painted over which is commonly done in our Stair Cases. Cedar is too brittle for that work at least where Negroes go up & down the Stairs but if there is any kind that will be acceptable to you please to point it out & I will spare no pains to procure it, & it shall go very hard with me if I do not send you a Turtle some time next Spring. I lost three lately by Cold Weather that weighed about 200 lbs. They came a little too Late either for Shipping or my own use.

I had rather have advanc'd three times £70 than have drawn on you for so much at an inconvenient hour. It was to serve Captain Holmes & some poor people that he had transacted business for & I asked it rather as matter of favour than right. At the same time I was very largely in Advance & am so still for the *Austin*'s last cargo as you will see by the Accounts. This is and always has been the Case in the Sale of dry goods in this Country unless you go wholly to Vendue which wou'd be next to giving the goods away. You will be Convinc'd that my Commission does barely perhaps not Quite compensate for the advance of my Money.

You must have the best Quality of Rice [&] you had it, but that preference I cou'd not secure without some consideration. This is ready Money or Money ready at all times when the Factor or Planter shall call for the ammount of his Rice. Second & third rate rice passes off by means of two or three Months Credit to customers in those classes. This is truely the case & if Money is so scarce at the fountain what must the little streams & Branches suffer? But, Sir, I shall always be as cautious of erring in this way as possible at the same time never doubting of your friendly Aid when I stand realy in need of it. It amazes me that you shou'd ask for an Invoice of the *Austins* last Cargo for I cannot think how it happens that you have not rece'd it, for I certainly sent you a full Invoice with a Bill Loading & one of Captain Holmes's receipts under the 8th March per Capt. Peel;[6] abstract of said Invoice & another Bill Loading & Receipt in the duplicate of said Letter per Capt. Doran. It appears so by my book & as none of the papers are now in the drawer where they are kept untill sent away I am hopefull that it is truely so & that you have mislaid them. Nevertheless I shall cause another Invoice to be made out & transmitted with the *Austins* other Accounts.

---

[6] The ship *Juno*, Benjamin Peel, sailed for Cowes on March 11. *Gazette*, March 12, 1763.

Sir, You have done both Mrs. Laurens & myself very great honour by your correspondence & her as high favour in the Roots & Seeds sent by Capt. Holmes & she has promised me to make the best acknowledgement in her power by the first Vessell for Liverpoole. That Lady has a wonderful inclination & some taste for Gardening but I am forced to check her Ardor a little now & then as I am not quite weary of her company nor satisfied with her services. If I was not to interpose I believe she wou'd soon become the Sextons property for Gardening in this moist uncertain Climate is often injurious & sometimes destructive to our good Women. However I shall rather encourage than hinder her to do credit to those articles which you have been so good as to transmitt & they shall have the first place in our little Plott. I Remain, &ca.—

P.S. Nine days gone, the *Austin*'s Salt not discharged, nor can be before the Holy days, in which time I cou'd have loaded her & sent her to Sea. What can I do in this Case?

SOURCE: Letterbook copy, HL Papers, S. C. Hist. Soc.; addressed "Liverpoole"; "per Brownett. Copy per Capt. White."

TO MEYLER & HALL

[Charles Town] 22d December 1763

Gentlemen,

I have read Original & duplicate of your favour under 13th August directing me to remitt the proceeds of your Havanna Sugar in a Good Bill to Hutchinson Mure, Esquire in London[7] which I shall duly observe but hitherto I have not finished the Sale by forty Boxes chiefly of the Seconds & untill very lately had not Cash to reimburse the freight & duty. The true reason of this is that I wou'd & have maintained my first prices which makes a difference in your favour at least 25 per Cent. I have therefore been obliged to sell it out by the Single Box at £12.10/ to £14 per Ct. for the inferior & £17.10/ for the best which can only be had of people that consume it in their own familys & such wou'd purchase no more than they use within themselves if you were to offer it at a lower rate. I have

---

[7] Hutchinson Mure was a West India merchant of French-ordinary-court, Nicholas Lane. *London Directories.*

offer'd it in Quantity at £14 round but never cou'd get a better price bid than £12 which I cou'd not consistant with my regard for your Intrest accept of. Then I caused 7 Chests to be started into Kegs & sent to Vendue hoping that housekeepers wou'd be induc'd to buy in small parcells who cou'd not take a Box at one time but as yet this scheme has not answer'd my expectations. However I shall continue to try that and every other method to finish the Account upon tolerable terms & in the mean time collect & remitt for what is allready Sold as speedily as possible & you may be assured that I shall in a few days send a Bill on your Accounts to Mr. Mure even if I advance for one half of it.

You will think this a tedious Sale & it is realy so but that is the case always in Charles Town unless you will accept of extreme low prices. I am sure that in the end you will be gainers by my delay which is some consolation & you may be assur'd that nothing on my part has been wanting to make a Quicker & a better Sale this country cannot afford.

I have now by me some Hogsheads of Jamaica Sugars Imported by A., L., & A. near four Years Since so slow is the Sale of that article except at some particular times which do very seldom come round.

Rice altho' we have as large a Crop as ever was made, open'd this Year & continues at 50/ per Ct. & Freight is very low only 50/ per Ton obtain'd by the London traders & 55/ to Holland.

Jamaica Rum sold daily at Vendue for 18/ to 19/, Leeward Island Rum at 14/ to 15/. Exchange 721 per Cent. I remain—

SOURCE: Letterbook copy, HL Papers, S. C. Hist. Soc.; addressed "Jamaica"; "per Capt. Dickinson. Copy per Craig."

TO COWLES & HARFORD

[Charles Town] 22d December 1763

Gentlemen,

Annex'd is duplicate of my last wrote Yesterday per Capt. White & I am now to address you by your own Brigantine *Favourite*, Capt. Brownett, who has greatly to my mortification been too long detain'd here partly owing to your not giving me previous advice of your intentions & partly to an uncommon run of ill Luck in not getting Pitch the article that you chiefly wanted to Town in time. I cou'd have got the preference of 2 or 300 Barrels more of Tar but the Casks in poor order, very full of water, & at the high price of 50/ discouraged me from touching it. After waiting for Pitch 'till my patience was worn out I resolv'd to fill the Vessel up with Rice & then I was for Eight days (in which time under 700 Barrels passed through my hands) before I cou'd meet with a Quality good enough for your Market & even now what I have Shipped is not altogether so fine as I cou'd wish. Now that the Vessell is quite Loaded I have both Pitch & Green Tar offer'd to me but at an extravigant price, 75/ for the former & 70/ for the latter. If I do not take them there are others ready to catch them up at once.

Please to receive inclos'd the following Papers, Vizt.

First—Mr. Applebys remarks on Austin, Laurens, & Applebys Account Current lately rend. with a memorandum directing any future Ballance due to them in consequence of said remarks & of the proceeds of their 7 Hogsheads Skins per *True Britton*[8] to be divided into thirds & passed to the Credit of their respective Accounts which I intreat you to do & advise me thereof without delay.

2d—Invoice & Bill Loading for 8 Casks Indigo per *Favourite* bought at Winyaw by Mr. Joseph Brown on his own & my account half each Amount £5,638.4.9 which you will be pleas'd to sell as soon as you can & remitt Mr. Brown's part of the proceeds to Mrs. Sarah Nicholson & Co. or send the Indigo up to them if you & they so agree, tho' I wou'd rather that you sold my half. I thought this purchase very dear & did not expect to have paid such prices. Therefore stoped my hand & wou'd not embark you in the concern—& Say a Bounty Certificate.

3d—Invoice & Bill Loading for 10 hogsheads fine purple & Copper Indigo & five Bundles fine Flora on our Joint Account with a Bounty Certificate for the latter parcell. The Planters Certificates are not all come to hand for the 10 hogsheads. As soon as they are I shall get the General one & transmitt to you. Part of this Indigo is a little too damp but I have an allowance made so as to average the price with all Charges below your Limitt 6d per pound which I think is more than sufficient & if I am not flatter'd by the opinion

---

[8] The snow *True-Briton* was cleared outwards on April 2, 1763 for Bristol. with 79 hogsheads of deerskins in the cargo. Naval Office Lists, 1757–1764, p. 130.

of other people and by my own judgment too, the whole is as well bought as any parcell shipp'd this Year & it does really appear so upon comparrison with other purchases. The Amount of these 15 Casks is £10,974.3.11 for which I debit (say one half of which) your Account Current £5,487.1.11 & I hope that it will turn out a good adventure to both of us. You will know very well what to do with it but permitt me to give this hint not to beleve implicitly all that Indigo buyers shall say of it. Tis a valueable article & gives temptation & scope for too much Artifice. If we succeed in this I shall be glad of early advice & much larger orders for another Year. I think I have a large acquaintance with Indigo makers & shou'd be glad of orders to do a good deal in that branch.

4th—Invoice for 2 Casks Indigo, 1,000 Mill'd Dollars, & 310 Ounces of Silver on my own Account included in the last mention'd Bill of Loading Amounting to £2,622.16.2. The Certificate to be sent with that (or included in it) for the 10 hogsheads on our joint Account. This Indigo was also bought for me by another hand, & seems to be but a bad purchase. Therefore you are not interested therein.

5th—Invoice & Bill Loading & Bounty Certificate for 138 Barrels & 13 half Barrels Rice, 228 Barrels pitch, & 317 Barrels Tar on your proper Account together with one of Capt. Brownetts receipts for the Brigantine's disbursments Amounting £4,482.7.11 charged to the debit of your Account Current. The whole of which I have endeavour'd to keep free from Error & hope that no mistakes will be found.

The Skins that Capt. Brownett hath on board are to pay 30/ per hogshead Freight but the Bills of Loading for three Hogsheads Ship'd by Mr. Thomas Smith are fill'd up at 25/ & being included in his Letter he desires you to rectify the mistake in the Account of Sale & then Charge 30/.[9]

Rice continues to Sell briskly at 50/ per Ct. & as Ships daily drop in the planters have a good Chance of holding it there for some time to come.

Indigo also goes of[f] at 27/6 for good Copper. Deer Skins are still above your Limitt & therefore I do not meddle with any.

---

[9] Thomas Smith, Nicholson & Bampfield, William Lewis, and Ancrum, Lance, & Loocock shipped deerskins on the *Favourite*. Public Treasurer, Journal B: Duties, 1748–1765, pp. 373–374, S. C. Archives.

There will soon be large quantitys of Pitch ready for Market but if Freight is low the prices will keep up. Exchange is 721 per Cent, but some Bills are sold under when people do not so well approve of the drawers.

I have said all that occurs to my mind to be needful at present. Therefore shall now conclude subscribing myself again, Your most Oblig'd humble Servant—

SOURCE: Letterbook copy, HL Papers, S. C. Hist. Soc.; addressed "Bristol"; "per Capt. Brownett. Copy per Smith with duplicates of Invoices, &ca. [*per*] the *Chance*."

TO HENRY BYRNE

[Charles Town] 22d December 1763
Sir,

The Snow *Austin* arrived here the 13th Inst. She has again brought an ill timed Cargo of Salt which detains the Vessell & is sold at such a price as will yeild no proffit to the Owners. I hope it will be all discharg'd & a beginning made for her Loading of Rice by the 28th Inst. & after that I shall soon fill her up. She is destin'd again for your market & by her I shall have the honour of writing to you further. Mean time be pleas'd to accept this previous notice from, Sir, your, &ca.—

SOURCE: Letterbook copy, HL Papers, S. C. Hist. Soc.; addressed "Esquire. Oporto"; "per Capt. Young. Copy per Capt. Candy."

TO JOSEPH BROWN

[Charles Town] 24th December 1763
Dear Sir,

I am indebted for your Sundry favours of 25 November, one without date, 11th & 14 December.

The 8 Casks Indigo per Cogdell are in my store & shall be Shipp'd on our Joint account per Capt. Barnes but they seem to require new packing. Your 10 Casks Indigo B No. 1 to 10 are also come to hand, the first three are Shipp'd & the latter Seven shall when Captain Barnes wants them. That Cask BG No. 1 is ship'd on board the *Favourite* as per Bill Loading inclosed. I wrote to Messrs. Lloyd & James to Insure £90 Sterling thereon & sent your Letters to them, one by that Vessel & one per Capt. White.

Your two Letters to Mrs. Nicholson & Co. shall go as you direct, one in Barnes & the other by the Vessel to sail before him as soon as the Bills of Loading are sign'd.

The Request that you make for my assistance to procure you a Small Cargo of Negroes I shall most readily comply with as far as 'tis in my power if you yourself will lay down a plan to proceed upon which I am affraid you will find attended with some difficulty & not a Little risque and danger to your own Interest; for the very reasons you assign will operate powerfully with the owners of Guinea Men against sending a Vessel to your port without a warrantee both as to the price & remittances. As there never have been an attempt of that kind made, the first adventure must be tempted by some sure promises especially while there is so fine a Markett for slaves in the Center of the province & in the old beaten Track. Then the people that you quote being as you say in General poor their honesty allowing to be greater then other folks will be no inducement to the Affrican Traders who love to go and allways seek for that Market where there is most money stirring & where there are men of Fortune who in Case of a Glutt will take of[f] a Cargo at some rate or other & pay for them. Now, Sir, the two points that you have to establish are assurence that in your new trade better prices than at Charles Town will be obtain'd & also better remittances & to give security for the performance of both for without something better offers you know that no Trade can be diverted from its' old Channel. But wou'd you make such offers? I think not. I wou'd advise you as a friend not to do it; at least before you have well consider'd the nature of such an engagement. Suppose you had a Cargo of Negroes arrived to you on one wing of the Province while there was another upon the right & two or three in the Center which in all probability will be the Case this year. How would you be perplex'd, how embarrass'd? forced to sell for long Credit in order to maintain the prices or to run off the Slaves very low for Money in order to comply with the terms of remittances; perhaps about the same juncture you may fall Sick & perhaps die. What a Situation wou'd your Widow and Children be in. More I cou'd say but may be I have said too much until I hear of or see your proposalls which are always to be laid down as the first step & therefore I suspend the Subject until I hear from you again.[1]

Capt. Holmes now here intreats you to sell of[f] his Hoes (if not already sold) at some rate or other or to return them now before he Sails again (10th January) & we both intreat you to think of Crofts House which seems to be a dormant Subject. Do advise me what I shall do to get rid of it before he departs.[2]

I have a melancholy Certificate from Mrs. Nicholson about Pikes[3] Pitch, a job that has cost me 40 lb. wt. of Pitch at 10/ Sterling & 40 times 12/6 Sterling for the freight besides all other Charges. I hope you will be able to come at the Knaves for me. My Love to Your family & be assur'd I am, &ca.—

SOURCE: Letterbook copy, Letter Book of Henry Laurens, Oct. 30, 1762–Sept. 10, 1766, Penn. Hist. Soc.; addressed "George Town."

TO JOSEPH BOWER[4]

[Charles Town] 24 December 1763

Sir,

My last to you was 15th July per Capt. Baker & Capt. Davis[5] since which & for a Long time before I have rece'd none of your esteem'd favours. You will no doubt think it now high time to have

---

[1] Only a few slaves were ever imported directly from Africa or the West Indies into the ports of Beaufort and Georgetown. The duties collected in these two ports are proof of this statement. At Beaufort £1,870 in duties were collected in 1736, £48.15 in 1756, and £190 in 1757. In 1755 £10 in duties were collected at Georgetown. After that date Joseph Brown himself collected at Georgetown £360.15 from March 25 to Sept. 29, 1764, £162.8.9 from March 25 to Sept. 29, 1765, £307.2.6 from Sept. 29, 1765 to March 25, 1766, £126.15 in 1769, £204.15 in 1771, £108.2.5 in 1772, and £765.7.6 in 1774. These figures indicate that Joseph Brown was the only merchant at either of the two outports who ever attempted to import many Negroes. The editor is indebted to Professor W. Robert Higgins of Murray State University, Murray, Ky. for these figures which were compiled from Public Treasurer, Journals A, B, and C: Duties (1735–1775), S. C. Archives.

[2] The house of John Croft in Georgetown. *HL Papers*, III, passim.

[3] The pitch of Mrs. Ann Pike. *HL Papers*, III, 144–146, 178.

[4] *HL Papers*, III, 99n.

[5] The snow *Charles*, John Davis, sailed on July 20 for Liverpool. *Gazette*, July 23, 1763.

the Sales of your goods per *Success*[6] clos'd & transmitted & tho' I am of the same opinion & have used all my endeavours yet it is not in my power to effect it. Your Cloths remain unsold notwithstanding they have been in the hands of the Vendue Master for Many Months past with orders to put them off at the Low rate formerly mention'd of 30 per Cent Less than they Cost as per Invoice & he has even try'd to retail them by cutting up a peice in pattrons of 3½ yards, &c., but all to no effect. Therefore I shall give him orders as you do not permitt me to send them elsewhere to sell them in the Course of next Month for what they will yeild for I think it will answer no good end to delay any Longer & then I shall transmitt your account. Mean time I am the greatest sufferer for as People will take the liberty of 12 Months Credit in this Country I have not collected enough to reimburse me above 1/3 of the amount of Capt. Dorans Cargo.

Rice broke & continues yet at 50/ per Ct. The Crop is certainly Very large & many more Ships than we have will be wanted to carry the whole away. Freight to Portugal 42/6, Holland 55/, London 50/. Naval Stores after a long & uncommon scarcity begin to come down. Pitch 75/, Green Tar 70/, Common 50/, Turpentine 15/, Indigo 25/ to 27/6. Exchange 721 per Cent. I remain—

SOURCE: Letterbook copy, HL Papers, S. C. Hist. Soc.; addressed "Bristol"; "per Brownett. Copy per Floyd."

TO ISAAC KING

[Charles Town] 24 December 1763

Sir,

Having had nothing important to trouble you with I have not wrote since the 20th September. Mean time your Sundry favours of 3d June, 26 July, 10 September, & 5 October have come to hand & I observe their several contents & thank you for such frequent inteligence. I was in great hopes to day of receiving an Account of the Sale of my Indigo as Capt. Mitchel[7] is arived but I have not the pleasure of a Line from you. Therefore I fix my hopes on the arival

---

[6] The snow *Success,* James Doran, was entered inwards on Jan. 11, 1763, from Bristol with sundry British goods. Naval Office Lists, 1757–1764, p. 116.
[7] The ship *Nancy,* David Mitchell, arrived from London on Dec. 24, 1763. *Gazette,* Dec. 26, 1763.

of Capt. Gunn & shall wait with patience. 'Tis buz'd about that Indigo was down at 3/[8] in your Citty & a Slow Sale. This if true will be bad news for our friend Brown at Winyaw who has been a bold purchaser both in Quantity & price. I have now ten Casks of his Ship'd on board your *Minerva*, Capt. Barnes, on which you may venture (to guard against accidents) to Insure four hundred Pounds Sterling to begin with & rest for his further orders for I don't know that he has wrote any other than one Letter now in my Custody to be sent after the Bill Loading is Sign'd & Inclos'd. Therefore this precaution may be usefull. I shall also Ship per the *Minerva* about £500 Sterling value in Indigo on the joint Account of said Mr. Joseph Brown on which be pleas'd to insure £250 on Mr. Browns Account but only £180 on my account leaving the remainder open to myself.

I have desir'd Messrs. Rawlinson, Davison, & Newman[9] to call upon you for £88.10.5 Sterling which be pleas'd to pay & take their receipt on my account.

Mr. James Poyas of this Town, Merchant,[1] lately signify'd to me his intentions of applying to you to Ship such goods as he imports for his trade here & desir'd me to recommend him to you which I think I can do with great safety as an honest punctual dealer. His Capital is unknown to me but I have great reason to belive he stands upon a good foundation & do not know a more frugal careful man in Charles Town & for my own part I wou'd trust him with any sum that he shou'd require & if you happen to correspond I wish it may be attended with mutual benefitt & Satisfaction. I remain—

SOURCE: Letterbook copy, HL Papers, S. C. Hist. Soc.; addressed "London"; "per Brownett. Copy per Smith."

TO DEVONSHEIR & REEVE

[Charles Town] 25 December 1763

Gentlemen,

Since my Last of 14 June I have receiv'd the favour of yours under the 21st May & thank you for it.

---

[8] Three shillings sterling.
[9] Sir Thomas Rawlinson, Monkhouse Davison, and Abram Newman were grocers of Fenchurch St. *HL Papers*, I, 12n; III, 138n.
[1] *HL Papers*, III, 32n.

I was agreeing on a price for your Bale Strouds but upon opening it there appears to be damage to several peices on the inside which
has baulk'd the Sale & I have no other chance of selling it now but
by Vendue which I shall do & transmitt you an account of it. This
sort of damage has been too common of Late. I have seen both
Negro Cloth & duffils in the same way which one wou'd think the
Packers must have been privy to.

You will oblige Mr. Appleby & myself very much by sending
all the Accounts of the late Partnership especialy the *Brislington's*[2]
by the first Vessell either from your Port or London. This will be
doing us a very great favour as Mr. Appleby will finally leave this
province in May next & we are both anxious to close our accounts
previous to that event, & we are so happy as to have scarcely another
obstacle to our wishes.

I have no great offers to make to you, Gentlemen, but if ever
you have occasion of my service here you may be assured of my
inclination to approve myself, Your, &c.—

SOURCE: Letterbook copy, HL Papers, S. C. Hist. Soc.; addressed "Bristol"; "per Brownett. Copy per Floyd."

TO JERMYN WRIGHT
[Charles Town, 26 December 1763]
Sir,

I am indebted for your favour of the 30th Ulto. which came
to hand no sooner than the 20th Inst. I am now to give the needful
reply.[3] Your sentiments & mine with respect to Mens *Opinions* be
they ever so learned in the Law are so much alike, that I am naturaly
disposed to think them perfectly just, none are infalable, & when any
two of them differ upon a Case whether they have *fully* consider'd

---

[2] The *Brislington* had made annual voyages from Bristol to Charleston, to
Oporto, and back to Bristol. *HL Papers*, I, passim; II, passim; III, 516.
[3] John Grayson, who was to deliver this letter to Jermyn Wright, was a
merchant of St. Helena parish. Judgment Rolls, 1767, No. 219A, S. C. Archives.
Grayson had come about 1750 from Yorkshire via the West Indies to Carolina.
He married Sarah Wigg on April 14, 1754. In June 1763 he received a grant
to 2,500 acres on the Little Satilla River in Georgia. He was the grandfather
of William John Grayson who wrote "The Hireling and the Slave." "The Auto-
biography of William J. Grayson," ed. Robert D. Bass (unpub. PhD diss., Univ.
of South Carolina, 1933), pp. i–iii, 6.

the merrits or hastily subscrib'd to their own opinions in the *hurry of their business* both cannot be right. At the same time it is necessary to remark to you that if your good Brother Mr. C. W. had not proposed to me an absolute Sale of those Lands & Marshes claimed by you at Ansonburgh & in which he seemed to be well warranted by the Case stated in your own hand writing* I shou'd have escaped an expence attending the advice of Council; nay he went further & offer'd to procure such advice at his or your own Charge in these words, "You may (said he to me) get the opinion of Council or if you please I will do it." Lawyers when they declare themselves honestly, as I hope they always do, are plain spoken Men & like good Pilots point out to the Less Skillful Mariner every distant Rock & Shelf from which the least danger may be foreseen or apprehended & I do suppose that the Gentleman to whome I apply'd upon the late occasion had in View or in contemplation that well known proverb "Fast bind fast find," & after he had delivered this thought left the matter with me to do therin as I shou'd think fitt.

I must confess indeed that I think your *Right* to the premises not altogether so remote as he seems to have put it from you; nevertheless I am perswaded that he did not mean to *prescribe* to you a *disreputable method* of conveyance but rather a method honourable, above-board, & safe to both parties. Be that as it may, permitt me, Sir, to assure you that I wou'd not purchase, nay more, that I wou'd not accept of your whole property upon dark ambiguous or disreputable terms; as I also beleve you incapable of attempting to offer such terms. Upon the whole therefore as you have for the present changed your Mind this business must for a while lay dormant, & when hereafter it shall become convenient to you to sell the fore mention'd Land, &ca. & to declare your price & conditions of Sale I shall be glad to be inform'd thereof. It is probable that I shall be willing to pay as large a consideration as any other person & if you think it not inconsistant with your own Interest to give me the first offer I shall be more obliged to you. Mean while as I have no inclinations toward hiring the whole or any part either on a building lease or otherwise I can only thank you for the hint & request you to loose no opportunity on my account to dispose of it in that way.

My Complments wait upon your Brother & I wish you both many happy returns of this Season. I Remain, Sir—

*"And the debt to Lord Anson being fully paid, the wharf &
Marsh remains the property of him the Said Jermyn Wright & a
Purchaser now offering, what method is most advisable for the said
JW. to take in prudence to *himself & his heirs,* & for the security of
such *Purchaser in his Title* to the said Wharf & Marsh."

Case Stated by Jermyn Wright, Esquire

SOURCE: Letterbook copy, Letter Book of Henry Laurens, Oct. 30, 1762–
Sept. 10, 1766, Penn. Hist. Soc. Endorsed: "Date omitted but must have
been done about 26th December & sent by Mr. Grayson 13 January
1764."

TO HENRY BRIGHT

[Charles Town] 26th December 1763

Sir,

I had the honour of writing to you as per annex'd duplicate
on the 12 Ulto. to which I beg leave to refer you. The price of Rice
has continued from the first opening of the Market to this time at
50/ per Ct. & some Vessells have obtain'd 55/ per Ton for Holland.
The Ships in the London trade from many hands & Laying by a
Long time 50/ for that port; & I have been offer'd Vessells at 40/
for Bristol or Portugal. This is poor encouragement for Shipping
with which our port abounds at present but as the Crop is undoubtedly very Large many more will be wanted to carry of[f] the
whole.

Last night I receiv'd a Letter from Capt. William Floyd of
your Ship *Sally*[4] who advices of his intention to come here to seek
a Freight & hopes to be with me in all this Month. By him 'tis
Probable I shall receive orders from you to which I shall pay due
regard & in every respect serve your interest as far as Lies in my
power, as I am with a true sence of your former favours, Sir, your,
&ca.—

Exchange 721 per Cent.

SOURCE: Letterbook copy, HL Papers, S. C. Hist. Soc.; addressed "Esquire. Bristol"; "per Brownett. Copy per White."

---

⁴ The ship *Sally,* William Floyd, arrived from St. Kitts on Feb. 3 and sailed
for Bristol on March 5. *Gazette,* Feb. 4, March 10, 1764. The *Sally* was entered
inwards from St. Christophers on Feb. 4 in ballast but with six slaves. Naval

TO JOHN COMING BALL

[Charles Town] 27 December 1763

Dear Sir,

I am indebted for both your favours of the 3d & 16th Inst. The first treats about the Wambaw Land & desires upon the whole that the consideration of that business may be deferr'd untill we meet again to which I have no objection as I realy do view that subject with a single Eye as much for your interest & ease as for my own, & indeed I wou'd rather sustain some considerable disadvantage than you shou'd be distressed about the Sale or division; at the same time 'tis necessary that some step shou'd be taken during the lives of us, who, I am persuaded do mean to act as good Fathers to our Children & friends to each other; I have been Candid & ingenuous in declaring my sentiments & you know as much of them now as I do myself, & I think a good & wholesome Lesson may be read from the little obstacles and differences that stand in our way, upon the Subject of what may & probably will come to pass if we adjourn our business over to posterity. An alternative from our last proposition will therefore remain with you for which I shall wait your leisure & if nothing extraordinary hinders me I shall strive to see you before the 20th January at Wambaw in your own Castle, but upon this I dare not depend.[5]

Mean time Abraham Shad[6] has been with me & requires as good wages as he can get in the Neighbourhood if he continues another year. I have promis'd him a positive answer in a forthnight. If the Plantation is to be carry'd on in the old way I shall leave the direction of him as heretofore pretty much or rather wholy to you but in case of a division or Sale my plan must naturaly be alter'd.

Office Lists, 1764–1767, p. 69. Thirteen Bristol merchants had underwritten a voyage of the *Sally* the previous year for £1,000 sterling at 12 guineas per centum for Africa and ports of discharge in America, mortality of Negroes by natural death excepted. Henry Bright's insurance policy, March 24, 1762, #16073, Bristol Archives Office.

[5] At the time of the division of the property there was a house on the plantation. Writs of Partition, 1754–1777, pp. 161–164, S. C. Archives.

[6] James Brenard and Abraham Schad were both overseers at Wambaw. Brenard was in charge. *HL Papers*, III, 426n. On June 27, 1764, Schad, who was a constable, petitioned the assembly for the payment of constable's fees of £37.12/ for apprehending a criminal slave, summoning a court of justices and freeholders, provisions, and mileage. On July 16, 1764, the assembly deducted a sum for what they considered an overcharge for mileage and awarded Schad £29.9.6. House Journal, xxxvi (Jan. 24, 1763–Oct. 6, 1764), 62, 138, 212, S. C. Archives.

The Wambaw Schooner Sail'd yesterday for her first load & carryed two pieces of duffles. I have not forgot the one piece more for you but have spoke of it twenty times now I think you may depend upon it the next opportunity & at the same time two & an half Hogsheads of Jamaica Rum being one half of five hogsheads just receiv'd from Jamaica on Account of Wambaw Plantation but the Account Sales of our Rice is not yet come.

I thank you for the Care of the Roan Horse sent down by Mr. Murry Lees[7] who informs me that you are going on both at Mepkin & home with my Bill of Scantling. I am glad of it. When the Ship arrives I can soon be inform'd by you what quantity is ready. I shall be a better judge too of her burthen, & more capable of giving directions for what more may be wanted. You will no doubt give orders for dispatch at both places.

All friends here are well. Your Sister & I were just going to make half a holyday at Rattray Green[8] in quiet while the whole Town almost seems to be using every means in their power to testify that they are—true Christians. We wish both houses many happy returns of this Season, & I remain, Dear Sir, your Aff., &ca.—

SOURCE: Letterbook copy, Letter Book of Henry Laurens, Oct. 30, 1762–Sept. 10, 1766, Penn. Hist. Soc.

TO JOHN TARLETON

[Charles Town] 27 December 1763

Sir,

My last was under the 3d Inst. per his Majestys Ships *Success* & *Bonetta,* Men of War. Soon after which I mett with an excelent parcell of Pork & receiv'd some very hard Pitch which enabled me to have every thing ready for filling up the *Elizabeth* but her people as I observed before worked slowly; & on some cold days not at all so that I cou'd not clear her out before the 22d Inst. which I did before the whole Cargo was on board in order to save them idle

---

[7] The editors have not been able to identify this person. The name was spelled many different ways in these letters: "Moorylees," "Merrywlees," "Merrilees." See HL to John Coming Ball, Feb. 10, March 3, and June 1764.
[8] HL referred to his newly acquired property in Ansonborough as Rattray Green. John Rattray had been a previous owner of the property.

holy days; & now at length she is full & under Sail with a fine wind & I wish her safe to a good Markett. Please to receive inclosed with this an Invoice & Bill Loading for her Cargo & Capt. Thornton's Receipt for disbursements the whole amounting to £5,390.1.3 to the debit of your account & as I am in advance for a great part & expect hourly to be call'd upon for the remainder, I shall in a few days take the liberty to reimburse myself by draughts on you at the most favourable exchange & Usance. The former I hope to procure £721 per Cent for which upon enquiry you will find to be 3 per Cent more than some bills do obtain. This I trust will not be inconvenient to you as I had many competitors for the articles of Pork, Corn, Pease, Lumber, & even the rice. There was no procuring the preference without prompt pay which you well know is the true means of procuring it in every place. The whole Cargo I will say is dear, much dearer than I did expect to have laid it in for, but the whole at the same time is bought upon the best terms our present Market admitts of & the Quality of each article is realy good.

If you shou'd hereafter think proper at any time to favour me with your business be so kind as to give or to order your Agent in the west Indies to give me some previous notice. It will enable me to serve you with more ease to myself & what is of more consiquence more advantage to you. Upon receiving such notice I might be looking out & securing the first offers of articles that shou'd be advis'd which otherwise slip by me. I am with great regard, &ca.—

SOURCE: Letterbook copy, HL Papers, S. C. Hist. Soc.; addressed "Liverpoole"; "per the *Union*, Smith. Copy per the *Chance*, Smith."

TO LACHLAN McINTOSH[9]

[Charles Town] 29th December 1763

Dear Sir,

Immediately upon the Receipt of your favour of the 15th

---

[9] In Volume III the editor assumed that Lachlan McIntosh of Georgia was the Lachlan McIntosh who had served as commander of Fort Prince George during the Cherokee War. *HL Papers*, III, 278n, 361n. There were apparently two men of the same name, a common occurrence in eighteenth-century S. C. By internal evidence the Lachlan McIntosh to whom this letter was addressed had obviously been engaged in the Cherokee campaign and had served as an advisor to the governors at the Augusta conference in November. Captain

Ulto. I waited on Mr. Harvey[1] to know if he had done any thing for you in hiring a proper plantation. His reply was that as soon as he had fix'd his eye upon such an one he wou'd aquaint me with it: & this has prevented my writing to you sooner; Yesterday he signify'd to me that he was in treaty with Mr. Jonathan Cochran for his plantation at Chehaw,[2] & that he expected to hire it at the rate of 20/ per acre per annum for every Acre planted by you. In consequence of this information I made some enquiry into the state & value of this plantation & have receiv'd so favourable an account that I most heartily wish Mr. Harvey may Engage it. I am told that there is about one hundred Acres cleared & under good Damms. The Land is good & there are a sufficient number of Houses for your own & the residence of an overseer & Negroes; in Short that every thing needfull is upon the Spot to enable you to set people to work both upon Rice & Indigo. If this be truely the Case as I hope it is for your sake, you are wise to hire instead of purchasing Land & all things consider'd you are certainly right in looking out for a retreat or at least to reallize some part of your loose money.

I wish you success & you may depend upon every thing in my power to contribute to it. I have heard not a sillable from Mr. Parsons.[3] The Cherokees you say were very humble. This is no more than I expected & I hope that after a few Years all the Gentry of their Complexion will find it consistant with their Interest to be so.

McIntosh did have a plantation in St. Andrew parish by January 1765 whence he shipped lumber to Charleston. *SCHM*, xv (1914), 44; HL to John Gray, Jan. 5–18, 1765. He married Elizabeth Smith, the daughter of Francis Smith of Stono River on Oct. 17, 1765. *Gazette,* Oct. 19, 1765. His will, dated June 18, 1787, was proved in England on Oct. 12, 1789. *SCHM*, vii (1906), 148. Mrs. Elizabeth McIntosh died on May 7, 1809, at the age of sixty-two. *SCHM*, xxxiii (1932), 72.

[1] Maurice Harvey who kept store at Bacon's Bridge on the headwaters of the Ashley River. *HL Papers,* iii, 413n.

[2] In 1714 Hugh Cochran had been granted lands at the head of Chehaw River and on Chehaw swamp. Index to Grants, S. C. Archives. Jonathan and Elizabeth Cochran had a daughter Mary born to them in 1761. He died on May 4, 1778. *SCHM,* x (1909), 150, 228. HL's son John was killed in 1782 on Chehaw Neck on the Combahee River, which site must have been near the plantation once owned by Jonathan Cochran. *SCHM,* i (1900), 13n.

[3] James Parsons, Irishman, was a leading lawyer of Charleston. He married Susannah Miles in 1753. He was a patriot and vice president of the new state of S. C. before his death in September 1779. His plantations were located in the parishes of St. Paul and St. Bartholomew in Colleton County. *SCHM,* xi (1910), 61; xvii (1916), 155; "Will of James Parsons," dated Feb. 20, 1779, proved ―――, Charleston County Wills, xviii (1776–1784), 344–355, S. C. Archives.

The good people in England seem to be in just such a ferment (only of more & of more dangerous consequence) about the late made peace in Europe, as our mistaken folks were here about the Cherokee Peace. It was either untimely for the Gratification of their hunger & thirst for Gold or power & Glory or they madden because so good a peace was made by Men they hate. Every day stares them in the Face with some new circumstance to brand their assertions with the Lye & yet the numbers of the Grumbletonians[4] increases daily. The meeting of the parliment must work some extrordinary Effect & we shall soon hear of it.[5]

God guide them in their deliberations, & may they by wise Measures do justice to an injured people or effectualy stop the tongue & pen of faction; may each crafty Knave & every knot of Knaves whether they are indebted to North or South, East or West for their first birth or their education meet with a reward adequate to their demerrit.

Mean while may we live in & strive to promote peace & friendship at home & as far as our example & Influence extends.

I wish you many happy returns of this season & am, Dear Sir—

SOURCE: Letterbook copy, Letter Book of Henry Laurens, Oct. 30, 1762– Sept. 10, 1766, Penn. Hist. Soc.; addressed "Esquire. Augusta."

T O J O H N A U G U S T U S S H U B A R T[6]

[Charles Town] 31st December 1763

Dear Sir,

I have been too long indebted for your very acceptable

[4] "A contemptuous designation applied in the latter part of the 17th c. to the members of the so-called 'Country Party' in English politics, who were accused by the 'Court Party' of being actuated by dissatisfied personal ambition; hence in later times applied to supporters of the Opposition." *OED.*

[5] After Parliament had reassembled on Nov. 15, 1763, the House of Commons did move quickly against John Wilkes who had been one of the chief critics of the treaty of peace and of the government. The house voted that No. 45 of the *North Briton* was a seditious libel, that parliamentary privilege did not cover Wilkes' case, and on Jan. 20, 1764, that he be expelled from the house. J. Steven Watson, *The Reign of George III, 1760–1815* (Oxford, Eng., 1960), pp. 100– 101.

[6] Doctor Shubart (Schubert) arrived at Bethabara on Sept. 26, 1760; he returned to Pennsylvania in 1765. *Records of the Moravians in North Carolina,* I, 228, 232, 488.

favours of the 10th May & 24th October but meeting now with a good opportunity by Mr. Mathew Lock[7] to send up the Gazettes, I shall at the same time do myself the pleasure of addressing you in a few Lines.

And first give me Leave to thank you for the drops & the Flower Roots that you were pleased to send me. I made no mention before of the former because truly tho I believe them to be very good yet, thank God, neither Mrs. Laurens nor I have had much, I may almost say, any, occasion to apply to them. We are both pretty stirring folks & find some easy manual employment from morning until Evening, & such people are seldom heard to complain of small ailments & in case of a severe attack, it is natural to call for the Physician, where he is so near at hand as in this Town, but as I observed above, our good state of health hath render'd your kind present useless, which I am sure will afford you at least as much pleasure as the most successfull applications could have done.

And as to the Flower Roots they were no novelty as we had such before in our Garden. Nevertheless your addition was very acceptable because we had not abundance but by an accident half of them were lost, the rest are put into proper ranks. Mrs. Laurens is greatly disappointed, as she is not yet able through the backwardness of Workmen, to get into our New House & become Mistress of that employment which she most delights in, the cultivating & ornamenting her Garden, but we have some hopes of taking possession before the next Month expires, & I flatter myself that upon some occasion I shall have the pleasure of seeing Doctor Shubart there.

I was not unmindful nor negligent of your order to send to Philadelphia for Glasses,[8] & from the exact description which I gave & the care of the person by whose hand I sent a duplicate of your draught of those Vessels; I was in great hopes that you would have receiv'd the very articles; but behold when they arrived they were no more than the same sort that I had formerly procured for you, however such as they were I transmitted them by the hands of Mr.

---

[7] Matthew Locke (1730–1801), born in Pennsylvania and settled near Salisbury, North Carolina by 1752, operated a wagon line between Charleston and the N. C. Piedmont. He was a "moral, provincial, uneducated, religious" man who became an "extreme Jeffersonian Republican." A. R. Newsome, "Matthew Locke," *DAB.*

[8] These were the "urinaria" which HL had ordered the previous spring. *HL Papers,* III, 375–376.

Steiner.[9] You will be so good as to accept of my endeavours to serve you altho they have not succeeded equal to my wishes, & I am determin'd to make another attempt to Philadelphia by a Vessel that will sail next Week & if such things as you want are to be bought in that Province I shall probably have some ready for the opportunity of your Spring Waggons; I have told you before that it gives me real pleasure to serve you & all your Brethren. Therefore I intreat you to trouble your self no more with appologies on one hand; nor to subdue me on the other by too many acknowledgements, but when you think that I can assist you & them inform me of it in your friendly manner & I hope you will always find me uniform in my professions & attachment.

While I am writing this Letter a Proclamation[1] is going about the Town, to call the House of Assembly to a meeting on Account of some new Outrages committed by the Creek Indians, of which certain intelligence is just now Receiv'd, Vizt. that they have crossed Savanna River & killed about fourteen of our planters on the Settlement called Long Canes.[2] This so soon following the late treaty shews their hearts to be equally full of malice & insolence & that the blow was premeditated. We have by our lavish presents enabled them to strike with more effect. The Cherokees continue firm in their profession of friendship & have now upon this occasion repeated the offers of their service declaring that if the Govournor will send them a painted knife they will immediately make use of it in our favour & I do believe they are very sincere. God grant that we may not, by keeping up our own domestick broils defeat their good designs & drive them to a necessity of joining the Enemy Tribes. This affair I am afraid will cause our Country much trouble & if it is not soon quas[he]d will also hinder the peopling of our new ceded provinces East & West Florida, in which I am told the Lands are very good &

---

[9] Jacob Steiner arrived in Bethabara June 13, 1755, married in 1766 Catharine Beroth, and died in 1801 at Salem. He took wagons to Bethlehem in Pennsylvania and to Charleston. *Records of the Moravians in North Carolina*, I, 121, 231, 246, 485, 490; *HL Papers*, III, 95n.

[1] Governor Thomas Boone issued a proclamation, dated Dec. 30, 1763, calling the assembly to meet on Jan. 4 "in Consequence of Information this day received, of many Persons being Murdered in the Long Canes Settlement by the Creek Indians." House Journal, xxxvi (Jan. 24, 1763–Oct. 6, 1764), 1 (2nd pagination), S. C. Archives.

[2] Accounts of the murders were published in the *Georgia Gazette*, Jan. 5, 1764, and the *Gazette*, Jan. 14, 1764.

that good indulgences will be granted to the first adventurers both as to the Land & proper means to improve their Plantations. Governor Grant is expected in a Month or six Weeks to preside over the former & he has happily engaged near two hundred french protestant families to come out with him.[3] These are useful inhabitants & will be some means of drawing forth other Emigrants to join them. For the division of those Southern Provinces I refer you to the News Papers as well as for other publick intelligence with which they abound;[4] and now after presenting my respects to the Reverend Mr. Edwin, Mr. Lash, Mr. Vangammern, & in short to all your family that will accept them, wishing you health & many happy Years I shall for the present take my leave assuring you once more that I heartily Love you all & that I am with great regard, Dear Sir, Your affectionate & Humble Servant—[5]

SOURCE: Letterbook copy, Letter Book of Henry Laurens, Oct. 30, 1762–Sept. 10, 1766, Penn. Hist. Soc.; addressed "Doctor. at Bethabara."

TO JOHN AUGUSTUS SHUBART
Saturday Evening [Charles Town] 31st December 1763
Dear Sir,
I had wrote to you fully this day by the hands of Mathew Lock & soon after I had Sealed up my Packet, your favour of the 29th Ulto. came to my hands by a Reverend Gentleman whom you have recommended to me but have not informed me of his name;

---

[3] The *Gazette,* Sept. 21, 1763, had mentioned the arrival in Plymouth, Eng., of 1,000 Huguenots from Bordeaux. James Grant had wanted to use these French Protestants as settlers in East Florida rather than persons from the slums of English cities. Gipson, *The Triumphant Empire,* p. 189. These Huguenots, however, were destined for S. C. where they arrived in April 1764 and eventually settled New Bordeaux in the upcountry. A. S. Salley, "The Settlement of New Bordeaux," *The Transactions of the Huguenot Society of South Carolina,* XLII (1937), 38–54.

[4] The Proclamation of Oct. 7, 1763, which established the boundaries and governments for East Florida, West Florida, the Grenadas, and Quebec, was published in the *Gazette* Dec. 31, 1763.

[5] "*Jan. 13* . . . A letter from Henry Laurens, from Charlestown, states that in spite of the recent peace treaty the Creeks have crossed the Savannah and have killed fourteen persons in Long Cane Bottom. Also that the Cherokees have offered to take the part of the English against the Creeks, but that opinions differ as to whether their offer should be accepted." "Extract from the Bethabara Diary, 1764," *Records of the Moravians in North Carolina,* I, 284.

I shall probably learn that to morrow evening when he is to be again at my House & such services as I can render to him to help his good designs shall not be wanting.[6] I repeat my Salutations to Bethabara & remain, Dear Sir, Your Affectionate friend & Servant—

SOURCE: Letterbook copy, Letter Book of Henry Laurens, Oct. 30, 1762– Sept. 10, 1766, Penn. Hist. Soc.; addressed "Doctor. at Bethabara in Wacovia, No. Carolina"; "per Mathew Lock."

TO LACHLAN McGILLIVRAY[7]

[Charles Town] 2d January 1764

Sir,

This covers a Letter from our good friend Mr. James Cowles of Bristol which he requests me to forward & also to use my interest with you to comply with the request therein which as I learn from him is for £92.1.9 Sterling due to him for Interest on your Account. I know him for many Years experience to be so reasonable a Man & so fair a dealer that I am persuaded he wou'd make no charge but what was strictly consistant with justice & the Custom of trade &

---

[6] Christian Frederick Post was a visitor in Bethabara on Feb. 15, 1761. He was again in Bethabara preaching from Nov. 19 to Nov. 29, 1763. *Records of the Moravians in North Carolina,* I, 277, 488. Post, who had been born in Germany in 1715, came out to Pennsylvania in 1742 where he lived among the Indians. He was married twice to Indian women. He returned to Germany in the period 1749–1752, went on a voyage with Moravian brethren to Labrador in 1752, and during the French and Indian War worked among the Indians on the Ohio to retain their friendship for the English. He was in 1763–1764 making his first voyage as a missionary to the Indians on the Bay of Honduras. In November 1767 he sailed from Philadelphia for a second visit to the Mosquito Coast where he still resided in 1775. The Schwenkfelders financed his missionary journeys. Selina G. Schultz and Andrew S. Berky, *The Mosquito Coast and the Story of the First Schwenkfelder Missionary Enterprise Among the Indians of Honduras from 1768 to 1775* (Norristown, Penn., 1953).

[7] Lachlan (spelled "Lachlin" here) McGillivray, who came from Scotland about 1738, had been an Indian trader settled for many years at Little Tallassie on the Coosa River among the Creek Indians. By 1763 he had amassed a large fortune part of which he invested in Georgia lands. His son Alexander, the child of Sehoy Marchand, Lachlan's Indian wife, was the famous Creek chief. During the Revolution Lachlan's estate was confiscated by Georgia. John W. Caughey, *McGillivray of the Creeks* (Norman, Okla., 1938), pp. 9–16. The *Georgia Gazette,* Oct. 6, 1763, announced his departure from the province in a few months. John Rae, George Galphin, and Lachlan McGillivray were in 1764 the surviving partners of Brown, Rae & Co., the great Indian trading company. *Georgia Gazette,* March 8, 1764.

indeed as he represents he will be rather a looser by your correspondence if this sum is not paid to him. On the other hand I know you for many Years experience too, to be a Man of so much honour & punctuality that I am sure you will not withhold a doit[8] from Mr. Cowles or any other Man that he has a just right to claim from you. Therefore I make no doubt your giving orders for Payment of the above mention'd Sum or assigning such reasons for not paying it as will be satisfactory to him.

As it is by particular desire that I have so far interfered in this matter I trust you will pardon me & beleve me to be upon all occasions, Sir, Your, &ca.—

SOURCE: Letterbook copy, Letter Book of Henry Laurens, Oct. 30, 1762–Sept. 10, 1766, Penn. Hist. Soc.; addressed "Savanna in Georgia."

TO JOHN COMING BALL

[Charles Town] 6 January 1764

Dear Sir,

I Rece'd your favour by Robbin & thank you for sending my Horse. I detain'd the Boy in Town Yesterday thinking to return a Horse by him but I have been too busy to call upon Doctor Garden[9] who is to have one of them & he happened not to come our way.

I leave every thing with respect to Wambaw until the period you name, Vizt. our meeting of which I shall next week write with more certainty. I send you a peice of Duffils. Your Sister & I send you with our Compliments—

One Barrel of Apples
One Rump of Beef—

in Mr. Linds Boat.[1] How goes on our Sawing work? I am yours, &c.—

SOURCE: Letterbook copy, Letter Book of Henry Laurens, Oct. 30, 1762–Sept. 10, 1766, Penn. Hist. Soc.

[8] A small Dutch coin—worth less than an English farthing. *OED*.
[9] Dr. Alexander Garden (1725–1791), physician and botanist, and HL were good friends, drawn closely together by their common interest in gardening. Edmund Berkeley and Dorothy Smith Berkeley, *Dr. Alexander Garden of Charles Town* (Chapel Hill, N. C., 1969), p. 200.
[1] This may be the schooner *Live Oak* in which Thomas Lind was to hold one-fourth share. *HL Papers*, III, 127n.

TO JAMES BRENARD[2]

[Charles Town] 6 January 1764

The Wambaw Boat brought down 96 Barrels of Rice & 12 half Barrels. Abram[3] wrote that 10 of them were yours but there appear'd to be 13 Mark'd JB so I have thrown them all into one & when the whole is brought down you shall have an equal proportion as to the weight & price. This I think is the fairest way & no doubt you will accept the indulgence.

I Rece'd your five Hogs, those not so good as last Year. Be so kind to send three or four more, some Turkeys, &c., &c., for I have had but poor fare this Christmas.

Tell Abraham that I have wrote to Mr. Ball according to promise but he deferrs giving me an answer untill we meet sometime before the 20th Inst. & he may depend upon it that he shall not be a sufferer by waiting untill Mr. Ball is at Leisure to determine.

I beg you will dispatch the Schooner & tell me how the Salt Account stands. Are we to have no Shingles this Year. Send the Wild Goose. Pray let me have some Summer Ducks.[4] I am yours, &c.—

SOURCE: Letterbook copy, Letter Book of Henry Laurens, Oct. 30, 1762–Sept. 10, 1766, Penn. Hist. Soc.; addressed "Wambaw."

TO FRANCIS STUART[5]

[Charles Town] 6th January 1764

Sir,

I Rece'd your favour of the 24 Ulto. with Thomas Myers[6] Receipt inclos'd for four Casks Indigo per Schooner *Blakney* on your Account. As I had comply'd with all the orders upon me for Indigo & had Shipp'd on my own Account as much as is convenient before

---

[2] Spelled "Breneard" in the letterbook.
[3] Abraham Schad.
[4] *HL Papers,* III, 217n.
[5] Merchant at Beaufort. *HL Papers,* III, 240n.
[6] Thomas Meyers was the master of Francis Stuart's schooner. On Jan. 12, 1764, Francis Stuart as owner registered the schooner *Success* of Port Royal, Thomas Meyers, master, a square sterned vessel of 18 tons, built in 1757. It had formerly been named the *Blakeney.* Ship Register, 1734–1765, p. 222, S. C. Archives; *HL Papers,* III, 358.

yours came to Market & have agreable to your directions Shipp'd said 4 Casks, Vizt. on board the *Union,* Capt. Smith,[7] for London as per Bill Load'g, here find inclosed consign'd to a House that transacts most of my business there Mrs. Sarah Nicholson & Co. to whome I shall give any further directions that you may think necessary, and as to the Sum to be advanced thereon to your Credit I trust that we shall accomodate that part to our Mutual Satisfaction when you come to Town & then I shall also assume your debt as you desire to A., L., & A. & bring the whole under one head in my Books.

I put you to the expence of a piece of paper & a stick of wax charged to your Account at Messrs. James Laurens & Co.[8] & I charge you for Certificate, Postage, Cooperage, & Wharfage 55/. I peep'd into one head of No. 1 & one of No. 3. The former looked well & free from mixture the Latter a Little adulterated; but is as you say a good shape & a tolerable good quality in general. You are Silent about Insurance therefore I have not wrote for any to be made on your Interest but I beleve you may have the whole done as cheap here as in London as you save the Commission for making it. Please to inform me with more certainty when I may send a Schooner for Indian Corn & at what price that I may engage one. I am—

SOURCE: Letterbook copy, Letter Book of Henry Laurens, Oct. 30, 1762–Sept. 10, 1766, Penn. Hist. Soc.; addressed "Beaufort."

TO ISAAC KING

[Charles Town] 7 January 1764

Sir,

The annex'd is duplicate of my last under the 24th Ulto. to

---

[7] The ship *Union,* James Smith, owned by John Beswicke of London, cleared outwards on Jan. 6 for London with a cargo of 572 barrels of rice, 23,462 pounds of indigo, 66 hogsheads and 152 bundles of deerskins, 11 otter skins, and 3 casks of seeds. Naval Office Lists, 1764–1767, p. 73. Two copies of the manifest of the cargo on board the *Union* are in Naval Office Lists, 1764–1767, pp. 1–2. The manifest states that HL shipped 4 casks of indigo (1,590 lbs.) to Sarah Nickleson & Co. The list reveals the consignees of many Charleston merchants.

[8] The firm of James Laurens & Co. had expired on Nov. 1, 1763. James Laurens and Isaac Motte signed a statement, Jan. 10, 1764, asking for the settlement of all accounts, which was published in the *Gazette,* Jan. 14, 1764. James Laurens, HL's brother, had formerly been a partner of Isaac's father, Jacob Motte. *HL Papers,* II, 285n.

which I beg leave to refer. You will find here inclosed a Bill Loading & Certificate for four Casks of fine Copper Indigo, Weight, &c. as below, shipp'd per the *Union*, Capt. Smith, on Account of Mr. Francis Stuart, Merchant in Beaufort, which you will be pleased to receive & sell in the best manner for his Interest. Pass the Net proceeds to the Credit of my Account Current with you & transmitt me an Account of the Sale as speedily after as you can that I may thereby account with that Gentleman & at present I have only to add that I remain with sincere esteem, Sir, Yours, &c.—

Account of the 4 Casks of Indigo referr'd to in the foregoing Letter

No. 1	481	69
2	450	68
3	460	71
4	471	64
	1,862	272
	272	

1,590 Net Weight Indigo

[*P.S.*] The Certificate was omitted in the above & I discovered it the 21st & forwarded it under a few Lines per *Mercury*, Man of War—[9]

SOURCE: Letterbook copy, HL Papers, S. C. Hist. Soc.; addressed "London"; "per Smith. Copy per Barnes."

TO JOHN KNIGHT

[Charles Town] 7th January 1764

Dear Sir,

The 22d Ulto. I troubled you with a long Letter per Capt Brownett & Capt. White to which please to be referr'd, & permitt me now to inform you that last Night your Ship *Hope*, Capt. Denison, arived here from Barbadoes & brought me your esteem'd favour of 6th August & Duplicate of 25 September. Her Cargo on your Account is only the article of Coal & a few packages of Earthenware & upon Freight about 20 hogsheads Rum. I am heartily glad that

---

[9] The HMS *Mercury*, Samuel Goodall, sailed over Charleston bar on Feb. 2 and arrived in the Downs on March 14. Ship's log, HMS *Mercury*, Adm. 51/4258; Samuel Goodall to Philip Stephens, March 15, 1764, Adm. 1/1836, Public Record Office, London.

she brought neither Rum nor Wine for you, but if 40 or 50 clever Negroes had been sent they wou'd probably have paid handsomely for their passages.[1]

I do not see any thing to be done with so good a prospect for your Interest in that Ship as to Load her imediately on your Account for Oporto, which I shall therefore do as expeditiously as I can with a Choice Cargo of Rice, Advertizeing in the mean time for Freight of part but without much hopes of success, for I cannot think of accepting 40/ per Ton nor do I beleve you wou'd commend me for it.[2]

The *Austin* after a detaintion that was very vexatious to me in the delivery of her Salt is now almost Loaded & Capt. Holmes I am sure will do me the justic to say that I have not spared the Labour of either my head or my hands to give him a good Cargo with dispatch & upon the best terms of purchase. I hope to clear that Snow out on the 10th Inst., & the moment Capt. Holmes back is turn'd I shall make up & transmitt a State of all your Account which I beleve will exhibit a proofe to you that however the Sale of dry goods, &ca. may not have answer'd the expectation of my friend yet that I have acted more upon a principle of friendship, Esteem, Gratitude to them than from any motive or view of Gain to myself for if I am not very much mistaken, the advance of my money (as Mr. Appleby kindly observ'd to Holmes) will absorb my whole commission but I entreat you to let this Matter rest between you & I. You will take nothing amiss that I write & there is nothing in my power that is too great for me to do to serve my dear & worthy Friend Mr. Knight, whose obliged & very Humble Servant always am—   HL

[*P.S.*] January 14, 1764. The *Austin* Loaded the 9th, Cleared the 11th, Now detain'd by nothing but Easterly Winds.[3]

SOURCE: Letterbook copy, HL Papers, S. C. Hist. Soc.; "per *Chance,* Smith. Copy per Brown."

---

[1] Laurens had expected the *Hope* to bring slaves. HL to John and Thomas Tipping, Dec. 15, 1763.

[2] The ship *Hope,* Thomas Dennison, was cleared outwards on Feb. 23 for Oporto with 600 barrels (317,149 pounds) of rice. Naval Office Lists, 1764–1767, p. 74.

[3] The snow *Austin,* Matthias Holme, was cleared outwards on Jan. 11 for Oporto with 558 barrels and 60 half barrels (303,442 pounds) of rice. Naval Office Lists, 1764–1767, p. 73.

TO JOHN TARLETON

[Charles Town] 9th January 1764

Sir,

The foregoing is duplicate of what I wrote you the 27th Ulto. which I now confirm & inclose herein a second Bill Loading, Abstract Invoice & receipt for the Cargo & disbursements of your Brigantine *Elizabeth* who did not get to Sea before the 1st Inst. Capt. Thornton being about an hour too late for the Tide on the day that he went from hence & was detain'd afterwards by fogs & Easterly Winds. I have taken the liberty under the 7th Inst. to draw on you at 40 days sight to the order of Messrs. Brailsford & Chapman[4] payable in London One hundred & twenty four Pounds Sterling at 721 per Cent Exchange to your Credit £894. This Exchange I hope will fully compensate any inconvenience that may attend the payment in London & you may rest assured of my endeavours to make my draught as advantageous to you as our plan admits of in which you will receive full satisfaction if you think it needfull to enquire. I remain—

SOURCE: Letterbook copy, HL Papers, S. C. Hist. Soc.; addressed "Liverpoole"; "per the *Chance,* Capt. Smith. Copy per *Union,* Smith."

TO THOMAS AUBREY

[Charles Town] 9th January 1764

Sir,

I am favour'd with yours of the 19th Ulto. & am glad to see that you were safe arriv'd at St. Augustine. Did you suffer any Loss of goods by Buckles Shipwreck?[5] You do not tell me.

---

[4] Samuel Brailsford and John Chapman. *HL Papers,* II, 212n; III, 122n.

[5] Thomas Buckle was the owner of the schooner *Harlequin* in which Thomas Aubrey had sailed for St. Augustine on Dec. 3. Buckle, a mariner, owned a number of sloops and schooners. Ship Register, 1734–1765, pp. 172, 194, 204, 231, S. C. Archives. Early in the Revolution Captain Buckle was instrumental in securing gunpowder from the West Indies for the patriots, but in 1780 he signed an address to Clinton for which gesture his estate was confiscated in 1782. *SCHM,* IX (1908), 10, 70–71; XXXIV (1933), 195. At the time of his death in 1787 he owned four slave ship carpenters. "Will of Thomas Buckle," dated March 17, 1787, proved Oct. 16, 1787, Charleston County Wills, XXII, Book A (1786–1793), 187–190, S. C. Archives.

Your Bills are drawn very methodicaly only the days of sight are rather long winded; however you are allowed the very highest exchange for them as per Inclos'd Account Ballanc'd by Cash paid for the Sundry Articles you desired me to send all which you will receive by Capt. Thomas Tucker except the Windsor Chairs an article that is not to be had at present in Charles Town.[6]

I thank you for your kind invitation & shall not forgett it when I come to Augustine. Meantime you may freely lay your Commands. Your, &ca.—

Cash paid or Receiv'd of Thomas Aubrey, Esquire.

1 Small Copper Sauspan	1.
1 Middle do.	2.
1 Large do.	3. 7.6
1 hand Spit	1. 5.
1 pr. Kitchen dogs	8.
6 Twin Small short pipes	1.17.6
1 Beaver Hatt	10.
2 lb. Hyson Tea	14.
	41.10.0
Cash paid Charles Warham[7] for 111 Dollars at 31/6	174.16.6
T. A. Bill for £30 Sterling at 721 per Cent is	£216. 6.6

SOURCE: Letterbook copy, HL Papers, S. C. Hist. Soc.; addressed "Lieutenant. Esquire. St. Augustine"; "per Capt. Tucker."

TO WILLING & MORRIS

[Charles Town] 9th January 1764

Gentlemen,

When this Vessell sail'd Last from hence[8] I had barely time

---

[6] The schooner *Hibernia,* Thomas Tucker, was cleared outwards for St. Augustine on Jan. 9 with 54 barrels of flour and sundry British goods. Naval Office Lists, 1764–1767, p. 73.

[7] Charles Warham, merchant and congregationalist, died July 20, 1779 at the age of 79. His partner in the 1750's had been Samuel Prioleau. *SCHM,* x (1909), 228; XII (1911), 139; Judgment Rolls, 1757, No. 70A, S. C. Archives.

[8] The brigantine *Charles Town Packet,* Thomas Mason, owned by George Noarth of Philadelphia and by Shirley & Martin and George Austin of Charleston, was cleared outwards on Nov. 11, 1763, for Philadelphia. It was cleared outwards again on Jan. 9, 1764. Naval Office Lists, 1757–1764, p. 135; 1764–1767, p. 73.

to inclose all Accounts Sale of your ten Casks o[f] Linced Oil[9] Nett proceeds £690.17.10 which now awaits your commands & have not since rece'd any of your acceptable favours. It often happens that people who have least to do not only do least but Less in proportion than other folks. This is in some measure verefyed in my partner G. Appleby who is so good as to wind up the Accounts of our Late House & save me no small addittion of Labour; I call'd on him just now for yours but he replyed they are not ready. You shall have them by the next opportunity. In the mean time I can inform you that he has by a stedy persevearence at length pretty well secured a large debt of £645, due by John Graham[1] who was long confined in Goal before he wou'd do the needfull part of it, is indeed still Lyable to a contest with another of Grahams Creditors but Mr. Appleby treats that with so much slight that he hopes you may have the Money whenever you call for it. He says [he] expects it soon from the Lawyer & will pay it into my hands then.

Rice is now at 40/ per Ct. & freight so Low as 55/ per Ton for Holland. Ships continue droping in so fast that no alteration can sudenly happen in their favour. West India Rum is here at 15/6 per Gallon in pleanty. Your produce is upon as bad a footing. Negroes sold extreamly high the last Year, the last Cargo advanced upwards of £36. The approaching season affords a fine prospect in that branch of trade. Exchange is 721 per Cent upon London & Bills not very pleanty. I am—

SOURCE: Letterbook copy, HL Papers, S. C. Hist. Soc.; addressed "Philidelpia"; "per Capt. Mason."

TO WILLIAM FISHER

[Charles Town] 9th January 1764
Dear Sir,

I am glad that I was so happy as to introduce Mr. Smith[2]

---

[9] HL had advertised these ten casks for sale on Aug. 27. *HL Papers*, III, 549.
[1] John Graham had been in debtor's prison. *HL Papers*, III, 214, 244, 512.
[2] The letter of introduction was dated July 16, 1763. *HL Papers*, III, 500–501. Benjamin Smith, former speaker of the Commons House of Assembly, had returned from his summer's trip to the North in the ship *Delaware*, Peter Creighton, which was entered inwards from Philadelphia on Nov. 22. Naval Office Lists, 1757–1764, p. 124; *Gazette*, Nov. 26, 1763; Rogers, *Evolution of a Federalist*, p. 34.

to your acquaintance since it has been attended with so much advantage to both parties. You express yourself to be highly pleased with him & he talks of you with great affection & respect. I have a parcell of narrow Cloths belonging to a worthy Friend in Liverpool[3] seemingly well bought at 3/3 to 4/6 Sterling per yard. With shalloons & trimmings they are quite unfitt for this overstock'd place. If you think that by Vendue or other Quick Sale you can obtain only the prime Cost in ready Money I intreet you to accept of the Sale of them. It will be doing me a very great favour as well as my friend in England & I will send them as soon as I have your permittion. I have one more favour to request & having so often intruded I am quite ashamed to be further troublesome to you. It is to send me by the return of this Vessell 6 peices of Glass call'd Urinalls such as are particularly discribed below.

Because I wou'd not be troublesome to you I desired James Verree[4] to bring one such but those he bought were with Necks & quite a wrong sort. These are for the use of some worthy people[5] Settled on our North West frontier three hundred & twenty Miles from this whome I now & then serve with as much pleasure (*because* they cannot help themselves) as ever I took in Loading a Vessell for a handsome Commission.

If you have no Money of mine in hand, you shall not long be in advance for this trifle. Rice is at 45/ per Ct. Freight to London 40/ per Ton, Holland 55/, Portugal 40/. Exchange 721 per Cent. I am—

N.B. The Glasses described in this Letter—

SOURCE: Letterbook copy, HL Papers, S. C. Hist. Soc.; "per Capt. Mason."

TO ALEXANDER DAVIDSON

[Charles Town] 13 January 1764

Sir,

You say that your Pitch is to go to somebody else. That I am

---

[3] John Knight. See HL to John Knight, Dec. 22, 1763.
[4] James Verree was a carpenter. *Abstracts of Wills, 1760–1784*, p. 193. In 1764 he was paid for repairing the fire engines. House Journal, xxxvi (Jan. 24, 1763–Oct. 6, 1764), 39, 101, 213, S. C. Archives.
[5] The Moravians in North Carolina.

very well content with since it is your wish, & be sure you may dispose of your own goods as you please expecialy as you can dispense with your promise.

I believe Mr. Dick has put your Indigo into Mr. Hutchins hands as I have no occasion for it. When you have satisfyed the *insistings* of your *Overseer, Cooper, School Master,* &c. 'tis possible you may think of one who has dealt with you as a friend & a Gentleman without *insisting even upon your keeping your own promise.* I mean your humble Servant—

SOURCE: Letterbook copy, Letter Book of Henry Laurens, Oct. 30, 1762–Sept. 10, 1766, Penn. Hist. Soc.; addressed "Black Mingo."

TO WILLIAM THOMPSON

[Charles Town] 13 January 1764

Dear Sir,

I have spoken to George Dick as you desired & hope he will bring your Pitch the next trip. My own schooner will probably come your way soon & you may make what use you please of her. I shall direct the Master to wait upon you & Mrs. Handlin[6]—& I am in the meantime, Dear Sir, Yours, &c.—

SOURCE: Letterbook copy, Letter Book of Henry Laurens, Oct. 30, 1762–Sept. 10, 1766, Penn. Hist. Soc.; addressed "Black Mingo."

TO ISAAC KING

[Charles Town] 14th January 1764

Sir,

My last to you was per the *Union,* Capt. Smith, with a Bill Loading for 4 Casks Indigo quantity 1,590 lb. Wt. on Account of Mr. Francis Stuart the produce to be passed to my Credit since which, Vizt. on the 11th Inst., I passed a Bill on you for One hundred pounds Sterling payable at 40 Days sight to the Order of William

---

[6] Mrs. Margaret Handlen, the widow of John Handlen. *HL Papers,* II, 138n.

Wragg, Esquire,[7] which be pleased to pay & make my Account Debtor for the same. I shall Ship Mr. Browns & my own Indigo per your *Minerva* in a day or two or when Capt. Barnes shall Call for it & by him shall write what may be further needfull. Mean while I remain, Your, &ca.—

SOURCE: Letterbook copy, HL Papers, S. C. Hist. Soc.; addressed "London"; "per Capt. Brown. Copy per *Mercury,* Capt. Goodall."

TO HENRY BYRNE

[Charles Town] 14 January 1764

Sir,

The 22d of last Month by Capt. Young for Lisbon & Capt. Candy for your River[8] I advised you of the *Austins* arival here & my intention to fill her with Rice on her owners Account to your address as usual. The Cargo of Salt was tediously taken out by the buyer, then the intervention of Holy days & much rainy weather hindred me from begining to Load her before the 2d Inst. & on the 9th I fill'd her up with 558 Barrels & 60 half Barrels of Rice as per Invoice of weight & Bill Loading here Inclosed which you will please to receive & dispose off on account of our Mutual good friends Messrs. John Knight & Thomas Mears from whome no doubt you have the needfull direction. I cannot compleat this Invoice at present because of one parcell of Ordinary Rice remaining on hand which in a day of scarcity & many purchasers I was obliged to take with a fine parcell as well as to bring the price from 50/ to 47/6 but if it is of any use to you please to be informed that except 49 of the half Barrels which cost 50/ per Ct. & some Loss that may attend the Sale of this ordinary Rice all the rest cost 47/6 per Ct. & I think that I may with great certainty assure you that the Quality is very good. Mr. Knights Ship *Hope,* Capt. Dennison, is here & I was

---

[7] William Wragg (1714–1777), who had inherited in 1750 a large fortune from his merchant father Samuel Wragg, was living at this time at Ashley Barony as a planter. After being suspended from the royal council of S. C. on Nov. 29, 1756, he was elected to the assembly in September 1760, where, during the winter of 1762–1763, he cooperated with HL. George C. Rogers, Jr., "The Conscience of a Huguenot," *Transactions of the Huguenot Society of South Carolina,* LXVII (1962), 1–11; *HL Papers,* III, 271.

[8] Oporto is on the Douro River.

boasting of getting her away for Oporto in 10 or 12 days but un-luckily She has sprung a Leake & in all probability must be hove down; this will detain her perhaps three or four Weeks & probably may occasion an Alteration of her Voyage. The Snow *Swift,* Capt. Duville, is Loading for Oporto.[9] The Brigantine *Hopewell,* Capt. Pitt,[1] will also Load for that Market & another small Brigantine is offering for Freight.[2] I strove to take up the whole or part of the *Hopewell* in order to thro' the Cargo into your hands but the Owner is here & Loads her himself.[3] If the last mention'd Brigantine persists in her resolution & I have the offer of her, I will Load her to your address. These are all that I know of yet to interfere with the *Austin's* Interest. Our Crop of Rice is certainly very Large & I begin to think that we shall rather want Ships to carry it off because Rice broke at so high a price & Freight so Low that timely Notice was given abroad & many Vessels diverted from their intended Voyages as seekers to this Port.

I shall keep you advised as oportunity offers & occasions require & be glad at all times to render you all the Services in my power. I am—

P.S. Meeting with a few Barrels Rice uncommonly fine I have put up some in small Barrels for my friends & beg your Exceptance of one marked HB per Capt. Holmes.

SOURCE: Letterbook copy, HL Papers, S. C. Hist. Soc.; addressed "Esquire. Oporto"; "per Holme with Bill Loading & Invoice. Copy per Lewis."

---

[9] The snow *Swift,* Thomas Deveulle, owned by Thomas Deveulle and Richard Trelswell of London, was entered inwards on Jan. 2 and was cleared outwards on Feb. 29 for Oporto with 733 barrels and 58 half barrels (389,478 pounds) of rice. Naval Office Lists, 1757–1764, p. 125; 1764–1767, p. 75.

[1] The brigantine *Hopewell,* Moses Pitt, owned by Young Green and Moses Pitt of Poole, was cleared outwards on March 6 for Oporto with 423 barrels and 55 half barrels (238,205 pounds) of rice. Naval Office Lists, 1764–1767, p. 75.

[2] The vessel was a snow not a brigantine. See HL to Henry Byrne, Feb. 9. The snow *Port Royal,* William Lewis, owned by Thomas Rock of Bristol, was cleared outwards on Feb. 9 for Oporto with 309 barrels and 43 half barrels (176,402 pounds) of rice. Naval Office Lists, 1764–1767, p. 74.

[3] H. E. S. Fisher uses Capt. Moses Pitt as an example of a master of a vessel in the rice trade who transacted business on his own account. Moses Pitt, how-ever, was more than the master of the vessel; he was also one of the owners. H. E. S. Fisher, *The Portugal Trade, A Study of Anglo-Portuguese Commerce, 1700–1770* (London, 1971), p. 70.

TO COWLES & HARFORD

[Charles Town] 14 January 1764

Gentlemen,

I wrote last to you per Capt. Brownett & Capt. White under the 22d Ulto. since which your favours of 26 October & 4th November are come to hand but at present I beg leave to pass them over & confine my Letter to one subject, Vizt.

I shall have on board the Brigantine *Barbados Packet,* Capt. William Harrop, for Cowes & Holland, Hamburgh, or Bremen about 450 Barrels Rice to sail sometime next week.[4] Be pleased to insure on said Adventure Seven hundred pounds Sterling on my Account. My interest will be upward of Eight therefore you may add another hundred if the Commodity will bear it at 45/ per Ct. for Rice & 55/ per Ton Freight. I shall recommend this Cargo to you for Sale in the Channel[5] or to send forward on my own Account as you shall judge most beneficial & in the meantime if you please you may look about you accordingly. I Remain—

SOURCE: Letterbook copy, HL Papers, S. C. Hist. Soc.; addressed "Bristol"; "per Brown. Copy per *Mercury,* Man of War." The first letter of this date copied into the letterbook was marked "This not sent." There was another letter of the same date with the same information which is printed above.

TO JOSEPH MANESTY

[Charles Town] 17th January 1764

Sir,

This Evening your Ship *Barter,* Capt. Gough, arived here from Barbadoes with fifty Hogsheads Rum & an order from Mr. John Haslin to load her with Lumber & rice on your Account which I shall do with the utmost expedition & upon the best terms that our place will admit of. I say this because the price of Lumber is greatly advanced in Carolina & there is at present an uncommon

---

[4] The brigantine *Barbados Packet,* Edward Nicholson, owned by William Harrop of Philadelphia, was cleared outwards on Jan. 17 for Cowes with 423 barrels and 63 half barrels of rice. Naval Office Lists, 1764–1767, p. 73. When the vessel was entered inwards from Antigua on Dec. 22, William Harrop himself was listed as master. Naval Office Lists, 1757–1764, p. 125.

[5] That is, at Cowes.

demand for it. I cou'd have wished both for your Interest & my own that not a drop of Rum had come in the Vessel for when I have done my best I shall procure no more than your own Money for it without one halfpenny for Freight & to obtain even so much for you I shall be obliged to give a Credit upon the Sale that will probably sink my Commission.

I am at present very unwell by an unlucky fall in my Stair case a day or two ago. Therefore after assuring you that nothing on my part shall be wanting to serve your Interest give me leave to conclude with great respect, Yours—

SOURCE: Letterbook copy, HL Papers, S. C. Hist. Soc.; addressed "Liverpoole"; "per Capt. Harrop. per *Mercury, Man of War, Goodall.*"

TO GEORGE McKENZIE & CO.[6]
[Charles Town] 18 January 1764
Gentlemen,

I had a few days since, Vizt. the 22d Ulto. the pleasure of receiving your favour of the 4th November & I heartily thank you for your kind assurances of your Inclinations to serve me. You must know that many years ago I received civilitys & marks of hospitality from our departed friend whose name still remains at the head of your firm, which with the regard I have for Capt. John McKenzie[7]

---

[6] Capt. George McKenzie had made at least six voyages from Bristol to Charleston during the 1730's as master and part owner with Graffin Prankard of the vessel *Baltick Merchant.* The *Baltick Merchant* on the return voyages stopped at Cowes for information on the northern markets. About 1738 George McKenzie settled down in Cowes as a merchant. Prankard-Dickinson Papers, Somerset Record Office, Taunton, Eng. Robert Pringle wrote to his brother Andrew in London on June 14, 1740: "It is pity there was not a Cliver Man at Cowes in the Room of Mr. Hope Deceas'd for I can't say I much like Mr. Mackenzie or take him to be a person much Conversant in Business or that is thankful to those that Employ him, being naturally a very stiff proud man & Mr. Reid is of the Same way of thinking." *Letterbook of Robert Pringle, 1737–1745,* I, 223. George McKenzie had handled some of HL's rice shipments. *HL Papers,* II, 390; III, 387, 393, 394. George McKenzie must have recently died, and HL was probably writing to his son James McKenzie who was 32 years old when he leased a quay and storehouses at the south end of Cowes on Jan. 1, 1766. E. G. Earl, archivist, County Record Office, Isle of Wight to editor, July 3, 1972.
[7] Capt. John McKenzie was buried on Jan. 4, 1766. *Register of St. Philip's Parish, 1754–1810,* p. 312.

here, must always lead me to give you a preferrence to any competitors in your branch whilst you can do business upon much the same terms with them which I make no doubt you will always do. I have made no inquiry into that particular but I take it for granted that you do because no complaints of the contrary have been made within my knowledge. I know your Wharfs & Warehouses well enough. They cost a great deal of money & are very comodious & fit for the purposes intended; my own consignments are very trifling but such as they are together with the small atmosphere of influence that I have you are heartily welcome to.

I am now to trouble you with an Invoice & Bill loading under cover of this for 423 Barrels & 63 half Barrels Rice per the Brigantine *Barbadoes Packet,* William Harrop, Master, for your Island[8] on my own Account which you will be pleased to Enter & Clear, following such other directions as may be given by Messrs. Cowles & Harford of Bristol who will be responsable to you for amount of your Account & tell you where to draw for the same.

There is in this Cargo 61 Barrels branded on the heads E.F.,[9] No. 1 to 61, & 60 Barrels branded on the heads G. AUSTIN No. 98 to 124 & No. 149 to 181. The Quality not so good as I generly Ship & indeed I was a little deceiv'd in both parcels but the remainder being all fine I hope when properly mix'd you will make it upon the whole as good a Cargo as most & better than many that is ship'd from hence. I am so particular in this because I wou'd have the fate of my rice as to it's Quality determin'd at Cowes & not Subject myself to the mercy of foreign Brokers by whome I have in two former Instances suffer'd a good deal. You say that I need not send you an Invoice. Nevertheless as it is not a great deal of trouble to make one here & that in some Cases I foresee how it may be useful on your side I have as abovemention'd inclosed one. I shall be obliged to you to drop me a line now & then advising the State of the Europian Markets, &ca. as you have frequent opportunitys of doing so, some days later than my friends above & when I can serve your Intrest here you may freely command me who are with great Respect, Your—

---

[8] Cowes was on the Isle of Wight.
[9] Elias Foissin was a rice and indigo planter in the parish of Prince George Winyah. Rogers, *History of Georgetown County,* pp. 49n, 60, 61, 86, 101, 102, 518.

SOURCE: Letterbook copy, HL Papers, S. C. Hist. Soc.; addressed "Cowes"; "per Capt. Harrop. Copy per Barnes or Harbison."

TO WATSON & GREGORY[1]

[Charles Town] 18 January 1764

Gentlemen,

I have sundry of your favours which I fully intended to have answer'd by this conveyance but unluckily got a fall a day or two ago and am now dictating this Letter abed. Therefore I beg that you will excuse me for confining myself at present to one subject only which is to beg your friendly countenance and aid if needful to the bearer of this, Mr. Frederic Post, a pious man & a teacher of the Gospel of Jesus Christ. I believe these are uncommon terms in Letters of recommendation to Jamaica but they are characterestics lovely in themselves & must meet with some friends in every country & I flatter myself that you will not dispise them.

This Gentleman was recommended to me by some of my friends to the Northward[2] & I find that he has credentials with him which will prove that he has been a very usefull man to and much respected by the late General Forbes, Collonel Bouquet,[3] & other officers commanding his Majestys troops in the back country, about Pittsburgh, Niagara, &ca.

His present design is to go down to the Musquito shore[4] with a view of propagating the Gospel among the Savage Natives thereabouts, & which he will further unfold to you if your curiosity or other motives shall lead you to inquire of him. I shall be very thankful to you to assist him to a passage to the continent & if some Money is necessary for that Purpose be so kind as to advance it on my Account & in fine any favours you are pleased to confer upon this Gentleman will be particularly obliging to, &ca.—

SOURCE: Letterbook copy, HL Papers, S. C. Hist. Soc.; addressed "Jamaica"; "per Capt. Craig."

---

[1] Formerly Watson, Gregory, and Delmestre. *HL Papers,* III, 219, 533.

[2] Dr. John Augustus Shubart. See HL to Shubart, Dec. 31, 1763 and HL to John Ettwein, March 13, 1764.

[3] Gen. John Forbes and Col. Henry Bouquet. *HL Papers,* III, 80n, 298n.

[4] The governors of Jamaica had always taken a special interest in the Indians who lived on the east coast of Nicaragua, which was known to the English as the "Moskito shore." Pares, *War and Trade in the West Indies,* pp. 97–104, 540–555, 602–603.

TO COWLES & HARFORD

[Charles Town] 20 January 1764

Gentlemen,

My last was under the 14 Inst. per Capt. Brown[5] & Copy per *Mercury,* Man of War, for Insurance of Seven hundred Pounds Sterling on my Account on Rice per the Brigantine *Barbados Packet,* William Harrop, Master, for Cowes & Holland, Hamburgh, or Bremen. This waits on you by that Vessell by which I have Ship'd 423 Barrels & 63 half Barrels Rice as per Invoice & Bill Loading transmitted to Messrs. George McKenzie & Company of Cowes who will enter the Cargo there & Clear it again for a foreign Market; apply to you for the payment of their Charges & follow such further directions as you shall give them & will also send you the Invoice if needful. The whole amount of this Cargo is £6,167.4.4 Currency. If you can obtain a price for it in the Channel so as to reimburse me reckoning the Exchange at 700 per Cent I wou'd rather you wou'd sell it there than send it upon my account to a foreign Market but you may do in this as may appear to you most promising for my Interest. If it shou'd go to Hamburgh on my own Account & that the House of William Burrows & Son[6] still exists & in good Credit, I beg the consignment may be made to them in preferrence to any other unless you shall have reasons to the contrary which I am not aware of. This Cargo of Rice is in General very good but 61 Barrels branded on the head E.F. & 60 Branded G. AUSTIN in both of which I was a little deceived are of Qualitys inferior to what I generaly Ship. I have pointed them out to the House at Cowes that they may if needfull be kept distinct & not impair the Value of the rest by an improper mixture. Nevertheless I am realy of opinion that if the whole was mix'd together it wou'd produce a Quality equal to most & better than many of the Cargos of rice Shipp'd from hence.

---

[5] The ship *Prince of Wales,* John Brown, cleared outwards on Jan. 10 for London. Naval Office Lists, 1764–1767, p. 73.

[6] The Burrows family was highly placed among the Merchant Adventurers at Hamburg from the early eighteenth century until the French forced these English merchants to renounce their privileges in 1806. One William Burrows married the heiress Alice Metcalfe in 1728. William Alexander Burrowes who was the last treasurer of the Merchant Adventurers was known as one who sold high-quality merchandise, specializing in colonial produce. Dr. Loose, ober-archivrat of the Hamburg Archives to the editor, March 21, 1972; William E. Lingelbach, "The Merchant Adventurers of Hamburg," *American Historical Review,* IX (1903–1904), 265–287.

I have twice suffer'd by abatements on exceeding fine Rice Ship'd by myself owing to inferior rice Ship'd by other people in the same Vessels. My Consignments were made over to Mr. Beswick[7] & the other time to Mr. Nutt.[8] Both those Gentlemen assured me that I was Sworn out of my property by foreign Brokers which I wou'd if possible Guard against for the future by fixing the Quality of my Rice together with the price at Cowes which I think it behooves all concern'd in that Article to endeavour to accomplish. And it wou'd give me more pleasure if you cou'd make sale of this Cargo by your own or thro' the means of one of your own Brokers than by the intervention of any of our friends in London who have Cargos consign'd to them for Sale in the Channel, but this between you & me. Do therein as you see fit.

Please now to receive Certificate for the 10 hogsheads Indigo *CJH* & 2 Barrels *CJH*, total Quantity Six thousand & thirty five pounds, Ship'd by your Brigantine *Favourite*, which I hope will reach you in good time to secure the Bounty. I shou'd go on to write you upon other matters but I met with an unlucky fall upon my Stair Case three or four days ago the effects of which confines me to my Chamber where I have dictated so far therefore I hope you will excuse me from adding farther than that, I am—

SOURCE: Letterbook copy, HL Papers, S. C. Hist. Soc.; addressed "Bristol"; "per Harrop. Copy per Harbinson."

TO JOHN KNIGHT

[Charles Town] 20th January 1764

Dear Sir,

I wrote you the 7th Inst. per Capt. Smith & Capt. Brown with a Postcript the 14th to which I beg leave to refer. You will see by my Letter of this date to the owners of the *Austin* that I have been for some days disabled to do business & that I am not capable of writing even this myself. Therefore to you, my good Sir, I shall make no further Apology for saying upon the present occasion only what is barely needfull.

---

[7] John Beswicke of London. *HL Papers*, I, 96n.
[8] John Nutt of London. For these instances of fraud see *HL Papers*, III, 259, 394.

I have sold the Coals on board the *Hope* at £6 to £7 per Ton & the last will be deliver'd tomorrow Morning. The Pilot unluckily Struck that Ship coming over the Bar the consequence of which is a dangerous leake. Capt. Dennison has enter'd a protest but must to his great mortification go to Hob Caw[9] & heave down the Ship. I am sure no diligence will be wanting in him to repair her and return to Town for he seems as anxious as if his whole happyness depended upon that one point. I have already put 50 Barrels Rice on board to keep the Ship on her Legs & I will take care to be prepared for her reception when she comes from Careening. Upon the whole if nothing extrordinary bad appears in her bottom I dare say her Lying here will not be more than the ordinary course of Ships in this Port that have met no disaster. Cap[t]. Dennison has Lodged with me 10 very shattred Casks of Earthen Ware & 9 of Bottled Ale & also 10 Crates of Yellow Ware;[1] these are Sold at £5 to £4.10 per Crate. The former I have solicited people to take at prime Cost & spent half a Morning myself, a Clerk, & three Negroes to retail one of them at Vendue but was forced to bring it home again. I am—

SOURCE: Letterbook copy, HL Papers, S. C. Hist. Soc.; addressed "Liverpoole"; "per *Mercury,* Capt. Goodall. Copy per Harrop."

TO JOHN KNIGHT & THOMAS MEARS

[Charles Town] 20 January 1764

Gentlemen,

After writing to you as I did on the 22 Ulto. per Brownett & White I continued my utmost endeavours to Clear the *Austin* of her Salt Cargo but I cou'd only endeavour & Wish not command all that I wou'd have done & thro' the slackness on the part of the purchaser together with intervening holydays & some rainy days I cou'd not begin to Load her with Rice before the 2d Inst. Then I began & finished her Loading the 9th with a Cargo of 558 Barrels & 60 half Barrels of very fine Rice & the Snow was Clear'd out upon

---

[9] Hobcaw was about three miles northeast of Charleston on the east side of the Wando River. It was the center for the careening and repair of vessels.

[1] Yellow ware was yellow earthenware or stoneware. *OED.*

the 11th. It wou'd have too much the Act of Vanity in me to talk of diligence in this affair to you Gentlemen who are so good judges of business & it wou'd Savour too much of a Querulous disposition. How sorry I am that the Vessel has been detain'd ever since by irisistable fate especialy as She has had only Neighbours for the Winds have been contrary & Detain'd her & many others.

The Cost of this Cargo except a few Barrels at 50/ will be 47/6 per Ct. Had I too implicitly follow'd your direction of buying Rice in haste without regard to price the whole wou'd have cost the former together with a heavy Charge of Storeage & your Vessel not one Moment earlyer at Sea. On the other hand If I had follow'd my own Inclination without any regard to your Orders I shou'd have purchas'd the whole at 45/ per Ct. and She would not have been a Moment later. This is a true state of the fact which I beg leave to submit to your consideration without any coment on my side. I cannot compleat an Invoice of the *Austins* Cargo because of one parcell of ordinary Rice which I was obliged to take in (tho' I wou'd not Ship it) to secure a fine parcell as well as to humble the price to 47/6. This has been in the Coopers hands for screening & Sale ever Since & he has not brought me in his Account & now I am by an unlucky fall upon my stair Case confined to my Chamber where I dictate this Letter but I hope to go abroad the day after tomorrow & then shall imediately forward that & all your other Accounts & perhaps they may reach you as soon as this.

After Selling about 10 hogsheads of your Rum upon very Long Credit from 17/ to 17/6 & seeing the same article daily Sold from 13/9 to 15/ per Gallon your Hogsheads being in very bad condition, new importations every day & advices of a large Crop coming on in the West Indies, I attempted to push yours of[f] by a private Auction at my own Stores offering two Months Credit and availing myself of my intention soon to remove from the Spot where I now live which I thought wou'd in some Measure take of[f] the appearance of necessity by my Scheme (tho' indeed it answer'd as well as I wou'd reasonably expect[)] yet it did not quite Succeed & no more than 9 Hogsheads were sold at 15/7 Upward. I shall leave no Stone unturned to get the remainder off upon the most advantagious terms as well as to finish the Sale of the dry Goods of which only a few are yet Sold. I have not Strength to go farther at present therefore I humbly beg you'll excuse me who are, Yours—

SOURCE: Letterbook copy, HL Papers, S. C. Hist. Soc.; addressed "Liverpoole"; "per *Mercury,* Capt. Goodall. Copy per Harrop."

T O   G R E Y   E L L I O T T[2]

[Charles Town] 21st January 1764

Sir,

After waiting so long for a final adjustment & discharge of the account of Negroes sold by Messrs. Elliott & Gordon on Account of the late Mr. John McQueen & Austin, Laurens, & Appleby & Mr. Applebys departure from this Province being now at hand, I can hardly restrain him from attempting other measures to procure justice than those humble applications which have hitherto proov'd inefectual. He was in great hopes that upon Mr. Gordons return from Augustine thro' Georgia[3] you wou'd have conveyed the Ballance of our Account or given orders for payment of it by that favourable opportunity, but upon application to that Gentleman he gives me no other satisfaction but that you promis'd to remit the Money very soon & desires that we will remind you once more.

You will pardon me therefore, Sir, for being again troublesome to you on this long spun Subject; I cannot avoid it without treating my late partner (who is so good as to wind up the affairs of our Late House as nearly as possible during his stay in this Province) with an ungratefull slight on one hand or consenting on the other to affront Mr. Gordon by an Action at Law, & he declares himself an innocent party free from blame or censure.

If you will be pleased for a few Minutes to make our case your own, I am perswaded that a Gentleman of your Honour will require no further arguements or expostulations to prevail on you to do now, what, consistant with the punctuality of a Merchant & the sacredness of your repeated promises shou'd have been accomplish'd several Years ago. I am, &ca.—

SOURCE: Letterbook copy, HL Papers, S. C. Hist. Soc.; addressed "Esquire. Georgia"; "per Capt. Tucker."

---

[2] *HL Papers,* III, 197n.

[3] John Gordon, who had been a partner of John McQueen in Charleston and then of Grey Elliott in Beaufort and Savannah, was in St. Augustine during December trying to record his deeds of purchase of Spanish property in East Florida.

TO DAVID GRAEME[4]

[Charles Town] 23d January 1764

Sir,

I have been Sick & confined to my Chamber all the last past Week & only a day or two before it was that I heard of your determination to go to Europe in the *Mercury* Man of War & I fully intended to have waited on you to offer my good wishes as well as to have inquired again what you had done with respect to those my Title deeds for 400 Acres of Land in St. John's Parish[5] put into your hands 8 or nine Years ago & said to be lost or mislaid by you, & which from Year to Year you have promised either to restore to me or to put me on a footing equal to the Possession of the original writings. I can clearly demonstrate that besides the danger I am in of loosing the Capital Value of that Land I have suffered damage of upward of £150 Sterling by the bare Interest of my Money for Want of those Titles.

Besides this there is the affair of the Widow Henderson's Passage due to Austin & Laurens for Messrs. Isaac & Zachary Hope of Rotterdam for which you had Money lodged in your hands & have over & over again promised to pay me [*and*] remains still unsettled.[6]

---

[4] David Graeme was the brother of James Graeme who had been chief justice of S. C., 1749–1752. David Graeme was appointed clerk of the crown and peace and of the common pleas on July 25, 1752. Miscellaneous Records, II, Part 1 (1751–1754), pp. 252–253, S. C. Archives. He lost his place to Dougal Campbell who was appointed clerk on Nov. 6, 1754. On July 27, 1757, David Graeme was appointed attorney general during the absence of James Wright, a position which he held until his departure for England in 1764. Miscellaneous Records, KK (1754–1758), pp. 113, 498, S. C. Archives. When he left for England in January 1764, he made out a power of attorney to William Graeme, James Skirving, and Joseph Glover. Miscellaneous Records, MM, Part 1 (1763–1767), pp. 243–244, S. C. Archives. He did not return from England until 1768. *General Gazette*, Oct. 21, 1768. He died on Nov. 14, 1777. *SCHM*, x (1909), 225.

[5] In 1768, HL advertised that these title deeds to 400 acres of land were still missing. He stated then that they had been lodged in David Graeme's hands about 1754. The land in question had been granted to John Alston March 4, 1705 and had been sold by John Alston to Elias Ball on July 30, 1720. *General Gazette,* May 6, 1768. John Coming Ball had inherited Dochuar ("Dockon") plantation of 400 acres from his father in 1751. "Will of Elias Ball," dated Feb. 1750, proved Oct. 4, 1751, Charleston County Wills, VI (1747–1752), 546–549, S. C. Archives. HL had apparently bought these 400 acres sometime between 1751 and 1754 from John Coming Ball.

[6] The widow Henderson must have crossed the Atlantic in a vessel owned by the Hopes of Rotterdam. Isaac Hope was buried in Rotterdam on April 11, 1767. Zachary Hope, who was born in Rotterdam in 1711, was buried in that

I will not doubt but you have left directions with some of your friends to do what is right & just in these several concerns tho in your hurry you have omitted to give me the needful information, therefore I trouble you once more hoping to find you now at Leisure to tell me to whom I must apply.

I wish Mrs. Graeme[7] & you a pleasent Passage across the Ocean & a happy meeting of friends on the further side, & I am, &ca.—

SOURCE: Letterbook copy, Letter Book of Henry Laurens, Oct. 30, 1762–Sept. 10, 1766, Penn. Hist. Soc.; addressed "Esquire. On board *Mercury*, Man of War. Reb. Road."

WILLIAM HEST TO JOSEPH BROWN

[Charles Town] 24 January 1764

Sir,

Mr. Laurens deliver'd your Bill of Loading to Mr. Appleby who took your goods from on board the *Hopewell* & put them on board Mr. Austins Schooner.[8] Mr. Laurens's Schooner[9] was not then in Town nor intended for Winyaw otherwise you shou'd have been welcome to the Freight. Inclos'd please to receive your Letter from Bristol. I have Ship'd all your Indigo on board Capt. Barnes by Mr.

---

city on March 21, 1770. They were the sons of Archibald Hope (born in Rotterdam in 1664) and Anna Claus. Their youngest brothers Thomas and Adrian Hope were the founders of the Amsterdam banking house which was known as Hope & Co. after 1762. Isaac and Zachary Hope were merchants and ship owners of great importance being ranked among the hundred most heavily taxed inhabitants of Rotterdam. They furnished madder to England and wheat and barley to Mediterranean countries. But they were most noted for the organization of the transport of German emigrants especially from the Palatinate to the British colonies in America. B. Woelderink, adjunct-gemeentearchivaris of the Gemeentelijke Archiefdienst, Rotterdam to the editor, Sept. 5, 1972. HL had been aware of the importance of the Hopes of Amsterdam as early as 1748. *HL Papers*, I, 198. Austin & Laurens had advertised the arrival of German servants from Rotterdam in the *Gazette*, Sept. 19, 1752. This advertisement, which was not printed in *HL Papers*, I, will be printed in the final volume.

[7] David Graeme had married Ann Mathews on Jan. 21, 1759. *Register of St. Philip's Parish, 1754–1810*, p. 153.

[8] Although George Austin had retired to England, he retained property in Carolina. Josiah Smith, Jr. registered on July 10, 1765, in Austin's name the schooner *Austin*, Thomas McCleish, which had been built in Carolina in 1765. Ship Register, 1734–1765, p. 249, S. C. Archives.

[9] *Wambaw*.

Laurens's order & also Eight Casks said to be on your Joint Account the Quality of which he & every body that has seen it complains of very much for the prices tho' he cannot forbare mentioning tho' he says he must submit to it. He likewise directs me to inclose you Mrs. Nicholson's Certificate of that Drossy Pitch which is double the Quantity he mention'd to you. He hopes you'll be able to do something to releive him in that affair. It lays entirely on you nor is it in his power to any thing in it but on your behalf. As soon as he is able he will send you some Money but he cannot help hoping that your contracts do not suffer, such Indigo & Such terms.

Mr. Laurens is very unwell occasion'd by a fall he got on his Stair case about a week ago who orders me to write this who am for Mr. H. L., Yours, &ca.—   W. H.[1]

A Copy of the original Certificate Inclos'd

This is to Certify that I have examin'd 104 Barrels Pitch part of HL 519 Barrels imported by Mrs. Sarah Nicholson & King in the *Elizabeth,* Capt. Mallard,[2] from So. Carolina and find many of them more than half Dross and on a computation think Eighty hundred weight to be only a reasonable allowance for Dross on the same which I have allow'd according to Messrs. Thompson, Sharp, & Thompson[3] and Mr. Richard Grundy.[4]

Witness my hand this 25th day of June 1763

William Purdy, Sworn Broker

SOURCE: Letterbook copy, Letter Book of Henry Laurens, Oct. 30, 1762–Sept. 10, 1766, Penn. Hist. Soc. This letter was copied into the letterbook after those of Jan. 6.

---

[1] William Hest was a native of Lancashire. HL to Shepherd, Langton, & Birley, May 9, 1764. He came out to Charleston in 1763, first acting as HL's clerk and then after December 1764 as the partner of William Price and Edmund Head. He remained in Charleston as a merchant and ropemaker until 1778, when, because he would not take an oath of allegiance to the new state, he was banished. He with Edmund Head and George Kincaid bought the ship *Hope,* James Gillis, filled it with rice that they had bought by selling their S. C. estates, and sailed in May for Rotterdam. After a number of misadventures they arrived in London in September 1778. In a memorial dated Dec. 16, 1783, he claimed that during his 15 years in Charleston his income ranged from £1,000 to £1,500 per annum. Loyalist Transcripts, LIII, 539–546.

[2] The ship *Elizabeth,* John Mallard, cleared outwards on Nov. 20, 1762, for London with a cargo which included 627 barrels of pitch. Naval Office Lists, 1757–1764, p. 103.

[3] Thompson, Sharp, & Thompson were New England merchants of Mill St., Bermondsey. *London Directories.*

[4] Richard Grundy was an oilman of East Smithfield. *London Directories.*

TO JAMES COWLES

[Charles Town] 24 January 1764

Dear Sir,

By the first good opportunity after the receipt of your favour of 4th November I convayed your Letter to Lachlin McGillivray in Georgia under cover of one from myself as per anexed Coppy which I hope will produce a good Effect. I beleve he will not be offended at my freedom & I shall in due time communicate what he may say in reply. I am—

SOURCE: Letterbook copy, HL Papers, S. C. Hist. Soc.; addressed "Bristol"; "per Harbison. Copy per Muire." The clerk started to enter this letter in the domestic letterbook but stopped and wrote the note "See foreign Letter Book."

TO COWLES & HARFORD

[Charles Town] 24th January 1764

Gentlemen,

The annex'd is duplicate of what I wrote you the 20th Inst. to which please to be referr'd. Today I have got into the accounting House again but not yet quite well enough for much business. The *Barbadoes Packet* is still here & probably will sail with this bearer. Please to receive inclosed a Second Bill Loading & abstract Invoice for the Cargo of Rice on board her & also a duplicate of the Indigo Certificate mentioned in the annexed which may probably be of use.

If I judge right your friends here are in general satisfyed with your account of the Causes of the extraordinary detention of their goods last Year. Every Man of any experience in trade must know that such crass accidents & unlucky circumstances will sometimes happen & every reasonable man will make reasonable allowances for them.

I remark what you say of a Ship for Capt. Baker[5] & have only to add on that subject that as long as I am in trade it will give me singular pleasure to serve you. Indeed to tell you the truth I wou'd much rather be without all business in the Commission way except from your own & four more Houses in England & tho' it is

---

[5] Capt. Richard Baker of the *Indian King*.

not wholey in my power to refuse yet I do not seek for more & let me beg that whatever commands you may have in that or other branches you will be so good as to give me previous Notice if you can more for your Interest then for my own Ease tho' I must confess I have this a little in View too.

If you please to look back to my former Letter you will see that any Shipping Pitch in uncommon packages was the effect of neccessity & not of Choice; a proper representation of this I shou'd think wou'd remove all doubt about obtaining the Bounty which is allow'd on the weight of the commodity; had I gone about to get new pitch Barrels made, the expence here in town wou'd exceed the Bounty. Besides the size of those are not fix'd or determinate. I see some people Ship Pitch of 280 Gross per Barrels & I as often as possible Ship them at 350 to 375 wt. Where then is the Criterion? The bounty I know is granted on the Tar of 20 hundred weight contain'd in eight Barrels of equal size but was there ever eight such pitch Barrels Ship'd? Yes by mere accident as there has been eight Rice Barrels or eight Rum hogsheads of equal size; & is there any Rule establish'd for indulging a deviation from the Letter of the Act? Again, in the Certificate sent from hence the Quantity of Barrels contain'd in the larger Casks was particularly expressed; but as this matter must be over before any argument can reach you & 'tis a thousand to one the like hapens not again in our day I ask pardon for taking up so much of your time with them.

The price of deer Skins holds up beyond your limits & our late advices from the Northward impart an inclination in the Indians there to be at peace rather than continue the War lately carryed on against us.[6] If Peace is establish'd the Skin & Fur trade will go on in the old Channel;[7] on the other hand our Creek Indians have committed fresh murders & Insults in this province & it is far from impossible that a general rupture with them may ensue which wou'd make a great abatement in our export of Skins from this Quarter. I shall be as attentive as I can to what may hereafter occur & act as appears most for your benefit whom am with great respect, Gentlemen—

---

[6] After Col. Henry Bouquet had defeated the Indians at the Battle of Bushy Run on Aug. 14 and relieved Fort Pitt, the Indians had become dispirited. Gipson, *The Triumphant Empire*, pp. 110–113.

[7] That is, with the Indians to the northward.

Rum 45/
Exchange 721 per Cent

SOURCE: Letterbook copy, HL Papers, S. C. Hist. Soc.; addressed "Bristol"; "per Harbison. Copy suppos'd by Barnes."

TO GEORGE WATKINS[8]

[Charles Town] 25 January 1764

Dear Sir,

I am indebted for many of your favours. The last was a Cheese per Capt. Harbison[9] which came to hand in pretty good order. Having a Barrel of very fine Rice I have divided it amongest four of my Bristol friends[1] & sent one part of it in a Keg mark'd GW by Capt. Harbison (who is so good as to give me the carriage) which I beg your acceptance of. I hope so small a package may be got a Shore by the indulgence of the officers & serve to make a Rice puddin duty free. I shall be always glad to hear of your welfare & to contribute thereto when in my power, who am, Sir, Yours, &ca.—

SOURCE: Letterbook copy, HL Papers, S. C. Hist. Soc.; addressed "Captain. Bristol"; "per Harbison."

TO RICHARD BAKER

[Charles Town] 25 January 1764

Dear Sir,

I thank you for your favour per Capt. Pitt & for the old News papers which tho' old are amuseing & sometimes edifying to me. I am never very eager in the pursuite of newes unless it be in my proper way of business & then my duty requires me to be both watchfull & vigilant to learn what is going forward & to improve upon the earlyest

[8] Captain Watkins may have been in the Bristol–Carolina trade, but there is no earlier mention of him in *HL Papers*. George Watkins was listed as a sailmaker at 25 Princes St. in *Sketchley's Bristol Directory* for 1775.

[9] The snow *True Britton,* John Harbison, was entered inwards on Nov. 10 from Bristol and was cleared outwards on Jan. 24 for Bristol. Naval Office Lists, 1757–1764, p. 124; 1764–1767, p. 73.

[1] George Watkins, Richard Baker, Edward Brownett, and most probably Cowles & Harford.

intelligence. As for other concerns I love to look them over after they have been garbled & sifted being of opinion with the old proverb that "the lame post brings the best inteligence." Therefore as often as you find a bundle of those old papers in danger of being condemned to the use of the pastery Cook's or perhaps a less sevoury Shop I beg you will pray to save them for transportation. Send them to me & you may [be] sure I will give them a kind reception & they shall never return to do mischif in their native Land again. I say mischeif because our late English papers seems to have been fill'd with very Little Glue, but even out of noxious herbs & flowers some sweets may be extracted.

I met yesterday with a Barrel of Rice of a Superior quality & thinking a Little Keg of it may be got ashore by indulgence I have sent one Mark'd RB by Capt. Harbison who is so kind as to give it the Carriage. I wish it may be acceptable to Mrs. Baker & I remain, Yours, &ca.—

SOURCE: Letterbook copy, HL Papers, S. C. Hist. Soc.; addressed "Captain. Bristol"; "per Harbison."

TO EDWARD BROWNETT

[Charles Town] 25 January 1764

Dear Sir,

I hope this will reach you safe under your own Roof, projecting a Plan for a better Voyage than your last both to yourself & Ship.

You will be anxious to know how your friend Clark[2] has gone on since your departure; slow I do assure you. He has had other jobs in hand & well he might poor fellow for if he had nothing else to depend upon but that one which you know he undertook for his honour, he wou'd be forced to live sometime upon that airy diet. He seems to do his work well & I will not let him be a Sufferer by Labouring to serve me. I met with a very unlucky fall going up my stair Case at home the most accidental thing that you ever heard of, but I am much indebted to a thick calabash under my Hat & to good strong bones, or I shou'd probably have fractured my Scull & broke

---

[2] This may be John Clarke, cabinetmaker, whom HL had to sue on Sept. 17, 1764, to recover £600 currency.

my Arm. Thank God I have escaped both & only been confined with pains all over my body for 8 days past but am now so well that I shall attempt a Visit at Noon to Mr. Clark & also to Mrs. Laurens who is gone up there[3] to make her annual Store of Hams & Bacon. I met with a Barrel of exceeding fine Rice in a parcell & thinking that a little Keg of it might be acceptable to Mrs. Brownett & got on Shoar in so small a Quantity by indulgence of the Guardians of the Revenue I have put up one mark'd EB which Capt. Harbison is so kind as to give me the carriage of.

Mrs. Laurens & my four little ones[4] Thank God are well & she desires me to present her Complyment to Mrs. Brownett & to you to which I beg leave to join my own & remain, Sir—

SOURCE: Letterbook copy, HL Papers, S. C. Hist. Soc.; addressed "Captain. Bristol"; "per Capt. Harbison."

TO TIMOTHY CREAMER

[Charles Town] 26 January 1764

Mr. Creamer,

I Expect to see you before Monday next. Mean time I send up a stout young Woman to be a Wife to whome she shall like best amongst the single men. The rest of the Gentlemen shall be served as I have opertunity. Tell them that I do not forget their request. I also send a Suite Cloth for Cudgo[5] & one for Caesar. The womans name is My Lady being her country name. I am—

SOURCE: Letterbook copy, Letter Book of Henry Laurens, Oct. 30, 1762–Sept. 10, 1766, Penn. Hist. Soc.; addressed "Mepkin."

---

[3] To Mepkin.

[4] John, Eleanor, Martha, and Henry.

[5] Cudgo (Cudjoe), an old man, took care of his fellow slaves. *HL Papers,* III, 203. HL paid £35 per year for his hire to his owner the Rev. Richard Clarke. Of Cudjoe HL wrote in 1770: "he is a quiet orderly old Man, not able to do much Work and therefore is never drove to Labour, but suffer'd to go on in his own way. I observe he makes larger Crops of Rice and Corn for himself than the most able Young Negroes, which I believe is greatly owing to their Aid for they all Respect and Love him. I give him more Cloaths and Shoes than is given to any other Negro, and he seems to be so perfectly satisfied with his Situation that I believe he has no Desire to change it. I shall order proper Care to be taken of him, if his Life shall happen to surpass his Strength for Labour without any Charge to you, and continue to make the same Annual Allowance during all the Time that he is able to perform any Work." HL to Rev. Richard Clarke, Aug. 25, 1770, HL Papers, S. C. Hist. Soc.

TO ISAAC KING

[Charles Town] 26th January 1764

Sir,

My last was on the 14th Inst. per *Prince Wales,* Brown, & *Mercury* Man of War advising of a draught on you for £150 Sterling to the order of William Wragg, Esquire. Some time ago I engaged to supply our friend Mr. John Hodsden[6] with Bills for One thousand pounds Sterling in this Month intending to have drawn upon Bristol but he was so extreamly pressing to have them in London urging that if I wou'd give him draughts on you they wou'd center in your own Books & take no money out of your hands that I was at last prevail'd on & the 24th Inst. made two Bills one for Seven hundred & one for three hundred pounds Sterling at 40 days sight to pay into yourselves as per his order, which I am now to request you will do & charge to my Account.

If my effects in your hands & what I have order'd to be remitted there do not greatly disapoint me you will have more than Money enough for that purpose, provided Capt. Courtain does not take above Nine Hundred pounds from you for the Ship *Flora,* which I think he will not, as Messrs. Cowles & Harford hold one fourth of her & that I sent him as much Silver & a Cargo of Naval Stores I expect will supply him with Six or Seven hundred pounds Sterling towards my three Quarters, but be this as it may you will not be greatly & shall not be long in advance for me & let me assure you that I wou'd not have been so bold as to have risqu'd the putting you one pound in advance if when I consented to gratify Mr. Hodsden I had not been fully assured of sending by this very Ship about Six Thousand Weight of Indigo the Crop of Mr. John Stanyarne[7] whose annual produce I have constantly had for many Years past until this, & Capt. Muir[8] had reserved a place to receive it but that Gentleman hapen'd to be sick when it came to town & I confined to my Chamber by the Effects of a fall & the person to whome he sent it differ'd with Mr. Appleby who was so good as to Act on my behalf in a manner that I think unreasonable & upon a point the value of which wou'd

---

[6] *HL Papers,* II, 211n.
[7] John Stanyarne of Johns Island. *HL Papers,* II, 407n.
[8] The ship *Little Carpenter,* William Muir, owned by Thomas and William Ellis, John Hodsden, Henry and Arthur Peronneau, and Isaac Holmes of Charleston and Grubb & Watson of London, cleared outwards on Jan. 24 for Lisbon. Naval Office Lists, 1764–1767, p. 73.

not have cost Mr. Stanyarne & myself a moments hesitation it was hastily carryed away from my Warehouse. I missed the purchase & you have lost the intended commission.

I am Loading one half a Brigantine for Oporto & shall order the proceeds to be remitted by Mr. Byrne[9] to you & if Mr. Manigault[1] & I meet with a proper Vessel we shall probably send you very soon a Cargo of Naval Stores. 'Tis likely too that the *Heart of Oak* will carry one fourth of her Cargo from me to your address. I mention these things because I am anxious lest you shou'd be troubled to advance money for me & therefore upon the whole if you find that my account is not so favourable on my part as I hope it is & that you cannot conveniently indulge me be pleased to apply to Messrs. Cowles & Harford who have money of mine & I am sure will assist you.

I have Ship'd for Mr. Brown[2] 10 Casks & on our Joint Account 8 Casks of Indigo per your *Minerva* & shou'd have been glad to put on board about 200 Barrels of Pitch & Green Tar but Capt. Barnes told me I was too late in my application for Freight. I shall endevour to write to you again by him & in the meantime remain with great respect, Sir, yours, &ca.—

SOURCE: Letterbook copy, HL Papers, S. C. Hist. Soc.; addressed "For Mrs. Sarah Nicholson & Co."; "per Capt. Muir. Copy per Barnes."

TO BENJAMIN JOHNSON

[Charles Town] 26th January 1764

Permit me to refer you to the Inclosed Copy of what I wrote to you the 19th October per Capt. Barker for St. Christophers.

Agriable to my resolution I proceeded to dismantle your Late Brigantine *Good Intent* & advertized her Hull, Sails, Rigging, Anchors, &ca. for Sale in Lots at Publick Auction[3] & by the assistance of Capt. Hardy in distributing them in small parcells the whole went

---

[9] Henry Byrne.
[1] Gabriel Manigault. *HL Papers,* I, 191n.
[2] Joseph Brown of Georgetown.
[3] This advertisement does not appear in the *Gazette*. It may have been published in Wells' *General Gazette* but there are no extant issues of this paper for this period. HL may also have advertised by means of broadsides.

of[f] beyond the prices I ever saw given for such articles as per account of perticulars here Inclosed.

I am now more satisfyed with my own conduct in this particular of selling your Vessel because it appears to me to be saveing you just so much Money as the Sale ammounts to instead of throwing it away. For the Poor Man who Bought the Hull has met with a total Loss; he design'd no more with her than to make the begining or head of a wharf but floating her towards his land she happen'd to touch the Ground of his Neighbour & down she went, became a wreck & is since gone almost to pieces & got nothing from her but her steering masts & Bowsprit out above the deck which in this Country is not so valuable as so much Oak-Tin-Wood, & will never repay him by ten or fifteen Pounds Sterling for his Expences in fruitless attempts to raise her again. Please to receive Inclosed Account Sales of your Rum & Molasses per said Brigantine. Net proceeds with the Amount of Vessel & Rigging £2,731.3.6. I was forced to sell of[f] the Molasses & part of the Rum in great haste on Account of the badness of the Hogsheads. Indeed If I had kept them Longer it wou'd have been worse for you. Molasses is not wanted in this Country & rum has long been a long time selling every day at Vendue from 14/ to 15/ per Gallon & now sells at 13/ to 13/9 for the best Antigua & Barbadoes & Northward Rum at 11/ to 11/6 but you see by giving a long Credit which is my Loss & your Gain I have obtained 16/ for the bulk of yours but the Gentlemen who bought it are extreamly angry & say they wou'd not have touched it if they had apprehended the Hogsheads were so bad. You'll remark that I am in advance on this account £1,228.12.0 besides £674, part of the Brigantine Sale but this I do not reckon upon because I ought to have made the Vendue Master pay it before now. The other Sum I think is in very good hands but shou'd it proove otherwise I cannot doubt your honour to save me from Loss by advancing my Money to serve you.

Inclosed you have also Invoice & Bill Loading for Sundrys Shipt on your Account by this Sloop *Crow Lain,* John Pruddin, Master, for Tortola[4] which I was in hopes when I engaged the Vessel

---

[4] The sloop *Crowlane,* John Prudden, was cleared on Jan. 26 for Tortola with 84 barrels and 127 half barrels of rice, 20 barrels of pitch, 10 barrels of tar, 6 barrels of turpentine, 78 barrels of beef and pork, 464 bushels of corn and peas, 6,000 feet of lumber, 1,000 staves, and 6,300 shingles. Naval Office Lists, 1764–1767, p. 73.

wou'd have been with you by this day but the Master who agreed to fill her up when your effects were shiped has been delaying ever since the 1st Inst. & at Length I am obliged to fill him up on my own Account to procur dispatch & save you from further Loss. My Goods are 25 half Barrels of Rice & three hundred & Seven Bushels of choice Indian Corn which I have consign'd to himself because he promises in return for my kindness to sell them free of Commission either in your Island or Else where & to moderate the Freight so that I may be no sufferer by an Act done merely to serve you & him & I flatter myself if it is in your power you will also assist me therein. I did not know how to return your Money in a better way than I have done. The rice was bought 2/6 to 5/ per Ct. under the Market price for best but by the Captain's long delay nothing in fact is saved. The Current price is now 45/. I thought it wou'd be throwing away your Money to send live stock in a strange Vessel & I happen'd to have judged very right for had I provided any the whole wou'd have been dead & lost by this time & I have forborne sending much Lumber on Account of the Freight & I know it is very cheap in the West Indies. Upon the whole I have done the best in my power to serve your Interest, & I hope you'll be pleas'd to think so. I inclose you Capt. Hardys Receipt for £310.10.1 disbursments & wages for the Brigantine & also a Receipt from Mr. James Stone[5] for £100 supply'd him as per his Letter herewith Inclosed.

Messrs. Johnson & Wylly[6] have promised to be security for this Sum in case you will not allow it. I advanc'd this Young Man a further Sum as he seemed to be in distress. God knows if ever he will return it but the time promis'd is already elaps'd. The two Sums above with my commission thereon are charged to your Account Current & also £67, for premium of £2,200 Insurance made on your Interest per the *Crow Lain* which I think consistant with your Interest & it seems to be likewise so with your orders. Lastly I inclose your said Account Current Ballance due to me if free from Error £43.9.1 past in course to the Debit of your new Account which Sum remitt me in any thing you please by Capt. Pruddin & when you think that

---

[5] James Stone, a friend of Isaac Pickering, was on his way to North Carolina. See HL to Isaac Pickering, Jan. 26, 1763.

[6] Lewis Johnson and Alexander Wylly. *HL Papers*, III, 136n. Johnson and Wylly, Savannah merchants, were commissioners of the pilotage at Savannah. *Georgia Gazette,* Jan. 19, 1764.

I can be further serviceable to you, your commands on me will meet with a ready complyance by, Sir, Your, &Ca.—

SOURCE: Letterbook copy, HL Papers, S. C. Hist. Soc.; addressed "Tortola"; "per Pruddin. Copy per Vesey with 2d Bill Loading inclosed." Endorsed: "Directed for Mr. Benjamin Johnson for himself & the Owners of the Brigantine *Good Intent.*"

TO ISAAC PICKERING[7]

[Charles Town] 26th January 1764

Dear Sir,

I duly rec'd your favour of the 2d August last inclosing an imperfect certificate for the discharge of Capt. Craigs[8] Cargo & therefore now earnestly request you to send me without delay, both for his sake & my own a proper one specifying every particular article mention'd in the clearance given him at our Custom House & then sign'd & Seal'd by your Governor & one other principle Officer. That certificate you sent had only one hand to it and will not be admitted by our Collector & now my Bond is near expiring & dare say you'll think properly of this business and save me both uneasyness & Expence. I deliver'd your Letters to the parties directed & show'd all the civility in my power to your friend Mr. Stone who was here sometime & is since gone to North Carolina.

My Family since you were here is increased by a fine Boy[9] & thank God all are very well except myself who met with an unlucky fall about 10 days ago which has made me almost as full of pains as my friend Pickering used to be in Carolina. If it had not been for this accident by which I have been confined to my Chamber I shou'd have treated you with a few Shotes & Ducks by this direct opportunity but I belive it is as well that I have not attempted it either to you & Zeagers[1] for I have some reason to fear by a strange kind of dela-

---

[7] Isaac Pickering had been in Charleston in the winter of 1762–1763. *HL Papers,* III, 210n.

[8] The ship *Hillary,* Thomas Cragg, owned by Thomas Cragg, Richard Hillary, John Scott, John Pickering, and Thomas Woolrich of Liverpool, cleared outwards on Jan. 8, 1763, for Tortola. Naval Office Lists, 1757–1764, p. 127. The certificate to cancel the plantation bond had to be returned in 18 months.

[9] Henry Laurens (1763–1821) was born on Aug. 25, 1763. *HL Papers,* III, 526n.

[1] Absalom Zeagers.

teryness in the Master of this Sloop who ought to have been gone a Month ago that nothing of that sort wou'd have out lived so long a passage & other fatal accidents to which Live Stock is but too Lyable.

Mrs. Laurens Joines in Good Wishes with Yours, &ca.—

P.S. Tell me if at any time a Voyage to be made to your Island by a small Vessel & I will send one with such articles as you shall advise me.

SOURCE: Letterbook copy, HL Papers, S. C. Hist. Soc.; addressed "Tortola"; "per Capt. Pruddin. Copy per Vesey."

TO ABSALOM ZEAGERS

[Charles Town] 26 January 1764

Dear Sir,

I thank you for your favour of 17th September last per the Brigantine *Good Intent,* Capt. Hardy, & beg leave to referr you to my Letter to Mr. Benjamin Johnson for Inteligence reletive to my conduct to that Vessel in which I have realy done every thing that I cou'd think of for your Interest & I shou'd be very unhappy if it does not meet with your approbation. From my knowledge & Experiance in trade I cannot be call'd quite a novice but yet I wou'd not trust to my own judgment wholly: I consulted Mr. Manigault, Mr. Savage,[2] & other experianc'd Men & have acted agreable to their advice & with a hearty concurrence of your Capt. Hardy who declar'd often that he was not hardy enough to risque another Voyage in the Brigantine without a full & thoro repair which cou'd not be effected in this Country or any where but at a greater expence than Building an entire new bottom in as much as it wou'd have cost a great deal to pull the Old one to peices & those peices not worth the labour.

Mrs. Laurens Joins me in best Wishes to & whenever you think

---

[2] Gabriel Manigault and John Savage owned jointly at least two vessels that were well known in the West Indies. Maurice A. Crouse, "Gabriel Manigault: Charleston Merchant," *SCHM,* LXVIII (1967), 223. John Savage, who had been born in 1715 in Bermuda, came to Charleston about 1735 where he established himself as a principal merchant. His stores were on Tradd St. He helped to establish the first Chamber of Commerce prior to the Revolution but took the King's side and left the province for England in the summer of 1775. *HL Papers,* I, 82n; Loyalist Transcripts, LII, 45–64.

that I can promote your Interest in this Quarter I shu'd be Glad to receive your comands who am with Great respect, Yours, &ca.—

SOURCE: Letterbook copy, HL Papers, S. C. Hist. Soc.; addressed "Esquire. Tortola"; "per Capt. Pruddin. Copy per Vesey."

TO JOHN PRUDDIN[3]

[Charles Town] 26 January 1764

Sir,

You have inclosed Invoice & Bill Loading for 25 half Barrels of Rice & three hundred & Seven Bushels of Choice Good Corn on board your Sloop *Crow Lain* consign'ed to yourself which being Ship'd merely to give you dispatch I rely upon your promises to sell the same for me at Tortola or Elsewhere in the West Indies to my best advantage. You offer to do this free of Commission but if the Sale & remittances will bear it I shall very chearfully make you the usual allowance & I am perswaded the Gentlemen to whome the rest of your Cargo is consign'd will assist you as much as is in their power knowing that I consulted their Intrest also in this Shipment.

As to the remittance for the net proceeds of my Goods make it in good Rum if you can but If you come directly from Tortola & that Limes are Cheap be pleased to bring me about twenty Barrels of the best sort carefully pack'd. Not doubting that you will do everything you can for my Interest I shall only add that I wish you a good Voyage & am, Your, &ca.—

P.S. Remember a Certificate to cancel your Bond exactly agreable to your Clearance & sign'd by two principle Officers.

SOURCE: Letterbook copy, HL Papers, S. C. Hist. Soc.; addressed "Captain."

---

[3] John Pruddin was master of the Bermuda sloop *Crow Lain*. Crow Lane was the vernacular name for the parish of Paget in Bermuda. Henry C. Wilkinson, *Bermuda in the Old Empire* (London, 1950), pp. 85, 132.

T O R O B E R T W A R I N G[4]

[Charles Town] 27th January 1764

Sir,

I observe in yours of the 23d Inst. that the pressing measures taken by Mr. Swinton[5] mislead you to give him that *very Money* that you had *promised* to me & that *your shame* therefore *restrained* you from coming to my House according to appointment.

I think you acted very wrong in giving the preference to any solicitous or troublesome Man, without first obtaining permission from one who had been so indulgent to you as I have been; well therefore might you be ashamed of your conduct. However, in hopes that this circumstance will operate in a right way upon your mind & that further indulgence will not meet with further abuse, I shall consent to wait six months Longer (you say a short time I suppose by that you cannot mean more than half a Year) for the money due by you to me & in the mean while you need not trouble yourself to add to the present security. I shall rest satisfied with what I have, relying on you not to give any body else a security to the prejudice of my demand. Sir, I am, &ca.—

SOURCE: Letterbook copy, Letter Book of Henry Laurens, Oct. 30, 1762–Sept. 10, 1766, Penn. Hist. Soc.

T O J O H N W I G F A L L

[Charles Town] 27th January 1764

Sir,

When your favour of the [*blank*] Inst. came to Town I was confin'd to my Chamber but soon as I cou'd move about I sent in search of your Tar and luckily found the whole 98 Barrels which in these times is very extraordinary as it is become too common for folks to Borrow such articles without leave. The Barrels are very indifferent being made of unseason'd stuff. However I have passed them to your

---

[4] Robert Waring was a tavern keeper of Prince George Winyah who obviously found it difficult to pay his debts. In 1768 the process server was warned: "The Defendant lives at Winyah Bay take good Bail." Judgment Rolls, 1768, Nos. 408A, 426A, 448A; 1769, No. 368A, S. C. Archives.

[5] Probably Hugh Swinton, who himself later kept a tavern in Charleston "upon the Bay." *HL Papers*, III, 484n; *Gazette*, April 6, 1769.

Credit at 50/ out of which is to be taken the Expence for filling, packing, &ca.

If nothing hinders me I am in hopes of being at your House about Tuesday next. Meantime I must inform you that I am in want of 15 or 20 Thousand of Scantling from 4 x 4 to 7 x 7 and wish it may be in your power to assist me with dispatch. If 'tis not I shall be oblig'd to you to recommend the Bill to any of your Neighbours who will undertake it deliverable in a forthnight. I Remain yours, &ca.—

SOURCE: Letterbook copy, Letter Book of Henry Laurens, Oct. 30, 1762–Sept. 10, 1766, Penn. Hist. Soc.; addressed "Esquire. St. Thomas's."

TO JOHN TARLETON

[Charles Town] 27 January 1764

Sir,

On the 9th Inst. per the *Chance*[6] & *Union* I advised you of a draught to the order of Messrs. Brailsfor[d] & Chapman for £124 Sterling & meeting this day with a purchaser for a £150 Sterling more at my price of 721 per Cent Exchange I have passed another Bill on you for that Sum to the Order of Christian Minnick[7] payable at 40 Days sight in London which bears to the credit of your Account Current £1,081.10. I know that Bills upon London directly which is some advantage & at 30 to 40 Days sight are sold here from 700 to 714 per Cent but I will rather remain a Month or two longer in advance than abate of my Exchange & I have no doubt that some people will give it to me within that time. I Remain, &ca.—

SOURCE: Letterbook copy, HL Papers, S. C. Hist. Soc.; addressed "Liverpoole"; "per Muir. Copy per Barnes."

---

[6] The ship *Chance*, Charles Smith, cleared outwards on Jan. 4 for Cowes. Naval Office Lists, 1757–1764, p. 136.

[7] Christian Minnick was a leading figure of Orangeburg District. Salley, *History of Orangeburg County*, passim. He was a justice of the peace for Colleton County in the commission of 1756. *SCHM*, xx (1921), 74. In 1757 he was a lieutenant colonel in Col. John Chevillette's regiment of Berkeley County militia. Council Journal, xxvi (Jan. 3, 1757–June 6, 1758), 87, S. C. Archives. The *Gazette*, Nov. 26, 1764, noted his recent return from London.

TO ISAAC KING

[Charles Town] 27 January 1764

Sir,

I confirm the proceeding Copy of my last per Capt. Muir & am now to forward herein a Bill Loading & Certificate for Eight Casks of Indigo per this *Minerva*, Capt. Barnes, on Account of Mr. Joseph Brown & myself & on the other side is a Copy of his Account of the weight & Costs by way of Invoice.[8] You will be pleased to dispose of this parcel in the best manner you can & pass the Net proceeds to our respective Accounts in Moiety. Your hint of Mr. Browns Judgment in Indigo led me to be concerned with him in some purchases this Year in which I shou'd have gone much deeper but I stop'd my hand as soon as this came to town finding that however good his luck or his judgment might be in other cases, as my factor he was by no means fortunate, of which you will have an oportunity of Judging. I remain, Your, &ca.—

Invoice of the 8 Casks of Indigo above mention'd per *Minerva*, Capt. Barnes—

B.					
9—539—79					
10—540—70					
11—546—73	Net				
12—314—55	Weight	1,906 lb.	at 27/6		2,620.15
13—292—48					
14—170—40		130	10/		130.
15—		313	7/6 to 10/		146.10
16—		213	25/		266. 5
					3,163.10

SOURCE: Letterbook copy, HL Papers, S. C. Hist. Soc.; addressed "for Mrs. Sarah Nicholson & Co., London"; "per Barnes. Copy per Wills."

---

[8] The ship *Minerva,* John Barnes, owned by Isaac King and Sarah Nickleson of London, cleared outwards on Jan. 31 for London with a cargo which included 23,653 pounds of indigo. Naval Office Lists, 1764–1767, p. 74. According to the manifest HL shipped 6,156 pounds of indigo on the *Minerva* consigned to Sarah Nickleson & Co. The manifest was signed on Jan. 31, 1764, at the Naval Office by John Barnes. Naval Office Lists, 1764–1767, p. 13.

TO JOHN PAGAN,[9]
ALEXANDER BROWN[1] & CO.

[Charles Town] 2d February 1764

Gentlemen,

It is now late in the Evening that Capt. John Francis of your Ship *Pearl*[2] has brought me your favour of 14th November & Copy of one of the 8th intended by the *Dennistoune*[3] not yet arrived, & tho he informs me that he had an opportunity of writing you a line as he was coming in over the Bar, yet I shall endeavour to reach a Vessel that will sail early tomorrow Morning with this to advise of your said Ships arrival & also to assure you that I shall do every thing in my power to serve your Interest in the disposal of her; to this end I shall regard your orders & not deviate from them without the greatest prospect of benefit to you.

Rice is at 45/ per Ct. & if Ships continue dropping in is more likely to rise than fall. The last Freight to Lisbon was 50/, to the Market 55/ per Ton. The latter is far short of the difference which you very justly calculate & point out, but I believe some difficulty may attend the procuring a full Freight to Lisbon for so large a Ship as the *Pearl,* but I shall exert myself to surmount all difficulties.

Your Coals will sell readily enough from £6 to £8 per Ton & upon the whole be pleased to rest satisfied that your concern will not suffer in my hands, who am with great regard, &ca.—

SOURCE: Letterbook copy, HL Papers, S. C. Hist. Soc.; addressed "Owners of the Ship *Pearl,* Glasgow"; "per Capt. Barnes. Copy per Brunett."

---

[9] *HL Papers,* III, 397n.

[1] Alexander Brown was an original member of the Glasgow Chamber of Commerce, chartered in 1783. Matthew Neil, secretary of the Glasgow Chamber of Commerce, to the editor, Nov. 10, 1970.

[2] The ship *Pearl,* John Francis, 150 tons, owned by John Pagan, Alexander Brown, Thomas Francis, and Hugh Melligan of Glasgow, was entered inwards on Feb. 3 from Glasgow with 62 chaldrons of coals and 14 packages of British goods. The *Pearl* was cleared outwards on March 17 for Lisbon with 984 barrels and 112 half barrels (551,636 pounds) of rice. Naval Office Lists, 1764–1767, pp. 69, 75.

[3] The snow *Dennistoune,* Hugh Porter, owned by James Dennistoune and John Stevenson of Glasgow, was entered inwards on Feb. 28 from Glasgow with sundry British goods. Naval Office Lists, 1764–1767, p. 70.

TO HENRY BRIGHT

[Charles Town] 4th February 1764

Sir,

The day after Christmas I wrote to you per Capt. Brownett & Capt. White, & this morning I am favour'd with both yours under the 26th September per Capt. Floyd who arrived very late last night in your Ship *Sally*[4] & by the hands of your Nephew Mr. Lowbridge Bright[5] who is come in the *Sally* & is in very good health, & you may be assured that nothing in my power shall be wanting during his sojourning here to make it both agreable & advantageous to him.

As to the Ship I shall advertize her for Bristol[6] & have some prospect of obtaining a Freight for her tho' a Low one, but as Good as times will afford & I shall have particular regard to dispatch. So many Vessels are gone & going for Portugal that considering the discouraging Accounts from thence I have no room to hope for offers either for Port[o] or Lisbon, nevertheless I shall strive to obtain a Load if better terms are to be had for one of those Markets than for Bristol, & I shall hold the Owners duly advised as I go forward. At present I beg the Gentlemens indulgence of this Letter to yourself only, as the Vessell in which I hope to convey it is already gone down & is ready to sail with the first fair wind.

Rice is at 45/. Freight to Holland 55/, London 42/6 & 45/. Many competitors for Naval Stores have raised the prices, Vizt. Pitch 75/, Tar 50/, Green Tar 77/, Turpentine 15/ to 17/6. Exchange 720 per Cent. I am, &ca.—

SOURCE: Letterbook copy, HL Papers, S. C. Hist. Soc.; addressed "Esquire. Bristol"; "per Capt. Barnes. Copy per Brunett."

---

[4] The ship *Sally*, William Floyd, was entered inwards on Feb. 4 from St. Christophers with 6 slaves consigned to HL by Smith & Baillies of St. Christophers. Naval Office Lists, 1764–1767, p. 69; HL to Smith & Baillies, Feb. 9, 1764.

[5] Lowbridge Bright, the nephew of Henry Bright, had come to Charleston to begin an American tour which would take him as far as Quebec. Lowbridge Bright was listed at 1 Charlotte St., Queen Square, in *Sketchley's Bristol Directory* for 1775. He died July 30, 1818, at the age of 78. *Bristol Lists: Municipal and Miscellaneous,* compiled by Rev. Alfred B. Beaven (Bristol, Eng., 1899), p. 326.

[6] The advertisement is printed below under the date Feb. 4.

ADVERTISEMENT
February 4, 1764
For BRISTOL or PORTUGAL, The Ship SALLY, WILLIAM FLOYD, Master, BURTHEN about 140 tons. If the said ship proceeds for Bristol, a considerable part of her cargo is engaged, and she may be soon dispatched, apply to

HENRY LAURENS

SOURCE: Printed in *Gazette,* Feb. 4, 1764.

ADVERTISEMENT
February 4, 1764
LARGE COALS, said to be of the best sort, from GLASGOW, Imported in the ship *Pearl,* John Francis, master. THE said ship or two thirds of her tonnage, to be lett to freight, for *Lisbon,* or *Cowes* and *Holland.* Enquire of

HENRY LAURENS

SOURCE: Printed in *Gazette,* Feb. 4, 1764.

TO JOHN WIGFALL
[Charles Town] 5th February 1764
Sir,
I have just rece'd your favour of the 2d Inst. advising of a Wraft of plank which the person you employ'd has brought to a little below the place intended and it is now late Saturday Evening so that I am almost affraid it cannot be got in a place of safety to night, but as he is very anxious to go home again I have prevail'd upon Capt. Gough[7] to send his Mate to endeavour to secure it that your people may return with as little delay as possible. I beg you will send the Inch boards & scantling as soon as you can. They are now much wanted & you will find Mr. Robert's Schooner[8] is already

---

[7] Capt. James Gough of the ship *Barter.*
[8] On May 30, 1767, Benjamin Roberts registered his schooner *Friendship,* 18 tons, built in Carolina in 1744. Ship Register, 1765–1783, p. 64, S. C. Archives. Many coasting schooners were registered in May 1767 when the customs officials began to tighten their enforcement of the navigation acts.

gone for that Scantling from Andrew Hasles Estate.[9] I have wrote to Mr. Thomas[1] & hope he will give such directions that I may not be disapointed in my expectation of it. I am, &ca.—

SOURCE: Letterbook copy, Letter Book of Henry Laurens, Oct. 30, 1762–Sept. 10, 1766, Penn. Hist. Soc.; addressed "Esquire."

TO JOHN RUTHERFORD

[Charles Town] 7th February 1764

Sir,

Your favour of 29th December per the hands of Mr. Dickson[2] I receiv'd & paid due regard to, by offering him my services & giving him a general & occasional invitations to my House where he often gave me the pleasure of his company on his first arrival & this might be of some service as it shewed that he was not quite a Blank. But he now seldom sees me; I can easily account for it; he is so deeply engaged with the Ladies, who swarm at this Season[3] as Bees do in the Summer, that half an hour's chat in a Counting House comes about soon enough within the course of one whole Week. He seems to be a genteel good natur'd Young Man & renders himself agreeable to gay company where perhaps he may luckily stumble upon something that may answer all the ends & save him all the trouble of plodding at a Desk twenty or thirty Years; if so, it will be very well. But otherwise, between you & I, he does not pursue those measures most likely to recommend him as a Factor or Merchant, & I am not so well acquainted with him as to think myself intitled to give him a friendly hint on this point.

Before the middle of December I Shiped near Six hundred pounds Sterling on your Account I mean to be applyed to your Credit

[9] Andrew Hasell, planter in the parish of St. Thomas, had lived at his home plantation of Mount Pleasant. He also owned 500 acres of pine land. He had named his wife Sarah, Samuel Thomas, Samuel and John Wigfall as the executors of his estate. "Will of Andrew Hasell," dated Nov. 29, 1758, proved Dec. 12, 1763, Charleston County Wills, IX, Book A (1760–1767), 416–418, S. C. Archives.

[1] Samuel Thomas of the parish of St. Thomas who had been named one of the executors of Hasell's estate. HL Papers, III, 204n.

[2] James Dixon or Dickson of Antigua. See HL to John Tally, Feb. 11, 1763; HL to Jeremiah Nibbs, Jr., Sept. 24, 1764.

[3] February was the height of the social season in Charleston.

with Messrs. Richard Oswald & Company in London & shall in the course of this Month make up a Thousand at least. In the present state of our affairs here this advance proves somewhat inconvenient to me but I shall struggle through it & perhaps more easily if you would move your pen in a proper stile to Mr. Saxby who pays me not one penny & yet he must surely have some Money in his hands which ought to be appropriated to your Account or demand on his Bank.

Mr. Appleby is near the point of leaving Carolina & talks often about his demand on you in behalf of Mr. Eveleigh,[4] nay yesterday he went so far as to say he would lay an attachment upon your effects in my hands but I have prevailed on him to forbear until I hear from you again.

The Gentleman who will deliver this Letter Mr. John Graham is an unfortunate Man, reduced almost to a state of want partly thro inadvertence & want of judgement in commercial affairs which he would dabble in, & partly thro some foul play of pretended friends. He is now going to North Carolina in hopes of collecting a few debts due to him in that country. If you can by a friendly word of advice or recommendation facilitate his endeavours it will be doing an act of humanity & will cost but little more than *the Cup of cold water* & I shall think myself further obliged to you also. I am, &ca.—

SOURCE: Letterbook copy, HL Papers, S. C. Hist. Soc.; addressed "Esquire"; "per Mr. John Graham."

TO JOHN STALLY[5]

[Charles Town] 8th February 1764

Sir,

I receiv'd your Letter of the 4th Inst. & a counterfeit Fifty Pounds Bill inclosed in it, which Bill I have advertised in the Gazettes[6] to prevent as much as possible further imposition upon unwary people;

---

[4] This may be George Eveleigh. *HL Papers*, I, 286n.

[5] John Stehely (Stally, Staley) was a German settler. Salley, *History of Orangeburg County*, pp. 170, 178, 186, 190. In 1768 he was granted 150 acres on Edisto River. Index to Grants, S. C. Archives. In 1773 John Staley witnessed the will of John Inabinet. *Abstracts of Wills, 1760–1784,* p. 203.

[6] The advertisement in the *Gazette* has not been found. There are no issues extant of the *General Gazette* for this period.

& I have lodged it in the Public Treasurer's office. I hope you will remember from whome you Receiv'd it; & you ought to do every thing in your power to discover & secure the forger & first curculater of the same.

I observe on the Back of the Bill the name of John Inabnet[7] is wrote, but I hope you will lay hold of the Knave that forged it & that neither you nor Abnet will sustain any loss by it. You will be pleased to find out some better Money & send to me as soon as you can & oblige, &ca.—

SOURCE: Letterbook copy, Letter Book of Henry Laurens, Oct. 30, 1762–Sept. 10, 1766, Penn. Hist. Soc.

TO CHRISTOPHER ROWE

[Charles Town] 8th February 1764

Sir,

I receiv'd in due time your favour of the 27th Ulto. giving me an Account of the situation of the inhabitants of your district.[8]

Their case is piteous enough, & calls loudly for public notice & relief; but God knows when they will receive either one or the other; therefore, I shall not much wonder if they should all go (as you say they talk of) to the Northward in a body.[9]

Our public disputes are still maintained & God only knows when there will be an end to them. One poor rash headlong Gentleman who has been too long a ringleader of people engaged in popular quarrels lately declared in full Assembly that he would rather submit to the distruction of one half of the Country than to give up the point in dispute with the Governor. His judgement must be very nice &

---

[7] John Inabinet was married to Marguretta Negly on Nov. 30, 1742, in Orangeburg by the Rev. John Ulrick Giessendanner. Salley, *History of Orangeburg County*, p. 97.

[8] Orangeburg District.

[9] These unfortunate inhabitants might have been some of the French Acadians. When the Acadians arrived in Charleston in 1756, they were divided into five groups, four of which were sent to outlying parishes. One group was sent by land to Orangeburg Township. *S. C. Statutes*, IV, 31–34; Council Journal, XXV (Jan. 2, 1756–Dec. 30, 1756), 313, S. C. Archives. Rowe had been one of those who had been paid to take care of the Acadians in his district. Salley, *History of Orangeburg County*, p. 33. In February 1760 HL had reported on the conditions of the Acadians living in Charleston. *HL Papers*, III, 560.

much refined to discover that just one half of our Lives would be a sufficient compensation for the loss of that point which he has in view, which perhaps may prove to be no more than the miscarriage of his own vain opinion, but it happens that he lives within the Walls of Charles Town. If he was a settler at long Canes or even had one Thousand pounds at stake then he would sing a different note. Our Frontier inhabitants are not very much obliged to him for his tenderness altho the Indians may be. This Gentleman could not have produced a stronger argument to convince me that he is not a fit person to judge of public affairs, but this being the uphappy situation or present circumstance of our Province we must all submit with patience until it pleases God to deliver us from the calamity of domestic broils, which we have long suffer'd under & which in my sentiments are more awful & more distressing than Fire, Pestilence, or Foreign Wars.[1] Your Company may justly complain of the hardship of marching 114 Miles from their family (nor do I know what right or authority you have for leading them such advance) without Pay.[2]

Please to read the inclosed Letter & then seal & Deliver it to John Stally & I dare say you will join with him to discover the Rogue that is in your Quarter counterfeiting Money. I am, &ca.—

SOURCE: Letterbook copy, Letter Book of Henry Laurens, Oct. 30, 1762–Sept. 10, 1766, Penn. Hist. Soc.

TO HENRY BYRNE

[Charles Town] 9th February 1764

Sir,

Please to be referr'd to the proceeding Duplicate of my last

---

[1] HL is undoubtedly referring to Christopher Gadsden who most probably made these remarks in the assembly on Jan. 6. On that day it had been moved that the resolution of Dec. 16, 1762, to do no business with the governor, should be vacated and discharged. On the motion should that question be now put, it passed in the negative. House Journal, xxxvi (Jan. 24, 1763–Oct. 6, 1764), 6, S. C. Archives.

[2] Captain Rowe had marched his militia company to the Long Canes, but without being ordered to do so. On Jan. 15, 1765, he asked the assembly to reimburse him for provisions impressed for his company going to the Long Canes. On March 5 the assembly rejected his petition inasmuch as the certificates he presented were all written in his own hand and not endorsed by those from whom the provisions had been impressed. Six months pay was granted for the rangers in Patrick Calhoun's company for service at the Long Canes. House Journal, Jan. 8, 1765.–Aug. 6, 1765, pp. 15, 45, 107, S. C. Archives.

trouble under the 14th Ulto. per Capt. Holme in the Snow *Austin* & now to receive inclosed an Invoice & Bill Loading for 86 Barrels & 43 half Barrels Rice on my own Account per the Snow *Port Royal*, Capt. Lewis, which you will be pleased to sell & remitt as early as possible the Net proceeds to Mrs. Sarah Nicholson & Co. in London. This is the Vessel called in my last a small Brigantine. The remainder of her Cargo is Shipt by Messrs. Brewton & Smith³ the consignment of which I have secured to you & that answers the good purpose intended by me better as to myself than if I had loaded the whole.

The Snow *Hopewell* is beginning to load & I have a few Barrels on board her but she will be very tedious in getting away & has already wasted much time. Capt. Deviel in the *Swift* is making a slow progress & will get away one of these days. Mr. Knight's Ship *Hope* will probably be next with you. I expect her at the Wharf in a day or two & if so she shall be loaden with about 500 or 600 Barrels in three Days after weather permitting. I am, &ca.—

SOURCE: Letterbook copy, HL Papers, S. C. Hist. Soc.; addressed "Esquire. Oporto"; "per Lewis. Copy per Dennison."

TO SMITH & BAILLIES

[Charles Town] 9th February 1764

Gentlemen,

I am indebted for your sundry acceptable favours of the 20th October, 20th November, 1, 3d, & 27 December in this period, & 2d Ulto. in the Current Year.

If I had not promised a draft on London for your part of the Barkers Cargo & been complimented with the very highest Exchange I shou'd at your request at any inconvenience to myself have withheld my Pen from a Draught made on Messrs. A. & J. Boyd for £150 Sterling on your Account & passed to the Credit thereon at 721 per Cent £1,081.10/ but I have remark'd to those Gentlemen your too late directions to me not to draw & at the same time pointed out where to send the Bill to be paid on my own Account if they think proper to do so. Therefore no great inconveniance can follow

---

³ The copartnership of Miles Brewton and Thomas Loughton Smith, the son of Benjamin Smith. Rogers, *Evolution of a Federalist,* pp. 17, 18, 47.

to you as it will return into my own hands again & I shall ask nothing more than to be made whole for the advance of Money which I am sure you will think reasonable.

I am glad to see that you have done so well with Barkers Cargo.[4] 'Tis hard to ship Rice at the latter end of our Crop free from Weavil. Those Vermin which you complain of more probably crept out of the Indian Corn than from the rough Rice. I think I may say without Vanity that I attend closely to my business & take as much pains to see it faithfully executed as most Men in trade but all the care & Watchfullness in the World will not exempt us from the common & Natural circumstances or effects of the Climate & I am heartily glad that we are no worse off. I was somewhat apprehensive of making but a Shabby adventure & therefore did the more readily offer to excuse you from any concern in it.

I shall send you in a few days a Sloop with about 200 Barrels & half Barrels of good Rice, 20 or 30 Barrels Pork, a few Barrels of Pitch, Tar, & Turpentine & as many shingles as can be got on our Joint Account which you may Sell as your Market best admits of. The Sloop is the *Molly,* Capt. Vesey[5] & Shall Insure our Interest here.

Of your five Negroes per the *Sally,* Capt. Floyd, I have sold four & hope to sell the other tomorrow so as to average upwards of £41 Sterling which you will say is very great considering this Country & that two of them were Little Boys, but let me beg of you not to be incouraged from this as to dabble too freely for our high prices will probably occasion vast Importations & soon knock down the Market.[6] But If you do send any more let them be young Men likely & healthy & none others & to come early in the Year & to have some Clothing & great care taken of them in the passage.

You must know, Gentlemen, that I have in general declined the Affrican business, altho I have had the most kind & friendly offers

---

[4] The brigantine *Nicholas & Mary,* Thomas Barker, had sailed for St. Kitts on Oct. 25, 1763. *HL Papers,* III, 537.
    [5] The sloop *Molly,* Abraham Vesey, owned by Thomas and Ephraim Gilbert and Abraham Vesey of Bermuda, was cleared outwards on Feb. 23 for St. Christophers with 240 barrels and 34 half barrels of rice, 20 barrels of pitch, 6 barrels of turpentine, 28 barrels of beef and pork, 50 pine planks, and 4,900 shingles. Naval Office Lists, 1764–1767, p. 74.
    [6] HL paid £50 duties on the six slaves imported in Floyd. Public Treasurer, Journal B: Duties, 1748–1765, p. 375, S. C. Archives. By an act of June 14, 1751, a duty of £10 currency was placed on slaves "four feet two inches and upward" and £5 for those "under that height, and above three feet two inches." *S. C. Statutes,* III, 739. HL had paid the duties on four adult slaves and two boys.

from my friends in London, Liverpool, & Bristol & do believe that I might have sold 1,000 or 1,500 last Year & more the Year we are now in if I wou'd ask for them but having no partner I do not chuse to embarrass & perhaps involve myself in concerns too unweildy for a single Man both on his own & his friends Account. However a few now & then of a good sort I can Manage well enough for you while the prices keep up of which I shall keep you advised. I remain—

SOURCE: Letterbook copy, HL Papers, S. C. Hist. Soc.; addressed "St. Christophers"; "per Capt. Nelme. Copy per Vesey."

TO JOHN COMING BALL

[Charles Town] February 10th, 1764

Dear Sir,

I Rece'd your favour by Smith Peter.[7] The Lumber that you sent in Mr. Lind's Schooner is all taken on board the Ship but I have not yet receiv'd the Captain's Account to compare with yours but I have heard him praise the Quality very much. Mr. Lind growles about the detaintion of the Schooner but I don't think if she had discharged at the Wharf a moment wou'd have been gain'd in this Weather & by his people but Peter will inform you that if there was any delay it was occasion'd as much by the neglect on one side as the other.

Diamond[8] insists upon it you order'd 10 Barrels of Salt after writing your Letter & bid him tell me so. Therefore I send it & here inclosed is the Account.

Inclosed also is an Account of our last 5 Hogsheads Rum, divided so that you gain half an empty Hogshead—thats all.

34 Barrels Pitch came to Town last week for you branded Jennerett.[9] I sent to Mr. Lind & to Mr. Moorylees but neither of them wou'd take charge of them. If they had remain'd three nights on the Wharf half or perhaps more wou'd have been Stolen. Therefore I have roll'd them into my Garden where they wait your order.

The Schooner is gone to Wambaw. Dickinson had a mind to Shuffle again—he wanted Ballest & said the Wind was too *sharp*

---

[7] A slave. See *HL Papers,* III, 481.
[8] A slave.
[9] Jacob Jennerette of Santee died on Sept. 14, 1792. *SCHM,* XXI (1920), 128.

to go into the Creek. Therefore I put 27 Barrels Salt on board & bid him be gone & If he cou'd not get into Wambaw go to Black Mingo, but I think the Devil must be in him if he does not go to Wambaw. You will be so good in that case to order some care to be taken of my Salt. My love, &c.

Compliments to all Friends & I remain, Dear Sir, Yours, &c.—

[*P.S.*] Hurry down the remainder of the Lumber.

SOURCE: Letterbook copy, Letter Book of Henry Laurens, Oct. 30, 1762–Sept. 10, 1766, Penn. Hist. Soc.

TO JOHN TALLY [1]

[Charles Town] 11th February 1764
Dear Sir,

Mr. James Dixon the Gentleman who bears this to you was introduced to me by a very worthy man in a Northern Collony;[2] & from a very short acquaintance I have conceived a favourable opinion of him. He is now extending his jurney as far as your province where he will be quite a stranger. Therefore I beg leave to recommend him to your countenance & protection during his stay there; a Liberty I flatter myself you will indulge me in, & when you think it in my power to make a return of kind offices to any of your friends be pleased to lay your commands on me who am with great respect, Dear Sir, Your, &ca.—

SOURCE: Letterbook copy, HL Papers, S. C. Hist. Soc.; addressed "Esquire. Savannah."

TO JOHNSON & WYLLY

[Charles Town] 11th February 1764
Gentlemen,

Agreable to your commands I supplied Mr. James Stone with

---

[1] John Tally was deputy secretary of Georgia. *Georgia Gazette,* July 7, 1763. When he petitioned for land on Sept. 2, 1760, he had been in Georgia for "some time." He was appointed justice of the peace for Christ Church parish on May 1, 1764. *Colonial Records of Georgia,* IX, 371–372; X, 179.
[2] John Rutherford of North Carolina.

£100 & charged that Sum to account of Mr. Benjamin Johnson of Tortola informing him at the same time that in case of his refusal you had engaged to make it good to me.

Mr. Stone fell short of Cash & afterwards I furnish'd at my own Risque with a Couple of peices of Gold to lay in a Sea Stock or some such matter in his way to North Carolina but I have not heard from him since he left this place.

Will you now permit me, Gentlemen, to Introduce Mr. James Dixon the Gentleman who beares this to your acquaintance & courtesy during a few days that he may sojourn in Savanna; he is recommended to me by a very worthy Man in a neighbouring province & from a short acquaintance I have conceived a favourable opinion of him as a genteel sensible Young Man. Your kind offices to him Shall be acknowledged whenever you have a similar occasion to lay your commands upon me who am, Yours, &ca.—

SOURCE: Letterbook copy, HL Papers, S. C. Hist. Soc.; addressed "Savanna"; "per favour Mr. Dixon."

TO MARTIN & STEVENS

[Charles Town] 11th February 1764

Gentlemen,

I had fully determin'd to write to you & transmitt your Account Current by this conveyence & I shou'd blush for the omittion of it was not owing to an extraordinary circumstance of a fraud attempted upon me which has diverted me from my accounting house all this day & Evening. [*It*] is now late on Saturday Night & I will not let Capt. Basset[3] go without this short appology & to assure you that I shall send your Account by Capt. Vesey who will sail in three or four days for St. Kitts or even by this conveyance if detained 'till Monday. Mean time as your Rum per Henderson is all in Casks I shall fall upwards of £300 Currency in your debt which is allways

---

[3] The brigantine *Porgy*, Jeremiah Bassett, owned by Richard and John Jennings and Jeremiah Bassett of Bermuda, was cleared outwards on Feb. 9, for Antigua. Naval Office Lists, 1764–1767, p. 74. In 1761 Jeremiah Bassett in the *Porgy* had managed after a seven-hour fight to escape from a French vessel of 12 guns. Henry C. Wilkinson, *Bermuda in the Old Empire* (London, 1950), p. 230.

at your Command & so are the best services of, Gentlemen, Yours, &ca.—

SOURCE: Letterbook copy, HL Papers, S. C. Hist. Soc.; addressed "Antigua"; "per Capt. Bassett. Copy per Vesey."

T O J E R E M I A H N I B B S , J R . [4]

[Charles Town] 11 February 1764

Sir,

You may very justly wonder at my silence by some late conveyences but when I inform you the cause I trust you will excuse me. Some of my Young Folks have deliver'd one of your 10 Hogsheads Rum without making an Entry for it & I have had the Imperfect Account Sales laying above two Months before me in hopes that from some circumstance we might recover the lost sheep but now I dispair of it & have no way left to do you justice but to pay for it myself which I shall do, transmit your Sale and Account Current, & remit the Ballance some day next week.

I had fully determin'd to do the whole this day but a most gross attempt made to defraud me has diverted me almost the whole day from my Counting House & also caused me a good deal of vexation. 'Tis now late Saturday Night but I will not let the opportunity of Capt. Bassett slip without this appology, relying upon your Indulgence for a day or two longer. I am with great regard, Your—

SOURCE: Letterbook copy, HL Papers, S. C. Hist. Soc.; addressed "Antigua"; "per Capt. Bassett. Copy per Vesey."

T O H E N R Y B R I G H T , J E R E M I A H A M E S , [5] F R A N C I S R O G E R S , [6] P E A C H & P I E R C E [7]

[Charles Town] 11th February 1764

Gentlemen,

I Acknowledged the receipt of your favour of 26th September in a Letter the 4th Inst. to Mr. Bright & I am now to inform you

---

[4] *HL Papers*, I, 100n.

[5] Jeremiah Ames was an esquire and an alderman living at 17 Lower Maudlin Lane in 1775. He married Phoebe Collins on March 2, 1731, was sheriff of Bris-

that after advertizing in both Gazetts & applying to every House where there was the least probability of procuring freight for your Ship *Sally,* I have obtain'd about 400 Barrels of Pitch at 40/ per Ton & 100 Barrels of Rice at 42/6 which you will find rather to exceed anything that is gone before besides the dispatch of your Ship which barring unforseen accidents I hope will be in 1/3 the time that other Vessels have met with because I have luckily enough in hand to fill her as fast as it can be Stowed away. I shall also procure a few Casks of Skins & Indigo.

I had provided about 400 Barrels Pitch & 120 Barrels Green Tar on my own Account to embrace the first opportunity of Shipping & accordingly offer'd it to Capt. Condon in the *Glostershire,*[8] but his Agents refused to take it upon Freight & I wou'd gladly put it on board the *Sally* on my own Account but as she is at my own direction & that you mention those Articles I think it my duty to give you the preferrence especialy as the Freight is low, at the same time as this exceeds your order in Number of Barrels I submitt it wholy to you Gentlemen to take to it yourselves or inform Messrs. Cowles & Harford that you shall reject it to the End that they may Insure on my account Two hundred pounds Sterling which is not the full Value but I shall say nothing to them upon the Subject until the Ship Sails. Besides these things as near as I can judge with the aid of Capt. Floyds opinion the *Sally* will require 150 to 200 Barrels Rice to fill her up which must be done on your own Account If I cannot prevail on somebody else to Ship it. [My] endevours shall not be wanting for that purpose nor advise of my proceeding before the Ship Sails for your Government about Insurance. I flatter myself with hopes of having

tol in 1742, and mayor in 1759. He died on April 3, 1779 at the age of 70. M. E. Williams, archivist of Bristol, to the editor, June 30, 1972.

[6] Francis Rogers, Jr. *HL Papers,* I, 323; II, 489.

[7] Samuel Peach (1715–1785) was the Bristol merchant in the firm of Peach and Pierce. Peach was a linen draper and a slave trader. One of his daughters married Isaac Elton; the other Henry Cruger (1739–1827). With Cruger, Peach led the radical movement in Bristol. Charles Henry Cave, *A History of Banking in Bristol from 1750 to 1899* (Bristol, Eng., 1899), p. 100; Wesley Savadge, "The West Country and the American Mainland Colonies, 1763–1783, with special reference to the Merchants of Bristol" (unpub. Litt Thesis, Univ. of Oxford, 1952), p. 110; "Henry Cruger," Namier and Brooke, *The House of Commons, 1754–1790,* II, 280.

[8] The ship *Gloucestershire,* Richard Condon, was cleared outwards on Feb. 21 for Bristol. Naval Office Lists, 1764–1767, p. 74.

her full & clear'd out by the 20th Inst. or perhaps a day or two sooner.[9] I remain with Great regard, Your, &ca.—

SOURCE: Letterbook copy, HL Papers, S. C. Hist. Soc.; addressed "Owners of the Ship *Sally* at Bristol"; "per Brunett. Copy per Stanfield which not being marked another Copy goes also by Condon."

TO JOHN PAGAN,
ALEXANDER BROWN & CO.

[Charles Town] 13th February 1764

Gentlemen,

You have preceeding this a duplicate of what I wrote upon the arival of your Ship *Pearl* the 2d Inst. since which she hath been delivering her Cargo of Coals & I endeavouring to procure a Freight of Rice for her, & she will be ready tomorrow or next day to be shifted, but I have not been able yet to engage more than 250 Barrels for Lisbon at the same rate that the general Cargo shall pay, which I am affraid will not go beyond 40/ tho' I shall try hard to get 45/ which was the last Freight for a small handy Vessel of 350 Barrels belonging to Dundee.[1] I told you it was 50/ but that was a mistake arising from the Master's giving out that he wou'd take no less. He got no more however than 45/ nor has any other to Lisbon. Our Accounts of Rice Sales there are very discouraging which makes people cautious of Shipping. At the same time, the highest Freight given for Cowes & Holland is 55/ to 57/6 for handy Vessels which Capt. Francis thinks is by no means an adequate advance for the difference of the Voyages & he presses very warmly for Lisbon. I will not determine either way untill he is upon calling for Rice & then with his advise I shall do that which shall appear most beneficial

---

[9] The *Sally* was cleared outwards for Bristol with 170 barrels of rice, 784 barrels of pitch, 129 barrels of tar, 54 barrels of turpentine, 3 hogsheads of deerskins, 1,271 pounds of indigo, 1 pipe of madeira wine, and 1 cask of rum. Naval Office Lists, 1764–1767, p. 74. The manifest, signed by William Floyd at the Naval Office on Feb. 23, stated that of the total cargo HL was consigning 70 barrels of rice, 479 barrels of pitch, 129 barrels of tar, and 54 barrels of turpentine to Henry Bright. Downes & Jones shipped 100 barrels of rice; Gabriel Manigault 305 barrels of pitch. Naval Office Lists, 1764–1767, p. 33.

[1] The brigantine *Dolphin,* James Rea, owned by Robert Stirling of Dundee, was cleared outwards on Jan. 23 for Lisbon with 361 barrels and 71 half barrels (213,781 pounds) of rice. Naval Office Lists, 1764–1767, p. 73.

to you and advise you immediately. Meantime I remain with great regard, Gentlemen, Yours, &ca.—

SOURCE: Letterbook copy, HL Papers, S. C. Hist. Soc.; addressed "Glasgow"; "per Capt. Brunett. Copy per Mitchel."

TO JOHN TARLETON

[Charles Town] 14 February 1764

Sir,

My last trouble was under the 27 Ulto. per Capt. Muir & Capt. Barnes advising of a draught on you to the order of Mr. Christian Minnick for £150 Sterling. This is intended to inform you that on the 9th Inst. I passed another Bill at 40 Days sight payable in London to the order of Messrs. Brailsford & Chapman for £473.11.8 Sterling which at 721 per Cent Exchange carries to your Credit £3,414.11.3 & closes your Account Current as per annex'd Coppy which I hope will be found free of error & receive your approbation.

Yesterday I rece'd a few lines from Capt. Hall inclosing me a certificate properly sign'd & Seal'd in the Custom House at Jamaica which will cancel our Joint bond given last Year for the *Clayton;*[2] he complains much of the Market in that Island.

Rice continues here at 45/. Naval Stores dear & rather scarce. Freight 40/ to England & Portugal & 55/ to £3 for Cowes & different Markets on the Continent.

Permit me, Sir, to repeat the tender of my best services & to assure you that I am with great regard, Your humble Servant—

SOURCE: Letterbook copy, HL Papers, S. C. Hist. Soc.; addressed "Liverpool"; "per Brunett. Copy per Stanfield."

TO COWLES & HARFORD

[Charles Town] 14th February 1764

Gentlemen,

The 24th Ulto. I wrote you per Harbison & sent a Copy per Barnes since which I am without any of your esteem'd favours.

---

[2] The ship *Clayton*, Charles Hall, owned by John Tarleton, Charles Hall, and Edward Parr of Liverpool, was cleared outwards on April 9, 1763, for Jamaica with 626 barrels and 6 half barrels of rice. Naval Office Lists, 1757–1764, p. 130.

On the 9th Inst. I took the Liberty to pass two Bills on you at 40 Days sight one payable to the order of Messrs. Brailsford & Chapman for Five hundred & thirty pounds Sterling the other to the order of Mr. Hugh Hughes[3] in London for one hundred pounds Sterling which be pleased to pay & charge my Account for the same. No variation in our Market since my last therefore I conclude without further troubling you. Gentlemen, Your humble, &ca.—

SOURCE: Letterbook copy, HL Papers, S. C. Hist. Soc.; addressed "Bristol"; "per Brunett. Copy per Stanfield."

TO SAMUEL THOMAS

[Charles Town] 16 February 1764

Dear Sir,

You make no mention to me about a difference in the price of your boards. Therefore I cannot agree to give the same price for that as for good Stuff. This I say because I wou'd always make a just distinction between good & bad. At the same time I do confess that you did me a favour in letting me have any or either of them. Therefore, Sir, I shall endevour to dispose of the inferior Class that you shall not suffer by indulging me & then if you please the matter shall rest two or three days.

In reply to your last favour of Yesterday I shall apply to Capt. Roberts[4] & urge him to send his Schooner for your Tar & hope I shall prevail on him. I am obliged to you for the Trees intended by Diamond & the Directions for planting them. I hope we shall one day or other have the pleasure of Mrs. Thomas's company & yours under the Shade of those pretty trees or of a Roof very near them. Mrs. Laurens joins with me in Complyments to you both & am with great regard, Yours, &ca.—

SOURCE: Letterbook copy, Letter Book of Henry Laurens, Oct. 30, 1762–Sept. 10, 1766, Penn. Hist. Soc.; addressed "St. Thomas's."

---

[3] Hugh Hughes was a druggist located in Bishopsgate. *London Directories.*
[4] Capt. Benjamin Roberts.

TO JAMES SANDERS[5]

[Charles Town] 17th February 1764

Sir,

I thank you very much for sending me the Shingles as you did for I was in great want of them. The Quantity proved to be only 29,060 of which many were worm eaten but I put 29,000 to your Credit at £6 per M. Be pleased to send me down the remainder & if you fill up the Boat with any kind of Cypress Boards I will take of you, I mean of the best quality but any Dimensions. Sir, I am, &ca.—

[*P.S.*] £6 & saving the wharfage with great dispatch is doing more than you expected but I have done all I could for you.

SOURCE: Letterbook copy, Letter Book of Henry Laurens, Oct. 30, 1762–Sept. 10, 1766, Penn. Hist. Soc.; addressed "at the Cypress."

TO JOHN FERDINAND MILLER

[Charles Town] 18 February 1764

Sir,

Capt. Nelson who brought me your favour of the 17th December has seen all the letters wrote by me on your Account since you left this province. I have hid nothing from him & therefore to him I shall referr you.[6]

I remark some essential differences in the Account that you have now transmitted to me of money & Bonds left in Mr. Waldrens hands & that Account Amount which he return'd to me after your departure, Vizt.—

You say the Cash deliver'd to him was £1,365, & this seems to be confirm'd by his original Letter that you have luckily preserv'd & sent to me but the Sum produc'd & payed to me was no more than £87.14. Again—

---

[5] James Sanders of St. George, Dorchester, who married Sarah Slann, died about 1784. *SCHM,* xxxvi (1937), 11; *HL Papers,* iii, 517n.

[6] Nicholas Neilson, who had been a witness to John Ferdinand Miller's letter of attorney, dated Dec. 17, 1763, swore on Feb. 18 to the signature before William Burrows, justice of the peace. See Letter of Attorney, Dec. 17, 1763. William Burrows, acting as HL's lawyer, advertised in the *Gazette,* Feb. 18, 1764, that all debts due to John Ferdinand Miller must be paid in to him (Burrows) before March 25 next.

Your Draught on Andrew Hunter[7] £100, Liston & Benfield Note £389.6.2, & Benjamin Godfreys[8] Note £81.12, mention'd in your schedule never came to my hands. However by means of your power I shall now enquire after & possibly discover these facts.

You desired in that hasty Letter wrote just before you quitted Charles Town that Mr. Waldren (& none other) shou'd have the bringing up & Settling of your Books. Therefore I applyed to him & often call'd again but hitherto he has done nothing therein.

You wou'd have acted more wisely to have made me your Confidant which you might have done with great safety. Since you have been so honest as to throw your effects into my hands a step of that sort wou'd have been of no disadvantage to you & must have proov'd very beneficial to your now distress'd friend Mr. De La Fontain.

I shall do all in my power to recover the Debts due to you but I have no great hopes of any except such as are under Bond & Seale. People in general are too much averse to paying other accounts than such as appear undenyably Clear & the bad state of your Books will rather indulge their inclinations & render it almost impossible to compell them to payment of simple contracts.

If any thing further occurs to you that is needfull please to let me hear from you & be assur'd that I shall truly inform you of all my proceedings in your affairs. I Who am, &ca.—

SOURCE: Letterbook copy, HL Papers, S. C. Hist. Soc.; addressed "St. Croix"; "per Capt. Nelson."

TO PATRICK WALDRON

[Charles Town] 20th February 1764

Sir,

Mr. John Ferdinand Miller from St. Croix has sent me an

---

[7] Andrew Hunter, deputy collector of customs at Charleston, died in August 1766. *SCHM*, XVI (1915), 34.

[8] Benjamin Godfrey was most probably a member of a family long established in St. Andrew parish. *SCHM*, XVI (1915), 57. Benjamin and Mary Godfrey had three children born in 1755, 1756, and 1758, all of whom were baptized by the Rev. Richard Clarke. *Register of St. Philip's Parish, 1754–1810*, pp. 102, 146. Benjamin Godfrey had been marshal of the first troop in Col. William Bull's Regiment of Horse in 1757. Council Journal, XXVI (Jan. 3, 1757–June 6, 1758), 80, S. C. Archives.

account of £1,365 Currency of Carolina, lodged in your hands to be deliver'd to me for the benefit of his Creditor & Friend Mr. De la Fontaine in London; & desires me to make a demand on you for that Sum. The Cash which you paid into my hands on this Account was only £87.14, which leaves a considerable Ballance in his favour. I am therefore to request payment of the same or that you will be so kind in case this apparent difference arises from any mistake as to explain the Accounts to me who am, Sir, yours, &c.—

SOURCE: Letterbook copy, Letter Book of Henry Laurens, Oct. 30, 1762–Sept. 10, 1766, Penn. Hist. Soc.; addressed "Charles Town."

TO JOHN COMING BALL
                    [Charles Town] 23d February 1764
Dear Sir,
        I take particular notice of what You say with respect to the payment to be made to Mr. Huger.[9]
        Mr. Manigault has deliver'd me £5,000 which Sum shall be paid to Mr. Huger as soon as he comes to Town & a proper receipt taken from him, the remainder to lay over of course untill the Titles for the Land are made unless you are pleased to pay it sooner.[1]
        By a very unexpected demand, instead of wanting Corn in August I shall be distressed for 1,500 or 2,000 Bushels to be deliver'd here on or before the 8th March. If you can by any means assist you will extreamly oblige me, & I intreat you to send me an imediate answer. Who am, Dear Sir, Your, &ca.—

---

[9] John Coming Ball was negotiating for the purchase of Limerick plantation from Daniel Huger, III. There is a record that Elias Ball, brother of John Coming Ball, made the purchase of Limerick containing 4,564½ acres on March 12, 1764. *SCHM*, XII (1911), 9. Irving also states that Elias Ball of Kensington bought Limerick from Daniel Huger, III. Irving, *A Day on Cooper River*, p. 176. When John Coming Ball wrote his will on March 28, 1764, he mentioned 61 acres next to Mr. Huger's Bridge "bought lately from my brother Elias." "Will of John Coming Ball," dated March 28, 1764, proved Nov. 23, 1764, Charleston County Wills, x, Book B (1760–1767), 578–585, S. C. Archives. Perhaps John Coming Ball was merely acting for his brother at this point. The plantation certainly passed to Elias Ball (1752–1810), the son of Elias Ball (1709–1786).
[1] Gabriel Manigault must have been lending £5,000 to the Balls so that they could make the purchase.

[*P.S.*] I have opened this letter again to desire your immediate assistance to procure all the Indian Corn that you possibly can to the amount of 20,000 say Twenty Thousand Bushels at the lowest rate possible not beyond 12/6 per Bushel & as I hope to gain some thing by it if bought under that you are welcome to an equale concern in the Bargain with me.

SOURCE: Letterbook copy, Letter Book of Henry Laurens, Oct. 30, 1762–Sept. 10, 1766, Penn. Hist. Soc.

TO HENRY BRIGHT & CO.
[Charles Town] 24th February 1764
Gentlemen,
The Annexed duplicate will shew you what I wrote the 11th Inst. relative to your Ship *Sally*. The Gentleman who promised to Ship about 400 Barrels of Pitch (if he could procure it) not receiving the quantity he expected has put only 301 on board. Besides this there are 100 Barrels Rice, 3 Hogsheads of Skins, 3 Casks of Indigo, & two or three of Wine & Rum on Freight.
The rest of her Cargo is on your Account, reserving to your selves a right of rejecting the whole or part of the Pitch, Turpentine, & Tar as before mentioned, 483 Barrels of heavy Pitch, 129 Barrels of Green Tar, 54 Barrels of exceeding fine Turpentine Value about £400 Sterling, & also 70 Barrels of fine Rice Value about £140 Sterling. If you do not take the Naval Stores be so good as to inform Messrs. Cowles & Harford & desire them to make up the Sum Insured for me on said Goods £300 Sterling. Two or three days lost by the bad Weather & the trifling of a person who promised an hundred Barrels of Rice upon Freight prevented my clearing out the Ship before yesterday. Capt. Floyd has some little matters to do about her rigging but hopes to Sail on Sunday the 26th. I shall write you again by him & at present only repeat that I am with great regard, &ca.—

SOURCE: Letterbook copy, HL Papers, S. C. Hist. Soc.; addressed "Owners of the Ship *Sally*, Bristol"; "per Capt. Condon. Copy per Coombs."

TO WILLIAM HODSHON

[Charles Town] 24 February 1764

Sir,

Your favour of the 15th November & duplicate of it I have duly Rec'd per Capt. Gun[2] & Capt. Coward[3] & since you are so kind as to take away the sting which your former Letters had left in my mind, I shall make no deeper retrospect than to my last of the 12th December per Capt. Ball with a remittance for 250 Dollars to cover Timberlake's protested Bill, & go forward to do you all the service in my power, sorry at the same time that I cannot do more on Account of the dilatoriness of the Gentlemen in Georgia[4] who have added to their former payments no more than £272.10.5 Sterling & that, all except £30 in paper Currency, was in Bills upon New York. This was a circumstance that affected me very much; I remonstrated upon the injustice of paying you in anything that would not produce you 20/ to the pound, refused to receive such Bills & at length brought them to refer the matter to four Gentlemen of undoubted judgement & integrity, Vizt. Gabriel Manigault, John Savage, George Inglis, & David Deas, Esquires who unanimously agreed that according to the tenour of the Conditions of the Bond you were obliged to take such Bills, tho at the same time they said it was not just in the Debtors to insist upon that advantage which was never intended by me to be given to them, for the Bond is filled up by Mr. Read[5] of Georgia contrary to my advice as well as *to a form which I gave him* for that purpose, but he thought that the words *"full Value in Gold Bills &ca."* would be sufficiently binding, & Upon my word I am so much of that opinion, from the groundwork & foundation of the debt & from the plain meaning of all contracts that were the Gentlemen to be come at in South Carolina, I would not submit to their arbitrary dictates, especially as everybody agrees that I have equity on my side. I would try & hope that justice would go a great way in obtaining a verdict from a Jury in my favour; but where they are situated, a Law suit would be gain to them as they would pay in the paper Lawfull Money of the province of Georgia & to you such payment wou'd be attended

---

[2] The ship *Heart of Oak,* Henry Gunn, was entered inwards on Feb. 14 from London. Naval Office Lists, 1764–1767, p. 70.

[3] The ship *King George,* William Coward, was entered inwards on Feb. 16 from London. Naval Office Lists, 1764–1767, p. 70.

[4] Johnson & Wylly.

[5] James Read.

with great loss. That you may be quite convinced that I do as much at least for you as I can do for myself, be pleased to read the inclosed Copy of a Letter lately wrote to an Honourable Gentleman in that Country upon the subject of a debt alluded to in mine of the 26th August which he has not yet found time to reply to altho many opportunities have offered.[6] As I do not mean to expose private business nor to injure Characters by that you will throw that Copy into the Fire soon as you have read it. Be pleased likewise to peruse the Copy of a letter which I sent to Johnson & Wylly of the 25th August which will further convince you of my hearty endeavours to serve you & of the trouble taken upon me on your Account.[7] But, Sir, these are now rather matters of Speculation, for having a good opportunity by the favour of a friend I exchanged the above mentioned Bills into Currency at 700 per Cent & for that Currency I have now Dollars that will yeild you rather more than they Cost, Vizt. 31/ to 31/6 per & I shall ship you that full Sum by the *Nancy,* Capt. Mitchel, for London some time within the present Month. I find my friend in New York had remitted you £129.9/ Sterling in a Bill of Exchange Isaac Man[8] on Neale & Pigau[9] of which your next will probably advise me. Be pleased (once more) to peruse the Award of the Arbitrators above mentioned which I also herewith inclose. These several papers will cost you some postage but I had rather pay ten times as much to shew you that I have truly been, Sir, Your Humble Servant—

SOURCE: Letterbook copy, HL Papers, S. C. Hist. Soc.; "per Coombs. Copy per Mitchel."

TO JOSEPH MANESTY

[Charles Town] 24th February 1764
Sir,

Since my last under the 17th Ulto. per two conveyances I have used my utmost endeavours to sell the Rum imported per your Ship *Barter* & to load her again & send her forward on her Voyage to

---

[6] HL to Grey Elliot, Jan. 24, 1764. *HL Papers,* III, 545.
[7] *HL Papers,* III, 535–537.
[8] Merchant of New York.
[9] Merchants of London.

Barbadoes.[1] In both I have succeeded as well as I could reasonably expect in the present state of our Market.

About one half of the Rum is sold from 15/6 upward which is really 2/ to 2/6 per Gallon more than the same article is sold for in great quantities per Hogshead on Tuesday & Thursday per Vendue in every Week. This difference arises from the indulgence that I give to the purchasers.

A Cargo of Lumber has been ready many days past & is now about one half with some Rice taken on board the Ship; but the work goes heavily on, not for want of diligence in Capt. Gough but principally owing to the awkwardness & difficulty of taking such good into a Ship that has no Lumber port, the want of which causes great delay & waste of time, &ca. Capt. Gough thinks it would injure the Ship very much to cut one.

She is now near full in the hold & I hope will get away before the 5th March. 'Tis not possible to ascertain the Value of the Cargo but as near as I can judge it will be about £450 or £500 Sterling & if it shall exceed you may depend upon having timely notice by future opportunities. Meantime I remain with great regard, &ca.—

SOURCE: Letterbook copy, HL Papers, S. C. Hist. Soc.; addressed "Liverpoole"; "per Capt. Condon. Copy per Mitchel."

TO JOHN KNIGHT & THOMAS MEARS

[Charles Town] 24 February 1764

Gentlemen,

My last was under the 20 Ulto. per Capt. Harrop & the *Mercury* Man of War since which I have not been able to do business with that chearfulness & constancy that had been usual to me. Every change of weather brought back the pains occasion'd by the fall that I mention'd to you & the Desk proov'd so unfriendly a resource that I was in a manner compeled to quit it for some days nor indeed have I been able to apply with proper spirit ever after. These circumstances I hope will excuse me for letting so much time pass without Writing

---

[1] The ship *Barter,* James Gough, was cleared outwards on March 14 for Barbados with 118 barrels and 48 half barrels of rice, 21 barrels of pitch, 20 barrels of tar, 9 barrels of turpentine, 50,000 feet of lumber, and 40,500 shingles. Naval Office Lists, 1764–1767, p. 75.

& the more as you have certainly suffer'd no loss or damage by the omition.

I now Inclose an Invoice & Bill Loading for the *Austins* last Cargo for Oporto, Vizt. 558 Barrels & 60 half Barrels of Rice & one of Capt. Holmes Receipts for money Supply'd him whole amount £8,545.17.9 carried of[f] in Moiety to the debit of your respective Accounts, Vizt. JK £4,272.18.10 & TM £4,272.18.11 & as Mr. Mears has inform'd me that he never rece'd the Invoice of the last Years Cargo of Rice I likewise Inclose you a Copy of that amounting to £7,301.10.9 to the debit of Mr. J. K. for one half £3,650.15.5 & to Mr. T. M. £3,650.15.4 but 'tis not in my power to send another Bill Loading or receipt for disbursements having sent two of each in due course & it is wonderfull how my Letters shou'd have reach'd you & those Contents have miscarry'd but If a notarial Copy of both is necessary please to give me notice & such proof shall be transmitted without delay. You have likewise here inclosed an Account of Sale of Sundry Rec'd per the *Austin* in February 1763 of which I shall say no more than this that I do not know a Merchant in this place who wou'd have made a Sale of the same Nature & effect upon the same terms & conditions. The Net proceeds being £6,108.0.11 is passed to your Credit, Vizt. one half thereof to Mr. John Knight £3,054.0.6 & for the other half Mr. Thomas Mears £3,054.0.5. Saving me harmless from any loss that may arrise from £3,780.0.7 of debts outstanding & by a sketch of each Account now transmitted in seperate Letters you will be pleased to observe that I am very considerably in advance.

I have Sold upwards of 20 Hogsheads Rum of those 40 Imported per the *Austin* & by means of giving Credit & taking much pains to Invite Customers have truely obtain'd 20 to 25 per Cent more than cou'd have been got if hastily turn'd into Cash. West India Rum is every Vendue day Sold from 12/6 to 13/ & I know of a large Quantity of New England Rum sold this Week at 10/ per Gallon which is less than it cost before it was put on Ship board. I shall endeavour to end your Sale as soon as may be without Squandering away your Interest & I know by long experience that the regard shewn on my part to that, will meet with a kind reception from you. As to the few dry goods they go as usual very dull indeed & are realy an Eye sore which only time & watching opportunitys can remove.

Salt is excessively low say 3/6 per Bushel & must soon be at 2/6 if the importations are continued. Nevertheless fine Salt is wanted

& a Cargo about September or October will probably pay some Freight. Coals also will be wanted for Fire wood becomes very scarce & dear in this Country & must be more so every Year. Besides these I do not recolect an Article worth mentioning to you but I shall continue to advise from time to time of the State of our Market & imbrace every occation to give further proofs of that attachment & regard with which I allways profess myself to be, Yours, &ca.—

SOURCE: Letterbook copy, HL Papers, S. C. Hist. Soc.; addressed "Liverpool"; "per Smith. Copy per Condon with Bill Loading Abstract Invoice & Receipt."

TO JOHN KNIGHT

[Charles Town] 24 February 1764

Dear Sir,

My last letter was dictated on a Sick Bed the 20 Ulto. on which I laid for some days by the effect of a fall which I cannot yet shake off nor can I expect to be exempt before the Spring weather setts steadyly in. Every change of Weather affects me greatly. To that Letter as well as to what I shall now write to the Owners of the Snow *Austin* I beg leave to refer you & shall proceed to say the needfull on your own concerns in the Ship *Hope*, &ca.

Capt. Dennison is a good judge of that Vessels quality's as well as of her imperfections. He has lately seen her bottom & caused what he thought requisite to be done to it. I have constantly advised him to be cautious of his proceedings & to consider your interest no farther than was consistant with your humanity & the preservation of his own & other Mens Lives. He returned from Hobcaw the 11th Inst. & assured me that his Ship was good for any Voyage provided she was not over Loaded upon which I recomended & he agreed to take only 500 Barrels Rice which he soon got in & then insisted upon having 100 more which after some objections on my part I complyed with, submitting to his better judgment. The Ship now lyes ready for Sea with 600 Barrels of as fine Rice as ever was seen at Oporto where I hope it will arrive in safety. If I can get Cap. Dennison to settle the Ships Accounts in time you shall have Invoice & Bill of Loading & his receipt by this conveyance but to guard against accidents please to take notice that the whole will ammount to something about £1,200 Sterling. Whatever he may think of the Sufficiency of the Ship his Old hands will not be of his opinion. They have droped away very fast & I am affraid will leave him almost to a Man but I am purswaded in my own Mind that they only make a pretence of the wariness of the Vessel to gloss over their real intentions of demanding Wages at a second delivery Port & ship themselves again upon better terms in other bottoms, which their Love & Respect for the Master seems to restrain them from confessing openly. I have advised him to give them the greatest encouragement by fair words & good usage that he can in which my assistance shall not be wanting, for I am in great pains when I think of the Consequences of such a general desertion. It will be extreamly dificult to replace a proper Number of hands & at best it cannot be done without much expence of time & Money. I have not been able to Sell one Hogshead of the Earthen Ware per the *Hope* nor a Bottle of the Ale. The place is quite overstock'd with both articles. The Amount of Sale of the *Hopes* last Years Cargo is about £7,200 & of that Sum upwards of £4,000 is outstanding & I dare say one half of that Will be so without one half penny Interest for many Months perhaps Years. This is the case continualy with dry Goods here except with those people who import every Article from the smalest to the largest of European & India Goods & retail & Book for twelve Months the Value of a Groat & bad enough is it even with some of them. There remains now 17 Peices of your Narrow Cloths & almost all the Shalloons, Buttons, & trimings. The Sale was so extreamly bad here that I was on the point of packing them up to send to Philadelphia when to my former discouraging advises the report of Cap. Gough of your Town who had been just selling a Cargo there was added which has made me resolve to push them off day by day per Vendue untill the beginning of April & then if any remains to send them away.

From this Account bad as it is you may discover two facts, that you cannot be a great looser & that 'tis impossible for me to be a gainer by that adventure; which will be further prooved too by a sketch of Account here Inclosed. I shall only say that I am glad to see it so near its Close & that it turns out no worse & for the present dismiss the Subject.

Capt. Devill & Capt. Pitt who both arived here long before Dennison still remain & will not sail for some time after him as things at present appear. All them with Cargos gone before will make about

3,540 Barrels for Oporto. Another little Vessel of 400 Barrels I believe is destin'd for that Market.[2] I strove hard to divert by offering a good Freight for Cadiz but it wou'd not do. However I strove [to get] as much as possible of what must go into the hands of Mr. Byrne which must be some advantage to your Sales.

Now I wish to see your *Pocock* or any of your Ships with Negros. I think people the least aquainted with that Branch wu'd not miss of making great Sales. A little Cargo unexpectedly sent to me from the West Indies averg'd £43 Sterling. I call it a Cargo tho there were only 14 in the Number but being too Old, too Swelled & Sick, & two Boys under Size the colection makes no bad epitome of a Cargo. Great prices you may depend upon it will be given untill we receive a full Supply. Rice is at 45/ slow Sale. Naval Stores very high. Freight 40/ to £3. Exchange 700 to 721 per Cent. Salt 3/6. I remain—

SOURCE: Letterbook copy, HL Papers, S. C. Hist. Soc.; addressed "Liverpool"; "per Capt. Smith. Copy per Condon."

TO THOMAS MEARS

[Charles Town] 24th February 1764

Dear Sir,

Give me leave to refer you to what I wrote yourself under the 22d December per Capt. Brownett & White & Yesterday to the Owners of the *Austin* as well as to the Sundry Accounts, &c. Inclosed in the Latter which I hope will all get safe to your hands & be found free from errors. I now inclose a sketch of an Account Current which I cannot finaly Ballance because the Sale of Rum, &ca., per the *Austin* is not closed & therefore only a Supposed Sum for one Moiety of the Net proceeds set down whereby a Ballance remains due to me of near £200 Sterling & it appears that I am in advance on your Account upwards of £750 Sterling. This added to Sums which I am unavoidably in advance for other friends at a time when Money is scarcer in Carolina than ever I knew it to be will oblige me to call on you soon for something about the said Ballance & I must trust to this Account together with your own goodness to be my appologists if any excuse is necessary.

---

[2] The brigantine *Hopewell*, Moses Pitt.

Rice continues at 45/. The sale grows slack as Ships for some days past have departed from our Port faster than others come into it. Near one half of the Crop is already carried off & the Planters will strugle hard to support their prices for the other.

The *Austin* will have a fine time at Oporto all the Lent season & at most only two Competitors for part of the time, perhaps but one, if my Neighbour tells me truth who say that one of those I alluded to is gone to Coimbra.[3] Two others who arrived here before the *Austin* & taken Rice for that Market are still here & will not Sail for there three or four days.[4] What think you of this? The *Hope* has 600 Barrels on board & will go to Sea tomorrow or next day but the *Austin*'s Cargo will be run off before she gets there.

No Turtle yet arrived. I shall not be unmindfull of your commands on that head at a proper season of the Year & at all times I am, Yours, &ca.—

SOURCE: Letterbook copy, HL Papers, S. C. Hist. Soc.; addressed "Liverpool"; "per Smith. Copy per Condon."

TO HENRY BYRNE

[Charles Town] 25th February 1764

Sir,

Annexed you have duplicate of my last under the 9th Inst. per Capt. Lewis to which & the Copy Bill of Loading here inclosed I beg leave to refer you.

This waits on you by the Ship *Hope,* Capt. Dennison, with Invoice & Bill of Loading for 600 Barrels of as good Rice as ever I Shipped, which you will please to receive & Sell on Account of our Worthy & good friend Mr. John Knight of Liverpool. The Master will more fully inform you how he came to take so light a Cargo & to be so much longer detained than we expected. The Brigantine *Hopewell,* Capt. Pitt, & the *Swift,* Capt. Davill, are still on this side. They may sail in a few days. Another small bark of 350 Barrels

---

[3] HL had written to Knight and Mears on Dec. 22 that the snow *Douro* and the ship *Caroline* had sailed for Oporto. The *Douro* had actually cleared for Figueira, which was the port of Coimbra. Naval Office Lists, 1757–1764, p. 136. Coimbra lies half-way between Oporto and Lisbon.

[4] The *Swift* and the *Hopewell.*

burthen offer'd for your port & considering the quantity of Rice gone & going thither I strove to divert her Voyage by offering a Freight for Cadiz but it was not accepted & I believe you will have her with you. On Board the *Hopewell* I have Ninety Barrels of Rice which go to your address but I could not succeed in procuring you the consignment of the whole, the Shippers being under some particular attachment to another very good House. I wish you all Happiness & remain, &ca.—

SOURCE: Letterbook copy, HL Papers, S. C. Hist. Soc.; "per Dennison. Copy per Pitt."

TO FRANCIS STUART[5]

[Charles Town] 28th February 1764

I now send my Schooner *Wambaw,* David Dickinson, Master, for one thousand Bushells of Corn which you said you could Supply me with at ten Shillings per Bushel. Be pleased to give such directions that the Schooner may meet with dispatch, the Corn be very Clean, & hold out the measure. If any unforeseen accident deprives me of my expectation either in part or whole of the Corn which would be a very great disappointment to me, be so good as to assist the Master in getting a load of something else. There are twenty Barrels of Salt on board the Schooner, Quantity 175½ Bushels, which I hope your house will take at 7/6 per Bushel, Barrels included. I am, your most obedient Servant—

SOURCE: Letterbook copy, Letter Book of Henry Laurens, Oct. 30, 1762–Sept. 10, 1766, Penn. Hist. Soc.; addressed "Esquire."

TO WILLIAM HODSHON

[Charles Town] 28 February 1764

Sir,

Referring you to what I wrote the 24th Insta. per Capt. Coombes[6] as per duplicate annexed, I come now to present you with

---

[5] Spelled "Stewart" in the letterbook.
[6] The ship *America,* William Coombes, was cleared outwards on Feb. 18, 1764, for London. Naval Office Lists, 1764–1767, p. 74.

a Bill of Loading for 1,212 Spanish Dollars Shipped on your Account
per this Bearer the *Nancy,* Capt. Mitchel,[7] which carries to the Debit
of your Account besides my Commission £1,898.12/, Vizt. 800 at
31/6 & 412 at 31/ per piece which you will be pleased to Note in
conformity to my Credit. I shall write a pressing Letter to your
debtors in Georgia & renew every argument in my power to prevail
on them to discharge the final Balance of their Bond before the Sailing
of the Ship *Heart of Oak,* Capt. Gunn, & shall convert at all events
what Currency is now in my hands into Dollars to Ship by that
Vessel to Sail sometime next Month of which I shall write more
particularly as the time approaches mean while, I remain, &ca.—

SOURCE: Letterbook copy, HL Papers, S. C. Hist. Soc.; "per Mitchell.
Copy per Floyd."

TO JOHN PAGAN,
ALEXANDER BROWN & CO.
                            [Charles Town] 29 February 1764
Gentlemen,
        The annex'd is duplicate of what I wrote you the 13th Inst.
since which I have ingaged from several hands in small parcells
about 300 Barrels Rice on Freight for the *Pearl* making in the whole
550 Casks & fixed the Freight at 45/ per Ton. These with 141
Barrels & 58 half Barrels on your own Account are chiefly on board
& the remainder promised to be shiped tomorrow & here I am left
aground wanting near 400 Barrels by the Masters computation to
fill up the Vessell. Capt. Francis is very averse to having that done
on your Account & myself by no means Inclined to do it but In case
of absolute necessity. What I have already Shiped is a little above
the price mention'd by you, but it was called for to keep the Ship
on her Legs after her Cargo of Coals were out & indeed was a means
of inviting others to Ship & of fixing the Freight at 45/ per Ton.
The half Barrels were given for Stowage & saves so much Freight.
        You may perceive the backwardness of people to ship for a
Market not very encouraging & in so large a Ship by the collection

---

[7] The ship *Nancy,* David Mitchell, was cleared outwards on Feb. 24, 1764,
for London. Naval Office Lists, 1764–1767, p. 75.

of this part of a Cargo being from no less than five different Houses. Rice seems Indeed to be on the decline & if more Vessels do not arrive within three or four days 'tis probable the price will fall & this may cause some alteration in your favour. Mean time the highest Freight to the Northern Markets has been 55/ to 57/6 according to the size of the Ship, save one small one agreed to go to Stettin for which £3 is given.

Be assured, Gentlemen, that I shall have a constant attention to your Interest & you shall hear from me as I go forward, who am with great regards, Yours, &ca.—

SOURCE: Letterbook copy, HL Papers, S. C. Hist. Soc.; addressed "Glasgow"; "per Mitchel. Copy per Floyd."

TO STEVENSON & LAIRD [8]

[Charles Town] 29th February 1764

Gentlemen,

Your favour of November last is come to hand by Capt. Porter[9] with a Bill Loading for 3 Casks Wine. If that Wine is as good as you think it & resembles Burgandy so nearly as to be little short of the best no doubt a few Dozens will sell here. You say 'tis from the Burgandy Grape therefore I shall call it by that name and give you the best & earliest Account I can of the Sale, who am with great Respect, Gentlemen, Your, &ca.—

SOURCE: Letterbook copy, HL Papers, S. C. Hist. Soc.; addressed "Port Glasgow"; "per Mitchel. Copy per Floyd."

TO DENNISTOUNE, MUNRO & CO. [1]

[Charles Town] 29th February 1764

Gentlemen,

Your favour of the 5th November after a very long Passage

---

[8] *HL Papers,* III, 172n.
[9] Capt. Hugh Porter of the *Dennistoune.*
[1] James Dennistoune (spelled "Dennistoun" here) and Ebenezer Munro (spelled "Monroe" here). *HL Papers,* III, 172n.

was deliver'd to me by Capt. Porter the day before Yesterday & I duly observe the Contents.

Since you are pleased to send your Snow *Dennistoun* again to my care I thank you for the honour you do me of leaving the management of her so much to myself, & you may rest satisfyed that I shall not abuse the confidence you repose in me, but as far as my judgement will reach, it shall be exercized for your Interest in which I heartily wish that I may not err.

Your Vessell is come at a critical time. Ships are going fast out of Port & come slowly into it & Rice is upon the latter. If some Ships of Burthen do not appear within a few days the price must fall to 40/ & Freight rise of course, but as this is a matter of uncertainty & a precarious dependence in this port I shall not trust to it too Long. My present thoughts are by no means to load one barrel upon your own Account if I can obtain even 50/ for Lisbon nay 45/ unless the price of Rice shou'd fall. At the same time I will not hastily accept off Freight at either of those rates but wait untill the Master has landed most of his Coals & begins to be in want of a foundation. This is just as I wou'd act if the Ship was my own & you shall hear in a few days what comes to pass. I belive Capt. Porter can dispose of the articles sent in his Snow full as well as anybody cou'd do & if my assistance is requisite he knows that he may always command it.

Now, Gentlemen, for your favour of the 9th September I am very much ashamed that it has lain by so long unanswered. It is owing wholly to that unlucky Ale brought in the Ship *Loudon*[2] which arrived rather too late in the season for Sale & my desire to support the price to £3.10/ per Dozen slackened the Sale, which I was in hopes wou'd revive again as this Winter came in, but such Quantity to that & other sorts of malt liquor have been imported that my expectations are quite baulked. I have used all the methods in my power to get it off but still a great deal remains which for your sakes to make an end of the account I lately offer'd at twelve Month Credit without Interest but cou'd not obtain my price. Some people complain that a good many bottles of this Ale in every Cask is thick & muddy & it is realy so. This has injured the Sale & then the late Imports have been sold at 50/ per Dozen. I say the hopes of making

---

[2] The ship *Loudon*, Andrew Lyon, had arrived from Glasgow on March 31, 1763. *Gazette*, April 2, 1763.

up this Sale from time to time has prevented my writing to you until I cou'd transmit the account. At length I have prevail'd on a Publican to take the remains at 50/ Six Months Credit the bottles to be counted. This is to be settled in some days hence & when done I shall transmit the Account & tho' I may be no gainfull one to you, you will see that I get nothing by it. Meantime I remain with great regard, Gentlemen, Your, &ca.—

SOURCE: Letterbook copy, HL Papers, S. C. Hist. Soc.; addressed "Glasgow"; "per Mitchel. Copy per Floyd."

TO SMITH & BAILLIES

[Charles Town] March 1st 1764

Gentlemen,

Inclosed is duplicate of a Letter wrote the 9th Ulto. intended to go by Capt. Basset Via Antigua to which I beg leave to refer. This covers Sale of your 5 Negroes per the *Sally* Net proceeds to the Credit of your Account Current £1,322, & I have also passed to your Credit for the Proceed of one Negro on Account of James Smith, Esquire[3] £228.17.6 both which I hope will be found free of Error & give content. I likewise Inclose you Invoice & Bill Loading for Sundry per this bearer the *Molly,* Capt. Vesey, on our Joint Account, Amount £4,096.2/ one half of which together with premium & policy of Insurance at £1,500 is charged to the debit of your Account Current £2,086.11/. I need not dictate to you what measures to pursue in the Sale of this Cargo. You will do what promises most for our mutual benefit & I shall be satisfyed with the issue.

Rum is exceeding low here. The produce of your Island Old & very good may be bought at 12/ to 12/6 per Gallon & Jamaica from 16/ to 17/6, New England 10/. There is such a vast quantity of every sort that I see little or no prospect of amendment very soon & probably not thro' the Summer. Therefore if I am so lucky as to have Cash in your hands together with the present Ballance of your own Account be pleased to invest the whole in New Negro men upon the best terms you can of any Country except Bite Slaves,[4] or in

---

[3] James Smith of Smith & Baillies.
[4] Calabar slaves came from the Bight of Biafra.

Young Boys & Girls not above 14 Years Old of Bites, having due attention to their health & freeness from blemishes & ship them by any good opportunity of a carefull humane Capt. coming to this Port.

I am making some efforts to have a parcell of clean sound Indian Corn at my Command about July or August next which is attended generaly with trouble & difficulty to collect at that season. Please to let me know if an assorted Cargo wou'd be acceptable to you in which you may if you please direct a Moiety or more on your Own Account.

Ships begin to be scarce & if many do not soon arrive Rice must fall & Freight Rise but our Planters strugle hard to support their produce & their circumstances are such as will admit of it. Capt. Floyd in the *Sally* now lies ready for Sea. I cleared him out a week ago but some of his Seamen Inlisted on board a Man of War & he has been detained to replace them with other Men.[5] I Remain, &ca.—

SOURCE: Letterbook copy, HL Papers, S. C. Hist. Soc.; addressed "St. Christophers"; "per Vesey."

TO MARTIN & STEVENS

[Charles Town] 1 March 1764

Gentlemen,

Annex'd is duplicate of what I wrote to you per Capt. Bassett the 14th Ulto. to which I refer. This incloses your Account Current ballance in your favour & carried forward to your Credit in a New Account £356.14.0 which I hope will be found free from error. There is a charge of Corn short accounted by Capt. Thomas in the *Prussian Hero*[6] which you formerly permitted me to make but I have not yet done it because the Gentleman to whome it belonged has not made a final Settlement of his Account but he promises next time he comes to Town & I shall lay that addition as lightly as I can perswade him to submit to.

---

[5] See HL to Henry Bright & Co., March 3, 1764.
[6] The brigantine *Prussian Hero*, Joseph Thomas, was entered inwards in ballast on Dec. 16, 1762, from Antigua. She was cleared outwards on Jan. 12, 1763, for Antigua with a cargo which included 1,600 bushels of corn. Naval Office Lists, 1757–1764, pp. 113, 127.

Rum is extreamly low here. The best of Leeward Island produce may be bought at 12/ to 13/ per Gallon, New England at 10/, Jamaica 16 to 17/6, & vast stores of every kind upon hand. Negroes are in great demand & sell high. I lately sold a few from the West Indies at an average of £37.10/ Sterling Net proceeds Duty, Freight, &ca. all paid, but no doubt we shall be fully supply'd & great abatement of prices before the Summer is over. Ships begin to be much wanted & if many do not soon arrive the price of Rice must fall & Freight rise from its late & present low ebb 40/ to 45/ per Ton for England & 55/ to Holland. I remain, your, &ca.—

P.S. I inclose another Copy of Mr. Martin's Account Current.

SOURCE: Letterbook copy, HL Papers, S. C. Hist. Soc.; addressed "Antigua"; "per Vesey."

TO JEREMIAH NIBBS, JR.

[Charles Town] 1st March 1764

Sir,

On the other side is duplicate of what I wrote you under the 11th Ulto. Please now to receive Account Sale of your 10 hogsheads Rum per Curlet,[7] Net proceeds £846.5.3 to the Credit of your Account Current which you will find to be in average 15 per Cent more than the Cash price of Rum, obtain'd by my selling it upon Credit in the usual Course of my Trade.

There is now £175.10/ outstanding on the Sale. All of it is good unless that part £101.10/ due by George Walker shou'd prove otherwise. He died about four days after I last wrote to you. I thought him very safe while alive & don't know that his Estate is otherwise. Of this I shall be more fully informed in the Course of this Week when an appraisement is to be made. If there appears to be enough to pay his debts I shall remitt the whole & rely on you to reimburse me in case of accident. If there is any great doubt, that part must lay over & I shall immediately remit the Ballance as you have directed in a Bill of my own draught.[8]

---

[7] The ship *Maria*, Patrick Curlett, was entered inwards on June 7, 1763, from Antigua with 9 tierces of sugar and 117 hogsheads and 2 tierces of rum. Naval Office Lists, 1757–1764, p. 120.

[8] George Walker, Sr., vintner, was buried on Feb. 19, 1764. *Register of St.*

Rum is now exceeding plenty here & the price is low at 12/ to 12/6 for the produce of the Leeward Islands nor do I see any prospect of amendment even if not one hogshead shou'd be imported for some months to come. Rice is 42/6 & rather declining. Exchange 714 to 721 per Cent. I remain, Yours, &ca.—

P.S. I paid your Bill to the order of Hedrington & Kinocke[9] £3.12.2 & passed the same to your debit at 400 per Cent, £14.8.8.[1]

SOURCE: Letterbook copy, HL Papers, S. C. Hist. Soc.; addressed "Antigua"; "per Vesey."

TO JAMES SMITH

[Charles Town] 1st March 1764

Sir,

I had the favour of yours 2d January per Cap. Floyd who delivered me one Gold Coast Man on your Account. The Man was Old discoverable by his Gray hairs & wither'd face & besides he had suffer'd on the Voyage by Cold & was not a little swell'd in the Legs. I caused proper care to be taken of him & after some days sold him as per Contra Account Net proceeds as you order to the Credit of Messrs. Smith & Baillies £228.17.6 which I think is a great price for such goods. As 'tis highly probable our Market will be very fully supply'd this ensuing Summer I dare not incourage your further attempts in Negroes unless prime Slaves can be bought very low with you I mean of Affrican Cargoes. As to those that you call season'd they pay a duty here of £60 per head[2] & therefore you cannot afford to send them. Whenever you think that I can serve you be pleased

---

Philip's Parish, 1754–1810, p. 306. Walker's estate consisted of personal property valued at slightly more than £3,000 currency plus 60 pages of open accounts in the day book. Inventories, 1763–1767, pp. 89–90, S. C. Archives.

[9] John Hetherington and Alexander Kynock, Charleston merchants, announced the end of their partnership in the *Gazette*, Oct. 29, 1763. John Hetherington borrowed large sums of money in 1763. Judgment Rolls, 1763, Nos. 66A, 80A, 81A; 1764, Nos. 15A, 64A, S. C. Archives. The provost marshal sold the goods of Hetherington & Kynock at their store on the Bay on April 26, 1764. *General Gazette*, April 18, 1764.

[1] £3.12.2 Antigua currency equaled £14.8.8 S. C. currency.

[2] There was a duty of £50 currency (in addition to the regular import duty of £10) on slaves imported from British colonies who had been in such colonies over six months. *S. C. Statutes*, III, 743. These were called "season'd" slaves.

to lay your commands on me, Who am with great regard, Sir, Your most humble Servant—

SOURCE: Letterbook copy, HL Papers, S. C. Hist. Soc.; addressed "Esquire. St. Christophers"; "per Vesey."

TO JOHN COMING BALL

[Charles Town] 2d March 1764

Dear Sir,

You & I have been so long aquainted that I shou'd have thought there was no room for professions of your willingness allways to serve your friends. My experience had made me take that matter for granted & therefore I craved your assistance in procuring Indian Corn for me without the least doubt of your serving therein as far as lay in your power.

I depend very much on you for a Thousand or fifteen hundred Bushels by the 10 or 12th Inst. Mr. Perdriau[3] who probably will take a bed with you will tell you the Case & Inform you that [we] have a much larger quantity in the Country but it cannot be brought to Town in time. I wou'd Chuse it to come in Bulk.

I have spoke to Watboo Johny[4] & he promises to bring down your Pitch this trip & If so I will take it off your hands, having room for it in the new Ship,[5] tho the price is falen & must go down lower as there is no Freight to be taken up in the Harbour the last let out today 50/ for London. Therefore I hope he will not fail to bring it down. I am glad you did not meddle with the Green Tar. I put a hogshead Rum marked J C BALL Quantity 113 Gallons on board Mr. Watts Schooner fill'd to the Bung as you directed. I must confess I did not mention the Freight to him 'till after it was on board & then he laugh'd at my offer of 10/ which for my own part I shou'd have thought a good Freight. As soon as Mr. Huger came to town

---

[3] Benjamin Perdriau, Jr., HL's clerk.

[4] The patroon of the Watboo schooner.

[5] John Edwards & Co. had advertised the ship *Heart of Oak* "To sail with all expedition" for London. *Gazette,* Feb. 18, 1764. The *Heart of Oak* must have cleared outwards during the period between March 20 and April 5, a period for which the clearances are lacking. The manifest, dated March 29, 1764, shows that only Gabriel Manigault shipped pitch on the *Heart of Oak.* Naval Office Lists, 1764–1767, p. 57.

I offered him five thousand pounds on your Account. He seem'd inclined to defer taking it until he shou'd go into the Country & return again saying he had no use for the Money 'till then[6] but as I knew it wou'd be satisfactory to you to have an acknowledgment of part of the consideration Money & a promise to make you Titles for his Land I proposed to him my own Note payable in ten days which was very agreeable to him & I here inclose you a Copy of his receipt. Your further Commands at this head shall be obeyed.

One Northerly Wind made me send Dickinson up Ashley River & he cleared a Freight of £30, in place of being Idle. The wind being Northerly when he return'd I order'd him away to Port Royal in hope he will soon be back again with a Load of Corn for me or Rice if he fails in the other.

The price of Rice is declining & indeed there is no demand for it at present therefore I am not Sorry that he did not go to Wambaw just now. I told you the price of the 7 hogsheads Rum to be paid for in Corn but not puting it down Imediately I cannot charge my Memory exactly with the odd pence but you will recollect & enable me to fill up the Blank. I am Yours, &ca.—

SOURCE: Letterbook copy, Letter Book of Henry Laurens, Oct. 30, 1762–Sept. 10, 1766, Penn. Hist. Soc.

TO TIMOTHY CREAMER

[Charles Town] 2d March 1764

I have sent by Wambaw Boat 37 Barrels Salt, Quantity 3,207 Bushels. Please [take] good care of it.

Let Mr. Perdriau have any of my Horses that he pleases & be very kind too & careful of that one that he will leave with you untill his return. Please to inform me if you can strip any Red Oak Bark this Spring. I am Yours, &ca.—

SOURCE: Letterbook copy, Letter Book of Henry Laurens, Oct. 30, 1762–Sept. 10, 1766, Penn. Hist. Soc.

---

[6] Daniel Huger was making plans at this time to sail for England. *Gazette*, Feb. 25, March 3, 1764. The date of the deed was March 12, ten days after the date of this letter.

TO JACOB COX[7]

[Charles Town] 2d March 1764

Sir,

Meeting with a Barrel Pork from my own Plantation which I know to be Corn fed & of the best kind I have under favour of Mr. Bedon[8] put it on board his Sloop marked in different places JC & tinn'd over the Bung. I beg your acceptence of the said Barrel of Pork. It is but a very small acknowledgement of a great many favours Rece'd from you & when you think of any thing this country produces that will be acceptable in your Island or of any services that I can render you, I shall be glad to receive your Commands, Who am with great regard, Sir, Your most humble Servant—

SOURCE: Letterbook copy, HL Papers, S. C. Hist. Soc.; addressed "Esquire. New Providence"; "per favour of Mr. John Bedon."

TO WILLIAM MANNING[9]

[Charles Town] 2d March 1764

Sir,

I have been very remiss & beg your pardon for not acknowledging the receipt of your favours under the 31 July & 12th November last & thanking you for your endeavours to recover the Amount of those protested Bills left in your hands by Capt. James Gilcrist. The Account you give of the drawers at St. Eustatia[1] is a bad one &

---

[7] The Cox family was a well-known family of Bermuda. One member Florentius Cox had moved to the Bahamas where he became in 1743 speaker of the assembly. Jacob Cox was probably a member of this family. Henry C. Wilkinson, *Bermuda in the Old Empire* (London, 1950), pp. 72, 191.

[8] The sloop *Betsey*, William Grime, owned by John Ross and John Raven Bedon of Charleston and registered on June 30, 1763, in Providence, was cleared outwards on March 3 for Providence. Naval Office Lists, 1764–1767, p. 75.

[9] This is HL's first extant (it may actually be the first) letter to William Manning, merchant of St. Kitts and later of London, who played such a large role in Laurens's career. Manning already had had mercantile connections with S. C. *HL Papers*, III, 202, 478. He must have moved to London late in 1767, for in 1768 he was a partner in Bannister, Hammond, & Manning at No. 15 St. Mary Axe. *London Directories.* Manning's daughter would later marry HL's son John. Wallace, *Life of Henry Laurens*, pp. 464–467.

[1] Messrs. Heileger & Hertun, Peter Cornelius & Docke Grober, merchants at St. Eustatius. See HL to James Gilchrist, June 22, 1763, *HL Papers*, III, 477–478.

if you have no better hopes of recovering from them be so kind to transmit the Bills & Acts of protest to me that I may make some attempt to come at the Endorsers Joseph & Shadlock Rivers[2] but I shall be extremely obliged to you since you have taken this troublesome affair in hand to make one more inquiry into the circumstances of the drawers. The Expence you have already been at or may farther be shall be thankfully repaid—either to any of your friends here or it may be that I may when you are pleased to encourage it trouble you to sell some of our produce for me. The Business of those Bills concerns me only as one of the late House of Austin, Laurens, & Appleby but as I am the only one of them now in Trade I think it my duty to do all in my power to serve the old friends of that House whose property the Bills are, as far as lays in my power. Your assistance therefore will be very obliging & always acknowledged as a particular favour to me, who am with great regard, &ca.—

SOURCE: Letterbook copy, HL Papers, S. C. Hist. Soc.; addressed "Esquire. St. Christophers"; "per Captain Vesey."

TO JOHN COMING BALL

[Charles Town] 3d March 1764

Dear Sir,

By this time you have what I wrote you by Mr. Perdreau. This morning I received yours by Mr. Merrywlees. Diamond is going up for the Corn & I have lent him two of the Wambaw Old Sails to dunnage[3] with. Pray hasten him with as much as you can possibly get in the Boat.

I this day rece'd from Mr. Manigault the further Sum of £2,000 & deliver'd him your Bond for £7,000. The good Old Gentleman insists upon making a Note in it that you shall pay no Interest on that Sum £2,000 before this day. I said do as you please, Sir. I am, dear Sir, Yours, &ca.—

SOURCE: Letterbook copy, Letter Book of Henry Laurens, Oct. 30, 1762–Sept. 10, 1766, Penn. Hist. Soc.

---

[2] Shadlock Rivers was the son of Capt. Joseph Rivers of Philadelphia who had died by May 1764. See HL to William Hopton, May 29, 1764.

[3] Dunnage was "Light material . . . stowed among and beneath the cargo of a vessel to keep it from injury by chafing or wet." OED.

TO HENRY BRIGHT & CO.

[Charles Town] 3d March 1764

Gentlemen,

When I wrote you last on the 24 Ulto. I was in great hopes that the *Sally* wou'd have been at Sea in a day or two after, but four of her Seamen after abusing Capt. Floyd in a most vilainous manner on board his own Ship, Entered on board His Majesty's Ship *Escort,* Thomas Foley, Esquire, Commander.[4] This embarassed us a good deal. To replace them was a dificulty that cou'd not be got over until last night & in the mean time Mr. Foley gave us some trouble by demanding about £11.10/ Sterling Wages due to those Seamen. I represented the case to him & remonstrated thereupon to shew the hardship there wou'd be if the Owners of the *Sally* shou'd be obliged to pay such wages to Men who had forfeited them to all intents & purposes, behaved in a piratical manner, & involved the Ship in New Expences & finally that as it was my duty so I was determin'd to defend & support Capt. Floyd's cause as far as Law & equity wou'd countinance my endevours. To these things that Gentleman was unpolitely Deaf for I rece'd no other answer from him than by his Lawyer who called upon me with notice that he had orders to Libel the Ship; hoping to alarm me into a complyance. I thank you for the Notice, Sir, but do as you please, was my reply, & then I sent Capt. Floyd to retain another Gentleman of the wrangling faculty & to offer me as his surety. Since that all has been silent. Therefore I conclude £10 Currency has Canceled the demand & that I shall hear no more of it.

Please now to receive Invoices & Bill Loading inclosed & also one of Capt. Floyds receipts for disbursments in which he has been remarkably frugal. First for Seventy Barrels of fine Rice, Amount with the disbursment £1,047.11.10 & secondly for pitch, Tar, & Turpentine on board the *Sally* on Account of your Good selves or my Account if you think that I have too far exceeded your orders

---

[4] Capt. Thomas Foley, who had taken command of HMS *Escorte* on Sept. 2, 1763 at Deptford, had arrived in Charleston harbor with his vessel on Jan. 7, 1764. This vessel remained on the Carolina station until June 17, 1767, when she sailed over New Providence bar for Spithead. For three and a half years Captain Foley was involved in the enforcement of the navigation acts. He had begun his work on Jan. 18, 1764, by sending his men on board two vessels in Charleston harbor. As this letter indicates, he had filled up his crew by taking seamen from the *Sally*. Ship's log, HMS *Escorte*, Adm. 51/323, Public Record Office, London.

in Amount £2,753.3.7, the whole charged to your Account Current & for the whole I shall take the liberty to pass my Bills on you, but if you deliver the Naval Stores to Messrs. Cowles & Harford, then you will also send my draughts for so much to them for payment. But I shall not draw altho I am in advance for the whole until I am in want of Money or can meet with the most favourable terms of running days & of Exchange.

I have done all in my power on this occasion to serve your Interest & so shall I exert myself to serve you upon every future occasion when you shall see it needfull to lay your commands on me, Who am with great regard, Gentlemen, Your, &ca.—

[P.S.] Rice 42/6 & on the Decline because we have few Ships remaining—

SOURCE: Letterbook copy, HL Papers, S. C. Hist. Soc.; addressed "Owners of the Ship *Sally,* Bristol"; "per Floyd. Copy per Hooper."

TO COWLES & HARFORD

[Charles Town] 3d March 1764

Gentlemen,

I advised you in my last the 14th February of 2 Draughts on you, one for £530 and one for £100 Sterling, to which please to be referr'd.

I have loaden on board the bearer the *Sally,* Capt. Floyd, 483 Barrels of very fine Pitch, 129 Barrels of Green Tar, & 54 Barrels of Turpentine which somewhat exceeds the order that was given to me by her Owners Henry Bright, Esquire & Co. & therefore if they do not chuse to indulge me they are at liberty to reject the whole & in such case will deliver it over to you on my Account & you will be pleased to sell it & pass the proceeds in due course to my Credit. I had been collecting these naval Stores for my own use having no orders for such & might have sold them to advantage, but while I act as a factor I am always open to the adress of my friends & except in very extraordinary cases, will always give them the preference. Upon this principle I have conducted myself in this present affair & am in no doubt of the Gentlemens taking to the goods; nevertheless as 'tis the first time I have done business for them, 'tis necessary that I shou'd use this precaution.

We have now but few Ships remaining in Port. Rice is at 42/6 & the demand very Little. Naval Stores will soon come to Market in pleanty & the price be govern'd chiefly by the Freight that may hereafter be given. I am loading about 800 or 900 Barrels on two Ships for London, part at 40/ & part 45/ per Ton, but 50/ is now offer'd. Good Copper Indigo still sells briskly at 26 to 27/6 per lb. & three days ago a parcell belonging to the Estate of one of the late Johnson's was sold at Auction[5] & yielded as high as 28/ for a quality in my Opinion 6d Sterling per pound inferior to that which I shiped per your Brigantine *Favourite*. These people who purchase are steady Men & must certainly have better inteligence than I have. For my part I dread to hear the fate of what I have Shiped. Deer Skins continue above your limits & indeed not many come to town. The Creek Indians have been pretty quiet since I last mention'd them to you, but our intercourse with them is greatly interupted if not altogether Stoped. Whither they mean to remain as they are or that they are only meditating another blow is quite uncertain. They may do as they please for ought that we (in a publick manner) are doing to repel them.

Messrs. Okill & Rigg[6] in a late Letter say they had offer'd to pay you £8.11.5 Sterling on Account of Austin & Laurens & that your reply was that you had no Bill. See Letter 4th March 1762 to Mr. James Cowles with a Bill at 10 Days sight & mine to yourselves the 12th October following.[7]

I have not to add now but that I am with true respect & Esteem, Gentlemen, Yours, &ca.—

SOURCE: Letterbook copy, HL Papers, S. C. Hist. Soc.; addressed "Bristol"; "per Floyd. Copy per Gunn."

---

[5] Archibald Johnston died on Dec. 13, 1762—"one of the first best, and most considerable Indico-makers, in this province." *Gazette*, Dec. 17, 1763. Andrew Johnston, Archibald's brother, died on Jan. 6, 1764. *HL Papers*, I, 29n. Although both brothers planted indigo near Georgetown, the parcel mentioned in the letter belonged to Archibald. John and William Allston and Thomas Lynch had advertised Archibald Johnston's indigo in the *Gazette*, Feb. 4, 1764, for sale on Feb. 28—"well known to be the best parcel ever made in this province."

[6] Okill & Rigg of Liverpool. *HL Papers*, II, 525n.

[7] No copy of the letter of March 4, 1762, has been found; that of Oct. 12 is printed in *HL Papers*, III, 131–132.

TO RICHARD OSWALD & CO.

[Charles Town] 3d March 1764

Gentlemen,

Since my Last 12 December per Ball & Brownett I have the favour of yours of the 5 November per the hands of Doctor Hugh Rose[8] & in consequence of your recommendation I have paid & shall continue to pay all due attention to that Gentleman. He hath rece'd a hearty welcome at my house & I will do him all the service in my power. At present he is in the Country; I may say to reconnoitre a certain district & make some acquaintance with the inhabitants, where his very good friend Dr. Garden advices him to settle. 'Tis a place about 35 Miles distant from this called Monks Corner in a very populous & good Neighbourhood, from whence Doctor Keith[9] is now retiring & will give place to Mr. Rose.

Please now to receive a Bill of Exchange of Yesterdays date Smith & Farr[1] on Sarah Nicholson & Co. at 90 Days sight to my order & by me endors'd to you on Account of John Rutherford, Esquire for £300 Sterling which Sum you will be pleased to apply to the Credit of his Bond. I have not been quite Punctual in remitting the Sum promised on his account because I had been amused with a promise of this & a larger Sum through the regular Channel of the Receiver General which wou'd be better on Mr. Rutherfords Account as well as mine. The remainder if I cannot coin it out of his own Stock I must advance & will remit by the *Heart of Oak* to sail some day in April.

I have an Inclination to send a small Vessel to your Factory at Bance Island for Negroes for my own Use provided I cou'd Ship Some Articles from hence that wou'd assist in paying the Purchase & the remains in Bills of Exchange. I therefore beg the favour of

---

[8] Dr. Hugh Rose, a Scotsman, lived for 18 years in the parish of St. John Berkeley. He was a tory and sailed with the British fleet in December 1782 for East Florida but was shipwrecked on the way. He estimated his professional income during his Carolina years at £500 sterling per annum. Loyalist Transcripts, LVI, 407–416.

[9] Dr. William Keith, who had lived at Keithfield near Moncks Corner in St. John Berkeley, died Aug. 13, 1777. Joseph I. Waring, *A History of Medicine in South Carolina, 1670–1825* (Columbia, S. C., 1964), p. 376; Irving, *A Day on Cooper River*, p. 123; *SCHM*, XXI (1920), 115; "Will of William Keith," dated Aug. 3, 1777, proved ————, Charleston County Wills, XVII, Book B (1774–1779), 642–644, S. C. Archives. He had married Anne Cordes before 1752. *SCHM*, XLIII (1942), 140–141.

[1] Robert Smyth and Thomas Farr, Jr.

your opinion of my scheme, & information of such Goods as will be acceptable at your Settlement & the Sterling price of prime Negroes delivered there, that if practicable I may provide in time for the next Season.

I shall have two Plantations to settle[2] & think I may procure hands by this means upon lower terms than purchasing here & this method of Selling Negroes if I remmember right is most consistant with the Plan laid down by yourselves.

This Winter I cou'd have ship'd New England Rum at 8/6 Currency per Gallon which is lower than it can be laid in for at Boston & West India Rum in proportion. A Cargo of Negros, about 120 Angolos from Antigua,[3] sold a few days ago at an average of £43 Sterling, but this cannot hold when the usual supplies arrive. I remain, Yours, &c.—

SOURCE: Letterbook copy, HL Papers, S. C. Hist. Soc.; addressed "London"; "per Floyd. Copy per Wills with 2d Bill of Exchange."

TO OKILL & RIGG

[Charles Town] 3d March 1764

Gentlemen,

I am indebted for your favour of the 31 October and agreable to your request have made further enquiry of Messrs. Brewton & Smith how much they had remitted Mr. Blaquin,[4] & Mr. Brewtons answer to me just now is they have already sent £2,500 Sterling in Bills of Exchange, have the Value of about £300 Sterling in Rice Ship'd & to sail next Week & that the whole Ballance will be remitted in two or three Months. I thank you Gentlemen for your kind offer of a Commission upon this occassion but the service affords no foundation for a Claim of that sort & you are most heartily welcome to it & more whenever you please to command me.

The Bill drawn on you for a trifling Ballance was to Mr. James Cowles & I have so reminded Messrs. Cowles & Harford of

---

[2] New Hope on the south side of the Altamaha River and Broughton Island on the north side.

[3] The brigantine *Hope*, William Royall had brought 117 slaves from Antigua. Naval Office Lists, 1764–1767, p. 70.

[4] See HL to Okill & Rigg, July 14, 1763. *HL Papers*, III, 492.

the circumstance that you will probably hear from them soon. I remain with great regard, &c.—

SOURCE: Letterbook copy, HL Papers, S. C. Hist. Soc.; addressed "Liverpool"; "per Floyd. Copy per Wills."

TO JOHN KNIGHT

[Charles Town] March 5th, 1764

Dear Sir,

The 24th Ulto. I wrote to you per Capt. Smith for your Port[5] & Capt. Condon Via Bristol, since which say on the 1st Inst. your Ship *Hope,* Capt. Dennison, Sailed well over our Bar. I have heard no complaints from himself nor the Pilot & am therefore hopefull that in her present trim she will go safely to your door where you will probably think of what is best to be done with such a crazy carcass.

Please to receive herewith Invoice & Bill Loading for 600 Barrels Rice on board the said *Hope* & one of the Masters Receipts for disbursements the whole amounting to £8,484.17.7 is placed to the debit of your Account.

The *Swift,* Capt. Devill, & *Hopewell,* Capt. Pitt, for Oporto who both arived just five Weeks before Dennison are still here, neither of them carry so much Rice by 100 Barrels as the *Hopes* present Cargo. This will give your Vessels some advantage perticularly the *Austin.* I am doing all in my power to make a tolerable end of your Accounts. I shou'd be glad to serve you to better effect but since my uttmost abilitys are exerted I am sure you will require no more from me. Rice is at 40/ & must go lower if Ships do not soon arive to take of[f] considerable Quantitys still on hand. I continue to be with much Affection Your, &c.—

SOURCE: Letterbook copy, HL Papers, S. C. Hist. Soc.; addressed "Liverpool"; "per Wills."

---

[5] The brigantine *Tryphena,* John Smith, was cleared outwards on Feb. 23 for Liverpool. Naval Office Lists, 1764–1767, p. 74.

TO HENRY BYRNE

[Charles Town] 7 March 1764

Sir,

On the other side is a duplicate of what I wrote you the 25th Ulto. per the *Hope,* Capt. Dennison, to which please to be referr'd. This waits on you per Capt. Pitt in the Brigantine *Hopewell* & Incloses Invoice & Bill Loading for 90 Barrels of very good Rice on board the said Brigantine on my own proper Account which you will be pleased to receive & Sell at such time and in such manner as you think most for my benefit & remit the proceeds as soon as you can to Mrs. Sarah Nicholson & Co. in London.

Capt. Devill sailed this day, the other Little Vessel is Loading & I know not of any more Rice destin'd for your Market this Season but some may unexpectedly Start up. Rice is now at 40/ per Ct., a few Ships in Port. I am with great Regard—

SOURCE: Letterbook copy, HL Papers, S. C. Hist. Soc.; addressed "Esquire. Oporto"; "per Pitt."

ADVERTISEMENT

March 10, 1764

TO BE SOLD at public vendue, on monday the 9th of *April* next, at the late dwelling house of Mrs. ANNE AIR,[6] deceased, in Tradd-street:

---

[6] Anne Air was the widow of William Air, mariner, who died in 1754. "Will of William Air," dated April 16, 1754, proved July 5, 1754, Charleston County Wills, VII (1752–1756), 241, S. C. Archives. Anne Air was buried on Feb. 25, 1764. *Register of St. Philip's Parish, 1754–1810,* p. 306. She had ordered HL and John Savage, her executors, to sell her estate and place the proceeds at interest which would be used to educate her two sons, William and James. "Will of Anne Air," dated Sept. 28, 1763, proved March 2, 1764, Charleston County Wills, x, Book B (1760–1767), 447–449, S. C. Archives. William was born April 12, 1749 and died Dec. 5, 1775. *Register of St. Philip's Parish, 1720–1758,* p. 96; *SCHM,* x (1909), 223. James, who was born Feb. 16, 1752, took his medical degree at Leyden, where he wrote his thesis *De Pleuritide,* dated July 8, 1775, and dedicated it to his Charleston teacher Dr. Alexander Garden, his Leyden professor John Frederick Gronovius, and Henry Laurens. In 1776 he became "Assistant to the General Hospital" in Charleston. He died June 19, 1777. Joseph Ioor Waring, *A History of Medicine in South Carolina, 1670–1825* (Columbia, S. C., 1964), p. 173.

ALL her SHOPGOODS, consisting of a variety of linens, callicoes, threads, ribbons, glass and stone ware, cutlery and other articles: Also, her NEGROES, among whom are a washer, another a seamstress, and 1 boy who is a good chimney sweeper, &c., all used to household work;[7] also the household furniture consisting of many useful particulars. The sale to begin at 10 o'clock A. M.—All such as have demands on the estate of the said deceased, are desired to give in their accounts attested; and those who are indebted, to make immediate payment to either of us, executors of her last will and testament.

JOHN SAVAGE.
HENRY LAURENS.

SOURCE: Printed in *Gazette,* March 10, 1764.

ADVERTISEMENT

March 10, 1764

For LISBON, or COWES and the MARKETS, The Snow DENNISTOUNE, HUGH PORTER, Master, (A stout handy Vessel). For freight apply to

HENRY LAURENS

N.B. About fifty Tons of COALS on board to be sold.

SOURCE: Printed in *Gazette,* March 10, 1764.

TO JOHN ETTWEIN

[Charles Town] 13 March 1764

Reverend Sir,

In the last Vessel from England I receiv'd the inclosed Letter which I have detain'd for some days untill I cou'd meet with a good opportunity to convey it & now transmit it together with all your

---

[7] The "Shop Goods," "House & Kitchin Furniture," and slaves were valued at £2,981.1.3 currency. There were five slaves: "Dinah (Old Wench) Cook" valued at £150, "Judith (Young Wench) Washer & Ironer" at £300, "Katy (well grown Girl) Needlework but very sickly" at £50, "Marriah (younger Girl) Ditto healthy" at £200, and "Toney (well grown Boy) Chimney sweeper much diseased" at £50. The appraisal, made by John McCall, Josiah Smith, Jr., Maurice Jones, and Edward Lightwood, Jr., was certified by HL and John Savage on May 18. Inventories, 1763–1767, pp. 91–95, S. C. Archives.

Gazetts and one Letter that I wrote in December last to Doctor Shubart which after some time was return'd to me by the hands of my friend Mr. Joseph Kershaw[8] in one packet directed to you which he will be carefull to foward.

I paid due regard to the Doctor's recommendation of the Reverend Mr. Frederick Post who after some days sojourning here took a passage for Jamaica. I expect soon to hear of his arrival there.

With respect to those *Urinals* which I had wrote for a second time to Philadelphia, please to read the following extract of a Letter from my friend Mr. William Fisher dated the 25th February & arriv'd Yesterday: "I have agreable to thy request endevour'd to get the Six peices of Glass called Urinals & have searched all through the City & cannot find any but with Necks such as James Verree took with him but am inform'd by a Gentleman that he expects such as those discribed in the Spring by some of the first Vessels from London. If they come shall be careful to send them per first opportunity after their Arival." W.F.

By this the Doctor may know that I have not forgoten his Commission & may still intertain hopes of being supply'd with the Article so much wanted.

I know too well how much an att[a]chment to the business of this World is apt to wipe out of our memories subjects of lesser importance. Besides this, Charity instructs me to make excuses for the delay of expected Letters from my friends. Accidents may happen to them on the Road & in a hundred other ways they may be detain'd or miscarri'd. Therefore I will not yet suppose that my Brother Merchant Mr. Vangammern has neglected his promise of writing to me & particularly upon two Subjects. One if I remember right was the Plan of Wachovia with the Towns of Bethabara & Bethany

---

[8] Letters had passed between Charleston and the Moravians via Joseph Kershaw of Pine Tree Hill. *Records of the Moravians in North Carolina*, 1, 277. Kershaw had come from Yorkshire to Charleston where he had served as clerk in the counting house of James Laurens & Co. In 1758 he established a country store for Ancrum, Lance, & Loocock at Pine Tree Hill. In 1763 he married Sarah Mathis, a Quaker. As the leading entrepreneur of his region, he was the founder of Camden. Kershaw changed the name of Pine Tree Hill to Camden in 1768 to honor Charles Pratt, Lord Camden, who had spoken out against the declaration of the right of Parliament to tax the colonies. Kershaw died in 1791 at the age of sixty-four. Thomas J. Kirkland and Robert M. Kennedy, *Historic Camden, Part One, Colonial and Revolutionary* (Columbia, S. C., 1905), pp. 375–381.

accurately marked thereon.[9] The other, a Letter recommending one of the Bretheren in Pensilvania who is curious in Workmanship & cou'd supply or procure for me a Neat Chamber Organ.[1]

I also mention'd to him the want of a Carravan, or better kind of Wagon, but this article I have determin'd to import from London.

The Plat of your Lands, since it was offer'd to me, I must confess I am covitous of & should be extreamly glad to obtain it.

Next Week please God we live Mrs. Laurens & all our family will remove to our new House where we hope such of yours as come to Charles Town will stop a few minutes as they approach to Town.

All the publick News that this place affords you will find in the Newspapers to which I shall endevour to add a few from Philadelphia & refer to them.

After this I have only to add the tenderness of my Love & good wishes to you, my Dear Sir, as well as to all your Bretheren, & remain Your Affectionate & most humble Servant—

SOURCE: Letterbook copy, Letter Book of Henry Laurens, Oct. 30, 1762–Sept. 10, 1766, Penn. Hist. Soc.

LETTER OF ATTORNEY
FROM EGERTON LEIGH

March 13, 1764

[Egerton Leigh, who was leaving South Carolina "in a short time,"

---

[9] For a number of maps of Bethabara, Bethania, and Wachovia, such as HL desired, see *Records of the Moravians in North Carolina*, I, 132, 273, 310, 364, 375, 433, 482.

[1] Entry in Bethabara diary, July 8, 1762: ". . . in the evening we heard an organ played for the first time in Carolina, and were very happy and thankful that it had reached us safely." *Records of the Moravians in North Carolina*, I, 247. "This small, one-rank organ was taken from Bethlehem, Pennsylvania, to North Carolina by a group of Moravian settlers led by Pastor Johann Michael Graff. The group left Bethlehem on April 20, 1762. . . ." This was a Klemm-Tannenberg organ. Johann Gottlob Klemm had arrived in Bethlehem in November 1757 where during the next four-and-a-half years he passed on to David Tannenberg the craft of organ building as he had learned it in Europe. The editors do not know if HL ever obtained an organ from Pennsylvania, but on Sept. 22, 1777, HL and other members of the Continental Congress having been driven out of Philadelphia by the British were entertained "with singing and playing on the organ" at Bethlehem. William H. Armstrong, *Organs for America, The Life and Work of David Tannenberg* (Philadelphia, Penn., 1967), pp. 12, 33, 87–88.

made out his power of attorney to HL, William Burrows, and Robert Williams, Jr., giving them authority to settle, collect, and pay his debts, to make remittances to him in Great Britain, and to act in his place as surveyor general.]

SOURCE: Copy, Miscellaneous Records, MM, Part 1 (1763–1767), pp. 95–97, S. C. Archives.

TO JOSEPH BROWN

[Charles Town] 15th March 1764

Dear Sir,

I have sundry of your favours now before me to which I shall briefly reply as far as is at present needful.

First I really am so distress'd for Cash because no body makes me payments & I have been oblig'd to make large purchases & every body expects punctuality from me, that I have three or four times broke in upon a Sum of Money laid by to send you. This I repeated yesterday & am now poor again. If you suffer any inconvenience on this Account, I must be answerable for it. Mean time I send you five fine Negroes for Sale. Each hath a Blanket & I hope will produce as much as the rest that I have sold here, Vizt. £330 to £320, payable in two Months, & some for Cash & in my opinion these are equal to any of them save the difference that fancy may make. You will sell these & pass the proceeds after deducting your Commission to my Credit.

I allow'd you the heigth of the Market, Vizt. 70/ per Barrel for the pitch you sent me, of which you shall have a particular Account when Mr. Perdriau returns. To have put it into the hands of any Factor would have been only to throw away 2½ per Cent Commission which you will find upon enquiry. Such Pitch as was only bare weight or lacked 5 or 6 lbs. per Barrel I bought for £3 to £3.3/, the latter fill'd up & Cooper'd. I never trust Capt. Dick nor others with any business that should be transacted only between you & me & I am afraid in saying that I was *enrag'd* about the Indigo, you have made use of too harsh a word. I was never in any rage about the matter, & whatever those people may have said to you must arise from their own ingenuity & from half words pick'd up in

my House for I am sure I never consulted them about it. Every body
that saw your purchases did say they were very badly made & I
can't help thinking so still, but our Sales will testify whether I am
right or wrong. 'Tis impossible to stop curiosity. People will be
peeping into Indigo & giving their sentiments & making comparisons
between one parcel & another & I do not know any thing more natural
than for Men [of] Trade to declare when a purchase is made for
them whether they think it a good & advantageous one or other wise,
but the construction you put upon this matter, that the Complaint
was made upon a falling Market is mean & beneath the Character
of a Merchant nay of every Man of common Candour & Honesty.
No Sir, the Moment I saw [the] Indigo, when every one was warm
in the pursuit of that article here in Charles Town, I said [it] was a
dear, a very dear purchase. Mr. Appleby was present then & so was
another Gent. & he join'd me in sentiments & was surprised at it. All
this may be, Sir, & yet no censure upon you only that I was mistaken
in your Judgment, or you was mistaken yourself. A Million of words
might be thrown away upon this subject to no purpose. If the Indigo
is badly bought We shall both be convinc'd of it by a small dash of
a pen. If otherwise a good Account will shew me how much I am
mistaken. This will by no means depend upon the fall or rise of
Markets, but by Comparison with other Sales of Indigo bought at
same prices & sold at & about the same time.

Be so kind to give me some description of Croft's Lot that
you have sold with other particulars necessary for making deeds of
conveyance & I will have the Titles drawn out imediately & executed.[2]
I am—

[P.S.] I cannot find out any Traces yet of your Hogshead of Tabacco.

SOURCE: Letterbook copy, Letter Book of Henry Laurens, Oct. 30,
1762–Sept. 10, 1766, Penn. Hist. Soc.; addressed "George Town."

TO ISAAC KING

[Charles Town] 15th March 1764
Sir,

Annex'd is duplicate of my last the 27th January per Barnes

---

[2] These documents have not been found in Deeds, S. C. Archives.

since which I am favour'd with yours of the 18th November per Capt. Gunn with Invoice for Sundry on my Account per the *Heart of Oak*, which are all come to hand except two spare setts of harness charged in Mr. Buck's[3] Bill £6.5/. These do not appear nor is the case said to contain them inserted in the Bill of Loading. You will be so kind to enquire into & set this matter to right for me. Every thing you have sent pleases me very well tho' the principle article will by no means answer my purposes, the Looking Glasses I mean, but that may be owing to my too general description of them. I do not know one House in Charles Town that can receive such Glasses to do justice to taste & be consistent with the House itself & its furniture; & I believe in the end I must send them back again.

Please to receive Inclosed a Bill of Loading & Bounty Certificate for 328 Barrels Pitch per this bearer the *Jupiter,* Capt. Wills,[4] on the joint Account of Gabriel Manigault, Esquire & myself & you will be pleased to apply the net proceeds of the Sale & bounty to our respective Accounts in Moiety. Mr. Manigault suggests that in filling up the Pitch Barrels here some dross may thro' the carelessness of Negroes go in & appear at the Bung of the Barrel & unfair advantage may perhaps be taken of that trifle & the whole Barrel represented as foul. I don't see any great reason to fear this in the Present Parcell. Nevertheless you will take the hint & make a proper use of it. I shipp'd on this *Jupiter* only 327 Barrels but the Mate return'd me an Account of 328 received on board which seems to account for one Barrel lost by Mr. Manigault in Shipping on Board another Vessel that lay along side of the *Jupiter*. However if only 327 Barrels shou'd be fairly turn'd out do not insist upon satisfaction for the odd one but explain the matter to Capt. Wills.

I shall write you more fully by Capt. Gunn. At present I am rather huryed in removing to a new Counting house & surrendering my Old one to Mr. William Price. Meantime I remain with true respect, Sir, Your, &ca.—

SOURCE: Letterbook copy, HL Papers, S. C. Hist. Soc.; addressed "for Mrs. Sarah Nicholson & Co., London"; "per Wills with Barnes's 2 Bills Loading. Copy per Gunn."

---

[3] William Beck of London. See HL to Grubb & Watson, April 7, 1764.

[4] The ship *Jupiter*, Joseph Wills, was cleared outwards on March 7 for London with a cargo which included 328 barrels of pitch. The manifest, dated March 7, showed that HL had consigned 328 barrels of pitch to Mrs. Sarah Nickleson & Co. Naval Office Lists, 1764–1767, pp. 43, 75.

TO THOMAS DANIEL[5]

[Charles Town] 15th March 1764

Sir,

It has been wholly for want of subject & not want of respect that I have not wrote to you since April in last Year. In the meantime your sundry kind favours of the 19th March, 25th May, 8th June, & 7th January are come to hand with Account Sales of my Goods & Account Current finally Balanc'd by Cash deliver'd me by Capt. Gilchrist. I thank you for the trouble you have taken in my trifling concerns & should you unexpectedly incur any bad Debts on my Account your indulgence for remiting before hand shall not be abus'd.

Hearing that the price of Rice had started in your Island I did about the middle of January engage A Sloop & intended to have sent her with about 200 Barrels Rice & other articles to your address & should have got her away in a very few days after but just at the Instant came in this Ship *Barter* to me with an order for Rice in part of her Cargo & being in hopes that she would be full & Sail before the 15th February. I diverted my own concern in another Channel lest my Interest should interfere with & prejudice that of my friends but as things are now circumstanced I have defeated my own purposes without any benefit to him. I shall be glad to embrace some future opportunity to pay my respects to you, & for this end the continuance of your advices will be very acceptable & obliging to, Sir, Yours, &c.—

Rice at 40/ per Ct. Few Ships in Harbour. Rum at all prices from 10/ to 15/6. Excellent Vidonia Wine selling today at £95 per pipe. Exchange 700 to 714 per Cent.

SOURCE: Letterbook copy, HL Papers, S. C. Hist. Soc.; addressed "Barbados"; "per Gough."

TO JOHN & THOMAS TIPPING

[Charles Town] 15 March 1764

Gentlemen,

Since I wrote to you on the 15th December per Capt. Seymour

---

[5] *HL Papers,* III, 228n.

your favour of the 14th of the same Month was deliver'd to me by
Capt. Dennison in the Ship *Hope*. You judg'd very rightly for Mr.
Knight's Interest to send no Wines to this Market, for they certainly
would not have yeilded prime Cost. On the other hand an hundred
healthy well chosen Negroes of any Country would have paid a fine
freight to the Ship. I have declin'd that branch of business in general
as being too Cumbrous & too important for a single hand for many
obvious reasons, but a few that came to my care from the West
Indias I sold at upward of £44 Sterling round. The best Men
brought from £320 to £330 Currency.

The *Hope* had the misfortune to touch the Bottom coming
over the Bar which shook her crazy Carcass so that after going thro'
the Carpenter's hands I thought it most advisable not to over burthen
her & therefore dispatch her for Oporto with only 600 Casks of Rice.

I have run off a little more than half the *Austin*'s 40 Hogsheads Rum from 15/6 to 17/6 which is 20 per Cent more than the
prices that West India Rum has been constantly selling for per Vendue
& also in private for Cash ever since that arriv'd. I must now push
off the remainder in the best manner I can for we may look for
importations of your new Crop every day.

The Ship *Barter* is just now ready to Sail. She has been a
long time unexpectedly detain'd here. I have done all in my power to
serve the Interest of your friend the Owner. The Commission will
be a dear bought one to me because of the advance I must be in to
keep his Rum from a destructive Sale, but if I give content I shall be
satisfy'd. I am with great regard—

SOURCE: Letterbook copy, HL Papers, S. C. Hist. Soc.; addressed
"Barbados"; "per Gough."

TO JOHN HASLIN

[Charles Town] 15th March 1764

Sir,

I beg leave to refer to what I wrote you the 15th December
since which, Vizt. on the 1st January I rece'd your acceptable favour
of the 15th & 24th December by the hands of Capt. Gough in Mr.
Manesty's Ship *Barter* with Invoice & Bill loading for 50 Hogsheads
Rum which have been deliver'd to me but in poor order on Account

of the Casks. These were of ordinary quality at first & then being stow'd in sand Balast hurt the hoops & staves more than a little. I have sold about twenty two Hogsheads from 15/3 upwards by giving Credit & Bartering part of it, tho' the common Sale per Vendue as well as in private for Cash hath been & now is from 12 to 14/ for West India & 10/ for Northward Rum but I will rather feel a part of the loss myself than by too precipitate a Sale lessen the Value of my friends goods so much as from 10 to 20 per Cent & I make no doubt that Mr. Manesty will consider this, & not let me be too great a sufferer from the regard I shew to his Interest. The Sale of Rum at those prices seems now to be over & we may expect every day Importations of the New Crop in the usual quantities. Therefore I shall try to run off the remains at the best prices the Market will admit of, as well because the Hogsheads are not sufficient to stand a Summer as because I see no prospect within that time of improving the Sale so as to pay for the keeping it.

Please now to receive Invoice & Bill loading for the Cargo on board the Ship *Barter* on Account of our mutual good friend Mr. Manesty Consign'd to you, the whole amount with the ship's Disbursements being £4,191.1, which will far exceeding the Value of the Rum and the Balance I must draw for as you have order'd which I shall do upon the most advantageous terms in my power.

The *Barter* has been detain'd here much longer than I expected & yet I know not any body to blame. I have been prepar'd for her ever since the 2d February & great part of her Lumber was provided & ready to come to Town from the day of the Ship's arrival. The whole has been along side & near the Ship these five Weeks past. At the same time I must say that Capt. Gough has not wanted industry. He was constantly from Morning 'till Night on board, but partly his unacquaintedness with the Stowage of a Lumber Cargo & principally the want of a Raft port has made his work go very heavily on which he can better explain to you than I can.

The quantity of Lumber taken into the Ship by the Mate's Account is vague & uncertain. In some parcels he is thousand over, in others a good deal short of the quantity undoubtedly deliver'd, one parcel not mention'd at all & upon the whole there seems to be a considerable difference between that return & the quantity that I must pay for but I do believe you will find the full quantity on board & with advantage to the Ship, for in one parcel provided at my own plantation I have inserted near 1,000 feet less of Scantlin than my Overseer assur'd me this very Morning he sent to Town, & called the difference as Inch & quarter Boards & Inch Boards which make a difference to my prejudice of above one half the Value. Had it been any body's else I could not have made so free with it. Some peices Capt. Gough informs me went adrift & were lost by the neglect of his people which he says they must pay for. I should have prevented all this trouble by sending a Man to be constantly on board both to inspect the quality & take particular Account of the quantity & I know by repeated instances that the expence would have been well bestow'd but the Captain thought that charge might be sav'd to the ship & the business done as effectually, & it would ill become me to crowd Charges on an Invoice, which with proper attention might be avoided. You will no doubt be very carefull in the receipt of this Cargo & I shall be thankfull to you to inform me how it turns out. The rice that is on board on the Ships Account is no great Matter & as Cap. Gough assures me is a saving of so much Freight being where he cou'd not store Lumber of any sort. Otherwise it was with reluctance that I put any in her, & he will also inform you that on this Account I realy diverted the Voyage of a Sloop which I was loading with Rice on my Own Account for Barbados & shou'd have been first at market by three or four Weeks with Rice after the price got up there, but as things have turned out now I might safely have reaped that benefit & done no prejudice to the *Barter*.

Upon the whole, Sir, I have done all in my power to serve & promote the Interest of this concern & shall think myself happy if I meet with the approbation of those friends that I act for.

Rice is now at 40/ and few Ships in Port, yet Freights do not advance as one might expect from such a scarcity—only 50/ given to London & 65/ for Holland. Negroes have Sold at very great prices. A small Cargo lately Averaged upwards of £43 Sterling.

I shall be glad to render you further Service & remain respectfully yours, &ca.—

SOURCE: Letterbook copy, HL Papers, S. C. Hist. Soc.; addressed "Barbados"; "per Gough. One copy sent to Mr. Manesty per Hooper and one per Capt. Gunn."

TO JONAS MAYNARD

[Charles Town] March 15, 1764

Sir,

I beg leave to refer you to the duplicate of my last Letter on the other side under the 14th December since which your favour of 30th December is come to hand, by which I am informed that you had rather have your effects in my hand, untill the day of *Judgement* than empower some impartial person to settle Accounts with me a proposition to which I shall by no means accede. I have great hopes of meeting you upon that day, & that we shall both after a suitable examination be order'd to file of[f] to the Right, but in order to secure so desirable an Event let us both in the meantime do strict justice tempered upon all proper occasions with generosity & Candour. On my part therefore, Sir, I shall within the Course of next week remit to your friend in London a Bill for the Sum mention'd in my last altho it shou'd be no further in Cash than it is at present which is about one half, for people here as in other parts of America are sometimes Slack in payment & I can Dunn with an Ill Grace when a man pays heavy Charges as in the present case. To this I shall also add the Sum to Ballance your Account Current with Austin, Laurens, & Appleby & afterward as heretofore I have done my uttmost endevours to procure Satisfaction for the Protested Eustatia Bill. I have wrote lately to Mr. Manning in St. Kitts to make another attempt at Statia & I shall try to get hold of the Endorsers at Philadelphia.[6] If I recover this the bad Debt made in Austin & Laurens time must be deducted; if not I shall submit the matter to you. If any errors have been committed by the Houses that you formerly employ'd, I am willing not only to take my part of blame but to pay my full quota of damages proved, but for Gods sake, Sir, lay not the faults of other people whether real or imaginary solely upon the shoulders of Your, &ca.—

SOURCE: Letterbook copy, HL Papers, S. C. Hist. Soc.; addressed "Esquire. Barbados"; "per Gough."

---

[6] Joseph and Shadlock Rivers.

TO JOHN CATTELL, SR.[7]

[Charles Town] 16th March 1764

Sir,

I have wrote twice to you about your Bond in my hands but have not been favour'd with an answer. The want of Money to support the Credit of People who are obliged to buy much Rice is uncommonly great this Year & I do in particular feel it very sensibly. I cannot bear to be Dunn'd & I hate to Dunn other folks but necessity has no Law. I am in fear every day of being call'd upon by the Sellers of Rice & I must therefore take time by the forelock & call upon my friends to assist me in purpose to meet these Gentlemen in good humour. I am persuaded that you can in five Minutes give me an order for the trifling Ballance due on your part to me, which will be some help & very obliging to, Sir, Yours, &c.—

SOURCE: Letterbook copy, Letter Book of Henry Laurens, Oct. 30, 1762–Sept. 10, 1766, Penn. Hist. Soc.; addressed "Esquire. Ashley River."

TO RICHARD BEDON[8]

[Charles Town] 16th March 1764

Sir,

I wrote to you some Weeks ago about your Bond in my hands but you have not been so obliging as to give me any answer altho you have been in Town & within a few paces of my Door. If every body was to use me in this way & every one has as good a right to do it, I shou'd loose my Credit & become Bankrupt in the midst of a large Pile of Bonds.

---

[7] John Cattell, the son of William Cattell who died in 1752, lived at Cattell Bluff plantation on the west bank of the Ashley River until his death on March 15, 1774. *SCHM*, xv (1914), 103; xx (1919), 108–109. His property passed to his nephew William Cattell who died in 1778. "Will of John Cattell," dated Oct. 24, 1771, proved ———, Charleston County Wills, xvi, Book A (1774–1779), 103–105, S. C. Archives.

[8] Col. Richard Bedon was a planter who lived at Ashley Bluff on the east side of the Ashley River. *SCHM*, xx (1919), 17. He married his second wife Martha Fuller on Oct. 17, 1745. *SCHM*, xiv (1913), 30. He was justice of the peace for Berkeley County in 1756. *SCHM*, xx (1919), 73. He was buried by an Anabaptist teacher on Dec. 26, 1765. *SCHM*, xv (1914), 44; "Will of Richard Bedon," dated Dec. 19, 1765, proved May 23, 1766, Charleston County Wills, xi, Book A (1767–1771), 214–215, S. C. Archives.

I don't care to affront any body nor even to be troublesomely importunate for what is my own, where I can with any tolerable convenience avoid it, but the demands on me for Rice & Indigo, Pitch & Tar are very considerable this Year & some of them near at hand that will be very pressing. Therefore I hope you will pardon my calling on you again to assist me with so much money as is due on your Bond & that you will be pleased to order payment to be made to me before the 25th Inst. which will much Oblige, Sir—

SOURCE: Letterbook copy, Letter Book of Henry Laurens, Oct. 30, 1762–Sept. 10, 1766, Penn. Hist. Soc.; addressed "Esquire. Ashley River."

TO JOHN PAGAN,
ALEXANDER BROWN & CO.
[Charles Town] March 17, 1764
Gentlemen,
Within a few days after my last of 29th Ulto. per Mitchel & Floyd the price of Rice declin'd to 42/6 & held not long there but fell to 40/. I embrac'd the opportunity & advertized the remainder of the *Pearls* Freight to be let at 47/6 per Ton which produc'd no more than the offer of One hundred & fifty Barrels.[9] This I accepted & after waiting so many Days as to make both Capt. Francis & myself think that your Interest wou'd suffer by any Longer delay I determin'd to fill her up on your Account & she is now full clear'd out & will probably sail in two Days. Your Interest in her is the Value of Two hundred & Seventeen Barrels & 112 half Barrels of very fine Rice, Say about Four hundred & Sixty pounds Sterling. Her whole Cargo consists off One Thousand & Forty Barrels Including half Barrels. This will serve for your government in making Insurance & my next shall convay you Invoice, Bill of Loading, & Account of Disbursments as well as Account Sale of the Coal. Mean while I remain with great regard, Yours, &ca.—

SOURCE: Letterbook copy, HL Papers, S. C. Hist. Soc.; addressed "Glasgow"; "per *Jupiter,* Wills. Copy per Gunn."

---

[9] The advertisement is printed under the date Feb. 4.

TO DENNISTOUNE, MUNRO & CO.

[Charles Town] March 17, 1764

Gentlemen,

I beg leave to refer you to my last under the 29th Ulto. & to Inform you that soon after as the Price of Rice was on the decline I obtain'd 60 Barrels upon Freight & the more readily accepted it because it served to fix the Freight at three pounds per Ton. Since that I have with some difficulty procured One hundred & fifty Barrels more at the same rate from the House here connected with Messrs. Mayne & Co. at Lisbon[1] but not a Barrel more can I yet get at that Freight & while Rice is at 40/, I think I ought not, I dare not, accept of Less, but I shall still move with caution and regard to Your Interest.

When Capt. Porter had discharged almost all his Coal it became absolutely Necessary & I therefore gave him fifty Barrels of Rice on the Ships Accounts to keep her upon her Legs & I have this Day purchas'd about One hundred & Forty Barrels More. When this & what is to go upon Freight is all on board, if no more is offer'd by other hands, I shall fill her up without further delay having in the meantime due regard to any alterations that may appear to be probable in Freight or the Price of our Produce & you may depend upon having timely advices of my proceedings.[2] I continue to be with true respect, Yours, &ca.—

---

[1] John and Edward Mayne and Edward Burne had been partners in the Lisbon firm of Maynes & Burne. *HL Papers,* I, 64n. By this date that firm had split into two partnerships: John and Edward Mayne (Maynes & Co.) and Edward Burne & Son. See HL to Maynes & Co., March 20, April 11, 1764. John Burn (or Burne) who had arrived in Charleston by May 29, 1760, must have been the son of Edward Burne. John Burn was permitted to act as executor of the estate of Charles Mayne, Charleston merchant and the brother of John and Edward Mayne. Judgment Rolls, 1760, No. 178A, S. C. Archives. John Burn purchased Charles Mayne's estate on July 28, 1761, for £20,500 currency which he secured in part by a mortgage to his "Uncle Mayne"—either John or Edward Mayne of Lisbon. John Burn immediately took his place as a man of consequence in S. C. He received a grant to 1,000 acres of land on the Altamaha River on May 18, 1763. He took his oath as a royal councilor on July 31, 1764. In 1767 he married Anne Baron, the widow of the Rev. Alexander Baron. He returned to Britain in 1773 where he remained until his death on Dec. 28, 1774. After his estate had been confiscated in 1782, his only son stated that his Carolina property had brought in £1,000 per annum. John Burn had owned two wharfs, each having a front of 100 feet with a dock of 74 feet between, two rows of storehouses opposite each wharf, weigh house, scale house, counting house, blacksmith shop, and cooper shop. The property itself extended 700 feet to Union Street. Loyalist Transcripts, LVI, 557-575; Index to Grants, S. C. Archives; Council Journal, xxx (Dec. 28, 1763–Dec. 24, 1764), 270-271, S. C. Archives; *Country Journal,* Oct. 27, 1767.

[2] The snow *Dennistoune,* Hugh Porter, was cleared outwards on April 7 for

SOURCE: Letterbook copy, HL Papers, S. C. Hist. Soc.; addressed "Glasgow"; "per *Jupiter,* Wills. Copy per Gunn."

TO JOSEPH MANESTY
[Charles Town] 17 March 1764

Sir,

I beg leave to refer you to my last under the 24 Ulto. per Condon & Mitchel & now to advise that your Ship *Barter* after a detaintion as gauling too as unexpected by me now lies ready in Rebelion Road³ for Sea.

The Amount of her Cargo & Disbursments for which I am every farthing in Advance is £4,191.0.1, which will oblige me to make a draught on you by and by for something about £250 Sterling. My next shall convay an Invoice, &Ca. for the above & Copy of what I have wrote to Mr. Haslin at Barbados. Meanwhile I remain with true respect, Your, &Ca.—

SOURCE: Letterbook copy, HL Papers, S. C. Hist. Soc.; addressed "Liverpool"; "per *Jupiter,* Wills."

TO MAYNES & CO.
[Charles Town] 20 March 1764

Gentlemen,

On the 16th Inst. your favour of the 28th January intended for the House of Austin & Laurens which expired near Six Years since & of which & the succeeding Partnership of Austin, Laurens, & Appleby I am the only remaining branch in trade in this province fell into my hands & Inform'd me of your having opened a New partner-

---

Lisbon with 539 barrels and 70 half barrels (301,719 pounds) of rice. Naval Office Lists, 1764–1767, p. 80.

³ *HL Papers,* I, 62n. Rebellion Road got its name in the following fashion according to a statement made in 1715: "The waters between Swillivans and James's Islands lie out of the reach of the guns of James Fort and for that reason are called Rebellion Road." "William Dry of Charleston, 1715," *National Genealogical Society Quarterly,* LX (1972), 17–19. "Swillivans" is, of course, Sullivans Island. "James Fort" was Fort Johnson which had been completed by 1709.

ship at Lisbon join'd with that Worthy Veteran in Commerce Mr. John Mayne of London.[4]

I shall as often as occasions demand it, give due Credit to your respective signatures & when it is in my Power contribute to the success of your House which I wish all manner of honour & Prosperity. Please now to receive a Bill of Loading for 217 Barrels & 112 half Barrels of Rice per this bearer the Ship *Pearl*, John Francis, Master on Account of Messrs. John Pagan, Alexander Brown & Co., Owners of the said Ship, Merchants in Glasgow, to be Sold to the best advantage on their Account. I think the Rice is of such a Quality as will recommend itself & I dare say you will do all the justice that is due to it. Capt. Francis has the Invoice & will put it into your hands if needfull & after your Purposes are serv'd will take it with him or otherwise convay it to the Owners to serve in case a duplicate is wanted. I have now in hand the Snow *Dennistoun* for Lisbon & She will be chiefly Loaden to your address & probably Sail hence about the last of this Month when I shall trouble you with another Letter.

Rice is at 40/ per Ct. & the rise or fall depends wholly on the Arival of Ships. At present there are very few in Port & there still remains near one half the Current Crop in the Country. I am with great regard, Your, &ca.—

SOURCE: Letterbook copy, HL Papers, S. C. Hist. Soc.; addressed "Lisbon"; "per Frances. Copy per Porter."

TO JOHN COMING BALL

[Charles Town] 21 March 1764

You have Credit for 1,492½ bushels Corn per *Speedwell*[5] at 12/6—£932.12.6—the precise Sum I rec'd for it. If any gain tis fairly your own.

The Money [is] ready. Cant with any face ask Mr. Manigault

---

[4] John Mayne, the eldest brother, was by this time in London with his younger brother William at New Broad St. *London Directories*. Edward Mayne must have been handling the Lisbon end of the business. *HL Papers*, 1, 64n.

[5] The sloop *Speedwell*, John Clark, was cleared outwards on Feb. 21 for Jamaica with a cargo which included only 766 bushels of corn. Naval Office Lists, 1764–1767, p. 74.

to take back £2,000, but if you please I will use it & allow Interest from this day until September or October & perhaps the whole Year.[6] Glad our Corn is not to be delivered till April or May. Would have it remain in the Ear until we give further Notice. If you agreed for Mr. Wright's Corn at 10/ I will pay no more.[7] Have engaged 3,000 bushels. Will cost in Charles Town in May next about 12/. Expect you'll be concerned in it. Hope for some profit. Am just moving House & find it very troublesome. Shall divert the Schooner a Month or two & not bring away our poor fragment of a short Crop just now unless you desire it. I remain, &ca.—

SOURCE: Letterbook copy, Letter Book of Henry Laurens, Oct. 30, 1762–Sept. 10, 1766, Penn. Hist. Soc. This letter was copied by HL.

TO HENRY TODD[8]

[Charles Town] 21 March 1764

Sir,

This covers a Bill of Loading & Invoice of the Weights of 36 Barrels & 30 half Barrels of very good Rice Shiped on board your Sloop *John*,[9] Consign'd to yourself for Sale at Barbados or at any of the Leeward Islands that you shall think best to stop at for the benefit of your Cargo in General. The Net proceeds if you sell at Barbados please to invest in the first & best Clay'd Sugars if to be had at a reasonable price otherwise in Rum, or if you can purchase likely little Negro Boys either there or to Leeward not lower than 48 to 58 Inches high for about £16 to £20 Sterling per head you may lay out my money in three or four such if it will extend so far, or in good Rum & in either case bring the produce of my Sale in your own Bottom.

---

[6] This may be proof that John Coming Ball did not purchase Limerick and therefore did not need the £2,000 offered by Gabriel Manigault as a loan.
[7] John Wright of the Cheraws. See HL to John Wright, Oct. 6, 1764.
[8] Henry Todd was a mariner of the parish of St. George in Bermuda. "Will of Henry Todd," dated May 6, 1786, proved Nov. 3, 1801, Charleston County Wills, XXIX (1800–1807), 429–430, S. C. Archives.
[9] The sloop *John*, 25 tons, built in Bermuda in 1760, was registered on Feb. 8, 1762, in Charleston by Henry Todd for the owners, John Jones, John Ward, and himself. Ship Register, 1734–1765, pp. 198–199, S. C. Archives. The sloop *John*, Francis Dickinson, owned by Henry Todd of Charleston, was cleared outwards on March 17 for Antigua with 210 barrels and 30 half barrels of rice and 550 bushels of rough rice. Naval Office Lists, 1764–1767, p. 75.

Alexander Fraser, Esquire[1] has likewise consign'd you 32 Barrels of Rice on his own Account as per Bill of Loading in your hands & the weight here Inclosed, the proceeds of which he desires you will return in good Rum. I wish you a prosperous Voyage & remain, Sir, Yours, &ca.—

SOURCE: Letterbook copy, HL Papers, S. C. Hist. Soc.; addressed "Captain. of the Sloop *John*."

PURCHASE OF LAND IN ANSONBOROUGH

March 24, 1764

[*HL bought from Jermyn Wright for £1,600 currency a certain wharf and marsh and high land east of the village of Ansonborough and partly east of land owned by the South Carolina Society. This property was the residue of certain lands conveyed by Jermyn Wright to Lord George Anson May 11, 1756, as security for a bond. Upon payment of the bond's principal and interest, the wharf had reverted to Wright. Laurens had purchased the land surrounding the wharf property on Sept. 7, 1762, from Philip Morison and his wife Helen. In the Morison-Laurens deed, the wharf property was described as a wharf, creek, and 35-foot entry reserved to Lord Anson. HL had been trying to buy Jermyn Wright's property ever since Nov. 1763. This deed was witnessed by William Hopton, William Hest, and John Bremar. William Hest swore to the signatures April 13, 1764, before William Burrows, justice of the peace. The deed was recorded April 24, 1764, by Fenwicke Bull, public register.*]

SOURCE: Deeds, BBB, pp. 193-195, S. C. Archives.

---

[1] Alexander Fraser (1722–1791) was the son of John Fraser (died 1754) who had come out to Carolina about 1700 from Wigton in Galloway, Scotland. John Fraser although an Indian trader among the Yemassees escaped the general slaughter of 1715. In 1744 he bought a plantation on Goose Creek which he called Wigton or Fraser's. Alexander Fraser married (1) Ann Harvey in 1749 and (2) Mary Grimké in 1755. Charles Fraser, the painter, was the fourteenth and youngest child of the second marriage. "Fraser Family Memoranda," *SCHM*, v, (1904), 56–58; xxix (1928), 18–20.

BILL OF SALE

March 24, 1764

[HL on this date purchased from Samuel Carne[2] of Charleston "One Negro Girl named Venus & one Negro Boy named Jack" for £579 currency. Norman Swallow and Maurice Jones witnessed the indenture. Norman Swallow swore to the signatures on May 17, before Jacob Motte, Esquire, justice of the peace. The transaction was recorded May 19.]

SOURCE: Miscellaneous Records, MM, Part 1 (1763–1767), p. 106, S. C. Archives.

TO JOHN PERDRIAU

[Charles Town] 29 March 1764

Dear Sir,

I heartily concur in the disposition made by my Aunt Savineau[3] in her last Will & Testament of those two female Negroes Sabena & Sarah which I did some Years ago purchase for her use during her Life; & that her bequests may be as complete as possible to her Children I beg you will inform me of the Amount of her debts & funeral Charges toward the payment of which I shall gladly contribute or perhaps pay the whole. I am—

SOURCE: Letterbook copy, Letter Book of Henry Laurens, Oct. 30, 1762–Sept. 10, 1766, Penn. Hist. Soc.

---

[2] Dr. Samuel Carne was preparing to sail for England in the *Heart of Oak. Gazette,* March 31, 1764.

[3] Jane Laurens, HL's aunt, who married John Perdriau on Feb. 21, 1721, had later married a Mr. Savineau, most probably the James Savineau who had received two grants of land on Lynches Creek in Craven County on May 11, 1739, and Oct. 9, 1741. Index to Grants, S. C. Archives. Jane Savineau of Georgetown named in her will her son John Perdriau and her daughters Lydia Morrall, Martha Savineau, Mary Ann Durant, Jane Brockinton, Judith Allin, Rebecca Savineau, and Susannah Minors. She freed her slave Sarey but ordered her other slaves November, Sabrina, and young Sarey to be sold to satisfy her debts with remainder to be divided among her heirs equally. "Will of Jane Savineau," dated 1763, proved May 19, 1764, Charleston County Wills, x, Book B (1760–1767), 509, S. C. Archives.

TO HENRY BRIGHT & CO.

[Charles Town] 29 March 1764

Gentlemen,

The Annexed is duplicate of what I wrote you the 3d Inst. per your Ship *Sally* & this incloses a duplicate Bill of Loading, Abstract Invoice, & Receipt for disbursements, to all which I beg leave to refer.

On the 7th Inst. I passed a Bill on you to the order of Henry Bright, Esquire for £52.5/ Sterling & passed the same to your Credit at 714 per Cent Exchange £373, & this day another Bill payable at 75 days sight to the order of Robert Raper, Esquire in London £336.11.9 Sterling which bears to your Credit at 700 per Cent £2,356.2.3. I strove hard to obtain a Little higher Exchange but scarcity of Money hath obliged some of the best Houses to offer Bills at 700 per Cent & particularly Messrs. Brewton & Smith sold yesterday £300 Sterling on London at 30 days sight at 700. Therefore I could gain you no further advantage than having more than double the time to pay my draught in.

Rice continues at 40/ per Ct. Freight to London 55/, Holland £3.10/, & very few Ships in port. I remain, &ca.—

SOURCE: Letterbook copy, HL Papers, S. C. Hist. Soc.; addressed "Owners of the Ship *Sally*. Bristol"; "per Capt. Hooper. Copy per Gunn."

TO JOSEPH MANESTY

[Charles Town] 30th March 1764

Sir,

My last was the 24th Ulto. per Capt. Condon & Capt. Mitchel, since which Capt. Gough compleated the load of your Ship *Barter* & sail'd over the Bar on the 16th Inst. Please to receive herewith inclosed an Invoice of that Ships Cargo also a Bill of Loading & one of the Captains' Receipts for disbursement whole amount to the Debit of your Account £4,191.1, & for further particulars I cannot do better than to refer you to the annex'd duplicate of my Letter to Mr. John Haslin which Capt. Gough read over before I sealed it & confirmed the contents.

I likewise inclose Account Sale of those 50 Hogsheads Rum imported in the Ship *Barter,* Net proceeds £3,037.10.9 to your Credit of which no less than £1,881.15/ is now outstanding & I do not expect to be in Cash for one half thereof within six Months. This circumstance curtails my Commission but I could not in these times have made a tolerable Sale without the assistance of some long winded customers. I know 'tis but a poor Account to you & am willing to submit to some inconvenience to make the most of it. You will remark that I have taken the last sixteen Hogsheads to myself in order to finish the Account which otherwise would have laid open some Months. The price that is affixed to it is such as I would now accept from any person who would be punctual in payment for it in a Month or 6 Weeks. Good West India, say St. Kitts Rum, sold yesterday at 12/6 per & the highest proof Jamaica I bought a single Hogshead at 17/6 per. Nevertheless if you incline & will be pleased to signify it the Sale of these 16 Hogsheads shall be on your Account & for this end I shall keep a distinct Account of the Sale of them.

I here inclose your Account Current, Balance due to me £1,153.10.3, for which I have taken the Liberty to pass a Bill on you at 75 days sight payable in London to the Order of Robert Raper, Esquire for £164.15.9 Sterling Exchange 700 per Cent. I was in hopes to have obtained 1 or 2 per Cent more but the want of Money hath obliged some people to offer Bills for Sale & there is some difference between that & being applied to for Bills, & I know that Messrs. Brewton & Smith Exchanged yesterday at 700 per Cent on London payable in 30 days. I mention them because they are of undoubted establishment. I have therefore been able only to gain for you in the days for payment which is something.

I have through the whole of this transaction studied your Interest & hope that my acts will be acceptable to you, & when I can be further serviceable your commands shall be carefully & duly executed by—

Rice 40/

SOURCE: Letterbook copy, HL Papers, S. C. Hist. Soc.; addressed "Liverpoole"; "per Capt. Hooper. Copy per Gunn with another Copy to Haslin & also Abstract Invoice, Bill Loading, & Receipt."

TO JOHN RUTHERFORD
[Charles Town] 31st March [1764]

Sir,

I beg leave to recommend the Gentleman who bears this Letter, to your acquaintance & friendly notice during his short Stay in your Province. Mr. Lowbridge Bright, for that is the Gentleman's name, is of a good family & fortune in Bristol & his Bills if he shou'd have occasion for any Money will be undoubtedly good. Those favours & civilitys that you allways shew to Strangers will in this case oblige a great many worthy persons of Mr. Brights friends & amongst the least of them, Sir, Yours, &ca.—

[*P.S.*] I forward three Letters by Mr. Bright lately rece'd for you & he will give you some Account of our friend Dickson.

SOURCE: Letterbook copy, HL Papers, S. C. Hist. Soc.; addressed "Esquire. North Carolina."

TO LEWIS DE ROSSET[4]
[Charles Town] 31 March [1764]

Sir,

I beg leave by this means to introduce to your acquaintance Mr. Lowbridge Bright. North Carolina will be but an Inn to him on his long Journey to Quebeck but during his halt there I request you to shew him that Regard that is due to a Stranger of good family & Fortune & what is more of great worth in himself & shou'd he have occasion of any money his Bills on me or upon his friends in Bristol will be duly paid. Your attention to this will particularly oblige me & be allways gratefully acknowledg'd by, Yours, &ca.—

SOURCE: Letterbook copy, HL Papers, S. C. Hist. Soc.; addressed "Honourable. Esquire. North Carolina."

---

[4] Lewis De Rosset was a member of the royal council of North Carolina from 1753 to the Revolution. His name was listed among those whose property was confiscated at the end of the Revolution. *Colonial Records of North Carolina,* v–x, passim; XVII, 145; *HL Papers,* I, 310n.

TO WILLIAM HODSHON

[Charles Town] 31st March 1764

Sir,

My last was the 28th Ulto. per Capt. Mitchel & Capt. Floyd. By the former I remitted you 1,212 Dollars charged to your Account £1,898.12, without Commission. I have not been Able to obtain any further payments from the Gentlemen in Georgia but my applications shall be repeated & particularly next week by a Neighbour of mine who is going to Savannah[5] & whome I shall prevail on, to call upon them. Meantime by the *Heart of Oak,* Capt. Gunn, to sail in four or five days I shall Ship you 500 Dollars more at 31/ per piece.[6] This week put me in advance for you somewhat about £150 besides Commission & if it depended wholly on me I wou'd not regard the advance to make a final end of so tedious an affair. As it does not I trust you will accept the will for the deed. I remain—

SOURCE: Letterbook copy, HL Papers, S. C. Hist. Soc.; addressed "London"; "per Addis. Copy per Gunn."

TO WILLIAM HODSHON

[Charles Town] 2d April 1764

Sir,

The annex'd is duplicate of what I wrote to you per Capt. Addis[7] the 31st Ulto. to which please to be referr'd, & now to receive the inclosed Bill of Loading for 500 Spanish Mill'd Dollars per this Ship the *Heart of Oak,* Capt. Gunn, charged to the Debit of your Account at 31/ per £775. I shall write by Mr. Brewton who goes tomorrow for Georgia to our friends there & inform you in my next what reply they are pleased to make but at present I have not to add, save that I continue to be your, &ca.—

SOURCE: Letterbook copy, HL Papers, S. C. Hist. Soc.; addressed "London"; "per Gunn."

---

[5] Miles Brewton.
[6] One Spanish milled dollar equaled 31 shillings currency.
[7] The ship *Prince of Bavern,* John Addis, was entered inwards on March 29 from Lisbon and was cleared outwards on April 28 for Lisbon. Naval Office Lists, 1764–1767, pp. 71, 80.

TO GEORGE CHISMAN[8]

[Charles Town] 2d April 1764

Sir,

I have both your favours of the 3d & 28th November, the latter deliver'd to me late the 31st Inst. by your Brother Christopher Chisman who arrived that evening in your Ship *Dorset.*[9] The Charter party[1] by this late arrival is vacated & you will be no looser thereby, which I am heartily glad of as it always gives me pleasure to see my friends fall on their feet. You may rest assured of my endeavours to secure the best Freight in my power for the Ship & I am under no great doubt of succeeding without troubling the Owners with any concern therein which I shall avoid if possible. I have no chance of getting a Barrel upon any terms to Oporto. Lisbon I may but very doubtful. If I can get £3 to London she shall go. Otherwise I must accept of an offer made of half her Cargo at £3.10/ to Cowes & Holland (shunning Bremen as you direct) & am hopeful of soon making up the other half, upon the same terms. Tis true there are but few Ships in Port but the arrival of three or four which may be hourly expected may work a pernicious alteration to the Ship. Therefore I shall not stand out Longer than tomorrow. This is the highest Freight that hath yet been given. Tis a very good one & ought not this Season of the Year to be Slighted. Upon the whole I shall act to the best of my judgement & act by your Ship as if the Interest was my own. You shall hear from me as I go forward. Meanwhile, I am, &ca.—

P.S. I shall have no objection to a concern with you in any Ship built at Poole or elsewhere if we can establish a plan to make the Interest of our money & serve a friend.

SOURCE: Letterbook copy, HL Papers, S. C. Hist. Soc.; addressed "Captain. London"; "per *Heart of Oak,* Capt. Gunn."

---

[8] George Chisman had for many years been master of a vessel in the Charleston–London trade. *HL Papers,* I & II, passim.

[9] The ship *Dorset,* Christopher Chisman, owned by George Chisman of London, was entered inwards on April 2 from Mobile with "a parcell of Arms belonging to 22d Regiment." Chisman is spelled "Cheesman" in the naval office records. Naval Office Lists, 1764–1767, p. 71. Major Robert Farmar, having proceeded from Havana with the 22nd and 34th regiments, took possession of Mobile on Oct. 20, 1763. C. N. Howard, "The Military Occupation of British West Florida, 1763," *Florida Historical Quarterly,* XVII (1939), 186–199.

[1] The terms under which a vessel was chartered usually specified periods of time for the performance of obligations.

TO THOMAS AUBREY

[Charles Town] 2d April 1764

Sir,

I now send you Six backed Windsor Chairs agreeable to your former order. They are the best that I have seen Imported & indeed tempted me to buy half a dozen for my own use in my new House & by taking a Dozen I got them cheap.

I likewise send you under the order in your favour of the 7th Ulto. one Cask of old Barbadoes Rum well Cooper'd & the Bung carefully secured to avoid loss or dulteration if possible. You have inclosed Capt. Rogers[2] Receipt for these articles & underneath an Account of the Cost charged to your Account.

You need not after what I have said make any further but as you have occasion for my services here freely command them. I wish you more society & a pleasant Summer & remain, &ca.—

6 Neat high back'd Windsor Chairs	
bought of Nowel & Co.[3]	£21. 7.6
23 Gallons old Barbadoes Rum at 20/	23.
1 Quarter Cask	1. 5.
to Mr. Aubreys Debit	£45.12.6

SOURCE: Letterbook copy, HL Papers, S. C. Hist. Soc.; addressed "Lieutenant. Esquire. St. Augustine"; "per Capt. Rogers."

TO JOHNSON & WYLLY

[Charles Town] 3d April 1764

Gentlemen,

Having but very short notice of this Opportunity I can barely

---

[2] The schooner *Tybee,* James Rodgers, owned by Thomas Tucker of Charleston, was entered inwards on March 13 from St. Augustine. Naval Office Lists, 1764–1767, p. 71. The *Gazette,* March 31, 1764, stated that the *Tybee* was nearly loaded for St. Augustine.

[3] The partnership of John Nowell, Edward Davies, and George Ancrum which was expiring. Judgment Rolls, 1765, No. 299A; 1766, Nos. 36A, 139A; 1767, No. 358A, S. C. Archives. In October John Nowell was contemplating a partnership with Richard Wayne, one of his clerks, but in February 1765 he formed with Andrew Lord the firm of Nowell & Lord. HL to Cowles & Harford, Oct. 10, 1764; *Gazette,* Feb. 9, 1765.

get time to thank you for your civilitys to Mr. Dickson at Savanna which I shall allways [be] glad to acknowledge by suitable returns & to request you to inform me when & in what manner I may expect to be paid the Ballance of the Bond given on the *Don Pedro*'s Account. The Gentleman to whome it is due in London is so exceedingly anxious, I had almost said troublesome, to get his money into his own Coffers that to get rid of more applications from him as well as to avoid making more excuses on my part I wou'd advance the remains for you provided you can put me into a state of Security to receive the same again in this Town in any reasonable time to suite your Convenience & mine, but chiefly your own. Be so good as to favour me with a Line by Mr. Brewtons return, & you'll Oblige—

SOURCE: Letterbook copy, HL Papers, S. C. Hist. Soc.; addressed "Georgia"; "per Mr. Brewton."

TO ISAAC KING

[Charles Town] 3d April 1764

Sir,

The above is duplicate of what I wrote you per Capt. Wills to which please to be referr'd & here receive second Bill Loading for the Pitch on board the *Jupiter,* Capt. Wills.

Mr. Manigault has Shiped [674] Barrels of Pitch & [182] Barrels of Green Tar on board this bearer the *Heart of Oak* in which he will inform you that I am one Moiety concern'd & that such proportion of the Net proceeds is to be passed to the Credit of my Account with you.[4]

---

[4] These figures were obtained from the manifest of the cargo on board the *Heart of Oak* which was signed by Henry Gunn in the naval office in Charleston on March 29. The cargo also included the following: Nathaniel Blundle shipped 92 barrels of rice, 104 pounds of indigo, 1 cask of pink root, and 1 cask of snake root consigned to John Beswicke & Co.; John Ward 100 barrels of rice and 774 pounds of indigo to Grubb & Watson; John Rose 104 barrels of rice to Sarah Nickleson & Co.; Moses Darquin & Co. 100 barrels of rice and 1,554 pounds of indigo to Grubb & Watson; Inglis, Lloyd, & Hall 100 barrels of rice and 1,480 pounds of indigo to Grubb & Watson; John Edwards & Co. 24,401 pounds of indigo to Sarah Nickleson & Co.; James Poyas 740 pounds of indigo to John Beswicke; Doctor Garden 1 barrel of earthenware to Charles Ogilvie; Carne & Wilson 4,445 pounds of indigo and 1 case of broad cloth to Doctor Carne; Darby Pendergrass 709 pounds of indigo to Mr. Brown; Henry & Arthur

I have urged Mr. Price to be very punctual in his remittance & rather make a Sacrifice of gain than of his Credit or put you to too much inconveniance by being in advance, & [I] am under no doubt of his doing all that the times will admit of to run off his late importation & to put you in Cash, but he will have some difficultys to strugle withal, because our Country is too fully stock'd with Europian goods insomuch that the Vendue House does afford twice in every Week goods of all sorts at less than prime Cost & many Country people of late have made that their Mart, which formerly was attended only by our own Shopkeepers.[5] Mr. Price from these discouragements is turning his thoughts to another branch & is about entering into partnership with Mr. William Hest a Young Gentleman who lately came well recommended from London & has been ever since in my Counting House. They will inform you of their plan & I shall write to you more about it when Mr. Hest goes to England some four or five Weeks hence.

Mr. Beck succeeded so well in the Windsor Chair that you got of him for me that I must trouble you once more to apply to him for a neat Single Horse Chair light & strong the body Not confined, but large enough for two persons who are neither of them Skeletons to sit easily in it, to be painted of a Strong Light Colour with a neat gilded bead down the corner & upon the back, not gaudy, Lined with a very good light Couloured Broad Clothe, the Reins of the Bridle to be part Worsted, no Cypher nor painted ornaments. One good set of Harness to be shiped in this Vessel when She returns. I am sorry that 'tis not in my power to offer you some better than these Troublesome Commissions, which I must endevour to make

---

Peronneau 184 pounds of indigo to Grubb & Watson; Thomas Smith 1,036 pounds of indigo to John Nutt; Booth & Webb 1 barrel of rice to Grubb & Watson; Hooper & Swallow 1,800 pounds of indigo to John Nutt; Alexander Kynock 2 bundles of deerskins to David Mitchell; William Kirkby 3,864 pounds of indigo to Charles Crokatt; William Poole 662 pounds of indigo to John Nutt; Liston, Benfield, & Jones 2,908 pounds of indigo to John Nutt; Moses Lindo 280 pounds of indigo to Grubb & Watson; John McCall 1,089 pounds of indigo to himself; Andrew Marr 3 hogsheads of deerskins to John Watson; Curtis 30 cedar posts to Grubb & Watson; John Deas 1 quarter cask of Madeira wine to himself; and "a Trunk Containing Books &c a part of the Library of Doctor Carn." Naval Office Lists, 1764–1767, p. 57.

[5] William Price had advertised in the *Gazette*, Feb. 25, 1764, European and East India goods, imported in the *Heart of Oak* from London and the *Hopewell* from Bristol, which he would sell reasonably "at the store lately possessed by Mr. *Henry Laurens*, on the Bay."

up by consignments from this side & shall do so as often as I can. The Garden Seeds & Roots that you sent by Capt. Gunn, came cheap enough 'tis true for I think you have charged nothing for them which I do not nor have any right to expect but they proove almost wholly useless. The Roots were all Rotton. This is to often the case with such things bought in the London Seed Shops.

I hope very soon to hear from you & to receive my Account. 'Tis a long time since we had a Vessel from London.

Egerton Leigh, Esquire, a Gentleman nearly allied by Marriage to me, goes a Passenger in this Ship.[6] If 'tis in your power at any time to be of service to him I shall be very thankfull to you for your favours tho' he does not know that I have mention'd his name to any body. I remain with great regard—

SOURCE: Letterbook copy, HL Papers, S. C. Hist. Soc.; addressed "for Mrs. Sarah Nicholson & Co., London"; "per Gunn."

TO GRUBB & WATSON

[Charles Town] 3d April 1764

Gentlemen,

My last trouble to you was under the 12th December per Capt. Ball & Capt. White since which I have rece'd your favours of the 31 October, 2d & 19th November. You judged right in sending the Ship *Heart of Oaks* papers to Mr. Edwards[7] as he takes upon him the trouble of her Accounts & therefore to what he has now wrote relative to that Ship I beg leave to referr you, only adding that it will for your own sakes give me a great deal of pleasure to see that she makes a tolerable Freight out & meets with quick dispatch the present Voyage through your means. I know it will fix the Ship more steadily & more profitably to your House in future. At present the Owners are not all so well satisfyed as partners shou'd be & I do confess frankly to you that from what I have heard & from what I

---

[6] Egerton Leigh had married Martha Bremar, HL's niece, on Jan. 15, 1756. *Register of St. Philip's Parish, 1754–1810*, p. 143. Egerton Leigh, Samuel Carne, David Deas, Robert Philp, John McCall, Jr., John Corrie, Thomas Lynch, Jr., Alexander Taylor, all sailed in the *Heart of Oak. Gazette,* March 31, 1764.
[7] John Edwards.

have seen too I am one of the disatisfyed ones fearing that you rather push too boldly upon your capital & have too many important concerns at one time upon your hands. If I am mistaken this sugestion cannot injure you but rather enable you by timely warning, to remove mine and all other jelousies. On the other hand if I am but too well grounded, I dare say you will improve this hint to your own benefit & in either case I intreat you do not be angry with me, but be assured you are spoken to by a person that heartily wishes & wou'd gladly contribute to the increase of your business.

I shall add no more at present but to desire that you will pass the remains of my fourth part of the Ship's Freights to London & out again to my Credit.[8] In future that is to say from this time I shall take upon myself the risque & make no further Insurance. I remain—

SOURCE: Letterbook copy, HL Papers, S. C. Hist. Soc.; addressed "London"; "per Gunn. Copy per Coward."

TO DENNISTOUNE, MUNRO & CO.

[Charles Town] 3d April 1764

Gentlemen,

The Annex'd is duplicate of what I wrote you the 17th Ulto. per Capt. Wills. Since which as no more Rice offer'd upon Freight I have been obliged, to keep the *Dennistoune* from Laying quite Idle, to give her to the Amount of 252 Barrels & 70 half Barrels of Rice on your own Account at 40/ per Ct., & as Capt. Porter had a great deal to do about the Ship in Sheathing her aloft I do not think there has been any time lost. I am in hopes all the rest of the Cargo will be upon Freight. She is pretty near full this Evening & will get away in a few days barring bad Weather. This may serve to govern you in making Insurance & by the next Vessel shall write you what further occurs. Meanwhile I remain, &ca.—

SOURCE: Letterbook copy, HL Papers, S. C. Hist. Soc.; addressed "Glasgow"; "per Gunn."

---

[8] Although HL, James Laurens, John Edwards, John Savage, and John Rose of Charleston and Grubb & Watson of London were listed as the owners, HL apparently held a one-quarter share. Naval Office Lists, 1764–1767, p. 70.

TO JOHN PAGAN,
ALEXANDER BROWN & CO.

[Charles Town] April 3d, 1764

Gentlemen,

My last to you was the 17 Ulto. as per Annex'd Duplicate to which I refer, & now Inclose you a Bill of Loading & Abstract Invoice for the Rice Shiped on your Account per the *Pearl* (She Sail'd the 22d) & also Capt. Frances Receipt for disbursments, the whole Amounting to £4,091.3.3 charged to the debit of your Account Current, the Ballance of which I shall not too hastily draw for & when 'tis proper to pass a Bill on you I shall send Account Sale of the Coals which as present lies unfinished by means of a mistake in the Mates Account of delivery. At least one person upon being apply'd to for payment avers that he neither bought nor rece'd a Coal from that Ship. I am in hopes this is only owing to wrong placing a Christian Name & that I shall soon have it clear'd up. I took all imaginable pains to avoid such mistakes by ordering none shou'd be sent away without a Ticket from me, but nevertheless there were some few Tons went away. It being very Cold at the time of Delivering some people wou'd even force the Carters to go with them when they were order'd another way.

Rice continues at 40/ per Ct. & Freight to Holland 70/ per Ton but people are not egar in taking the few Ships that are lately come in. I am, &ca.—

SOURCE: Letterbook copy, HL Papers, S. C. Hist. Soc.; addressed "Owners of the Ship *Pearl,* Glasgow"; "per Gunn."

TO HENRY BRIGHT

[Charles Town] 3 April 1764

Sir,

My last trouble to you the 11th February per Barnes & Brunett[9] since which I supply'd your Nephew Mr. Lowbridge Bright with £630 Currency for which he has given me a draught on you

---

[9] The brigantine *Tryton,* John Brunet, was cleared outwards on Feb. 10, for Cowes. Naval Office Lists, 1764–1767, p. 74. HL had helped John Brunet purchase the *Tryton,* a New England-built vessel. See HL to Nathaniel & George Bethune, May 28, 1764.

for £190 Sterling, Exchange at 700 per Cent, at which rate some good houses have drawn & do now to raise Cash still draw.

The 7th March I rece'd the Value of £52.5/ Sterling from Capt. Moses Pitt & gave him a Bill on the Owners of the *Sally* payable to your order. He took the first with him & left the other under Cover of a Letter at my Counting House to be forwarded when I shou'd have further occasion to draw upon those Gentlemen. That Letter hath been officiously and without my knowledge forwarded or otherwise lost in my late removal from one House to another & lest this Latter shou'd be the case I have made out a third Bill & here Inclose it.

I gave Mr. Bright two Letters to the best sort of folks in North Carolina & shall meet him with others at Philadelphia. He set out on his Journey in very good health the 31st Ulto. During his sojourning here he was much respected & gave great satisfaction to every body that was acquainted with him & I dare say he will reap great benefit from this Tour which is better Worth the notice & attention of Young Gentlemen in England than is generaly thought of. I am Yours, &ca.—

[*P.S.*] 13 April. Have rece'd your favour of 26 January & forwarded the Letter for Mr. L. Bright to Philadelphia, & shall send the Pitch pine Plank by the first Ship that will take it in.

SOURCE: Letterbook copy, HL Papers, S. C. Hist. Soc.; addressed "Esquire. Bristol"; "per Gunn. Copy per Gibbes." The postscript was copied by HL.

ADMINISTRATOR OF ABRAHAM CARDOZO VERSUS HENRY LAURENS

April 3, 1764

[*On February 23, 1764 on motion of John Rutledge for the plaintiff and with the consent of Egerton Leigh for the defendant the issue in this case was placed under the arbitration of George Inglis and William Wooddrop who were to return an award before the first day of May term next. The arbiters' award was entered by the court on April 3, 1764 and made binding upon the litigants.*]

SOURCE: Journal, Court of Common Pleas, 1763–1769, pp. 55, 57, S. C. Archives.

TO JOHN MITCHELL[1]

[Charles Town] 5th April 1764

Sir,

Beef is not to be had at this time of day but in the Morning I shall see you in the Road[2] & bring what is needfull. Therefore 'tis unnecessary to add more than that I shall do all in my power to serve the Interest of the Concern'd in your Cargo & make the Voyage agreable to you. Meantime I am, &ca.—

SOURCE: Letterbook copy, Letter Book of Henry Laurens, Oct. 30, 1762–Sept. 10, 1766, Penn. Hist. Soc.; addressed "Captain of the *Mary Ann*. Rebellion Road."

TO GEORGE CHISMAN

[Charles Town] 7th April 1764

Sir,

Since writing you per this Ship 2d Inst., I have let to Freight 900 Barrels of your Ship *Dorsett's* Tonnage at £3.10/ per Ton to Cowes & Holland or Hamburgh (not Bremen) & five per Cent primage each Shipper to furnish his Quoto of half Barrels, about 8 or 10 to the hundred. This Freight was taken by no less than five Houses by which you may see there is no great eagerness to Load

---

[1] The sloop *Mary Anne,* John Mitchell, owned by James Smith, William Henderson, Alexander and James Baillie, and Samuel Phillips of St. Christophers, was entered inwards on April 16 from St. Christophers with a cargo of 50 slaves. Naval Office Lists, 1764–1767, p. 77. Captain Mitchell needed food for his human cargo while the vessel sat out the quarantine period which was ten days. The quarantine period explains the delay between the date of arrival and the date of entry at the naval office. *S. C. Statutes*, III, 773–774. HL paid £490 in duties on these slaves brought by Mitchell. Public Treasurer, Journal B: Duties, 1748–1765, p. 401, S. C. Archives. For the sale of these slaves see HL to John Knight & Co., April 14, 1764.

[2] Rebellion Road.

upon such terms.[3] Three or four more Vessels have since dropt in which has induced the Rice Factors to lock up their Stores & this day there is not a Barrel of good Rice to be bought at 40/. Therefore I am well pleased that our business is done & I shall urge our Freighters to give the *Dorset* good dispatch. In the meantime this may govern you to make the needfull Insurance, & I remain—

SOURCE: Letterbook copy, HL Papers, S. C. Hist. Soc.; addressed "Captain. London"; "per Gunn. Copy per Coward."

TO GRUBB & WATSON

[Charles Town] 7th April 1764

Gentlemen,

As this Ship is detain'd by contrary Winds give me leave to add a few lines to what I troubled you with by her under the 3d Inst. Mr. John Savage requests that you will pass all the charges both Debit & Credit relative to his one eighth part of the said Ship *Heart of Oak* to my Account & 'tis my request that you will enable me to settle Account with Mr. Savage by the earliest advices of such entries. And further I desire you to bespeak to William Beeck Six Windsor Chairs exactly such as Mrs. Sarah Nicholson & Co. bought of him on my Account in November last described more particularly on the other side by a Copy of his Bill excepting only that I wou'd not have all of them painted of *One Coulour* nor all the Linings to be of one Coulour, but let there be a Variety of Stone blue, Green, & be pleased not to forget to direct him to make the Chairs very strong, & One Inch or two wider in the Seat than the Last. Please to have them ready to come in our own Ship & they will pay a little Freight—

SOURCE: Letterbook copy, HL Papers, S. C. Hist. Soc.; addressed "London"; "per Gunn." A letter of the same tenor, dated April 5, was crossed out in the letterbook and noted "not sent."

---

[3] The *Dorset* was cleared outwards on May 2 for Cowes with 793 barrels and 69 half barrels of rice. Naval Office Lists, 1764–1767, p. 80. Primage was a small payment made by shippers to the captain of a vessel for his special care of the goods. In 1755 it was usual to give 5% primage. *OED*. The 69 half barrels were approximately 5% of 793 whole barrels.

GEORGE AUSTIN & HENRY LAURENS VERSUS EDWARD DANNELLY[4]

April 7, 1764

[*On April 7, 1764, William Burrows, attorney for the plaintiffs, filed suit in the court of common pleas against Edward Dannelly, planter of St. Thomas parish, for recovery of a bond, dated April 6, 1762, in the sum of £618 currency. The defendant through his attorney James Grindlay confessed judgment. The judgment was signed on the same day and recorded by Dougal Campbell, clerk of the court.*]

SOURCE: Judgment Rolls, 1764, No. 117A, S. C. Archives; Judgment Docket, Court of Common Pleas, Book 2 (1755–1773), p. 86, S. C. Archives.

TO MAYNES & CO.

[Charles Town] 11 April 1764

Gentlemen,

Annex'd to this you will see a duplicate of what I had the honour of writing you under the 20th Ulto. to which please to be refer'd.

This will be deliver'd to you by Capt. Hugh Porter of the Snow *Dennistoune* & you will find inclosed an invoice & Bill of Loading for 252 Barrels & 70 half Barrels of Rice Shiped on the said Snow on her Owners Account to your address. I hope that it will arive at a good Market. There is not at present another Vessel offers for Lisbon. If none appears before my own Vessel the *Flora* arrives here & that Rice does not advance in price 'tis highly probable that I shall wholly Load her on my own Account for that Market & Consign the Cargo half to yours & the other half to Mr. Edward Burn & Son's House, because I wish you both alike prosperity. If this shou'd not take place, some future occasion will assure you that I am with great regard, Gentlemen, Yours, &ca.—

SOURCE: Letterbook copy, HL Papers, S. C. Hist. Soc.; addressed "Lisbon"; "per Porter."

---

[4] Edward Dannelly described himself as of Christ Church parish in his will. "Will of Edward Dannelly," dated June 12, 1776, proved ———, Charleston County Wills, XVIII (1776–1784), p. 260, S. C. Archives.

BILL OF SALE

April 11, 1764

[HL purchased on this date from Charles and Susannah Lorimer[5] of Charleston "a Mulatto man named Samuel, a Brick layer by Trade," for the sum of £1,200 currency. Charles Lorimer acknowledged the receipt of the purchase money from HL on April 12. Robert Rawlins, who had witnessed the transaction, swore to the signatures on April 16, before William Burrows, Esquire, justice of the peace, and the deed was recorded the same day.]

SOURCE: Miscellaneous Records, MM, Part 1 (1763–1767), pp. 88–89, S. C. Archives.

TO THOMAS ROSE[6]

[Charles Town] 12 April 1764

Sir,

I shall be ready at any time to pay the Balance of your Account but cannot consent to let the Money lay over that I advanced for you to Mr. Elliott. I have a family to provide for as well as you have, & the distress of yours is wholly owing to your own folly, madness, & extravagance after many repeated indulgences & acts of friendship from me, & I am sure that if I was to aid you again, you would again fall into the same errors. Therefore I think it would have been doing you an act of kindness if I had held my hand some years ago. You would by this time have come to your senses, & now I am resolved to do nothing more for you until I see by a thorough change of life you are once more that Thomas Rose that Mr. Gadsden[7] recommended

---

[5] Charles Lorimer had advertised for sale on April 4 "as good a bricklayer as any in the province." General Gazette, April 18, 1764. Charles Lorimer was minister of the Scots Presbyterian church in Charleston from the early 1750's until October 1754 and pastor of the Johns Island Presbyterian church from April 1755 until shortly before he sailed for England on July 8, 1764. Gazette, Oct. 8, 1764; George Howe, History of the Presbyterian Church in South Carolina (2 vols.: Columbia, S. C., 1870, 1883), I, 271, 278–279, 321. He married after 1754 Susan Fraser, the daughter of John Fraser of Wigton or Fraser's plantation at Goose Creek. SCHM, xxix (1928), 19. His estate was confiscated in 1782. SCHM, xxxiv (1933), 195. Susan Lorimer died in Kent, England, on June 16, 1785. SCHM, v (1904), 56.

[6] Thomas Rose pursued the "Cooperage Business" at his shop on Motte's wharf. The copartnership of Rose & Thomson had ended on Sept. 30, 1763. Gazette, Feb. 10, 1757, Oct. 1, 1763. Rose, who had been elected packer every year except one from 1750 to 1763, was not reelected in 1764.

[7] Most probably Christopher Gadsden.

to me 13 or 14 Years ago, a diligent, careful, *Sober* Tradesman. Then & not until then can I consent to have any further connexion with you, for I am certain that if you do not receive some such Check to your Carreer, nothing but death to your self and grand losses to the few that befriend you will put a stop to it.

This may seem to you to be a bitter potion but I intend it to do you service & hope you will make such use of it as to experience & shew me its wholesome effects. I am, &ca.—

SOURCE: Letterbook copy, Letter Book of Henry Laurens, Oct. 30, 1762–Sept. 10, 1766, Penn. Hist. Soc.; addressed "Cooper. Charles Town."

TO NICHOLAS GERISSON[8]

[Charles Town] 12 April 1764

Sir,

Under this cover you will find Capt. Dingee's[9] Receipt for a small Box put on board his Schooner & also a Letter referring to said Box both which I forward at request of our Friends at Bethabara. I wish them safe to your hands & remain Yours, &ca.—

SOURCE: Letterbook copy, HL Papers, S. C. Hist. Soc.; addressed "Philadelphia"; "per Capt. Dingee." This letter was copied into this letterbook after the letter to Joseph Bower, Aug. 25, 1764. The copy was endorsed: "This was by mistake Copied in the Inland Book & not discover'd in time." This letter, therefore, can also be found in Letter Book of Henry Laurens, Oct. 30, 1762–Sept. 10, 1766, Penn. Hist. Soc. where it was endorsed: "N. B. This Letter is Copied in the Foreign Letter Book."

---

[8] Nicholas Gerisson (1701–1781) as captain of the *Little Strength*, owned by the Moravian church, brought the "Second Sea Congregation" of Moravians to Pennsylvania in 1743. After serving for many years as "a sea-captain of repute," he selected in 1763 Bethlehem as the home for his declining years. *Pennsylvania Magazine of History and Biography*, x (1886), 207n; xxxiii (1907), 231–232. Gerisson may have brought to America some of the Moravians who later moved to North Carolina.

[9] The schooner *Susannah & Hannah*, Daniel Dingee, was cleared outwards on April 12 for Philadelphia. Naval Office Lists, 1764–1767, p. 80.

TO LOWBRIDGE BRIGHT

[Charles Town] 13th April 1764

Dear Sir,

    I was extreamly sorry that your punctuality in observing the moment of your appointment for commencing your Long journey & mine to be the same morning at James's Island[1] rendered it impossible for me to have the pleasure of taking you by the hand & seeing your first embarkation in a Ferry Boat.[2] Nevertheless my good wishes did & do attend you & I hope they will be successable, that you may make a pleasant & advantagious tour thro' North America, & that you may arrive before the Winter setts in, in the embraces of your many good friends in England, for I must not confine you to Bristol only.

    If you shou'd on this or the other side of the Atlantic find an Idle half hour to give me some Account of your travels, you will oblige me very much & the fuller you are upon the Subjects that offer the more agreable.

    Yesterday Capt. Deas[3] arrived from Bristol & brought me the inclosed Letter which I forward without delay. Very Little news we hear & that Little will be stale by the time you receive this, therefore I shall not intrude a recital of any part upon your time. Yet I must tell you one thing that gives me much concern. Our Petition or as I shou'd say the Petition or representation or Address of the House of Assembly in Carolina to the King has been read & *thats all*. We are therefore in dolefull plight, no province in his Majesty's Dominions in so bad a situation.[4] Mrs. Laurens & all my family thank God are well & all often mention your name with affection & respect.

---

    [1] James Island lies south and west of Charleston across the Ashley River. As there were shipyards on the island, HL may have been attending to his commercial affairs.

    [2] If Lowbridge Bright left Charleston by ferry, he must have crossed the Cooper River to Hobcaw whence he would make his way overland to the Santee and to Georgetown. John Bartram used Hobcaw ferry in 1765 as he was returning from Cape Fear and Georgetown: "came to lamprees at hobcaw ferry. paid 20 shillings for ferriage & 30 shillings for a dish or two of tea. passage 3 mile, landed at Charles town." Bartram, *Diary of a Journey*, p. 19.

    [3] The brigantine *Industry*, David Dease, was entered inwards on April 13 from Bristol. Naval Office Lists, 1764–1767, p. 77.

    [4] The assembly had drawn up an address to the King denouncing Governor Boone which they had accepted on Sept. 13, 1763. Charles Garth, the agent for South Carolina, presented the address to the Privy Council on Nov. 18. On the advice of the Board of Trade, the Privy Council had decided to postpone consideration of it until Boone returned to England. Boone did not sail until May 11, 1764. Garth on June 25, three days before Boone's arrival in London, asked the Privy Council to act on the address. The Board of Trade ultimately

The House & Gardens go on as quick & as well as I can expect all things considered, & I am generally as well disposed for a Nap at ½ past ten as you have known me to be. Labour in the day & an undisturbed conscience at night procures sweet rest to Man, & health ensues.

I hope that I need not tell you over again that I shall always be glad to serve you, but permit me to repeat that, I remain with great regard—

SOURCE: Letterbook copy, HL Papers, S. C. Hist. Soc.; addressed "Philadelphia"; "per Capt. Dingee."

TO GRUBB & WATSON

[Charles Town] 14th April 1764

Gentlemen,

The preceeding is duplicate of what I wrote you per Capt. Gunn since which the Coppy of your favour of the 14th January by way of Bristol is come to hand, but the original said to have been sent by Chisman[5] does not appear consequently I am without a Receipt from Mr. William Roberts & unluckily it is wanted by Mr. Mansel[6] to settle an Account with the Gentleman by whose order the £70 Sterling was paid. I fancy the Letter was never put into the *Dianna*'s Bag, because I have rece'd exclusive of that, the exact number inserted in the List.

The arival of four or five Sail this week has almost stagnated the Sale of Rice. Almost every parcel that comes down is put into Store & the Factors are divided in their Opinions whether to keep it for 45/ or 50/ & truly a few Ships more will enable them to obtain the former at least & I begin to be apprehensive that Ships will be in almost as bad a plight this Year as they were the last.

I beg leave to recommend all possible dispatch to be given to the *Heart of Oak* & I remain with great regard—

took a position unsympathetic to Boone's position. Jack P. Greene, "The Gadsden Election Controversy and the Revolutionary Movement in South Carolina," *Mississippi Valley Historical Review*, XLVI (1959), 485–488.

[5] The ship *Diana*, Isaac Cheesman, was entered inwards on April 13 from London. Naval Office Lists, 1764–1767, p. 77.

[6] Walter Mansell, a tailor, had branched out into merchandizing. He came out to Charleston in 1752 and returned to England in 1770. *HL Papers*, II, 160n; Loyalist Transcripts, LV, 352–358.

SOURCE: Letterbook copy, HL Papers, S. C. Hist. Soc.; addressed "London"; "per Gibbs."

TO DENNISTOUNE, MUNRO & CO.

[Charles Town] 14 April 1764

Gentlemen,

My last was under the 3d Ulto. per Capt. Gunn & on the 7 Inst. I clear'd out the *Dennistoune* since which she has been lying in readyness for Sea with the first wind that offers. Please to receive Inclos'd Invoice & Bill of Loading for 252 Barrels & 70 half Barrels Rice on your Account per said Snow together with one of Capt. Porters Receipts for disbursments. The whole amounting to £4,136.12.5 is placed to the debit of your Account also Sale of 78 Tons of Coals Net proceed to your Credit £411.7.6. Besides these the Capt. hath left in my hands Nineteen Casks of Bott'd Ale & three of Claret which I shall Sell for you as speedily & upon as good terms as the trade of this place in it's present circumstances will admit. The former is very good & I cou'd have sold it ere now if I wou'd have taken less than 60/ per dozen which people do not care to give at this time of Year. The Claret is by no means approved of or I shou'd have sold it upon tryal & I know not what to do with it.

A few Ships have droped in within this Week past which has set our Rice Factors aloft & they refuse to accept 40/ per Ct. for their Rice but put all in Store that comes to them & Freights are therefore at a Stand & must fall if two or three more Ships come in. I do not know of any that has obtained so high a Freight as your *Dennistoune* within 10/ per Ton & I begin to think that none will after this time during the Current Year.

I must observe one thing to you which my duty as a Factor & friend prompts me to & which I cannot resist, but as it is a subject that shou'd be treated with the utmost delicasy I rely upon your prudence, Gentlemen, to make a proper use of it if you see needfull for your own Interest without subjecting me to unjust imputations. The Rice that I have Shiped for you I know to be of a good quality & in good Barrels & as well Cooper'd as our Rich & busy Coopers can be made to do them. The quality of the Rice & Cask I always judge of myself & depend upon no other eyes than my Own; but I do know that some Rice & some Barrels Shiped in the same bottom are not so good. Great care therefore shou'd be had at Lisbon that a good parcel does not Suffer in the Sale by being connected to such as is inferior. I have the greatest Reason in the World to believe that I have sustain'd some disadvantages more than once by Shipping Rice to a foreign Market promiscously with many other people.

I have talked to Capt. Porter & desired him to give a hint to Messrs. Maynes to shun if possible any Mistakes that might otherwise be made thro' inadvertience or inattention of their Brokers or Servants.

SOURCE: Letterbook copy, HL Papers, S. C. Hist. Soc.; addressed "Glasgow"; "per Gibbs. Copy per Higgins with duplicate B. L., Invoice, & Receipt & Sale of Coals." Note added in letterbook by HL: "The remainder of this Letter Mr. Hest has omitted."

TO JOHN KNIGHT & CO.

[Charles Town] 14th April 1764

Dear Sir,

I have very little to add to the foregoing duplicate of my last under the 5th March & this serves chiefly to convey Copy of Capt. Dennison's Bill of Loading & Receipt & Abstract Invoice of his Cargo. I had a Message from him three days after he went over this Bar all well.

The fragments of the *Hope*'s goods inward are still on hand. I sent them to Vendue & there offer'd them at 6 for 1 but nobody would bid.

I should be glad for your sake that some of your Affrican would drop in. I sold as wretched a fifty Ebo Slaves this week as ever I saw here at £34.6/ Sterling round. They were sent to me by a friend in the West Indies contrary to my will as well as expectation. Had they been tolerable they would have yeilded £8 or £10 more but there were no less than 31 scrawney females amongst them & none except 4 Boys that Could be called passable.[7]

Upon the arrival of a few Ships Rice begins to Look up again & most of the Factors refuse to sell at 40/ per Ct. Freight of course, altho there are not many empty Ships in Port, is at a Stand.

---

[7] These were the slaves whom Capt. John Mitchell had brought from St. Christophers.

The last given was 50/ to 55/ for London & 70/ to Holland. I remain with most sincere esteem, &ca.—

SOURCE: Letterbook copy, HL Papers, S. C. Hist. Soc.; addressed "Liverpoole"; "per Capt. McGee."

TO WILLIAM THOMPSON

[Charles Town] 17 April 1764
Dear Sir,

A few Hours after you took leave of Charles Town a Vessel arived from London & brought me an account of the Sale of your Indigo & a very good one I think it is considering the bad Quality of the Indigo. The Net proceeds is £420 to the Credit of your Account which with a Copy of the Sale I here inclose.

I beg you will inform me as soon as you can about the payment on your Account to Mr. Baxter[8] for nothing relative to it appears in my Books.

I have allowed you 55/ for your last parcel of pitch which is really 5/ more than is given for any other & I pay it on Account of the Weight & goodness of the Barrel but as I hinted to you before this should be only to our selves, because other people without knowing the true reason & without judging upon right principles, may be offended that they have not the same Price for Pitch that is not worth it. Indeed it is at present only an expence to me being all in Store but I am looking out for a Ship every moment.

I cannot be certain as to the Number of Barrels. They were hurryed into Store without my knowledge but they shall be counted when they come out. I am with my Compliments, &ca.—

[P.S.] 18th April. Added a few Lines per Dick & inclosed the several Accounts, Viz. Account Current Balance to W. T. £161.15.10. Account Sale & the Old Account with A., L., & A., which had been omitted in the foregoing.

SOURCE: Letterbook copy, Letter Book of Henry Laurens, Oct. 30, 1762–Sept. 10, 1766, Penn. Hist. Soc.; addressed "Black Mingo"; "per Dickinson." The postscript was copied by HL.

---

[8] John Baxter. *HL Papers*, III, 223n.

TO ALEXANDER DAVIDSON

[Charles Town] 17th April 1764

Sir,

I have both your favours of the 16th & 22d March, with 80 Barrels of pitch per Capt. Williams Schooner,[9] which did not prove to be quite so heavy by about 20 lb. Weight per Barrel as a parcel that I bought of Mr. Marr[1] which came in the same Schooner. It was the Weight & goodness of the Latter that induced me to give 60/ per Barrel when I was buying other pitch from 50/ to 42/6, & I have allowed you the same price without any difference which I would not have done if you had been upon the spot because I am sure you Could not have got so much from any body else. I shall be ready at any time to discount your Bill on me to Mr. Swinton[2] & you know I never scruple to advance Cash for you if I can do it with any tolerable convenience to myself.

I thank you for the received offer of your Pitch & have only to repeat that I shall be upon every occasion careful either to allow or to procure for you the highest price of the Market.

Weight of Mr. Davidsons Pitch	Mr. Swintons	
325	355	346
337	337	340
333	360	335
995	1,052	1,021
331 Average	350 Average	340 Average

Your pitch fared well by coming down in good Company—

SOURCE: Letterbook copy, Letter Book of Henry Laurens, Oct. 30, 1762–Sept. 10, 1766, Penn. Hist. Soc.; addressed "Black Mingo"; "per Dickinson."

---

[9] John Williams registered the schooner *Molly* of which he was the master on Nov. 24, 1763 for himself "of North Carolina" and Joseph Turpin of Charleston. Ship Register, 1734–1765, p. 221, S. C. Archives.

[1] Andrew Marr. *HL Papers,* III, 523n.

[2] Hugh Swinton.

TO JOHN GREGG[3]

[Charles Town] 17 April 1764

Sir,

I Receiv'd per Mr. Dick's Schooner 90 Barrels of your pitch which is to your Credit at 50/ per Barrel, being the price given to the Factors for heavier pitch as you may see below. Your Barrels & Pitch were good but you [were] covetous of the quantity which shou'd not be for you will never loose by making the Barrels full size & filling them to the Bung. You will always receive a price or some advantage in proportion.

Weight of Mr. Gregg's Pitch
 Weight 320 Average short 2 lbs. per barrel
Weight of 2 parcels of Pitch Bought of William Logan[4] at 50/ per barrel.
 331 lbs. Average of one parcel
 337 Ditto the Other
Another parcel bought of William Parker[5] rather heavyer than the above.

SOURCE: Letterbook copy, Letter Book of Henry Laurens, Oct. 30, 1762–Sept. 10, 1766, Penn. Hist. Soc.; addressed "Black Mingo"; "per Dickinson."

TO JOHN BROCKINGTON[6]

[Charles Town] 17 April 1764

Sir,

I Rece'd your favour of the 5th per *Wambaw* Schooner with 32 or 33 Barrels of Pitch—you say 32, Dickinson says 33—but as there was no Sale for it nor Freight to be had the Wharfinger wou'd not allow it to lay in his way & before I was aware he put it with

---

[3] John Gregg was elected overseer of the poor for the parish of Prince Frederick on April 12, 1762 and on April 4, 1763. *Register Book for the Parish Prince Frederick Winyaw*, pp. 175, 179. John Gregg, who had settled on Cedar Swamp in 1752, called himself a planter in 1775. Boddie, *History of Williamsburg County*, pp. 31, 86; "Will of John Gregg," dated Oct. 3, 1775, proved ———, Charleston County Wills, XVIII (1776–1784), 152–153, S. C. Archives.

[4] *HL Papers*, I, 141n.

[5] *HL Papers*, III, 31n.

[6] William Brockington, who lived on the south side of Black Mingo Creek and died in 1741, left three sons, William, John, and Richard. John, a merchant, became one of the three Williamsburg tories. Boddie, *History of Williamsburg County*, pp. 74, 77, 102, 129; Rogers, *History of Georgetown County*, p. 164.

other parcels in Store. When it comes out I shall reccon it again. The price is 50/ for such Pitch as yours & I have bought near 450 Barrels that were a little light at 42/6.

I am obliged to you for giving me the preference of your Pitch, but in such cases it will always [be] more agreable to me that you appoint some friend to fix the price at delivery. If the Schooner goes to Black Mingo you may put what you please on board of her. I am—

SOURCE: Letterbook copy, Letter Book of Henry Laurens, Oct. 30, 1762–Sept. 10, 1766, Penn. Hist. Soc.; addressed "Black Mingo"; "per Dickinson."

TO DAVID FULTON[7]

[Charles Town] 17 April 1764

Sir,

I Rece'd your favour of the 4th per *Wambaw* Schooner with a parcel of Pitch said by you to be 95 Barrels but there being neither Sale nor Freight for it the Wharfinger wou'd not allow it to lay in his way but hurryed it into store & had put a good deal in before I knew it so that I cou'd not reccon them. I have passed the Amount to your Credit at 50/ per Barrel being the same price that I gave to Mr. William Parker for Mr. Carrs[8] & to William Logan for Mr. Grier's Pitch & for other parcels. Indeed at present I wou'd rather be without it as it only puts me to an expence of Storage. When it comes out I shall count it & hope to find the Number agree with yours. I shall be obliged to you to consider it & make up some further payment in order to cancel your debts which have been so long standing as to become exceedingly inconvenient to me.

SOURCE: Letterbook copy, Letter Book of Henry Laurens, Oct. 30, 1762–Sept. 10, 1766, Penn. Hist. Soc.; addressed "Black Mingo"; "per Dickinson."

---

[7] *HL Papers*, III, 373n.
[8] Isaac Carr. *HL Papers*, III, 146n.

TO JOHN WIGFALL

[Charles Town] 17 April 1764

Sir,

I am sorry that so many little circumstances in our late bargain for Lumber have fallen out to give occasion for complaints but the worst of all is what is now come to my knowledge of the Wraft of 2½ Inch plank, Vizt. that the Plank in Average are marked about 20 per Cent more than they realy measure for proof of which I here Inclose you the Contents of 12 Plank. These things cause me a good deal of uneasyness, from an avertive that I have & allways have had to disputes & altercation in Accounts which I have ever shuned with the most studious care & I must say that in the course of 15 Years dealing in Timber which at best is a troublesome Article I have not had so much dissatisfaction as in this one contract. You have I hope been in too much hurry of business & that after some recollection you will be able to set these things to right but I must desire that you will as soon as possible send somebody down to re-measure what remains of the Wraft before referr'd to. I am yours, &ca.—

SOURCE: Letterbook copy, Letter Book of Henry Laurens, Oct. 30, 1762–Sept. 10, 1766, Penn. Hist. Soc.; addressed "St. Thomas's."

GEORGE AUSTIN & HENRY LAURENS VERSUS JOHN MILES[9]

April 17, 1764

[On April 17, 1764, James Moultrie,[1] attorney for the plaintiffs, filed suit in the court of common pleas against John Miles of Ashley River for recovery of a bond, dated May 11, 1762, in the sum of £663.5.9 currency. Miles through his attorney James Parsons entered a plea on August 22, 1764, that the debt was not his. The docket does not indicate if any further action was taken in this case.]

SOURCE: Judgment Rolls, 1764, No. 167A, S. C. Archives.

---

[9] John Miles of St. Andrew parish died on Nov. 11, 1772. SCHM, x (1909), 169.

[1] James Moultrie was attorney general of S. C. in 1764 before becoming on Oct. 31, 1764, chief justice of East Florida. W. Roy Smith, South Carolina as a Royal Province, 1719–1776 (New York, 1903), p. 412; HL Papers, III, 423n.

TO DANIEL CROKATT[2]

[Charles Town] 23d April 1764

Sir,

A few days ago I receiv'd a Letter from my dear friend the Reverend Mr. Clark which I cannot give a suitable answer to before I see or hear from you; therefore I shall subjoin an extract from that Letter that you may be apprized of the subject & inabled to give me your own sentiments thereupon; which I shall be glad to receive as soon as possible but not before you have thought upon & considered the matter properly.

The regard that I bear to Mr. Clark will not suffer me to deny any thing that he asks if tis in my power with any tolerable convenience to gratify him & this leads me to repeat the offers of my service which I made to you in consequence of a former Letter from him & altho I am not in want of a Clerk nor shall be for this Summer & perhaps never again & especially of one whose services will be of uncertain duration & but short at most, yet I can furnish you with some employment which I think you may make both advantageous & reputable to yourself. 'Tis needless to add more until I hear from you. Therefore I take leave & remain, Sir, Your most Humble Servant—

P.S. Since writing as above I have looked over Mr. Clarkes Letter & think 'tis better to send you the very Letter[3] than any extract; you will find it under cover with this & will be pleased to return it to me in your answer.

SOURCE: Letterbook copy, Letter Book of Henry Laurens, Oct. 30, 1762–Sept. 10, 1766, Penn. Hist. Soc.; addressed "Monks Corner."

---

[2] Daniel Crokatt was most probably the son of James Crokatt. HL referred to him as a little boy in 1747. In 1776 he would be in the employ of the East India Co. *HL Papers*, I, 5n, 76. The Reverend Richard Clarke, who did tutor the sons of Carolina merchants, may have taught Daniel and was recommending him as clerk to HL. Perhaps Daniel was at Moncks Corner visiting his mother's relations the Gaillards, who lived along the Santee and in St. Stephen parish.

[3] The letter from Richard Clarke was not copied into the letterbook.

TO THOMAS YOUNG & OTHERS[4]

[Charles Town] 28 April 1764

Sir,

As the debt due to Austin & Laurens by the late Capt. John Gray deceased remains unpaid, & hath lain dormant a much Longer time than that which you required when you engaged to pay it to me, I hope you will not think me unreasonable in that I now request you either to comply with your promise & cancel the Bond by a full payment or that you give me or lodge in my hands sufficient security for the amount thereof. The nature of the case together with the uncommon indulgence that I have shewn will I am perswaded induce you to do now what ought to have been done some Months agone without further delay & you will thereby very much oblige, Sir, Your, &ca.—

SOURCE: Letterbook copy, Letter Book of Henry Laurens, Oct. 30, 1762–Sept. 10, 1766, Penn. Hist. Soc.; addressed "for himself & other Administrators of the Estate & Effects of John Gray, Esquire Deceas'd. Broad St."

TO DANIEL DOYLEY[5]

[Charles Town] 28 April 1764

Sir,

Mr. Appleby being upon the point of embarking for London I shall be glad to embrace the opportunity of writing by him to my friends Messrs. Wilson[6] in London to advise them of having recovered

---

[4] See Memorial of the Creditors of Captain John Gray Deceased, Nov. 8, 1762, *HL Papers*, III, 153–156.

[5] Daniel Doyley was appointed deputy provost marshal on April 5, 1760 and reappointed by Bull in June 1764. Miscellaneous Records, LL, Part I (1758–1763), pp. 261–262; MM, Part I (1763–1767), p. 117, S. C. Archives. Roger Pinckney, however, arrived on June 27, 1764, to assume the position of deputy provost marshal having been appointed by Richard Cumberland, the patent holder. *Gazette*, Oct. 8, 1764; *Documents Connected with the History of South Carolina*, ed. Plowden C. J. Weston (London, 1856), pp. 105–107. Doyley was appointed an assistant judge on March 1, 1766. *SCHM*, XXXI (1930), 216. He had married Ann Pinckney, the daughter of commissary William Pinckney, on Jan. 18, 1756. *SCHM*, XXXIX (1938), 30. He died in 1770 while in Rhode Island. *SCHM*, XVI (1915), 130.

[6] Samuel Wilson and Samuel Wilson, Jr., were hardwaremen. *HL Papers*, I, 13n; II, 377, 396, 482, 486. In 1763 Samuel Wilson, Jr., merchant, was at Mrs. Hammond's, Fenchurch Buildings. *London Directories*.

their Money from Thorpe's Estate[7] & at the same time make provision for Lodging the Money in their own hands upon their giving me a proper Security & indempnity. The Charges set forth in the Writt were paid, say £49.6.10 of them, were paid by me to James Wright, Esquire in December 1757. Therefore, Sir, I request you to Inform me when & where I may wait on you to receive the said Money & to give you such security as you required in the Case? I remain, &ca.—

SOURCE: Letterbook copy, HL Papers, S. C. Hist. Soc.; addressed "Esquire. Broad Street."

TO WILLIAM MANNING

[Charles Town] 28th April 1764

Sir,

Since writing to you as per duplicate annex'd I have been informed by different hands that altho the House of Heyleger & Hertson of Eustatia was hurt by some misadventures in the eve of the present peace, yet it stands and is able to pay all demands upon it; & that the House of Peter Cornelius & Docke Grober is undoubtedly firm; therefore I am in great hopes that if you will be so good as to renew & repeat your application to them you will succeed & recover the amount of their protested Bills in your hands together with all Charges.

I do not know of any title I have to take this freedom with you nor can I think that the commission that may arrise in case of success will compensate your trouble; nevertheless from that tender regard that one Merchant shou'd bear to the Interest of another as well as from the necessity there is of doing all that can be reasonably expected from us to encourage & give spirit to commerce & negotiation I am under no doubt of your doing every thing in your power to assist the proprietors of those Bills. Therefore presuming that we have the same feelings I shall trouble you with no further appology, but give me leave to repeat that your services herein will very much oblige me altho I am as little concern'd as you are in the issue, & that I remain, Yours—

---

[7] The estate of Robert Thorpe. *HL Papers,* II, 197n.

SOURCE: Letterbook copy, HL Papers, S. C. Hist. Soc.; addressed
"Esquire. St. Christopher"; "per Mitchel."

GEORGE AUSTIN, HENRY LAURENS,
& GEORGE APPLEBY VERSUS
DAVID OLIPHANT [8]

April 28, 1764

[On April 17, 1764, Robert Williams, Jr., attorney for the plaintiffs, filed suit in the court of common pleas against David Oliphant, a Charleston physician, for recovery of a bond, dated June 9, 1761, in the sum of £1,260 currency. The case was ordered for judgment on April 28, 1764 and settled without further action as the defendant paid the debt and court costs.]

SOURCE: Judgment Rolls, 1764, No. 207A, S. C. Archives.

TO SMITH & BAILLIES

[Charles Town] 30th April 1764

Gentlemen,

On the 6th Inst. I rece'd your favour of the 21st March per the *Mary Ann* Sloop with Bill of Loading for 50 New Negroes on your Account which came in all alive but extreamly meagre & thin. I viewed them with great attention over & over again & likewise took the opinion of a Gentleman[9] who had formerly lived with me and Assisted at the Sale of many Thousands, & upon the whole was convinced that the ordinary course of this Market would by no means turn them out to your advantage, & having that Solely in view I had project'd a voyage to George Town Winyaw in which I should have Subjected my Self to no small risque, & had given Capt. Mitchel orders to deliver the Slaves on board a Schooner which I had engaged for that purpose but the Wind coming suddenly round to North &

---

[8] Dr. David Olyphant (1720–1805) was a native of Scotland who emigrated to S. C. after the battle of Culloden. He practiced medicine in the parish of St. George Dorchester. During the Revolution he was director of hospitals for the army of Gen. Nathanael Greene. Joseph Ioor Waring, *A History of Medicine in South Carolina, 1670–1825* (Columbia, S. C., 1964), pp. 274–275.

[9] Perhaps William Price who had been a clerk in HL's counting house.

blew fresh & put an end to that Scheme. I then proposed to send
them to Port Royal but could not agree upon terms to induce me as
I do not so well like the payments in that quarter; & at length Mr.
Francis Stuart of Beaufort made me an offer of £11,200 for the
whole which I rejected [*and*] at the same time told him he might
have them for £12,000, which after a day or two he agreed to give
but then we parted on Account of the time of Payment which he
would have to be 1st January next. He went out of Charles Town &
left directions with a House here to agree with me if I should come
to new terms. And after placing your Negroes in the most advantageous light that I could, Vizt.

5	Men not extraordinary at	£300	£1,500.
10	inferior 3 of them very ordinary	£280	2,800.
15	Women chiefly small & very thin	245	3,675.
16	Girls very thin & slender	£200	3,200.
4	Boys small	£240	960.
			£12,135.

& considering the very great probability of a large abatement from
these prices by the arrival of African Ships I thought it most for
your Interest to accept of Mr. Stuart's offer which with some difficulty
I got the Gentlemen here who were grown very cool to confirm, & I
think myself very Lucky in effecting the bargain, because I could not
have sold upon so good terms above one half of them before the
arrival of a Ship from the Windward Coast with 410 which would
have knocked the Sale of the remainder on the head.[1] Upon the
whole I have done the utmost in my power to make a good Account
of them & should have been very glad to have got any body else to
have accepted the sale upon the same conditions. The Credit that I
have been obliged to give may probaly be attended with some inconvenience to you, its evidently so to me by the advance that I am
obliged to make for the Sloops Cargo & for the Duty which you are
heartily welcome to.[2] Please now to receive Accounts sale of said

---

[1] The ship *Minories,* Peter Bostock, was entered inwards on May 3 from
Africa with 394 slaves. Naval Office Lists, 1764–1767, p. 77. The ship would
have arrived in Charleston harbor at least ten days prior to the entering since
a quarantine period would have been necessary. Brewton & Smith sold this
cargo of slaves. See HL to John Knight, May 7.
[2] The sloop *Mary Anne,* John Mitchell, was cleared outwards on April 28 for
St. Kitts with 244 barrels and 62 half barrels of rice, 8 barrels of beef and
pork, and 5,000 shingles. Naval Office Lists, 1764–1767, p. 80.

Negroes Net proceed to the Credit of your Account £10,905 which Account is also charged for Amount of 244 Barrels & 62 half Barrels Rice & 5 M Shingles Shipped on your own Account per the *Mary Ann* & his disbursements £3,536.1.7 as per Invoice Bill of Loading & one of Capt. Mitchells Receipts here inclosed. I advertised[3] the Sloop during her Ten days of quarentine & applyed to Messrs. Smith and Farr[4] & every other probable place to procure freight but could not obtain one Cask. Those Gentlemen said they had a Vessel of their own upon hand for the West Indies. Indeed the sudden demand of Cash for Rice & the great prospect of an advance of price frighted people from entering into new engagements & I thought it would be distructive to your Interest as well as repugnant to your orders to keep the Vessel by the walls. I am already so deeply in adventures in the West Indies & shall have a considerable Sum to advance in a few Weeks for the Indian Corn that I have engaged that prudence forbids any further entanglements for the present Summer. Your next acceptable favour of the 3d Instant came to hand 8 or ten hours after the Sloop was cleared out; therefore it is not in my power to send any Pork in her but in fact there remains little or none in the Province of such quality as I would chuse to Ship.

Your request to remit £1,000 Sterling to be in London in July I should most readily comply with if I had as much money there as I had there & in Bristol some ten days ago, but the great want of Cash in this Town & the extream backwardness of payments has compelled me to draw for almost all that I had in both Cities merely to raise Currency to keep my Credit, which I have been forced to stake to a large amount on account of your good selves & several other friends whose orders I have complied with in the course of the last Winter to this time. But if your affairs do so pressingly require it, you have time enough to advise me & I will upon receiving directions borrow the Money for you & remit without delay.

An accident (melancholy enough to us who are nearly concerned) in my family, the sudden & unlooked for death of my eldest daughter on the 18th Instant,[5] filled my mind with so much grief & concern & employed me so much to compose & quiet her distressed

---

[3] The *Gazette* was not published between March 31 and Aug. 25, 1764.
[4] Smyth & Farr.
[5] Eleanor, born 1755, died on April 18, 1764. She was buried on April 20. *Register of St. Philip's Parish, 1754–1810*, p. 306.

Mother upon whose health the Life of another child greatly depended that I must acknowledge all business was for some days put out of my head as if I had been altogether unconnected with trade.

During that space I find that one or two Vessels Sailed for Antigua & your Island by which I ought to have wrote. As Capt. Mitchel Luckily did write to you I think my remisness will be attended with no ill consequence. The same circumstance hath caused me wholly to neglect your orders for the Accounts of repairs to the *Mercury*[6] per Mr. John Rose. I beg pardon for both & assure you that I shall send the Account in the most authentic manner that I can prevail on him to extend it, by the next opportunity or even by this if any accident prevents the Sailing of the Sloop today which I hope will not be the case for here is a fine Wind as ever filled Sails & Capt. Mitchel & I am equally anxious to embrace it. Many people here are eagerly purchasing Rice & Storing it upon speculation which keeps the price at 40/ Cash & the arrival of 3 or four Ships will start it. Rum continues extreamly dull & indeed no Sale for it but per Vendue from 11/ to 14/ per Gallon. Freights are rather on the decline. Exchange on England at 721 per Cent for good Bills.

I remain with true esteem & respect, Gentlemen, Your oblig'd humble Servant—

SOURCE: Letterbook copy, HL Papers, S. C. Hist. Soc.; addressed "St. Kitts"; "per Capt. Mitchell."

TO BELLAMY CRAWFORD[7]

[Charles Town] 2 May 1764

Dear Sir,

It is utterly imposible for me to comply with your request for the Loan of £2,000 because I not only have not that Sum at command but truly I can but just collect Money enough to keep my

---

[6] For the fortunes of the *Mercury*, William Robertson, see *HL Papers*, III, passim.

[7] Bellamy Crawford was born in Christ Church parish on Oct. 18, 1739. *SCHM*, XVIII (1917), 173. He was commissioned an ensign in the Provincial Regiment on Sept. 25, 1760. *SCHM*, III (1902), 205. He married Sara Pepper on Dec. 24, 1765. *SCHM*, XXII (1921), 34. He was exiled by the British from Charleston in 1781. *SCHM*, XXXIV (1933), 79. He died in Charleston in February 1784. *SCHM*, XVIII (1917), 148.

Credit whole & to ward of[f] a repetition of Duns, I am some times forced to submit to the first.

But besides this if I had money in never so great plenty I must repeat again what I candidly told you sometime ago that I should not think it consistent with your Interest to Lend you that Large sum that is necessary to extricate you from your present Load of debts & therefore should not hastily do what I am so well convinced would only tend to involve you more & more.

You talk of doing things with a better grace by & by, than could be done at this period. Beleive me, Sir, your unhappy circumstances & the dread of what the World will say, makes you view the advice of your friends as well as your own Interest & honour thro a flattering & delusive medium, & if you persist in your late & present resolutions, you may & probably will in the event be compelled to do what will neither be graceful to your Self nor satisfactory to anybody that wishes you well tho it may serve some busy Idle ones as a Subject for sneering at you. My advice is short. I think it is salutary. I would give it to my Brother. I would pursue it myself in like circumstances. Sell off your whole Estate (if necessary for the purpose) & pay off all your debts. My reasons are these & appear to me to be well founded. Your expected produce will not cancel the growing Interest upon your debts. Your Negroes in all probability will not sell so much by 10 per Cent or more next fall when you say you are resolved to sell them as they will at this time. To pay off all your debts while you have 20/ to the pound will be an act graceful, Honourable, commendable & will beget you some friends, more confidence, & the applause of every thinking Man.

To defer paying your debts until you may by some intervening misfortune be incapable of giving each Creditor his full demand will be it self, an act presumptuous, unwarrantable, & not quite honest, will put it out of the power of any friend you have to say a Word in excuse for you, will make every thinking Man withdraw his confidence, & will render you a subject for Laughter & redicule to those whom you now fear, but who in fact are not worthy of notice. I am, Dear Sir, &ca.—

SOURCE: Letterbook copy, Letter Book of Henry Laurens, Oct. 30, 1762–Sept. 10, 1766, Penn. Hist. Soc.

APPOINTMENT AS A COMMISSIONER
FOR REGULATING OF PILOTS

May 3, 1764

South Carolina

By His Excellency Thomas Boone, Esquire, Capt. General & Governor in Chief in & over the said Province, & Vice Admiral of the Same—

To John Savage, Henry Laurens, John Forbes, & John Torrans,[8] Esquires—

I reposing especial trust [&] confidence, in Your Loyalty, Integrity, & Circumspection have Constituted & Appointed [& by] these presents do Constitute you the said John Savage, Henry Laurens, John Forbes, & John Torrans, to be Commissioners for Regulating of Pilots for the Port and harbour of Charles Town giving [&] thereby Granting to you [*torn*] of You full power, & Authority to discharge [*torn*] as Commissioners as well as full & Ample Manner, as the Commissioners [*torn*] by An Act of Assembly of the Province aforesaid Passed the Ninth day of April 1734 Might or Could do.[9]

Given under my Hand & Seal at Charles Town this Third day of May Anno Domini 1764 in the fourth Year of his Majesty's Reign.

Thomas Boone

By his Excellency's Command
George Johnston, Deputy Secretary

SOURCE: Miscellaneous Records, MM, Part 1 (1763–1767), p. 95, S. C. Archives.

---

[8] John Torrans was born in Derry, Northern Ireland, settled in Charleston in 1758, flourished as a merchant, and died in 1780 at the age of seventy-eight. *SCHM*, xxix (1928), 149–150. He was a partner in the firm of Torrans, Greg, & Poaug. *HL Papers*, iii, 70, 195n, 408n. He owned in 1780 a one-third share in a distillery and with Alexander Rose property on the Pee Dee and Waccamaw Rivers. "Will of John Torrans," dated Jan. 14, 1780, proved ———, *Abstracts of Wills, 1760–1784*, p. 306. John Torrans was one of three Charleston merchants to marry daughters of Judge William Smith of New York (1728–1793), the historian and loyalist. John Gordon married Catherine Smith on March 10, 1767. *SCHM*, iii (1902), 177; Marriage Bond, dated March 10, 1767, signed by John Gordon and John Torrans, S. C. Broadsides, Rare Book Room, Library of Congress. John Torrans married Elizabeth Smith, the third daughter of William Smith. *SCHM*, xxix (1928), 149. Alexander Rose married Margaret Smith on Jan. 21, 1779. *SCHM*, xi, (1910), 168.

[9] *S. C. Statutes*, iii, 399–402.

TO JOHN WIGFALL

[Charles Town] 4th May 1764

Sir,

In answer to your favour of the 2d Instant in writing of which you have put your self to too much trouble; it appears to me needful to say only a few words.

You & I, Sir, made one clear & plain bargain for a certain quantity of Lumber at certain prices, to be delivered within a certain bound near my Land & in certain good order & condition.

I am inclined & determined as nearly as you will permit me, to comply on my part with each & every branch of our agreement; therefore if there is (as you say) any *difference* between us it must lay wholly on your side; & in order to remove such difference and reconcile you to your own propositions made at our first entring upon this troublesome engagement give me Leave to say this altho I am not under the least obligation, & that I do not perceive the least necessity for doing so in the present case, yet I am willing to submit this matter to the final determination of any two Men of Honesty & experience in the Trade to be indifferently chosen by us. But I am almost persuaded that upon further reflection a Gentleman of your candour & Veracity will not call in third & fourth persons to confirm an engagement which may so easily be done only by an adherence to your own repeated promises, bothe verbally in presence of witnesses & in writing.

Your to much haste has led you to say very unnecessary & I think very unjustifiable things of the absent plank from the wraft of 2½ Inches. Those plank are very safe and if you had enquired or said a word to me you would have been informed that Mr. Cannon[1] had them & thereby the error in measurement was discovered & who after such egregious mistake found the wraft would not possibly be at my

---

[1] Joseph Johnson called the carpenter Daniel Cannon "the oldest and most influential mechanic in Charleston." He was also one of the richest because he became the owner of Cannonsboro, one of the earliest suburbs of Charleston. Joseph Johnson, *Traditions and Reminiscences chiefly of the American Revolution in the South* (Charleston, S. C., 1851), p. 34. Daniel Cannon married (1) Martha Winn on March 8, 1750 and (2) Mary Doughty on Oct. 30, 1755. *Register of St. Philip's Parish, 1720–1758,* p. 191; *Register of St. Philip's Parish, 1754–1810,* p. 142. He was a founder of the Fellowship Society in 1762 and first president of the Carpenter's Society in Aug. 1783. Richard Walsh, *Charleston's Sons of Liberty, A Study of the Artisans, 1763–1789* (Columbia, S. C., 1959), pp. 29, 131. He died in 1803. "Will of Daniel Cannon," dated June 24, 1802, proved Jan. 21, 1803, Charleston County Wills, xxix (1800–1807), 390–393, S. C. Archives.

risque & your own Letter will prove that; yet I took as much care of
it as if had to all intents and purposes mine, & assure you that neither
you nor any body else shall ever suffer Loss thro wilful default or
negligence of, Sir, Your most humble Servant—

SOURCE: Letterbook copy, Letter Book of Henry Laurens, Oct. 30,
1762–Sept. 10, 1766, Penn. Hist. Soc.; addressed "Esquire. Cainhoy."

TO DUNBAR, YOUNG & CO.

[Charles Town] 4th May 1764
Gentlemen,
    This Morning Your favour of yesterday's date was brought to
me & I found it covered the Bill therein mentioned for £85.1.1 Sterling. The draught of Constantinus Zweerts on Messrs. Hall & Zweerts
in Jamaica which I shall send to that Island & endeavour to recover
the amount the Net proceeds whereof together with that of Sir John
Colletons[2] Note shall in due time be passed to the Credit of Mr. John
Gray's Bond.[3] Meantime to guard against disappointments I intreat
you to provide for payment not only of the ballance but in case of need
the whole Amount, which I shall apply for immediately after I hear
from Jamaica, according to the fate of this Bill which at best will give
me an additional trouble that ought not to have been put upon me.
I remain with great regard, Gentlemen, Your most humble Servant—

SOURCE: Letterbook copy, Letter Book of Henry Laurens, Oct. 30,
1762–Sept. 10, 1766, Penn. Hist. Soc.; addressed "Messrs. Charles
Town."

TO NATHANIEL PAICE[4]

[Charles Town] 4 May 1764
Sir,
    I wrote to you under the 30th March in the Late expired Year
with a remittance per John Lindsays Bill on William Bordon for

---

[2] Sir John Colleton of Fairlawn who died in 1777.
[3] See HL to Thomas Young & Others, April 28, 1764.
[4] HL Papers, III, 213n.

£111.1.2 Sterling on Account of Jonas Maynard, Esquire since which I have rece'd none of your favours but the said Bill came Back to me through the hands of Mr. Maynard. I now forward under this cover on his Account a Bill of my own draught the 2d Inst. on Messrs. Cowles & Harford, Bristol, payable at Sixty days sight in London to your order for £194.13.9 Sterling which includes £123.12.6, the produce of the Protested Bill above said & £71.1.3 for Ballance of his Account Current with Austin, Laurens, & Appleby. Your acknowledging the Receipt hereof in a single line will be very obliging to, Sir, Your, &ca.—

SOURCE: Letterbook copy, HL Papers, S. C. Hist. Soc.; addressed "Esquire. London"; "per Chisman. Copy per Higgins with 2d Bill."

TO THOMAS ELLIS[5]

[Charles Town] 4 May 1764

Sir,

You will receive under this cover a Bill of my own draught on Messrs. Cowles & Harford, Bristol, payable in London at 60 days sight to your order for £109.15.7 Sterling which I remit on Account of Mr. Jeremiah Nibbs, Junior, Merchant in Antigua being the Ballence of his account with me. Your acknowledging the Receipt hereof in a Line or two will much oblige, Sir, Your, &ca.—

SOURCE: Letterbook copy, HL Papers, S. C. Hist. Soc.; addressed "Esquire. London"; "per Chisman. Copy per Higgins with 2d Bill."

TO HUTCHINSON MURE

[Charles Town] 4 May 1764

You will find under this cover a Bill drawn by me this day on Messrs. Cowles and Harford, Bristol, payable at 60 days sight in London to your order for £300 Sterling on account of Messrs. Meyler & Hall, Merchants in Jamaica to whose account you will be pleased to pass the produce of said Bill & I shall be very thankful to you for a Line or two acknowledging the Receipt of it. I am Sir, Your, &ca.—

---

[5] Thomas Ellis was a merchant of Savage Gardens. *London Directories.*

SOURCE: Letterbook copy, HL Papers, S. C. Hist. Soc.; addressed "London"; "per Chisman. Copy per Higgins with 2d Bill."

TO COWLES & HARFORD

[Charles Town] 5th May 1764

Gentlemen,

Since the date of my last Letter, Vizt. the 3d March, I have received your sundry favours of the 20th & 26th January & 18th February inclosing the sundry Sales therein mentioned which appear to be right tho I have not fully examined them. The discount on the Navy Bills for the bounty on Navel Stores is really too much & beyond anything that I have experienced in your house before for the course of fifteen Years. Would it not have been Better worth your while to have kept them on your own or on my Account than to have paid so heavy an Interest for money that was not really wanted?

The case of Capt. Kerr,[6] relative to his primage differed very widely indeed from Capt. Green.[7] The first was a Sin of pure ignorance which you see I disdain'd to take an advantage of; the latter was the effect of obstinacy & self sufficiency in Capt. Green against all the expostulations & explanations that I could make use of, & his pretending that he was not apprized of the manner in which the Bill of Loading was filled up, was making bad worse, for I not only repeated the contents to him but assured him so often of what would be the consequence that I was at length ashamed to say any more lest he should think I meant to deceive him.

You gave me some hopes the 20th January of receiving my Account Current but to my no small mortification neither that nor my account with my good Friend Mr. Cowles is come in any of your Letters which occasions very disagreeable uncertainties & Chasms in my Accounts on this side. I must therefore once more intreat you to send them by the first opportunity in which you will do me a very great favour & I must beg in the most pressing manner that you will not disappoint me again. I want to know of several remittances which I hope are made to you from Philadelphia & Portugal which I am now ignorant of. Meantime according to my reckoning I must have

---

[6] Capt. Alexander Ker of the *Minerva*.
[7] Capt. Young Green of the *Susannah*.

in balance of Account & effects sold or unsold in your hands enough
to intitle me to draw on you for upwards of Three Thousands pounds
Sterling. And therefore in these times of necessity when money is
scarser than ever was known in Carolina I am necessitated and have
made Free to draw on you for a large sum, vizt. £2,193.1.4 Sterling
as per account below & which I have done with the less reluctance
because so great a part of it will fall into the hands of my Friend &
late partner George Appleby who I know will wait if needful to a
time convenient to yourselves for payment. I have very Large Sums
due to me in this Country but cannot without much plague & trouble
collect enough to carry on Business in the way that I chuse & I have
been & am largely in advance for several friends on your side. If I
should be again streighted for Cash shall draw on you in the next
Month for seven or Eight hundred pounds which if Harrop's Cargo
came safe to your care will still be within bounds of my own Accounts.
I mean not to put you in advance beyond what you have in hand.
You will observe that I have marked opposite to each Bill the Exchange but I think the most equitable way will be to charge the whole
to my account Current & make that in Credit by your account Current
for one half at 7 14 per Cent Exchange & so I shall enter untill I hear
from you.

Capt. Courtin does not yet appear. I am surprized you have
not taken the least notice of his Ship in any of your Letters & fearing
that he may be gone around about Voyage I am just Shipping off a
Cargo of Pitch & Green Tar laid in for him. Rice is at 40/ & freight
to Holland £3 per Ton. We have an exceeding dry spring which gives
a dismal prospect to many of our planters of the growing Crop of Rice
& Corn & worse of Indigo.

Date	days sight	to order of		Sum	Exchange
1764 April 28	75	Geo. Appleby	£	380.	714
"	40	ditto		970.	700
May 1	60	ditto		238.12	721
2d	60	Nathaniel Paice, Esquire		194.13.9	721
4th	60	Thomas Ellis, Esquire		109.15.7	721
"		Hutchison Mure, Esquire		300.	721

2,193. 1.4

SOURCE: Letterbook copy, HL Papers, S. C. Hist. Soc.; addressed
"Bristol"; "per Higgins. Copy per Chisman."

TO HENRY BRIGHT & CO.

[Charles Town] 5th May 1764

Gentlemen,

My last was on the 29th March per Capt. Hooper[8] & Capt. Gunn to which please to be refered.

Yesterday I passed a Bill on you to the order of Mr. George Appleby at 40 days sight payable in London for £148.12.9 Sterling for which I obtained 721 per Cent & passed the same to your Credit £1,071.13.2 as per this annexed Account Current balanced thereby. I hope you will find the same free from error & upon enquiry that my draughts on you have been made upon the most advantageous terms. If I have done well in this transaction you may rely upon the same endeavours for your Interest in all future commands that you shall be pleased to lay upon, Gentlemen, Your, &ca.—

SOURCE: Letterbook copy, HL Papers, S. C. Hist. Soc.; addressed "Esquire. Bristol"; "per Capt. Higgins. Copy per Chisman with duplicate Account Current."

TO GEORGE CHISMAN

[Charles Town, 5 May 1764]

Sir,

My Last was the 7th April per Capts. Gunn & Coward[9] since which the *Dorsett* is fully Loaden & now lies ready to sail with the first Wind. I have supplyed your Brother with Cash for the Ships Disburse which with my Commission thereon amounts to £174.9/ as per his receipt inclosed & I shall one of these days pass a Bill on you for the Value. Besides this I am entitled to a Commission for procuring freight for the *Dorsett*, Vizt. 840 barrels Rice at 4/ per barrel being the customary Charges in this place £168, but as you are heartily welcome to any such services that I can do for you be pleased to deduct so much thereof as your proportion of the Ship is liable to pay & appropriate that part to yourself & the remainder to be paid by the other owner or owners I present to your Brother Christopher, Master

---

[8] The ship *Fortune,* Daniel Hooper, sailed for London on March 31. *Gazette,* March 31, 1764.

[9] The *Gazette,* March 24, 1764, listed the ship *King George,* William Coward, as "near loaded & may sail next week" for Portsmouth.

of the said Ship & desir'd it may be paid to him. When I can be further useful to you in this place be pleased to lay your commands on, Sir—

SOURCE: Letterbook copy, HL Papers, S. C. Hist. Soc.; addressed "London"; "original per Higgins. Copy per Chisman with duplicate receipt."

TO JOHN KNIGHT

[Charles Town] 7th May 1764

Dear Sir,

The preceeding is Copy of what I wrote the 14th Ulto. since which I have attempted to finish the Sale of the *Hopes* Cloths, &c., even at 5 for 1 per Vendue but all in vain. Nay I applyed to a Taylor to get him to make the whole up into Waistcats & Breeches & mend the sale per Vendue in that Shape but upon a Calculation I found that scheme would not answer and from my advices from Philadelphia I have not the least room to hope for amendment of the Sale in case I should send them to that Market. Therefore I am necessitated to accept of an offer of 5 for 1 here upon a long Credit of four months certain & as much longer as the purchasers affairs will admit of, paying me Interest after 4 months. They are already injured by Moth & would be much worse in the Course of this Summer if I should keep them on hand for another Winter. I shall deliver them tomorrow or next day & soon after transmit you the Amount. You will be no gainers by that adventure; I shall be rather a looser by the long advance of my money but that I do not set in comp[et]ition with any services that I can do or cause to be done to my good Friend & benefactor Mr. Knight.

I have kept the *Austins* Rum too in hopes of better times but my hopes are fruitless. West India Rum is every day sold at 13/6 & 13/ per Gallon & there is not only a prodigious Stock upon hand but new imports are made every day. I shall therefore advertize to sell what remains at 15/ per Gallon which perhaps the name of age may entitle it to & if that cannot be obtained accept of the best price that is offered & put an end to that Account.

When any thing is to be done here I believe I can do it as well as most of my Neighbours & I think that what I have hitherto sold will bear a comparison with any accounts in Charles Town, but it Chagrins me a little for the sake of your self & Mr. Mears to look back & see that I have not been able to do better. Mr. Appleby will forward this & when he sees you will explain the situation of our Trade in this place & of my own affairs particularly.

I continue to wish for some of your Africans to partake of the advantages of this Market. Brewton & Smith averaged Capt. Bostock's Cargo of 410 Windward Slaves last Week at £36. I never saw them But am told they were not a fine Cargo & many little ones. The average is just now sent to me by themselves. This is probably the flower of the Market & I wish your Factors had gathered it. I remain, Dear Sir—

SOURCE: Letterbook copy, HL Papers, S. C. Hist. Soc.; addressed "London"; "per Higgins. Copy per Kendal."

TO ISAAC KING

[Charles Town] 7th May 1764

Sir,

Since my last of the 3d Ultimo as per Copy inclosed I have received your acceptable favour of the 12th January inclosing the Sale of Indigo per Jenkins[1] on Mr. William Thompsons account & on my own account which I have not examined & am advised of the Sale of part of my Indigo per Strachan[2] which affords no satisfaction to the covetous eye. But as I am perswaded you have done all in your power to procure the best terms, please to be assured that I am & shall be contented with the event. I also observe the remittance made to you by Messrs. Bewickes, Timmerman & Co. £108.13.5 & of the draughts made by Capt. Courtin which shall be duly noted to your debit & Credit as they ought to be. Tis surprising to me that no body had said a word about the time when the Ship *Flora* would probaly sail. This I could not so much look for from you as from Bristol & from the Capt. & their silence together with the delay of the Ship has brought about a new consignment of Pitch & Green Tar which I had laid in for that Vessel & am now Loading on board the Ship *Hope*,

---

[1] The ship *Boscawen*, David Jenkins, had sailed for London on Jan. 31, 1763. *Gazette*, Feb. 5, 1763; HL Papers, III, 206, 220, 222, 225.

[2] The ship *Union*, James Strachan, sailed for London on April 3, 1763. *Gazette*, April 9, 1763; HL Papers, III, 372, 379, 388, 406, 410.

Capt. Bowers,[3] on the joint account of Mr. Gabriel Manigault & myself, say about 800 barrels. The Ship will Sail for London about the 20th Instant. Mr. Manigault has wrote to you for Insurance of his part. Mine I shall either risque or Insure a part of it here in hopes of making the premium Sterling in your hands.

I am half concerned in 750 Barrels of Pitch Shipped by Mr. Manigault a few days ago per the Snow *Charles Town,* Capt. Simpson, for London[4] to your address. I was at that time under a Cloud of affliction & did not write to you but I believe that good man said & did all that was needful upon the occasion. The risque of my part of that adventure is likewise my own or may perhaps be Insured here.

Mr. William Price has Entred into a partnership with Mr. Hest as intimated in my last. They are a couple of sensible active young men & I do think will do very well in trade. I hope in a few Years to see them rise and establish a reputable House, towards which I shall very freely contribute the little ade in my power & beg leave to recommend them to your friendship & correspondence. I have hinted to them to be very cautious in their first outset in order to gain Credit by punctuality in their engagements & you may be assured that as far as I can consistantly with good manners, I shall advise & assist them as they go forward & that security which I formerly offered on Mr. Price's Account I now beg leave to remove & confirm on behalf of the new House, the former contracts being first fulfilled. Mr. Hest will be with you in a day or two after this & tell you more of this plan than is needful from me.[5]

---

[3] The ship *Hope,* Philip Bowers, was cleared outwards on May 17 for London with 305 barrels of rice, 535 barrels of pitch, 268 barrels of tar, and 1 hogshead of deerskins. Naval Office Lists, 1764–1767, p. 80. Moses Lopez, who had arrived on the *Hope* from Rhode Island with instructions to sell the vessel in Charleston, wrote his brother Aaron, the owner, on May 3 stating that he had been unable to sell the *Hope* and had therefore advertised her to take freight for London. "At last Mr. Laurens offer'd 500 bb. Pitch provided we would take 400 of Green Tarr at 50/ p Ton of 8 bb. After due consultation accepted to take the 500 of Pitch & as much of the Tarr as could be taken in, leaving room for 300 casks rice for your Acct. It is computed this freight is better than rice at 55/ p. Ton because it will store to better advantage." "Charles Town in 1764," ed. Thomas J. Tobias, *SCHM,* LXVII (1966), 70.

[4] The snow *Charles Town,* John Simpson, was cleared outwards on April 25 for London with a cargo which included 860 barrels of pitch. Naval Office Lists, 1764–1767, p. 80.

[5] Hest, according to the source note to this letter, sailed with Capt. Kendall. The ship *Reward,* William Kendall, was cleared outwards on May 4 for Cowes. Naval Office Lists, 1764–1767, p. 80. Hest returned to Charleston in December. *Gazette,* Dec. 10, 1764.

I was not full enough in my last respecting Mr. Leigh, therefore I request the favour of Mr. King to call upon or write to that Gentleman & offer if his occasions require to supply or procure for him as much money as my Credit will stand good for with you. I do not immagine that he will have the least call for any money & yet my offered service is not a mere compliment. God knows what may happen & I should endeavour to guard against every inconvenience & ward off as far as possible every embarassment to a Gentleman of his worth & one for whome I bear the heighest regard. It falls so offten to my Lot to give you trouble of this sort that I am quite ashamed of it, but be assured that it will give me great pleasure to embrace every opportunity of making proper acknowledgements of your favours. Mr. Appleby will be with you soon after this. To him & Mr. Hest I refer you for the State of our Markets & other intelligence which my present state of mind will not permit me to enlarge upon. Therefore I conclude with repeated assurances of being, Sir, Your—

SOURCE: Letterbook copy, HL Papers, S. C. Hist. Soc.; addressed "For Mrs. Sarah Nickleson & Co., London"; "per Higgins. Copy per Mr. Hest per Kendal."

TO COWLES & HARFORD

[Charles Town] 8th May 1764

Gentlemen,

I wrote you per Higgins[6] & Chisman the 5th Instant to which please to be refered. This addition is first to inform Mr. Cowles that Mr. Lachlin McGillivray is going to London in the Ship *Polly*, Capt. Ratsey,[7] to sail some day in this week. Therefore tis needless for me to urge him, Mr. McGillivray, further to a compliance with Mr. Cowles's just demand as he will probably have a much better opportunity of doing it in Bristol & I am in hopes there will be no obsticle to success, for if I am not much mistaken in that Gentleman he will

---

[6] The brigantine *Portland*, George Higgins, was entered inwards on Jan. 23 from St. Christophers and was cleared outwards on May 5 for London. The *Portland* was listed as a snow when cleared outwards. Naval Office Lists, 1764–1767, pp. 69, 80.

[7] The ship *Polly*, Edward Ratsey, was cleared outwards on May 10 for Cowes. Naval Office Lists, 1764–1767, p. 80.

not refuse to do what he ought to do both as an honest Man & as a generous Merchant.

The next subject that offers is to recommend to your correspondence & favours the New House of Messrs. William Price & William Hest of which no doubt Mr. Price hath advised you & Mr. Hest will soon after this be in your City. I am in hopes these Gentlemen will set out upon a very good footing. They have both of them understanding & Industry & they shall have all the favour & assistance that I can reasonably extend to establish them in Trade which by means of their own application & the aid of their friends & acquaintance I dare say will soon be effected. I have strongly recommended to them to be wary in their engagements & punctual in fulfilling their part of every one that they enter into, & as long as it is needful they shall have my best advice for their further proceedings. I think if any of your friends who have not a Correspondent here should apply to you to recommend one as does sometimes happen you might with great safty name these young Gentlemen & in such case I should take a particular pleasure to see that the orders they receive were expiditiously & advantageously complyed with. And after a little introduction of this kind they will be very well able to answer for themselves. I remain—

SOURCE: Letterbook copy, HL Papers, S. C. Hist. Soc.; addressed "Bristol"; "per Mr. Hest per Kendal."

TO JOHN RUTHERFORD

[Charles Town] 8th May 1764

Dear Sir,

I acknowledge myself much obliged to you & to Mr. Duncan[8] for his friendly reception & hospitality to Mr. Bright Who had informed me in a letter accompanying your favour of the 26th Ulto. that he was highly satisfied with & much indebted for Mr. Duncan's polite behaviour towards him during his stay at Wilmington. I have

---

[8] Alexander Duncan, a Scotsman from Edinburgh, was a partner of John Rutherford from 1762 to 1766. He returned to Britain in 1767. *Journal of a Lady of Quality*, pp. 295–299, 319. He was justice of the peace for New Hanover in 1763 and commissioner of the pilotage in 1764. *Colonial Records of North Carolina*, v, 1121, 1197.

now another favour to request in Behalf of Joseph Sparkes, Esquire & Joseph Cator, Esquire, two Gentlemen from Jamacia on a tour thro our Southern Colonies to Boston. Be so kind to give them your countenance & aid if requisite as they pass by your door. They are warmly recommended to me & from thence as well as from the little acquaintance that I have with them in Charles Town I am sure they will do honour to their friends wherever they go. I am not apprised of any probability of their being in want of money but to guard against unforeseen accidents (tho I say this without their Knowledge) if they have occasion for Cash their Bills upon me shall be duly honoured.

The former Letter which you allude to must be one of the 7th February sent by the hands of a poor distressed old Man John Graham who I suppose kept it close to have the Honour of delivering it with his own hands. Tis of no great importence but for your satisfaction I shall send you a duplicate of it with this.

Mr. Saxby & his Lady⁹ are going in a fortnight or so to London. I shall adress him once more before his departure, but having no orders from you to proceed further I can only adress him in terms of supplication & I am really inclined to beleive that other Language is not only necessary but would Also have a good effect. You talk of coming this way as soon as your public affairs will permit. I wish that may be before Mr. Saxby's departure for your presence & your knowledge of his branch of the Revenue would certainly work some advantage & accelerate the Receipt of the sum due to you. A Cargo of 410 Negroes not very prime sold last Week at an average of £36 Sterling. I am—

SOURCE: Letterbook copy, HL Papers, S. C. Hist. Soc.; addressed "Esquire. No. Carolina"; "per Mr. Sparkes."

TO LEWIS DE ROSSET

[Charles Town] 8th May 1764

Sir,

I took the Liberty of troubling you with a Letter the 31st March per the hands of Mr. Lowbride Bright who informs me that

⁹ George Saxby married Elizabeth Seabrook on Dec. 13, 1741. They sailed for England on May 16, 1764. After Saxby had been made stamp inspector, he returned to Charleston on Oct. 26, 1765. Mrs. Saxby died much later in England. *SCHM*, XVII (1916), 20; *Gazette*, Oct. 8, 1764, Oct. 31, 1765.

you were abroad when he arrived at Wilmington. Your repeated kind offers of service emboldens me again to trouble you with a request in favour of Joseph Sparkes, Esquire & Joseph Cator, Esquire, two Gentlemen lately arrived from Jamacia with an intention to make a tour thro North America & are now beginning their long journey. I beg leave to introduce them to your acquaintance. If they should require any advice or direction about their Journey I am sure you will administer such as will be useful to them, & if thro any unforeseen accidents Cash shall be wanted to carry them forward which I am morally certain will not be the case as they are well provided, their Bills on me shall be duly paid.

You will receive under cover with this a letter from Mr. Abraham Parsons[1] of Bristol who desires me to Charter a Vessel to Load at Cape Fear with Naval Stores which you are to supply upon his account & I presume his Letter to you is to the same effect. If you will be pleased to inform me what burthen the Vessel should be of & in what space of time you can engage to load her, I shall use my best endeavours to procure one suitable to the purpose, but at present we have no empty Vessels in our Harbour. Be so kind to inform early the state of your Market particularly the price of Tar, which by my late advices, is excessively Low in London & when I can be serviceable to you in this Quarter please to lay your commands upon me who am, &ca.—

SOURCE: Letterbook copy, HL Papers, S. C. Hist. Soc.; addressed "No. Carolina"; "per Mr. Sparkes."

TO WILLIAM FISHER

[Charles Town] 8 May 1764

Dear Sir,

Lest I should not have opportunity to write to you by Sea to meet two Gentlemen Joseph Sparkes & Joseph Cator, Esquires now begining a long Journey by land to our Eastermost American Settlements I trouble you with this short line by their hands requesting your favours & friendship to them during their abode in your City. These Gentlemen are very warmly recommended to me by friends

---

[1] Abraham Parsons. *HL Papers,* III, 28n.

in Jamaica upon whome I can rely & from my own observation I am assured that they will not discredit their friends in any place. If they should want Money which I believe will not be the case you may safely supply them & depend upon their own draughts for payment. This I shall set down amongst many other debts that I have contracted with you & you may rest assured of my readiness to acknowledge tho I am never to able to cancel, the whole whenever you shall be pleased to lay your commands upon, Dear Sir, &ca.—

SOURCE: Letterbook copy, HL Papers, S. C. Hist. Soc.; "per Mr. Sparkes."

TO JOHN KNIGHT

[Charles Town] 8th May 1764

Dear Sir,

Refering to what I wrote you yesterday as per duplicate annexed, permit me now to request the favour of your countenance & advice to Mr. William Hest who will forward this & soon after follow it to Leverpoole. He is a native of your Country, has been a few months at my House, & is now entred into partnership with Mr. Price who lived several years with A. & L. & A., L., & A. & my self & I have great hopes of their establishing a good House after struggling thro some difficulties that young adventurers must expect to encounter; & which I shall use my endeavours to make light to them. You may have it in your power, good Sir, to recommend them to some of your neighbours & even if the first offer of a small Guinea Man was made to them here, I would if they thought proper to take her up be answerable for the true & exact performance of their engagements & do every thing that they would expect from me to assist in making a good Sale. But I do not mean by this to recommend away any Little business that you may think proper To entrust me with. No, Sir, my gratitude is such that as long as I continue in Trade I shall rather transact the business of Loading a Vessel or two that you may send this way in a year for nothing than loose the pleasure of corresponding with you & shewing forth my thankfulness upon every occasion of rendering you my best services. But I have no desire or inclination to make new connexions and some businesses which your goodness might (as heretofore) Lead you to throw in my way you may now turn down this New Channel, & I hope the young Gentlemen will acquit themselves so as to give all their friends satisfaction & me no cause to repent of having been so warm in their Interest, but be that as it may, I beg leave to Repeat that I am & always will be, Dear Sir, Your obliged & faithful Servant—

SOURCE: Letterbook copy, HL Papers, S. C. Hist. Soc.; addressed "Leverpoole"; "per Mr. Hest, per Kendal."

GEORGE AUSTIN & HENRY LAURENS VERSUS GASPER AKERMAN[2]

May 8, 1764

[On April 17, 1764, James Moultrie, attorney for the plaintiffs, filed suit in the court of common pleas against Gasper Akerman, planter of St. Bartholomew parish, for recovery of a bond, dated August 7, 1760, in the sum of £291.8.4 currency. The case was ordered for judgment on May 8, 1764.]

SOURCE: Judgment Rolls, 1764, No. 21A, S. C. Archives; Journal, Court of Common Pleas, 1763–1769, p. 60, S. C. Archives.

GEORGE AUSTIN, HENRY LAURENS, & GEORGE APPLEBY VERSUS HANS McCULLOCH[3]

May 8, 1764

[On April 17, 1764, James Moultrie, attorney for the plaintiffs, filed suit in the court of commons pleas against Hans McCulloch of St. Bartholomew parish for recovery of a bond, dated Sept. 3, 1760, in the sum of £1,000 currency. The court ruled for the plaintiffs, and the case was ordered for judgment on May 8, 1764.]

---

[2] Gasper Akerman was granted 200 acres on a branch of the Saltcatcher on Aug. 1, 1758 and 200 acres on Saltcatcher Swamp on March 8, 1763. Index to Grants, S. C. Archives.

[3] Hans McCulloch was granted 600 acres in Colleton County on Sept. 25, 1766. Index to Grants, S. C. Archives. On July 1, 1768, he was appointed an administrator of the estate of Francis Sarragosia of St. Paul parish. *SCHM,* xxvi (1925), 127.

SOURCE: Judgment Rolls, 1764, No. 168A, S. C. Archives; Journal, Court of Commons Pleas, 1763–1769, p. 60, S. C. Archives.

TO RICHARD HEATLY

[Charles Town] 9th May 1764

Sir,

Since my last the 9th December per the *Bonetta* Man of War I have continued my endeavours to close the Sale of your Wine by frequent attempts at the Vendue but there still remains 8 or 9 dozen bottles & 1 quarter cask unsold. These I shall by Vendue or some other means dispose of next Week & transmit you an Account of the whole with a remittance for at least as much as I shall be in Cash perhaps for the full amount. Meantime permit me to introduce Mr. William Hest (a young Gentleman who will forward or deliver this) to your acquaintance. He has just entred into a partnership with Mr. William Price & I am in hopes that they will thro their own industry & the help of friends establish a good House in this Town. The little assistance that I can give they shall always be welcome to & for further perticulars I beg leave to refer you to Mr. Hest himself who is a native of England and no stranger in London and I remain with great regard, Sir, Your most obedient Servant—

SOURCE: Letterbook copy, HL Papers, S. C. Hist. Soc.; addressed "London"; "per Mr. Hest."

TO SHEPHERD, LANGTON, & BIRLEY

[Charles Town] 9 May 1764

Gentlemen,

I wrote to you the 20 December per two Vessels that I see are arrived since when I have sold upwards of 90 peices of your Sail Cloth all upon Credit tho' at a low price but the payments begin to come due. I shall collect in as much as possible & remit within the Course of this Month & for the remainder I can only promise the continuance of my uttmost endevours to get them off upon saveing terms.

Soon after this reaches you 'tis probable that Mr. William Hest a native of Lancashire will wait on you with the offers of his

service in this Country where he hath inter'd into partnership with
Mr. William Price, & I have great hopes that they will soon lay the
foundation of a good House. They are sensible Young Men, understand business, & will apply very closely to it & they shall allways command that little assistance that I can give them. Mr. Hest will further
apprise you of their plan & if you Incline to do any thing more in this
trade I wish he may recommend himself so as to procure your favours
& I make no doubt but he will merrit the countenance of them. You
shall soon hear from me with a remittance & also an Account of Sale
if to be affected. Mean while I remain, Yours, &ca.—

SOURCE: Letterbook copy, HL Papers, S. C. Hist. Soc.; addressed
"Kirkham"; "per Mr. Hest in Kendal."

TO THOMAS HARTLEY & SON [4]

[Charles Town] 9 May 1764

Gentlemen,

It is a long time since I had the honour of writing you a
Letter in the Late house of Austin, Laurens, & Appleby & as I do not
recolect ever to have wrote or rece'd one from you in my own Name
I know not whether I have any Interest with you or not. Nevertheless upon our former correspondence & to serve two worthy Young
Men, I presume to trouble you with this in order to recommend to
your acquaintance Messrs. Price & Hest who have just enter'd into
partnership & I hope will soon establish a good House in this town
but Mr. Hest will be present when this is read. I beg leave to refer
you to him for further particulars & think it needfull only to add that
if the offer of any Guinea Men shou'd be made to them by Vessels
that may come hither to try the Market I shall give them my best
advice & assistance and be responsible for their punctual performance
enter'd into with my knowledge and concurrance. I have declin'd that
branch myself but I am sure it is still in my power to do them great
service in the Sale of Negroes. You will conclude that I hold a good
opinion of those Gentlemen & I declare to you that I have not the

---

[4] A., L., & A. sold a cargo of slaves in October 1760. They had been brought
from Africa in the snow *Betty* which had been owned in part by Thomas
Hartley & Son of Whitehaven. *HL Papers*, III, 52n.

least Interest in view by recommending them save only that pleasure which is the Natural result of doing kind offices. If at any time you see occasion please freely to command the Services of Your, &ca.—

SOURCE: Letterbook copy, HL Papers, S. C. Hist. Soc.; addressed "Whitehaven"; "per Mr. Hest per Kendal."

TO ZACHARY VILLEPONTOUX [5]

[Charles Town] 11 May 1764

Sir,

I shall want a large quantity of good Bricks deliver'd at my Wharf, opposite to Ansonburgh where your Boat may come in & go out the same Tide if she does not draw above five feet Water. Please to let me know if you can supply me One Hundred to Three Hundred Thousand & your lowest price, observing that there will be no Wharfage to pay & that I shall make you Payments upon the usual terms or as soon as you shall please to name in case we agree. I request your Answer as speedily as possible & also that you will order one Boat Load to be delivered at the above mentioned place next Week. I am, &ca.—

SOURCE: Letterbook copy, Letter Book of Henry Laurens, Oct. 30, 1762–Sept. 10, 1766, Penn. Hist. Soc.; addressed "Esquire. Goose Creek."

TO JOSEPH BROWN

[Charles Town] 11 May 1764

Dear Sir,

I have paid your Bill on me to Mr. Thomas Smith, Junior [6]

---

[5] Zachariah Villepontoux was born at New Rochelle, N. Y., in 1698 and died at Goose Creek about 1780–1781. His home was at Mount Parnassus plantation on Back River in the parish of St. James Goose Creek where he supplied from his kilns bricks for many Charleston buildings, most notably for the construction of St. Michael's Church. "The Villepontoux Family of South Carolina," compiled by I. Heyward Peck, SCHM, L (1949), 34–36; Irving, A Day on Cooper River, pp. 18–21; George W. Williams, St. Michael's, Charleston, 1751–1951 (Columbia, S. C., 1951), pp. 135, 137, 140, 149. He may have supplied the plans as well as the brick for Pompion Hill Chapel which was rebuilt in 1763 with features copied from St. Michael's. Samuel Gaillard Stoney, Plantations of the Carolina Low Country (Charleston, S. C., 1955), pp. 67–68.

[6] Thomas Smith, Jr. was also known as Thomas Smith of Broad St.

£120 & charged to your account, and tendered the sum of £480 to Mr. John Neufville[7] as you directed on Account of Mr. George Pawly, Senior,[8] but he refused to receive it, saying that the whole must be paid off together & that the Interest is not due. I am—

[P. S.] I want the best discription that you can give of the Land belonging to Crofts Estate in order to have the deeds of conveyance made.

SOURCE: Letterbook copy, Letter Book of Henry Laurens, Oct. 30, 1762–Sept. 10, 1766, Penn. Hist. Soc.; addressed "George Town."

TO PETER MOUZON[9]

[Charles Town] 17 May 1764

Dear Sir,

I beg your attention to a few facts relative to your 69 barrels

---

[7] *HL Papers*, II, 212n.

[8] George Pawley, Sr., who died in 1774, had been colonel of the Craven County regiment and adjutant general of the province. He was the head of a family with extensive holdings in land on the Waccamaw River. Rogers, *History of Georgetown County*, passim. On July 3, 1764, he and Samuel Wylly were appointed the S. C. commissioners to run the line between North and South Carolina. Miscellaneous Records, MM, Part 1 (1763–1767), p. 121, S. C. Archives.

[9] Peter Mouzon, a planter in the parish of St. James Santee, had married Judith Laurens, the daughter of HL's uncle Angustus. Augustus Laurens was born October 1700. Wallace, *Life of Henry Laurens*, p. 502. He was a planter on the Santee in Craven County who sold to his nephew John Perdriau 863½ acres on Wambaw Creek April 24, 1745. *Transactions of the Huguenot Society of South Carolina*, LXVIII (1963), 79–80. The will of John Snow, dated March 23, 1749, mentioned Augustus Laurens and his two daughters: Judith and Susannah (under 21). When Augustus wrote his will in 1755, he called himself planter of Craven County and mentioned his daughters Judith (then married to Peter Mouzon) and Susannah. His will was proved Oct. 1, 1757. *Abstracts of Wills, 1740–1760*, pp. 145, 232. Peter and Judith Mouzon had five children: Peter, born Aug. 6, 1758 (died Nov. 16, 1758), Judith, born May 14, 1760, Eleanor, born April 15, 1762, Peter, born Sept. 18, 1764 (died Oct. 3, 1764) and Susannah, born Aug. 6, 1765. Judith Laurens Mouzon died Feb. 2, 1767. *SCHM*, XVII (1916), 34, 36, 38, 40, 42, 76. When Peter Mouzon, then of Christ Church parish, wrote his will in 1787, his three daughters were still living: Judith Lesesne, Eleanor Wragg (married Joseph Wragg of Georgetown Oct. 23, 1783), and Susannah Mouzon. "Will of Peter Mouzon," dated June 30, 1787, proved Aug. 29, 1787, Charleston County Wills, XXII, Book A (1786–1793), 170–171, S. C. Archives; *SCHM* XVIII (1917), 143. Augustus Laurens' daughter Susannah married Daniel McGregor of St. James Santee on Feb. 25, 1768. *SCHM*, XV (1914), 201.

of Green Tar lately sold to me by Mr. Thomas Legare which I shall here lay before you.

The Barrels that contained that Tar was in such exceeding bad order that after I had them rolled down on the Wharf to be Shipped on board the *Hope*, Capt. Bowers (the Master of said Ship) absolutely refused to receive them on board, alledging that they were unmerchantable and insufficient for a Voyage across the Sea; & he called in two or three indifferent persons whose opinions confirmed his own & to say the best, the Tar was running about the wharf in such quantities as to give the most undeniable evidence of the Truth of his allegations.

Hereupon I applyed to Garret Kain, who had packed that parcel of Tar and asked how he could consistantly with his duty fix his Brand of office upon such bad Casks & more especially as he had before possitively and repeatedly refused to do so.[1] He answered that it was utterly against his inclinations to brand it & that he had persisted in his refusals untill he was promised an *indempnification*. When he told me of this extraordinary circumstances I pitied the man & resolved in my own mind to make the most that I could of the Tar without more delay & loss & to give neither Mr. Legare nor yourself, trouble about it, untill the whole was disposed of in some way or other.

I was so fortunate as to meet with a parcel of good empty Tar Barrels in the hands of John Nipper[2] another packer or as I should say *Sworn Packer* & therefore employed him to run off your Tar into his Barrels which he did & repacked the whole upon terms that appeared to be very moderate: You will here find on Account of your said Tar Stated at £8 per parcel & charged with the new expences & loss per Nipper's Account. The difference between that Account & the amount as first charged to me by Mr. Legare at 57/6 per Barrel is only £15.4.6 which is not equal to the trouble, loss, and

---

[1] Garret Cain was a cooper who had been elected to the office of packer on Easter Monday in 1762, 1763, and 1764. Six packers were elected annually for the port of Charleston. The duties of the packers were set forth in "an act to prevent frauds and deceits in selling rice, pitch, tar, rosin, turpentine, beef, pork, shingles, staves, and fire wood" which had been passed on June 17, 1746. *S. C. Statutes*, III, 686–691.

[2] John Nipper (Naper) was a cooper who was elected to the office of packer in 1764, 1767, and 1768. Michael Thompson, also a cooper, requested on Feb. 10, 1769, that he be permitted to administer the estate of John Naper, as next of kin. On Feb. 25 Hannah Naper, the widow, asked that she be appointed. The governor appointed Michael Thompson as administrator on March 3. *SCHM*, XXXI (1930), 155–156.

expence that would have attended the Tar if you had returned it to your Landing and put it in merchantable order there as you did once purpose to have done.

I have not the least doubt of my right to insist upon this difference being made good to me & that any impartial men upon hearing the foregoing facts will give an award in my favour, but as I perswade myself that you will require no arguments to induce you to do as you would be done by, I shall add no more but to request your directions to Mr. Legare upon this head and remain, Dear Sir, Your most humble Servant—

SOURCE: Letterbook copy, Letter Book of Henry Laurens, Oct. 30, 1762–Sept. 10, 1766, Penn. Hist. Soc.; addressed "Santé."

TO HUGH SWINTON

[Charles Town] 17 May 1764

Sir,

I have placed £167.14.9 to your Credit for Mr. Alexander Davidson's Bill in your favour as you directed me to do for which payment I thank you & shall be looking for the balance due me in a few days the receipt of which will further oblige, Sir, Your most humble Servant—

SOURCE: Letterbook copy, Letter Book of Henry Laurens, Oct. 30, 1762–Sept. 10, 1766, Penn. Hist. Soc.; addressed "Black Mingo"; "Per Mr. Gregg."

TO WILLIAM THOMPSON

[Charles Town] 18 May 1764

Dear Sir,

I thought there would be a better opportunity of purchasing Negroes for you some time after the last Sale that was made & therefore deferred that business.

No Guinea Ship arrived since but you may rest assured that I shall be mindful of your order whenever there appears to be a proper time to execute it, & I remain, Dear Sir—

SOURCE: Letterbook copy, Letter Book of Henry Laurens, Oct. 30, 1762–Sept. 10, 1766, Penn. Hist. Soc.; addressed "Black Mingo"; "per Mr. Gregg."

TO JOSEPH BROWN

[Charles Town] 19 May 1764

Dear Sir,

I have but five minutes to acknowledge your favour of the 16th Instant which is this moment come to hand & Dickinson waiting at my Elbow to be dismissed. I believe your discription of Crofts Land is enough to the purpose intended.

I thank you for your favours to Mr. Sparks & his companion and if I do not mistake the Men they will seek some opportunity to cancel the debt which they have contracted by your civilities. I shall endeavour to do all that you desire me with respect to Mr. Pawleys bond, the pitch, and your account but don't hurry for the latter is your fault that they were not settled long ago & now they may be kept open thro my misfortune for I have been every day sick for a month and business is really most irksome & distasteful to me especially that of sitting down in a Counting house which exposes me a little too much to thought & now at this instant, I feel such a gloom & weakness over whelming me that if I had even more time & more matter to write it would be necessary for me to lay by the pen & move abroad a little, but I hope a few days or Weeks may recover me.

Mrs. Laurens & two of our Children are in St. John's. Jacky & I present our Love to Mrs. Brown & all yours & to Miss Becky & I remain, Dear Sir, Your affectionate Servant—

SOURCE: Letterbook copy, Letter Book of Henry Laurens, Oct. 30, 1762–Sept. 10, 1766, Penn. Hist. Soc.; addressed "George Town."

TO ISAAC KING

[Charles Town] 21st May 1764

Sir,

I wrote to you the 7th Instant per Capt. Higgins & Capt.

Kendal to which I refer and this is intended per the *Hope,* Capt. Bowers, in which Ship I have Loaden 526 Barrels of Pitch & 268 Barrels of Green Tar both articles in very good condition on the joint account of Gabriel Manigault, Esquire and myself as per Bill of Loading here inclosed, which Pitch & Tar be the same more or less you will be pleased to dispose of to our best advantage & carry the Net proceeds to the Credit of our several accounts in moiety.

You will remark by the Bill of Loading that the Capt. or his Mate rather has decleared to have rece'd 289 Barrels of Tar. This I am morally sure is an error & Absolutely certain that it is so with respect to my own Tar, because I really had no more than 268 barrels in possession. Therefore if more is found in the Ship it does not belong to me. On the other hand there ought to be instead of 526 barrels of Pitch as per Bill of Loading 535 barrels of Pitch & I hope so many will be found. If not they were either stolen in the Shipment per Capt. Simpson or now upon the wharf where Capt. Bower suffered them to lay too many nights after they were turned out at his own request, but I believe he is an honest Man & will Faithfully deliver all that are on board the Ship to which you will no doubt pay some attention and we must be satisfied with the event.

Two of the makers of this Green Tar having neglected to send down their Certificates, I must defer the general Certificate to another Opportunity. Mean while please to receive one under this cover for the pitch.

Many of our Plantations had suffered much by a very long continuance of dry Windy Weather but within a Week past we have had refreshing & plentiful Rains. Nevertheless I will at this distance of time venture to prognosticate that our Crop of Indigo which has suffered most will fall short & if I had of that Commodity on hand I should pay some regard to the present bad prospect. Rice continues at 40/ & tho we have very few Ships in port the planters & Factors are taking measures to get a better price. I remain with great regard, Sir—

SOURCE: Letterbook copy, HL Papers, S. C. Hist. Soc.; addressed "For Mrs. Sarah Nickleson & Co., London"; "per *Hope,* Capt. Bowers."

TO ISAAC KING

[Charles Town] 22 May 1764

Sir,

I wrote to you Yesterday per the Ship *Hope,* on board of which I am Interested about Two hundred pounds Sterling per one half of Pitch & Tar as per inclosed Bill of Loading & abstract Invoice. This Vessel[3] will sail with the *Hope* or possibly a day or two before her & in Case she shall also arrive before her please to Insure One Hundred Guineas on my part of said Goods, the remainder I shall risque, and continue to be, Sir, &ca.—

SOURCE: Letterbook copy, HL Papers, S. C. Hist. Soc.; addressed "For Mrs. Sarah Nickleson & Co., London"; "per the *Betty,* Capt. Coil." HL added: "Note the above mentioned abstract Invoice is Copied on the Bill of Loading in the Book."

TO GEORGE APPLEBY

[Charles Town] 22d May 1764

My Dear Sir,

Mr. Mansell & I with your God Son Jack made more than a faint effort to wait on you the morning that the *Portland* got to Sea, but our Bark the *Wambaw* was foul. She once missed stays near the breakers & we could not recover our Loss. Your Snow sailed much better too than we imagined she would have done & soon bore away from the Bar. Therefore after Loading you With good wishes we put about & came home again; & a few hours af[t]er, your very Obliging Letter dated at Sea came to hand by the Pilot. Let it suffice that I say by way of answer, it is laid by as one of my most valuable deposits.

In this short Interval nothing very important has come to pass in our Little Town, unless the Death of our old Friend John Guerard, Esquire,[4] the meeting of the House of Assembly,[5] & the

---

[3] The snow *Betty,* James Coile, was cleared outwards on May 18 for Cowes. Naval Office Lists, 1764–1767, p. 80.

[4] Appleby had sailed on May 9. See HL to Willing & Morris, May 29. John Guerard, Charleston merchant and member of the S. C. royal council, had died on May 14. *HL Papers,* I, 218n.

[5] Lt. Gov. William Bull issued a proclamation on May 12, the day after Governor Boone's sailing, calling the general assembly to meet on May 22. When the assembly met on May 22, Bull sent a message "that some Members

cap[t]ure of one of the murdering Creek Indians are events of Note.[6] The first happined with circumstances alarming to every man that is in danger of dying at any time & may give rise to a moments retrospection of your own annals. That Gentleman was standing at his door in a powdered Wig at 8 oClock A.M. and an hour before Noon his very capacious Scheming Head was of less value than a good Calabash. He had some previous intimation of the violent Shock that carried him off, called hastily for his Will which had been brought home but 48 Hours before, had sense enough to order the Blank left for the date to be filled up, and to subscribe & publish it but time did not permit him to discover a most unlucky mistake of Mr. Lamboll's who drew it up & has left out the name of One of his Sons & twice inserted that of another giving to the latter what was by his Fathers minutes intended for his Brother. This they say must be remided by an Act of Assembly.[7] The House met Yesterday, but the Old Colonel's indisposition[8] & the want of Counsellors by Death & absence[9] render'd

---

of the Council being Sick there was not a Board" and asked them to meet the next day for business which they did. House Journal, xxxvi (Jan. 24, 1763–Oct. 6, 1764), 14–15, S. C. Archives.

[6] Two Creek warriors had killed a Long Canes settler on May 4. They fled to the Cherokee towns, where they were seized by the Cherokees and sent to Fort Prince George. One escaped, but the other, known as "the Evil Doer," was carried to Charleston, tried, condemned, and executed. Bull and two members of the council considered the documents on May 22. Council Journal, xxx (Dec. 28, 1763–Dec. 24, 1764), 189–192, 196, S. C. Archives. See also John R. Alden, John Stuart and the Southern Colonial Frontier (Ann Arbor, Mich., 1944), pp. 190–191.

[7] Thomas Lamboll drew up Guerard's will on May 4 from Guerard's own notes. Lamboll wrote out the will on May 9. On May 12 he read it to Guerard who approved it as read. Guerard died on May 14 "of a Fit of Apoplexy." In his will he had left his fourth son Isaac a messuage and a town lot on the Bay as well as a plantation of 1,064 acres near Port Royal which he had intended, according to his notes originally given to Lamboll, to leave to his son Richard. Richard Guerard (spelled "Garrard" in the journal) petitioned the assembly on Aug. 14 asking for a bill to rectify the mistake in his father's will. The petition was referred to a committee of seven which included three of the ablest lawyers in the province, John Rutledge, James Parsons, and Thomas Bee. On Aug. 18 Richard was permitted to withdraw the petition. The records do not reveal how the mistake was remedied. Guerard was survived by his wife, seven sons, and a daughter. "Will of John Guerard," dated May 14, 1764, proved May 18, 1764, Charleston County Wills, x, Book B (1760–1767), 481–492, S. C. Archives; House Journal, xxxvi (Jan. 24, 1763–Oct. 6, 1764), 229–231, 239, S. C. Archives; Council Journal, xxx (Dec. 28, 1763–Dec. 24, 1764), 222–224, S. C. Archives.

[8] As Col. Othniel Beale, the senior member of the royal council, was ill, the board met on May 22 "at the Honourable Othniel Beales." Bull and Charles Shinner, the chief justice, were present. Council Journal, xxx (Dec. 28, 1763–Dec. 24, 1764), 189, S. C. Archives.

[9] There were only seven members of the council at this time. They were

it impracticable for the Leiut. Governor to offer us any Business. I
believe if his honour thinks it essential to have the aid of that Board
he must enter upon the arduous work of Creation.[1] The Indian it
seems was taken by the famous Cherokee call'd Young Warrior, and
sent down prisoner to the Governor which is surely a further and
indeed the best and most unanswerable answer to all the fits & fears
and frights of Philopatrios.[2] This incident will probably ripen the
bickerings of those two Indian Tribes into an open and inveterate
War, a circumstance that will be attended with no Evil consequence
to Carolina or Georgia.

Within 10th days past we have had many refreshing Showers
of Rains which have put the articles of Rice & Corn upon a tolerable
good footing, but from the best Accounts our Indigo has suffered so
much by the dry weather & Vermin that the produce of this Year
will fall short.

Mr. Williams[3] the other day offered me three or four hundred
pounds of your Money but I desired him to keep it till he could make
up about £100 Sterling and then I shall remit it immediately.

I beg you to urge Mr. Cowles & his House to transmit our
Companies & my own Accounts. Their unreasonable delay has
hitherto sat lighter than most other people's would do, but at Length
it is intolerable & I must confess it is vexatious to me.

Your Aunt is at Roscoby[4] & your friend Mrs. Laurens with
Harry & Patty at Hyde Park.[5] Jacky & I keep a sort of House here
at Rattray Green & truly I find it expedient to keep the house pretty

---

(with the dates of their appointments): William Bull, Jr. (1748), Othniel
Beale (1755), Henry Middleton (1755), Egerton Leigh (1759), Charles Shinner
(1761), John Drayton (1761), and Daniel Blake (1761). M. Eugene Sirmans,
"The South Carolina Royal Council, 1720–1763," *William and Mary Quarterly,*
XVIII (1961), 392.

[1] Bull appointed Thomas Skottowe a councilor on May 23, and Skottowe
took his seat that day. On July 31, Bull announced that John Burn had received
a mandamus, dated Nov. 10, 1763, appointing him a councilor, and John Burn
appeared that day and took his seat. Council Journal, XXX (Dec. 28, 1763–
Dec. 24, 1764), 193, 220, S. C. Archives.

[2] Christopher Gadsden, as Philopatrios, had argued that Grant's campaign of
1761 had not been successful in crushing the spirit of the Cherokees. *HL Papers,*
III, 270–272.

[3] Robert Williams, Jr., the lawyer.

[4] Roscoby was the plantation of John Moultrie who had married Mrs. Austin's
daughter. See HL to John Moultrie, Jan. 28, 1768. Roscoby was the name of
the ancestral home of the Moultries in Scotland. *SCHM,* v (1904), 239–245.

[5] Hyde Park was the plantation of Mrs. Laurens' brother, Elias Ball.

much on account of the little disor[d]er that I had which is not yet removed tho I have at least consented to take physic for it but as I shall shun a good many hot walks thro the Sun I hope it wont hold many days.

Jacky presents his duty to you & I pray you to make my compliments to your Mama[6] & present them to any other Friends that may enquire after me, & be assured your self that I am with great affection, Dear Sir—

[*P.S.*] Since writing above Abraham Schad has been with me & at his request I intreat you to enquire of Mr. Austin & to inform me as soon as possible how much Money he had in his hands of Mrs. Schad's[7] Father's, & into whose hands & when he afterwards lodged the same.

SOURCE: Letterbook copy, HL Papers, S. C. Hist. Soc.; addressed "London or Shifnall"; "per the *Hope*, Capt. Bowers. Copy per Reeves." The postscript was copied by HL.

TO CHARLES CROKATT[8]

[Charles Town] 23d May 1764

Sir,

Hearing that you were considerably Interested in the New Ship *Queen Charlotte*[9] & perceiving that your Friends on this side

---

[6] Mrs. Appleby lived at Shifnal in Shropshire to which place George Appleby was making his way.

[7] Mary Anne Schad. *HL Papers,* III, 426n.

[8] Charles Crokatt (1730–1769) was the eldest son of James Crokatt. *HL Papers,* I, 5n, 7n. In 1763 Charles and his father were listed as Carolina merchants at Old Bethlem. *London Directories.*

[9] The ship *Queen Charlotte,* Henry Reeves, was registered on April 18, 1764, as having been built in S. C. in 1764. This vessel of 280 tons was owned by Cathcart & Wooddrop of Charleston and Charles Crokatt of London. She was cleared outwards on June 6 for Cowes with 1,400 barrels and 35 half barrels of rice and 479 mahogany plank. *Naval Office Lists, 1764–1767,* p. 81. The *Georgia Gazette,* May 17, 1764, stated that the *Queen Charlotte* had been launched by "Mr. Emrie." John Imrie, shipbuilder, came to Charleston in 1761. He was a loyalist who escaped to East Florida in May 1778. By 1774 he had built a wharf on the south side of Charleston on the Ashley River which had a front of 60 feet and length of 250 feet and was valued at £120 sterling. In 1776 the patriots took away from him his Negro shipwright and caulker, valued at £100 sterling, whom he had purchased as a boy and trained. *Loyalist Transcripts,* LV, 32–45.

would be under some difficulty at this advanced Season to procure a full Freight for so large a Vessel, I took the Liberty to offer my aid in dispatching her from a Port in which a long detention would endanger her Bottom to much damage by the Worms,[1] & that offer being accepted I have Shipped on board her all the Rice that was in my possession, that is to say 253 Barrels, Value about £400 Sterling. You know the intended Voyage for said Ship is to Cowes & from thence to Holland or Hamburgh, & I am promised that she shall not be detained longer than the 10th June. My present business therefore is to desire you to Insure upon goods on my account in that Vessel a sum to Net in case of Loss Three hundred Guineas or thereabouts & the remainder of my Interest shall run at my own risque. I shall request the House of George McKenzie & Co. to Clear my Rice at Cowes & you to sell it deliverable at a foreign Market which shall be the subjects of my Letter by the Ship. Meantime I remain with great regard, Sir—

SOURCE: Letterbook copy, HL Papers, S. C. Hist. Soc.; addressed "Esquire. London"; "per the *Hope,* Capt. Bowers. Copy per Reeves."

TO NATHANIEL & GEORGE BETHUNE[2]
[Charles Town] 28th May 1764

Gentlemen,
        I am favoured with yours of the 18th Ulto. & duplicate of the 5th which Informes me that One of the Bills endorsed by me & paid by the purchaser of that Vessel of yours which Capt. Cathcart sold here last Winter,[3] Amount £42.10.5 Sterling, is under protest & on its way hither, but as the Original of your first favour hath not reached

---

[1] *HL Papers,* I, 40n.

[2] Nathaniel (spelled Nathanael here) Bethune (1715–1771) and George Bethune (1720–1785) were Boston merchants of Scottish descent. Both were graduates of Harvard. They owned ships, sold military and marine supplies to the provincial and royal governments, and "specialized in exporting provisions for the Newfoundland fishery." They were accused of violating the non-importation agreements of 1769. George first took the side of the Crown but then returned to the American cause, making money from the war. Clifford K. Shipton, *Sibley's Harvard Graduates* (Boston, 1956, 1958), IX, 386, 389; X, 466.

[3] The brigantine *Tryton,* John Cathcart, owned by Nathaniel and George Bethune of Boston, was entered inwards on Nov. 22, 1763, from Boston with 79 hogsheads of rum and 80 bundles of hay. Naval Office Lists, 1757–1764, p. 124.

me I can at present say nothing more than to acknowledge the Truth of Capt. Cathcart's Assertion that my endorsing that Bill solely induced him to take it in part payment as I very well remember what I said to him upon the occasion & therefore, Gentlemen, you may rest assured that whenever the Bill & protest reaches me I shall do the needfull for you in Exchanging it together with the accustomed charges into a better and remit it to you without delay & without expence too. I observe what you say confirming the Sale of your Brigantine *Tryton*. I had not the least Interest or concern in the purchase of her, any further than to assist one Capt. Brunett[4] who came over to this Province in order to take possession of an Estate which had been left in my care by an Uncle of his[5] & as he was a stranger to everybody else, he naturally asked my advice and assistance which you may see by the transaction with Capt. Cathcart I gave him without reserve, & I believe he is very well satisfied with his Bill of Sale & possession. Nevertheless when I do write to him I shall recite that part of your Letter. I am—

SOURCE: Letterbook copy, HL Papers, S. C. Hist. Soc.; addressed "Boston"; "per Capt. Mason."

HENRY LAURENS VERSUS *ADMINISTRATORS OF GEORGE WALKER*

May 28, 1764

[William Burrows was the attorney for the plaintiff. Judgment was issued on May 28.]

SOURCE: Judgment Docket, Court of Common Pleas, Book 2 (1755–1773), p. 86, S. C. Archives.

---

[4] When the brigantine *Tryton,* John Brunet, was cleared outwards on Feb. 10, 1764, for Cowes, she was owned by John Brunet and Philip Winter of Jersey and Samuel Lightfoot of London. The *Tryton* had been registered on Jan. 12, 1764, in Charleston as having been built in New England in 1761. Naval Office Lists, 1764–1767, p. 74.

[5] His uncle was Esaie Brunet, carpenter. *HL Papers*, III, 122, 156.

TO WILLIAM FISHER

[Charles Town] 29 May 1764

Sir,

I rece'd your favour of the 9th Instant per Capt. Mason & the two Bales of Strouds therein mentioned per his Brigantine *Charles Town Packet*[6] are come to hand in pretty good order, but truly to a bad Market. I believe there is not a worse for the sale of all kinds of Goods than this at present is & by the continual supplies see no prospect of a sudden change. Woolen goods are every Vandue sold at $\frac{1}{2}$ to 2/3ds of the first cost in the London and other Warehouses & publickly advertized to be sold at & for less than cost and Charges. I cleared my hands lately of a Quantity of well bought Cloths, Shalloon, &ca. at 5 for 1 after trying for a Year & an half every measure to do better with them. From this Account you cannot think it adviseable to send any of your Woolens here for Sale. As to these two Bales I shall follow your directions & sell them for the most they will Yeild & pass the Net proceeds accordingly. I am extremely glad you did not send the Ship *Ann*[7] to Charles Town, where it would not have been in my power to obtain above 50/ Freight & very likely not more than 40/ for London or Bristol. The former was the last given but upon the arrival of only three or four Sail of Ships, all the Rice is locked up & Naval Stores stopped in the Country untill higher prices can be obtained & these very Vessels will probably be very Long detained at this bad Season of the Year before they are Loaded.

This goes in company with our good friend Mr. Hopton[8] to whom I beg leave to refer you for the News in this quarter & remain with great regard, Dear Sir—

SOURCE: Letterbook copy, HL Papers, S. C. Hist. Soc.; addressed "Philadelphia"; "per Mason."

---

[6] The brigantine *Charles Town Packet*, Thomas Mason, was entered inwards on May 22 from Philadelphia with a cargo of bread, flour, gammon, oil, paper, and iron work. Naval Office Lists, 1764–1767, p. 77.

[7] HL would sell the ship *Ann* in 1765. See Advertisement, April 13, 1765.

[8] William Hopton was sailing for Philadelphia in the *Charles Town Packet* which was cleared outwards on May 31. Naval Office Lists, 1764–1767, p. 81.

TO WILLING & MORRIS

[Charles Town] 29th May 1764

Gentlemen,

The 22d Instant Capt. Mason brought me your esteemed favour of the 4th covering a Bill of Loading for three Caskes of Linseed Oil which are since come to hand but not quite in good order, One Cask lacking near 30 Gallons. Therefore I declined paying freight untill the Capt. assured me that you had used a part of that Cask to fill up the other two, that it was delivered in the same order to me that you Shipped it in, & signed a Receipt subjecting himself to an Adjustment with you in case you shall be dissatisfied. You may depend upon it that I shall think it no trouble to sell this Oil for you upon the best terms in our market which perhaps may be a better one for that than for almost any other article & when sold I shall transmit you an Account thereof together with your Account Current. Meantime let the balance lay on which side it may you have not done amiss in passing a Bill on me to Mr. Bache[9] for five hundred Milled Dollars or the Value thereof in Currency. I shall pay due honour unto it when ever it appears.

As to your Account with A., L., & A., I beg leave to refer you to Mr. Appleby's Letter which will go by this conveyance. He wrote it seperately because he had something to say on Mr. Austin's Account with you. He Sailed for England the 9th Instant, after having settled all our Accounts which were to a very considerable amount to our mutual satisfaction. We have at present not more than four or five empty Vessels in Port & even these will find no small difficulty in obtaining full Loads either upon freights or purchase, not because there are not commodities enough in the Province but because the Holders of Rice & Naval Stores are not content with the present prices of those Articles. Therefore I am glad that your Ships are better provided for. The arrival of a dozen Sail more in a Short space of time would make sad work, tho I am morally sure there remains goods to Load Thirty Sail of 160 Ton each at least. Rice is nominally at 40/, but none good to be sold at that price. Pitch 60/, Tar 45/, Turpentine 12/6, Exchange 721 per Cent.

---

[9] This may be Theophylact Bache (1735–1807), a merchant of New York, who had come from Yorkshire in 1751. His younger brother Richard Bache (1737–1811) came out to New York in 1765, then moved to Philadelphia where on Oct. 29, 1767 he married Benjamin Franklin's daughter Sarah. Edmund K. Alden, "Richard Bache," "Theophylact Bache," *DAB*.

I thank you heartily, Gentlemen, for your Cordial invitation
to keep our correspondence alive & I do assure that I shall make use
of every occasion to confirm to you that I am with great regard,
Gentlemen—

SOURCE: Letterbook copy, HL Papers, S. C. Hist. Soc.; addressed
"Philadelphia"; "per Mason."

TO WILLIAM HOPTON
                              [Charles Town] 29th May 1764
Dear Sir,
        At Your Leisure in Philadelphia I entreat you to inquire as
minutely as you can into the circumstances of the late Capt. Joseph
Rivers of that City deceased & also those of his Son Mr. Shadlock
Rivers; where the Latter is settled, & if there is any hopes of recovering about £300 Sterling from the Estate of either or both of them,
& inform me of your discoveries as early afterward as opportunity
may permit.
        I most heartily wish you a perfect state of Health & a happy
return to your family & friends in Charles Town & during your
absence I shall do every thing in my power to confirm to you my
professions of being Dear Sir, &ca.—

Added a few Lines the 31st May. If W. Fisher has Money of mine
in hand to draw as much out as will purchase two of the best light,
strong, broad wheeled Waggons if to be laid on our Wharf exclusive
of Insurance at £120 Currency per peice with Harness & send per
Mason. Transmit an Account of Regulations of cleaning & lighting
Streets in Philadelphia.[1] Also if you can procure one send a clear

---

[1] In 1762 the Pennsylvania assembly had passed an act for "Regulating,
Pitching, Paving, and Cleansing the Highways," which set up a board of street
commissioners to contract for and supervise the paving of the streets of Philadelphia. In 1764 a suitable plan for paving High Street was worked out, and
within a few years Philadelphia had the best streets in America. HL, being
aware of these civic advances to the northward, provided leadership for urban
changes in Charleston. He was particularly interested as he lived in one of the
new suburbs which must be linked with the town. Charleston at this time did
lay out streets to the suburbs of Ansonborough and Coming's Point, contracted
for new drains and sewers, and paved sidewalks. Carl Bridenbaugh, *Cities in
Revolt, Urban Life in America, 1743–1776* (New York, 1964), pp. 28–32,
236–245. HL had been appointed by the assembly on May 25 to a seven-

sensible Account of their method of making Wharfs in Deep Water. Call on Mr. Robinson at Road Island.[2]

SOURCE: Letterbook copy, HL Papers, S. C. Hist. Soc.; addressed "Bound to Philadelphia." The postscript was copied by HL.

TO JOHN CATHCART

[Charles Town] 30th May 1764

Sir,

This Morning your favour of the 14th Ulto. was brought to me. I observe what you write of Bains Robinsons protested Bill for £42.10.4 Sterling & very well remember what I said to you upon the Subject when you rece'd that & the other Bills from Capt. Brunett & you may rest assured that as soon as the Bill appears I shall replace

---

member committee to bring in a street cleaning bill for Charleston. See Appendix. "An act to impower certain commissioners therein mentioned to keep clean and in good order and repair the streets of Charlestown, and for establishing other regulations in the said town" was passed on Aug. 10, 1764. By this law Isaac Mazyck, Gabriel Manigault, John Savage, Thomas Smith, Jr., Henry Peronneau, John Scott, Hopkin Price, Daniel Cannon, and William Glen were appointed commissioners of the streets for a term of five years and then to the end of the next ensuing session of the assembly. Upon a vacancy they could coopt new members. They had the power to contract with scavengers for the cleaning of the streets, to supervise the laying of sewers and drains, to issue licenses for every cart, wagon, and dray, to set the rates of haulage, and to fine whites for speeding and to whip Negroes for the same offense. They were to enforce the law that no one could hire out more than two slaves nor could a slave be trained to practice as a mechanic by himself (white masters could train Negro artisans, however). They received £1,400 from the general tax each year to carry out their duties, but they could levy special taxes in the parishes of St. Philip and St. Michael for street improvements. Manuscript Act No. 927, S. C. Archives.

[2] Matthew Robinson (1709–1795) was born in Newport, R. I., the son of a searcher of customs. He became a lawyer, prospered, and about 1750 moved to Narragansett where he bought an estate. He was known for his library and for his literary accomplishments. His wife was the daughter of Mr. Lucas, a French Huguenot, who had been married first to a Mr. Johnston and was the mother of Augustus Johnston, the stamp agent for Rhode Island and later judge of the Vice Admiralty court in Charleston. "Matthew Robinson," *Biographical Cyclopedia of Representative Men of Rhode Island* (Providence, R. I., 1881), pp. 105–106. HL's grandfather André Laurens had married Marie Lucas. Marie Lucas had three brothers, one of whom was named Augustus. *Publications of the Huguenot Society of London*, XVIII, p. 148. Mrs. Robinson was probably a niece of Marie Lucas Laurens, perhaps a daughter of Augustus Lucas. If so, HL would have been Mrs. Robinson's first cousin once removed.

it together with the usual charges in the hands of Messrs. Bethune to which effect I wrote to them Yesterday, but the Bill being sent by way of New York does not yet appear. I had no Interest nor connexion in Capt. Brunetts purchase. My promises were made on his behalf merely to serve him as a Stranger & to facilitate his business with you which without such promises might have been much more difficult for him to transact & I am glad that I come so cheaply off as with only the trouble that may attend the recovery of this Bill & perhaps some trifling expence. You need not be under the least anxiety about your Bond to Brunett. The penalty was only to guard against a Claim to the Brigantine *Tryton* by her proper owners or their Assigns & they having now confirmed your Act & deed in the Sale of her; Your obligation can never operate against you & is become thereby as harmless as Your Indentures of Apprenticeship. I shall acquaint Capt. Brunett in a few days of this circumstance. Meantime wishing you health & another good Ship I remain, Sir, your most humble Servant—

SOURCE: Letterbook copy, HL Papers, S. C. Hist. Soc.; addressed "at the House of Nathaniel & George Bethune, Boston"; "per Mason."

TO MATHEW ROBINSON

[Charles Town] 30th May 1764

Dear Sir,

I have had the pleasure of hearing from Mr. Lopez,[3] the Gentleman who is so kind as to bear this to you, that you & my Cousin Robinson were alive & well when he left New England. He likewise informed me that you would have taken the trouble of Writing to me but that you alledged there had been great remissness for Years past on my part. The civilities which I rece'd from you some Twenty two Summers since[4] did demand a more early acknowl-

---

[3] Moses Lopez had arrived in Charleston on April 13 from Newport. With the aid of Isaac Da Costa, the family friend and merchant in Charleston, he had obtained freight for the *Hope* and was now returning by way of Philadelphia to Rhode Island. He sailed on the *Charles Town Packet* on May 31 and arrived in eight days in Philadelphia. "Charles Town in 1764," ed. Thomas J. Tobias, *SCHM*, LXVII (1966), 63–74.

[4] HL may have been in Rhode Island in the summer of 1742. Very little is known of HL's life prior to 1747.

edgement. I cannot therefore long pause upon your charge. My Conscience is an Evidence against me & my Integrity will not admit of a plea even in paliation of my fault. I do confess at Large that I have been too careless of my Friends & must intreat you to accept as the best attonement of what is past a promise of more respectful deportment in future & I have great encouragement to hope for your forgiveness from that very remembrance that you were pleased to have of me to Mr. Lopez which convinces me that you are not inexorable.

Since I parted with you in the Year 1742 I have traveled thus far through the Vicissitudes of human life in various scenes, terminating upon the whole to my advantage, far beyond my merrits & more than adequate to my most Sanguine hopes. I shall not obtrude upon you a tedious detail of my Journey. Let it suffice to inform you in brief that after three or 4 Years Adventuring across the Atlantic, great part of which time I spent in an exceeding good Counting house in London[5] to further that knowledge in Mercantile affairs which I had acquired here, I returned to Carolina in the close of 1748 & sat myself close to business in a Copartnership which hath produced me very extensive, honourable, & valuable connexions.[6] In the Year 1750 I enter'd into a Matrimonial partnership & in this state have alternately enjoyed the blessings & felt the Afflictive hand of divine providence. But as I remarked above the former does greatly preponderate & demands my incessant thanks. I have indeed been shocked & almost ready to murmur at the Death of some very promising Children, particularly an improved Boy of Six and a clever Girl of Eight Years old,[7] losses that to me who may be called a fond parent proved almost insurmontable but thank God I have two Sons remaining one of Ten Years Old, another of One, and a lively Girl in her fifth Year.[8] Mrs. Laurens with the two Youngest is now in the Country at the Houses of some of our Relations. I keep the eldest in Town to apply to his Books in which he makes no bad progress.

I am at this middle state of Life retreating by gradual Steps from that bustle & hurry that my attention to commerce had unavoidably led me into and in order to accelarate my plan have relinquished

---

[5] That of James Crokatt.
[6] That of Austin & Laurens.
[7] Henry died Aug. 1, 1758 and Eleanor died April 18, 1764.
[8] John, Henry, and Martha.

some of the most lucrative branches of trade which thro the partiality of my friends were at my command in whole or in part to suit my own convenience but I do not mean wholly to retire. It is at present incumbent on me for several obvious reasons to shun a state of inaction: some duties that I owe to my Country, the necessary improvements of my Lands in & near Charles Town, a few Vessels in which I am concerned or own, & the transaction of business for particular old friends in England will at the same time keep me from Idleness & maintain a Select correspondence which may be beneficial hereafter to some worthy young Man or to my Sons if they should live & incline to improve their Talents in merchandize, by and by, when these considerations which now induce me to draw a little of my attention from the *Busy World* may ripen into injunctions to detach my mind intirely from those fleeting runs which are the daly product of it. Thus, Dear Sir, I have given you an abstract of some of my former annals & future intentions. I must beg leave to refer you to this good Old Gentleman for more particulars. He can tell you where I live but as to the manner I must suffer from his discription unless he is very indulgent (for he came at a time when my Wife and I were in distress under the loss of our eldest Daughter) but I will venture to say that tis hospitable & I strive to make it decent. If any other of your friends should come this way you may freely command my respects to them & upon any other occasion you will find me ready to wait upon you. I beg, Sir, that you will present my Love to Mrs. Robinson in which I cannot say that Mrs. Laurens joins me because she knows nothing of my writing but this I can with truth assure you that she esteems all my friends as her own & therefore I may add that she will unite in my good wishes to both of you & bear a part in that satisfaction which your felicity will always produce to, Dear Sir, your affectionate & obliged Servant—

SOURCE: Letterbook copy, HL Papers, S. C. Hist. Soc.; addressed "Esquire. Rhode Island"; "per Capt. Mason for Philadelphia."

TO WILLIAM KEITH

[Charles Town, June 1764]

Dear Sir,

I have a large quantity of Old Barbadoes Rum in Store which

I think is in general as good as any in this Province. The price is 17/6 per Gallon which it absolutely stood me in some Twelve months ago.

Mr. Rhind[9] did Speak to me about a Young Gentleman[1] who was desirous he said of Writing in my Counting House but I could then give him no encouragement to hope for a place there nor can I say more at present than this, that to shew my regard for Mr. Keith & Mr. Rhind if that Young Gentleman cannot engage himself in a better way between this & the time that I shall be settled in a new Counting House which is now building at home say about a Month hence he shall be heartily welcome to write there and receive such advantages as the knowledge of my old & new Books & also of the little business that I shall transact may afford him & he may diet with me. This may be better for him than total inaction, but I really have not nor do I expect to have employment for more hands than are already engaged in my service, & tho I do not mean to retire wholly from Trade but nevertheless my determination not to increase my business but to retreat (barring accidents) by gradual steps from that hurry & bustle which a Long & close application had unavoidably led me into. When I have the pleasure of seeing Your self I shall add what may be needful upon the subject. Meantime I beg pardon for omitting this Answer to your favour in the Morning but I was in the Middle of a Long Letter for Philadelphia when Your Boy came to me & the Vessel by which it was to go being upon the point of Sailing I was streightened in time to finish & get it on board. Therefore I trust you will excuse me & believe me to be with great regard, Dear Sir—

SOURCE: Letterbook copy, Letter Book of Henry Laurens, Oct. 30, 1762–Sept. 10, 1766, Penn. Hist. Soc.; addressed "Charles Town."

TO JOHN COMING BALL

[Charles Town, June 1764]

Dear Sir,

I rece'd your favour of 28th May by Carolina[2] who with all

---

[9] David Rhind was a physician. *HL Papers*, III, 18. Beaufain, the collector of customs in Charleston, left his books and his share in the Charleston Library Society to Dr. Rhind. *SCHM*, XI, (1910), 132. The patriots banished him from Charleston during the Revolution. *SCHM*, XXXIV (1933), 198.

[1] This may have been Daniel Crokatt who had been at Moncks Corner near which place Dr. Keith resided.

[2] Perhaps a slave.

of my Negroes came that day to Town. It would have done me great service if our affairs had permitted you to indulge me with the number that I asked for & I believe would have been much time saved upon the whole.[3] Mr. Creamer writes pressingly for a dozen broad Hoes which I now send by Mr. Bonneau's Boat,[4] must send to Mr. Bonneau's for them.

Last Week came in 10 Hogsheads of Jamaca Rum on Account of Wambaw. My Store being quite full I ordered 5 to be carted up here to Rattray Green & the other 5 to be Lodged at your own House with Mr. Merrilees who promised to take care of them. As soon as I pay the duty & Freight I shall state an Account of these & send you a duplicate.

I thank you for your kind invitation to Hyde Park where I wish to be for a few days but this baulk about the hands will keep me at home a fortnight longer than I expected for I cannot think of leaving this gang here to the Government of a Stranger who seems to be no great manager neither. The work that they are about promises well & if I do not succeed this attempt it will be merely for want of strength. One week more with 6 or 8 additional hands would make all that is to follow very easily performed. My Love to Sister Ball & all the Young folks & I remain, Dear Sir—

SOURCE: Letterbook copy, Letter book of Henry Laurens, Oct. 30, 1762–Sept. 10, 1766, Penn. Hist. Soc.; addressed "Hyde Park."

TO GEORGE DICK

[Charles Town, June 1764]

Sir,

I consign to you for Sale at Winyaw a Negro Man named Abram, Carolina born & aged about 34 to 36 Years & believe not

---

[3] HL undoubtedly needed this gang of slaves to do some heavy labor at his new home, wharf, and counting house at Rattray Green in Ansonborough.

[4] Samuel Bonneau (1725–1788), who lived at Bonneau's Ferry on the Eastern Branch of the Cooper River, had married Mary Boisseau, a widow. Their daughter Floride married John Ewing Colhoun and their granddaughter Floride married John C. Calhoun. W. Allan Moore, Jr., "The Bonneau Family," *The Transactions of the Huguenot Society of South Carolina*, LII (1947), 38–39; Irving, *A Day on Cooper River*, pp. 133–134. There is no registration for a vessel owned by Samuel Bonneau.

more than 36 for having owned him these 12 Years know he was when he first came to me a Boy or just entring upon Manhood. From my experience of him I will venture to give him the following character.

His good qualities	His bad Ones
SOBER.	He will deceive you as often as he can.
A very good boatman.	
A very good hand at the Whip Saw or any other Plantation Business.	Will pilfer trifles but always carefully keeps out of greater scrapes.
A Jobbing Carpenter so far as to thorough work & to be a great assistant to a better hand.	Fond of Women.
A tolerable good Cooper can White wash & do little plaster work.	Ungrateful & disobedient to any Man that uses him well and does not keep him close to work.
Very active, alert and Strong when he pleases.	Will feign himself Sick when he is not so.
Very healthy in general, a good horseman, and very well acquainted all over the Province.	
Much afraid of chastisement & will exert himself to ward off Whipping if he is sure of having it in case he fails.	

I have here said so much of him in order to do justice to his Character. However this I must observe that when he is away from some pernicious connexions that he has made with Slaves in Charles Town I do believe he will behave much better and become a Valuable Slave, and upon the whole if I could be sure of his amendment or even that I could resort to compel him by chastisement to behave as well as he can I would not part with him for One Thousand pounds as indeed I would bare with all his faults if I was not apprehensive that his example will have a very bad effect upon the manners of other of my Negroes—and in hopes that this kind of banishment will alarm them. I beg you to sell you[5] for ready Money or upon Bond & security with Interest for about Six or Seven hundred pounds & if you cannot obtain that amount leave him with my Friend William

---

[5] The clerk undoubtedly should have copied "him."

Smith[6] and put this Letter into his hands or bring him to Town again as you please. I wish you well and am—

SOURCE: Letterbook copy, Letter Book of Henry Laurens, Oct. 30, 1762–Sept. 10, 1766, Penn. Hist. Soc.; addressed "Captain."

T O   B E L L A M Y   C R A W F O R D
[Charles Town] 1st June 1764
Dear Sir,

Mr. Jackson[7] who is the Bearer of this has now called upon me a second or I believe a third time for the Amount of your Bond in which I stand bound to him as your surety & he informs me that he has likewise called upon you to no purpose. This Young Gentleman is very pressing for his Money & I think since it was lent to you you have not even paid one farthing for the use of it. It is not in my power by any means at present to advance the sum that is due & I must even subject myself to those inconveniences which a suit will draw upon me before I am drove to greater to raise the Money— inconveniences which I would not if I was in Mr. Crawford's place put any Gentleman to who had acted so disinterested & friendly a part to me as I have done to Mr. Crawford & which I hope he will while it is in his power avert & ward off from, &ca.—

SOURCE: Letterbook copy, Letter Book of Henry Laurens, Oct. 30, 1762–Sept. 10, 1766, Penn. Hist. Soc.; addressed "Charles Town."

T O   C O W L E S   &   H A R F O R D
[Charles Town] 4th June 1764
Gentlemen,

I wrote you the 5th Ulto. per Higgins & Chisman & the 8th per Kendal since which, Vizt. Yesterday, your acceptable favours of the 21st March are both come to hand with duplicates of the 20th

---

[6] As William Smith was a merchant of Georgetown, HL had obviously instructed Captain Dick to sell the slave there. *HL Papers*, III, 107n, 124, 144, 475, 482, 484, 508.
[7] This may be John Jackson who had requested HL to be his guardian in 1759. *HL Papers*, III, 15.

& 25th January & of sundry sales; an Invoice & Bill of Loading for 4 bales of Oznabrug per *Susanna*[8] is likewise come under the same cover; but to my great grief none of these Accounts that I have been so many Years praying for make their appearance yet.

Since the consignment of the *Barbadoes Packet* Cargo is not unacceptable I may take the Liberty when their is a proper opening to make you another of the same sort & if you can do as well in such sales as the London Factor's do (& I have hopes that you will do better than some of them) it will be in my power to procure consignments now & then from other hands. The premium you paid was high but you have had a dreadful Winter. The accident that I met with & which you was so kind as to take notice of has introduced such pains as I was never subject to before. I have been ever since it happened more or less invalid, & if I do not get much better in the course of this Summer I shall think seriously of crossing the Atlantic the ensuing Spring. We should not suffer disorders to hang long upon us in this climate, but I flatter myself with hopes that there will be no necessity for such a change. If there is I shall advertize all my Friends in due time.

You will see George Appleby & he is the Man to talk to about those Accounts of A., L., & A. What I wrote was at his request & whatever you & he may agree to will be well pleasing to me. The error that you have discovered & noted in the bounty Bill per *Minerva* shall be mended in the Account sent to me.

Our Indigo Account will prove an unprofitable one I observe by your minutes of what is sold. If you could have seen with my eyes you would have paid a Little longer Ware house Room. The prices were mending a little in London & will no doubt get up when they hear of the very bad prospect of our Crop on the ground which must have some effect upon your Markets. The Accounts of Sale & Bounty will be very acceptable when they are ready.

The Hot Well Water[9] that you mentioned I know nothing of further than by conjecture. There did lay in my Store two Buckets of that Water, whether left by Capt. Baker I know not but being at a loss for a claimant & the Subject of no great Value, I fancy they

---

[8] The snow *Susannah*, Young Green.

[9] The Hotwells was a radioactive spring near the Avon River below Bristol which attracted crowds of visitors in the eighteenth century and in 1939 supplied the Grand Spa Hotel. *The Blue Guide to England*, ed. L. Russell Muirhead (London, 1939), p. 150.

were used by my two partners who as they were going to Sea each took one. Mr. Appleby can better inform you.

Now for the *Flora*—I am glad that you have at length brought her out of that long concealment which had totally hidden her from my knowledge. What you have determined to do with her is not only perfectly agreeable to me but I think calls for my thanks which please to accept; but good Sirs, if you had reverted to the Latter part of my Letter under the 15th October last, the necessity for making any appology or for offering to take the risque of any blame upon yourselves, must have vanished, nor can I see how Capt. Courtin could hesitate one moment to do whatever you should require when he reflected upon these words in My Letter to him the 19th May Last—"If Messrs. Cowles & Harford (for Mrs. Sarah Nickleson & Co.) should give you any orders respecting the Ship please to receive & follow the same as if they were from me."

I had provided as much Pitch & Tar at different times since the Month of February as would have three times Loaded the *Flora,* the Latter part of it I had engaged to Ship on board the Brigantine *Rose,* Henry Gray, Master for Bristol (as hinted to you the 5th Ulto.) for which I request you to Insure as much as will Net two hundred Guineas & the over Value I shall risque. This Vessel will Sail sometime in July.[1]

But to return to the *Flora* I am now utterly at a loss what sort of Cargo to purchase for her. The price of Pitch will soon be high again. There is a great deal in the Country but it is kept back & the demand begins now to be very considerable. Rice is got up to 45/ & here are several empty Vessels in port. I have the offer of upward of 600 Barrels of Rice of the very best sort to be had at this Season which I sometimes think of purchasing & send the Ship away to Lisbon. I could wish to have had the aid of Your advice, but you may rest assured of my determining as shall appear most advantageous for the General Interest & (as I have your permission to do so) that I shall Interest you in any provision that I shall make for her. Meantime I remain with great regard, Gentlemen—

---

[1] Henry Gray, owner and master, registered the Brigantine *Rose,* 60 tons, on May 16, 1764. It had previously been registered at New Providence on Feb. 5, 1764, as the sloop *Advice,* where it had been condemned as a lawful prize on Aug. 16, 1762. Gray had transformed it from a sloop into a brigantine. Ship Register, 1734–1765, p. 232, S. C. Archives.

SOURCE: Letterbook copy, HL Papers, S. C. Hist. Soc.; addressed "Bristol"; "per Reeves. Uncertain if a Copy of this was ever sent. See my Letter 17th July."

TO JOHN BRUCE[2]

[Charles Town] 6th June 1764

Sir,

When I wrote to you a day or two ago the Person who brought your favour of the 2nd Inst. & carried that in answer to it could not wait until I might make out Mr. Dannelly's[3] Account, but according to promise I send it inclosed, Amounting with Interest to the 5th July next to £785.14.3 for the payment of which I am now to look upon you as surety & may request the favour of you to call upon me in order to acknowledge the same by your hand upon the back of Mr. Dannellys Bond the next time you come to this Town. I am, Sir, &ca.—

SOURCE: Letterbook copy, Letter Book of Henry Laurens, Oct. 30, 1762–Sept. 10, 1766, Penn. Hist. Soc.; addressed "Christ Church."

TO EDWARD MARTIN

[Charles Town] 10th June 1764

A Ship belonging to Mr. Knight in Liverpoole arriv'd yesterday with about 260 to 280 Slaves from Whyda[4] & orders to call on me & put the Cargo into my hands if I would undertake to dispose of it. This I am determined not to do unless I find it necessary for

---

[2] John Bruce (1732–1765) of Christ Church parish, planter, married Ann Sanders on Feb. 14, 1751. *SCHM*, II (1901), 132; "Will of John Bruce," dated Sept. 15, 1764, proved June 7, 1765, Charleston County Wills, x, Book B (1760–1767), 680–684, S. C. Archives.

[3] Edward Dannelly of Christ Church parish.

[4] The ship *Jenny*, George McKie, owned by John Knight of Liverpool, was entered inwards on June 18 from Africa with 290 slaves. Naval Office Lists, 1764–1767, p. 78. Whyda (Ouidah) was the port of Dahomey on the Bight of Benin, which because of a developed network of trade routes to the interior, was capable of exporting from 1,000 to 6,000 slaves annually during the 1770's. Fluctuations in the trade occurred during the eighteenth century because of political changes taking place in the interior. Philip D. Curtin, *The Atlantic Slave Trade, A Census* (Madison, Wisc., 1969), pp. 226–227.

my friends Interest to interfere. I see the Captain has an alternative in case of my refusal; & the name of Your House Messrs. Shirley & Martin is Mentioned. He informs me that his orders are to have remittances for the whole Amount in the Bottom, Vizt. a Load of Rice & some Deer Skins & the remainder in Bills at 3 & 6 Months. If you incline to take him up be pleased to inform me directly & take as soon as you can the necessary steps for making a good Sale. Let who will sell them, my regard to Mr. Knight will oblige me to offer my best services upon that occasion & the more as he Seems to require it in very pressing terms.[5] I am, &ca.—

SOURCE: Letterbook copy, Letter Book of Henry Laurens, Oct. 30, 1762–Sept. 10, 1766, Penn. Hist. Soc.; addressed "Charles Town."

TO BREWTON & SMITH

[Charles Town] 10th June 1764

Gentlemen,

I believe you have not been explicit with Capt. McKee.[6] Offer him as good terms of remittance for his Cargo as any that have been made the present Year & you need not doubt of having the Sale of the Cargo of Negroes on board his Ship. Let who will sell it if they will accept of my best Services they may be assure[d] of having them. Your Answer before 6 oClock is necessary & will oblige, Gentlemen, Your well wisher & most Obedient Servant—

SOURCE: Letterbook copy, Letter Book of Henry Laurens, Oct. 30, 1762–Sept. 10, 1766; addressed "Charles Town."

---

[5] Brewton & Smith sold the cargo as they paid the duty of £2,362.10/ currency on the cargo. Public Treasurer, Journal B: Duties, 1748–1765, p. 401, S. C. Archives.

[6] Capt. George McKie of the *Jenny*.

TO WILLIAM FRIERSON[7]

[Charles Town] 11th June 1764

Dear Sir,

The Cargo of Negroes for Sale as per inclosed Advertisements[8] to be sold by Messrs. Brewton & Smith belongs to a particular friend of mine in England.

The Negroes are from that part of Africa which people in the West Indies esteem most for producing the best Slaves. Please to disperse the Advertisements as quick & as generally as you can & I wish it may suit you & many others of my old friends in your Quarters to attend the Sales.

My Complements to Mrs. Frierson & good wishes to all your family are offered by, Dear Sir, &ca.—

SOURCE: Letterbook copy, Letter Book of Henry Laurens, Oct. 30, 1762–Sept. 10, 1766, Penn. Hist. Soc.; addressed "Captain. Williamsburgh."

TO DANIEL HEYWARD[9]

[Charles Town] 11th June 1764

Dear Colonel,

A Cargo of Negroes belonging to a very good friend of mine is offer'd to Sale by Messrs. Brewton & Smith as per inclosed advertisement, which I take the Liberty to forward & recommend to your consideration. You have often complimented me with enquiries when I should have Negroes & promises of further favours which add to the obligations that I am under for all past ones. Now, Sir, your aid

---

[7] *HL Papers,* III, 22n. William Frierson had been lieutenant of the Williamsburg Township company in the Craven County militia on May 4, 1757. Council Journal, XXVI (Jan. 3, 1757–June 6, 1758), 84, S. C. Archives. He had apparently been elected captain of that company since that date.

[8] These were broadsides announcing the sale and were to be distributed among prospective purchasers.

[9] Daniel Heyward (1720–1777), who was lieutenant colonel of the Granville County regiment, lived just south of the Combahee River in the Indian Land at "Old House" plantation which he had begun to develop at age twenty-one. He founded one of the great rice-planting dynasties of Carolina. His great-great-grandson in recording the family story wondered how the Heywards had acquired their slaves. This letter provides one answer. Duncan Clinch Heyward, *Seed from Madagascar* (Chapel Hill, N. C., 1937), pp. 45–52.

at this Sale of my friends will oblige me as much as if I made the Sale myself & if I can but win you to come & see them I am under no doubt that the Country will tempt you to make a small purchase. I am, &ca.—

SOURCE: Letterbook copy, Letter Book of Henry Laurens, Oct. 30, 1762–Sept. 10, 1766, Penn. Hist. Soc.; addressed "Colonel. Indian Land."

TO CHARLES CROKATT

[Charles Town] 11th June 1764

Sir,

Annexed is a duplicate of what I wrote to you the 23d Ulto. per Capt. Bowers. I wait on you now per the Ship *Queen Charlotte* & present under this cover an Invoice & Bill of Loading for 253 Barrels of Rice of as good a quality as can be Shipped at this Season of the Year, & such as would pass examination at any time. Be pleased to sell it in such manner as you shall think most advantageous & pass the Net proceeds to my Credit.

Having upon two occasions suffered very considerably from disputes about the quality of my Rice sold in the Channel when I knew that it was of the very best, I had made a general resolution never to ship Rice for a foreign market but in Vessels Loaden wholly by myself or in conjunction with some friend upon whose attention to the quality of his goods I could depend. Nor would I have deviated from my plan at this time but for reasons assigned in my last.

My friends who sold the Rice alluded to, told me that I was sworn out of my property by Dutch Brokers. That might have been the case, but I am rather inclined to believe that I suffered in it thro the hurry of expeditious Cowes-Factors who for the sake of dispatch tumble the several parcels of one Cargo into a promiscuous heap from whence the Barrels were filled again. If this be their method & I believe it was in time past, my loss is easily accounted for. We have people amongst us as there are in all countries who are not very nice in their choices & others whose circumstances oblige them to put up with goods of inferior quality for the sake of two or three Months Credit. I have formerly wrote as fully upon this head to Messrs. George McKenzie & Co. to prevail upon them to let my Rice be Shipped distinctly from other parcels & take its chance according to its own merit, & if the same method could be pursued in the Sale & delivery, each shipper would have his own, but according to the present Rule a whole Cargo may be sold at any given rate, say at 10/ deliverable at Hamburgh & part of it not worth within 13d per Ct. of the Market price, the abatement demanded by the purchasers is made on the whole; so I understand it by my friends allegation that I was sworn out of my property. These are hints that I take the Liberty of giving to you but probably you may be aware of all these things & that I have taken up your time unnecessarily, if so, I beg your pardon & that you will believe me to be with great regard, Sir, Your obliged humble Servant—

SOURCE: Letterbook copy, HL Papers, S. C. Hist. Soc.; addressed "Esquire. London"; "per Capt. Reeves."

TO JOHN KNIGHT

[Charles Town] 12th June 1764

Dear Sir,

I wrote you the 7th & 8th Ulto. per Higgins & Kendal since which I have sold off all your goods per the *Hope* except the Hogsheads of Earthen Ware which were in such a shattered condition that they have already cost more porterage for unpacking, carrying to Vendue, returned home over & over again, & Cartage than I beleive they will ever repay. At Length I have put them into the hands of a poor industrious Woman to retail. If I can get an Account from her, at any rate soon, it shall be inserted in the general Sales. Otherwise I shall send all your Accounts leaving that Article out until the whole is sold & paid for.

Last Saturday Morning the 9th Inst. Your Ship *Jenny*, Capt. McKie, arrived here with 269 Slaves on the Ships Account & 26 upon Freight from Whydah. Capt. McKie wrote to me that he had orders to make an offer of his Cargo to me, for which Additional favour I beg leave to repeat my most grateful thanks. Upon inquiry I found that you had given the Capt. an alternative in case of my refusal & named the Houses of Messrs. Shirly & Martin, Brewton & Smith, or any other that I should recommend & that the terms in case I did not take up the Ship were remittances for the whole per

Bills in the bottom payable at 3 & 6 Months save the Amount of a
Cargo of Rice & some Deer skins. This I say was the information he
gave me. My reply was that nothing should tempt me to touch her
but an absolute necessity to serve you & therefore I desired him to
apply without delay to those other Houses. He asked me which? &
I could not help on your account recommending him to the latter
for many evident reasons which I assigned to him & shall here repeat
some of them, vizt. the same objections lay against the other House
that I make to myself. Mr. Martin is at present alone[1] & consequently
not so capable of going thro business of this importance as those two
partners with the assistance of the Elder Mr. Smith[2] whose extensive
acquaintance & ability in dispatch of business as well as influence
with the Planters are at least equal to those of any other Man in the
Province. Sudden Death or even a Sharp disorder to a single person
would greatly injure your Interest for I am sure by experience that
it cannot be so well taken Care of by any Substitute. Again Mr.
Martin's acquaintance is not very extensive yet & indeed his name
scarcely known by a great many very good customers for Negroes
who are very cautious of bonding themselves to strangers & therefore
he must be under some disadvantage in case of one or more competitors although he might if there were no other Cargoes at Market do
very well & here lay the weight of my arguments. We had upon
your Ship's arrival the *Sally* of Bristol with [*blank*] Slaves to Smith &
Brewton,[3] a small Cargo of 90 to Middleton, Liston, & Hope,[4] the
Sales of both to come on within these eight days, besides several Little

---

[1] His partner Thomas Shirley returned from England in July. *Gazette,* Oct.
8, 1764.
[2] Benjamin Smith who had been senior partner in the firm of Smith, Brewton,
& Smith.
[3] The ship *Sally,* Thomas Gullan, owned by John and Robert Gordon of
Bristol, was entered inwards on June 18 with 320 slaves from Africa. Naval
Office Lists, 1764–1767, p. 78. Brewton & Smith paid £2,335 in duties on
these slaves from Angola. Public Treasurer, Journal B: Duties, 1748–1765,
p. 401, S. C. Archives. Thomas Gullan had brought the *Roebuck* to Charleston
from Africa in 1760, the *Roebuck* to Virginia in 1762, and would bring the
Constantine to Charleston in 1768. Donnan, *Documents Illustrative of the Slave
Trade,* IV, 229, 375, 624. Donnan did not mention the slavetrading voyage of
1764.
[4] The schooner *Ann,* John Darrell, owned by Benjamin Butterfield, Benjamin
Lightbourn, John Darrell, etc. of Bermuda, was entered inwards on June 13
with 80 slaves from Barbados. Naval Office Lists, 1764–1767, p. 78. Middleton,
Liston, & Hope paid £705 in duties on these slaves brought from Barbados.
Public Treasurer, Journal B: Duties, 1748–1765, p. 401, S. C. Archives.

scattered parcels from West Indies and more daily expected,[5] as well as a Cargo of 500 from Angola which B. & S. have late advice of & hourly expect its arrival.[6] These are too powerful opponents for a new House and must distress one greatly, besides on the other hand since it falls out so & there is really a demand for the whole confining them to one House or nearly so, does undoubtedly enable that House to maintain its prices & I am morally sure it will have that effect in the present case. Capt. McKie hereupon wrote to those Gentlemen whose reply was that they would comply with his terms except in point of remittances which they could not make better than at 3, 6, & 12 Months being the stated periods for other Cargoes sold by them. Then I wrote to Mr. Martin but found that all my reasonings with the Capt. were unnecessary because Mr. Martin was out of Town & not to return before tomorrow, a delay which I could by no means subject your business to. Next I offered the Cargoes to Mr. Thomas Savage a Young Gentleman of exceeding good connexions here & for his encouragement told him he might depend upon my utmost assistance to make a good Sale, that I would undertake to procure him all the Bills wanted & he should have the whole Commission but he had not resolution to encounter the terms. In the meantime McKie became anxious to fix with B. & S. & to avoid further loss of time. Nevertheless I made one effort more & that was with Messrs. Brailsford & Chapman making them an offer of the Cargo upon the terms prescribed (or I believe more properly squeezed) by your Captain assuring them that I would make no further attempts if they would comply but those Gentlemen would come no nearer than 3, 6, & 9 Months, which made me turn once more to the Other House who at length agree'd to remit in 3, 6, 9, & 12 Months. The difference here lays wholly in the Interest of the last paid portion

---

[5] The sloop *Carolina*, Clement Conyers, owned by Josiah, George, and Thomas Smith and William Dandridge of Charleston and William Manning of St. Kitts was entered inwards on June 1 with 8 slaves from St. Kitts. The schooner *Mary*, William Brown, owned by Shirley & Martin and Robert Boyd of Charleston, was entered inwards on June 1 with 10 slaves from Providence. The sloop *John*, Francis Dickinson, owned by Henry Todd of Charleston, was entered inwards on June 8 with 9 slaves from St. Kitts. Naval Office Lists, 1764–1767, pp. 77–78. Samuel Peronneau paid £90 in duties on the slaves brought by Todd from St. Kitts. Public Treasurer, Journal B: Duties, 1748–1765, p. 401, S. C. Archives.

[6] The ship *Queen Barra* would bring about 300 slaves from Sierra Leone to Brewton & Smith in August. See HL to Richard Oswald & Co., Aug. 10.

which in my opinion is greatly over weighed by some of the considerations above mentioned. Therefore I closed with them & your Cargo is advertised for sale on the 19th Inst. the same day with the *Sally*'s.

I have wrote Letters to some of my old Friends & if needful my utmost services shall be exerted on the day of the sale but I am very sure those Gentlemen will do every thing in their power to serve you & that they can do much more than I a single Hand could do even barring the accidents of Sickness, &ca., which are no small consideration in this Climate where one Man is obliged to bustle thro a great deal of business. I know these things very well from some experience & observations & must confess that, I have not resolution & avarice enough to endanger either my good Friends who would intrust me on one hand, or my Family on the other to great disappointments & Losses, upon the precarious Tenure of my Life or health & indeed I must Inform you that I have not been quite well ever since that Fall in my Stair case mentioned to you in January last. I feel frequent visits of pains in my bones & particularly at this time I am hardly able to walk about which is a great mortification to me who have enough to employ me & am naturally inclined to exercise. In short if I do not shake off these complaints in the course of this Summer I shall think seriously of a Voyage to England the ensuing Spring & perhaps a change of Air & manner of Life for a few Months in that fine Climate may recover me.

I took notice just now of the probability of your Captain's having squeesed the terms of 3 & 6 Months for I cannot think that a Man of Mr. Knight's judgement & generosity would lay such heavy & unprecedented Bonds upon honest Men, nor expose himself on the other side to the danger of being made the dupe of his own policy by the rapaciousness of designing Men who will Lick themselves whole under any terms.

But, Dear Sir, I now talk of this. Did you ever find any inconvenience attending the mode of remittances made by the houses of A. & L., & A., L., & A.—vizt. according to the times of payment set forth in the Sales? Surely you did not or, if ever you did, they were small in comparison of the difference of prices obtained for a few months Credit, but I beleive upon the whole you had your remittances made in a shorter time than those Gentlemen who had tied up their Factors to certain Rules for remitting the whole in the bottom, & I have known the time when some of our Neighbours under those Limitations have pocketed by gain of Interest a Commission of 12 or 13 per Cent when we have made barely 9 per Cent, averaged more money upon the Cargo sold by us, & remitted the whole or within a trifle of the whole in the Course of 7 to 9 months & the bulk of it in the bottom & in 3 to 6 Months of which I think I can produce more than two or three instances. Now in the present case Your Negroes will all or almost all be paid for in Cash, or an Interest of 8 per Cent running upon the deficency within 4 or 5 Months of the Sale. This is a benefit which in my sense of things ought to be wholly yours but yet there is no prevailing upon Gentlemen tied down to remit in the bottom to give it. They argue & with great plausibility, the difficulty of purchasing Bills for the Amount of a whole Cargo of Negroes & the risques they take upon themselves in Shipping the produce of the Country to raise a Bank & make some compensation to their friends who in the mean time give Credit to their draughts by accepting them without effects in hand. If indeed the advantage of handling & negotiating those long sighted bills are more than adequate to those other considerations in moving the great Wheel of unfathomable commerce round, which you know best, the case is greatly altered. Upon the whole, I shall be as strenuous as I dare to be with these Gentlemen not to crimp the average merely for the sake of speedy payment.

I have talked very freely to you, Sir, & long enough upon the present occasion you will perceive that your service only & no Interested views hath prompted my pen & if my thoughts are inoffensively impertinent the paper to which they are committed may still be made useful in various ways & you will pardon my Zeal.

I shall have my eye upon your Interest as long as my services are acceptable & I shall receive great pleasure upon every fresh opportunity of testifying that I am with the utmost gratitude, Dear Sir, Your much obliged humble Servant—

SOURCE: Letterbook copy, HL Papers, S. C. Hist. Soc.; addressed "Leverpoole"; "per Reeves. Copy per McKie."

TO GEORGE McKENZIE & CO.

[Charles Town] 12th June 1764

Gentlemen,

My last trouble to you was per the *Barbadoes Packet,* Capt. Harrop, since which I have none of your favours. I lately let to Freight the Ship *Dorset,* Capt. Christopher Chisman, for a foreign Market & made a point of clearing her at Cowes of which I gave Capt. John McKenzie timely notice that he might use his endeavours to have the Cargo cleared at your House in which I hope he succeeded.

This goes by the *Queen Charlotte,* Capt. Reeves, for Cowes & Holland or Hamburgh having on board on my proper Account 253 Barrels of as good Rice as this advanced Season affords, contents as below. I have consigned it for sale to Charles Crokatt, Esquire on whom you will be pleased to Value for amount of your Account & upon all occasions in my little course of business you will find that I am with great esteem, Gentlemen—

HL 1 to 253 Barrels of Rice
Gross Weight	152,076	
Tare	15,622	
Net	136,454	

This if I understand you is what you directed in yours of the 4th November last.

SOURCE: Letterbook copy, HL Papers, S. C. Hist. Soc.; addressed "Cowes"; "per Reeves."

TO JOHN WIGFALL

[Charles Town] 13th June 1764

Sir,

I rece'd your favour of the 11th Inst. per your Brother[7] with whom I would have settled your Account but as there [*is*] some

---

[7] Benjamin Wigfall of St. Thomas parish, planter, mentioned his brothers John, Elias, and Joseph in his will. "Will of Benjamin Wigfall," dated Oct. 15, 1773, proved ———, Charleston County Wills, XVII, Book B (1774–1779), 619, S. C. Archives.

evident mistake he chose to decline it. In the meantime I have accepted your draught on me to Doctor Oliphant payable in one Month. I shall be at all times ready to call on you to make an end of this account whenever it is convenient to Your self & if I should happen to be out of Town the accounts will remain with my Clerk. I am, &ca.—

SOURCE: Letterbook copy, Letter Book of Henry Laurens, Oct. 30, 1762–Sept. 10, 1766, Penn. Hist. Soc.; addressed "Esquire. St. Thomas."

TO JOHN SAVAGE

[Charles Town] 14th June 1764

Sir,

I have deliver'd Money on Account of Mrs. Ann Air's Estate To Messrs. John Dutarque, Junior & Senior,[8] vizt. £1,000 & to Mr. Thomas Scott[9] £1,500 and taken Bonds for repayment dated the 1st June which was as early as I could with propriety say the Cash was waiting for them because Mr. Warham[1] had settled his Accounts but 2 or 3 days before. Mr. Scott had added to his own Bond a Mortgage of 20 Negroes by way of security & I have entred the same Upon record at the Secretary's Office.[2]

Mr. Nathaniel Green[3] has been soliciting me to Lend him £700 upon his own Bond & a Mortgage of 9 Negroes which he assures me is his own & free from all incumbrance (but this I must

---

[8] The Dutarques were Huguenots who had long been settled in the parish of St. Thomas. John Dutarque, Sr., born June 19, 1707, was buried on his own plantation on Oct. 11, 1767. His brothers-in-law were Stephen Fogartie, Lewis Mouzon, Alexander Brown, Henry Bonneau, and Stephen Miller. His son John, born June 1, 1734, married (1) Mary Serré in 1753 and (2) Lydia Gaillard in 1774. Annie B. Hasell, "Early Generations of the Dutarque Family," *Transactions of the Huguenot Society of South Carolina*, LXVII (1962), 57–60. John Dutarque, Jr., died in 1779. *SCHM*, x (1909), 229.

[9] Thomas Scott was an Ashley River planter.

[1] Charles Warham, vendue master, had sold the property of Ann Air at the request of HL and John Savage, the executors of her estate.

[2] HL was now putting the proceeds of the sale out at interest to the Dutarques and to Thomas Scott. Scott mortgaged twenty Negroes to secure his bond. On July 14, 1770, HL and John Savage conveyed the Negroes to Agnes Scott, widow, for £1,635 currency. Mortgages, BBB (1766–1771), pp. 408–409, S. C. Archives. Agnes Scott died on Sept. 1, 1778, at the age of 68. *SCHM*, x (1909), 226.

[3] *HL Papers*, III, 435n.

further inquire into if needful). The security seems to be enough for the Sum to be Lent on the Estate's Account & I shall be obliged to you for your approbation or dislike just as the case may appear to you, either of which will govern the proceedings of, Sir, Your most humble Servant—

SOURCE: Letterbook copy, Letter Book of Henry Laurens, Oct. 30, 1762–Sept. 10, 1766, Penn. Hist. Soc.; addressed "Esquire. Charles Town."

TO GEORGE APPLEBY
[Charles Town] 14th June 1764
Dear Sir,

After confirming the above to be a duplicate of what I wrote you the 22d Ulto. I shall only add that Mr. Williams has brought to me on Your Account £1,017.5.4 which sum I have passed to Your Credit & shall remit you a Bill for the same the first day that I can sit down to make out some Accounts & draw for balances due to me. I continue in a poor way as to my health not well yet in my bowels & constantly in Slow pains in my bones which I impute to the fall that I got last Winter. Mrs. Laurens & our two Youngest are still in the Country and very well. Jackey is well with me at home. Our house begins to be in order, & when tis quite so then I shall invite the Mistress's return & not before, that she may be as free from trouble as I can make her. I am, my Dear Sir—

SOURCE: Letterbook copy, HL Papers, S. C. Hist. Soc.; "per Reeves."

TO WILLIAM THOMPSON
[Charles Town] 19th June 1764
Dear Sir,

I have agreeable to your Order paid Mr. Potts[4] One Hundred pounds & charged the same to your Account.

---

[4] Thomas Potts had come to Charleston to qualify as executor of his father's will which was proved on June 15, 1764. Thomas Potts left his son Thomas a 430-acre plantation near the Black River and his son John the home plantation of 500 acres. "Will of Thomas Potts," dated May 23, 1757, proved June 15, 1764, Charleston County Wills, x (1760–1767), 502–504, S. C. Archives.

I have also charged your Account with Five Hundred & Sixty pounds for two Young Negroes a Male & a Female which are part of a Lot that I was tempted to buy in order to secure two for you, for otherwise I certainly should not have purchased one. The price is high enough but they are likely & Mr. Potts & I are both of opinion that they are cheaper by £20 per head than they could have been bought singly for in the Negro Yard.

I am in want of pitch & beg that you will recommend all you can to me for which I shall be always willing to give the highest prices according to the quality of Pitch & Barrels, & also remember that I shall be a purchaser of Indigo this ensuing Year. I remain, &ca.—

SOURCE: Letterbook copy, Letter Book of Henry Laurens, Oct. 30, 1762–Sept. 10, 1766, Penn. Hist. Soc.; addressed "Black Mingo"; "per Mr. Thomas Potts."

TO JONATHAN DONNOM[5] OR JAMES DONNOM[6]

[Charles Town] 19th June 1764

Sir,

Agreable to your direction I here inclose an Account of your debt to me for that Bond of yours which I paid or assumed to Austin, Laurens, & Appleby Amount as per inclosed Account with Interest calculated to the 31st of next Month £1,265.11.2 for which Amount your Brother & yourself according to the proposition in your favour of the 6th Inst. will be pleased to execute the inclosed Bond & the party by whome you shall transmit me this duly executed shall receive the former Bond with a Receipt thereon to discharge you. I am, &ca.—

SOURCE: Letterbook copy, Letter Book of Henry Laurens, Oct. 30, 1762–Sept. 10, 1766, Penn. Hist. Soc.; addressed "Ponpon."

---

[5] *HL Papers,* III, 487n.
[6] *HL Papers,* III, 486n.

TO BENJAMIN BAKER[7]

[Charles Town, 19–25 June 1764]

Sir,

I relyed so much upon your promise to spare a good hand for a Little Carpenters work for two or at most three Days, that I could not have beleived that you would have disappointed me in the manner that you have done & assign no other reason but that your people have a *heavy peice of work in hand,* because I did not think that any peice of work could be so heavy as to out weigh your promise, and as you do not even tell me when I may expect your assistance I must conclude that something has happened to give you offence, and if so it is more than I know of and more than I can account for, but taking this for granted I ought not to remain in you[r] debt. I therefore send money by Mr. Hopton[8] out of which I beg you will satisfy yourself for so much time as you have lately wasted on my account & then it will not be wholly wasted to you & I shall remain by so much the less, Sir, Your oblig'd Servant—

SOURCE: Letterbook copy, Letter Book of Henry Laurens, Oct. 30, 1762–Sept. 10, 1766, Penn. Hist. Soc.; addressed "Queen Street." This letter which was undated appears between those dated June 19 and 25 in the letterbook.

TO PAUL TRAPIER[9]

[Charles Town] 25th June 1764

Sir,

At the request of Mr. William Price who has embarked

---

[7] Benjamin Baker, a carpenter, was "the Builder" of St. Michael's Church. George W. Williams, *St. Michael's, Charleston, 1751–1951* (Columbia, S. C., 1951), pp. 192, 200, 221, 245. He lived on the north side of Queen St. near Thomas Elfe, the cabinetmaker, for whom he sent out goods from England in 1768–1769. Elfe left him £1,000 currency and made him one of the executors of his estate. *SCHM,* xxxv (1934), 14, 67, 96, 155. Three of Baker's houses on Queen St. were destroyed by fire in 1774. *Country Journal,* Dec. 22, 1774. Baker's estate was confiscated in 1782. *SCHM,* xxxiv (1933), 195. He died before June 18, 1784. "Will of Benjamin Baker," dated Feb. 24, 1780, proved June 18, 1784, Charleston County Wills, xx (1783–1786), 413–414, S. C. Archives.

[8] John Hopton who may by this time have been HL's clerk.

[9] Paul Trapier (died 1793) was the leading merchant of Georgetown during the three decades prior to the Revolution. Rogers, *History of Georgetown County,* passim.

himself & me in a purchase of Negroes which he intends to sell at George Town, I take the Liberty of requesting your countenance & friendship to him upon that occasion. I tell Mr. Price that I do not know of any right I have to make so free with you, and to yourself permit me to say that whatever favours you are pleased to shew him shall be thankfully acknowledged whenever it is in the power of, Sir, Your most obedient humble Servant—

SOURCE: Letterbook copy, Letter Book of Henry Laurens, Oct. 30, 1762–Sept. 10, 1766, Penn. Hist. Soc.; addressed "Esquire. George Town."

TO WILLIAM SMITH

[Charles Town] 25th June 1764

Sir,

I have rece'd your favour per Mr. Dickinson with 72 Barrels of Pitch, our agreement for which you have some how or other mistaken and therefore I send a true Copy inclosed herein, by which you will see that the Pitch was to be subject to pay Freight & Wharfage but no hoops if the barrels were good. However if you have made a mistake & that the loss will fall upon you I will not insist upon my bargain to do you an injury.

Mr. Price will apply to you & I beg your best assistance to him. My late disorder returned upon me last Night & has left me as week as an Infant. If it should come back with the same violence I shall not have strength to stand it. I am, dear Sir, Your friend & humble Servant—

SOURCE: Letterbook copy, Letter Book of Henry Laurens, Oct. 30, 1762–Sept. 10, 1766, Penn. Hist. Soc.; addressed "George Town."

TO WILLIAM FRIERSON

[Charles Town, 25–26 June 1764]

Dear Sir,

Mr. Dickinson the Master of my Schooner declares that he

delivered your two Barrels of Salt at Black Mingo to Mr. William Thomson of whom you may have them at any time.

If he misinforms me please to let me know that I may make him accountable & send you up two Barrels more the first opportunity. Will you please to remember that I shall be a purchaser of Indigo the ensuing Winter if I Live to see that time. I remain, Dear Sir—

SOURCE: Letterbook copy, Letter Book of Henry Laurens, Oct. 30, 1762–Sept. 10, 1766, Penn. Hist. Soc.; addressed "Capt. Black Mingo." This letter which was undated appears between those of June 25 and 26 in the letterbook.

TO JOSEPH BROWN

[Charles Town] 26th June 1764

Dear Sir,

I here inclose you three Letters. One of them being in a packet with mine I had cut the Paper of the outside Wafer taking it to be my own but discovered my mistake in time & went no further.

Your Account is not yet settled but it shall be this Week please God I Live and sent to you per first opportunity. Neither have I taken up that Bond of Mr. Pawley's but that shall be done too as soon as any of my neighbours will enable me to spare so much money which I hope will be in a few days, for I have several of them largely in arrears, but they all complain of the want of Cash & every body calls upon me for Money for Rice, Pitch, &ca., as if I kept the Treasury.

Mr. Price has made a purchase of a parcel of Negroes & thinking it a large concern asked me to hold a part which I have agreed to. If you can be of any aid to him or the Sale I make no doubt of your friendship therein. My Love to Mrs. Brown, Miss Becky, and the Children & I remain—

SOURCE: Letterbook copy, Letter Book of Henry Laurens, Oct. 30, 1762–Sept. 10, 1766, Penn. Hist. Soc.; addressed "George Town."

TO TIMOTHY CREAMER

[Charles Town] 26th June 1764

Mr. Creamer,

I send home eleven Negroes namely Caesar, Taff, George, Jack, Tom, Bennet, Billy, Tanner, July, Charles, Adam.[1]

My Boat will be with you tomorrow. Please to put about one hundred or two hundred Bushels of the best fresh Water sand for making Mortar on board of her & then fill her up as much as she can take with pine Wood and dispatch her down again. Send also the Scaffolding poles. What Corn you may want Mr. Ball can easily supply you with & you will please to get it of him. I am, Sir, &ca.—

[P.S.] Dont let the Boat Negroes go amongst the Plantation Slaves.

[P.P.S.] The Names of Eleven New Negroes sent in the Schooner *Baker*[2] to the care of Mr. Creamer at Mepkin having each a blanket, an handkercheif, & 3 Yards Oznabrug. The Men & Boys have one hat & there is near 50 Yards of Negro Cloth to Cloath them immediately. I recommend them to Mr. Creamer's Care.

1	Othello	7	Juliet
2	Goodson	8	Lavinia
3	Tully	9	Rachael
4	Mentor	10	Matty
5	Valerius	11	Melissa[3]
6	Claudius		

SOURCE: Letterbook copy, Letter Book of Henry Laurens, Oct. 30, 1762–Sept. 10, 1766, Penn. Hist. Soc.; addressed "Mepkin."

TO EDWARD MARTIN

[Charles Town] 27 June 1764

Sir,

I inclose you a Letter from our friend Mr. John Knight and refer to that part of it relative to the Brigantine *Pocock*, which you

---

[1] These plantation slaves had been working on HL's town house.

[2] John Gray was captain of the schooner *Baker*. See HL to John Gray, Jan. 15–18, 1765.

[3] These Negroes must have been bought at the recent sales. Laurens may have given the new Negroes their classical names.

see he insists upon my taking up, at the peril of nothing less than his Friendship. This I would not forfeit for Twenty *Pocock* Cargoes, but I cannot think that he will inflict so heavy a penalty upon me for continuing to refuse the consignments, when he hears my further reasons for doing so. The principal one I shall mention to you & is this: that after having made a full & clear surrender to your House as you know I did some Months ago of that Vessel, I would not upon any account (but such as I then reserved) deprive or baulk you of your expectations, which indeed may be more injurious to your credit than the loss of double the Amount of commission, arising by another kind of misadventure, for when tis given out that a House expects such a Cargo of Negroes & that same consignment is seen to go by to another House it must occasion whispers & conjectures amongst Trading Men to Lessen the reputation of the first.

And in order to give my very kind friend all the satisfaction in my power I beg leave to offer in case your partner does not in the mean time arrive to lend you a helping hand, my utmost assistance to obtain good customers & to make a profitable sale of the *Pococks* Cargo & even after his arrival if he and you shall think that I can be of any service.[4] I am not very well & therefore could not write this Letter through with my own hand which I beg you will excuse. I remain—

SOURCE: Letterbook copy, Letter Book of Henry Laurens, Oct. 30, 1762–Sept. 10, 1766, Penn. Hist. Soc.

TO JOSEPH BROWN

[Charles Town] 29th June 1764

Dear Sir,

I herewith inclose you a Letter rece'd per Capt. White.[5] I observe that you had not sold my three Negroes when you last wrote, that your Customers had greatly altered their notions since last Winter. Let me take occasion from hence to remark how you would have been embarrassed & how I should have been put to the blush, if I had recommended and you had undertaken the Sale of a Cargo.

---

[4] The *Pocock* did not arrive as it had been cut off on the coast of Africa.
[5] The ship *Carolina Packett,* William White, was entered inwards from London on June 28. Naval Office Lists, 1764–1767, p. 78.

For if the Sale of three proves so difficult how must a Man be puzzled to sell & remit for 300. But by the by this is a Little strange too, because I see people come from all quarters & give £320 to £325 per head for Negroes not superior to those you have & I did a few days ago put a small parcel of Ten into the hands of a Young House here.[6] They were Ebo,[7] two of them guy headed,[8] & one a Boy & they produced me £515 round pay'ble in Cash for more than half & the remainder pay'ble in 60 days. If they remain unsold when this reaches you be so good as to deliver them to Mr. Price on my Account unless you can obtain about £320 per & I will thankfully repay all the expence you have been at on this Account.

I cannot discover in my Waste Book, Landing or Shipping Book the Least trace of 67 Barrels of Pitch Rece'd from you or by your order in April 1763 nor does your Letters in that Month mention any such Goods. Mr. Price then Lived with me & he was generally very exact in noting the receipt of all goods that came to me. I am therefore inclined to believe there is some mistake in this Article & it will depend upon some further proof which you will be so good as to give me in your next & immediately after this is Cleared up I will settle your whole Account.

I find upon the 7th April 1763 Entered to the Credit of Joseph Hutchins 67 Barrels Pitch & as there is a Winyaw parcel, vizt. 33 G G P,[9] Entered at the same time possibly the mistake may lay there but Hutchins says it does not for that parcel of 67 came down Cooper River. May be some of my Letters or some memorandum from Capt. Cogdill[1] may clear this up.

I shall enquire of Capt. White if any goods for you are on board his Ship & either Mr. Lind or I will take care of them. I remain, Dear Sir—

P. S. I have been examining my Wharfage Accounts. I can make no discovery of the 67 Barrels of Pitch, but in April 1763 here is a

---

[6] That of William Price.

[7] The Ebos who came from Calabar (sometimes called Calabars) in the Bight of Biafra were undesirable slaves in the Carolina market. Philip D. Curtin, *The Atlantic Slave Trade, A Census* (Madison, Wisc., 1969), pp. 155–158, 161; *HL Papers*, I & II, passim.

[8] A guy-headed person was one of grotesque appearance. *OED.*

[9] George Gabriel Powell, at this time a planter on the Pee Dee, played an important role in the Regulation and in the pre-Revolutionary years in S. C. Rogers, *History of Georgetown County*, passim.

[1] Capt. John Cogdell.

parcel of 35 barrels sent per Mr. Richard Brockington[2] in Cogdill's Schooner recommended by you but it was so exceeding ordinary that I was obliged to put it into the hands of Mr. Lind & after he had it near a month & no body would buy it, & the pitch wasting every day, I bought it of him as per his Account Sales 28th May 1763.

Net proceed £55.7.9. I might as well have taken it at first and saved all the charges paid to him but I acted as I thought it was most canded & ingenuous.

I shall be in want of Pitch for my new Ship expected from Bristol in about three weeks. Please to recommend such good parcels as may fall in your way.

SOURCE: Letterbook copy, Letter Book of Henry Laurens, Oct. 30, 1762–Sept. 10, 1766, Penn. Hist. Soc.; addressed "George Town." The postscript was written on a separate page headed "P.S. to his Letter of 29th June per Mr. Davidson."

TO SAMUEL WRAGG[3]

[Charles Town] 29th June 1764

Sir,

I have rece'd your favour of the 26th & thank you for the purchase of Pitch on my Account therein noted & you may depend upon punctuality on my part in discharge of your draughts.

As I have advice that my Ship[4] was gone round to Bristol from Poole tis probable she may not arrive here before the 20th July & this has induced me to Ship off the provision lately made for her & I must begin to lay by again; & thereby save some expence of Storage and waste; tho I am not yet resolved upon a Voyage for her, having some thoughts of sending her to Portugal with a load of Rice, but in order as far as I can to have both commodities Rice & Naval

---

[2] Richard Brockinton was a brother of John Brockinton.
[3] Samuel Wragg (1721–1787), the son of the great merchant Joseph Wragg (d. 1751), married Judith Rothmahler, the sister of Job Rothmahler, who was his partner in Georgetown. Rogers, *History of Georgetown County*, pp. 49n, 50, 88, 95n, 105, 115, 123; *SCHM*, XIX (1918), 121.
[4] The ship *Flora*.

stores at my option I must request your further endeavours to procure me about one Thousand Barrels of good Pitch or 1,200 Barrels or any part thereof to arrive here on or before the first September, as much sooner as possible, for which I am willing to pay Three pounds Sixteen shillings per Barrel, the customary charges of Freight, Wharfage, hoops to be taken off. This I believe is a greater price than any other person & I offer it to secure my quantity in time & to be sure of good hard Pitch, full weight, & in good barrels. If you can purchase such at a Lower rate I shall beg Leave to insist upon your taking all the benefit of such purchase to your self & I shall be glad to have it in my power by other means to thank you for your favours. Please to make your draughts on me as favourable as you can but draw at three days sight rather than loose any very good parcel of Pitch. I am, Sir, &ca.—

SOURCE: Letterbook copy, Letter Book of Henry Laurens, Oct. 30, 1762–Sept. 10, 1766, Penn. Hist. Soc.; addressed "George Town."

TO WILLIAM PRICE

[Charles Town] 29th June 1764

Dear Sir,

I herewith cover three Letters to you which came Yesterday per Capt. White, there are two for your partner Mr. Hest which shall be delivered to you when you come to Town. I shall be obliged to you to secure for me all the right good Pitch that can be got but let it be in your own name at something about 70/ to 75/ delivered here, the customary charges to be deducted. The *Flora* was got round to Bristol & I shall look for her arrival here about the 20th July. I am not determined on a Voyage for her but would willingly have the command of both Rice and Naval Stores. The former I have pretty secure that is to say the offer of it. Do spur Mr. Brown to make an end of the Sale of my Negroes or endeavour to do it for me. I hope you have had a good Sale and will soon return to Charles Town. I remain—

SOURCE: Letterbook copy, Letter Book of Henry Laurens, Oct. 30, 1762–Sept. 10, 1766, Penn. Hist. Soc.; addressed "George Town."

TO JOSEPH BROWN

[Charles Town] 30 June 1764

Sir,

Please to deliver to Mr. Alexander Davidson or his order two of those three Negro Men which are in your hands belonging to me & in case they are sold before he gits to George Town which we shall fix to the 2d July then please to advise me that I may cancel Mr. Davidsons Note or procure two other Negro Men for him. I am, Sir, &ca.—

SOURCE: Letterbook copy, Letter Book of Henry Laurens, Oct. 30, 1762–Sept. 10, 1766, Penn. Hist. Soc.; addressed "George Town."

TO WILLIAM PRICE

[Charles Town] 30th June 1764

Sir,

If Mr. McDowell[5] should agree with you for any two of the Negro Men that you have to sell or for one & one of those in Mr. Brown's hands please to deliver him such two or one as he likes & charge the same to my Account provided the price is not above £320 per head which you may accept of or benefit by the bargain made with him, Vizt. One hundred & Ten Barrels of good hard Pitch, Weighty & in good Barrels, per Negro to be delivered one half before Christmas & the other half before the 10th March next. Both to be free from Freight, Wharfage, & Cooperage, these to be paid by the Maker of the Pitch. This is a sort of guess contract which you may partake of or charge me your Current selling price. I am, Sir, &ca.—

SOURCE: Letterbook copy, Letter Book of Henry Laurens, Oct. 30, 1762–Sept. 10, 1766, Penn. Hist. Soc.; addressed "George Town."

---

[5] This may be John McDowell who lived at Black Mingo to whom HL wrote on April 8, 1765.

TO JOHN WIGFALL

[Charles Town] 5th July 1764

Sir,

Mr. Perdriau waits on you with Accounts of three parcels of your plank deliver'd here which have fallen short of measure & on which Account I have had very great complaints & more uneasiness (as I have never been us'd to hear such in my dealings) than I would submit to for the value of the Lumber ten times Fold. Whenever therefore you will please to appoint a time & proper person to measure over what remains upon hand I shall either attend or order some person to attend to see it done & take Account of it & after that I shall settle the whole as soon as possible, hoping at the same time that you will without any hesitation make a proportionable abatement of the measure of such parcels as are Ship'd under the original marks as these several parcels shall fall short, but these mistakes have so confused my Accounts that it will give me more trouble to settle now than it would have done before they were discover'd.

Therefore if I should not be able to attend a final settlement at this time I am sure you will not think me blameable & the less so as your not coming at your own appointed time, Vizt. the 11th June, prevented my going into the Country untill yesterday when I went having no item of your intention to call on me tho I enquired of your Negroes two days ago, & I am this hour returned from the Country. [I] must attend the House of Assembly & have several businesses to transact in the intervals. Nevertheless nothing on my part shall be wanting to close our Accounts which I most heartily long for after the measure of your plank, &ca. is adjusted. I am, &ca.—

SOURCE: Letterbook copy, Letter Book of Henry Laurens, Oct. 30, 1762–Sept. 10, 1766, Penn. Hist. Soc.; addressed "Esquire. Charles Town."

TO JAMES DENNISTOUNE, JOHN PAGAN & CO.

[Charles Town] 6th July 1764

Gentlemen,

After trying every rational method to get off your Ale which arrived in the Ship *Loudon* in April last Year at a better price, I have thought it for your Interest to close the Sale as you will see by Peter Horn[6] an industrious Young Man who promises to make me payments as quick as he can. If he makes them at all which I have not the Least doubt of the loss shall be wholly mine by the advance of my money which if I was to reckon upon would reduce my Commission almost to a Cypher. If any accident happens to him I can only say that I have trusted the same person with goods of my own & in some measure to induce him to take the trouble of the Ale & that you shall always be upon an equal footing with myself, but this I trust is quite an useless anticipation. Your Ale was as I informed you complained of by many of the purchasers particularly by James Marshall[7] who stands in the Account for 7 Casks. He really suffered both in the quality and number of bottles as he took his per Invoice. He avered to me that he would rather give 80/ per dozen for such as Capt. Sterland[8] & Capt. Porter[9] brought than touch the *Loudon*'s at any price. Nobody would buy of it a second time. The Town I may say was overflowed with Malt Liquor, a great deal of Bristol Beer selling at 40/ to 45/ per dozen All conspired to quash the Sale of yours. Please now to receive Account Sale of said Ale, Net proceeds to your Credit £1,500.14/ & also your Account Current, Balance carried forward to a New Account £71.7.9 where if you please as it is such a trifle it shall rest untill I collect the Money due by Peter

---

[6] Peter Horn was a tavern keeper. Later HL had to go to court to collect. Judgment Rolls, 1766, No. 133A, S. C. Archives.

[7] James Marshall ran an "Old and Noted Tavern" on the Bay. *Gazette,* Dec. 3, 1764. He was buried on Sept. 16, 1764. *Register of St. Philip's Parish, 1754–1810,* p. 307. His wife, the sole administratrix of his estate, advertised for sale ten valuable slaves (including "waiting men" and "good Cooks"), a fine billiard table, and a large stock of liquors. *Gazette,* Oct. 15, 1764. Robert Dillon, another tavern keeper, helped to assess the value of his estate, which included, among other items, 5 beds, bedsteads, and pavilions complete, 9 night caps, 1 warming pan, 55 billiard sticks, 1 billiard table with cover (value £80). The stock of liquor included porter, cider, claret, Madeira, Lisbon, gin, brandy, rum, and wine. The slaves were valued at £500 for Ben, £400 for Edinburgh, £300 for Dundee, £350 for Betty, £300 each for Peggy and Maria. The total value was £6,048.3.10½. Inventories, 1763–1767, pp. 462–464, S. C. Archives.

[8] Capt. Robert Sterling. *HL Papers,* III, 26, 440. Capt. Robert Sterling was again in Charleston the following winter with a cargo consigned to Hogg & Clayton. Alexander Strachan & Co. of Dundee shipped 100 dozen bottles of Bells Ale, 79.5 dozen bottles of Hunters Beer, and 22.3 dozen bottles of Mundells Beer on the *Minerva,* James Rea, to Hogg & Clayton late in 1765. Invoices, Nos. 29, 39, Invoice Book Inward, Robert Hogg Account Books, 1762–1775, #343, SHC.

[9] Capt. Hugh Porter.

Horne which I hope will be soon after the time of agreement. If these Accounts are right be pleased to enter in conformity thereto & if any error appears it shall be rectified upon the first Notice.

Rice is got up here to 40/ per Ct. & Freight tho' not many Ships in port may be had to London & Bristol for 35/ to 40/ per Ton. I think that I may now venture to say that our growing Crops will not, cannot, be very large, & may if we have not plentiful Rains in a few days be very small. The Indigo & Indian Corn has suffered greatly already & altho Rice will endure much more hardship yet the produce of it must be stinted by this Iron burning Weather that we have had for some Weeks past. The generality of Planters are too discreet to complain openly of any of these disasters untill the Ships are fairly harbour'd in the Winter & then we are told the Crop is short and that the prices must be in proportion. Tis my duty to hold you advised and I shall continue to transmit you further Accounts to the best of my knowledge as I am with great regard, Gentlemen, Your obliged humble Servant—

SOURCE: Letterbook copy, HL Papers, S. C. Hist. Soc.; addressed "Owners of the Ship *Loudon,* Glasgow"; "per Capt. Bostock. Copy per White."

TO DENNISTOUNE, MUNRO & CO.

[Charles Town] 6th July 1764

Gentlemen,

My Last trouble was under the 14th April per Capt. Gibbs[1] & Capt. Higgins with the needful documents & duplicate thereof, of Rice Ship'd on your Account per the Snow *Dennistoune* & also Sale of Coals imported by her, since which by advice from Lisbon I have reason to believe that said Rice will pay you rather a better Freight than the remainder of her Cargo was let out for.

Please to receive inclosed Account of Sale of the Strong Beer & Claret left in my hands by Capt. Porter Net proceed to your Credit £532.4.3, barring any Loss to me by outstanding debts, or those 2

---

[1] The brigantine *Ceres,* John Gibbs, was cleared outwards for Cowes on April 9. Naval Office Lists, 1764–1767, p. 80.

Casks of Claret not yet delivered to Robert Dillon[2] as noted on the Sale. Being now in want of money I have taking the Liberty to reimburse myself in part for the Invoice per your Snow *Dennistoune* by passing two Setts of Bills on you the 4th Instant as below, £300 Sterling to the Credit of your Account Current £2,135. That Bill to Robert Deans I had engaged sometime ago when Bills were selling upon London at 7 for 1 & thought I did very well in obtaining 60 days sight & payable in Glasgow, nor indeed could I get more than that Exchange now for Bills payable in Scotland. Therefore I thought it must be most for your advantage to make them payable in London for the difference of 2½ per Cent which it cannot cost you to raise a sufficient Fund there. I have bought this week for a Friend £500 Sterling of Mr. Manigault in his own draughts upon London at 721 per Cent & am selling of my own occasionally at the same rate which considering the difference of Sight, time for acceptance, postage, &ca. is certainly worth more than ½ per Cent.

The balance of your Account Current is now about £1,058.1.11 supposing no alteration by the outstanding debts or the Claret for which sum I shall draw on you very soon if I have occasion of money. Otherwise you shall not be troubled with a call for some weeks longer but people grow more & more backward in their payments here, which I experience every day & this hinders me from giving all the indulgence that I could wish to give to my friends. Rice is got up to 47/6 per Ct. & will in a few days more be at 50/. I am morally sure of it & probably higher before the Month of September. The Crops on the ground have already undergone some pernicious seasons & tho' not so much injured as to make the planters cry out yet I may venture to aver they will not be so plentiful as last year, this I mean chiefly of Rice & Indian Corn. As to Indigo our produce will be very short of our expectations at planting for in almost every part of the province the Weed has suffered Much by dry weather. I am, &ca.—

---

[2] The most famous tavern in Charleston had been kept on the northeast corner of Broad and Church streets. Charles Shepheard was at this location in the 1730's and 1740's; John Gordon in the 1750's. Robert Dillon who was a witness to John Gordon's will took over the tavern after Gordon's death. "Will of John Gordon," dated Jan. 13, 1762, proved Jan. 22, 1762, *Abstracts of Wills, 1760–1784,* p. 20. The annual gatherings of the Masons, as well as many other important events, were held at this tavern. Albert G. Mackey, *The History of Freemasonry in South Carolina, From its Origin in the Year 1736 to the Present Time* (Columbia, S. C., 1861), pp. 15, 16, 19, 21, 26, 32, 35, 40, 45.

SOURCE: Letterbook copy, HL Papers, S. C. Hist. Soc.; addressed "Owners of the Snow *Dennistoune*, Glasgow"; "per Capt. Bostock. Copy per Capt. White." Endorsed: "Note that both on the original & duplicate the Bills were described tho omitted in this Book."

TO JOHN PAGAN, ALEXANDER BROWN & CO.

[Charles Town] 6th July 1764

Gentlemen,

On the other side is a duplicate of what I wrote to you the 3d April since which I have had a Young Man for a great many days employed to collect as much money as possible for Coals per the *Pearl* but you will see by the inclosed Account of sale what a poor progress is made & may form some judgement of the trouble attending such a transaction in a place where not many people are punctual in their payments even for their meat & fires. Some have forgotten, others do not recollect that they had any Coals, & not a few have sworn down the price from £7 to £6 per Ton & I expect still that some of them will never pay but that shall not be for want of dunning. Meantime the Net proceed of the said Sale as it stands £832.7.6 is passed to the Credit of your Account Current. The Mate of the *Pearl* (Mr. Service) Rece'd money on board for 9 Tons as noted at foot of the Sale the Amount of which I believe he gave to Capt. Francis for the Ship's use. It does not appear that he ever brought it to me & as I remember he did not, but having left the Account open in order to collect as much more as possible & besides being a good deal taking off from business first by a Stroke of Providence in the death of my eldest daughter and afterward by more than a Month's indisposition of Body I cannot pretend to be precise in this circumstance. My Cash was not settled & my Clerk has a poor memory & in this case seems to have been rather more inattentive than ordinary; therefore I must refer the matter wholly to Mr. Service or to Capt. Francis. They know the fact & their declaration will set this affair to right. I have (vizt. on the 4th Inst.) passed a Bill on you at 60 days sight to the order of Brewton & Smith payable in London for £300 Sterling which at 717.10/ per Cent carries £2,152.10/ to the Credit of your Account Current which Account shall be transmitted when I have occasion to draw on you for the balance about £1,106.5.9. The premium that I have obtained on my Bill together with the days between sight & payment I hope will amply compensate any inconvenience that might or may arise by the payment in London. If I had confined the payment to Glasgow I have not hitherto had any offer above 700 per Cent for my draught & indeed several Bills are daily picked up at that Exchange payable in London while I have obtained so much more for a Bill that is to be sent so far for acceptance.

Rice is advanced here to 47/6 per Ct. & will soon be higher as the quantity remaining is not very great & there will be a continual demand even to the very eve of the New Crop. That new Crop I may now venture to pronounce will be but a middling one even if all our future seasons thro which it must pass to the end of October, should prove propitious. It was chicked in the beginning & must suffer in some measure from the present spell of dry weather.

The Crop of Indigo I am sure will be short because a great part of what was planted hath suffered & more than a Little is destroyed beyond redemption. Our Town continues to receive a super abundance of European Merchandizes which are almost every day both by private & public Sale, sold for about the prime cost & offten below that. Rum & Wine are very plenty & Cheap. Great Losses sustained by the Sale of Both articles. Negroes only support a saving price. These have sold so far in the Season most extravagantly. The general average is about 2,000 since the Month of February is as nearly as I can collect about £36 Sterling per head. Except this one article of commerce it would seem as if mankind by the high prices given for our exports & the Low rates of almost every specie imported amongst us, were conspiring the prosperity of Carolina. This is pretty nearly a just state of our Markets & commerce & I hope the information will not be altogether useless to you. I remain, &ca.—

SOURCE: Letterbook copy, HL Papers, S. C. Hist. Soc.; addressed "Owners of the Ship *Pearl*, Glasgow"; "per Capt. Bostock. Copy per White."

TO STEVENSON & LAIRD

[Charles Town] 7th July 1764

Gentlemen,

Since I wrote to you on the 29th February per Capt. Mitchell

& Floyd I have not been able to sell a single dozen of your Wine called Burgundy. The quality of it does by no means answer your discription nor the Accounts that I had given of it from yours and the Gentlemen who came to taste it, expressed much dissatisfaction & said I was surely bantering to call that Wine Burgundy. It is not fine nor bright, tis ropy & has a harshness upon the palate that is very disagreeable & being inferior is dispised here where we have for some Years past drank Maderia, Vidonia, Fajal, Lisbon, Oporto & other Wines at Less than prime Cost & charges. Had it been fine burgundy or nearly deserving that Character here are a few people who would nevertheless have catched it up at almost any price. I shall advertise it once more under the name you give it (tho it is pretty well known) & if in a few weeks that does not produce me a Sale upon terms near to the Cost I shall think it for your Interest to obtain the best price I can for it & make & end of the Sale of which you shall be duly advised. Meantime I continue to be with great regard, Gentlemen—

SOURCE: Letterbook copy, HL Papers, S. C. Hist. Soc.; addressed "Port Glasgow"; "per Capt. Bostock. Copy per Capt. White."

TO RICHARD OSWALD

[Charles Town] 7th July 1764

Sir,

On the 29th Ulto. your much esteem'd favours of the 24th March & 14th April were deliver'd to me by Messrs. Rossell & Gervais,[3] two Gentlemen who arrived here in Capt. Whites Ship

---

[3] James Theodore Rossel and John Lewis Gervais were of French Huguenot descent. Their families had been living in Hameln near Hanover since the 1690's. Theodore Rossel, a stocking manufacturer from Nîmes in Languedoc, died in Hameln in 1747 at the age of seventy-five. His son Jean, who had married for the second time in 1737 Adrienne Villeneuve, died in Hameln in 1754. James Theodore Rossel was born about 1740. John Lewis Gervais (1741–1795) was most probably a grandson of either François or Jean Gervaix, brothers who had come from Ganges in Langedoc. François Gervaix, a chamois dresser, married for a second time in Hameln in 1693 Louise Trapier. He died in Hameln in 1715 at the age of forty-eight. She was the daughter of Isaac Trapier, chamois dresser from Grenoble in the Dauphiné, who died at Hameln in 1711. Jean Gervaix, a dresser of white leather, died at Hameln in 1740 at the age of sixty. Wilhelm Beuleke, *Die Hugenotten in Niedersachsen* (Hildesheim, Germany, 1960), pp. 46–49. HL must have been eager to help Rossel

from London. They found me a good deal indispos'd which together with an indispensible attendance upon some public affairs has hinder'd me from sitting down earlier to write to you, & will hinder me at present from being so full in my reply as otherwise I should have been. But nothing could prove an impediment to a hearty & friendly reception on my part to those Gentlemen so warmly recommended by Mr. Oswald, nor has anything else but the subject matters of your Letters employ'd my thoughts at every proper interval of time since they came to hand.

I thank you, Sir, for the confidence you have repos'd in me. You may be assur'd that I shall never abuse it, & altho an application to your extensive schemes may run me a little devious from that plan of Life which I had Laid down & was endeavouring to establish for my future conduct, yet I shall do every thing in my power to serve your Interest & think my time well spent in contributing to forward your Laudable designs.

I have but about two hours to write in by the present opportunity[4] therefore I shall not loose any of the minutes in a longer preface but proceed to touch briefly on the several matters recommended in your letter & by the next opportunity shall add what may appear to be needful.

Your views of establishing a Farm, plantation & Vineyard in our back settlements, are commendable, Generous, & the principles upon which they are extended, truly noble; nevertheless, I must not flatter but plainly tell you that the carrying of them into effect, tho not impracticable, will be attended with more difficulty & more ex-

---

and Gervais whose families had a history so similar to that of the Laurens family. These two young men, who had already been on many military campaigns in Europe, arrived in Charleston on June 28, having been sent out by Richard Oswald to establish a plantation for him in the backcountry of S. C. Rossel died in Georgia at HL's Broughton Island plantation on May 12, 1767, of an "Appoplectic fit." *Gazette*, June 1, 1767. John Lewis Gervais was to play a prominent role in the career of HL. Gervais became first a planter in Ninety Six District, then a merchant in Charleston, and finally a patriot during the Revolution. While HL sat in the Continental Congress, Gervais looked after his property interests in S. C. Richard Maxwell Brown, *The South Carolina Regulators* (Cambridge, Mass., 1963), pp. 16, 75, 134, 184, 208; Emily Bellinger Reynolds and Joan Reynolds Faunt, *Biographical Directory of the Senate of the State of South Carolina, 1776–1964* (Columbia, S. C., 1964), p. 221; "Letters from John Lewis Gervais to Henry Laurens, 1777–1778," ed. Raymond Starr, *SCHM*, LXVI (1965), 15–37.

[4] Capt. Peter Bostock had cleared his ship *Minories* for London on June 29. Naval Office Lists, 1764–1767, p. 81.

pence of Money than you seem to apprehend; & therefore I shall, after giving you the fullest & clearest intelligence & advice that I am capable of attaining to by my own & the knowledge of more experienced & more judicious Men who I have the honour of freely consulting upon this occasion, partly in this & partly in my next Letter, leave you to give due consideration to what I shall lay before you & wait your final orders & determination thereon, taking in the meantime every step in my power to secure you a good entrance in case you should resolve to carry your original projections with some amendments & additions into execution.

The first difficulty that you will have to encounter is that of obtaining a Sufficient quantity of good land in one body; sufficient I mean for doing honour to yourself. Almost all the lands within that limited space agreed upon to be our western boundaries in the last treaty with the Cherrokee Indians in 1761 is Granted to divers people who have become settlers in our province since the peace establis'd with those Savages.[5] The last considerable tract was to those French protestants lately arrived amongst us & alluded to in your letter.[6] To go beyond those boundaries would be running counter to a Royal instruction lately given to our Governor & proclaim'd here the 20th June 1763,[7] strictly inhibiting all encroach-

---

[5] The treaty of peace with the Cherokees signed in December 1761 fixed the boundary at an undefined point forty miles east of Keowee. The *Gazette,* April 2, 1763, reported that over 1,000 families from the northward had settled in the debatable area between the forty-mile boundary and the Long Canes. The actual line between the whites and the Indians was not marked until 1766, a line which was ratified by the Treaty of Hard Labour on Oct. 14, 1768. Louis De Vorsey, Jr., *The Indian Boundary in the Southern Colonies, 1763-1775* (Chapel Hill, N. C., 1966), pp. 123-235.

[6] These were the French Protestants whom James Grant had hoped to lure to East Florida. They had arrived in Charleston on April 14. After staying for a while at Fort Lyttelton near Beaufort, they made their way into the back-country to the town of New Bordeaux in the township of Hillsborough which Patrick Calhoun at the command of Lt. Gov. William Bull had laid off for them just below the junction of Long Canes Creek and Little River. The first group was escorted to their new homes in July by Patrick Calhoun. "Journal of Pierre Moragne" in W. C. Moragne, *An Address Delivered at New Bordeaux* (Charleston, S. C., 1857), pp. 44–46; A. S. Salley, "The Settlement of New Bordeaux," *The Transactions of the Huguenot Society of South Carolina,* XLII (1937), 38–54; Robert L. Meriwether, *The Expansion of South Carolina, 1729–1765* (Kingsport, Tenn., 1940), pp. 252–254. The London mercantile community must have been particularly interested in these French immigrants as each step of the journey was noted in the London *Daily Advertiser,* June 19, 21, Sept. 11, Nov. 15, 1764.

[7] On June 17, 1763, Boone had received instructions, dated Dec. 9, 1761, to restrain provincials from settling on or purchasing lands claimed by the Indians

ments upon lands ceded to Indians by our several Treaties, as well as forbidding the purchase of such lands even from the Indian-proprieters themselves, & commanding the immediate removal of all persons set down or settled thereon. This renders any attempt to make a settlement near to Fort Prince George or within many Miles Eastward of it wholly fruitless. The Lands thereabouts I do agree with Colonel Grant are exceeding fine & I call that place & its environs the Paradise of America, & Indeed I am very doubtfull whether any Lands Westward of it will produce Grapes with so much certainty as those, in quantities sufficient to make the production of Wine an object worthy of notice. This difficulty may nevertheless be got over, & the Kings orders as well as the remoteness of the Land from Market (at least 280 Miles) may enable you to surmount it with so much the greater facility as the attention of other people will be diverted by both these considerations. Propositions for settling & cultivating those Lands would undoubtedly meet with countenance & encouragement from the Ministry & any assurances that might be depended upon for making such settlement, obtain a Royal Grant of so much as could fairly & clearly be purchased of the present thin scatter'd possessors & nominal-proprietors thereof. And this purchase I apprehend may be effected upon very easy terms when once the sanction of His Majesty can be procured. This will probably employ your contemplation for some time & as I can pretend to say nothing of the necessary means to enlighten you, shall return again to the more interior parts of our province.

There is a large almost wholly-unoccupied Tract of about One Hundred Thousand Acres of fine Land at the place commonly called *Ninetysix* formerly run out & I believe granted to one Hamilton,[8] now the property or within the claim of Mr. Joseph

---

without lawful authority. Boone issued a proclamation to this effect on June 20, 1763. *Gazette*, June 25, 1763.

[8] In 1737 John Hamilton of London petitioned the crown for 200,000 acres of land in S. C. The Board of Trade opposed the grant. In 1747 Hamilton petitioned again, this time with the support of London Jews who were looking for a place to settle their poor, and in 1749 succeeded. He proceeded to America where in November 1751 the Surveyor General George Hunter surveyed 200,000 acres of "Hamilton's Great Survey" in four plats of 50,000 acres each. The tract nearest to Ninety Six was bought in 1755 by William Simpson and Dr. John Murray. Two tracts lying on the Saluda River were sold at the same time to Joseph Salvador of London. Robert L. Meriwether, *The Expansion of South Carolina, 1729–1765* (Kingsport, Tenn., 1940), pp. 125–127.

Salvador & Co.,[9] which at present is a *nuisance,* as it lies vacant & hinders the establishment of a great many useful settlers. I fancy Doctor John Murray[1] has the charge or care of that Tract & I had intended to speak to him about it but he has been & is still out of Town. You may learn something of this parcel whether for Sale or what is intended to be done with it (& probably with more certainty than I can do) from the Gentlemen in London.

The next parcel or body of good Lands that I can yet discover has been pointed out to me by Lieut. Governor Bull & Lies within 25 or 30 Miles of that plat mark'd out for the French Refugie's, but more Frontier & nearer the Banks of *Savanna River,* much expos'd to incursions by the Indians, tho it is not very distant from Augusta & Fort Moore. This Tract I have heard much extold by another Gentleman who spent the last Evening with me & knows it well & therefore I do intend to have my eye upon it as I shall presently inform you. But now give me leave to say a word or two upon the subject of the expected productions from any of these Lands & to start some new difficulties thereon as well as upon the means of establishing a *reputable* and an *advantageous* settlement upon them.

---

[9] Joseph Salvador (1716–1786) was an eminent merchant who reputedly furnished the British government with a million pounds on two hours notice in the crisis of 1745. On Nov. 28, 1755, he bought from John Hamilton of St. George, Hanover Square, London, 100,000 acres, bounding northeast on the Saluda River, for £2,000 sterling. Deeds, FFF, pp. 133–137, S. C. Archives. Salvador lost large sums by the Lisbon earthquake of Nov. 1, 1755. Francis Salvador, his nephew and son-in-law, who came to S. C. on the eve of the Revolution to look after the family property, was the first Jew to be killed in the American Revolution. Joseph himself came out in 1784 and died in S. C. two years later. *SCHM,* III (1902), 59–64; Barnett A. Elzas, *The Jews of South Carolina* (Philadelphia, Penn., 1905), pp. 108–118.
[1] Dr. John Murray and William Simpson bought 50,000 acres of land from Hamilton on Nov. 28, 1755, bounding northeast on the Saluda River and northwest on Salvador's lands. On July 7, 1758, Murray bought Simpson's share. Deeds, TTTT, pp. 490-501, S. C. Archives. On Feb. 17, 1764, Dr. John Murray had married Lady Anne Mackenzie, daughter of the Earl of Cromartie, who had been the wife of Edmond Atkin, the superintendent of Indian affairs for the Southern Department, who had died on Oct. 8, 1761. *Gazette,* Oct. 16, 1761, Feb. 18, 1764. Lady Anne Murray died on Jan. 17, 1768. *SCHM,* XX (1919), 206. Dr. John Murray and Andrew Williamson were partners in 1761 in the firm of Andrew Williamson & Co. Judgment Rolls, 1765, No. 313A, S. C. Archives. They were contractors for supplying the provisions to the troops. Gavin Cochrane to Fenwick Bull, Oct. 1, 1764, enclosure in Cochrane to General Gage, Jan. 4, 1765, Gage Papers, WLCL. Dr. John Murray was made an assistant judge and died on Jan. 12, 1774. *Gazette,* Jan. 17, 1774.

First as to Vines: these are the spontaneous growth, in no small variety & in the greatest Luxuriancy of all the above mention'd Soil; yet the higher up, the better the Land, & the more steady the Climate; but whether Wine of a good quality could be produced from those Grapes & after produced whether it would quit the cost of making & transporting to Market by such tedious Land carriage are questions which I cannot answer with any precision.

The first may be answer'd in the affirmative allowing time enough for experiments & perseverance. I do believe that good Wine may be produced from good Grapes, & I am quite sure that good Grapes may be produced & kept up *even in the Lower parts of Carolina*. I have the most undeniable evidence of this fact in my own Garden, where grows a Vine planted by the late John Rattray, Esquire in a Bed of Asparagus cultivated & improved by me with some care which now has on it by a moderate calculation 100 bunches of Grapes many of the bunches weighing 8 to 10 lbs. each & the whole about 400 lb. Weight or say 300 lbs. at the very least. The Grapes are white, clear, & transparent very delicious to the palate & each grape of a well grown cluster is of the size of those Musket Balls that carry 24 to a pound. This Vine of mine has given Spirits to our New French incomers; 'tis said by many Gentlemen to be as fine as any they have seen in Lisbon or Spain & the French cry out, *C'est beau et bon,* and neither the Stock nor its fruit hath hitherto suffer'd those disasters which Mr. Austin hinted to you, tho we can scarcely ever have a more unfriendly Year than the present. From this Vine I have propagated some others which already produce Grapes very fine but not equal to the Stock from whence they sprung; however I do not therefore announce a degeneracy—No! by no means—but I clearly discover that a different foundation in planting occasions the present difference in the produce & will cause the dissolution of these Young ones while the main Stock shall continue in vigour; at least I think so; which may be guarded against in future attempts. I conclude from hence, that if one Vine is brought to such a degree of perfection any number may by the same means & methods used with that one, be brought to the same or nearly the same standard, but whether they will ever repay the Labour & expence is an essential question in & near Charles Town, but may admit of no question at all in better Lands & better Air. Thus much at present upon the subject of the Vines.[2]

My next remarks must be on the obstacles of settling a considerable Plantation in those remote parts of the Country & my doubts whether an advantageous return can be made for Wine (admiting that *a tolerable good sort* may be produced) subject to the expence of so vast a carriage by Land before it can be brought to Market; but these I shall reserve for my next Letter when I shall resume the subject. It is now near Saturdays Midnight & my Letter must be deliver'd at 4 oClock tomorrow morning.

Meantime I shall go on to say, that I am under no doubt that *good Silk, fine Indigo,* large herds of *Cattle,* a valuable breed of *Horses,* abundance of *Hemp* & many less valuable articles (but *no Cotton* worth notice) may be expected in due time from an establish'd Plantation in those parts, for which end a certain Sum of Money will be requisite, not less in my opinion for the first outset than One Thousand pounds Sterling as a bank to be occasionally applied for, over & above the cost of many essential implements for Agriculture which must be sent from London. That Sum will produce no returns in the first Year, And none in the second, but some samples of production & hopes of future success, which samples in the third Year may grow to a Larger bulk of the several species for Sale at Market, & your hopes of success be confirm'd by an advantagious prospect or wholly quash'd, & the capital Stock almost absorb'd.

A less Sum than £1,000, join'd to the needful tools & plantation implements I think will not do, & you may increase it as you see fitt or shall receive encouragement to do so.

I have recommended to Mr. Rossel & Gervais to make a journey to *Ninetysix, Long Canes,* & if they conveniently can to

---

[2] A brief summary of the attempts to make wine in S. C. during the late colonial period are set forth in Lewis C. Gray, *History of Agriculture in the Southern United States to 1860* (2 vols.: reprint, Gloucester, Mass., 1958), I, 189–190. John Bartram described HL's vine as it stood in 1765. See Diary of John Bartram, July 12, 1765. David Ramsay, the historian and son-in-law of HL, mentioned HL's successful attempts to grow "vines which bore abundantly of the choice white eating grape called Chasselates blancs." David Ramsay, *History of South Carolina From its First Settlement in 1670 to the Year 1808* (2 vols.: Charleston, S. C., 1858), II, 124–125, 128. HL must have experimented with making wine from rice since he wrote Richard Grubb, Dec. 28, 1772, that rough rice "Malts extremely well & produces a Spirits by distillation Superior to the English Brandy. . . ." HL Papers, S. C. Hist. Soc.

Keowee[3] & particularly to ride over & attentively view that Vacant Tract above mention'd & they are to begin it in a few days. The Lieut. Governor has promis'd to give them Letters to the principal people in those parts & particularly to order a detatchment of Rangers[4] to escort them & I shall write to two or three substantial Men there, upon whose aid I can depend.[5] If they transmit me good Accounts of the Soil I shall not wait for your orders but proceed to take up as many acres as my remains of family right will extend to,[6] which with what the Governor will grant to those Gentlemen may inclose five or Six Thousand, & which I shall again relinquish in case you do not persevere in your plan, for I abhor the thoughts of engrossing vast bodies of Land to the exclusion of useful settlers & greatly therefore to the prejudice of the Colony.

As these Gentlemen have brought no Money with them your Credit is rather a scanty allowance but they shall not suffer as they descend from you. They are in want of almost every article requisite for such an undertaking & it is absolutely necessary for[7] them to preserve that *first appearance* that they have made amongst us, which however must be done with great prudence & economy; therefore they will reside chiefly in the Country at an easy expence until I have the honour of your further commands.

As to their entring just now into any retail Trade in those parts I cannot admit of it, because it would be mean, would Lessen them in the esteem of people whose respect they must endeavour to attract, & without which they will be exposed to encounter with tenfold hardships & hindrances. They are no Planters I can easily perceive, but I can also discern that they have understanding & industry enough to make very good ones in a short time, under the tuition & assistance of a capable overseer for one or two Years & when once they are set down in a Creditable manner as Planters they may carry on the Sale of many specie of European & West Indian goods to some advantage & with a good grace.

---

[3] Fort Prince George was at Keowee.

[4] Capt. Patrick Calhoun commanded the rangers who had protected the Long Canes settlement. *S. C. Statutes,* IV, 225.

[5] The substantial men to whom HL wrote letters were John Geiger, David Webb, Thomas Bell, Andrew Williamson, and Edward Wilkinson.

[6] HL's family rights would include fifty acres for each member of his family including each slave that he had acquired. As HL had been purchasing slaves, he would have been increasing the total of his family rights.

[7] HL copied the letter from this point.

I have suffered many interuptions in the course of writing this Letter which together with the haste in which it is wrote you will be pleased to receive as an appology for its imperfections, but I must not close it until I have informed you that Mr. Rose[8] cannot undertake to build you a Snow before the ensuing Winter, nor can any other Carpenter because none of them have proper Timber nor can they provide such Timber before the Month of November or December next to do you justice in the Frame. You will therefore have time to transmit your resolutions on this head also, after being told that the price of building here is £6 to £6.6/ Sterling per Ton including all material of Wood & Iron, whereas I have lately built a Ship at Poole which I am told is a very complete & good Vessel for £5.18/ per Ton. I expect her arrival here in a few days, the whole cost including the Masters Wages & expences will not Amount to £2,000 Sterling. He writes only about £1,800 & I am sure that such a Bark as she is described to be in the builders contract & advices from several persons who have seen her would cost more money here without the decorations which I have ordered to be very ample.

Now, Sir, tis past midnight & I shall beg leave to retire after assuring you that I am with great gratitude & the most perfect esteem, Your much obliged & faithful Servant—

SOURCE: Letterbook copy, HL Papers, S. C. Hist. Soc.; addressed "London"; "per Capt. Bostock. Copy per Tayler." Part of this letter was copied by HL.

RECOMMENDATION FOR APPOINTMENT TO COUNCIL

July 10th, 1764

To the King's most Excellent Majesty
May it please your Majesty

There being but nine persons Members of your Majesty's Council of the Province of So. Carolina by Your Majesty's appointment: We humbly beg leave to propose, that Sir John Colleton Baronet[9] & Henry Lawrens, Esquires, who have been recommended

---

[8] John Rose of Hobcaw.
[9] Sir John Colleton, the fourth baronet, was head of the Colleton family. Sir John Colleton, first baronet (1608–1666), had three sons: Peter, Thomas, and James. Sir Peter Colleton, second baronet (died 1694), had been granted

to us as persons every way qualified to serve your Majesty in that Station, may be appointed of Your Majesty's said Council.[1] Which is most humbly submitted.

Hillsborough[2]

Geo. Rice[3]

Bamber Gascoyne[4]

J. Dyson[5]

Fairlawn Barony on the west side of the Western Branch of the Cooper River. Sir John Colleton, third baronet (1679–1754), had lived at Exmouth in England while his son John (1701–1750) lived at Fairlawn in S. C. Sir John, the fourth baronet, inherited Fairlawn from his father and his title from his grandfather. He returned to Carolina with his wife (Anne Fulford of Devon) in Nov. 1759. *Gazette*, Nov. 17, 1759. They had a daughter Louisa Carolina born in 1763. As head of the Proprietary family and son of a royal councilor (his father John had been a member of the council from 1736 to 1750), it was fitting that Sir John Colleton should be appointed to the council. "The Colleton Family in South Carolina," *SCHM*, 1 (1900), 325–341.

[1] Lt. Gov. William Bull had written to the Board of Trade on May 16 to announce that John Guerard had died and to recommend Sir John Colleton, Henry Laurens, and David Deas for appointment to the council. Hillsborough wrote Bull, July 13, 1764: "We have received your letter to us, dated the 16th of May, acquainting us with the death of Mr. Guerard, one of the Council, and We have in consequence thereof recommended Sir John Colleton and Colonel Laurens to supply two of the Vacancies." The Board of Trade endorsed the recommendation of Colleton and Laurens on July 9 and so reported to the Privy Council on July 10. On July 11 the recommendation printed here was referred to a committee of the Privy Council which reported with approval on July 17 to the Privy Council. BPRO, xxx, 6–7, 143–144, 170, 171. On July 20, the King in Council approved these two appointments. *Acts of Privy Council, Colonial*, IV (1754–1766), 798. HL wrote Richard Oswald on Oct. 10, 1764 that he would refuse the appointment and gave the reasons why he would do so. Bull did not read Hillsborough's letter of July 13 to the members of the S. C. council until Dec. 10, 1764. Council Journal, xxx (Dec. 28, 1763–Dec. 24, 1764), 379, S. C. Archives. The information that Laurens had declined was slow in reaching the royal authorities for he and George Austin were both mentioned as councilors in the instructions made out for Lord Charles Montagu on Feb. 19, 1766. BPRO, xxx, 310. Lord Charles Montagu wrote Hillsborough on March 1, 1769, that HL had "declined acting." BPRO, xxxII, 74.

[2] Wills Hill, first Earl of Hillsborough (1718–1793), was appointed president of the board of trade on Sept. 10, 1763, which office he resigned in July 1765. George F. R. Barker, "Wills Hill," *DNB*.

[3] George Rice (1724–1779) was appointed a lord commissioner of the board of trade on March 21, 1761, a position he held until April 1770. William R. Williams, "George Rice," *DNB*.

[4] Bamber Gascoyne (1725–1791) was a lord commissioner of trade from April 1763 to August 1765. Namier and Brooke, *The House of Commons, 1754–1790*, II, 486–491.

[5] Jeremiah Dyson (1722–1776) was a lord commissioner of the board of trade from April 1764 to Jan. 20, 1768. William P. Courtney, "Jeremiah Dyson," *DNB*.

SOURCE: Copy, BPRO, xxx (1764–1765), 143, 170, 171, S. C. Archives. Another copy is in CO 5/404, p. 224, Public Record Office, London.

TO SAMUEL WRAGG

[Charles Town] 13th July 1764

Sir,

I receiv'd two days ago your favour of the 29th Ulto. which was the date of what I wrote last to you.

I now send you per the Schooner *Susanna,* William Smart, Master the consignment of thirteen Gold Coast Negroes just arrived from the West Indies, Vizt.

4 Men	all in good health, tho one of the
1 Boy	
7 Women	Women has Guinea Worm in her
1 Girl	Leg which is of no great injury.[6]

I beg you will sell these as speedily as you can to good safe Men for ready money or produce of Pitch or Rice deliverable presently or upon Bonds bearing Interest. The prices shall be left to you not doubting but you will do as much for me as your Market will admit of & transmit me an Account of the Sale, &ca. as soon as you can.

If this consignment is not acceptable be pleased to transfer it to William Smith (but observe he knows nothing of it nor will without you inform him) with an extract of this Letter for his direction, & if you have no dislike to it I shall endeavour hereafter to make you some of the same kind & perhaps more valuable, I am—

Note. All these are really Gold Coast Negroes bought at Anamaboo & the little Boy a very fine one. I am expecting an answer to the Subject of mine the 29th Ulto. If you think it necessary please to give each of these a Blanket.

SOURCE: Letterbook copy, Letter Book of Henry Laurens, Oct. 30, 1762–Sept. 10, 1766, Penn. Hist. Soc.; addressed "Esquire. George Town."

---

[6] These slaves may have come in the snow *Fanny,* Ralph Samson, which was entered inwards on July 8 with 35 slaves from St. Kitts. Naval Office Lists, 1757–1764, p. 83.

PAYMENT FOR AN EXECUTED SLAVE

July 13, 1764

*[On this date the Commons House of Assembly allowed Austin &
Laurens £200 plus £16 interest on a certificate that had been
presented on May 25, 1764, for a Negro who had been executed.[7]]*

SOURCE: House Journal, XXXVI (Jan. 24, 1763–Oct. 6, 1764), 36, 94,
127, 211, S. C. Archives.

TO ZACHARY VILLEPONTOUX

[Charles Town] 14th July 1764

Sir,

Yesterday your Nephew[8] called upon me with an order for
£1,000, which sum I advanced upon your Account altho the order
is not expressive of your promise, Vizt. to allow Interest on the same
untill it should be repaid to me in specie, Vizt. the first 100,000[9] at
£5.10/ to be discounted as the first payment in bar of Interest when
you shall have delivered that quantity.

And the second payment to stop Interest when the second
delivery of 100,000 shall be compleated. This was your proposition
& as I have advanced this sum with some inconvenience to myself &
merely to oblige you, I beg that you will by the first opportunity
acknowledge the same in conformation of what you proposed to do
in this case. I am, Sir—

SOURCE: Letterbook copy, Letter Book of Henry Laurens, Oct. 30,
1762–Sept. 10, 1766, Penn. Hist. Soc.; addressed "Esquire. Goose
Creek."

---

[7] There were 215 payments to masters for execution of their slaves between
1700 and 1776. This was the only payment made to HL. For a table listing all
the payments, see John D. Duncan, "Servitude and Slavery in Colonial South
Carolina, 1670–1776" (unpub. PhD diss., Emory Univ., 1972), pp. 707–713.

[8] Benjamin Villepontoux (died 1792) was a son of Peter Villepontoux (1685–
1748). He was a Charleston factor who married Jane Dupont on April 1,
1766. "The Villepontoux Family of South Carolina," compiled by I. Heyward
Peck, *SCHM*, L (1949), 38–39.

[9] The first 100,000 bricks at £5.10/ per thousand.

TO COWLES & HARFORD

[Charles Town] 17th July 1764

Gentlemen,

The 4th Ulto. I wrote to you per Capt. Reeves & believe a duplicate of it went by Bostock or some Vessel that sailed a little before him tho it is not so marked in my Copy Book. Please now to receive Invoice, Bill of Loading, & two Certificates for 354 Barrels of Pitch & 160 Barrels of Green Tar on my Account per this bearer the *Rose,* Henry Gray, Master & to sell the said Pitch & Tar in such manner as you shall think most beneficial to me & pass the Net proceed to my Credit. These Goods were delivered in exceeding good order and knowing of them to be so I did the more readily agree to asscertain the Freight previous to Shipping to be every 8 Barrels Ship'd to make one Ton, which I should never have acquiesced in if I had apprehended so much carelessness in taking in as well as in stowing as I have since discovered, & therefore I must beg leave to engage your attention to the unloading of this Vessel that you may judge properly who ought to bear or pay for the Loss in case of any great deficiency; I know that one Barrel of Pitch leaked wholly, and several others part out of being left one night with their bungs downward. Mr. Gray does indeed tell me that he filled them up again with Pitch of his own, but if the Contrary shall appear to you I will not submit to the Loss.

Mr. Gray sometime ago applied to me to recommend him to you & upon my promise to do so assured me that he would write to you to make Insurance upon his Vessel, Freight, &ca. but yesterday informed me that he had been prevailed upon to address his Little concerns to Mr. Edward Neufville[1] who is a distant relation of his Wife's family. Nevertheless he presses me to introduce him to you & to request the favour of your Notice & acquaintance at Bristol. He has been a resident in this Country in the planting business some 18 or 19 Years in which time he has not only brought up a large family in a very decent & reputable way but has likewise added to his capital which was not a very inconsiderable one when he first set down here. His present plan is to fix in some cheap country in the West

---

[1] Edward Neufville, the brother of John Neufville of Charleston had recently moved to Bristol. *HL Papers,* II, 212n. He had written HL a letter on Nov. 8, 1763, from Bristol offering his services. See HL to Edward Neufville, Sept. 7, 1764. On Feb. 21, 1764 John Neufville shipped items to Edward Neufville in the ship *Gloucestershire.* Naval Office Lists, 1764–1767, p. 32.

of England & to do a great many fine things in the farming way & dabble a little now & then in commerce & to seek some good establishment for his Children. The plain English of all which in my opinion is, that he is leaving good Wheat Bread to take up with Rye, 10 or 12 per Cent (& a great deal more considering the expence of his family) on his money & Labours for 3 or 4 per Cent. A Country where he was known & might have rubbed thro the wane of his Life with ease & satisfaction to begin anew Life with Grey Hairs in some place where he will be an utter stranger & subject to many, many inconveniences; & from whence he will probably return to us after a year or two of fruitless & vexatious toil with a Lighter prize toward which he has made a large step in his first outset by a very injudicious purchase of this Vessel but I hope if he is in error that he will make a timely discovery of it for his own & his family's sake, & if he is not, my observations can be of no prejudice to him as they are intended to be wholly confined to you & me. Mr. Austin always professed a friendship for this Gentleman & for my own part I have so great a regard for him that I would do him any reasonable service in my power & therefore I take the Liberty of intreating your favours in any thing that he may apply to you for, as advice, assistance, & direction in his new way of Life which you must be better qualified to give him than Mr. Neufville who is yet but a stranger in Britain.[2]

The Bales of Oznabrug per *Susannah* are charged uncommonly high & the quality of the Oznabrug so bad that it will not sell for my own money.

I shall this day pass three Bills on you . . . . Vizt.

to the order of James Poyas at 60 days £300
of John Hodsden . . . 40   180
of Nathaniel & George Bethune . . . 60 . . .   50
                                                        ————
                                                        £530
                                                        ————

---

[2] Henry Gray had married Anna Villepontoux, the sister of Benjamin Villepontoux, on April 24, 1745. *SCHM*, L (1949), 36–37. He had advertised in the *Gazette,* Oct. 8, 1763, that he was leaving the province the next spring. He had for sale 1,000 acres of pine land near Bacon's Bridge, two schooners, and 60 slaves ("sawyers, squarers, boatmen, coopers, and jobbing carpenters"). Henry Gray and his family and "Zachariah Villepontoux (son of Peter)" sailed for Bristol on July 19. *Gazette,* Oct. 8, 1764. Gray returned to Carolina at a later date for he died at Goose Creek in August 1772. *SCHM,* XXXIV (1933), 154.

which sum be pleased to pay & charge to my Account. Mr. Manigault & myself are Shipping about 300 Barrels of Pitch the fragments of several parcels in which we were concerned, per the *Charles Town,* Capt. Bampfield,[3] which will be consigned to you. Please to insure Fifty Guineas on my moiety thereof.

I am now making provision for the *Flora* having engaged a good deal of Pitch & some Green Tar & also the first offer of several parcels of fine Rice that I may be prepared to act as shall appear most for her Interest when she arrives. Whatever Loss or gain may attend these engagements I shall hold you to be one fourth concerned therein & myself three fourths. I remain—

SOURCE: Letterbook copy, HL Papers, S. C. Hist. Soc.; addressed "Bristol"; "per Capt. Gray. Copy per Mr. Poyas to forward with B. L. & Ab. In."

TO JOHN GEIGAR[4]

[Charles Town] 20th July 1764

Dear Sir,

Messrs. Rossel & Gervais will deliver this to you & I request you again to shew them all the civility in your power. You will find them worthy of your services, & if they have proper encouragement to make a settlement in our back Country, it will be of general benefit & therefore I think every Man that bares any love to the Country should contribute with chearfulness those favours & marks of humanity which are due to all strangers to these Gentlemen who are likely to become such useful members of our Community. I am, Sir—

SOURCE: Letterbook copy, Letter Book of Henry Laurens, Oct. 30, 1762–Sept. 10, 1766, Penn. Hist. Soc.; addressed "Congree."

---

[3] The ship *Charles Town,* William Bampfield, owned by Thomas Rock of Bristol, was entered inwards on June 5 from London. Naval Office Lists, 1764–1767, p. 77. Clearances for the period of July 6, 1764 to July 6, 1765 are missing from the naval office lists. Thomas Rock who had long had Charleston commercial ties went bankrupt late in the summer. London *Daily Advertiser,* Sept. 10, 1764.

[4] John Jacob Geiger had been settled in Saxe-Gotha Township on the west side of the Congaree River since 1737. *HL Papers,* III, 356n; Salley, *History of Orangeburg County,* p. 71.

*TO DAVID WEBB*⁵

[Charles Town] 20th July 1764

Sir,

I informed Mrs. Webb⁶ a few days since that two Gentlemen of my acquaintance who are going to Ninetysix & Fort Pr. George, would call at your house & probably make that their headquarters as they may make more than one journey to the upper Country.

These Gentlemen, Vizt. Mr. James Theodore Rossel & Mr. John Lewis Gervais, will deliver you this Letter & from the encouragement that Mrs. Webb gave me I have assured them that they may depend upon a comfortable Lodging at your house during their abode at Congree & that you will not only entertain them hospitably but do all in your power to assist them in the prosecution of their Journey. They are going at present to look over vacant Lands about Ninetysix & Long Canes. If you are acquainted with any good spots not yet granted I beg that you will point them out to them. These Gentlemen have some thoughts of establishing a very large Plantation in those parts of our Country & if they carry their plan into execution it will be of general benefit to the province. For my own part I think they are intitled to all encouragement that we can give them & therefore I do most chearfully contribute all in my power to serve them & I beg leave to recommend them to your favours also. If they should have occasion for Horses or anything else their draughts on me shall be duly honoured & one favour more I shall request of you

⁵ Although addressed as "Webb," this is certainly David Webb who had come from Virginia to S. C. and had served as a lieutenant of the Rangers in the Cherokee War. *Gazette*, July 5, 1760; "Will of David Webb," dated May 10, 1772, proved ———, Charleston County Wills, XVI, Book A (1774–1779), 59, S. C. Archives.

⁶ Mrs. Elizabeth Webb was first married to George Haig, deputy surveyor, who had laid out lands in the backcountry as early as 1732. Her home was often used as a place for religious services in Saxe-Gotha Township. Salley, *History of Orangeburg County*, pp. 23, 25, 28–29, 63, 226, 231, 237. In 1748 George Haig had been carried off the path from the Catawbas to the Congarees by French Indians and was dead by the next year. *The Journal of the Commons House of Assembly, January 19, 1748–June 29, 1748*, ed. J. H. Easterby (Columbia, S. C., 1961), pp. 190, 335; *The Journal of the Commons House of Assembly, March 28, 1749–March 19, 1750*, ed. J. H. Easterby (Columbia, S. C., 1962), p. 148. Her second husband was Lt. Peter Mercier of the Independent Company who was killed at the battle of Great Meadows in Virginia in 1754. "Will of Peter Mercier," dated June 27, 1754, at Camp in the Great Meadow, proved Jan. 10, ———, Charleston County Wills, VII (1752–1756), 279, S. C. Archives. Her third husband was David Webb. She outlived him, and died in May or June 1783. *SCHM*, XVIII (1917), 85.

before I close my Letter, that is to give them your advice & direction about the Roads & of the sort of people that they are to meet with in the way & as much as in you lies to prevent any impositions being offered or put upon them, that they may not be disgusted nor conceive any unfavourable opinion of the Country in their first attempts.

I present my compliments to Mrs. Webb & am, Sir, &ca.—

SOURCE: Letterbook copy, Letterbook of Henry Laurens, Oct. 30, 1762–Sept. 10, 1766, Penn. Hist. Soc.; addressed "Congree."

TO THOMAS BELL

[Charles Town] 20th July 1764

Dear Sir,

I shall take the Liberty without giving you the trouble of an appology to recommend Messrs. James Theodore Rossel & John Lewis Gervais to your favours during their abode at Ninety Six, assuring you that I shall hold myself indebted for every instance of kindness & civility that you shall be pleased to shew them & if they should be in want of money their draughts on me shall be duly honoured.

These Gentlemen have some thoughts of settling of Plantation some where about Ninety Six, Long Canes, &ca. & if they are encouraged to carry their plan into execution it will be a very extensive work & of general Utility as I am persuaded it will lead other Men of worth & fortune to follow their example. They want first to fix upon a spot of good Land. If you know of such an one not yet granted I beg that you will point it out to them & I have been so bold as to tell them that I made no doubt of your taking a ride for a day or two with them about the Country. They intend if nothing extraordinary prevents them to make one journey to Keowee, but this I would not have them undertake unless there is some tolerable good company going that way or that they can hire a very honest careful fellow for a guide.

One thing I intreat you to ward off from them as much as possible that is imposition either in dealings or on the Roads. The Gentlemen are strangers, very sensible genteel Men, & any Little frauds & tricks in their first attempts might tend to give them a general disgust to the Country. I shall write much to the same effect as this to Mr. Williamson[7] relying very much on the friendship of you both in the present circumstance. If these Gentlemen determine to settle in your parts I shall not hesitate to make a beginning of a Farm very near to theirs. I am, Dear Sir—

SOURCE: Letterbook copy, Letter Book of Henry Laurens, Oct. 30, 1762–Sept. 10, 1766, Penn. Hist. Soc.; addressed "Esquire. Ninety Six."

TO ANDREW WILLIAMSON

[Charles Town], 20th July 1764

Dear Sir,

This will be delivered to you by Messrs. Rossel & Gervais two Gentlemen who are now bound on a tour to your parts & probably as far as Keowee with some design to fix on a spot of good Land for establishing an extensive Farm & Plantation. Their scheme deserves the encouragement of every Man that wishes to see our back lands well settled & particularly of those whose Interest lies there. I have taken the Liberty to assure them of your friendship & assistance in their present undertaking & now beg leave to recommend them to you in the warmest manner that my Interest in your esteem will intitle me to. I beg that you will provide them some where or other the best Lodging that the place affords & every other necessary entertainment. At the same time I must inform you that altho these Gentlemen have been used to polite company & the genteelest manner of Living yet they are not strangers to the coarser & roughest fare, having been more than one Campaign in Germany they have seen variety of Life & experienced the vicissitudes of human affairs, which I say, that you may not mistake me & look upon them as Beaux or petit Maitre's. If they have occasion for money their draughts on me will be paid on sight and I hope they will from their present journey be induced to return again & perhaps induce me more than once to visit that part of our Country which I think will be by far the most delightful when once we can prevail upon a few Men of Honour & wealth to give it their countenance. Mr. Gervais will trouble you to execute a small Commission that I have given to him

---

[7] Andrew Williamson.

for Pacoon,[8] dryed Rattle Snake, Bears Oyl, & some wild flower Roots & I remain, Dear Sir, &ca.—

SOURCE: Letterbook copy, Letter Book of Henry Laurens, Oct. 30, 1762–Sept. 10, 1766, Penn. Hist. Soc.; addressed "Ninety Six."

TO EDWARD WILKINSON[9]

[Charles Town] 20th July 1764

Sir,

His Honour The Leiutenant Governor has favoured Messrs. Rossel and Gervais, the Gentlemen who will deliver this, with a recommendatory Letter to you, which I cannot doubt will secure to them your countenance & friendship during their short stay at Keowee, but as some thing more than we could presume to ask of the Governour may be wanting I shall beg leave to add a few lines to your trouble.

These Gentlemen have some remote intentions of settling a very extensive Farm, Vineyards, & Plantations in our back Country provided they can meet a proper spot of Land for their purpose, & in order to explore the vacant Tracts they have now undertaken this long journey. I call their intentions remote because I myself have said so much to them about the difficulty of carrying their plans (formed in England) into good effect, that their first hopes are not a little damped; at the same time I have not gone so far as wholly to discourage them, but rather recommended caution and wariness; to make themselves in some measure acquainted with that part of

---

[8] Puccoon was the Virginian Indian name of a North American plant which yielded a red dye. Capt. John Smith had written in 1612: "Pocones is a small roote that groweth in the mountains, which being dryed and beat in powder turneth red." OED. From the practice of painting themselves with this dye, the Indians became known as "Redskins." Wesley Frank Craven, *White, Red, and Black, The Seventeenth-Century Virginian* (Charlottesville, Va., 1971), p. 41.

[9] Edward Wilkinson was the son of Francis Wilkinson of Colleton County. *Abstracts of Wills, 1760–1784*, p. 61. After the Commons House of Assembly established the Directors of the Cherokee Trade on May 29, 1762, the Directors on July 19, 1762 appointed Edward Wilkinson "Factor, to attend and carry on the Trade" with the Cherokees "at the Factory, at Fort Prince George, Keowee." When the original act was repealed on Oct. 6, 1764, Wilkinson's position as factor was abolished. McDowell, *Documents relating to Indian Affairs*, pp. 510, 512, 569–572, 594.

the Country in which they design to live, as well as with the people who Live thereabout & their manner of Living too, before they run into great expences upon a scheme which they may soon be weary of & Let fall to the ground as some too-hasty adventurers have done before them.

If after they have viewed our Lands & are a Little better acquainted with the Rude way in which the inhabitants of our New World are obliged to Live they shall persevere in their resolutions, no expence will be spared by their friends in England to settle & establish such a plantation as will deserve the name of a Little Colony and soon become of general utility as other Men of Merit & wealth will no doubt be induced to follow their Laudable example. I know their plan to be grounded on a good Basis & that it is not merely a chimerical Land Hunting project & therefore I have been the more earnest in my dissuasives against their attempts before they had taken these previous steps, which will enable them to act from conviction & their own judgment; at least, prevent their running blindfold upon an enterprise that may prove worse than fruitless. From what I have here offered I am sure that you will join in opinion with me that these Gentlemen merit at least that notice & attention from every good Man that is due to honourable Strangers, & the experience that I have had of your humanity & politeness leaves me not the least room to suspect a deficiency in Mr. Wilkinson but it is necessary as I observed above to inform you that if thro any accident they shall be in want of money their Bills upon me shall be punctually paid & I must request the favour of you to supply them with Cash or Credit in case of need for I have advised them not to take too large a sum with them lest as they are Strangers a bait might thereby be put in the way of bad Men.

Messrs. Rossel & Gervais will soon discover themselves to be well bred Men & if occasion requires they will shew too that they are not unacquainted with the coarser and rougher manner of Living upon a Campaign, as they have been upon more than one or two of greater importance than the present one. I shall therefore only add that whatever civilities or favours you are pleased to extend to them will be particularly obliging to, Sir, &ca.—

SOURCE: Letterbook copy, Letter Book of Henry Laurens, Oct. 30, 1762–Sept. 10, 1766, Penn. Hist. Soc.; addressed "at Fort Prince George, Kiowee."

TO AUGUSTUS & JOHN BOYD

[Charles Town] 20th July 1764

Gentlemen,

Since I last troubled you, Vizt 7th December per *Bonetta* & *Success* Men of War, I have not rece'd any of your favours. This serves to convey Gabriel Manigault's 1st Bill for £500 Sterling dated 10th Inst. on Sarah Nickleson & Co. payable at 10 days sight to your order on Account of Messrs. Smith & Baillies which you will be pleased to pass to their Credit. I had sold a parcell of Negroes for those Gentlemen payable the 1st January next & had their direction to borrow in the mean time £1,000 Sterling to remit to you which I should have done, but I not only found some difficulty in borrowing Sterling, but the Exchange being 3 per Cent above the common par together with 8 per Cent Interest, would have [been] such a load upon their Account as I think you would not desire, & therefore I have taken the Liberty to keep back one half, hoping that you will be content to wait a few Months longer from the above considerations & also from my assurances of punctuality so soon as their own Money will begin to bear an equivalent Interest. Whether it be fair or not I will undertake to remit it to you & besides this our Imports of Negroes are not so large as was expected. Tis highly probable that they will then save 2 or 3 per Cent more in the Exchange. This I do confess is a Step taken by me for the Interest of Messrs. Smith & Baillies not exactly in pursuance of their orders but as I have advanced them on the same Account full £500 Sterling already I trust that I shall not incur their censure & that the forbearance for such a Sum for a few Months can be no great inconvenience to your Affairs. I remain—

SOURCE: Letterbook copy, HL Papers, S. C. Hist. Soc.; addressed "Esquires. London"; "per Capt. Bampfield. Copy per McKie with Second Bill."

TO WILLIAM PRICE

[Charles Town] 21st July 1764

Dear Sir,

In answer to your favour of the 10th Inst. the short notice that is given of this opportunity will permit me only to say that what

Negroes may remain upon your hands when this reaches you I would sell them (if I was in your place) to good Men for a barely saving price rather than keep them longer upon hand, & next to that attempt in case it should fail I would bring them to Charles Town again rather than let designing people compass their ends of getting them at their own prices. This that you experience is always the case at little Markets, they must be fed sparingly & then they pay the dearer for their meat, but if you put any large quantities in their way, they triumph & will not purchase even what they stand in need of unless at their own prices and terms.

A parcel of about 20 Hogsheads porter came in Capt. Muir[1] for Mr. Hest which I have given directions about & they are in your back Store. If any Letter came for him it is taken up by some Curious or too careful hand. I am, Dear Sir—

[P.S.] Just as I had subscribed to the foregoing Mr. Dickinson brought me your favour of the 16th. I have no more to add respecting the Negroes but that you may leave them in such hands as you like best. I should certainly have sent the 13 Negroes that went to Mr. Wragg to your address to avoid that clashing of Sale which you apprehend if I had not flattered myself with hopes of your being on the point of returning to Charles Town, but be not discouraged neither be talked out of reasonable demands by people who may design to tire you out. The business you mention at your Store shall be done without fail, by Mr. Perdriau if he is able, but poor fellow, he is this minute fallen into a most violent convulsion which probably will debilitate both his body & mind for some days. If there is any body that you can rely upon or bind down to deliver as good Pitch & Weighty as Mr. Clegg[2] generally makes & as I hope he will make now under contract & as good Barrels too to be delivered in Charles Town half on this side & the other half on the other side Christmas before the 1st April at 60/ per Barrel—but no charges to be paid by me—you may make contracts for 2 or 3,000 barrels, but not a penny more. Take care of the Men you deal with & oblige them to

---

[1] The ship *Little Carpenter*, William Muir, arrived June 15. She brought "a fine peal of bells" and a clock which the vestry of St. Michael's had ordered from London. The owners of the *Little Carpenter* had shipped the bells and clock without charging freight. *Gazette,* Oct. 8, 1764; George W. Williams, *St. Michael's, Charleston, 1751–1951* (Columbia, S. C., 1951), pp. 239, 243, 244.
[2] Samuel Clegg. *HL Papers*, III, 145n.

deliver it (say their Pitch) on or before a certain day. This you will find very difficult for they will have two strings to their Bow & leave a hole to creep through as occasion may serve but I will submit to no more such Pye Crust bargains unless I know my Man & have tried him. I have many unperformed contracts for Pitch, Rice, Corn, & Lumber in which the contractors are all uniform in their excuses of some accident preventing a compliance on their part when a better price offered than the contract stipulated.

SOURCE: Letterbook copy, Letter Book of Henry Laurens, Oct. 30, 1762–Sept. 10, 1766, Penn. Hist. Soc.; addressed "George Town."

TO JOSEPH BROWN

[Charles Town] 21st July 1764

Dear Sir,

Having but very short notice of this opportunity I cannot be very full in reply to your favour of the 7th Inst. but shall endeavour to say the needful.

You have really mistaken my remarks upon the subject of Negroes for Sale at George Town & from thence put yourself into a very unnecessary heat. I cannot see that there is one word *cruel* or *hard* or even inclining to either in my whole Letter, & I am sure there was nothing of that nature intended by me. What I suggested there still appears to me to deserve attention; that if instead of a few prime Negroes you had, had a mixed Cargo of good & bad Old & Young you would have been embarassed & I should have been put to the blush if I had recommended such a Cargo to you & you had been as much puzzled to sell it as you were to dispose of the few that I troubled you with. You may say & insist upon what you please about peoples' notions of every Negroes being a refuse that goes from Charles Town; but I am sure with submission to you that it is not invariably the case; & I need not go further than your own Letter for a proof. Is there a more wary Man in dealing than Mr. Davidson? Has he not given me a very good price for those very Negroes which you found unsaleable for so long a time? Why did he as you say "*go out of your House & somewhere into Town*" & then return & take my Negroes? I am no conjurer but yet with the small share of penetration that is fallen to my Lot I will venture to answer that question. He delivered you my order to secure the preference of my Negroes to himself then he went *somewhere into Town,* that is to say to take a view of Mr. Prices Cargo or perhaps some others, & when he had satisfied himself he returned & took those from you. Is not this a full proof that he could easily discern the difference between the negroes in one place & the other? 'Tis too true that many refuse Slaves are sent to George Town which no doubt does make people thereabouts cautious of buying such as go in general from Charles Town & some times even shy of good Slaves, but that must be according to the experience & knowledge of different Men as occasions offer, & sometimes the most knowing are deceived or deceive themselves. But now, Sir, what does all this prove but that you have not (being on one wing or in a corner of the Province) so good a chance of selling a Cargo (in which there is always some refuse & sometimes a good many) in George Town as the Merchants have in Charles Town the Center of the Province & where purchasers for every sort & size are to be found & this you will be convinced of either to your own or the cost of your New-England friends. Let the Cargo that you expect come when it will, unless they happen to be all fine Slaves which can hardly be suppos'd or expected, & the less if they are to be purchased on the Coast in the manner you talk of, for let the Salem Gentlemen[3] be never so sober or never so careful, Rum & their Bar Iron will not command fine Slaves if any better Cargoes are in the way. I had nothing more in view when I first attempted to disuade you from interfering in the African Trade than your Interest. I am sure you have not a proper idea of the difficulties attending it, when a Man acts in such a manner as not to injure himself and family & at the same time to preserve his reputation & do justice to his constituents, in which there must always be a dash of generosity over and above bare starved justice, & if you had not applied to me upon the occasion I should not have been so impertinent as to have troubled you with my opinion. You must know from other parts of my conduct that it was not owing to a want of Friendship for or inclination to serve you that I declined giving that recommendation that you desired, & you will excuse me for saying that your neglect of answering what I kindly & candidly wrote upon that

---

[3] When HL had told Brown that it would be difficult to sell a cargo of slaves at Georgetown, he must have contacted merchants at Salem, Mass., in the hope that they could send him a cargo.

subject because I was not so happy as to chime into your sentiments, was neither Mercantile, friendly, nor Genteel & your applications to New England discovers too plainly that you were miffed with my candour, & here I might very justly retort that it is "*cruel hard*" to be thus treated, in return for one's advice & opinion given to a friend in the most open & unreserved manner, & not without being first asked for them. But let me once more & for the last time recommend to you to forego the shew of profits on the African Trade rather than stake your peace, perhaps your Character, & fortune to attain to it, unless in the way that you talk of making a purchase now & then in Charles Town in which there may some times be profits made, and the Basis upon which you deal is more certain—& now drop this troublesome subject.

Capt. Cogdill must be mistaken with respect to the Freight paid him for that Pitch per Hoggart. I never did pay it to him, but I believe Mr. Lind who sold the Pitch did & I shall look further into that affair.

I was going on upon another sheet but poor Perdriau is tumbled down in a most violent fit & three people waiting in the Counting house hastens me to conclude upon this with presenting my Love to all your family & assuring you that I am, Dear Sir—

SOURCE: Letterbook copy, Letter Book of Henry Laurens, Oct. 30, 1762–Sept. 10, 1766, Penn. Hist. Soc.; addressed "George Town."

TO SAMUEL WRAGG

[Charles Town] 24th July 1764

Sir,

Whatever you do in the Sale of the 13 New Negroes lately consigned to you (as I am satisfied of your designs to do what promises most for my Interest) will content me. This I say in reply to your favour of the 14th just come to hand, & I am obliged to you for giving them Blankets which would have been done here but this neglect was omitted.

I cannot go beyond my former Limit for Pitch if I was sure by such means to procure all the Pitch made & to be made within three months in the Province. I am generally & may be allowed to say always at a word in my offers either as buyer or seller never purposely asking a higher or bidding a Lower price that I mean to take or give. Mr. Manigault had informed me before I wrote to you of his application (& terms) to Mr. Godfrey[4] & said he made it from a hint that I had given him, but he did not think that Mr. Godfrey would have communicated it to anybody. That Good Gentleman does not regard a few Shillings per barrel when giving them will procure his business to be done without much bustle, but he is so much of a Merchant as to be tenacious in not doing any thing that may tend to injure his Neighbours. Please to continue your endeavours (without taking too much trouble) to secure some good parcels of Pitch on my Account & I shall acknowledge myself equally obliged to you whether you succeed or fail. I remain, Sir—

SOURCE: Letterbook copy, Letter Book of Henry Laurens, Oct. 30, 1762–Sept. 10, 1766, Penn. Hist. Soc.; addressed "George Town."

TO NATHANIEL & GEORGE BETHUNE

[Charles Town] 25th July 1764

Gentlemen,

Since I wrote to you under the 28th May of which a duplicate is now unnecessary, your favour of the 5th April & 20th Ulto. with Barnes, Robinson's 1st & 2nd Bills & the Act of Protest there upon are come to my hands. The former reached me per this bearer Capt. Schermerhorn[5] at a time when I was very sick. Otherwise I might & should have wrote to you by one earlier opportunity which I find has unavoidably escaped me. I make the Amount of said protested Bill & all charges thereon to be £50.10/ Sterling, Vizt.

The Bill protested for non payment 20th March 1764	£42.10.5
Noting & protesting 18/ York Currency	9.5
Re-exchange at 15 per Cent	6. 7.6
Interest to 20th July 1764 at 8/ per Cent per Annum	1. 2.8
	£50.10

from which I deduct no Commission but for the full Sum herein

---

[4] Thomas Godfrey of Georgetown.
[5] The sloop *Sally*, John Schermerhorn, was entered inwards on June 28, from New York. Naval Office Lists, 1764–1767, p. 78.

transmit you my own Bill dated 17th Inst. being the day on which I advised of this amongst other draughts on Messrs. Cowles & Harford, Bristol, payable to your order at 60 days sight. You will find the 1st & 2d of the set under this Cover & may send both forward if you please as I shall in two or three days per Capt. McLain[6] convey to you a 3d & 4th.

If I am guilty of any error in my calculation be pleased to point it out and be assured that I shall be ready to rectify the mistake upon the first notice. I remain, Gentlemen—

Rice 47/6 to 50/ per Ct.
Freight 32/6 to Britain, 42/6 to Holland.

[*P.S.*] The Crops of Rice on the ground are in flourishing circumstances & will be large barring tempestuous weather in the Harvest.

SOURCE: Letterbook copy, HL Papers, S. C. Hist. Soc.; addressed "Boston"; "per Schermerhorn. Copy per McLean with 3d & 4 Bills. Original per Capt. Schermerhorn for New York delivered into his own hands per B. P."

TO COWLES & HARFORD

[Charles Town] 25 July 1764

Gentlemen,

I beg leave to refer you to what is wrote on the other side & then to desire that you will pay to Capt. Young Green[7] upon sight hereof the difference between what you paid him Last Year on his Cargo for primage & what he would have been paid thereon for Average according to the custom of Bristol if the Bills of Loading had been filled up in the ordinary way; provided he will receive the same as a favour & not of right. He has asked it as a favour of me but I am told that he does sometimes in my absence say that he did not understand the nature of the Bill of Loading. I do believe that he did not understand that he was doing an act which would subject him to receive a less sum than he aimed at, but I am very sure that the Bills of Loading were read & explained to him & he gave me

---

[6] This may be John McClaine who sailed between Charleston and New York in the schooner *Success*. *Gazette*, Oct. 1, 1764.

[7] The snow *Hannah*, Young Green, owned by Young Green of Poole, was entered inwards on June 14 from Bristol. Naval Office Lists, 1764–1767, p. 78.

good reason to believe that his view was to get a larger Sum from me than was really his due, for which he now apologizes *to me* by alledging that he was in a Combination of Masters & under a penalty of Ten Guineas to sign no Bills of Loading for Bristol without inserting the above mentioned primage in them & if the truth of the Story was known he had not given himself time to consider at the signing of mine the 2½ per Cent upon Freight of 34 or 35/ per Ton would not amount to quite so much as 2½ per Cent upon a Freight of £4 or £5 per Ton altho it was 2½ per Cent still. I have said so much upon this occasion because I would not suffer Capt. Green by any means to extort Money from me that was not his due & at the same time shew him that I have no desire to keep an Farthing of what ought & should have been paid to him if he & I had not been overruled by his own superior knowledge. I remain, Gentlemen—

SOURCE: Letterbook copy, HL Papers, S. C. Hist. Soc.; addressed "Bristol"; "per Capt. Green. Copy deliver'd to Capt. Green to be forwarded."

TO ZACHARY VILLEPONTOUX

[Charles Town] 28th July 1764

Sir,

On the 20th Inst. I rece'd a Letter from you dated the 28th which I suppose must have been intended for the 18th. It inclosed a promissary note for One Thousand pounds, the Sum advanced by your desire to Mr. Benjamin Villepontoux. Your order for that Sum shall be delivered when we settle Accounts or when you come next to Town if you think it of any consequence to have it sooner but this is a sufficient acknowledgement to take away any improper effect that it might have by mistake. The terms of discount which you propos'd to me were certainly as noted in my last & very good terms I think they are on your part considering the uncommoness of advancing Money in this way & that I put myself to some inconvenience merely to oblige you. I do assure you that the Interest was no temptation to me to do what I did in that case. However I never was known to be very strenuous in my demands & if you are dissatisfied with your own proposition I shall give the Subject a further consideration altho it is not strictly due. The number of Bricks hitherto Rece'd from you is 32,550, Vizt.

May 26	....	6,550
31	....	6,500
July 3	....	6,500
14	....	6,500
28	....	6,500 32,550

Please to let me know in your next if this is agreeable to your Account. I think it is all but ten Bricks which are not worth notice upon either side. A person desired me today to let him have your next Boat load which may be as you think proper, but the two next following I shall want for my own use & all the remainder at your own convenience without too much delay. I am—

SOURCE: Letterbook copy, Letter Book of Henry Laurens, Oct. 30, 1762–Sept. 10, 1766, Penn. Hist. Soc.; addressed "Goose Creek."

TO TIMOTHY CREAMER

[Charles Town] 31st July 1764

Mr. Creamer,

I send you two of the very best Whip Saws

1 Sett
6 Files
1 Cotton Line
Sundry Medicine as per account below
3 bundles baby Cloths
Mrs. Creamer's Bowl & some Tomawtoes

I hope when I come which will be when the House of Assembly adjourns[8] that I shall find a good quantity of Lumber Sawed as well as fire Wood & that you will at Leisure cause all the Pine Wood to be collected but not cut to short.

I send you three or four pine Laths for a pattern. Set one hand to make as many such as you can. 100,000 will be wanted and may always be sent upon Deck. The very worst pine is good enough. I am, Sir—

---

[8] This session of the Commons House of Assembly did not end until Aug. 25. House Journal, XXXVI (Jan. 24, 1763–Oct. 6, 1764), 254, S. C. Archives.

SOURCE: Letterbook copy, Letter Book of Henry Laurens, Oct. 30, 1762–Sept. 10, 1766, Penn. Hist. Soc.; addressed "Mepkin"; "per Watboo Schooner."

TO ARNOLD, ALBERT, & ALEXANDER NESBITT [9]

[Charles Town] 7th August 1764

Gentlemen,

Since I had the pleasure of writing to you 11th October 1762, I have not received any of your favours. Mr. Sommervilles Estate[1] I have learned is sufficient to pay all his debts & therefore hope you will be no sufferer by your connexions in that quarter.

Yesterday came to my hands 15 New Negroes a consignment from Messrs. Day & Welch of St. Christophers,[2] the Net proceed whereof they order me to remit to you. The Negroes are of an ordinary sort only one remove from refuse, nevertheless I shall find means to put them off at about Five hundred pounds Sterling Net not much over or under provided no accident happens to prejudice the Sale & as soon as in Cash I shall remit to you which I think necessary to advise you of as it may have some effect in the concerns of our said friends with you. I remain, &ca.—

SOURCE: Letterbook copy, HL Papers, S. C. Hist. Soc.; addressed "Esquires. London"; "per Capt. Bampfield."

TO COWLES & HARFORD

[Charles Town] 10th August 1764

Gentlemen,

This serves to convey a Bill of Loading & bounty Certificate

---

[9] *HL Papers*, II, 381n.

[1] Edward Somerville of Savannah, Ga. *HL Papers*, III, 130n. John Rae and Thomas Eaton, the executors of Somerville's estate, had warned that those who did not pay their debts to the estate would be prosecuted at law. *Georgia Gazette*, April 7, 1763. A Negro woman and two mulatto children, belonging to the estate, after having been sold by the provost marshal at public auction, had run away. *Georgia Gazette*, May 10, 1764.

[2] HL paid £150 in duties on slaves brought in the *Manchester*, Gilbert Livingston, from St. Kitts. Public Treasurer, Journal B: Duties, 1748–1765, p. 401, S. C. Archives.

for 291 Barrels & 1 Tureen of Pitch & 41 Barrels of Tar, shiped by Gabriel Manigault, Esquire per this Bearer the Ship *Charles Town,* William Bamfield, Master for Bristol consign'd to you which you will be pleas'd to receive & Sell on Account of that Gentleman & myself & pass the net proceed to our respective Accounts, half to each.

Capt. Courtin arriv'd this evening.[3] I shall reply to your favours by him & some former ones in my next. Meantime I remain with great regard, &ca.—

SOURCE: Letterbook copy, HL Papers, S. C. Hist. Soc.; addressed "Bristol"; "per Capt. Bamfield. Copy per Capt. Farnsworth."

TO ISAAC KING

[Charles Town] 10th August 1764

I have sundry of your favours to reply to which shall be done in my next. At present please to receive under this cover a bounty Certificate for 268 Barrels of Green Tar per the Ship *Hope,* Capt. Bowers, & to be advised of my Draught the 4th Insta. for £500 Sterling to the order of Mr. William Gibbs[4] payable at fifty days sight for which I trust I have a sufficient fund in you[r] hands. I remain, &ca.—

SOURCE: Letterbook copy, HL Papers, S. C. Hist. Soc.; addressed "For Mrs. Sarah Nickleson & Co., London"; "per Capt. Bamfield. Copy per Capt. Farnsworth."

TO RICHARD OSWALD & CO.

[Charles Town] 10th August 1764

Since I wrote to you the 3d March last & for sometime before I have not receiv'd any of your esteem'd favours.

The day before yesterday your Ship *Queen Barra,* Capt.

---

[3] Capt. Thomas Courtin in the *Flora.*

[4] William Gibbes, Charleston factor, advertised in the *Gazette,* Jan. 7, 1764, that he continued to sell country produce on commission. *HL Papers,* III, 31n.

Taylor, arrived here from Searralion[5] with about 300 Slaves of which 106 were Shiped by Mr. Aird on your Account & the rest are upon Freight partly Shiped by that Gentleman & partly by Mr. James Tweed[6] at £6 Sterling per head.

Mr. Aird in his Letter to me of the 11th June desires me to recommend some proper Person here. I have therefore agreed with Messrs. Brewton & Smith to sell your Negroes & those which he Shiped upon Freight to remit the whole proceeds in the Bottom in Bills payable at three, Six, & Nine Months, after deducting Charges & the Cost of a Cargo for the Ship, which I shall direct to be in such articles as may promise to pay the best Freight. These in my oppinion are good terms & I am sure that House will make at least as good a Sale as any in Charles Town for it has undoubtedly the most extensive Correspondence & is upon a par with any other in point of knowledge & application to Business. If I had thought it had been in my power without a partner to do so well for you I should not have let the Commission pass by me. At present I have no other Interest or advantage therein but the pleasure of making a Greatfull acknowledgement for your repeated favours to me & which I shall continue to do as often as opportunity presents. Captain Taylor has been very sick the whole Voyage & is now in a very low state under my roof where I have obtained permission to lodge him while the Ship performs her Quarrintine. Mr. James Tweed is well but necessarily confined on board. If Mr. Aird is in London be so good as to assure him that I shall have a friendly eye to his concerns & that I shall pay my respects to him in a few days. I am—

SOURCE: Letterbook copy, HL Papers, S. C. Hist. Soc.; "per Capt. Bamfield. Copy per Capt. Taylor."

RECEIPT FOR SALE OF SLAVE

August 10, 1764

Received 10th August 1764 of William Hopton, Esquire,

---

[5] The ship *Queen Barra*, Alexander Taylor, sailed for London about the first of Oct. *Gazette*, Oct. 1, 1764. Brewton & Smith paid £2,520 in duties on the slaves brought from Africa by Taylor. Public Treasurer, Journal B: Duties, 1748–1765, p. 401, S. C. Archives.

[6] According to two invoices of 1759 and 1760 Messrs. Aird and James were merchants at the factory at Bance Island in the Sierra Leone River. Perhaps the James of the invoices was actually James Tweed. *HL Papers*, III, 12, 43.

two hundred & ten Pounds Current Money in full for a Negro Boy lately Sold & delivered to Mrs. Hopton for the use of Thomas Hoyland a Minor.
                                                                Henry Laurens

£210

I Acknowledge that I have Received of Mrs. Ann Maria Hoyland the above mentioned Sum of two hundred & ten pounds Current Money and am Witness that the above mentioned Negro Boy (who is now Called Bob) is the sole property of her Son the above Named Thomas Hoyland.[7]
Recorded 13th May 1765   William Hopton

SOURCE: Miscellaneous Records, MM, Part 1 (1763–1767), p. 259, S. C. Archives.

TO JOSEPH BOWER

[Charles Town] 11th August 1764
Sir,

The second Copy of your favour of 16th April & original of the 17th May came to hand only the 29th Ulto. per Capt. Harbinson.[8] The original & duplicate of the former have not yet appeared, & as it happens their delay or miscarriage is rather beneficial to you than otherwise for had either reached me in the ordinary course I should by your orders have purchased Pitch not only at the very dearest rate but the Storage & waste thro the Summer Months would have made the Cost excessive. I shall now be looking out to make the provisions that you order for your Snow *New Success*,[9] Vizt. 200 barrels Green Tar, 200 barrels best Pitch, & 50 Barrels of Turpentine, but I doubt whether I shall be able to procure the Green Tar

---

[7] The father Thomas Hoyland had been a butcher in Charleston. Judgment Rolls, 1755, No. 111A, S. C. Archives. The widow Anna Maria Hoyland, the niece of Mrs. Sarah Hopton, lived in Charleston for over fifty years. *Abstracts of Wills, 1740–1760,* p. 141; "Will of Anna Maria Hoyland," dated July 12, 1801, proved Jan. 19, 1816, Charleston County Wills, XXXIII, Book C (1807–1818), 1027–1028, S. C. Archives. The Hoptons purchased the slave from HL for young Thomas Hoyland and were reimbursed by the boy's mother which made the slave the property of young Thomas Hoyland.
[8] Capt. Thomas Harbison of the *True Briton.*
[9] The snow *New Success,* James Doran, sailed for Bristol on Nov. 12. *Gazette,* Nov. 12, 1764.

which is become very scarce & probably the other articles may not come to Market before the time Limitted by you will expire, Vizt. 1st September & if so I shall not engage you in a purchase before the Snow arrives when I may expect your further commands as you intimate in your Last an order for other Goods without which it will be extremely difficult to make up a Loading. Capt. Gallen[1] & Harbison are taking in at 35/ per Ton for Bristol & because there is nothing better to be done I am sending the new Ship *Flora*, Capt. Courtin, to Oporto. Upon the whole you may depend upon my best endeavours to serve you. If your orders are strict I shall obey them as nearly as the times and circumstances of our market will admit of; if you leave an opening for the exercising of my own Judgment, I shall in that Case act for you as if the profit or Loss of the Voyage was to be wholly my own.

Our Crops of Rice upon the Ground are very fine & barring a bad harvest the produce will be as great as Last Year. This prospect will lower the price of Naval Stores about a Month hence. I remain—

SOURCE: Letterbook copy, HL Papers, S. C. Hist. Soc.; addressed "Bristol"; "per Capt. Bamfield. Copy per McKie."

TO SAMUEL WRAGG

[Charles Town] 13th August 1764

Sir,

I remark your Sales of 6 of those Negroes lately consigned to you as advised in your favour of the 6th Inst. & make no doubt of your endeavours to get rid of the rest the sooner the better (so as to avoid precipitation) because I shall probably trouble you with a few more by George Dick. As to the Article of Pitch I cannot extend my former Limit as to time, as the price is more than I would give if I had not already offered it. My Ship is arrived but the price of Naval Stores here & in England are so in[a]dequate that I can see no prospect of making a saving Freight upon such goods. Therefore I have resolved either to send her to Oporto or to lay by for the New Crop. That point I shall determine while she is Caulking which I find necessary to do over again as it most commonly is in New Ships.

---

[1] Capt. Thomas Gullan of the *Sally*.

I am morally sure that the price of Pitch will be lower in a few Weeks, for as the Crop approaches so Light Ships will be encouraged to wait for it rather than accept of the paultry Freights of 32/6 to 35/ per Ton which are now & have for some time past been given. These circumstances affect each other very sensibly. They are always in motion & the gain of one is inevitably the Loss of the other. At the same time I shall take it as a great favour if you will be pleased after the 1 September to recommend the first offer of any parcels of Pitch that fall in your way to me. I generally am a purchaser at Market prices & strive to make good payments, &ca.—

SOURCE: Letterbook copy, Letter Book of Henry Laurens, Oct. 30, 1762–Sept. 10, 1766, Penn. Hist. Soc.; addressed "George Town"; "per favour of Mr. William Smith."

TO HENRY BYRNE

[Charles Town] 13th August 1764

Sir,

I am indebted for a great many of your favours which should not have been the Case if I had not been a good deal interupted this Year by Sickness, removing my habitation, & a melancholy accident in my family of the death of my eldest daughter. These several circumstances have conspired to make me more remiss than I was wont to be but thank God I am (in appearance at least) recovering my former vigour & ability. This serves to advise you that I shall Load the New Ship *Flora*, burthen about 700 barrels of Rice, 1/4 belonging to Messrs. Cowles & Harford of Bristol & 3/4ths to myself, with the very best Rice that the Season affords & hope to dispatch her to your address for Oporto about the 10th September, say the Ship *Flora*, Thomas Courtin, Master will wear off port Bar a Jack[2] at her Fore-top-Gallant Masthead which signal I shall direct that your orders may reach Capt. Courtin in time to prevent his going over the Bar in Case you have no Sale or a bad one for his Cargo & in such an unlucky event you will be pleased to advise him to go to Lisbon or Cadiz as you may judge most for our Interest[3]

---

[2] *HL Papers,* II, 114n.
[3] This procedure was used in order to avoid paying the duties at Oporto. *HL Papers,* II, 88, 92.

which will lay the owners under great obligations to you & you may depend upon it they will make the best acknowledgement in their power, but I will hope for better things, that your Market will be open & afford such a price for our Rice as will pay us a saving Freight for the Ship, & also that you will have it in your power to recommend to her a good Freight from Oporto to London or Bristol for which end I trust this previous advice will be useful. I recommend it to your attention & shall not add to your trouble untill Capt. Courtin Sails when I shall write fully & in the meantime take leave with assuring you that I am with great respect, Sir—

SOURCE: Letterbook copy, HL Papers, S. C. Hist. Soc.; addressed "Esquire. Oporto"; "per Capt. Barnes."

TO HENRY BRIGHT

[Charles Town] 13th August 1764

Sir,

I am indebted for your sundry obliging favours of the 8th, 17th, & 17th May & pay due regard to their several contents.

I shall write tomorrow to Messrs. Smith & Baillies my opinion of Freights the approaching Crop under which they may govern the proceedings of your Ship *Sally.* There is nothing to be done for her at present nor will be before October or November as you will know by the paultry Freight that this Ship the *Charles Town* now makes as well & Gullen & Harbison for Bristol. Pitch is very dear just now & probably will continue to be so untill the eve of the New Crop when Freights must begin to advance.

Your two Casks of Copper per *True Britton,* Harbison, are come to hand & shall be disposed of on Account of the Estate of Mr. Allen Bright[4] as speedily as possible but it will take sometime to reallize so large a Sum in a place where that Specie is rather disliked. As soon as the Amount is converted into other Money I shall remit the proceeds in the way that you direct.

---

[4] Allen Bright was a pewterer who became a freeman of Bristol on Nov. 2, 1742. When he was apprenticed to William Watkins and Mary his wife on Nov. 1, 1735, he was identified as the son of Henry Bright of Hereford, gentleman, lately deceased. M. E. Williams, archivist of Bristol, to the editor, June 30, 1972.

I am sorry that you have not had a Cargo or two of fine Negroes here this Year which has afforded great prices. I transfered a consignment of about 300 from Whyda a few days ago to Messrs. Brewton & Smith which they turned out at about £36 Sterling round & have just now resigned the like number in a Ship from Bance Island to the same house which I hope will yeild as good an average.[5] I should not let these commissions slip me if I thought that I could in my present circumstance single & without a partner do as well for my friends, but I think it better to forego my own Interest than to stake theirs upon my own health which for some time past had failed me a good deal but, thank God, I have now recovered my wonted vigour & am very well, Sir—

SOURCE: Letterbook copy, HL Papers, S. C. Hist. Soc.; addressed "Esquire. Bristol"; "per Capt. Bamfield. Copy per Capt. Harbison."

GEORGE AUSTIN, HENRY LAURENS, & GEORGE APPLEBY VERSUS JOHN MILES

August 13, 1764

[On August 13, 1764, James Moultrie, attorney for the plaintiffs, filed suit in the court of common pleas against John Miles of Ashley River for payment of a promissory note in the sum of £250 currency. John Miles through his attorney James Parsons entered a plea on August 22, 1764, that the debt was not his. The docket does not indicate if any further action was taken in this case.]

SOURCE: Judgment Rolls, 1764, No. 166A, S. C. Archives.

TO LACHLAN McINTOSH

[Charles Town] 14 to the 15th August 1764

Dear Sir,

I own myself indebted for a great many of your favours which have lain dormant with much of my other concerns, owing

---

[5] Captain McKie had brought a cargo of slaves from Whydah in June, and Captain Taylor had just arrived with a cargo from Sierra Leone. Brewton and Smith sold the four largest cargoes during the summer of 1764. Donnan, *Documents Illustrative of the Slave Trade*, IV, 386.

to several accidents in my family conspiring to make me more remiss in business than ever I was wont to be. The severest stroke of all was the sudden death of my dear Little improved Girl Nelly, but thank God I have pretty well recover'd my former health & vigor & my family are once more in a state of order & tranquility.

The Deeds which you sent to me for Broughton Island are imperfect for want of Mrs. McIntosh's Renunciation but if that cannot with great convenience be procured I would not have you think of it until I have the pleasure of seeing you at my Cottage where I hope you will stop in your way to Charles Town & you may be assured of a hearty welcome & the best entertainment for Man & Horse that the place affords.

I am in treaty with Mr. Pendergrass for your favourite 1,200 Acre Tract upon Altamaha. He offer'd it. He has this moment agreed to sell it to me for One Thousand pounds Currency & I hope he will be as good as his word. I shall endeavour to get the platt & Grant from him in order to prevent fallbacks if possible for he seems to be very unsteady & in fact has no will of his own.[6]

I was obliged to leave this Letter open for concluding the above paragraph to the very last & now Mr. Loockerman[7] calls upon me for the fourth & last time I can only add that Mr. Deas,[8] on behalf of his Brother,[9] Mr. Hopton,[1] himself, & me, has entered into an agreement with this Gentleman to Settle our Altamaha Lands. I refer you to the agreement & shall be glad of your opinion thereon as well as of your aid in our present undertaking. I shall strive hard to pay you a visit in November next but dare not promise because I know the difficulty of shaking loose from so many attachments as have laid hold of me & that I have on my part too.

---

[6] HL purchased this tract from Pendergrass on Nov. 28, 1764 and sold it to McIntosh on Oct. 9, 1765.

[7] Jacob Lookerman had received a grant in 1757 to 350 acres on the north side of Midway River in Georgia. *Colonial Records of Georgia*, VII, 145, 687. On March 16, 1762, he sold a herd of cattle for £50 sterling in St. John parish, Ga. Miscellaneous Deeds, Book J, p. 493, microfilm, Ga. Archives. On Aug. 15, 1762, calling himself a planter of Sunbury, he mortgaged 3 tracts of land and 10 riding horses. Mortgages, Book E, pp. 444–449, Ga. Archives. On Feb. 5, 1765, he received a grant of 400 acres on the north side of the Little Satilla in Georgia. *Colonial Records of Georgia*, IX, 279.

[8] John Deas.

[9] David Deas.

[1] William Hopton.

The Titles from Pendergrass will be in my own name but you shall have a reconveyance if you please when you come to Town & in order to make it as easy as possible I have obtained a Credit free of Interest to the first day of March next. Make my best compliments acceptable to Mrs. McIntosh & your fire side & be assur'd that I am, &ca.—

SOURCE: Letterbook copy, Letter Book of Henry Laurens, Oct. 30, 1762–Sept. 10, 1766, Penn. Hist. Soc.; addressed "Esquire. at Darien in Georgia."

TO TIMOTHY CREAMER
[Charles Town] 18th August 1764
I Send you by Mr. Philps Boat[2] another Cotton Line, 1 oz. sweet Mercury, 2 Carpenters Compasses, 1 lb. Blue Stone, which are the articles Mr. Ball told me you were in want of.

I have also sent up a Sample for Larths[3] but I should think you might have proceeded in that sort of work without a Sample as there is no great nicety in it.

Mr. Philps Boat must be loaded again with the same quantity of Fire Wood as last Trip.

Let me know now what quantity of Wood will remain & also what Lumber is ready, & if Mrs. Creamer can undertake to make the Negro Cloths this Fall. I am—

SOURCE: Letterbook copy, Letter Book of Henry Laurens, Oct. 30, 1762–Sept. 10, 1766, Penn. Hist. Soc.; addressed "Mepkin"; "By Mr. Philps Schooner."

---

[2] On March 29, 1764, Robert Philp had registered the schooner *Thomas,* William Phillips, owned by himself and Thomas Caw, a minor. Ship Register, 1734–1765, p. 227, S. C. Archives. Robert Philp had qualified as an executor of David Caw's will on Dec. 1, 1758. Thomas was the only child of David and Rachel Caw. "Will of David Caw," dated Sept. 21, 1758, proved Dec. 1, 1758, Charleston County Wills, VIII (1757–1763), 275–278, S. C. Archives. David Caw had owned a schooner which with sails, anchor, etc. was valued at £350 currency. Inventories, T (1758–1761), 185–188, S. C. Archives.
[3] Laths.

TO JOSEPH BAIRD

[Charles Town] 18th August 1764

Dear Sir,

In case Mr. Carver[4] shall make any demur to paying my draught on him in your favour for £250 Sterling, you will be pleased after the needful expostulation to cause the Bill to be Noted & Protested for the whole or part as the case shall require & then present it to Mrs. Sarah Nickleson & Company In London who will pay the same with all charges on my Account.

I wish you a prosperous Voyage & happy meeting with all your friends in Europe & if at any time you have occasion for my services in this Quarter I shall be ready to execute your commands to the best of my ability, who am, Dear Sir—

SOURCE: Letterbook copy, Letter Book of Henry Laurens, Oct. 30, 1762–Sept. 10, 1766, Penn. Hist. Soc.; addressed "In Charles Town bound on a Voyage to London."

TO ERASMUS CARVER[5]

[Charles Town] 18th August 1764

Sir,

I am indebted for your sundry favours of the 4th June, 7th September, & 17 November in the expired year & the 24th February & 10 March in the present which are now before me with your Account Sales of the Pitch & Turpentine consigned to you in the Brigantine *Portsmouth,* Capt. Page[6] & my Account Current with you, Balance in my favour £208.7/ Sterling, to which Sum I presume I may now add an uncertain proceed between £50 & £60 for Amount of the Bounty Bill which you have receiv'd as Mrs. Sarah Nickleson & Company have not advised me of the receipt of it from you & in consequence of this & your advice of the Balance of the Account being ready I have this day passed a Bill on you at 30 days sight to the

---

[4] Erasmus Carver of Gosport. *HL Papers,* III, 509n.

[5] The Company of Merchants trading to Africa used Erasmus Carver as agent for the shipping of supplies to their posts in Africa. T 70/29, passim; T 70/69, pp. 1, 3, Public Record Office, London.

[6] HL shipped 337 barrels of pitch and 112 casks of turpentine in the brigantine *Portsmouth,* William Page, which sailed for Poole on July 29, 1763. *HL Papers,* III, 509–511.

order of Mr. Joseph Baird for £250 Sterling which I recommend to your accustomed punctuality & if it shall so happen that you have remitted the Bounty Bill, or the said Balance or both to the said Mrs. Nickleson & Co. in such case you will be pleased to recommend my Bill to them also for payment in whole or in part as the case shall be. But, Sir, will you give me leave to make a few remarks upon your Account of Sale in which I think there are some errors & some articles that require explanation? Vizt.

1st. Of the Sale; you advise me the 17th November that you had sold all the Turpentine at 8/ & half the Pitch at 10/ whereas the Account shews 251 Barrels Pitch & 110 Barrels Turpentine sent to London & the proceeds of both are Lumped in your Account & admit of no examination but it is evident from the said Lump that both articles have incurred double Charges & Commission. It would have been kind upon failure of your own Market if you had sent my Goods to that House which I had informed you transacted my business in London & to whome therefore you were to have sent the Bounty Bill.

2d. The 25 Barrels stove in the hold & used to fill up the rest have paid or charged for full Freight & charges.

3d. The Freight, primage, & port Charges at Poole seem to be above my agreement but require explanation.

4th. The 2d, 3d, 4th, 5th, 6th, 7th, 8th, 10th, & 11th articles of charges Amounting to £24.6.5 are excessive & near threefold of what is charged on the like services in Bristol.

5th. The Duty & Fees seem to be out of proportion when compared with other Sales, that I have by me.

6th. Postage £1.2.6 is equal to a correspondence of 70 Single Letters & upwards at 3d to 4d per Letter.

7th. Commission for advance of Freight & charges is, (to say the least) quite uncustomary but if insisted upon by Mr. Carver, surely 2½ per Cent is inadequate or rather too high; & 'tis hoped that the use of my Money since that time will sufficiently compensate that advance & remove this charge.

I beg the favour of you to retrospect the Account & if you perceive that my remarks are well founded make the needful alterations in my favour & then remit the final Balance to my said friends Mrs. Sarah Nickleson & Company in London & upon future occasions I shall with the more chearfulness renew our correspondence.

If I am wrong in these observations please to convince me thereof in your next & to excuse me for the mistake; but in all events I intreat you to settle the Account with them & their Receipt shall be as effectual as my own could be. You who are so largely concern'd in commerce need not be informed that the want of this Balance which was appropriated to so particular a purpose as Ship Building might have been injurious to my Plan & perhaps to my Credit, & that it must have put me to an expence to procure other Money in place of it therefore I shall not trouble you with expostulation but take it for granted that you will upon Receipt of this be so good as to do what would have been very right to do many Months before. I am, Sir, Your most Obedient Servant—

SOURCE: Letterbook copy, HL Papers, S. C. Hist. Soc.; addressed "Gosport"; "per Capt. Farnsworth."

TO GRUBB & WATSON

[Charles Town] 18th August 1764

Gentlemen,

Since I wrote to you in April last per Capt. Gunn, Gibbes, &ca. your sundry favours of the 13th November 1763, the 6th March, 19 April, 11th & 22d May are come to my hand together with my Account Current Balance 31st December last in my favour £186.17.6 which I have not examined but I can see a Blank for your Commission on paying Bills which I intreat you to fill up in the usual manner in next Account. In consequence of that Balance & hoping that you will have a sufficient fund from 5/8th of the freight home & out per *Heart of Oak* I have presumed this day to pass a Bill on you at 40 days sight to the order of Mr. Joseph Baird for Two Hundred pounds Sterling which I recommend to your accustomed punctuality.

I lately Received some pretty things thro the hands of my Brother[7] of China, Arrac,[8] & Tobacco all which I am told are derived from your Bounty & intended for a present to me. The articles are truly such as I like & very acceptable provided you will

---

[7] James Laurens.

[8] Arrack was the "name applied in Eastern countries to any spirituous liquor of native manufacture; especially, that distilled from the fermented sap of the coco-palm, or from rice and sugar, fermented with the coco-nut juice." *OED*.

be so good as to charge them full Value to my Account which I intreat you to do, for I am sure it has not been in my power hitherto to merit so genteel an acknowledgement from you, nor indeed would I ever expect anything of this kind from my friends. I hope you will receive this as it is meant & intended; not to affront your friendy offers & at the same time to avoid putting you to needless expence & trouble for articles that are just such as I should have been glad to buy & shall therefore with many thanks pay you for.

I was on the point of Shipping about 27,000 feet of Jamaica Mahogany to your address in this bottom but differing about 5/ per Ton in the Freight have sent it to Bristol. Our Crops of Rice barring Hurricanes will be large & the folks talk as if the Indigo fields had mended very much of late. I remain with great respect, &ca.—

SOURCE: Letterbook copy, HL Papers, S. C. Hist. Soc.; addressed "London"; "per Capt. Farnsworth."

T O C O W L E S & H A R F O R D

[Charles Town] 18th August 1764

Gentlemen,

The above is Copy of what I wrote to you the 10th Inst. This serves to advise of my draught on you this day to the order of Mr. Joseph Baird payable in London at 40 days sight for £150 Sterling & I must beg your excuse for not writing more fully as I have been closely confined to some public business for many days past & tis now Saturday Evening. On Monday I shall write by another or perhaps this same conveyance. Mean time I remain with great regard, &ca.—

SOURCE: Letterbook copy, HL Papers, S. C. Hist. Soc.; addressed "Bristol"; "per Capt. Farnsworth."

T O S A R A H N I C K L E S O N & C O .

[Charles Town] 18th August 1764

Sir,

When I wrote to you the 10th Inst. as per Copy above I had fully intended before this day to have replyed to your several un-

answered favours in my hands but being closely confined to some
public business all the past Week I must defer it a day or two longer.
At present I take leave to inclose you a Copy of an Account Sale &
Account Current lately Rec'd from Mr. E. Carver of Gosport & also
of my Letter of this date to him to which I beg leave to refer & request
you to pay my Bill to Joseph Baird in case he should refuse it but
not before it undergoes the form of noting & protesting & if he pays
the Bill that you will do me the favour to persuade him if you can
to remit to you what shall appear to be further due to me. I am,
&ca.—

SOURCE: Letterbook copy, HL Papers, S. C. Hist. Soc.; addressed
"London"; "per Capt. Farnsworth."

TO SAMUEL WRAGG

[Charles Town] 21 August 1764

Wrote to him per Capt. Smart. Sent him 9 Negroes, Vizt. 4
Men 5 Women. They belong to a person in West Indies who praises
them much & expects high prices, but in my opinion they are refuse.
Sell them to safe Men payable in January upon the best terms you
can & send me the Account soon that I may close mine.

SOURCE: Letterbook copy, Letter Book of Henry Laurens, Oct. 30,
1762–Sept. 10, 1766, Penn. Hist. Soc. This letter was copied by HL.

TO JOSEPH BROWN

[Charles Town] 21st August 1764

In answer to what he lately wrote advised him of 3 Guinea
Men being here. If he is inclined to purchase I will be surety if
required or be concerned if he desires it. His Account shall be made
soon as the House adjourns but cannot sooner for want of help.

SOURCE: Letterbook copy, Letter Book of Henry Laurens, Oct. 30,
1762–Sept. 10, 1766, Penn. Hist. Soc.; addressed "per Smart." This
letter was copied by HL.

GEORGE AUSTIN, HENRY LAURENS, & GEORGE APPLEBY VERSUS DAVID MILLER[9]

August 23, 1764

[On July 2, 1764, Robert Williams, Jr., attorney for the plaintiffs, filed suit in the court of common pleas against David Miller, planter of St. Bartholomew parish ("now or lately overseer to Mr. Josiah Perry at Horse-Savannah"), for recovery of a bond, dated September 4, 1760, in the sum of £270 currency. The case was ordered for judgment on July 14. The judgment was signed on August 23 and recorded by Dougal Campbell, clerk of the court. The judgment was reissued on October 16, 1764, and again on January 16, 1765.]

SOURCE: Judgment Rolls, 1764, No. 161A, S. C. Archives; Judgment Docket, Court of Common Pleas, Book 2 (1755–1773), p. 92, S. C. Archives.

TO MATHIAS HOLME

[Charles Town] 24th August 1764

Dear Sir,

I am indebted for your obliging Letter of the 9th April from Oporto & am glad that notwithstanding the ill luck you had of being detained here a few days extraordinary by bad weather, you had arrived at so good a Market which I think must pay your Snow a very Living Freight. If you come here again as you seem to expect I hope you will be early, so early that this will be opened by Mrs. Holmes & not by you.

I had sold Mr. Crofts George Town Lott & House at public Vendue made by Mr. Brown for Eight hundred pounds & was on the point of making Titles to it when Mr. Brown advis'd me that he had just rece'd intelligence that a Nephew of Croft's in whose favour he had made a Will & who is heir at Law was alive & resident in Virginia but expected soon into this province. This report whether true or false is of some prejudice to the good people on your side

---

[9] David Miller, Elizabeth Miller, and Mary Gould of St. Bartholomew parish were granted letters of administration on Nov. 16, 1768, to the estate of William Gould of St. Peter parish, planter, as next of kin. *SCHM*, XXXI (1930), 63, 64, 154.

under whose power I was to have conveyed the Land. If true they will not only be deprived of the benefit arising from this Sale but must think of refunding what has already been paid to them & admitting it to be groundless, it will require some time to quiet the apprehensions of the purchaser who will not pay the purchase money nor will he accept of such Title as they can make to him by me their Attorney. There is therefore an unavoidable necessity for Letting this matter lay dormant a few months which (if the Lad is living) will no doubt bring him upon the Stage. In the meantime I shall make all the enquiry in my power to find out the truth & hope to receive satisfactory Accounts by the time you land here.

We have lately had excellent Seasons for our Rice whereby the Crops are greatly refreshed and barring Hurricanes will be very large, I mean the Crops of Rice. Those of Indigo are much better too than was expected a Month or two since.

Mrs. Laurens, Jacky, Patty, & Harry are well, my once Dear Nelly is no more mine, but I must forbear. I remain with great regard for you & Yours, &ca.—

SOURCE: Letterbook copy, HL Papers, S. C. Hist. Soc.; addressed "Leverpoole"; "per Capt. McKie."

TO THOMAS MEARS
[Charles Town] 24th August 1764
Dear Sir,

I have not troubled you with a Letter since the 24th February last per Smith & Condon nor has any of your esteemed favours come to hand. In that Letter I told you that I should soon call on you for Balance of your Account but have managed my affairs so as to keep away untill now that after passing to the Credit of your Account Current £1,277.14.3 for half Net proceed of 40 Hogsheads Rum per *Austin,* Holme, & £810.11.6 for half Net proceeds of sundry, Salt, & dry Goods per said Vessel as per Account Current here inclosed I have drawn upon you for £45.15/ Sterling to the order of Capt. George McKie & for £148.3.8 Sterling to the order of Brewton & Smith, both Bills at 40 days sight, the Exchange of the former at 700 & the Latter at 721 per Cent is £1,388.12.10 Current Money which if free from error does close our Accounts to this time save only in case of any part of the large Sum that is still outstanding for goods sold on your Account proving bad in which case I am sure you will reimburse me, but I shall endeavour to avoid any call upon you on that Account.

Our Crops of Rice are in exceeding fine order just now & if bad weather does not interrupt the Harvest it will be very large & the grain early at Market, the Indigo Planters have also tolerable good prospects being greatly favoured by Latter Seasons & in general our Planters are in a state of prosperity which was pretty clearly evinced by their purchase at a Sale of Negroes this Week. There the first 230 of the Cargo averaged £41 Sterling & the whole will turn out near £40 remitted for in the bottom at 3, 6, & 9 Months.[1]

I assure you, Sir, it gives me a good deal of concern that I am disappointed of a Turtle which I had hoped to have sent you under the care of Capt. McKie. We have not had a Vessel from Providence for several Weeks past & indeed those Animals make their appearance much seldomer than in former days from whence I conjecture that our Rich Neighbours from Virginia Northward are grown more fond of them & encourage the importation more than they were wont to do before their acquaintance with those great folks which the late War introduced among them. Whenever opportunitys of purchasing and Shipping shall present I shall be sure to embrace it, but the Season is nearly over for this Year again, for unless you can Send them under the Care of some old Friend who will not grudge a Little trouble tis in vain to attempt to after this month for so long a Voyage as from hence to England the Cold nights in the Channel is more than their strength can bear unless they are warmly covered in woolen.

We have a flying report that Salt is become very dear in the West Indies & not to be had at St. Martins & Anguilla. If this be fact & you should send out the *Austin* in the usual way, you may chance to make a good Freight but you will undoubtedly have heard of this in time for your Government. I remain—

SOURCE: Letterbook copy, HL Papers, S. C. Hist. Soc.; addressed "Leverpoole"; "per Capt. McKie."

---

[1] This must be the sale of the Negroes brought by Captain Taylor in *Queen Barra.*

TO JOHN KNIGHT

[Charles Town] 24th August 1764

Dear Sir,

I herewith transmit a duplicate of my last long Letter under the 12th June per Capt. Brown to which please to be refered, & as I foresee that this will be a pretty long epistle too, I shall touch briefly upon each needful subject & endeavour to avoid tediousness.

First to reply to your sundry obliging Letters under the 20th March, 4th & 30th May, permit me to return you my thanks again for the repeated offer of the *Pococks* Cargo of Slaves. I would not forfeit your friendship for a great deal more than the Value of the whole but I will not suffer such a thought in my breast, as that you will inflict so heavy a penalty upon me for acting according to the dictates of reason & principles of generosity which now oblige me to adhere to my first resolution of not selling that Cargo. I had with your permission assigned it to Messrs. Shirly & Martin. They no doubt had fixed some dependance upon that & have talked among their friends of their expectations, after that to be disappointed I should think would not only be galling to them but might create injurious whispers from some people whose envy leads them to do mischief whenever they have opportunity. From this consideration I have told those Gentlemen again that I shall not deprive them of the benefit of that Sale & assured them of my best services in every respect to make a good one, which they have expected & were so genteel as to offer me a share of the Commission which I declined with a hint of the impropriety of making Sale of my Friends favours & that as they would have the trouble & risque attending that transaction I thought they were intitled to all the benefit arising from it & indeed I would by all means hold myself detached & independent that I may do you in case of need the more effectual service.

I am sorry that as some other of your Ships do not appear I resigned a Cargo from Bance Island this Week of which about 230 are sold at upwards of £40 Sterling & the general average will be within a few shillings of that Sum.

If Mr. Austin's *Black Joke*[2] comes here as her Cargo will not embarass me much I shall take proper Care of it & hope to render him a satisfactory Account if the Negroes are well chosen and healthy.

---

[2] The *Black Joke,* Robert Riddle, which arrived in May 1765 with 90 slaves may have been George Austin's vessel. *Gazette,* June 1, 1765.

I observe your commands for the frame of a House to be Shipped
in her to which I shall pay particular attention. I know something
of that sort of business from my own experience but I have asked
for Mr. Manigault's aid upon this occasion who will do every thing
needful to serve you therein but I believe I shall send you little or
no Cedar or Red Bay. The former is become very scarce & dear in
this Country, almost as dear as Mahogany, & Red Bay is not easily
to be had & at best is a course grained, ill coloured Wood.[3] Mahogany
is the thing by all means for your Stair case. (I believe you would
agree in opinion with me if you saw mine.) The expence is very
little more than of Cedar in the first Cost & in time it becomes
abundantly cheaper, as it is firm, durable, & gains beauty whether
you will or not with age, whereas Cedar is brittle, splintery, & without
an excess of rubbing & waxing fades & loses its colour in a very few
Years. Cypress is the best & Cheapest Wood with us for Wainscot,
but your Oak is in my judgment infinitely preferable. I have painted
one Room in my House Wasinscot colour & pattern upon a coat of
brown Plaister. It stands very well & is much admired.

I had almost forgot what should have ended the former
paragraph that I wish my Cousin George[4] would (as you say he
intended to do) write to me. It will give me a great deal of pleasure
to serve him in any of his commands & it will take off not only the
appearance of an unnecessary coolness but the imputation too of
breach of promise, or rather too long a delay in complying with his
promise.

Your intelligence of the *Hope*'s safe arrival at Oporto gave
me a most sensible pleasure. That Ship was scarcely ever out of my
thoughts after She Sailed from hence. You are happy in having (&
more so in deserving) a great many good Servants, but without
disparagement to any of them, there is none excells Capt. Dennison—
none can; for he does all that is in his power to serve you, & I was
under a good deal of anxiety upon his Account. In short he was to
me a Man condemned & with little hopes of a reprieve. May he get
safe to Leverpoole & never go to Sea in that Ship again.

---

[3] The cedar had been the principal tree found in Bermuda. As it was valuable
for shipbuilding, it was quickly exhausted. By the mid-eighteenth century the
Bermudians were searching for substitutes. Henry C. Wilkinson, *Bermuda in the
Old Empire* (London, 1950), pp. 16–17.
[4] George Austin.

I most heartily wish that the Tour you were upon when you wrote your last favour may prove beneficial to your health & delightful to the young ladies. I make a most respectful Bow to them & after assuring them of my best wishes at all times I must, merchant like, beg pardon for Entring abruptly upon business again, as I have a great deal to say & not a great deal of time to say it in.

Capt. McKie has just been with me & laid before me Messrs. Brewton & Smith's Account of Sale of the *Jenny*'s Cargo & your Account Current. The former I believe is as good as any body would have made it in this place but the mode of remittances set forth in the Latter disgusts the Captain not a little. He is much to be commended for his watchfulness of your Interest but this is the consequence always of Bargain-making. Each party thinks himself justifiable if he complies with his engagement. This the Gentlemen have certainly done in point of time and a little more, but yet as the Account would have admitted of it I should have been highly pleased with a dash of generosity. The same time they have done as much as any other House would have done in that way. The course of Exchange is certainly as they charge 721 per Cent in general. Nevertheless if they have purchased any Bills lower I think you should at least share the benefit. This is too delicate a point to be broached abruptly but at a proper Season you may depend upon it that I shall speak to them and advise you of what passes.

Please now to receive an Account Sale of the 40 Hogsheads Rum per *Austin* last Voyage the Net proceed to your Credit £1,277.14.5. Also Sale of Salt & dry Goods per ditto ½ proceed to your Credit £810.11.6 also Sale of Earthen Ware & Ale per the Ship *Hope* last Voyage left in my hands per Capt. Dennison Net proceed to your Credit £[blank] & if possible I shall put in the Sale of sundry per the *Hope* her first Voyage together with your Account Current. The Sale is finished but tis a tedious Account & requires examination which my Clerk is now about. If he does not go thro it in time for this it shall go with your Account Current in three or four days. Meantime I have taken the Liberty to pass a Bill which I know will fall into your own hands for £151.16.4 Sterling at 40 days sight to the order of Messrs. Brewton & Smith Exchange 721 per Cent, is Likewise to your Credit £1,094.12/ which will come near to our Balance & leave not much over or under when you are so good as to let me know what the Lumber per *Upton*[5] yeilded which you say is sold for its full Value. Indeed I am ashamed to think of having troubled you with such an Article. I need not expatiate on the several Accounts above mentioned but leave each Account to Speak for itself & content myself with saying that I am very sorry that all my endeavours could make them no better.

The latter End of our last vast Crop of Rice in the face of another apparently great is running off at 45/ to 47/6 & much has been as high as 50/. Our stage will be quite clear of the old by the time the new comes to Market which will be very early if we have no violent Stormes to break in upon the Harvest. If the *Austin* comes this way again I hope she will be so early as to be a first Ship at Oporto where I find the Market has been pretty good thro the Month of June & not much if any is gone since but here is one Ship now Loading for that place with 6 or 700 Barrels will Sail in 10 or 14 days.[6] I am to load a part of her with Rice belonging to Gentlemen in Bristol & myself. I endeavour'd to divert the Voyage but without effect. Therefore I shall throw as much as possible into Mr. Byrnes hands. We hear a rumor of a great scarcity of Salt in the West Indies. If it is founded in truth I shall for her owners make certain the Snow *Austin* may bring the usual Ballast.

Having now run thro all private concerns that have occured as needful to mention at this time, I must beg your patience while I detain you with an Account of a Law just passed in this province which I think is of importance to the public both on yours & this side of the Water, regarding it either as a Salutary or a pernicious Act. The Law that I mean is one that has passed three Readings in both Houses of Assembly, laying an additional Duty or Tax upon all Negroes imported into this province for the term of three Years from the 1st January 1766 of One hundred Pounds Current Money which amounts to a prohibition. You will receive with this a Copy of the Bill with some remarks upon it to which I refer. It stuck sometime with the Council or Carolina House of Lord's & would have remained there I do believe till doomsday if it had not been a necessary instrument to save appearances & take off the imputation of outragiousness in a quarrel that the two Houses are unhappily engaged in & which I fear will be attended with many disadvantages

---

[5] The ship *Upton*, Hugh Maxwell, which sailed for Liverpool on Sept. 26, 1763.
[6] The *Flora*.

to those whom we represent. As it now stands it awaits only for the Governors assent which there is no doubt of,[7] & therefore receiving it as a Law I think it my duty to apprize yourself & other Gentlemen in the African Trade of the Tenour of it as well as to trouble you with my opinion of it which I have sketched upon the Bill & under those heads I took up the time of the House both at the second & 3d readings with many arguments, which with myself were honest & of great weight, & I made some comments but we were outvoted by four voices, tho none of my arguments were answered.[8] We have only two Merchants besides Myself in the House, Mr. Benjamin Smith & Mr. Brailsford,[9] from neither of whom I rec'd any assistance. The former had said out of Doors that he was against the importation of more Negroes & he uniformly voted for the Bill. The other Gentleman who countinanced it with his voice at the Second reading, but as if his conscience & his Interest were at variance he would vote on neither side at the third, but retired when the question was going to be put. I think it necessary to say so much to you upon this occasion because if the Law is (as I apprehend it to be) unnecessary with regard to the local circumstances of the Country in which it is intended to Operate & at the same time a stroke at the Trade of his

---

[7] On Aug. 25 Bull assented to "An act for laying an additional duty upon all Negroes hereafter to be imported into this province, for the time therein mentioned, to be paid by the first purchasers of such Negroes." *S. C. Statutes,* IV, 187–188. For the quarrel between the two houses see HL to Joseph Brown, Aug. 30, 1764.

[8] Thomas Smith presented the bill on Aug. 14 for its first reading in the lower house. When it was moved on Aug. 15 that the second reading of the bill be postponed, the motion passed in the negative. HL obviously spoke in favor of the postponement. The bill, however, was read a second time and sent to the council. Christopher Gadsden and Thomas Lynch took the bill to the council where it was read the first time on Aug. 16 and the second time on Aug. 17. The bill was returned to the lower house where on Aug. 18 it was announced that the bill would be read a third time on Aug. 21. On that date in spite of HL's opposition, the bill was read a third time. On Aug. 25, Dr. John Murray took the bill to the council where, after it was examined, the governor gave his assent to it. House Journal, XXXVI (Jan. 24, 1763–Oct. 6, 1764), 231, 233, 238, 239, 242, 251, S. C. Archives; Upper House Journal, XXXI (Jan. 4, 1764–April 9, 1768), 47–49, 63, 65, S. C. Archives. When the committee of correspondence wrote on Sept. 4 to Charles Garth, the agent of S. C. in London, they sent a copy of this act and asked "that should any application be made, or endeavors used to procure a repeal of it, that you will oppose to the utmost of your power any such attempt." HL, although a member of the committee, did not sign this letter. *Documentary History of the American Revolution,* ed. R. W. Gibbes (3 vols.: New York, 1853–1857), I, 5–6. News of this law was published in the London *Daily Advertiser,* Nov. 16, 1764.

[9] Samuel Brailsford.

Majestys British Subjects, you might otherwise wonder how such a Law could pass in a Town abounding with commercial Men, but indeed as the generality of them alledge that their own respective branches of Trade are injured by the free importation of Slaves, which to me is a meer Chimera, so you may be assured very few of them were Enemies to this new & extraordinary measure. I shall forbear to add to this long Letter which has been wrote in too much haste and suffered too many interuptions to be very correct but leave what I have here offered to your disposal & conclude with assurances that I am with great respect, Dear Sir—

SOURCE: Letterbook copy, HL Papers, S. C. Hist. Soc.; addressed "Leverpoole"; "per Capt. McKie. Note only the 2 Sales per *Austin* sent per McKie. The other two & A/Current were omitted. The law sent."

TO JOSEPH BOWER

[Charles Town] 25 August 1764

Sir,

The annex'd is duplicate of what I wrote to you under 11th Inst. since which, Vizt. the 20th Inst., Capt. Doran in your Snow *New Success* arrived here & brought me your further favours of 6th & 23d June the contents of which I shall pay due regard to, by endeavouring to dispose of the goods you have Ship'd in her upon the best terms & Loading the Vessel again as nearly to your order & with as much dispatch as possible for I cannot obtain any Freight near your Limit. A Ship for London is now taking in Pitch at 32/6 per Ton. I shall write you more fully when the Snow has unloaden her inward Cargo which I shall hurry Capt. Doran to effect & meantime I remain with true respect, &ca.—

SOURCE: Letterbook copy, HL Papers, S. C. Hist. Soc.; addressed "Bristol"; "per Capt. McKie."

TO WILLIAM HUGHES[1]

[Charles Town] 28th August 1764

Sir,

Your favour of the 15th Inst. is just come to my hand and I sit down to reply to it without delay because I discover an instance of negligence on my part which should be explained as soon as possible.

I must acknowledge, Sir, that I am totally ignorant of any propositions made by me to Mr. McDonald[2] to engage your Pitch, over & above the Copy of that agreement between Mr. Potts[3] & me. I say if I made any addition to that agreement by way of proposition to you which your Letter seems to imply, the particulars have escaped my memory, which has been so much taken up for some Weeks past with public affairs that those of my own private concerns have suffered more than a few inconveniencies as I have no partner & my Clerk not very happy in his state of health, a circumstance that often interrupts his attention to business. I must therefore beg leave to refer you to a Sketch or model for an agreement which I shall here inclose. It comprehends the substance of that with Mr. Potts, and as far as tis in my power, extends to & takes in your particular purposes. If this is agreeable to you, please to cause a fair Copy to be made & to execute the same on your part & upon receipt thereof I will interchange it with and under my hand & seal.

Nothing is more evident than the disadvantage which lays on my side in this agreement. Nor would I enter into such an one for any apparent profits but with a Gentleman whose integrity & candour I absolutely confide in. Indeed I have frequently eshewed contracts of this nature; as subjects that sometimes prove stumbling blocks in the way of a friendly correspondence, tho this ought not to be, nor can it possibly happen where the parties mutually act upon principles of honour & uprightness; nevertheless it does wear something of the aspect of gaming, & for these reasons it would be more agreeable

---

[1] William Hughes, born Nov. 12, 1726, was the son of Meredith Hughes, the most important Indian trader and militia leader in the early history of the settlement on the Black River. William Hughes married Sarah Potts on June 2, 1747. *Register Book for the Parish Prince Frederick Winyaw,* pp. 4, 53; Rogers, *History of Georgetown County,* passim. In 1764 he was one of those who distributed the *Gazette* at Williamsburg. *Gazette,* Aug. 25, 1764.

[2] Perhaps John McDonald who was churchwarden in 1757 while Hughes was a vestryman. *Register Book for the Parish Prince Frederick Winyaw,* p. 146.

[3] John Potts. See HL to William Hughes, Sept. 28, 1764.

to me to engage to take all the Pitch that you should make in any giving time at the highest Market price. But if you rather approve of a contract according to my present plan, I shall hope to see some of your Pitch very soon as I am more in want of that article now than I may be through the whole Year; & in that case I hope you will fill every Barrel up to the bung & put a bung to each Cask to guard against loss which often happens to very good Pitch by careless stowage in Schooners. Also put your brand quite plain upon the bung Stave of each Cask & you may depend upon having a just account of the over weight. I am—

SOURCE: Letterbook copy, Letter Book of Henry Laurens, Oct. 30, 1762–Sept. 10, 1766, Penn. Hist. Soc.; addressed "Williamsburgh."

TO THOMAS MITCHEL[4]

[Charles Town] 29th August 1764

Dear Sir,

I most heartily congratulate you on the Marriage of your Daughter[5] a circumstance which I hope will introduce many felicitous events in the Evening of your Day.

Mr. Bell[6] whom you were so kind as to engage to throw up a

---

[4] Thomas Mitchell was a planter of the parish of Prince George Winyah. He had a son Anthony and a daughter Mary by his first marriage. His second wife, whom he married after 1751, was Esther Marion, the widow of John Allston, by whom he had six children, four of whom (Thomas, Edward, Sarah, and Elizabeth) were living at the time he wrote his will in 1767. Rogers, *History of Georgetown County*, pp. 82, 101n; *SCHM*, XLIII (1942), 142; "Will of Thomas Mitchell," dated Dec. 12, 1767, proved Jan. 11, 1768, *Abstracts of Wills, 1760–1784*, pp. 94–95.

[5] On July 19 Maurice Simons had married in Georgetown Mary Mitchell, the daughter of Thomas Mitchell by his first marriage. *Gazette*, Oct. 8, 1764. Edward Simons (1742–1775) and Maurice Simons (1744–1785) were younger sons of Benjamin Simons (1713–1772) who lived at Middleburg plantation which lay on the east side of the Eastern Branch of the Cooper River above French Quarter Creek. Benjamin Simons, the Huguenot immigrant, had built in 1699 at Middleburg a wooden house which still stands, the oldest wooden house in South Carolina. *SCHM*, XXXVII (1936), 144–145, 150; Irving, *A Day on Cooper River*, p. 154; Samuel Gaillard Stoney, *Plantations of the Carolina Low Country* (Charleston, S. C., 1955), pp. 48–49. As the second Benjamin Simons had fifteen children, his younger sons had to find their way in Charleston. Maurice and Edward Simons announced in the *Gazette*, Oct. 15, 1764, the continuation of the "Factorage Bussiness" in all its branches on Colonel Beale's wharf.

[6] Duke Bell. See HL to Duke Bell, Feb. 4, 1766.

Dam or Bank for me perform'd the Work tolerably well considering the disadvantages that he Laboured under from incessant Easterly Winds which made every days flood as high as the Spring Tides and also from Rain. In short the Elements seem'd to conspire against him & he was obliged to quit his undertaking before he had perfected it. This leads me to be troublesome to you once more to assist me with a proper hand to compleat my design of banking in the whole of my Marsh which I believe may be done with more ease & certainty in the Month of October or November than at any other time of the Year. I would chuse, if it were at my option, to pay a good price to some person to undertake & finish the whole according to a plan to be laid before him & within a Certain time with his own hands, rather than to bring my Negroes to Town again, because it is attended with some inconvenience while I plant in partnership as I do at present with Mr. Ball. Permit [me] to recommend this matter to your consideration & request your assistance therein. I have advertised for some Weeks past in Wells's *Gazette*[7] that such a Dam or Bank was wanted but have not had any application. Perhaps the people up your way may not have seen it. I remain, Dear Sir, &ca.—

SOURCE: Letterbook copy, Letter Book of Henry Laurens, Oct. 30, 1762–Sept. 10, 1766, Penn. Hist. Soc.; addressed "George Town."

TO THOMAS POTTS

[Charles Town] 29th August 1764

Sir,

I thank you for your good intentions in recommending 43 Barrels of Pitch to me the other day by George Dick, but they were quite too light for Shipping some weighed not above 270 lbs. I was therefore obliged to have the whole parcell weighed & what was under weight I sold as per Account below which I hope will prove satisfactory to the Owner as he himself nor any body else could have done better with them. I begin to be very much in want of some of your own or any other parcels of good Pitch & hope to receive some from you very soon. I remain, Sir—

---

[7] April 18, 1764, is the only issue extant for this year of Wells' *General Gazette.*

43 Barrels of Pitch Receiv'd per George Dicks Schooner 10th August 1764 from Mr. Thomas Potts at Colonel Beals Wharf.[8]

21 Sold to Mr. William Parker weighing from		
275 upwards but underweight at 60/	£ 63.	
10 ditto very light Shiped before the Cooper		
had informed of their Lack of Weight	30.	
12 ditto weight but indifferent Barrels at 10/	42.	
	———	
	£135.	
Wharfage & Weighing the whole £ 2. 3		
33 Hoops 33/. Cooperage of those		
21 Barrels sold to Mr. Parker 21/ 2.14		
Freight to George Dick at 8/6 per 18. 5.6	£ 23. 2.6	
	———	
Net proceed £111.17.6		

SOURCE: Letterbook copy, Letter Book of Henry Laurens, Oct. 30, 1762–Sept. 10, 1766, Penn. Hist. Soc.; addressed "Williamsburgh."

TO JOHN HANDLIN[9]

[Charles Town] 30th August 1764

Sir,

Mr. Perdriau has made a Mistake in sending the Negro Cloth & Green plains which you ordered to go by George Dick to Mr. William Thomson. Be so kind as to speak to Mr. Thomson about it & if he chuses to keep those articles I can send your quantity the next return of the Schooners. Otherwise you may order them to your own House. Mr. Thomson can shew you the Account of it. My compliments to your Mother & all the Family & I remain, Sir, &ca.—

SOURCE: Letterbook copy, Letter Book of Henry Laurens, Oct. 30, 1762–Sept. 10, 1766, Penn. Hist. Soc.; addressed "Black Mingo."

---

[8] The wharf of Colonel Othniel Beale where Maurice and Edward Simons had their factorage business.

[9] John Handlen was the son of Margaret and John Handlen. *HL Papers*, II, 138n.

TO WILLIAM BRUCE[1]

[Charles Town] 30th August 1764

Sir,

For some time past there seems to have been a total suspension of our correspondence whereas I had good reason to expect that you would have made some effort either by Money or goods to cancel *your very old debt.*

I think, Sir, that I have borne with you as Long as you can possibly expect I should & will be bold to say that you would have found no such forbearance as I have shewn from the Generality of Merchants & perhaps from none; & I do think that you have worn my Lenity thread bare—even abused it. I hear every now & then that one Mr. Bruce is sawing Cypress & Oak & the Lord knows what, for me. If you are the Man pray where are the Goods that you have prepared? But in short I will wait no longer than 4 Weeks more & then if you do not pay off your whole debt or give me good security for it, I must be obliged to put you to trouble and altho you could have no cause to complain of being surprised yet I cannot forbear to give you this one more notice. I remain—

SOURCE: Letterbook copy, Letter Book of Henry Laurens, Oct. 30, 1762–Sept. 10, 1766, Penn. Hist. Soc.; addressed "Black Mingo."

TO SAMUEL WRAGG

[Charles Town] 30th August 1764

Sir,

The last that I Troubled you with was by Mr. Smart in whose Schooner I sent you Nine Negroes which I hope you have sold or will sell without delay. They do not deserve & therefore I do not expect high prices for them. At the same time you will obtain the most you can, & send me the Account of your Sale. This is nearly a repetition of what I have already said and it will serve to shew you an un-usual desire to have the Account closed. The Gentlemen

---

[1] William Bruce, a carpenter, was paid £93 in 1766 for repairing the parsonage and building a stable. *Register Book for the Parish Prince Frederick Winyaw,* p. 189. When Samuel Wragg sued William Bruce in 1768, the deputy provost marshal wrote on the summons that "The Defendant is a Carpenter & lives at Black Mingo. Take good Bail." Judgment Rolls, 1768, No. 49A, S. C. Archives.

who own those Negroes are very anxious to have their Money reallized in London where probably their affairs do require a Lift & I would not subject myself (if possible to avoid it) to be called upon by them again.

I am desired by a particular friend[2] in England to procure for him a parcel of Ceder & Red Bay for inside work in some parts of a House that he is about Building. If you can therefore purchase for me a quantity of Logs of each that will saw into boards of about 10 Inches & upward I shall take it as a great favour that you will send me as soon as you can get them about 20 Logs of each. Order them to be of the very best that can be had & allow a proper price for such. The Red Bay I think should have the Barke squared off to save stowage & Labour. If you are not under any engagement for purchasing Indigo this approaching Crop & think it worth your while to buy on mine or our joint Account, be pleased to inform me & of your terms. I remain, Sir—

SOURCE: Letterbook copy, Letter Book of Henry Laurens, Oct. 30, 1762–Sept. 10, 1766, Penn. Hist. Soc.; addressed "George Town."

TO JOSEPH BROWN

[Charles Town] 30th August 1764

Dear Sir,

A very unhappy difference of opinion between our House of Lords & House of Commons respecting the Salary or gratuity (usually allowed to Governours) to be provided in or left out of the Estimate, for our present Governor Boone has, after a good deal of altercation, brought forth a proroguation, annihilated upwards of Twenty five essential Laws the existance of which depended upon the Session of the House of Assembly, created much animosity amongst People who make a Cloak of patriotism merely to hide self-Love & ambitious views, & upon the whole procured me a short respite untill the 18th September.[3]

---

[2] John Knight of Liverpool. See HL to John Knight, Aug. 24, 1764.
[3] The assembly received a message from the council on Aug. 22 which expressed surprise that the assembly had struck out the first item in the schedule, £7,000 for the governor's salary for two years. On Aug. 23 the lower house refused to restore the item. On Aug. 25 Bull prorogued the assembly until Sept. 18. The

I shall improve my time at home & amongst the first of my undertakings the Long Account between you & me shall employ my attention & I hope some day in next Week to return it to you in order to make a final end of it.

I shall be obliged to you if you conveniently can to purchase & send me Ten or Twenty of the Larges[*t*] Ceder Logs that grow in your part's as strait free from Knotts & wrents as possible & therefore I must expect to pay a proper price which I shall do with thanks.

My Ship *Flora* will Sail early in November for Bristol & will be glad of your favours if you have any Freight for that City and be so kind to speak to some of your Neighbours & you will oblige, Dear Sir, Your most humble Servant—

SOURCE: Letterbook copy, Letter Book of Henry Laurens, Oct. 30, 1762–Sept. 10, 1766, Penn. Hist. Soc.; addressed "George Town."

T O   I S A A C   D A   C O S T A[4]

[Charles Town] 31st August 1764

Sir,

I have an order from Nassau Senior, Esquire[5] to call upon

work of the assembly actually resumed on Sept. 19 and on Oct. 6, the day of adjournment, the Great Seal was affixed to the money bill but without the reinstatement of the governor's salary. House Journal, XXXVI (Jan. 24, 1763–Oct. 6, 1764), 244–247, 253–255, 271, 276, S. C. Archives. After the repeal of the Stamp Act, the Commons House of Assembly did appropriate £8,273.12.2 under "extraordinary expenses" in the Tax Act of 1766 to pay the back salary of Thomas Boone. *S. C. Statutes*, IV, 253; Jack P. Greene, "The Gadsden Election Controversy and the Revolutionary Movement in South Carolina," *Mississippi Valley Historical Review*, XLVI (1959), 489.

[4] Isaac Da Costa (spelled "De Costa" here) (1722–1783) came to Charleston from London in 1750. He began as a shopkeeper, later becoming a merchant, and after 1758 a partner of Thomas Farr, Jr. Da Costa & Farr sold two cargoes of slaves between 1760 and 1763. *SCHM*, LXV, (1964), 208. In 1764 Da Costa resigned as reader of the Congregation Beth Elohim, a position he had held since 1750. After business reversals Da Costa & Farr had to assign their goods to their creditors. *Gazette*, Aug. 3, 1765. Joseph Da Costa, merchant of St. Mary Axe, London, went bankrupt that winter. London *Daily Advertiser*, Dec. 9, 1765. Da Costa took the side of the patriots during the Revolution, was banished by the British in 1781, returned to Charleston in 1783, and died there at the age of sixty-two on Nov. 23, 1783. Barnett A. Elzas, *The Jews of South Carolina* (Philadelphia, Pa., 1905), pp. 33–37.

[5] Nassau Senior had been president of Cape Coast Castle in 1758, serving the Company of Merchants trading to Africa. In 1761 he was residing in Margaret St., Cavendish Square, London. T 70/29, pp. 136–140, 238, Public Record Office,

Messrs. De Costa & Farr for the proceed of Nine Negro Slaves Shiped on his Account per Mr. Muller of Cape Coast in the *Greyhound*, Capt. Pinnegar,[6] & which they sold. Be so kind as to inform me how that Account Stands & to whom I ought properly to apply upon this occasion whether to Mr. Farr or your self or both. Please to excuse this freedom & believe me to be, Sir, &ca.—

SOURCE: Letterbook copy, Letter Book of Henry Laurens, Oct. 30, 1762–Sept. 10, 1766, Penn. Hist. Soc.; addressed "Union Street."

TO THOMAS FARR, JR.[7]

[Charles Town] 1st September 1764

Sir,

I informed Mr. Decosta yesterday as the eldest partner of the late House of Decosta & Farr that I was directed to call upon the said House for the Net proceed of Nine Negroes rec'd by them from on board the *Greyhound,* Capt. Pinnegar, Shiped at Cape Coast by Mr. Muller on Account of Nassau Senior, Esquire.

London. Cape Coast Castle had been the headquarters of the Royal African Company. A. W. Lawrence, *Trade Castles and Forts of West Africa* (London, 1963), pp. 183–198. The editors have not been able to establish the family connection with Nassau Senior (1790–1864), the economist.

⁶ The brigantine *Greyhound,* William Pinniger, owned by Aaron Lopez of Newport and Jacob Riviera of New York, arrived Jan. 6, 1763, from Guinea. Isaac Da Costa and Thomas Farr advertised the slaves for sale on Jan. 25 at Charleston. The vessel was entered inwards on that date with 134 slaves. *Gazette,* Jan. 8, 1763; Naval Office Lists, 1757–1764, p. 116. No duties were entered as having been paid for the importation of these slaves.

⁷ Thomas Farr, Jr., was first the partner of Isaac Da Costa, 1758–1763, and then of Robert Smythe, 1763–1765. He may have been the son of Richard Farr of Bristol who was master of the Society of Merchant Venturers, 1762–1763, and mayor, 1763–1764. A Thomas Farr, Jr., had been warden of the Society of Merchant Venturers of Bristol in 1757. Wesley Savadge states that Richard Farr's son Thomas was in America from 1761 to 1765. *Bristol Lists: Municipal and Miscellaneous,* compiled by Alfred B. Beaven (Bristol, Eng., 1899), pp. 126–128, 289; Wesley Savadge, "The West Country and the American Mainland Colonies, 1763–1783, with special reference to the Merchants of Bristol" (unpub. B. Litt. thesis, Univ. of Oxford, 1952), p. 120. The fact that he was known in Charleston as Thomas Farr, Jr., would indicate that there was another Thomas Farr in Carolina at this time. The other Thomas Farr was the Stono River planter who died after May 27, 1775. "Will of Thomas Farr," dated May 27, 1775, proved ————, Charleston County Wills, XVIII (1776–1784), 224–226, S. C. Archives.

Mr. Decosta sent me a Verbal answer that he would speak to me before Sunset but I suppose something hindred him from coming abroad for I have neither seen nor heard from him since. This is his Sabbath[8] and therefore I must not obtrude business upon him on this day but as I am writing to London by a Vessel that will Sail tomorrow or on Monday, I beg the favour of you, Sir, to inform me what is the Amount of said Net proceed and what expectations I may give Mr. Senior of remitting him his Value for the same. I remain, Sir, &ca.—

SOURCE: Letterbook copy, Letter Book of Henry Laurens, Oct. 30, 1762–Sept. 10, 1766, Penn. Hist. Soc.; addressed "Charles Town."

TO JOHN RUTHERFORD

[Charles Town] 1st September 1764

Dear Sir,

I am indebted for sundry of your favours which should at this time be replyed to & other matters communicated but I have had such a pain in my head for 36 hours past that I have not been able to sit to writing & can now only hold it up to inform you that by this Snow the [blank], Capt. Brison, I forward a Brown paper Bundle & Letters in a pacquet for you. The bundle was a long time coming round by way of Georgia. If the Wind detains this Vessel till Monday which may be the Case I shall add a few Lines provided I am in better health. Meanwhile, I remain, Dear Sir, &ca.—

SOURCE: Letterbook copy, HL Papers, S. C. Hist. Soc.; addressed "Esquire. North Carolina"; "per Capt. Brison."

TO ROSS & MILL[9]

[Charles Town] 1st September 1764

Gentlemen,

Your favours of the 31st Decem. & 10th April reached me

---

[8] September 1, 1764, was a Saturday.

[9] Ross & Mill were not listed in the London directory for 1763 but were listed in 1765 and 1767 as merchants in Fenchurch St. *London Directories.* This is the first of many letters that HL wrote to this London firm which apparently

only Yesterday as they came a tedious way about in the *Suffolk,* Packet Boat.[1] I shall pay due regard to your respective signatures whenever I am called upon, but besides my good wishes I have not much to flatter you with as contributary to your success in Trade, seeing my business is now drawn within a very contracted sphere, which I shall never extend unless some Maladventures shall render it necessary for the good of my Family to bustle in commerce again & in such an event it will become my duty to bestir myself even under Gray hairs, a Badge of honour which I have not yet merited. Nevertheless I thank you Gentlemen for this opening to a correspondence; you may be assured that it shall not be slighted on my part & I beg that you will make use of me as a Friend as often as you have occasion for my services in this Quarter of the World.

Annexed you have duplicates of two Notes which I wrote Yesterday & this morning to Mr. DeCosta & Mr. Farr. This appeared to me to be the most effectual way for obtaining an answer to the enquiry made by your friend Nassau Senior, to which I have subjoined an answer from Mr. Farr. How satisfactory that answer will prove I know not, but the plea of outstanding debts for Negroes

---

was just beginning business. Gilbert Ross and James Mill, undoubtedly the partners in this firm, each received a grant of 10,000 acres in East Florida in May 1767. *Acts of Privy Council, Colonial,* v (1766–1783), 590.

[1] On Jan. 4, 1764, the Postmasters General petitioned the Lords Commissioners of the Treasury to establish packet boats on a southern route. These vessels would be run on the same plan as the New York packets but would be ten tons heavier. In the *London Gazette,* Jan. 7, 1764, the Postmasters General announced that there would be three packet boats established at Falmouth of 140 tons and 18 hands each for conveyance of mails, expresses, and passengers to Barbados, Grenada, St. Christopher, Jamaica, Pensacola, St. Augustine, Savannah, and Charleston, and back to Falmouth. The cost for each packet was £1,572.14.6 per year. The first packet would leave on Feb. 23rd, the second on April 12th, and the third on June 14th; following the first voyage mail would be dispatched once in two months or thereabouts. *Georgia Gazette,* April 19, 1764. The first packet to arrive in Charleston was the *Grenville Packet* on July 29. She sailed on Aug. 23 for Falmouth. The authorized call at Charleston was 14 days, the longest in the voyage, to permit repairs to the vessel. The *Suffolk Packet* arrived on Aug. 30 and sailed for Portsmouth on Sept. 16. *Gazette,* Oct. 8, 1764. In 1765 the Postmasters General put on two more packets so that mail could be sent out once a month. The vessels were increased from 140 tons to 170 tons as they had been found to be too light "for the dangerous navigation in Southern waters." In 1768 it was decided that the southern voyage was too long so four new vessels were requested for Falmouth to Charleston and return. In 1770 two more vessels were put on between Jamaica, Pensacola, and Charleston. The English Treasury was willing to make these large outlays to assist the commercial interests of these southern colonies. Ruth Lapham Butler, *Doctor Franklin, Postmaster General* (Garden City, N. Y., 1928), pp. 120–124.

is quite a new thing to me. This very circumstance alone is a strong proof that their Company affairs are embarrased, & how clear or firm their seperate Interests are I cannot inform you because I know nothing of them. As for the Letter which you inclosed I presume it was left open to be at my disposal & therefore I have locked it up & chosen to pursue the present method of application which I hope Mr. Senior & your good selves will approve of. I shall expostulate with Messrs. DeCosta & Farr to make a remittance immediately but if it shall become necessary for Mr. Senior to use compulsary means pray advise him to accompany his Letter of Attorney with the Bill or Bills of Loading for his property & every other essential proof in his possession or power.

Our Crops of Rice will be very Large this Year if no Hurricanes interupts the Harvest and the great demand at present for old Rice will leave a clear stage for the New. I remain with great respect, &ca.—

SOURCE: Letterbook copy, HL Papers, S. C. Hist. Soc.; addressed "London"; "per Capt. Ball. Copy per Capt. Harbison."

T O   J O H N   W I G F A L L

[Charles Town] 3d September 1764

Sir,

When I settled the Lumber Account with you in July I reminded you of near [*blank*] feet of Sheathing Boards that should have been delivered but was not & that was an Article more wanted by me than any other. Your reply was that the remains of our contract should be ready whenever I should call for it. Therefore I send Capt. Courtin to wait on you for the said Sheathing which you will be pleased to send to Hobcaw as speedily as you can & the amount I shall pay you on demand.[2]

I need not remind you of the extreme bad bargain that contract proved to me. Let it suffice that I have fully performed all that was due on my part and put myself to some trouble & inconvenience to save you from either & that all I ask for now is the completion of your part of the engagement which I am perswaded will be done without hesitation. I am, &ca.—

---

[2] The sheathing was needed for the *Flora.*

SOURCE: Letterbook copy, Letter Book of Henry Laurens, Oct. 30, 1762–Sept. 10, 1766, Penn. Hist. Soc.; addressed "Esquire. Bullhead."

TO JOHN DUTARQUE, SR.

[Charles Town] 3 September 1764

Sir,

I have an order from a friend[3] in England to send him a frame for a House according to the inclosed Bill of Scantlin, which I shall be glad to have provided by you as I shall then be sure of having the very best pine in every piece without exception, for I would have none other.

If you can supply me I beg that you will set your hands about it so that I may have the whole delivered in Charles Town by the 15th October. The quality & prices of this frame if approved of will be a means of increasing the demand for our Pine, & it will be both honourable & beneficial to supply our Mother Country with materials for building. I remain, Sir, &ca.—

SOURCE: Letterbook copy, Letter Book of Henry Laurens, Oct. 30, 1762–Sept. 10, 1766, Penn. Hist. Soc.; addressed "Cainhoy."

TO ROSSEL & GERVAIS

[Charles Town] 4th September 1764

Gentlemen,

Your several very acceptable favours of the 30th July, 10th & 26th Ulto. came duly to hand & have afforded me great pleasure, as I perceive from your Accounts that your long journey will not be quite fruitless altho' it may not be productive of all the good ends that we could wish for.

The Account you give of the Country are no more than I expected, admitting you to be Lucky in point of health which, thank God, you have been, nor are they as large as I expect to have at your return under the fume of a Friendly pipe which we can smoke here as well as your new Indian Allies.

---

[3] John Knight.

I have as yet forborn to take up our family rights of Land & shall forbear until I have the pleasure of seeing you in Charles Town. No ill consequence I think can attend this delay; & to tell you truth an impolitic & partial Act which has been for some time in agitation & is at length passed into a Law to prohibit the importation of Negroes has made me the more indifferent about that matter in the present juncture, for I am almost certain that if that Law is approved of or not repealed in Britain, Vacant Lands will abound in the Year 1767 more than they do in the Current Year.

Permit me to tell Mr. Gervais in plain Words that he is in some things a bad appologist. To excuse himself or desire to be excused for imperfection & in such Masterly Epistles too is carrying the assertion in one hand & its confutation in the other; in Short, Sirs, he writes wonderfully well, well enough I do aver for a Carolina Secretary of State at least & better by far than many a Carolina Senator, but I will not therefore say that there is no room for improvement.[4]

Under cover with this you will receive three English Letters which came to my hands lately & will I hope go to yours welcome messengers.

As to public News we have none of importance enough to trouble you with, none however that I can recollect just now & what you are deprived of at present will be the more entertaining by & by, for 'tis ten to one that you have Leisure hours sufficient in the Course of the advancing Winter to read all the News papers Imported & printed here.

Early in October or sooner if you are tired of the Country or have compleat'd the purposes of your emigration I shall hope to take you by the hand at Rattray-Green or within some Miles of it if I have previous notice of your approach & repeat the assurances of being with great regard, Gentlemen, Yours, &ca.—

SOURCE: Letterbook copy, Letter Book of Henry Laurens, Oct. 30, 1762–Sept. 10, 1766, Penn. Hist. Soc.

---

[4] Gervais may be writing his letters for the first time in English.

TO ISAAC KING

[Charles Town] 6th September 1764

Sir,

I wrote you the 10th [*Ulto.*] per Banfield[5] & Farnsworth advising of a draught in favour of Mr. William Gibbes since which I have been importuned by him to give more than three Bills to the set, appologising that he had bought them for or sold them to some other person who would not be satisfied without forwarding at least three of the Bills. There must be a good deal of caprice, and jealousy, or some unseen stratagim in this extraordinary demand. However as I rather believe it to be owing to the former I have got rid of the solicitation by adding a fourth & Fifth Bills which I should observe are for Five hundred pounds Sterling & payable at 50 days sight & if there is any design (which I do not suspect) this may enable you to guard against it. I likewise wrote to you the 18th per Capt. Farnsworth as per Copy herewith to which please to be referred.

Your sundry favours of the 13th February, 8th March, 16th April, 9th & 23d May come now before me to reply to.

I have looked over my Account Current which you transmitted in the first & make the balance in your favour £842.10.5 the articles of which appear to be right enough, except that of Interest of which I cannot be as compleat a judge untill I consider some others which must follow soon after the close of that Account or perhaps might have been with a Little pains included within it. Therefore this must rest as it stands now until I receive my Account of the present Year which I beg may be as early after your day for closing Accounts as opportunity will permit. I had laid a good foundation & was therefore in hopes of always having money in your hands & under no apprehensions of your being in advance, which in future I shall guard against. At the same time my acknowledgements are due for your kind offers which I shall remember in a proper manner upon every opening to do you service.

I have Likewise examined the Sales of Indigo Shiped by the *Union,* Strachan, in which there appears a most extraordinary loss in weight of 635 lbs. about 9 per Cent on the quantity sold of HL. That parcel was remarkably dry nor do I remember that you ever hinted the contrary. I packed it with my own hands & used no

---

[5] Capt. William Bampfield of the ship *Charles Town.*

means to moisten it, but how comes such a Loss now which was unknown upon Indigo some Six or Seven Years ago & thank God is still unknown (except where it has really been tampered with) in Bristol & Liverpoole? There must be some pilferage which you have not yet detected or some allowances of weight for price, or some other cause which is still a Secret to me, for I am sure by experience in this hot drying Climate, that well cured Indigo (as that was) will not waste quite half that proportion in one whole Year & therefore I cannot think that the loss which I sustain is merely owing to evaporation or to drying in your Warehouses. I do not say this to lay any imputation upon you. No, by no means, but the loss is uncommon. I feel is sensibly & I complain in hopes of warding off the like in future. The Loss upon the Indigo ALA is very extraordinary too. That was made up chiefly of John Stanyarnes Crop, always as dry as Indigo can possibly be & both parcels were Shiped after they had stood here a whole Winter drying & curing. Tricks of this sort are played by the dealers in Pitch who *amuse you* with crying that *the Weight of a Barrel is owing to the quantity of Dross in it*. The assertion carries its confutation with it, for what Dross is so heavy as solid Pitch, surely not chips, sand, and Pine Leaves which are always the Dross found in our Pitch? The weight of a Barrel of pitch is owing to the contents of the Barrel & to the quantity of pitch put into it. The standard content is 31½ Gallons which if filled up will be about ⅛ of a Ton but the makers are careless. Some make their Barrels smaller & others Larger up to 34 or 36 Gallons. Again some careful Merchants Ship Pitch just in the order that it comes to Town wanting perhaps 6 Inches of being full. Others less mindful of their Interest will cause every Barrel to be filled up to the bung. The Causes of difference in weight in these Cases is too obvious to require a Note upon it, but this is a fact not to be denied that if you divide a parcel of pitch weighing in Average 360 lbs. Grose per Barrell or thereabouts when Shiped send one half to Bristol and the other half to London the former will hold its weight & produce a full Credit in your Account Sale & the latter will fall short at least 15 per Cent often 20. Take a Barrel of Pitch of the above given weight in Carolina carry it to London, Weigh it at a Grocers Scales & it will still weigh 360 lbs. a pound or two more or less. Suppose that one Barrel to be Multiplied into 500, & sold in the ordinary way in that City & it will yield no more than about 310 or 315 lbs. Grose. Purchase the very same barrel & transport it instantly to Poole & it will there be as ponderous as it was in Carolina. This difference may be owing to Local custom as well as to the beneficial *Labours* of the London Pitch Dealers in their proper *Vocation,* & if so it must be submitted to by those who traffick with them & on their part a proper price must be and generally is paid where if no amendments can be obtained each party must rest satisfied; but they should not attempt to talk us out of our senses. From hence I begin to apprehend that Indigo is sinking into the like subjection. Indulge me with one question more & I shall dissmiss this subject. How comes it that I paid Freight on the above cases upon 248 lbs. weight of Indigo more than it appears by your Sale I was possessed of? This is also new.

I am very sorry too that Mr. Brown was so largely concerned in the purchase of Indigo last Year and rather the more because I was concerned with him in too great a part of what he bought. You say that per Barnes was very indifferent. I believe it was. I thought so before it was Shiped, I told him so, but he either was not or affected not to be of the same opinion. If those purchases made wholly on his own Account (of which you only can judge) were as injudiciously performed as those on our joint Account he will be too great a sufferer. You are pleased at my escape from the purchase of Mr. Stanyarnes Indigo last Year, but how so when he assures me that he is a gainer by Shipping it on his own Account & he is a Man full of honesty & candour.

The looking Glasses which you sent me per Gunn were truly elegant & worthy a place in my dining Room occupied by a Merchant. Their fault with me I wrote last about them was their fineness. They are too fine, I will rather say too large for my dining Room. I had then seen, but one of them, Vizt. the Peer or the Chimney Glass. But now that I have opened all the Cases much greater faults appear than I was aware of, all the Carved work & gilded ornaments by bad gluing or moisture at Sea is come off & what is worse (I mean of the two Sconces) by exceeding bad and careless Package the Paste Board back was squeezed so near as to take the Quick Silvering off in several places which the packer or the Workman ought really to be answerable for. I shall return those two in the Ship *Queen of Barra,* Capt. Taylor, to be exchanged for two somewhat smaller.

I have now my eye upon that part of your favor of 23d May in which you tell me of Mr. Poyas's application to you & of the reasons for refering or transfering his order, &ca. unto his old correspondents, namely that you should insist upon his entering into such a Bond, as those Gentlemen had proposed to him, & which proposition or demand was the only cause of his retiring from them, that therefore the same impediment would remain in his way, upon which you are pleased to ask for my sentiments. Upon this subject I shall give you my opinion with great candour and in as few words as the subject can be contained in. And first, for Mr. Poyas himself, I do think that you did not treat his addresses with that delicacy that they were intitled to, & that the Punctilio which you pursued with Messrs. John Beswicke & Company wears two aspects, one of which looks fully to the establishment of a point for your selves, & savours too much of combination. I know he views it & feels it in this Light & sense & that your conduct has mortified him more than a Little. This I say is his & I am morally certain would be the construction or interpretation of every impartial Man who should give his voice upon the occasion.

What more relates to him let him say for himself. I will go on to tell you what I think of the Demand & of the Bonds demanded from our poor, Necessitous Merchants of this Town.

The demand in itself is an unjust innovation upon Trade & an Affront to the Character of a Merchant. It is an innovation because such a demand has been unusual, is uncustomary, and was not made upon your Carolina debtors at the commencement of their correspondence nor will be made even now, upon any Man whose circumstances puts him one step above dependance and further because it is made at a time when the necessities of some among the number may compel them to submit to terms which they would have disdained when they were out of debt. This may not be exactly the case between you & Mr. Poyas but it will hold good with respect to the generality of the Importing Retailers in Carolina.

It is an unjust innovation because the Carolina Agents or Factors to a Man have sustained as few Losses by their Trade to this Colony as have been felt or known in any trade whatever to America & also because they have in general & almost to a Man by means of their Commissions & profits arising from such Trade, risen from humble & moderate Fortunes to great affluence, from walking upon foot to the command of Conveniencies which render their Legs & feet almost useless. These are Facts very notorious & upon which I need not enlarge. It is an affront to the Character of a Merchant, because every Merchant ought to be a Man of strict Honour & every Man of strict honour must receive it as an affront, from any one of his Creditors who should ask him without some extraordinary reason to give him a preference to all or to a Majority of his other Creditors. So much for the demand.

As to the Obligation demanded it carries (I do acknowledge) a specious face of equity almost through it, but it is nevertheless big with dangerous effects to the poor Bonds Man & puts more power into the hands of the Obligor than a Man ought to trust himself or another with & more than is intended to be countenanced by the Laws of the Land. The engagement to pay in London & with Interest, &ca. seems at first view to be all very fair & may be consistent with Late practice, tho by the by, the modern mode of calculations & accumulations of Interest & Interest upon Interest is Illegal & not quite so equitable niether, for every sum should be at use a full Year before the Stipulated Use or premium for a Year should be demanded or paid, but to pass over this & come to the power of "Demanding and Recovering your money due in this Country, *or any part of it,* whenever it shall be *necessary*" together with all the Unlimitted & indefinite additions of Commissions, Interest, & other reasonable charges as shall fully indempnify you, not only from the Loss but also from the *disadvantage* of receiving the same in America & moreover (as if the Bonds were too weak before) shall be also fully sufficient to put you in the same state & condition as if the same had been duly paid in London of which you the demandants are also to be the judges.

Alas, Sir, is not this taking too much power into your own hands? Is not the advantage of proving your debts upon Oath before the Lord Mayor of London which is to be received in our American Courts as ample Testimonials of the Sums due to you without canvassing of Books & examination of Witnesses, enough? Must you also bind the Estates of many in this Province to secure the debts which you claim from a few. I could put several cases that would further prove the danger of Entering into such Bonds, & shew how easily a Man might be ruined thereby but enough is already said to shew you my sentiments, & you must have penetrated into the nature & tendency of every case that can be put, before you were pleased to appeal to me on this subject. Let me therefore proceed and repeat, that I believe you will find no Man who is above dependance that will (in good earnest) acquiesce in your demands & add that you yourselves would not do so if you were in the situation of your debtors. That the few necessitous ones that must submit, will ascribe it to a just cause, & look upon it as so great a hardship that they will never think you intitled to an equality with more generous Creditors, if at any time they should find themselves on the verge of Bankruptcy & will if they can, slight you accordingly; (but here say you we shall have our Agents upon the Spot & a Judgement shall be the Associate of the Bond after a few months delinquency or upon the least appearance of a Failure. There lays one of the very dreadful Shelves that I would point at, a Man is not only to be within your power but exposed also to the Caprice or Ill nature of some body here too who may imprudently sap his Credit by foolish or malicious whispers & at length blast it for some imaginary slight). Further that people on this side of the Water will of course take every method in their power to gain an advantage over you which will be very natural after the example that you shall have set them, & that you will find in the end, that no benefit will result to yourselves from such an unprecedented & very extraordinary attempt to fortify & hedge in your debt in Carolina. For my own part I frankly declare that whenever I know of a House having intered into such Bonds I will not Credit that House but by the day, without some permanent Security or some Obligation a Little more coercive than that given to you, for why should I? At the same time some two or three good Houses may possibly out of mere compliment to you and by way of Leading on others comply with your demands, but I trust not. I hope none will pay you a compliment at so great an expence that may in the end prove the ruin of some of his Neighbours & not a Little injure the reputation of our Traders in general. I know that I would not, I know that I refused to execute a bond of this sort Sixteen years ago & the more strenuously when I was soothed with declarations that the request (not demand) was made to me in hopes that from my example other people would the more readily be perswaded to do the same.

You may reply, & I am sure you may very justly reply that you have no such deep designs, no such destructive views as I seem to apprehend. Granted you have not, I believe you to be too honest, generous, humane but (speaking as one of your debtors) what have I to do with your designs or your present intentions?

As a prudent Man it becomes me to guard against every evil tendency, every dangerous consequence that may lay hidden & at present unseen under your demands, or why should I by vesting you with an unreasonable *power* tempt you or your Heirs to Acts that would tarnish those bright Characteristics? You will not say now that I have not been full enough in giving my opinions. You were pleased to ask for them & such as they are you are welcome to them. I am not confident of being altogether in the right but I am very much so, of my honesty and disinterestedness upon the Subject matter & also of my regard for those before whom my thoughts are Laid. However I have not done yet & must beg your patience for a few words more. You say you are determined to give up the dry goods *Trade intirely* rather than continue it without such obligations. Why so? Have you lost by that Trade to Carolina in general, or have you a clear view of Entering into any other that is totally exempt from danger of Losses? I dare give an Answer for you that neither one nor the other is the Case.

It may be that you have lost or are in danger of Loosing by some individual of your Correspondents here, but be not therefore disgusted with the whole body. Reflect a Little upon times past & particularly recollect whether you have not Staked your Credit I had almost said Wantonly for persons against whom you have been warned. If this be the truth of the case, proceed with more circum-spection in future, know your Men, both the recommenders & rec-ommended, & take not everyone by the hand who makes his Exit from Charles Town where with great difficulty he might have ob-tained Credit for One hundred Barrels of Rice, & his appearance in your Counter where you eagerly give him or procure for him a Credit for the Value of Five Thousand, lest one of these days you find yourselves catching at a Shadow & loosing the substance. At the same time I would observe here that Mens Characters for Integrity & the hands of Fortune, Industry, & frugality are often & indeed always more to be esteemed & should intitle a Man to Confidence & trust more than a Little ready money where those essential ingredients are deficient. Now, Sir, I have done & I beg you will receive this as it is intended the offering of one who has uniformly preserved a friendship for your House & tho his services have been very small they have always been chearfully performed, of one who wishes you well & who upon all occasions professes himself to be with great regard, Sir, Yours, &ca.—

Post Script. 10th September 1764. Since writing as above I have had occasion to write to our friends Messrs. Cowles & Harford upon the Subject of a Large debt due to them in this Country & I beg leave to trouble you with an extract of my Letter which will further shew you my sentiments upon the manner in which Sterling Accounts ought to be paid, Vizt. "but I hope you have some written promise from him, & from everybody else that you are in advance for to allow you Interest upon the Sums advanced. I do not know that you will ever be in advance for me nor is it my design to put you to any such trouble, but to guard against accident in case I shall at any time fall in your debt, be pleased to receive this Voluntary promise as obligatory upon myself, my Heirs, & Executors—That for any & all such sums of Money as you may or shall hereafter advance by my direction I will allow you thereon the customary Interest of five per cent per Annum & also make good & pay in Bristol such sum & Sums or the Balance of my Account in Sterling Money. This I think you ought for your own sakes to exact from each of your debtors & that they should chearfully comply with your demand." Which extract of my Letter to Messrs. Cowles & Harford may be applied by Mrs. Sarah Nickleson & Company to any future Account between them & me in case it shall so fall out that they are or shall be in advance for their most humble Servant.

SOURCE: Letterbook copy, HL Papers, S. C. Hist. Soc.; addressed "for Mrs. Sarah Nickleson & Company, London"; "per Capt. Ball."

TO THOMAS AUBREY

[Charles Town] 6th September 1764

Sir,

I am indebted for your favour of the 2d July per Capt. Rogers[6] who did return to Augustine notwithstanding his doubt but

---

[6] James Rodgers of the schooner *Tybee*.

I omitted to write or send by him what you had wrote for, for which I ask your pardon.

The goods which I received from England & sent you by Rogers were not chargeable with any Freight here. I suppose Mr. Carter[7] paid the Freight in London nor is there any other charge upon them.

I have put on board this bearer the Schooner [Mary], Capt. Adam Bachop,[8] One Quarter Cask of best old Barbadoes Rum Value to your Debit as below. I hope it will reach you in good order because I think Bachops care may be depended upon.

If you can be of any service to Dennis Rolle, Esquire[9] who goes passenger in this Vessel, I beg that you will, & charge the obligation upon, &ca.—

SOURCE: Letterbook copy, HL Papers, S. C. Hist. Soc.; addressed "Esquire. St. Augustine"; "per Capt. Bachop."

TO GEORGE RICHARD CARTER

[Charles Town] 7th September 1764

Sir,

I am indebted for your favour of the 16th April which inclosed a Bill of Loading for two Cases per the *Union,* Capt. Smith,

---

[7] George Richard Carter of Chilton in Buckinghamshire and of Warlies in Essex, married Juliana Spilman, the daughter of a director of the Bank of England. Their elder daughter married Sir John Aubrey, baronet. K. C. Newton, county archivist, Essex Record Office, to the editor, June 30, 1971. Carter resided in Conduit St., London, at the time he was a member of the Society for the Encouragement of Arts, Manufactures, and Commerce, 1758–1761. Subscription Book, 1754–1763, Royal Society of Arts, London.

[8] The schooner *Mary,* Adam Bachop, sailed for St. Augustine on Sept. 7. *Gazette,* Oct. 8, 1764.

[9] Denys Rolle (1725?–1797) had arrived on Aug. 10 in the *Two Friends,* Ball, from London. *Gazette,* Oct. 8, 1764. He was a member of the House of Commons for Barnstaple in Devon, 1761–1774. In May 1764 he had received a grant of 20,000 acres in East Florida provided he settled 200 persons in 10 years. On June 10 he had embarked with 14 settlers for Charleston. This was the beginning of an ill-fated attempt to settle Rollestown on the St. Johns River about a mile from the present-day town of San Mateo. Namier & Brooke, *The House of Commons, 1754–1790,* III, 371–373; Mowat, *East Florida,* pp. 50–51, 60–61, 71; "Denys Rolle and Rollestown, a Pioneer for Utopia," *Florida Historical Quarterly,* VII (1928), 115–134.

from London directed to Mr. Thomas Aubrey at St. Augustine and consigned to my care.

I rece'd the said Cases & forwarded them the day after they were Landed here the latter end of June & I have rece'd a Letter from Mr. Aubrey acknowledging that they were delivered in good order to him.

Your Nephew,[1] Sir, brought me a Letter from Messrs. Richard Oswald & Co. which commanded my best services upon his first arrival in Carolina & I am under no doubt that his own merit will make it honourable to me to correspond with him in future. I am with great regard, Sir, &ca.—

SOURCE: Letterbook copy, HL Papers, S. C. Hist. Soc.; addressed "Esquire. at Warlies near Watham Abby, Essex"; "per Capt. Harbison. Copy per Capt. Ball."

TO EDWARD NEUFVILLE

[Charles Town] 7th September 1764

Sir,

I thank you for your favour of the 8th November & for the offers of your services in Bristol where you inform me you intend to fix yourself in business.

My commercial concerns are drawn within a very narrow Compass & such consignments as I now make are hardly worth any body's notice but such as they are they ought to, & must, go where you know my connexion has been for a great many years & where gratitude, as I have always been well used, will oblige me to continue it. Nevertheless I do most heartily give you my good wishes & you may be assured that if a proper opportunity shall present I will embrace it, to contribute to your prosperity.

If you have Leisure to advise me of the State of the European Markets you may depend upon suitable returns & perhaps such a correspondence may produce a more beneficial one in time. I remain with great regard, &ca.—

SOURCE: Letterbook copy, HL Papers, S. C. Hist. Soc.; addressed "Bristol"; "per Capt. Harbison. Copy per Capt. Gullan."

---

[1] Thomas Aubrey.

TO COWLES & HARFORD

[Charles Town] 7 September 1764

Gentlemen,

I advised you the 18th Ulto. per Capt. Farnsworth of a draught on you for £150 Sterling at 40 days sight to the order of Mr. Joseph Baird since which I have passed another Bill, Vizt. the 24th, to the order of Messrs. Brewton & Smith for £200 at the same sight. I come now to acknowledge your favours of the 30th May & 22d June & to advise of some of our Affairs which I have too much neglected by some late conveyances, but the neglect was unavoidable & I hope will be attended with no bad effects.

The several Accounts that you have transmitted seem to be right but I have not examined them minutely nor have I made out your Account Current. Both shall be done very soon.

All that I can say in Answer to your Advices about the Ship *Flora* is that she has not had a Lucky beginning but she is a good Vessel & I hope will in time yield us satisfaction. The Tyles & Empty Bottles that you Shiped in her had much better been left at Bristol. The former Article is a very dull one, almost all those that Capt. Brownett[2] left here are still upon hand altho I have offered them at about prime Cost. There are a great many in Town & there is no Forcing a Sale for them with any but our Bricklayers, one of whom had the modesty to offer me £50 per thousand one with another and smiled at me for refusing it. Every body knows that I have them & some will send for them when they are in want but it may be two or three Years before they are all sold. The Bottles are very troublesome & really will not pay for the detention of the Ship which I think was at least four days to take them out but they are selling off daily.

Now for the Ship: She arrived here in a very leaky condition on the 8th Ulto. & by successive Rainy days was detained at the Wharf to unload her untill the 25th & then there was an absolute necessity according to Capt. Courtins report to heave her down & new Caulk her, the first Oakum being Caulked in the Winter were observed out of many seams so that the Pumps even in the Harbour were kept going almost continually & tis really a Wonder how the Ship got here if Courtin's Account be genuine which no doubt it is. When the Ship arrived I had for a foundation of her Load about

---

[2] Capt. Edward Brownett of the *Favourite*.

five hundred Barrels of Pitch & Tar, I should say 330 Barrels having just before Shiped 171 Barrels on board the *Sally* as you shall hear presently. I had also an offer made of 45/ per ton for one half of her Load to Oporto & also load the other half on the Owners Account which I accepted of provided the Ship could be got ready in any tolerable time & had purchased 140 Barrels of Rice towards our moiety to make dispatch. Meantime another Ship sets up for Oporto at 40/ per Ton[3] & the *Flora* lying so Long at the Wharf the probability at this quarter of the Year of her being also detained at Hobcaw together with the Lowness of freight both to Bristol & Oporto as well as the consideration that if both Ships went to the latter we should probably suffer greatly at this late Season by the Sale of our half of the Cargo, I say these several considerations induced me rather to Ship our effects in other bottoms upon low terms & keep the *Flora* for the first of the New Crop which will make no more difference in time than Six Weeks at the very most for with our utmost dispatch she could not have been got away before the middle perhaps latter end of this Month & unless some cross accidents betide us again I shall have her Loaded & away early in November as early as I can pick up a Little New Rice & prevail on my friends to Ship Skins & Indigo. In the meantime that necessary work of Sheathing her will be performed & is to be done as cheap as in London & will come the Cheaper to us by all the expence of heaving down, Caulking, &ca. which must have been done at all events & now will be included in the Sheathing Account. I expect to have her ready to take in goods by the 1st October & shall go on to load her as good parcels of Pitch come to my hands & I expect a Large quantity in this & the next Month & as I go on solicit for the Freight of Light goods & then with the earliest of the New Rice dispatch her in November. This I say is my present plan but circumstances unforeseen may cause me to change it of which in such case I shall give you timely notice. Meanwhile please to Insure on her Bottom for my 4th £1,200, say Twelve hundred pounds Sterling at & from this port to Bristol & upon Goods on my Account Three hundred pounds Sterling that I may not have the whole Harbour risque upon myself, & if her Voyage for any good reason shall be altered you shall be informed in time to Stay the Tenour of the Policy.

---

[3] The *Pensacola Packet,* Nicholas Jackson.

Of the 500 Barrels of Pitch & Tar to be provided on our joint Account, I have Shiped 171 Barrels of Pitch on board the *Sally,* Capt. Gullan, for Bristol & 262 Barrels Pitch & 65 of Green Tar (& sold here) on board the *True Briton,* Capt. Harbison. Both will Sail next Week & I shall run the risque of my share in both, but I have on board the *Sally* a more valuable article on my own Account in which I request you to Insure as much as will net me in case of Loss Three hundred & Sixty Guineas, Vizt. on one half a quantity of exceeding fine Mahogany. I had bought the whole but Mr. Brewton prevailed on me to spare him one half which I would not do without his promise that you should sell the whole which he has so far made as to write to the Gentlemen for whose Account he purchased it that Was his agreement & I shall be very sorry to hear of a disappointment of my wishes herein. The Rice that I provided, Vizt. about 140 Barrels for the *Flora,* is partly Shiped on board a very fine Bermuda built Ship, The *Pansacola Packet,* Capt. Jackson, for Oporto at 40/ per Ton. The remains will either be Shiped or sold at the price it Cost. Please to Insure on my ¾ths One Hundred pounds Sterling. The Vessel will Sail in Six or Eight days.

Now to return to the Subject matter of your Letters, I heartily thank you for the honour you have paid to my draughts & your kind offers to advance for me in case of need but 'tis not my design to put any of my friends to that sort of inconvenience, at least not without having first Large effects in their hands. The explanation you make is quite unnecessary about the Sales of the Bounty Bills for Naval Stores sold by you last Year & I wish I had held my peace rather than have caused you so much trouble. The discount I said was paying a high Interest for money it certainly is so, but if you had said in answer to it, that you thought there was no great difference between such discount and the disadvantage of laying out of my money a long time, it would have been sufficient for me. I take the liberty to speak my mind but I do not mean to censure or to make you uneasy. I have a Bounty or Navy Bill & more than one laying in Mrs. Nickleson's hands & would always rather take my chance of being paid sooner or later than discount more than 18 Months Interest, for you must know that tho I am exceedingly sorry to hear of your public feuds in Britain, yet the reports of them make no impression upon my mind as to the rise or fall of public Credit. These are effected by cunning Men who make these the Instruments to work their wicked purposes of cozening the Simple & the Honest, but I have observed in my short experience that all those Court broils as well as in these diminutive States in America (where we are very apt to Ape great folks in every thing that makes a sound or a shew) as in the Mother Country subside as soon as the patriotic party have seated themselves in the Chairs of the old Ministry, where they soon become Ministers too & then the play begins again.

The last thing that I have to take notice of is the Letter of Attorney that you have sent as you say in order to recover any debt that may be due to you in Carolina which shall be too long standing or may appear to be dubious, but you point out at present only the House of McQueen & Gordon who I perceive & am really very sorry to see it are Largely indebted to you. Dear Sirs, I think my capital nearly as large or perhaps equal to theirs & yet I should be both afraid & ashamed to ask for so large an advance & 'tis not impossible but you have sums here in a still more precarious situation. You may be assured of my utmost endeavours to serve you whenever you shall be pleased to require it. Upon the present occasion I must observe to you that Mr. Gordon has been some Months absent on a Voyage & Journies to the Floridas & his return is uncertain, else I think it will be most for your advantage so I shall untill I hear from you again conceal from him the knowledge of my having your power to call upon him, (unless some unforeseen circumstance shall make a disclosure of it necessary). Meantime permit me to recommend to you to write to him your inclination & desire that he should adjust & close his Accounts with me on your behalf & intimate that you have wrote to me to that effect, & his retiring or seeming to retire from business, his long absence from Charles Town, & longer omission of writing to you, will conspire to furnish you with arguments that must be void of offence & then I shall pursue your directions or Act as shall appear most for your Interest if you leave such an opening to me. Mr. Gordon I believe to be a Man of Honour & hope that upon reflection he will do every thing that becomes an honest Man but perhaps a hasty demand by the Mouth of an Attorney might occasion a disgust & represent things in such a Light as to make him avail himself of every plausible argument to escape the payment of Interest & therefore I think these few Months untill I have your further orders will prove to be no more than a prudent delay. But, by the by, I hope you have some written promise from him & from everybody else that you are in advance for to allow you Interest for such advance. I do not know that you will ever be in advance for me nor is it my design to put you to any such trouble, but to guard against accidents in case I shall at any time fall in your debt be pleased to receive this promise as obligatory upon myself, my Heirs, & Executors, That for any & all Sums of Money that you may hereafter advance by my direction, I shall allow you thereon the Customary Interest of five per Cent per Annum & also make good such sum & Sums or the Balance of my Accounts in Sterling Money to be paid in Bristol. This I think you ought for your own sakes to exact from each of your debtors & that they should chearfully comply with your demands.

I am Shipping a parcel of excellent Mahogany on board the Ship *Queen of Barra,* Alexander Taylor, Master for London will probably Sail in this Month & be little more than as a Set of Ballast. Be pleased to Insure on my Account Three hundred pounds Sterling on the said Wood which may be taken at as Low a premium as is given upon any goods not Liable to damage by Salt Water.

I have now wrote you a very Long Letter & as no more business occurs to my thoughts I shall take my leave for the present assuring you that I remain with great regard, Gentlemen, &ca.—

SOURCE: Letterbook copy, HL Papers, S. C. Hist. Soc.; addressed "Bristol"; "per Capt. Ball. Copy per Capt. Bull."

TO COWLES & HARFORD

[Charles Town] 10th September 1764

Gentlemen,

I refer you to a Long Letter under the 7th Inst. per Capt. Ball & duplicate accompanying the present. Please to receive inclosed Invoice & Bill of Loading for 262 Barrels Pitch & 65 Barrels Green Tar both exceeding good quality with Certificates to recover the bounty on the same per this Snow the *True Briton,* John Harbinson, Master for Bristol ¼th on yours & ¾th on my Account, being part of the provision for our Ship *Flora* & your Account will be debited for one quarter of the Amount £1,355.8.4. The goods are high but I think the Freight is Low in proportion & I hope to do somewhat better with our own.

I must trouble you again tomorrow per Capt. Gullan & therefore shall only add to this that I remain with great respect, Gentlemen, &ca.——

SOURCE: Letterbook copy, HL Papers, S. C. Hist. Soc.; addressed "Bristol"; "per Capt. Harbinson. Copy per Capt. Gullan, Abstract Invoice & Bill of Loading."

TO DAY & WELCH

[Charles Town] 10th September 1764

Gentlemen,

With your favour of the 23d June per the *Manchester,* Capt. Livingston, I receiv'd fifteen Negroes, Vizt. seven Males & Eight females, which came in most wretched plight. They were in general Aged, some quite Grey, others maim'd but you know better than I do what they were when they were Shiped at St. Kitts, & you may imagine how much they were improved by a long Voyage & very short provision, for the Capt. of the *Manchester* alledged that the provision you had laid in was exhausted in a few days & that he had spared to them as much as he could of his own for which he made a small charge in addition to his Freight.

Such Negroes as those will not sell here upon the best terms nor can it be expected. I think I have been exceedingly Lucky in what is already done & I hope soon to close the Sales & transmit to You, Vizt. I have sold Three Men & three Women at £280 per head & one Boy very ill made at £262.10/ the whole to be paid in a few days or Weeks. But the first lot gave such dissatisfaction to the purchaser after viewing them deliberately at home that he return'd or rather attempted to return two of them upon my hands & I declare upon my Honor if I had been dealing for myself I would have receiv'd them but I did not think myself at liberty to use the same freedom with your Interest. However it will still occasion me some trouble & perhaps the loss of an acquaintance merely because he has made a bad bargain for I practice no artifice.

As to the other eight I could not get them off here at any rate, at any tolerable rate. One of them is deaf & dumb & truly they all seem to be proper subjects for an Alms House. I have sent them a little way in the Country where I think there is a better chance of

Selling them than here & I expect an Account of the Sale every day for it can answer no good end to keep such goods upon hand, & thereupon I have given proper orders to end the Sale without much delay & you may depend upon it that I shall forward your Money into the hands of Messrs. Nisbett as speedily as possible to whome I have wrote upon this Occasion & given them reason to expect a remittance from me on your Account.

Negroes have sold extremely high even to an Average of £40 Sterling for a Cargo of 320, & £36 for another of about the same number but inferior in Quality, & I do believe that prime Negroes will yield a great price thro the ensuing Winter but refuse Slaves will not yield any satisfaction. I am, &ca.—

SOURCE: Letterbook copy, HL Papers, S. C. Hist. Soc.; addressed "St. Kitts"; "per Capt. Stafford Dickenson. Copy per Capt. Emery."

TO COWLES & HARFORD

[Charles Town] 11th September 1764

Gentlemen,

I wrote you yesterday per Capt. Harbinson as per duplicate annexed to which I beg leave to refer. In all my late Letters I have forgot to make a complaint to you which there is too much room for of the Oznabrug that you Shiped on my Account per the *Susannah,* Capt. Green. It is very bad indeed, so bad that I would not chuse to have it at any price because I never deal in goods of such quality. There is no satisfaction results from the Sale of such & indeed I have so used myself to buy & sell the best only that it is become repugnant to me to offer a bad commodity for Sale & when any such falls unavoidably to my Lot I hurry them away to Public Vendue where purchasers may judge for themselves & give according to their own Judgement & that I foresee must be the Channel for the Sale of this abominable stuff called or miscalled Oznabrug. I sold one Bale of it not inspecting the quality & sent it 45 Miles by Water to a Worthy friend, who in a few days returned it, a circumstance that vexed me a good deal. I had charges to pay & a Long appology to make which with every body might not have excused me. I have opened another Bale & it is equally bad. Besides this, several pieces in each Bale is damaged which have quite the appearance of damage received before the bales were Shipped & I do believe that to be really the Case with these & many other goods from Bristol. I have offered this Oznabrug for Sale at prime Cost & cant obtain it. Indeed its quality suffers greatly by comparison with the cost which is uncommonly high. Upon further inspection I find all four Bales are alike. I can hardly think that you ever saw this parcel, but please in future if I should trouble you to send me any more goods, to make it a rule to purchase none of a bad or ordinary quality on my Account.

Inclosed you have Bill of Loading, Invoice, & Certificate for 171 Barrels of Pitch per this bearer the *Sally*, Capt. Gullan, part of the provision made for our Ship *Flora*, ¼th amounting to £639.16.10 is to the Debit of your Account, the other ¾ths on my own. I never saw the quality of this Pitch. It was purchased for me in the Country & being in a Boat of my own I caused her to put it directly on board the *Sally* three or four Miles up the River where I sent a Cooper to attend it & saved the Wharfage, porterage, & pillferage. I am told that it is in general very good, heavy, & filled up & hope it will prove to your satisfaction & our advantage.

Please likewise to receive Invoice & Bill of Loading on my seperate Account for one undivided Moiety of 197 Logs & square blocks of Mahogany on board the said *Sally*. The other half is on Account of Mr. Deane of your City to whom Messrs. Brewton & Smith assured me they have wrote in pressing terms to let the whole fall into your hands for Sale & I hope that Gentleman will have no objection to it, for let it be a good or a bad bargain I spared it in a Neighbourly way to oblige Mr. Brewton (tho he half attempted to extort it in on Account of giving me room to Ship the other half but I convinced him that I could Ship it upon the same terms to London & have Shiped one parcel but I chose to have some at each Market). I would not have done so if I had not been pretty well assured that my intended consignment should not be altered. The Mahogany I am assured by our best judges is as good as ever was Shiped & I have seen a Letter from one of the concerned in it at Jamaica to their Factor here to purchase the whole on his Account at Three pounds Sterling per hundred feet & to Ship it for London at 1½ or 2d per foot besides which he would have had commission & charges to pay. It cost me as you see only £20 Currency and charges & the measure is so advantagiously made that I cannot doubt of its yielding the full contents per Invoice & even hope for some gain in Bristol (tho none in London). The Freight is settled as noted on the Bill of Loading which I think leaves no opening for dispute & to avoid all occasion I have inserted the Freight to be on the quantity that you shall Sell in Bristol which I really believe to be greater than that paid for here & will in that case come to a trifle more than Three farthings per foot.

You say nothing about Dear Skins nor Indigo from whence I must conclude that you have nothing to say about them & yet I find people eagerly catching at one and bespeaking the first offers of the other when it shall come to Market.

We have a pretty good Season for Harvest which keeps up our prospect of a very Large Crop of Rice. I remain with great regard, &ca.—

SOURCE: Letterbook copy, HL Papers, S. C. Hist. Soc.; addressed "Bristol"; "per Capt. Gullan. Copy per Harbison with Abstract of Invoices & Bills of Loading."

TO SMITH & BAILLIES

[Charles Town] 11th September 1764

Gentlemen,

As it is uncertain whether this Sloop will touch at St. Kitts or not I shall confine myself at present only to two subjects and write you more fully per next oportunity.

I have remitted to Messrs. Boyds on your Account £500 Sterling & assigned them such reasons for not sending another sum equal to it, Vizt. the rise of Exchange 3 per Cent together with our high Interest of 8 per Cent & also given them assurances of remitting £500 more in January when I hope you will save in both those articles, that I am perswaded they will be satisfied. It was really cutting to me to think of sending your money upon such bad terms & yet I thought it might be necessary to send a part of it.

If Capt. Floyd in Mr. Bright's *Sally* is with you & nothing to be done for him there please to tell him that we have a prospect of a very large Crop of Rice & early at Market & you & he will think of this and govern the Ship accordingly.

I lately resigned two Cargoes of Negroes from the Windward & Gold Coast which were consigned absolutely to me but I did not care to undertake the Sale, one of 320 Averaged £39.19/ Sterling, the other about the same number averaged £36 & I do believe as we have passed a Law to prohibit the importation after January 1766 that prime Negro Men will continue to sell very high all through the ensuing Winter. We shall probably have abundance brought in, in the Spring. I am, &ca.—

[*P.S.*] Please to forward this packet to Messrs. Martin & Stevens at Antigua. I tie it on the outside lest the Vessel should not touch at your Island.

SOURCE: Letterbook copy, HL Papers, S. C. Hist. Soc.; addressed "St. Kitts"; "per Capt. Stafford Dickenson. Copy per Capt. Emery."

TO DANIEL DOYLEY

[Charles Town] 12th September 1764

Sir,

As from the hopes that you once gave me of receiving a dividend of Thorpe's Estate on Account of Mr. Wilsons Judgement I did give him some expectation of a remittance. It becomes me now to inform him clearly how my mistake happened & from whence the misinformation sprung, otherwise he may form unfavourable conjectures upon my conduct, the least of which will be carelessness & inattention to a trust that I had undertaken. I therefore request the favour of you to furnish me with a fair Account of the receipts & payments on Account of the several Judgements that have passed thro your hands against the Assets of that Estate; a Copy of which I shall transmit to London & put a final end to that affair. I am, Sir, &ca.—

SOURCE: Letterbook copy, Letter Book of Henry Laurens, Oct. 30, 1762–Sept. 10, 1766, Penn. Hist. Soc.; addressed "Esquire. Broad Street."

TO JOSEPH BOWER

[Charles Town] 12th September 1764

Sir,

Since writing to you the 25th Ulto. as per duplicate above, Capt. Doran has discharged the Snow of all but his own & part of your goods & begun to take in some Pine Plank & Hogshead Staves. Only one parcel of Pitch is come to Town & that of so bad a quality both as to the Pitch & Cask tho I had the first offer I was forced to decline it, which I did too with somewhat less reluctance because the Snow could not take it in these three or four days in which space it will waste a good deal more & I have no doubt of procuring a sufficient quantity full as soon as she will be ready. There is but one parcel of Mahogany of Providence[4] in Town & that is very ordinary in general & I cant bring the proprietors to consent that I should pick it, without which it would really be picking your pocket to Ship it at £28 per Ct. I am sorry you forbid Logs. I had Bought & Shipped one parcell in Capt. Gullen before your Snow came in which you will probably see at Bristol & one parcel since which am Shipping to London. Out of this Latter I could have conveniently spared the quantity you order or the whole if it had been consistent with your direction.

I have wrote into the Country for Sassafras but hardly expect to receive any as every body is now busy in Harvest & cannot take off their hands these four or Six Weeks. The Deer Skin which you sent me as a pattern & mentioned in your favour of the 23d June is undoubtedly a good one but unluckily our Deer in this part of the World are so far like the Men in your part that everyone has not so good a Coat as his Neighbour & we are forced to take them as they run without examination & if one was to wait until they could select ten Hogsheads of just such Skins as that it would take a great deal of time & require a very large purchase to cull out the quantity, indeed to be plain it is impracticable. I have always Shiped very good Skins, at least as good as the best & better I am sure than 9/10ths that are Shiped here but with all my care & labour I could not avoid putting in many a worse Skin than that. I have governed myself in purchasing or rather not purchasing that article for some time past by Messrs. Cowles & Harford's advice & tho I am very

---

[4] Four vessels had brought mahogany from Providence in May and June. Naval Office Lists, 1764–1767, pp. 77–78.

much obliged to you for the offer of a concern with me yet it is not in my power to accept it while I am so connected with these Gentlemen, & I would observe the same rule with you & with everybody else, but if you please to give me orders I will endeavour to purchase in the best manner on your Account. I shall do my utmost to dispatch your Snow & advise you as I proceed but I am afraid the goods you have sent in her, I mean the Beer and Cyder, will be some hindrance to her Loading. I remain, &ca.—

SOURCE: Letterbook copy, HL Papers, S. C. Hist. Soc.; addressed "Bristol"; "per Capt. Harbison. Copy per Capt. Gullan."

TO DEVONSHEIR & REEVE

[Charles Town] 12th September 1764

Gentlemen,

I have the honour of yours of the 4th June & it is before me to reply to. Capt. James Doran rightly informed you that he had lodged ten Kegs of Red Lead in my Cellar, which I should have retained for a proper claim, but the Kegs were in exceeding bad order, hardly mendable by any Cooperage. Therefore I judged it most for the proprietors Interest be who he would to sell them & accordingly I did sell them to Abraham Vangammern[5] 9th November 1763, Net Weight 1,220 lbs. at £8 per Ct., £97.12/, & he has given for some time passed orders to pay me but I have not called for the money because it did not belong to me. I shall remit you that & the Amount of some other Articles by Capt. Courtin. Meantime, a Grapnel, Box of Pipes, & one piece of damaged Strouds which I think remains upon hand shall be disposed of.

As to the Accounts of Austin & Laurens & Austin, Laurens, & Appleby The *Brislington* included, I shall leave them all to be settled with you by Mr. Appleby with the concurrence of Mr. Austin who are now both in England & whatever you & they agree to will be satisfactory to me.

I heartily thank you, Gentlemen, for your kind offers of service, but as for reciprocality of favours, which you most esteem, there can hardly be any between us because of inability on my part,

---

[5] The Moravian.

for what have I to offer from this part of the World even if I was in the Rigour of Trade that is or would be worth your attention, but the case is quite otherwise. I do very little business & shall probably do less in the Commission way for I desire none but from my old friends whom I will as long as I am able & my services acceptable, serve from a principle of gratitude, & in order to serve them the better as I must have some time for myself, I have declined & will more decline new connexions. I live at a Little distance from that throng of business that I was once acquainted with & yet within Town & near enough to acquit myself with satisfaction in such things as I take upon me to transact. I wish I could hear that my good friends Devonsheir & Reeve had lessened their attachments to the Counter & the Quays reaping the Harvest of their past Labours in the enjoyment of themselves & of their friends, still continuing to be friends to commerce & beneficial to Mankind without bearing the Yoke so taught upon their necks as might have been necessary some Twenty Years since. Think not from hence that I pretend or affect to be very Rich; that is not the Case. I have enough to procure contentment & yet my attention is not so widely diverted as to leave me an unwatchful prey to misfortunes. If such, which are the common Lot & inheritance of the Sons of Men, shall betide me, I shall not have business to begin as it is not my plan to quit it altogether, but I would not anticipate misfortune & I think there can hardly be a greater than for a Man either thro' habit or necessity to be drudging all his days in a constant hurry of Trade.

This a freedom which I hope you will not be offended at & that you will please to permit me to rank you amongst those friends whose commands, when I can be of real service to them, I always hold myself ready to receive & to obey.

We have exceeding fine Harvest weather & the Hurricane Season steals off in smiles. A fortnight more will secure a very large Crop of Rice, Corn, & pease & a tolerable good one of Indigo. I remain with great regard, &ca.—

SOURCE: Letterbook copy, HL Papers, S. C. Hist. Soc.; addressed "Bristol"; "per Capt. Harbison. Copy per Gullan."

TO HENRY BRIGHT

[Charles Town] 12th September 1764

Sir,

Above you are troubled with a duplicate of what I wrote you the 13th Ulto. since which I have not been able to get off any of your half pence in quantities tho I have offered 2½ per Cent abatement on them & three Months Credit. This Town is rather too full of that sort of a distorted specie & People begin to be cloged with it. I proposed as many to my Baker as would pay for a Years Bread advance but he wont touch them therefore I must vend them in smaller Sums & you will be a little the longer out of your money.

I lately wrote to Messrs. Smith & Baillies desiring them if nothing could be done for Capt. Floyd at St. Kitts[6] to inform him that we have a prospect of a very large & early Crop of Rice in this Country but this is all that I dare to say, for Freights at present are very low as you will learn by these Vessels now going to Bristol.

Your Nephew[7] transmitted me a little order from the Northward for some pine plank & pieces of Timber for Window frames which did not come in time to go by this Vessel but I shall endeavour to procure & send them soon.

The Cargo of Negroes from Bance Island mentioned in my last has Netted £39.10 Sterling but this branch of Trade if you Gentlemen are content[8] will cease in a few Months & be prohibited for three Years by a Law lately passed in our Assembly. It was introduced & hurried through in a manner uncommon, unexpected, & without argument to support it. I strove hard to have it deferred until the meeting in December that in the meantime the general Voice of our constituents might be heard but the Junto by which it was planned & introduced knew that would not countenance their designs & so depending upon a Majority in a thin House they pushed it forward & succeeded. I transmit you a Copy of the Law with a few Notes on the back of it & leave it to your disposal. I remain with great regard, &ca.—

SOURCE: Letterbook copy, HL Papers, S. C. Hist. Soc.; addressed "Esquire. Bristol"; "per Capt. Harbison. Copy per Gullan."

---

[6] Capt. William Floyd in the ship *Sally* on a new voyage out of Bristol.
[7] Lowbridge Bright.
[8] HL was indicating that the English merchants could use their influence to bring about the disallowance of the law by the King in Council.

TO FRANCIS STUART

[Charles Town] 13th September 1764

Dear Sir,

I have this Moment Rece'd your favour of the 11th and am very glad to see that you have a consignment from our friends Smith & Baillies that is so agreeable to your self & likely to prove so advantageous to them.

I dare not claim the merit of their present address to you nor am I conscious of having said any thing to them that could have induced it, unless it was through their Capt. Mitchell[9] who did ask me some questions about your Trade, &ca. to which I replied in the integrity of my heart just what I thought of you, but there is no thanks due for this.

You certainly judge right to dispatch the *Mary Ann* immediately with Corn, Rice, & Shingles & not to wait for Pork which you cannot expect to get these two Months. I wish I had her here to Load with Corn that partly belongs to those Gentlemen.

'Tis impossible to tell you what a parcel of Negroes will sell for in Charles Town without knowing whether they are Men, Women, or Children or what Number & proportion of each; which particular information relative to those you have remains a secret to me but this I can inform you, that the last Cargo which I put into the hands of Messrs. Brewton & Smith which truly was not the finest I ever saw, averaged £39.19/ Sterling at 721 per Cent Exchange and I have no reason to think that a Cargo of equal or superior quality would yield less but rather more.

Mrs. Nickleson has not yet transmitted the Sale of your Indigo. Whenever I receive it you shall soon be furnished with a duplicate or the original. I shall be very glad to see you when you come to Charles Town & am with great regard, Dear Sir, &ca.—

SOURCE: Letterbook copy, Letter Book of Henry Laurens, Oct. 30, 1762–Sept. 10, 1766, Penn. Hist. Soc.; addressed "Beaufort."

---

[9] Capt. John Mitchell of the sloop *Mary Ann,* owned by Smith & Baillies of St. Kitts.

TO JOHN TARLETON

[Charles Town] 13th September 1764

Sir,

Your favour of the 25th February Via London stuck a good while by the way & came to my hands but a few Weeks ago & no Letters with it for Pensacola. Therefore I presume a more direct conveyance was found.

I observe what you say of the impracticability of your giving me previous advice for the Loading of any of your Vessels. I hope your factors in the West Indies will do it as often as opportunity will permit that I may have a chance of giving you good Goods and with dispatch.

We are now in full prospect of Large Crops of Rice, Corn, & pease, & a better one of Indigo than was sometime ago expected. The Harvest is Entering upon & the Hurricane Season wearing out in fine Weather. A fortnight more will secure the produce of most plantations in the Country.

It gives me a pleasure to serve, & I count it an honour to correspond with a gentleman of your integrity & generosity. Therefore I remain with great regard, Sir, &ca.—

SOURCE: Letterbook copy, HL Papers, S. C. Hist. Soc.; addressed "Leverpoole"; "per Capt. Harbison. Copy per Capt. Gullan."

TO ISAAC KING

[Charles Town] 13th September 1764

Sir,

Under the 6th & 10th Inst. per this conveyance I wrote you a very Long Letter & postscript which I have been reviewing, & reconsidering the subject matter, I mean of the Latter part relative to the Bond that you demand of some of your debtors in Charles Town & altho I do not see cause to make any alteration therein, nor do I vary my sentiments in the smallest degree, yet I fear that I may have been much too free in the manner of delivering them, for even truth itself will make different impressions upon our minds according to the various methods taken to introduce it to us. If I have erred in this respect, I beg your pardon & that you will be pleased to impute it wholly to that unreservedness which I allways discover when I speak to persons in whom I confide, & further that you will believe that I had not least design to offend.

I am just now applied to by a worthy Young Woman who is left a Widow in a strange land & is strugling with fortune for a Livelihood, to assist her with Forty pounds Sterling to purchase a few small articles in London for Sale here; which I have consented to & must therefore request you to pay to Miss Hetty Havercam the above mentioned Sum when she shall call for it taking three receipts on my Account for the use of her Sister Mrs. Mary Stokes[1] in Charles Town & transmit me two of the receipts, Sir, &ca.—

P.S. We have a continuance of very fine Harvest weather. The Hurricane Season is wearing off with a favourable aspect. A fortnight more will secure a very Large Crop.

SOURCE: Letterbook copy, HL Papers, S. C. Hist. Soc.; addressed "for Mrs. Sarah Nickleson & Company, London"; "per Capt. Ball. Copy per Capt. Taylor."

TO JAMES WRIGHT

[Charles Town] 14th September 1764

Sir,

I have the honour of forwarding to you by Mr. Brewton's Schooner[2] a Red Sealed case & a small packet under cover with this which I received two days since from Governor Grant at Augustine.[3]

I wish it safe to your Excellency's hands & remain, Sir—

SOURCE: Letterbook copy, HL Papers, S. C. Hist. Soc.; addressed "His Excellency Governor. Georgia."

---

[1] The widow of the Reverend Joseph Stokes.

[2] On Feb. 8, 1763, Miles Brewton had registered the schooner *Jonathan*, Jarvis Williams, which was owned by himself and Thomas Loughton Smith. Ship Register, 1734–1765, p. 211, S. C. Archives.

[3] Grant had gone on board HMS *Ferret*, Capt. Bremer, at Portsmouth on June 17. London *Daily Advertiser*, June 20, 1764. He landed on Aug. 29 at St. Augustine from HMS *Ferret*, which sloop arrived in Charleston on Sept. 12. *Gazette*, Oct. 8, 1764.

TO JAMES BOX[4]

[Charles Town] 14th September 1764

Sir,

I have the pleasure of forwarding you under this cover with this a small packet which I received two days ago from Governor Grant, which will inform you of his arrival in East Florida & probably hasten your steps to the same place in which I wish much Honour & prosperity & remain with great regard, Sir, &ca.—

SOURCE: Letterbook copy, HL Papers, S. C. Hist. Soc.; addressed "Savanna."

TO ABRAHAM PARSONS

[Charles Town] 14th September 1764

Sir,

I am sorry to see that I have so many of your esteem'd favours laying by me unanswered as the 11th October, 12th February, 12th & 21st March but thro a variety of causes chiefly death & Sickness in my family has made me thus remiss, yet I have not been unmindful of the business that you had given me in charge.

The Sheathing Boards provided by your order I disposed of again without loss & the purchase & portage you are welcome to. I wrote to Mr. De Rossett the 8th May offering my service to Charter a Vessel for you. His answer was dated the 25th June but did not reach me before the 9th August & then he wrote me so discouragingly, Vizt. that Mr. Parson's Naval Stores were in some Gentleman's hands to be delivered thirty days after demand & did not exceed five or Six hundred Barrels, that I was afraid on your Account to Charter such Vessel as were offering, tho very low for I believe I might have got one to go there for 45/ per Ton, but how was the remainder to be filled up? If on your Account you must have been a great sufferer since Mr. De Rossett in his P.S. says Tar is very dear here at present not less than 12/ per Barrel besides Shipping

---

[4] James Box, a lawyer in Savannah, was appointed by Grant attorney general of East Florida on Oct. 31, 1764. Box, who was an original member of the royal council of East Florida, died in 1770. Mowat, *East Florida,* pp. 15, 162. Box sailed from Savannah to St. Augustine in the sloop *Hope,* Nicholas Neilson. *Georgia Gazette,* Nov. 1, 1764.

charges. I presume this great price must be owing to a great demand & that there must be many Ships at Cape Fear & Freight Low of course, (tho he does not mention a word about that) & in that case no doubt Mr. De Rossett has engaged enough to transport your effects. There are so many delays, demurs, & disappointments in that Country that no Ship will remove from here under 7/6 or 10/ per Ton Extra, & then not without a Bondsman here which few People for those very reason chuse to be. I have not yet heard whether the Gentlemen whom you were establishing at St. Kitts had arrived there. If they are fixed & will please to let me hear from them, I will endeavour to recommend them, but my own business is very much contracted & indeed all that is done between this & that place except to one or two of the old Houses is a very trifle & hardly worth any Mans notice.

Your Guns which Lay in the hands of A., L., & A. were become so exceedingly rusty that I was forced to put them all into a Gunsmiths hands to clean. I had made him an offer of them at £3.7.6 per Gun rusty as they were sometime before your order for Shipping them came which upon telling him that I had such an order, he accepted of & I believe it is more for your Interest than any thing else that could have been done with them for some of them were greatly injured & the purchaser has since assured me that if he had been fully apprized of the badness of many he would not have given so much by a good deal. Please to receive inclosed the Account of Sale & when the Cash comes to hand which I believe will be punctually paid a remittance shall immediately follow. Said Net proceed is £209.18.3 to the Credit of your Account Current.

We have very favourable weather for the Harvest. If this continues ten or fourteen days longer a very large Crop of every kind except Indigo will be procured & the Crop of Indigo will not be a despicable one. I remain with great regard, Sir, &ca.—

SOURCE: Letterbook copy, HL Papers, S. C. Hist. Soc.; addressed "Bristol"; "per Capt. Tayler. Copy per Capt. Marshall."

TO WILLIAM HOPTON

[Charles Town] 15th September 1764
Dear Sir,

I return you a great many thanks for your favour of the 26th

June & the papers which accompanied it. One more favour I have to request in that way which is that you will procure for me one or more of the general Tax Laws in New York & Pensilvania, that I may form some judgement of their several modes of Taxation of Real Estates in the Country as well as in Town.

I here Inclose you James Wrights first Bill dated 28th May 1764 on Abraham Mortier, Esquire[5] in New York for Three Hundred pounds Sterling payable at thirty days sight to John Milledge[6] & endorsed by him & Johnson & Wylly. If you are at New York when this reaches you & that you can by discounting the days Interest procure another good Bill for its Value after such discount & your Commission be pleas'd to do so & remit such Bill to Mr. William Hodshon, Merchant in Fenchurch Street, London, advising him that it is the product of the Inclosed Bill transmitted by me. If you are at Philadelphia please to convert it into Sterling & remit it as above provided you can do so upon no greater a deduction than 3 per Cent altogether, & if that cannot be effected I must beg the favour of you to lay it out in any articles that you think will yield me 12d for a Shilling to come in the *Charles-Town*[7] & among other things that I recollect if good West India Rum can be purchased as I see it quoted at 2/6 or under per Gallon you may send the whole in that, taking care of the quality both of Rum & the Hogsheads.

If this attempt of mine to make you a Man of business is disagreeable be pleased to transfer my Letter to any of your friends only be so good as to see that my orders are executed for this Bill is the fragment of a long & troublesome Account that I have had to settle for Mr. Hodshon & am now subjecting myself to the danger of a Loss or some disadvantage to bring it to a final end.

You will hear from Mrs. Hopton & Jack[8] the state of your family affairs & we have nothing here of public news but what may as well remain hidden from you until you return.

---

[5] *HL Papers*, III, 415n.

[6] John Milledge had come out with James Oglethorpe in 1732–1733. He represented Savannah district in the first provincial assembly of Georgia in 1751. He was a captain of rangers who supported Governor Wright during the Stamp Act crisis. His son John was to be a leading patriot and future governor of Georgia. J.H.T.M., "John Milledge (1757–1818)," *DAB*; W. W. Abbot, *The Royal Governors of Georgia, 1754–1775* (Chapel Hill, N. C., 1959), pp. 76, 114, 152.

[7] *Charles-Town Packet,* Thomas Mason.

[8] John Hopton.

Please to present my Compliments to Miss Polly[9] & to accept my best wishes for your safe return to Charles Town. I remain, &ca.—

SOURCE: Letterbook copy, HL Papers, S. C. Hist. Soc.; "per Capt. Mason."

TO HENRY BYRNE

[Charles Town] 15th September 1764

Sir,

Mr. Laurens being much indisposed (just at the time of Capt. Jacksons sailing) & not able to write himself hath given directions to me in his behalf.

You will be pleased to receive per this bearer the Ship *Pensacola Packet,* Nicholas Jackson, Master, Invoice & Bill of Loading for 140 Barrels & 7 half Barrels Rice, & dispose of the same ¼ on Account of Messrs. Cowles & Harford of Bristol & ¾ on Account of Mr. Laurens, & remit the Amount as Speedily as possible to said Messrs. Cowles & Harford. The Rice has all been Winnowed & is as good as can be at this time of Year.

There is another Vessel put up for Oporto to Sail in 8 or 10 days. Mr. Laurens will use his utmost endeavours to procure the whole of the consignments to you, & rather than not he will Ship a part therein himself, if he cannot obtain the having her Voyage diverted to Cadiz, imagining that your Market is full or rather over stocked with Old Rice, which may be prejudicial to some of his friends who may send an early Vessel with New.

Mr. Laurens hopes to write you fully by said Vessel. Meantime I remain for him, Sir, &ca.—

SOURCE: Letterbook copy, HL Papers, S. C. Hist. Soc.; addressed "Esquire. Oporto"; "per the *Pensecola Packet,* Capt. Jackson. Copy per Capt. Summers." This letter was written for HL by his clerk.

---

[9] William Hopton had three daughters: Alicia, Sarah, and Mary. *HL Papers,* I, 102n. Alicia was born on Jan. 4, 1749 and Sarah on July 28, 1752. *Register of St. Philip's Parish, 1720–1758,* p. 103.

TO JAMES GRANT

[Charles Town] 15 September 1764

Sir,

Four days ago I had the honour of receiving your Excellency's Letter of the 31st Ulto. & 2d Inst. together with a little square Box for Governor Wright & a packet of Letters for this & other places by the *Ferret* Sloop.

I beg leave to offer my congratulations upon your safe arrival in your Government, where I sincerely wish that every thing may conspire to make the weight sit Light & the trust prove equally honorable & beneficial to you & if my best services in this corner will in any degree contribute to effect those good ends your Excellency may rely upon them.

Your several dispatches are distributed in the following manner: those for Georgia in a Schooner, one Williams, Master,[1] whose receipt I have taken, the Letters for England in the *Suffolck Packet,* & those for General Gage[2] & Colonel Robinson[3] in a Brigantine for Philadelphia[4] & all will be moving forward tomorrow. Your Letters for the Major & Mr. Chief Justice Moultrie[5] & that for Wells I deliver'd within Ten minutes after they reached me, & altho I did not reply to your favour of the 25th October because I expected that

---

[1] Capt. Jarvis Williams of Miles Brewton's schooner.

[2] Major-General Thomas Gage (1721–1787) had succeeded General Amherst as commander-in-chief of the British forces in North America on Nov. 17, 1763 upon Amherst's departure from America. Gage was formally commissioned commander-in-chief by the King on Nov. 16, 1764. John R. Alden, *General Gage in America* (Baton Rouge, La., 1948), pp. 61, 63.

[3] James Robertson was a Scotsman who rose through the ranks to become a major general in the British army during the American Revolution. In August 1763 General Amherst had ordered Lieutenant Colonel Robertson, one of his staff officers, to inspect the regiments and posts at St. Augustine, Pensacola, and Mobile. Robertson was at this time returning to the northward after completing his assignment. He worked for a stricter Quartering Act and for the concentration of British troops in the Middle Colonies, steps which increased the tensions between England and her colonies. John Shy, *Toward Lexington, The Role of the British Army in the Coming of the American Revolution* (Princeton, N. J., 1965), pp. 71–72, 135, 179–180, 268, 351.

[4] *Charles-Town Packet,* Thomas Mason.

[5] Major John Moultrie would be appointed lieutenant governor of East Florida in 1771. James Moultrie, S. C.'s attorney general, was appointed chief justice of East Florida on Oct. 31, 1764. Mowat, *East Florida,* p. 162. James Moultrie carried HL's letter to Grant, sailing in the *Wambaw* to St. Augustine. HL to John Coming Ball, Oct. 6, 1764.

you was very soon to have followed it yet Mr. Dunnett[6] will inform you that the little business committed to my charge did not lay unnoticed.

Mr. Cox does not yet appear. It is very unlucky that he did not outsail the *Ferret*. The Chief Justice has been very anxious to get away from the moment that I delivered your commands to him, & I have been officious to accelerate his flight for I can so sensibly feel the awkardness of your situation as to know that the Multiplication of his Sleeps will remind you of those which you experienced in the delays of certain great Men in 1761. The remembrance of those may indeed fortify your mind in the present case, & the more when you are assured that there is not an hour trifled or squander'd away here. But be that as it may I interest myself so much in your happiness that I am more than a Little sorry for the disappointment you have suffered.

Almost every minute since I received your Excellency's Letters have been employed in Act or thought how to procure just such a Vessel as you want & within the scanty Sum limitted for the purchase. I have talked to Mr. Rose,[7] to Mr. Tucker,[8] & consulted the Masters of some Vessels of my own. I have likewise applied to a Shipwright to undertake the building of one in which Mr. Rose joined & assisted me, & upon the Whole find it cannot be effected within the Limits of time or money. Such a Vessel cannot be compleated here before the Month of March nor for a less Sum than £350 Sterling. My next Step was to consult the Connoissuiers in that branch what such a bark could be built & compleatly rigged & fitted for in Philadelphia & am very well satisfied from the information given me, that it cannot be done there for less £300 Sterling & the Vessel not worth half so much (the hull of her) as one built of our Live Oak & Pine & possibly by some real or imaginary accidents the Bill run up to half

---

[6] John Dunnett had come out to S. C. in 1757 with James Grant. Dunnett was surgeon's mate and then ensign of the First Highland Battalion. *Papers of Henry Bouquet,* I, 320–321. Grant in a letter of Dec. 12, 1757, written from Charleston, mentioned that Dunnett was from Capernach in Scotland. Ms 1284, ff. 145–146, National Library of Scotland. Dunnett was appointed a lieutenant in the Independent Companies in place of John Gray, just made captain, on Aug. 20, 1761. *SCHM,* XXXIII (1932), 295. The *Georgia Gazette,* Dec. 22, 1763, announced that he was to be secretary of East Florida. He was appointed secretary and clerk of the council on Nov. 17, 1764, was an original member of the council, and died on June 12, 1776. Mowat, *East Florida,* pp. 14, 162.

[7] The shipbuilder John Rose of Hobcaw.

[8] Thomas Tucker, the mariner.

as much more. I know my late partner Austin paid very dearly for a Schooner that he built there. After this I turned my thoughts to the purchase of a Schooner not quite new & have two of that sort in view. One of them is well known to Mr. Tucker & he will give you some Account of her. Therefore, Sir, altho I have not already succeeeded, dont despair; my diligence shall be continued & your further orders may bring me some aid; for if a Schooner must be had let's have her at once. You will be no gainer by procrastination. But it may be, that you do not describe the Vessel you want so clearly by her Tonnage, as you might have done & may still do from the burthen and appearance of some other little Vessel, or from the quantity of Cask of Beef, Bread, Flour, or Rice that she is to carry. Please to cast your eye upon this Thing[9] that the Chief Justice goes in & by all means consult this Mr. Tucker who waits upon Mr. Moultrie as his Pilot but merely to oblige him for he is a Man of an easy fortune in this Country & by no means dependent upon such little jobbs. He is a clever fellow & in my opinion peerless in his way of Life. He can give you a tolerable Account of your own Coast & Southward of it to this Bar & I do believe that an hour spent with him will yield you some satisfactory informations. I have not seen your Mr. Smith[1] yet, but he is to call upon me this Evening & if our meeting produces any thing to the purpose I shall add it in a postscript.

Your Bar, Sir, is indeed a great Bar to the rise of East Florida, but the Coast must be explored & some better Navigation may be discovered.[2] Another Bar will be the Soil, if it is no better than report makes it. Upon these two essential points will very much depend the Fate of the Colony & determine it only a Frontier Garrison or a flourishing Country of Merchants and Farmers. Your Excellencys plan for avoiding the danger of sudden irruptions by the Indians is extreamly good; to be upon our gard is to be strong; & watchfulness answers all the ends of power & saves the expence attending it. But I am afraid the delay in determining that important point about the Lands purchased from the late proprietors or supposed Owners will

---

[9] The schooner *Wambaw*.
[1] Mr. Smith was master of the *Ferret*. See HL to James Grant, Oct. 10, 1764.
[2] For a map and description of the bar at St. Augustine and for comments on the soil of East Florida, see *DeBrahm's Report of the General Survey in the Southern District of North America,* ed. Louis De Vorsey, Jr. (Columbia, S. C., 1971), pp. 204–205, 209–229.

greatly impede your settlement & postpone the necessity for building Stockades. People will not go to any new Country especially a frontier one, but upon inviting prospects of mending their fortunes, & those who have anything to risque will be more cautious of improving Lands tho granted by the Crown with usual Solemnity if there is the least apprehension of being removed from or even disturbed in their possessions by a Dormant Claim. There should be a speedy ecclaircissment upon this head otherwise your province will dwindle even from its present Littleness. I have a great regard for & wish the purchasers of that vast Tract of Land very well as Neighbours & as Men, but in the light they now stand in I view them as impediments to the Welfare of one of His Majesty's plantations where a friend of mine happens to preside as Governor, whose Glory & Honour may & probably will very much depend upon his Success in the Establishment of that plantation.[3]

I accept your kind hint of becoming a planter in East Florida & shall have no objection to transpose a Thousand or Fifteen Hundred Guineas for a beginning upon a tolerable prospect of receiving the Interest of my money & if my affairs dont run very perversely I shall have the Honour of paying my respects to you at St. Augustine sometime within the Course of this Winter. In the meantime I have desired the favour of Mr. Chief Justice to cast his eye upon some well wooded Island as well as upon a good tract upon the Continent which I shall be glad to hold & to settle if such there are to spare & that I can comply with the terms & conditions of your Grants.[4]

I shall endeavour to prevail upon some Workmen in Wood & Stone to wait on you. One that wrought for me (a Mason) had promised to go down in this Boat but the poor Man was seized suddenly with our Fall Fever & lies very ill.

I beg leave to refer your Excellency to Mr. Moultrie for intelligence of public Affairs in this very disturbed state. That Ebullition which a commander in Chief seemed to have raised in our

---

[3] When Lord Adam Gordon reached St. Augustine in December 1764 he recorded in his journal: "The Land for thirty Miles round this Bay, is claimed by John Gordon Esqr., as a Spanish purchase." "Journal of Lord Adam Gordon," p. 392.
[4] HL did petition for Florida land. At the court of St. James on July 20, 1764, a warrant of survey for 2,000 acres was ordered for HL. And on Dec. 9, 1766, the Florida council ordered a warrant of survey for 500 acres for HL. CO 5/548, pp. 351, 355, Land Registry, Public Record Office, London.

Bloods some three Years since does not yet subside. A Grant, A Boone, or A Bull have each in their turns administred fuel to our Fires & I have heard some of our Partisan-patriots say "of two Evils chuse the least. We would even submit to *Grant* rather than have this Man, *Boone,* to Govern us." In some instances, like Gallio, I care for none of those things;[5] in others I answer stiffly as long as truth will support me, but I often find even that too weak to oppose invincible ignorance, prejudice, & obstinacy. I have the Honour to be, Sir, &ca.—

SOURCE: Letterbook copy, HL Papers, S. C. Hist. Soc.; addressed "Governor. Augustine"; "per James Moultrie, Esquire."

REGISTRATION OF
THE SCHOONER WAMBAW

September 15, 1764

[*On this date Benjamin Perdriau registered the schooner* Wambaw, *David Walker, master, 15 tons, built in South Carolina in 1760, for himself, HL, and John Coming Ball as owners.*]

SOURCE: Ship Register, 1734–1765, p. 241, S. C. Archives.

HENRY LAURENS VERSUS *JOHN CLARKE*

September 17, 1764

[*On September 17, 1764, William Burrows, attorney for the plaintiff, filed suit in the court of common pleas against John Clarke, Charleston cabinetmaker, for recovery of a bond, dated May 2, 1764, in the sum of £300 currency. Clarke through his attorney John Rutledge confessed judgment. The judgment was also signed on September 17 and recorded by Dougal Campbell, clerk of the court.*]

---

[5] Junius Gallio was the brother of the philosopher Seneca. During the reign of Claudius he was proconsul of Achæa where in 53 A.D. he dismissed the charges brought by the Jews against the apostle Paul. His statement ("But Gallio cared for none of these things") showed the impartial attitude of the Roman officials towards Christianity in its early days. "Junius Annaeus Gallio," *Encyclopedia Britannica,* 11th edition.

SOURCE: Judgment Rolls, 1764, No. 58A, S. C. Archives; Judgment Docket, Court of Common Pleas, Book 2 (1755–1773), p. 91, S. C. Archives.

TO SAMUEL WRAGG

[Charles Town] 19th September 1764

Sir,

I have just now received your favour of the 10th Inst. You will oblige me very much to procure the preference of good parcels of Pitch as they shall fall conveniently in your way. I shall begin to be in want for my own Ship early next Month. The Cedar & Red Bay Logs will come acceptably at any time in January but would be most so if I could have them for a certain Vessel[6] that will Sail (if she ever arrives) before Christmas & now that I mention this Vessel let me inform you she is a Guinea Man & may bring 80 to 120 Gambia Negroes, which for some very particular considerations I shall dispose of. Do you think, Sir, from the experience that you have had that I might expect any advantage by removing such a Cargo to George Town, I mean as well in payments as prices? Your sentiments hereon may induce me to ask your assistance in the Sale if you encourage it to be made there.

I am quite satisfied with the Sales that you have made of the Negroes so far as you have informed me & I do think you have bid full enough for the quiet Woman; was she my own I would surely make you an abatement but it being your own offer & the property a third person's I dare not pay you such a compliment. Please now to close & forward the Sale of those & if you can of the former parcel, also that I may Enter them accordingly.

The difficulty which you are pleased to start upon a method to be taken to convince me that you shall make no unfair or undue advantages in the purchase of Indigo on my Account compared with what you may buy for your self, is no difficulty at all in my view. I have not the Least cause to suspect that you will do anything of that sort & I never suspect any body without some good cause & then my Rule is to avoid dealing with them any further than necessity obliges.

---

[6] This may be a reference to the *Austin* which arrived on Nov. 25. It brought, however, only three slaves. See HL to John and Thomas Tipping, Dec. 4, 1764.

I know by some fifteen or sixteen Years experience that to purchase the same spicie of Goods upon a friends & upon ones own Account at the same time are by no means incompatible with strict Honesty & that rectitude of conduct which every Merchant should preserve. 'Tho I have more than once found such mixed purchases not the most conducive to my own Interest, that is to say upon the first appearance, therefore it was that I enquired of you again if you were under any engagements, & you inform me that you are so far engaged as to purchase on your own Account. This will be no obstacle with me if it is none on your part & the proposition that you make of buying & Shipping upon our joint Account in proportion to our respective Value is quite agreeable to me because it is the least liable to exceptions. My aim is to have good Indigo at a price, all charges included, not exceeding the price that may be given in Charles Town with a chance of having a superior quality. The Sum that I shall advance upon this occasion will be about the same that you set down, Vizt. £1,000 to £2,000 Sterling, & therefore if you please we shall go hand in hand & I shall thankfully allow you Commission on the Amount of my share & pay your draughts as they shall appear & become due in which you will give as Long time as you can that I may not suffer the inconvenience of a dunn to which I am hitherto a Stranger. You are very good to submit the Sale of such Indigo as shall be purchased on our joint Account to *my* correspondent. This leads me to remark that I do not think my old correspondent, & still my correspondent in every thing else, the best hand for the Sale of Indigo. I mean Mrs. Nickleson. I dont say this from one instance only but from repeated observation & comparisons but after all I may be mistaken & would beg that this may not be noticed to the prejudice of that House. I think to take a method this Year that will convince me upon that point whether I am right or wrong & we may think further & determine on that part of our business time enough.

I have a very strong firm Ship commanded by a clever Master, Vizt. the *Flora*, Capt. Courtin, will Sail for Bristol early in November. If you have any Freight to offer her I shall be thankful for your favours.

I shall be a large purchaser of good Pork in the Season & beg that you will recommend some parcels to me. I remain, Sir, &ca.—

SOURCE: Letterbook copy, Letter Book of Henry Laurens, Oct. 30, 1762–Sept. 10, 1766, Penn. Hist. Soc.; addressed "George Town."

TO JOHN MAYRANT[7]

[Charles Town] 19th September 1764

Sir,

To forward & conclude an agreement upon the subject that engaged us this Morning, be pleased to consider & inform me the several prices of the articles of Lumber underwritten, observing one main point that I set out upon, Vizt. the quality of each specie to be unexceptionably good of which I myself will not desire to be sole judge but some other person or persons that we shall previously fix upon shall determine in every case where I happen to be dissatisfied. This method will avoid disputes.

¾ Inch Boards 20 to 30 feet long chiefly the latter & upward
    if convenient to you
1 Inch Boards—all Lengths from 15 feet up
1¼ Boards from 15+, 20+, 25+, to 35 feet
1½ ditto—20 feet upwards to 30 feet
2 Inch plank ⎤
2½ Inch plank ⎬ from 25 feet to 40 feet as you can get
3 Inch plank ⎦ them but chiefly 30 feet
Scantlin 3 by 4—4 by 5—to 6 + 8 an equal quantity
Clean smooth barked spars from 8 Inches diameter to 18 Inches
    clear of the Bark Sap I mean that will work so large—for
    I would have the Bark remain—& from 40 to 66 feet Long
At what landing to be delivered?
When any part & what part or parts will be ready for delivery?
Your people always to assist in Loading my Schooner.
When to be paid for after delivery of each Boat Load?

& some other particulars that may occur to you & me before a written agreement is Entered into. If you answer these several particulars in such a manner as to encourage me I will take of your pine the Value of One or Two Thousand pounds Sterling which will make it the better worth your attention.

One thing more, I would add that altho I am to receive the Goods at your Landing by which I mean to take the Freight & risque to Charles Town upon myself yet the quality & measure is not to be determined before they are landed here & in case of any inferior

---

[7] John Mayrant (1726–1767) was a planter on the Santee River. His mother was a sister of Mrs. James Crokatt of London. His second wife, whom he married on Oct. 25, 1758, was Ann, the daughter of William Wooddrop and Elizabeth Crokatt. *SCHM*, xxvii (1926), 81–84; Rogers, *History of Georgetown County*, p. 56.

pieces being put in; the same to be valued by an impartial judge in proportion to the prices of the best & then I am to Account for such inferior goods, which will be rather a benefit to you as such might otherwise be wafe & waste at your Pits. I remain, &ca.—

SOURCE: Letterbook copy, Letter Book of Henry Laurens, Oct. 30, 1762–Sept. 10, 1766, Penn. Hist. Soc.; addressed "Esquire. Charles Town."

TO WILLIAM WHARTON[8]

[Charles Town] 19th September 1764

Sir,

I was very glad to receive your favour of the 24th Ulto. per Capt. Mason[9] giving some directions about a parcel of Hats in my custody & had fully determined to answer it per same hand but was a good deal fatigued the Evening before Mason sailed & trusted to his waiting the next day as the wind was then contrary but it came suddenly about & he slid away.

When Capt. Harrop[1] left those hats which he called yours in my hands I was sick abed & whether I signed the Receipt that was given to him for them or not I am not certain; but believe it was signed by a Clerk who is since gone to England, & in whose blotter I find so much of a Copy of said Receipt as is subjoined, together with Copy of Mr. Harrops order, by which you will perceive that he left fifty three hats in my Store which are all said to be on your Account whereas you Claim but Eighteen. The Captain's orders given in my absence were to send the Hats to you, which when I was informed of in Bed I desired the Clerk to tell him that I thought it impracticable & should not care to attempt such a measure & if I remember right his reply was that he would write a Letter to you &

---

[8] Joseph Wharton (1707–1776), a very successful Philadelphia merchant who retired to his country seat Walnut Grove, had three sons: Samuel (1732–1800), Joseph (1734–1816), and William (1740–c. 1805). Joseph who married Sarah Tallman was "an active & successful merchant" before the Revolution. William married Susannah Medcalf in 1767. *Pennsylvania Magazine of History and Biography*, 1 (1877), 326–327, 457–458. Samuel, the most famous of the brothers, was a great land speculator. Wayne E. Stevens, "Samuel Wharton," *DAB*.

[9] Capt. Thomas Mason.

[1] Capt. William Harrop of the *Barbadoes Packett*.

that I should soon hear from yourself. I shall now by virtue of your orders send the hats to Vendue for I know of no other method of disposing of them & that cannot be done in less than three or four Weeks, two days in a Week, for if they were all to be put up at one Sale I suppose they would not yeild above half as much as if only five or Six are produced in one day.

You will be pleased if you can to give me some further direction relative to the Supernumerary Hats, but at the same time from the tenor of the order & receipt I am accountable to you only & tho (I keep no Store of Merchandize) the Sale of such goods is a Little out of my way yet I shall do the best in my power with them for your Interest. I remain, Sir, &ca.—

Copy of Capt. Harrops order.

Sir,

Be so good as to send the Four dozen & five Beaver Hats you was so good as to take into your Store to Mister Wharton, Merchant in Philadelphia. Sir, &ca.—

Signed William Harrop

Charles Town, 21st January 1764—Copy of a receipt (except the Signature) given to Capt. Harrop—

Received of Capt. William Harrop 21st January 1764: Four dozen & five Beaver Hatts some cut at the edges which are to be sent to Mr. Joseph Wharton, Merchant in Philadelphia, or to be sold for his Account & the proceeds remitted to him by order of Capt. Harrop.

SOURCE: Letterbook copy, HL Papers, S. C. Hist. Soc.; addressed "Philadelphia"; "per Capt. McLean. Copy per Mason."

TO JOHN HALLIDAY[2]

[Charles Town] 22d September 1764

Sir,

Messrs. Brailsford & Chapman inform me that they are about an application to you to transact some business of consequence for them in Antigua.

---

[2] *HL Papers*, III, 381n.

You may rest assured that they are Gentlemen of Fortune & that you will be perfectly safe in executing their orders.

I remain here always ready to receive your commands & with great respect, Sir, &ca.—

SOURCE: Letterbook copy, HL Papers, S. C. Hist. Soc.; addressed "Esquire. Antigua"; "per Capt. Dickenson."

TO MEYLER & HALL

[Charles Town] 22 September 1764

Gentlemen,

Your favour of the 25th March by Mr. Sparkes & Mr. Cator reach'd me at a time when I was in a good deal of distress occasioned by the sudden death of my eldest daughter. That circumstance with some others of sickness in my family has made me very remiss in writing foreign Letters but the business which I had to transact for my friends has by no means suffered, & I believe those Gentlemen in particular will inform you that I did every thing in my power to do honour to your recommendation.

On the 4th May I remitted to Hutchinson Mure, Esquire a Bill for £300 Sterling on your Account to which it is charged at 721 per Cent Exchange & 5 per Cent Commission £2,271.3/ which was at that time Fifty pounds Sterling more than I was in Cash on Account of your Havanna Sugars, the Sale of which I have at length finished & now inclose you the Account, Net proceed to your Credit £3,448.7.11. I say at length because I might have made an end of it a long time ago but not so much to your advantage by 20 to 25 per Cent for the best offer that ever I had for it in quantity was £12 per Ct. the difference to you in gain near One Hundred pounds Sterling for which I would take a little extra trouble to myself & some additional expence of Storage. You will perceive by said Account that there is now £800.14.5 outstanding & probably the greatest part of it will be so until January or March next but as I am not apprehensive of one dubious debt in the Sale I shall in a few days remit Mr. Mure a Bill for about that Value. Meantime please to receive a Bill here inclosed for Eighty five pounds, one Shilling, & one penny, £85.1.1 Sterling, the draught of Constantine Zweerts 14 March 1764 on Messrs. Hall & Zweerts at Kingston payable at 30 days sight to Dunbar, Young, & Simpson & by them to Dunbar, Young, & Co., endorsed to you which I am assured you will receive without the least demur & in this case after deducting your Commission you will be pleased to pass the Net to the Credit of your Account with me & advise me thereof otherwise to return it under protest & in either event I shall immediately after finally Balance said Account.

We have a large Crop of Rice now gathering in as fine a Harvest Season as ever was seen. Negroes have sold very high all the past Summer. The general Average has been upward of £36 per head. Some Cargoes run as high as £39, & Remittances in the Bottom at 3, 6, & 9 Months.

I shall be always glad to receive your Commands being with great regard, &ca.—

SOURCE: Letterbook copy, HL Papers, S. C. Hist. Soc.; addressed "Jamaica"; "per the *Ferrett*, Man of War. Copy per Capt. McCormick."

TO JEREMIAH NIBBS, JR.

[Charles Town] 24 September 1764

Since I wrote to you the 1st March Last I remitted the Balance of your Account £109.15.7 Sterling to Mr. Thomas Ellis of London who has acknowledged to me the Receipt of the same. For that outstanding debt £101.10/ due by George Walker I have received a dividend of his Estate £35.8.6 & shall never be able to recover any more. Therefore you remain £66.1.6 in my debt which Sum you may repay as most convenient to yourself.

In March last Mr. James Dickson of your Island who had brought me Letters from the Northern Colonies which introduced me to the Honour of his acquaintance went from this Province about £30 Sterling in my debt for Money advanced merely to keep him out of the Marshall's hands which he promised to remit immediately upon his arrival at Antigua & I have since been informed by him that he was on the point of embarking for Britain & had ordered his Attornies to make a remittance of my Money in Rum but he neither told me their names nor have they yet complied with his orders. I shall therefore be obliged to you to make some inquiry & advise me if Mr. Dickson has left any effects behind him & in whose possession.

This will be forwarded to you by Messrs. Brailsford & Chapman who have some business of importance to transact in Antigua. I have told them that you will execute their orders very faithfully & you may be assured on your part that you will be perfectly safe in making any draughts by their direction.

We have fine Harvest Weather & our Crops will be large & early at Market. I remain, &ca.—

SOURCE: Letterbook copy, HL Papers, S. C. Hist. Soc.; addressed "Antigua." This letter was copied by HL.

TO THOMAS POTTS

[Charles Town] 26 September 1764

Sir,

A Letter was brought to Me by Mr. Joseph Burch[3] for the Balance of Your Pitch which I have paid to the said Burch, Vizt. One Hundred & Eleven pounds 17/6, tho' there is some reason to doubt whether the said Letter was wrote by you or not, but as he Assures me that You were unwell & that Your Sister wrote the Letter, I presume it was done by your Order & therefore will not detain the Money, tho' I have not rec'd the Amount of said Pitch which You know I informed you was Sold in part at 60/ per Barrel, it being too light for Shipping.

In looking over our Agreement dated in June I see that You encouraged Me to hope for some part of the 1,000 Barrels of Pitch before this day & in dependance of that I have neglected to look out elsewhere by which I am now Suffering some Inconveniences which I hope You will think of and remedy as soon as your health will permit. I remain, &ca.—

SOURCE: Letterbook copy, Letter Book of Henry Laurens, Oct. 30, 1762–Sept. 10, 1766, Penn. Hist. Soc.; addressed "Black River."

---

[3] Joseph Burch obtained grants along the Pee Dee River in 1767 and 1771, that for 150 acres on April 10, 1771 was at Cat Fish River. Index to Grants, S. C. Archives. Francis Marion signed a treaty with the tories at Burch's Mill on the Pee Dee in June 1782. Alexander Gregg, *History of the Old Cheraws* (Columbia, S. C., 1925), p. 375. By act of Dec. 21, 1792, the state legislature established a ferry over the Pee Dee near Cat Fish Creek in the name of Joseph Burch. *S. C. Statutes*, IX, 347.

TO SAMPSON NEYLE

[Charles Town] 26 September 1764

Sir,

It is so long since You last Spoke to Me about the *Elisabeth,* Capt. Smith, that I have really forgot what passed between us upon that Occasion, but let that have been as it may, the Proposition made in Your favour of this date is such an One as I never refuse to Listen to. If the Case is clear on my Side I can have no fears from Submitting it to the Determination of Indifferent persons, if it is doubtfull I ought to have no Objections. Therefore, Sir, be pleased to Tell me the Story once more & name anyone Man or More Men of Probity and Judgement & I shall wait on You & them when and where You please to Appoint. In the mean Time I shall be Glad to Talk with You upon the Subject, that I may not be quite so Ignorant of an Affair that I once Transacted as I profess myself to be at this Time, & for this End will wait on You whenever I know it will be Convenient. I am, &ca.—

SOURCE: Letterbook copy, Letter Book of Henry Laurens, Oct. 30, 1762–Sept. 10, 1766, Penn. Hist. Soc.; addressed "Charles Town."

TO ANDREW BROUGHTON[4]

[Charles Town] 26 September 1764

Sir,

I thank You for the Offer of Your Plantation which You Intend to Sell, and the more as You are pleas'd to give Me the Preference of Two other Persons, but altho Your Land is so Contiguous to mine I am Ignorant of its Qualities and its Value. If You will therefore be pleased to Inform Me how many Acres it Contains, how much Swamp, & how the high Land is Covered with pine &

---

[4] Andrew Broughton owned Stafford plantation which had belonged to his father Andrew, the son of Thomas Broughton, the lieutenant governor. When he wrote his will in 1779 he was living in the parish of St. George Dorchester. *SCHM,* xv (1914), 171–172, 185; "Will of Andrew Broughton," dated June 7, 1779, proved April 11, 1783, Charleston County Wills, xx, Book A (1783–1786), 80–81, S. C. Archives. On Aug. 6, 1764 Andrew Broughton, whose plantation was just to the north of Mepkin, stated that he owned 13 male slaves between 16 and 60. Minute Book of Commissioners of Roads, St. John Berkeley, 1 (1760–1798), S. C. Hist. Soc.

other woods, & what proportion of both sorts of Land is Cleared, what Buildings & fences, &ca. and Your very lowest price, I shall not detain you many Days without a final Answer on my part. Meantime I remain, Sir, &ca.—

SOURCE: Letterbook copy, Letter Book of Henry Laurens, Oct. 30, 1762–Sept. 10, 1766, Penn. Hist. Soc.; addressed "St. Johns."

TO JOHN HANDLIN
[Charles Town] 26 September 1764

Sir,

I Duely received Your favour of the 8 Inst. per Capt. Dick who deliver'd Me Your 100 Barrels of Pitch for which I have allowed You the highest Market price, Viz. £3.15/ per Barrel & pay for overweight, but I am very sorry Yours proves so much underweight as You will see by the Inclosed Account. It is a great Loss to Me for that 4 Barrels & ¾ will pay so much dead freight and Charges in England at least 30/ Sterling in the whole. You did not use to make such Barrels & I hope You will not do so again.

I have sent You in Mr. Dicks Schooner 1 piece white plains and charge you for the piece of Green that went up the last Trip £69.14.2 as per Account Inclosed.

Please to make my respects Acceptable to Your Mother and to Your whole Family & I remain, Sir, &ca.—

SOURCE: Letterbook copy, Letter Book of Henry Laurens, Oct. 30, 1762–Sept. 10, 1766, Penn. Hist. Soc.; addressed "Black Mingo."

TO WILLIAM THOMPSON
[Charles Town] 26th September 1764

Dear Sir,

Mr. Dick deliver'd me 60 Barrels of Your Pitch. Your Favour of the 13th says there were 61 Barrels but no more than 60 is come to hand for which You have Credit as per Inclosed Account.

I have sent You by his Schooner one piece White Plains and One piece of Green, also 9 large Duffel Blankets, Amounting as

Account herewith £89.19.2. The White Cloth is a little more then you Order'd, but if I had gone to buy just so much it wou'd have Cost You 1/3 or perhaps 2/ for Cutting.

The piece of White Plains that was wrong sent the last Trip is left at Mr. Nesmiths.[5] It contains 93 yards at 11/3 per yard comes to £52.6.3. I beg you will be so good as to Sell it for Me, and if You cant readily do that, return it by Mr. Dick.

Please to Sell none of my Salt after this Time under 12/6 per Bushel & to pay for the Barrels or 15/ per Bushel & nothing for the Barrel. I believe that Salt is going to be Scarce and Dear.

I shall be Obliged to You to recommend all the Pitch You can to Me who am, Dear Sir, Your, &ca.—

SOURCE: Letterbook copy, Letter Book of Henry Laurens, Oct. 30, 1762–Sept. 10, 1766, Penn. Hist. Soc.; addressed "Black Mingo."

TO SAMUEL NESMITH

[Charles Town] 26 September 1764

Sir,

I am informed that Mr. George Dick left in your hands 1 piece of Negro Cloth, quantity 93 yards. The price is 11/3 per yard and amounts to £52.6.3. It was intended for Mrs. Handlin, but my Young Man it seems neglected to Mark it. If You have Occasion for it & like the price (which it really cost me) please to keep it and Inform me thereof, otherwise be so Good as to Send it to Mr. William Thompsons or to return it by the first Opportunity and You will oblige, Sir, &ca.—

SOURCE: Letterbook copy, Letter Book of Henry Laurens, Oct. 30, 1762–Sept. 10, 1766, Penn. Hist. Soc.; addressed "Black Mingo."

---

[5] Samuel Nesmith, a justice of the peace who lived at Black Mingo, was a brother-in-law of John Brockinton. He had four sons who fought with Francis Marion. Boddie, *History of Williamsburg County*, pp. 77, 84, 92, 127; *Register of the Parish Prince Frederick Winyaw*, pp. 202–205.

TO WILLIAM HUGHES

[Charles Town] 28 September 1764

Sir,

Mr. John Potts[6] has deliver'd me your favour of the 25th together with one part of a Contract between us for Pitch executed by You, in which the Alterations that you have made from the Original seems to Me to be very Material, for the Quantity of Barrels shou'd be specifically set forth or at least the Quantity of Hundreds, otherwise I may be Obliged to receive & pay for 2,000, whereas you are Obliged to deliver only so many as shall be Convenient to You to make. This will be throwing too great a disadvantage on my Side & therefore I return you your part again desiring that these Words may be wrote on the Back *"the Quantity of Barrels of Pitch to be deliver'd by Me under the Contract within is to be at least ———— hundred Barrels"* wrote in Your own hand & Signed & the Blank filled up with the Quantity afterwards.

I have not the least doubt of your good designs whether the Contract be so perfected or not, but for both our Sakes let us Avoid every thing that may hereafter Occasion disputes & perhaps Lawsuits. If we enter into Contracts and Written Agreements let them be Clear & free from all Ambiguity—if merely upon the Honour of each other—be it so—Hands & Seals are unnecessary. I have executed my part & will Transmit it to You as soon as I receive Yours with this Amendment. The Number of barrels is of no moment to Me, nor am I Anxious to have Two thousand (more) then Two hundred, but it is absolutely necessary that You shou'd be Oblig'd to deliver Me so many as You may Compel me to take. Besides that, without such Specification, I shall not know with any Certainty what Freight to Engage, nor whether I may with Safety make further Bargains for the same kind of Goods. Waiting Your favour in reply I remain, Sir, &ca.—

SOURCE: Letterbook copy, Letter Book of Henry Laurens, Oct. 30, 1762–Sept. 10, 1766, Penn. Hist. Soc.; addressed "Captain. Williamsburgh."

---

[6] The younger brother of Thomas Potts.

T O   A L E X A N D E R   D A V I D S O N
[Charles Town] 2d October 1764

Sir,

I Receiv'd your favour of the 24 Ulto. & am obliged to you for the offer of your Pitch per George Dick which your Nephew[7] very Genteely made to me, but it has so fallen out that I am not the purchaser of it. I proposed to give him £3.16.3 per Barrel for it as it lay which was a very high price & I thought it a very generous offer too because there was not another buyer (that I knew of) in Charles Town. However one did start up & I was told that he had given Mr. Dick £3.15 per Barrel for a parcel that he had & to pay for over weight. Soon as I heard this, & it was from Dick himself, I offer'd your Nephew the same terms for yours & he told me that "I might depend upon having it." Afterwards when I went to take possession of it I was inform'd that Mr. Dick had sold it previous to your Nephew's engagement which astonished me because Mr. Dick had repeatedly sent me word that he had nothing to do with it & particularly because it was in consequence of his telling me that he had sold his Pitch at so much but that yours was not sold—that he had nothing to do with it, & that your Nephew was going to Ship it—that I applied to your Nephew & proposed to pay what Mr. Dick had established as a Market price.

However I have the satisfaction of being confirm'd in opinion that my first offer was a generous one since 'tis evident that there was no pitch Buyer of any consequence but myself, for even the person who bought yours be who he will could have no great stomach or he might & would have purchased both parcels at the same time, whereas it is clear that whatever pretences may be made Your Pitch was not sold to any other person when I bought it of your Nephew. He is well satisfied of this & seems to be under some concern about it. For the rest I refer you to my friend George who seems for the present to have fallen out with truth & gratitude & even with decency itself.

If you have not the Pitch ready for me by the time appointed it will be of some importance to me & probably of some to yourself & therefore I make no doubt of your endeavours to comply with your contracts. I remain with great regard, &ca.—

---

[7] Robert Davidson.

P.S. I also beg leave to refer you to my Letter of the 17th April last. If I had this pitch at even £3.15/ it would have been no more than returning what I then lent to you.

SOURCE: Letterbook copy, Letter Book of Henry Laurens, Oct. 30, 1762–Sept. 10, 1766, Penn. Hist. Soc.; addressed "Black Mingo."

TO PETER MOUZON

[Charles Town] 4th October 1764

Dear Sir,

If Mr. Halsey[8] had either called upon me or met me according to appointment at Mr. Legares Wharf[9] I should have wrote to you by him. I shall be obliged to you to ask him if he will come & take charge of my Boat which I shall keep ten days for his answer and then either by him or some other hand if he will not accept of her I shall send her immediately to your Landing. In the mean time I shall be extremely obliged to you to send down the Green Tar if by any possible means you can do it, as I have a Vessel that now almost waits for nothing else.

My Boat was out of Town when Mr. Halsey was at my House. I am in hopes if he will undertake the management of her that she will serve his purpose as well as mine. Pray between you & I, is not he a little addicted to tipling? If he is I shall be obliged to you to mention it that I may talk to him upon the subject & set out with a clear understanding in case he shall think proper to come.

My love to my Cousins[1] & I remain, Dear Sir, &ca.—

SOURCE: Letterbook copy, Letter Book of Henry Laurens, Oct. 30, 1762–Sept. 10, 1766, Penn. Hist. Soc.; addressed "Santé."

---

[8] James Halsey, widower, married Frances Grant, widow, at her house in St. James Santee on July 12, 1764. *SCHM*, xv (1914), 143. John Bartram lodged with James Halsey at Santee on July 16, 1765, on his trip from Charleston to the Cape Fear and again on Aug. 14 on his return to Charleston. Bartram, *Diary of a Journey*, pp. 14, 19.

[9] In the *General Gazette*, April 17, 1769, Thomas Legare advertised for rent the wharf and stores on the Bay which he had been occupying. In the *Gazette*, Oct. 26, 1769, he announced that he was resuming the factorage business in his countinghouse on Eveleigh's (commonly called Dandridge's) wharf.

[1] Peter Mouzon had married Judith Laurens, HL's first cousin. See HL to Peter Mouzon, May 14, 1764.

TO WILLIAM SANDERS[2]

[Charles Town] 4th October 1764

Dear Sir,

I here inclose you a Bill for the frame of a House which I want to send to England. If you can supply me with the whole both pine & Cypress I shall be much better pleased than to seek elsewhere, but if that is inconvenient please to take off such articles as you like best & send me an extract of the Bill containing what you reject. I beg, Sir, that you will be so good as to attend to this one point that I must have every piece of the very best & free from all exceptions. Please to inform me when I may expect the whole or such part as you accept, and the prices if you can. I am, Dear Sir, &ca.—

SOURCE: Letterbook copy, Letter Book of Henry Laurens, Oct. 30, 1762–Sept. 10, 1766, Penn. Hist. Soc.

TO HENRY BYRNE

[Charles Town] 4th October 1764

Sir,

I had wrote to you the 13th August advice of my intention to Load the Ship *Flora* with about 730 Barrels Rice to your address but another Ship, Vizt. the *Pensacola Packet,* Capt. Jackson, offering at a low Freight suppressed my plan & I have laid by the said Ship *Flora* for the New Crop when if I was sure it would not clash with the Interest of my friend Mr. Knight she should be with you very early. By the *Pensacola Packet,* I shiped 140 Barrels Rice part of the Provision made for the *Flora* in proportions on Account of Messrs. Cowles & Harford & my own as we hold in that Vessel, which you will observe by the inclosed Copy of the 15th Ulto.

This waits on you by the Brigantine *Delight,* Capt. Summers,[3] in which Vessel Mr. Manigault has Shiped One Hundred Barrels

---

[2] William Sanders, planter of the parish of St. George Dorchester, was the son of Col. William Sanders (died 1742) and of Margaret Moore (1707–1775), a daughter of Governor James Moore. William Sanders married Ann Broughton, the sister of Andrew Broughton of Stafford. *SCHM,* XXXVI (1935), 11. He died in 1776. "Will of William Sanders," dated Aug. 2, 1775, proved May 3, 1776, Charleston County Wills, XVIII (1776–1784), 11–12, S. C. Archives. He was the brother of James Sanders "at the Cypress."

[3] The brigantine *Delight,* John Somers, sailed for Oporto on Oct. 7. *Gazette,* Oct. 8, 1764.

of Rice on our joint Account & has wrote to you thereupon. I was partly induced to take up this late Freight from a promise of Messrs. Brewton & Smith that the rest of the Cargo Shiped by them should also fall into your hand which must be of service to your first Sales of the approaching Crop. You will be pleased to remit my part of the Net proceeds of this 100 barrels to Messrs. Cowles & Harford also. Tis time now that I should acknowledge the Receipt of your favours of the 21st January & 14th April which lay before me & make the needful reply to them.

I am perfectly satisfied with the Sales that you made of my Rice per Schonsevar & Addis[4] (some trifling errors indeed do appear but upon the whole not worth Notice & so I shall Enter in conformity to the several Net proceeds established by you) & I do believe that no person in Oporto has a better opportunity of disposing of that commodity to advantage than you have, but my opinion is better testified by the continuance of my consignments than by verbal declarations. However I must add that it is a matter of great pleasure to me to hear Mr. Manigault express his good will towards you, as well as others whom I have recommended.

Your Bill upon Mr. William Guerin[5] came to hand & was accepted the 15th June & fell due the 18th July last at which time I charged it to his Account & you in course have Credit in my Account Current for 144$126.[6] Mr. Guerin is a very good Young Man both as to his fortune & his principles, but you see that we give Credits in Carolina as well as you do in Oporto.

Our Crop of Rice upon the Ground or rather in Harvest was in the most flourishing state that ever I knew one to be until five days past when one of our Autumnal Gusts of Wind & Rain set in which must do some considerable damage to the Grain but if it goes

---

[4] The brigantine *Fox-Hunter*, George Addis, was cleared outwards for Oporto on March 21, 1763, and the snow *Oporto Packet*, Robert Schonswar, on May 6, 1763. *HL Papers*, III, 254n, 420n.

[5] The partnership of John Logan, William Guerin, and Elias Vanderhorst expired in July 1765. *HL Papers*, III, 31n; *Country Journal*, April 15, 1766. When William Guerin wrote his will on Aug. 13, 1765, he referred to himself as merchant. When he died on Jan. 20, 1768, he was a planter of St. Andrew parish. *SCHM*, x (1909), 156; "Will of William Guerin," dated Aug. 13, 1765, proved March 29, 1768, Charleston County Wills, XI, Book A (1767–1771), 323–325, S. C. Archives.

[6] For the rate of exchange between sterling and Portuguese money see *HL Papers*, II, 8n. The sum mentioned here was 144 milreas 126 reas Portuguese money.

over within a day or two the whole produce will still be very great, full as much Rice will be made as we shall find Markets for & no doubt yours will be fully supplied & you may expect some very early as here are more than one Vessel with a Licence.[7]

You observe in the Postscript of your Letter the 14th April some damage in the Cargo of Rice per Lewis.[8] I was very ill used by that Man both as to the soundness of the Ship & the terms of Freight which will in the end be no great advantage to him. I remain with great regard, Sir, &ca.—

P.S. I took great pains to Winnow every Barrel of Rice that I ship'd in the *Pensacola Packet* & made quite clean & free from Vermin. I think there must appear an essential difference between the quality of that & the rest of the Cargo of which I shall be glad to be informed for my own satisfaction for if there shall be no great odds I may upon a future occasion save some expence.

SOURCE: Letterbook copy, HL Papers, S. C. Hist. Soc.; addressed "Esquire. Oporto"; "per Capt. Summers. Copy per Capt. Dennison."

TO JOHN WRIGHT

[Charles Town] 6th October 1764

Sir,

I have receiv'd two Letters from you excusing yourself for not complying with your contract for Corn to be deliver'd to me in May last which I shall accept of & release you from any apprehensions on Account of the Penalty which is no less than Five Hundred pounds; at the same time let me ask you one question an answer to which will be sufficient from yourself to yourself, that short answer to be made by Conscience, will be more pertinent & more to the purpose than a whole Volume of written appologies. If the price of Corn at the time that you came down to George Town had been only 5/ per Bushel would you have sold it at that rate & returned contentedly home again without calling upon me? I am, &ca.—

---

[7] A license which permitted rice vessels to call at ports south of Cape Finisterre.
[8] Capt. William Lewis in the snow *Port Royal*.

SOURCE: Letterbook copy, Letter Book of Henry Laurens, Oct. 30, 1762–Sept. 10, 1766, Penn. Hist. Soc.; addressed "Cherraws"; "per George Dick."

TO JOHN COMING BALL

[Charles Town] 6 October 1764

Dear Sir,

As Mr. Fleming[9] is quite a stranger to me I think he can't be angry, if I should say that I would have believed you without the evidence of his Letter. Besides it produces nothing new. I had heard all that more than once in different words. At the same time I am heartily sorry to put Mr. Fleming or you or anybody else to trouble & I do assure you I had not been forgetful or neg[ligent] of that affair that he writes about. I told you my reasons for letting the Corn remain in the Country as long as possible, but I began this Week to reflect that it might become very troublesome & therefore have been endeavouring to hire Schooners to send for it. I applied two days ago to Mr. Lind & this day to Capt. Hutchins & neither of them happen'd to have an idle Boat, & I should have gone further but our *Wambaw* came in this Morning & I had determined to send a Boy this very evening to inform you that she should proceed immediately for that Corn & bring it away as quick as possible. I am much oblig'd to the people for indulging me so long. I have no desire to impose upon their good nature & am willing to make any reasonable compensation for what is past. I suppose I am to order the Boat to Mr. Gaillard's Landing.[1]

The *Wambaw* went to Augustine the 19th September & sailed from thence again the 22d. I had a prospect of her being here eight

---

[9] The Flemings were planters in the parish of Prince Frederick. William Fleming had been a justice of the peace. *Register Book for the Parish Prince Frederick Winyaw*, pp. 95–109. John Fleming, a planter in Williamsburg, died in 1768. "Will of John Fleming," dated March 23, 1768, proved May 11, 1768, *Abstracts of Wills, 1760–1784,* p. 105.

[1] Theodore Gaillard received grants to ten tracts of land on the south side of the Santee River between 1735 and 1769. Index to Grants, S. C. Archives. On April 13, 1756, acting at the request of the people of Williamsburg Township, the assembly had established a ferry from Theodore Gaillard's plantation on the south side of the Santee to Murray's Landing on the north side of the river. *S. C. Statutes,* IX, 187–189. By sending his vessel to Gaillard's Landing, HL could secure the corn that Mr. Fleming of Williamsburg Township had stored for him.

days ago, otherwise on Account of this very Corn I should not have suffered her to go (altho she has made a tolerable good Freight of £150).

I intended also to have wrote to you about the Wambaw Negro Cloth, which I wonder'd you had remain'd so long silent upon. If you will be so good as to inform me as you have always done in former Years, what is wanting either for the whole or for my part I shall send the quantity that you direct as usual.

Your Sister was taken so sick last Sunday that I found it necessary to get her Nurse home, but tho she is confin'd to her Chamber she still walks about & really seems to be more cheerful today than she has been for two Months past. I wish this suspense was over that I might have leave to come up your way which I shall do immediately after.

I present my Love to all friends & remain, Dear Sir, Your affectionate & humble Servant—

SOURCE: Letterbook copy, Letter Book of Henry Laurens, Oct. 30, 1762–Sept. 10, 1766, Penn. Hist. Soc.; addressed "Hyde Park." This letter was copied in the letterbook after those of Feb. 16, 1765.

FROM JOHN SAVAGE

Charlestown, So. Carolina, October 8th, 1764

It is requested that Enquiry be made whether there is any safe Harbour for Vessels on the East Side of Florida, Southward of St. Augustine, & what depth of Water at the Entrance from Sea, and if there is such an Harbour, whether there is any Communication from it within Land, near paralel with the Coast, whether Northward or Southward, and whether any Rivers or Creeks fall into it from the Westward and from what Distances.

What sorts of Land are Contigous and with what sorts of Timber it is covered particularly whether there is Quantities of Live Oak & Cedar or good Sawing Pine, and whether the latter is situated with Convenience for Transportation by Water.

Whether the Governor of East Florida could reserve convenient to such Harbours, Rivers, or Creeks, as are above enquired after, about Ten Thousand Acres of Land tollerable good, for a few Months, and if people from abroad should propose to take them up and Settle, what Quantity may be granted to each Person or Family & What Tenor & Terms such Lands will be granted.

It is proposed if Satisfactory Answers are received, that they shall be communicated & made publick in Bermuda, from whence many people may be glad of an Opportunity of transporting themselves and Family for a Livelihood & possessions, and no Country seems better adapted to them than the Southern Coasts of Florida, as such of them as have never been abroad, have not seen Frost, so that a cold Climate may not be agreeable to them.

It is proposed that as an Encouragement there shall be payed at the Charge of people here, the Sum of Five pounds Sterling per head for Men, Women, & Children as far as the Number of two Hundred, which Bounty shall be payed immediately after arrival at the place where they shall chuse to Settle within the province of East Florida above said, provided they the parents, Guardians, or Trustees declare on Oath or otherwise as may be satisfactory to the Administration, that it is their real Intention to settle in the Said province, or if it should be more suitable or agreeable that the said Bounty should be laid out in Provisions, Utensils, or necessarys in any other Country and sent th[ere] it shall be done in the most careful Manner & they furnished therewith without any charge of Commission by the purchaser. Possibly [the] above sums may induce the Number above mentioned to come over. It is very probable their Passages may be obtained with [no] charge to themselves, which the people here will use their endeavours to procure.

Perhaps some people of property for the Sake of good Lands may also remove, but for any such the above Bounty is not designed.

If any comes and the Climate agrees with them, possibly a Considerable Number may follow, and likely very useful people, such as good Carpenters and other handy craftsmen, besides Mariners, & in General they know enough of Agriculture to plant provisions very well. About October may be the best Time for their Landing as then they'l have the Winter to settle, clear Ground, and be in Order for planting in Season.[2]

---

[2] To answer Savage's questions about the lands south of St. Augustine, Grant dispatched Major John Moultrie and an engineer to search for a suitable tract. On their recommendations, Grant proposed to settle the Bermudians on the river which flowed into Mosquito Inlet sixty miles south of St. Augustine. Grant told the Board of Trade that this was the best natural harbor yet located and that

SOURCE: Copy, CO 5/540, pp. 293-295, Public Record Office, London. Endorsed: "Proposal Made for Settling a Tract of Land in East Florida by John Savage, Esquire To Henry Laurens, Esquire, To be laid before Governor Grant." Enclosed "In the Governor's letter of 22 November 1764."

---

the land surrounding it resembled that of the West Indies. The soil was good as was the timber which consisted of live oak, hickory, cypress, and pine. He sent this same report to HL (the date of Grant to HL is not known), who passed it to Savage. Grant to Board of Trade, Nov. 22, 1764, Savage to Grant, Feb. 23, 1765, CO 5/540, pp. 353-354, 369-371, Public Record Office, London.

The second issue raised by Savage, the terms under which lands would be granted, was answered by Grant's proclamation of Oct. 31, 1764, which he sent to American newspapers. Each family head was entitled to 100 acres for himself plus 50 acres for members of his family including slaves and indentured servants. Quit rents were to be only ½ pence per acre and were to begin two years after the land was granted. *Gazette,* Dec. 3, 1764.

While Grant was getting the project underway in East Florida, Savage was busy trying to stimulate interest in Bermuda. He wrote a series of letters to members of his family and other men he knew on the island. One letter went to two members of the Bermuda council, Francis Jones and Cornelius Hinson. In his description of the potential value of East Florida, Savage emphasized that the land was supposed to abound with the "best live Oak Timber," "a great deal of good Cedar, and vast numbers of Pine Trees fit for sawing and other purposes." Cedar which was used as framing timber for ships was particularly valued by the Bermudians. He also noted that the climate and soil should be suitable for rice, indigo, and perhaps cotton and coffee. Savage enclosed an extract of the letter from Grant to Laurens which contained Grant's report on the Mosquito Inlet. Savage asked the two councillors to recommend his project so that a delegation from the island would visit the area for a first hand appraisal. Savage's Bermuda contacts did publish his proposal and the terms under which land would be granted in East Florida. Savage to Jones and Hinson, Dec. 14, 1764, CO 5/540, pp. 365-368, Public Record Office, London. (The extract of Grant to HL is mentioned but not found with the Savage letter.) Alexander Heron commented on the value of cedar in a letter to Benjamin Martyn, May 18, 1750, as did James Habersham to Benjamin Martyn, Feb. 6, 1752. *Colonial Records of Georgia,* XXV, 489; XXVI, 343-344.

Two Bermuda merchants, Ephraim and John Gilbert, wrote Savage Jan. 26, 1765 to propose the removal of 100 families to East Florida. They planned to inspect East Florida to find a suitable location, and they asked Savage to recommend them to Governor Grant. Their prerequisite for settlement was a good harbor which would serve as a place of trade. The two brothers did journey to East Florida in the spring or early summer of 1765. After exploring the coast, they decided that their settlement should be between the St. Mary's (the southern boundary of Georgia) and Nassau rivers. They petitioned Grant and the East Florida council for a reserve of 40,000 acres, claiming to represent 500 persons who would settle in the area. Grant complied with the request, but not without having to ask first several men to vacate their lands in the area. Within the reserve, 10,000 acres was set aside for a township which was located about 13 miles from the mouth of the St. Mary's River. William Gerard De Brahm, surveyor general for the Southern District of North America, made a plat of the town which he called "New Bermuda." Ephraim and John Gilbert to John Savage, Jan. 26, 1765, Grant to Board of Trade, July 16, 1765, Petition of Ephraim and John Gilbert, n. d., CO 5/540, pp. 377, 415-418, 425-426, Public Record Office,

TO JAMES GRANT

[Charles Town] 10th October 1764

Sir,

Four or five days since your Excellency's favour of the 22d Ulto. reached me per the hands of Capt. Tucker, & yesterday that of the 24th August under cover from Jacob Cox, Esquire of New Providence with two Turtle of 60 lbs. each came also to hand. Capt. Tucker seems to want words to express his satisfaction with his late Voyage to East Florida. He extols the Governor & says a great many fine things of the Government, which, by the by, tho from a Tom Tucker is no disadvantage to either.

After my last Letter per Mr. Chief Justice Moultrie was closed I had two or three visits from Mr. Smith, Master of the *Ferret,* who appears to be the proper Man for your purpose. He discovers a clearness of understanding in the Branch that you would wish to enter him, & withal a solidity inviting confidence, but I am more than half afraid you will see that Gentleman no more, from a hint droped by him of the opposition that he apprehended would attend his application for a discharge from the King's service, & also from some little qualms visible enough about the propriety & utility of the proposed Exchange. As to the first he had not disclosed his thoughts to Capt. Bremer,[3] but wou'd as soon as he Arrived at Jamaica & Imme-

---

London; De Brahm's "Plan of St. Mary's Inlet . . . with part of St. Mary's Stream as far west as the intended Town of Bermudas, Surveyed Anno 1770" appears opposite p. 200 in *De Brahm's Report of the General Survey in the Southern District of North America,* ed. Louis De Vorsey, Jr. (Columbia, S. C., 1971).

The Gilberts reached Savannah in the latter part of 1765 with the first contingent of Bermudians who planned to settle in East Florida. This arrival went virtually unnoticed during the Stamp Act crisis. Governor Grant was elated with the news that the Bermudians were enroute to East Florida, though this first contingent numbered only 90 persons. Grant predicted that they would be followed by "hundreds" more from the tiny island. By the spring of 1766, the Bermudians had moved only as far south as Sunbury on the Midway River in Georgia. Grant was annoyed at the delay but continued making plans for their ultimate arrival in East Florida. He asked the Board of Trade to provide a bounty on all ships built in East Florida, which he hoped would give new encouragement to the Bermudians. Grant had good reason to worry: the Bermudians had already decided to settle in Georgia. According to De Brahm the Bermudians "all found their Graves in that Province [Georgia] in a short time." Grant to Board of Trade, Jan. 26, 1766, Aug. 5, 1766, CO 5/540, pp. 505–506; CO 5/541, pp. 113–115, Public Record Office, London; *De Brahm's Report of the General Survey in the Southern District of North America,* ed. Louis De Vorsey, Jr. (Columbia, S. C., 1971), p. 199.

[3] Captain Bremer of the *Ferret.*

diately apprize you of the Issue. Upon the Second point I endeavour'd to remove His dread of Sinking by Introducing my own remembrance of a present celebrated Admiral who was in the very same sort of employ or rather Station at the same place, meaning Mr. Tyrrel, in a small Armed Boat or Schooner attending Capt. Warren at the Siege of St. Augustine in 1740.[4]

Lord Albemarles[5] Two Turtle are already reimbark'd and luckily on Board a Ship of our Friend Oswalds to Sail tomorrow. The Master is a Clever Man. I can rely upon his Care & Attention & I have Great hopes that his Lordship will receive them, notwithstanding the Season is so far Advanced.[6]

Now that I name Mr. Oswald it Occurs to me that I have his Commands to purchase Negroes & Utensils for a plantation in Your Country whenever I have the Honour of your directions thereupon.[7] Perhaps You may not like Me so well for such Service from the Specimen that Mr. Dunnett carried from hence, but Indeed the whole of that purchase was not Consistent with my good Will nor with Mr. Dunnetts neither, but rather the Effect of Obedience to your peremptory Orders.[8]

I observe the Orders you have given that Your Wines and some other Articles shou'd be directed to my Care which shall be

---

[4] Richard Tyrrell (1717?–1766) entered the navy in 1730 as able seaman on board HMS *Solebay,* commanded by his uncle Peter Warren, and stationed at New York and Charleston. He also served on board HMS *Squirrel,* Peter Warren, at Boston and Charleston. In 1740 Lieutenant Tyrrell had been given command of a large schooner, the *Pearl,* which S. C. had fitted out to assist Oglethorpe and Warren in their assault against St. Augustine. Tyrrell with his 54 officers and men in the *Pearl* led the attack in June 1740. After 1740 his naval career was largely in the West Indies. After his marriage in 1747 to an Antigua heiress, he for a time forsook the navy for the sugar trade. In 1762 he was promoted to rear admiral. The *Georgia Gazette,* Dec. 29, 1763, announced that Admiral Tyrrell had arrived in Barbados as commander in chief of all His Majesty's ships on the Leeward Island station. HL was obviously impressed by his advance from able seaman to rear admiral. Julian Gwyn, Professor of History, University of Ottawa, who is completing a biography of Peter Warren, supplied the editor with the above information. Also see *Journal of the Commons House of Assembly, March 18, 1741–July 10, 1742,* ed. J. H. Easterby (Columbia, S. C., 1953), pp. 92, 112, 123, 246.
[5] George Keppel (1724–1772), who became third earl of Albemarle in 1754, commanded the ground forces in the attack on Havana in 1762. His share of the prize money was £122,000 sterling. Henry Manners Chichester, "George Keppel," *DNB.*
[6] The ship *Queen Barra,* Alexander Taylor.
[7] Richard Oswald had received a grant in London in July 1764 to 20,000 acres of land in East Florida. *Acts of Privy Council, Colonial,* IV (1745–1766), 814.
[8] HL had helped John Dunnett purchase slaves for Grant.

extended upon every Occasion to make the Channel of Conveyance Safe and easy to you.

Major Moultrie will tell your Excellency how my Family Affairs are at present Circumstanced, & what probability there is of my waiting upon you soon, which I am determined to do, if nothing Extraordinary hinders & Honest Tom Savage says he will Accompany Me, or go without Me if I delay, for He must pay his Respects to *Governour Grant.*

John Savage, Esquire, elder Brother of the Gentleman just named, an Israelite in whom there is no Guile, has turn'd his Mind upon one Scheme (among many others) full of Benificence in itself, promising great Advantage to the Natives of that Island where he was Born, as well as a Considerable Acquisition to your Infant Colony. For particulars I beg leave to refer to the Inclosed Writing in his own hand.[9] The Major who has one of the same papers & some Explanations from the Worthy Author, will be Able to say more to you on this Head. I shall be Exceeding Glad if you can give Satisfactory Answers to every one of Mr. Savages Enquiries. The Bounty propos'd for these the most Indigent Emigrators, I do believe is to be every penny paid from his own purse. He has the Completion of his project much at Heart & I am perswaded will Exert his Interest & Influence to encourage many others of somewhat more property in the Summer Islands[1] to remove from thence to Your Government. The Establishment of such people will Invite many more of the most valuable Subjects but the very Rumour of their Intentions will quicken the pace of some.

That poor Fellow the Mason mention'd in my last died three or four days after. I shall Speak to other Tradesmen as Occasions Offer & hope to prevail on some to go to Augustine, but I Have the less Chance of Succeeding as I shou'd encourage none but good Men, & such have Work enough here.

I have been as Industrious as was necessary to propagate your Opinions about the late purchase of Lands from the Spaniards in East Florida, & find the doubts and fears of many are remov'd in Consequence of which you will soon have some Adventurers from this Quarter. For my own part, tho' I pay the greatest defference to your Judgment & Agree in the General as to the Inequity and un-

[9] John Savage to HL, Oct. 8, 1764.
[1] Bermuda.

reasonableness of the thing, yet if the purchases are made in Terms of a Treaty Subsisting between the Crowns of England & Spain and the Title deeds of Conveyance receiv'd & in due form recorded in the Courts or Archives of the Latter, I can't see how the Purchasers can be Ousted. But I can very Clearly perceive Immense Obstacles in the way of an attempt to divest them of their Claims, so long as that piece of parchment call'd Magna Charta exists for I Conceive the proof will not lay so much upon the purchasers that the Spanish Vendors were possessed of and held those Lands by a Good Right & so forth, as upon other Claimants (be who they may) that they (the Spaniards) were not possessed, a proof hardly attainable after the Solemn Evidences Presupposed. The Quantity of Land purchased tho' it may stagger & vex the Ministry can make no difference, because the Validity of the Purchase of One Million of Acres & of one Rood will Stand upon the same Base.

The first and the other Lords of Trade Heard with equal Indignation of the Grants of the Altamaha Lands made to the Carolinians by Mr. Boone where by the way I hold some fine Specks; Governor Wright and all the Wise people in Georgia were certain that his Conduct wou'd be highly Censur'd & his Acts Annull'd. His Steps upon that Occasion, I believe gain'd him no Applause from the Ministry, but his Grants are Irrevocable.

I presume too much upon Your Excellencys patience, these things are only Entre nos & I wish rather to discover my own Ignorance & Mistakes then to be Confirmed in my present Sentiments. Be that as it may, I shall find some Corner Sufficient for my purpose, even if I purchase it from the Grand Proprietaries, which I wou'd chuse to do at a reasonable Rate, sooner than Subject myself to Certain Troubles or Expences that I do, or Dream I do, foresee, in case of a Contest with these Barons.

I wait Your further Commands, and in the Mean Time remain with great regard and Attachment, Sir, Your Excellency's most obliged & Obedient Servant—

P.S. I herewith forward a Letter lately from England left at my house. Your four Letters for Europe to the Earl of Sutherland, Mr. Oswald, Mr. Forbes, & Mr. Brodie[2] go with the Turtle in the Ship

---

[2] James Grant throughout his years in America hoped for a seat in Parliament. These four letters were addressed to persons who could use their influence to further his ambitions. Grant on his first visit to Charleston had written a long

Queen of Barra, Capt. Taylor, that one for Virginia per the first Oppertunity.

SOURCE: Letterbook copy, HL Papers, S. C. Hist. Soc.; addressed "Governor. Augustine"; "per Major Moultrie."

TO DENYS ROLLE

[Charles Town] 10th October 1764

Sir,

The Inclosed Letter tho' directed to the Care of other Gentlemen was sent to my House & I take this first Oppertunity of Conveying it to you.

I shall be extreamly Glad to hear of Your health & Success in Your present enterprize, & you will do me a very Great favour if you will give me some Account of the Lands you have seen, as I have thoughts of making a Voyage next Month to East Florida, & of Establishing a plantation there upon proper Encouragement.

If you have any Commands for me in this Quarter You will find me upon all Occasions, Your, &ca.—

SOURCE: Letterbook copy, HL Papers, S. C. Hist. Soc.; addressed "Esquire. St. Augustine"; "per Major Moultrie."

---

letter on Dec. 12, 1757, in which he mentioned that Lord Sutherland would exert himself to bring him into the House of Commons. Ms 1284, ff. 145–146, National Library of Scotland. The Sutherland interest dominated Sutherland and the Tain (Northern) Burghs. William Gordon, 18th and last earl of Sutherland (1735–1766), had succeeded to the earldom in 1750. Grant had been his tutor in 1752 when they made the grand tour. The Earl married Mary Maxwell on April 14, 1761. Their only child Elizabeth (born May 24, 1765) successfully claimed the title as Countess of Sutherland on March 21, 1771. Her husband would be created the first Duke of Sutherland. When Grant did enter Parliament in 1773, he did so "on the Sutherland interest" from the Tain Burghs. Henry Paton, "John Gordon, 16th earl (1660?–1733)," *DNB*; Namier and Brooke, *The House of Commons, 1754–1790,* II, 530. Richard Oswald with his wealth and his new estate in Scotland would have had immense influence. The Brodies had long had influence in Elginshire (Morayshire). The eldest son of James Brodie of Spynie, Elginshire, became Laird of Brodie in succession to a cousin in 1759. His younger brother Alexander Brodie (1748–1812) would enter Parliament in 1785. Namier and Brooke, *The House of Commons, 1754–1790,* II, 119–120.

TO ISAAC KING

[Charles Town] 10th October 1764

Sir,

The foregoing is duplicate of my last under the 13th Ulto. since which I have received your favours of the 2d & 20th July per Coombes[3] & Grant.[4] You complain that the Pitch Ship'd by Mr. Manigault per Gunn & Simpson was thin. It arrived with you in the very hottest Season which no doubt had some effect upon it. What I have now Shiped on our joint Account per this bearer the *Queen of Barra,* Capt. Taylor, Vizt. 108 Barrels as per Bill of Loading & Certificate here inclosed, goes thin from hence but will probably appear of a different quality with you in December next. You will be pleased to pass the Net proceed of this Pitch to our several Accounts in moiety as usual.

Please also to receive per said Ship & to sell on my Account One hundred & eleven pieces of exceeding fine Mahogany included in the above mentioned Bill of Loading & per Invoice inclosed.

I have Ship'd in the same Vessel the two Sconce Glasses in their original package which you sent me per the *Heart of Oak.* Please to return & Exchange them upon the best terms you can for two others ornamented pretty nearly the same as those to suit the Pier Glass, but one or two sizes smaller & send them per first Vessel. They were certainly packed very badly at first which should be considered by Mr. Bay if he makes the Exchange.

I have passed a Bill on you the 9th Inst. at 40 days sight to the order of Charles Garth, Esquire for £392.6/ Sterling which please to pay & charge to my Account Current.[5] I have examined the Sale of Mr. Stuarts[6] Indigo & pass the Net proceed to your debit £309.8.2 Sterling. The loss in Weight on this parcel is not quite 4 per Cent & yet I am as sure as I can be of any thing of this nature

---

[3] The Ship *America,* William Coombes, for London. *Gazette,* Oct. 1, 1764.

[4] The ship *Sea Nymph,* John Grant, arrived from London on Oct. 6. *Gazette,* Oct. 8, 1764.

[5] In the "Schedule of the Charges of this Government" from Jan. 1, 1762 to Dec. 31, 1763, there were allowances for public officers which included £1,512 for "The Agent in Great Britain his Salary" and £1,234.2/ "For his Bill of Disbursements and other Services." This total of £2,746.2/ currency equaled £392.6/ sterling. HL had therefore been asked to make this sum available to Charles Garth. House Journal, XXXVI (Jan. 24, 1763–Oct. 6, 1764), 199, S. C. Archives.

[6] Francis Stuart.

that it was moister, & might be called damp compared with the parcel that I Ship'd in the same Vessel the Voyage before. I do not mention or repeat these things to censure you but to apprize you of facts which if they have escaped you may make you more watchful in future. Our Crop of Indigo will prove better than was expected early in the Year but will not be large. No body talks of prices yet. If I can purchase upon saving terms I shall be a large adventurer otherwise will have nothing to do with that Article this Season. I remain with great regard, &ca.—

[*P.S.*] Having by me a duplicate of the Certificate for Green Tar per the *Hope* I put it into this packet.

SOURCE: Letterbook copy, HL Papers, S. C. Hist. Soc.; addressed "for Mrs. Sarah Nickleson & Company, London"; "per Capt. Taylor. Copy per Hart."

TO COWLES & HARFORD

[Charles Town] 10th October 1764

Gentlemen,

My last was the 13th Ulto. per Capts. Gullen & Harbison since which I have none of your favours. Please to receive an Invoice & Bill of Loading for 140 Barrels & 7 half Barrels Rice on our joint Account per the *Pensacola Packet,* Capt. Jackson, for Oporto Amount £1,843.5.4, ¼th whereof being £460.16.4 is to your debit & I have desir'd Mr. Byrne to remit my ¾ths of the proceed together with one Moiety of the proceeds of 100 Barrels Rice between Mr. Manigault & me per the Brigantine *Delight,* Capt. Summers, into your hands. Please also to receive a Bill of Loading & abstract Invoice for the Mahogany per Gullen.

Our Ship *Flora* is still lying at Hobcaw but I shall this day send up as much Pitch as with her Water & other heavy articles will stiffen her to come to the Wharf. Capt. Courtin has been long sick & now lies dangerously ill which does in some measure retard business but not much as goods do not come to Town in any quantities yet. Pitch keeps up at the enormous price of 75/ per barrel & to pay for all overweight. I have suffer'd two very fine parcels to slip by me on Account of this demand but there were others ready to take my refusal, wherefore I must submit. If I determine to Load her for

Bristol which I shall not until the next return of Schooners from Winyaw when if I am likely to get so much Pitch & Green Tar as will enable me to dispatch her very soon after, she shall proceed there. Otherwise I shall load her with New Rice in part & let out part if 60/ per Ton can be obtain'd for Portugal. In either case I shall have the general Interest at heart & hope my endeavours will meet your approbation & after this stumbling unlucky outset we may with regular advices be able to keep her moving to more advantage. This is a time of Year when your opinion of the prices of Deer Skins & Indigo would be very acceptable & might be made very useful & you have been a long time silent upon both. I find many people eagerly purchasing the former & I should be glad to enter the lists with them but I have not heard so much as the price of that article from you & your former Limits are below the present value on this side.

I am applied to by Mr. Nowell the first in the late House of Nowell, Davis, & Ancrum. He is Entring into a New Copartnership with Mr. Wayne late one of his Clerks, a sober discreet Young Man, & of some Capital.[7] Mr. Nowell is a good hand in business very diligent & must have a tolerable foundation unless he has been more unlucky than I am aware of, but you will hear their proposals & judge for yourselves accordingly. I have advised them by all means to address you in case they ask for Credit with a promise obligatory upon their Heirs & Executors to pay you in Sterling in Bristol & with Legal Interest. I remain, &ca.—

SOURCE: Letterbook copy, HL Papers, S. C. Hist. Soc.; addressed "Bristol"; "per Capt. Tayler. Copy per Marshall."

---

[7] Richard Wayne apparently formed a partnership with Edward Davies rather than with John Nowell. Miscellaneous Records, MM, Part 2 (1763–1767), pp. 654–656, S. C. Archives. Richard Wayne married Elizabeth Clifford of St. Bartholomew parish on Sept. 14, 1769. *SCHM*, xi (1910), 37. He received a grant of 500 acres in St. Bartholomew on May 17, 1774, and of 600 acres on Feb. 3, 1775, as well as other grants in the province. Index to Grants, S. C. Archives. His estate was confiscated in 1782 because he had petitioned to be armed as one of the loyal militia. *SCHM*, xxxiv (1933), 196.

TO THE EARL OF ALBEMARLE

[Charles Town] 10 October 1764

My Lord,

Three days ago I receiv'd from New providence Two Turtle mark'd *IG* & weighing about 60 lbs. each, which at the request of Governor Grant of East Florida, I have caus'd to be reimbark'd & directed to your Lordship on board the Ship *Queen of Barra,* Alexander Taylor, Master, for London, who has promis'd to take uncommon care of them & I think he may be relied on, in return for which I have engaged that your Lordship will gratify him with Three pounds, twelve shillings for each Turtle deliver'd alive. I have sent a large quantity of Purslain[8] for their food & the Master assures me that he will add other necessary articles as he goes along. I have the honour to be, with great respect, My Lord, Your Lordships Most Obedient Servant—

SOURCE: Letterbook copy, HL Papers, S. C. Hist. Soc.; addressed "The Right Honourable. Berkly Square, London"; "per *Queen of Barra,* Capt. Alexander Tayler."

TO RICHARD OSWALD

[Charles Town] 10th October 1764

Sir,

You have preceeding this duplicate of a Long Letter wrote per Capt. Bostock the 7th July to which I had intended to make some addition very soon after but was delayed some days for assistance from a friend or two in those particulars that I said should be enlarged upon as well as for a schedule of implements necessary for a farm. Afterward I defered writing until I should receive some Account from Messrs. Rossel & Gervais who set out on their long journey the 21st. I shall now enter upon the subject again tho it

---

[8] Purslane was a "low succulent herb . . . widely distributed throughout tropical and warmer temperate regions, used in salads, and sometimes as a pot-herb, or for pickling." "Formerly cultivated in English kitchen gardens, but now rarely met with." *OED.* When Robert Pringle sent his brother Andrew Pringle a turtle in 1743, he provided Indian corn for its food. *Letterbook of Robert Pringle, 1737–1745,* II, 562. The *Georgia Gazette,* June 8, 1768, stated that a live turtle (370 pounds) from the West Indies had brought a half guinea per pound when sold in London.

seems needless to be very full since I have received your favour of the 28th May which tho wrote so long ago came to hand only the 7th Inst. per Capt. Grant, in which you express some inclination to defer the prosecution of your original plan.

The Obstacles to settling so remote a Plantation are chiefly the distance from a Sea port & at the same time the vicinity of a capricious & barbarous neighbour. The first is no more than the inhabitants of Pensilvania have to encounter with in order to bring a commodity to Market of much less Value than Wine in proportion to the bulk & Weight of each, & this difficulty may easily be surmounted as the whole expence of transportation will after the first Year center within yourself. The late Duty on Wine will enhance the Value of it within Land & must have the effect of a Bounty upon all that is produced amongst ourselves & be so far an encouragement that comes unlooked for.[9] Mr. Murray[1] has offered to sell me a Tract of Land at Ninety Six of about 50,000 Acres which he calls very good & I believe it is so, at about Ten Shillings Currency per Acre. This offer & a desire to hear from the Young Gentlemen induced me to lay aside the thoughts of taking up a Warrant to survey any Vacant Tract which would have been attended with a considerable expence & leave me uncertain of the goodness of the Tract as I must have depended much upon the faith of a Deputy Surveyor who are in general mere hirelings. When they return I shall be capable of forming a clearer judgement as they have been as far as Fort Prince George, from thence across the Country to Agusta, all over the Long-Cane Settlement, & Ninety Six. I enjoin'd them to be very circumspect, to keep an exact journal of their proceedings, & to make very minute Notes of the quantities & qualities of the several Tracts of Land that they should pass over, as well vacant as appropriated & from the purport of two Letters Received from them[2] I expect great satisfaction in those particulars & I look for their return every day. No time will be lost by this delay, but an exceeding good end will be answered thereby as I shall be able to act with my Eyes

---

[9] Parliament had levied in the Sugar Act of 1764 a duty of £7 per ton on Madeira wines and ten shillings per ton on Portuguese and Spanish wines imported into the British colonies. The duties were effective after Sept. 29, 1764. *British Statutes*, XXVI, 33–34.

[1] Dr. John Murray.

[2] The journal and the two letters have not been found.

open whereas if I had gone more hastily to work, it must have been in a great measure blindfold & as the vacant Spots which I had in view will still be at my command no time would have been gained. So far I trust you will approve of my conduct.

As to the Indians which is the next obstacle, they are now & have been for some time past very quiet & must become less formidable every day as their numbers decrease & ours are increasing in much greater proportion. The Cherokees I am morally sure will never enter upon a formal War with us again, & the Creeks will very soon be so hem'd in that it must be consistent with their own Interest to keep upon good terms with the English. This they begin to see very clearly & confess it, & these tho at present the most numerous will from the Situation of their Country & our hasty approaches upon them sooner become Vassals than the others who have inaccessible Mountains to fortify a very fine Country Westward of them.

The French Refugees are highly pleased with their New settlement,[3] & the Irish are satisfied[4] & I am in hopes of seeing in a few Years a fine Colony rising upon the Spots where they are fixed.

I apprehend Messrs. Rossell & Gervais will be a good deal disappointed if you should wholly lay aside your intentions of establishing a Plantation in this Country nor do I know what scene of business they can immediately enter upon with Credit to themselves or to you. The sum that you order'd me to advance is exhausted. Nevertheless they shall not suffer want & I beg, Sir, that you will be so kind as to let me hear from you upon this point explicitly. In the mean time I shall talk to them about Trade & if they give me encouragement, I will enter them upon anything that they think eligible, so good an opinion do I entertain of them, & I must support them in the expectation of hearing from you about the Month of January upon the Farming plan.

---

[3] New Bordeaux.

[4] In 1761 the assembly offered to pay four pounds sterling for the passage of each poor Protestant brought to S. C. This act was printed in the *Gazette*, Aug. 1, 1761. John Poaug, John Greg, and John Torrans were eager to take advantage of this bounty and made plans to bring out settlers from Belfast. They petitoned for a survey of two townships in June 1762. Two townships were laid out in December: Boonesborough of 20,500 acres at the head of Long Canes Creek and Londonborough of 22,000 acres on Hard Labor Creek. In Feb. 1763 about 70 persons arrived from Belfast and settled in Boonesborough. Robert L. Meriwether, *The Expansion of South Carolina, 1729–1765* (Kingsport, Tenn., 1940), pp. 250–252.

I shall subjoin a list[5] of some articles that are thought to be necessary for a Farm & that may be sent from London upon better terms than I can procure them here & now I shall leave this subject & go on to that of building a Snow for you.

In my last I had in some measure postponed this business until Winter or till I should hear again from you but now receiving your further directions together with a sketch for the Scantling & the Season for falling timber being at hand I have applied to Mr. Rose & he after some hesitation has undertaken to build a Vessel as near to your discriptions as can be done & where he perceives any obvious defects as you rely so much upon him I shall consent to his making some alterations. The first Variation must be in the beam which Capt. Stephens[6] makes 19.6. This is undoubtedly too narrow for the length & absolutely contradicts your direction not to pinch her in the Beam. Mr. Rose says she will be ruined if he complies with that dimention & thinks it is calculated to save in the measurement of Tonnage. The depth in the hold is another error if calculated to take as you say for two rounds of Rice, because nine feet will receive Three tier of whole Barrels upon high Dunnage & leave vacancy enough aloft for very near an half Barrel under the Beams. I therefore think it must be greatly for your Interest to add nine inches to the depth & then she will take easily three heights And half barrel under the beam & be of good dimensions for Sugar in any of the windward Islands. The expence of building will not be increased & her draught of water will be nothing or a mere triffle more on that account.

Mr. Rose undertakes this job more to oblige you & me he says than for the sake of profit alledging that he can always imploy his people to more advantage in old work, & I believe him. His lowest price for building; finding every material of Wood, Iron, Oakam, Pitch, Tar, Turpentine, Masts, Yards, Bowsprit, to make the Hull & Masts perfectly compleat as to Carpenters work to a cleat is Six pounds Sterling per Ton, payments to be made at three periods & the risque of Fire to be yours, so far as the payments are made. The Vessel to be deliver'd in good order afloat. But he desires me to try some other builders & only to conclude a bargain with him in

---

[5] The list is missing.

[6] Capt. John Stephens had brought Oswald's vessel *Bance Island* to Charleston in 1760 and 1761. *HL Papers*, III, 35n, 43, 71, 78, 194. He was expected again in Charleston, but did not arrive.

case that I cannot succeed elsewhere. You will now be so good as to send out a Master as soon as you can to oversee & inspect the work as that goes forward & also such rigging & materials as you shall judge proper. The length of the Keel shall be as you direct. The Beam must be 21 feet or 20 feet 6 Inches at the least. Rose says he will rather give you the difference of Tonnage than to build her narrower. The depth of the hold from plank to plank, 9 feet 9 inches. All your other directions shall be adher'd to as nearly as possible. From hence you may form a just idea of what Sails, Anchors, Cables, & Cordage will be necessary.[7]

Mean time I must inform you that here is Landed from on board the Ship *America,* Capt. Coombes, a quantity of long Iron bolts, Rudder Irons, &[8] two Casks of Iron ware all seemingly calculated for a Vessel about 100 or 110 Tons marked RO which no person claims & which the Master says he signed no Bills of Loading for. I think tis highly probable that these were shiped by your order. I shall therefore at the Captains request pay him the Freight & what charges hitherto attend them & keep the whole in my possession until I hear from the true Owner. If they are your property you will have no use for them as Mr. Rose is to find every specie of Iron for the Hull but such articles will generally sell for full cost & charges.

I have heard nothing yet from Governor Grant (tho I have receiv'd three Letters from him) relative to the purchase of Negroes for your plantation in E. Florida. He will get a Letter from me to morrow by the *Tryal* Man of War[9] sailed this Morning in which I have hinted that subject & both of you may depend upon my best services in all your commands.

I wish Capt. Stephens may arrive here with an early & fine Cargo. 'Tis probable he will make a very great Sale.

You will see what has been done with those few ordinary Negroes imported per *Queen of Barra* which I hope will give your House satisfaction. I shall send you by Capt. Coombes some day next Week state of our imports & Exports for four Years past which will throw further light upon an Act of Assembly lately passed here calculated to prohibit the Importation of Negroes, a Copy of which with

---

[7] The editor has found no evidence that this vessel was built for Oswald.
[8] HL copied the letter from this point.
[9] HMS *Tryal,* James Wallace, sailed for St. Augustine on Oct. 12. *Gazette,* Oct. 15, 1764.

a few crude Notes on the back I now send by Capt. Taylor & refer you thereto.

You were pleased to intimate to me a promise that my good friend Colonel Grant had obtained that I should be appointed one of his Majesty's Council in this province. I find the Lieutenant Governor has also named me to the Lords of Trade & some other friends have Interested themselves upon this occasion in my behalf. Much am I indebted to them all for their kind intentions, but I wish they had previously consulted my own inclinations it would have saved some trouble, for I am determined not to be prevailed upon by any argument to accept that honour. I have many reasons to urge why I ought not, but I shall trouble you with only two which to me are invincible. The first, that I cannot attend the Duty of the Council consistently with my plan of Life & business & I always make a consequence of discharging faithfully every trust reposed in me, at least I would set out upon that principle. Second, I am not qualified for a reputable & Honorable discharge of that Duty & upon my word, Sir, I am & have been sorry to see that Honorable Board so much slighted as it has been at some times by certain appointments which hath reduced its character with some people almost below contempt, but I have nothing to do with this at present.[1] My design by what I have said is to request you in the most earnest manner to prevent, by a timely notice of my resolution a Mandamus in my Name. If one is already issued I must pay the expence but will never make use of it. At the same time I profess great obligations to my friends for their good will but I am sure when they seriously reflect upon my several circumstances they will, they must applaud my resolution.[2] I ask pardon for giving you this trouble & remain with great regard, Sir, Your faithful & obliged Servant—

P.S. Note the Schedule of plantation Tools, Tradesmen, &ca., &ca. from Mr. Moultries list sent in the Original & Copy—

---

[1] HL must be referring to the recent appointments of placemen such as Egerton Leigh in 1759, Charles Shinner in 1761, Thomas Skottowe in 1763, and also perhaps John Burn in 1763 who had so recently come to Carolina. M. Eugene Sirmans, "The South Carolina Royal Council, 1720–1763," *William and Mary Quarterly*, XVIII (1961), 373–391.

[2] "Mandamus's, we hear, are come over in the last ship from London, for appointing Sir John Colleton, Bart., and Henry Laurens, Esq; members of his majesty's council in this province." *Gazette*, Oct. 15, 1764. The same news was printed in the *Georgia Gazette*, Nov. 1, 1764.

SOURCE: Letterbook copy, HL Papers, S. C. Hist. Soc.; addressed "Esquire. London"; "per Taylor. Copy per Capt. Hart." HL copied part of this letter.

TO WILLIAM DONNAM

[Charles Town] 11th October 1764

Sir,

It is very surprizing to me that a Gentleman of your principles, should after such long indulgence as you have experienced from Austin & Laurens, leave your Bond unpaid, & now, without even the least notice of it, as if time instead of strengthning the obligations upon you, had cancell'd the debt, or that you thought, *that,* a sufficient plea for never paying it.

While you were under difficulties we waited with patience; now you are in circumstances to pay off old scores;[3] surely this that I have mention'd, which is a very old one, should rouse your attention; & I hope that you will give immediate orders to some of your friends here to discharge it. At least that you will inform me by a Line when I may expect to be paid. I recommend this to your serious consideration & remain, &ca.—

SOURCE: Letterbook copy, Letter Book of Henry Laurens, Oct. 30, 1762–Sept. 10, 1766, Penn. Hist. Soc.; addressed "at New Port, Georgia"; "per favour Mr. Lockerman."

TO LACHLAN McINTOSH

[Charles Town] 11th October 1764

Dear Sir,

I have received both your favours of the 15th & 17th Ulto. inclosing a Bill on Capt. Prevost[4] for £25.13.6 Sterling which is

---

[3] William Donnam was an example of a South Carolinian who made a fresh and successful start in Georgia. For the story of the South Carolinians who moved into the coastal regions of Georgia see David R. Chesnutt, "South Carolina's Expansion into Colonial Georgia, 1720–1765" (unpub. PhD diss., Univ. of Georgia, 1973).

[4] Capt. James Marquis Prevost had arrived in S. C. on Nov. 22, 1763 in HMS *Arundel* from Virginia to take command of the three companies of Royal Americans (the 60th Regiment) who were to replace the three Independent companies which were being disbanded. *Georgia Gazette,* Dec. 8, 1763.

accepted by Capt. Cochran[5] & shall be passed to your Credit in course. I am very sorry that your Brother[6] & Mrs. McIntosh were interupted by such an accident in their Voyage. I hope your Brother is now recover'd & well again. I am very much obliged to you for what you have done in the Caldwell's affair[7] tho I believe it will turn to no great Account if the Negroes are Mortgaged elsewhere which I have not looked into. Their Bond or Bonds did lay in the hands of James Box, Esquire, now Attorney General of East Florida. I shall write to some person in Savanna to get them & to transmit them to you & shall be obliged to you to get any thing from the Debtors that they will pay on Account unless you think it will be better to let the Bonds lay dormant until they are in better circumstances.

I wish you had mentioned something of your opinion relative of the engagement we are Entring upon with Mr. Lookerman. I submit the whole to the management of Mr. Deas & we had not gone so far but amendments & additions might have been made without prejudice or umbrage to any body & I shall be glad to hear from you still upon that very head, indeed from Mr. Lookerman's Account I have hopes of seeing you soon in Town which will really at this time be an agreeable event, & if you have any thoughts of coming this way pray hasten your steps.

As to your determination about Pendergrass's land, when you reflect a Little farther, you will see that it can by no means be obligatory upon you. Indeed to adhere to it would be to violate what I am sure Mr. McIntosh will forever hold sacred. I purchased it at your earnest request & within your Limitation & surely you would not because I have not your orders under hand & Seal involve me in a purchase which I should never have made but on your Account. My only difficulty upon that subject was to vest you with the property

---

[5] Capt. Gavin Cochrane of the 60th Regiment had arrived on May 21, 1764, to replace Capt. Prevost who promptly sailed for New York. Gavin Cochrane to Thomas Gage, May 25, 1765, Gage Papers, WLCL; *Georgia Gazette,* June 14, 1764.

[6] George McIntosh.

[7] On April 4, 1764, John and Henry Calwell had given a bond for £300 sterling with due date of Jan. 1, 1765; on Sept. 15, 1764, John Calwell, planter of the parish of St. John in Georgia, gave a bond for £250 sterling with due date of Jan. 1, 1767, and on Jan. 17, 1765, a bond for £76.6.6 sterling with due date of Jan. 1, 1766. Miscellaneous Deeds, Book O, pp. 166, 212, 265–266, Ga. Archives. If either of these men had mortgaged slaves to HL, the mortgage has not been found.

without paying one penny of the purchase which I think is the least that can be done for you by the proprietors of those valuable Tracts in its environs which you procured by a vigilance & activity not to be found in any hireling but only in the Acts of a Friend. This I am in hopes of effecting when we come together again & I will be quite plain with you. Having that in view I put a stop lately to an acknowledgement that was going to be made which according to my notions was paultry, compared with your merit.

I have not the least objection to your doing acts of Generosity nor would I presume to dash your munificince with a cool reception, but, Dear Sir, let every thing have its due cause & this time be content to receive a small token acknowledging that you have been to us extremely generous. All this I say only between you & me. If other Gentlemen are not quite of my way of thinking we shall accomodate matters to our mutual satisfaction but I really believe they will all chearfully come into my sentiments which I do not declare until we are together again. At present Mr. Hopton & Mr. Deas are off the Province. My best wishes attend you & yours & I remain, Dear Sir, Yours, &ca.—

P.S. Be so good as to peruse the inclosed Letter & then Seal & send it as directed & give me your opinion of the Debtor & his circumstance. His debt is £149.4/ per Bond 5th September 1755 due the 1st January 1756. (See Letter to Donnam[8] in Country Letter Book.[9])

SOURCE: Letterbook copy, HL Papers, S. C. Hist. Soc.; addressed "Esquire"; "per Mr. Lockerman."

TO JOSEPH BOWER
                                    [Charles Town] 11th October 1764
Sir,

My last letter was on the 12th Ulto. per Captains Harbison & Gullan, since which I have been doing every thing in my power to get your Snow *New Success* away, but she is still here. After waiting several days for Green Tar the only parcel that I know of in the

---

[8] In HL to James Donnam, July 9, 1763, HL mentioned a bond "of a very old date 1755 by Mr. William Donnam. . . ." *HL Papers*, III, 486–487.
[9] The "Country Letter Book" is the one in the Penn. Hist. Soc.

Country the Owner informs me that he cannot run off his Kiln until his Harvest was over. I have on board of Her 200 Barrels of Pitch, 105 Barrels Turpentine, a considerable quantity of pine plank, & about 1,000 Foot of Mahogany plank. I had offered a few days ago no less than Three pounds Sixteen & three pence per Barrel, for near 200 Barrels more of Pitch which I thought was a very long price but it was Snap'd out of my hands at about Four pounds before I had time to recollect myself. Finding this to be the case on that hand and that on the other Freight is let out for London at Twenty Seven & Six pence per Ton I had come to a resolution of filling up the Snow with Mahogany, pine plank, & a parcel of Cedar Logs which the Captain has purchased he says by your order & to have got her away within these Five or Six days. Hitherto I perceived that no time has been lost by waiting for any part of Her Cargo as Capt. Doran has but just made an end of the Sale of his & your goods which I believe he precipitated too because I told him the Vessel must go away at any Rate. However he says it will take him some days to collect his money yet, but what is worse than all this, the Snow made last night no less than Seventeen Inches water which gives me extreme concern on Your Account. I have advis'd Capt. Doran to give her a large heel hoping to find the leak in her upper works & easily to stop it, but if it proves otherways it will be a very troublesome & expensive job, & if the Snow must be hove down it will be more for your Interest that she should wait the New Crop which now comes on very fast than to be so long detained & to land & reload such a ragged Cargo as she has in her at present. Upon the whole, I shall do everything in my power to serve you as far as your orders & the State of our Market will admit of & you shall here further from me by Capt. Coombes who will Sail in two or three days. In the mean time I remain with great regard, Sir, &ca.—

SOURCE: Letterbook copy, HL Papers, S. C. Hist. Soc.; addressed "Bristol"; "per Capt. Marshall. Copy per Capt. Hart."

TO RICHARD OSWALD & CO.

[Charles Town] 12th October 1764

Gentlemen,

The foregoing is a duplicate of what I wrote you the 10th

August since which you have heard often from Messrs. Brewton & Smith whose Accounts of Sale & remittances for the Negroes per the *Queen of Barra,* I hope will give you satisfaction. If not I beg that it may be my duty to see any errors or wrong charges rectified. I have relied upon them as Men of Honour & not taken upon me the invidious task of prying into their proceedings, & I flatter myself that they have not done any thing to disappoint my hopes.

I am now to acknowledge the Receipt of your very obliging Letter under the 12th April which reach'd me no sooner than the 1st Ulto., so long was it coming round by the packet which is a bad conveyance in time of peace for Letters as those Vessels go so far round & are not in a Violent hurry to leave a good port.

I am much obliged to you for keeping my Silver a little while upon hand. When the Sale is ended, be so kind as to let me know what remains of Mr. Rutherfords debt that I may immediately discharge it or at least take some needful steps towards it for his money comes in so slowly that I continue to be in advance for him.

Gentlemen, I thank you for accepting my services to any of your friends, and I intreat you do not restrain your recommendations for fear of incommoding me. All that I have done are but small returns of acknowledgement for your great favours, besides I am a plain Man & a pretty plain dealer. I live in one nearly uniform course & endeavour to avoid all extraordinary airs upon the first appearance of any person, which must be troublesome to every one that merits the Name of Gentleman, & for such of your friends I cannot do too much when I consider whence they derive their claim.

I had no extensive scheme in my head by an African Voyage, only to serve my own demand for Negroes or very little more & am quite satisfied with what you have said upon this subject. I hope Capt. Stephens will be here with an early Cargo. The prospect I think is much in his favour.

Our Crop of Rice is large & just at hand. The price will probably break so high as to keep Freights down. The last let out was Coombes for London at 27/6 per Ton & I dont imagine that the first in the New Crop will be above 45 or 50/ unless 2 or 3 early Ships for Portugal may possibly obtain £3. I remain with great regard, &ca.—

SOURCE: Letterbook copy, HL Papers, S. C. Hist. Soc.; addressed "Esquire. London"; "per Capt. Tayler. Copy per Hart."

GEORGE AUSTIN, HENRY LAURENS, & GEORGE APPLEBY VERSUS JAMES ATKINS[1]

October 13, 1764

[On October 13, 1764, Robert Williams, Jr., attorney for the plaintiffs, filed suit in the court of common pleas against James Atkins, planter of St. Bartholomew parish who resided at Chehaw, for the recovery of a bond, dated September 3, 1760, in the sum of £550 currency. The court records do not indicate that the case was ordered for judgment or that a judgment was signed. The defendant did, however, pay the debt and court costs.]

SOURCE: Judgment Rolls, 1764, No. 20A, S. C. Archives.

TO JOSEPH BOWER

[Charles Town] 18th October 1764

Sir,

Refering to what I wrote you the 11th Inst. by this conveyance & Capt. Hart,[2] give me leave to add that Capt. Doran informs me he has discover'd the leak of his Snow & stop'd it & he now promises to fill up without further delay so that I hope to write you by him in five or Six days. Mean time I must inform you that the quantity of goods Ship'd by me are as at foot Value about £3,000 currency. Bad enough this is, but I know not how it could be amended consistent with your orders nor is it worse than the cases of some of your neighbours. This Vessel I believe has no more than 30/ & here is

---

[1] James Atkins married Ann Grey on Oct. 30, 1760. *SCHM*, x (1909), 234. He was granted a total of 3,000 acres in Colleton County in 1766, 1768, and 1771. Index to Grants, S. C. Archives. He was dead by January 1774. "Will of James Atkins," dated Sept. 4, 1771, proved Jan. 5, 1774, Charleston County Wills, xv, Book B (1771–1774), 665–666, S. C. Archives.

[2] The ship *Prince George*, Benjamin Hart, sailed for Cowes. *Gazette*, Oct. 8, 1764.

another Loading for your City (the *Tryton*) at 27/6 per Ton, which not only keeps up the price of Naval Stores but it has made the holders of it so indifferent or rather proud that they wont send any down till after their Harvest & Indigo works are over, thinking to suit their own convenience in every respect as well as to obtain their own price. This is truly the case with the generality of them, & therefore the little parcels that have been brought to Town have been sold at the extravagant rates before quoted. In these circumstances I have no just ground for complaint having procured more than my quota in proportion to the whole demand altho I have been Jockyed in one or two instances but that is a trade I do not understand & am content to put up with disappointments rather than learn it.

I am heartily chagrined that I cannot get the Green Tar for you, even that would have afforded me some consolation but it cannot be in Charles Town before the middle of November. I have only 81 Barrels of Pitch yet on board the *Flora* & perceiving how many difficulties there are in the way of making a tolerable Voyage for her to Bristol I am determined to take them out again & send that Vessel with New Rice to Portugal. I may therefore with great truth aver that I have done at least as much for you as I have done or can do for myself, with this difference only, that your Vessel is not so absolutely at my disposal. I remain with great regard, Sir, &ca.—

265 Pine & Cypress Plank
—— ditto not yet adjusted the whole about   £ 600
305 barrels Pitch & Turpentine   1,150
613 Mahogany Plank   300
with charges the whole may Amount to about £3,000

SOURCE: Letterbook copy, HL Papers, S. C. Hist. Soc.; addressed "Bristol"; "per Capt. Marshall. Copy per Capt. Moth."

TO COWLES & HARFORD

[Charles Town] 18th October 1764

Gentlemen,

The annex'd is duplicate of what I wrote you the 10th Inst. per Capt. Taylor, ever since which we have had (as well as for many days before) one series of Easterly Winds whereby the Schooners are all detained on this side & may be kept ten days longer for aught I can tell. Besides this, Freight for your port was Yesterday let out at Twenty seven & Six pence per Ton & one Ship going round to Winyaw to load there all which conspires to keep up the demand & price for Naval Stores & at the same time to suffer them to come to Town in very small quantities. Upon the whole therefore I have determined to take out 81 Barrels of Pitch which I had in the *Flora*'s bottom & to Ship them on board the *Tryton*[3] at 27/6 & to let out about five hundred Barrels on board the *Flora*, at the highest Freight that shall be given for the first Ships for Lisbon or Oporto & fill the remainder upon our joint Account. I am offered fifty Shillings per Ton but think it better to take our chance the other way & I am induced to let out some part of her Loading for the sake of dispatch. This appears to me to be the only step to be taken with her in the present circumstances of our port & Market. Capt. Courtin poor Man continues very sick. God knows if he will ever be better. I think his case extremely dangerous & if he recovers, he will not be able (according to present appearances) to proceed in the Ship as I shall not stay her any longer than to be loaden. All these things have been & are against us but 'tis better still than if I had attempted to load her for Bristol or sent her on the Voyage to Oporto.

Please now to receive your Account Current with a sketch of my Account with you which if you find right you will conform thereunto & if any errors point them out to be rectified immediately & I shall be obliged to you to transpose any additional articles that may be to my debit or Credit with you & Not here taken notice of to my new Account so that we may proceed in future with uniformity.

I have an old & long Account with my worthy friend Mr. Cowles. He will do me a very great favour in causing it to be adjusted & a Copy transmitted to me.

I shall take the Liberty tomorrow to draw on you for about four Hundred pounds Sterling.

[P.S.] 12th November. So far I had gone when the Sudden death of Mr. John Coming Ball obliged me to leave Charles Town.[4] The same circumstance puts it out of my power to perfect those Accounts which I intended to inclose here. I am compel'd by the strongest

---

[3] The brigantine *Tryton,* Nicholas Doyle, sailed for Bristol on Dec. 9. *Gazette,* Dec. 10, 1764.
[4] John Coming Ball, "an eminent planter" of St. John Berkeley, died on Saturday evening, Oct. 20. *Gazette,* Oct. 22, 1764.

necessity to go into the Country again for three or four days. When I return I hope to make amends for what is now deficient in the advices of, Gentlemen, Your obliged Servant—

SOURCE: Letterbook copy, HL Papers, S. C. Hist. Soc.; addressed "Bristol"; "per Doran. Copy per Moth." The postscript was copied by HL.

TO GEORGE APPLEBY

[Charles Town] 18th October 1764

My Dear Sir,

Since I wrote you last under the 14th June I have made several attempts to sit down again upon the like occasion but one thing or other has hindred me, some times ailments but oftener attendance on the House of Assembly, from both of which, thank God, I have now some respite. I have been very well & intend to keep so as long as possible, & the House is adjourned until January next. The mean time shall not be wasted, & hope soon after to have a final adjournment from that Duty. Those my friends who recommended me as a proper person to sit in Council here, did not consider so well as they ought to have done the subject matter of their application or they would have consulted at least my own inclinations to say nothing of my abilities. I thought it had been a new affair & a secret almost to myself as I had imparted it to none but Mr. Manigault; to whom I said that effectually to put a bar to such an appointment I should desire you without further delay to signify at the board of Trade in the most respectful manner my fixed resolution not to serve. To this purpose I have already closed a Letter & its duplicate to Mr. Oswald when behold just as I was entering upon this to you in comes Capt. Ball[5] with a packet containing a Mandamus, a present disagreeable to me from a twofold consideration, first that the Lords of Trade have been put to unnecessary trouble & secondly myself to a very unnecessary expence for I am determined not to accept of the Honour proposed to me. None of my friends can be justly offended with me on that Account since they omitted that ceremony of asking my opinion upon a matter of so much consequence & in which I was to

---

[5] The ship *Friendship,* Samuel Ball, Jr., arrived from London on Oct. 17. *Gazette,* Oct. 22, 1764.

be so materially interested. Now it will become me to pursue a more methodical plan & declare myself to the Lieutenant Governor who will in due course advise their Lordships of this Abortion.

The reasons upon which I found my refusal are invincible, at least they are so in my own mind. I shall trouble you with only two. In the first place it is utterly inconsistent with my plan of Life & business to give up so much more of my time as will be necessary to discharge my duty as I ought & would wish to do & you know that I do exercise some conscience in accquitting myself in every trust reposed in me, & I cant at this age new model that plan, so suddenly after an establishment that I have been seeking for & am pretty successful in. Next & more to the point, I am not qualified for that important charge. Some Folks laugh at this, & endeavour to point out my mistake by setting me up to my own view in an invidious light of comparison, but this instead of inflaming my vanity, convinces me more powerfully that it is absolutely necessary to have the present Vacancies filled with able Men—Men conversant with the Laws of the Realm, familiar with those of this Coloney, experienced in affairs of Government in general & the particular constitution of this, cool, sedate, wise, capable of giving wholesome Advice to the King's Representative, well qualified to judge & determine upon cases in Chancery, &ca., &ca. Such Men ought & some such may be found to fill that Honourable Board, which has already by injudicious appointments dwindled in the estimation of some people almost below contempt. Enough upon this head between you & me as I am quite sure that you will use no persuasives to alter those sentiments in which I declare my conduct is fixed.

I now begin to discover that this will be a long epistle & not the most correct one that ever was wrote but having taken it in hand I must go through with it, & first to begin with your very kind favours of the 5th & 30th July. The first gave all your friends notice of your safe arrival after a short passage which they were all glad to hear & I know that some of them, it being just Supper time, drank your health & one went so far as to smoke an additional pipe upon the occasion which must have had as good an effect upon you as if he had fired three rounds of 18 pounders. No doubt you will have your eye upon Governor Debatt.[6] He has not behaved genteely to us, in return for which I am watching the arrival of some Negroes of his

---

[6] Governor Debat of Gambia.

that are expected here. He will have no ground for complaint if I should avail our late House of the benefit of the Attachment Act.[7]

I shall apply to the other Owners of the *Lyttelton*.[8] No doubt they will readily pay their several quota of the charge you exhibit, if not readily they must & will at last.

As to the affairs of Capt. Stephens, & other Guinea concerns mentioned in both your Letters I'll tell you what I have done this Summer & what I may possible do in future. When Mr. Knights *Jenny* arrived here it was really not in my power to do him justice in the Sale of her Cargo. I was wholly unprepared & so unwell that I could not have exerted myself to my own wishes for his Interest. Brewton & Smith undertook the Sale upon good terms somewhat the better by the falling under my disposal. Capt. McKie complain'd a little of their remittances but I am sure they were just, tho I might allow there was some room to be generous too, but that is a principle whose legitimate issue freeborn only is valuable in my eye & therefore I cannot go about to extort its effects.

Another Cargo from Bance Island belonging to Mr. Oswald & Co., Mr. Tweed,[9] and others they sold too under my direction, & in both they certainly have made better averages than any other House. They have as great advantages as any and greater than almost every other in the Town. Mr. Oswald writes that Capt. Stephens will come here. If his or any other Cargo should be Lodged under my care, I will assuredly do as shall appear most for the benefit of the Owners by undertaking the Sale if I can do so with Honour to myself & advantage to them or by making the best bargain I can with somebody else. I am tied to none in particular, for I gain nothing by that sort of business—you know I scorn it—unless my friends the Owners are pleased to thank me. I am very loth to touch business of such

---

[7] The attachment act was passed May 29, 1744. Its title was "An act for the better securing the payment and more easy recovery of debts due from any person or persons inhabiting, residing or being beyond the seas, or elsewhere without the limits of this province, by attaching the moneys, goods, chattels, debts and books of account of such person or persons, if any he, she or they shall have within this province; and to impower and enable a feme covert that is a sole-trader, to sue for and recover such debts as shall be contracted with her as a sole trader, and to subject such feme covert to be arrested and sued for any debt contracted by her as a sole trader." *S. C. Statutes*, III, 616–621. For the identification of this law as the attachment act, see *S. C. Statutes*, IV, 92.

[8] For the owners of the *Lyttelton Frigate*, see *HL Papers*, III, 4–5.

[9] James Tweed.

importance without the assistance of a partner, & I neither see the fit Man nor feel inclination to seek for one on this side.

Your junction with Mr. Knight I hope will be a very happy one[1] but if the Law lately passed in Carolina is not repealed at St. James's you must look out for other Markets for your African Cargoes. This in all probability will be quite over stock'd next year & then for three succeeding Years that Law will operate to prevent a further importation. I transmitted a Copy of that Act with some notes on it to Mr. Knight, Mr. Oswald, & Mr. Bright & I now send you a state of the Trade of this province for the last four Years from whence you may form some further opinions of the propriety of & necessity for such a Law. I thought myself at Liberty to speak boldly against it & made use of arguments & introduced proofs which could not be controverted. Nevertheless the Law being artfully introduced did pass & I may say was cramm'd down in the latter end of a Session after other business had been requested for no other reason but because it was the latter end of a Session & many members gone home. Our once neighbour Brailsford[2] acted two droll parts upon this occasion, first in voting & whispering strenuously in favour of the Bill & afterward when I told him that I hop'd he intended to sell no more Negroes at the Crisis, he retired from the House & withheld his Vote as if his patriotism & his Interest were in strong debate. He may nevertheless be very honest & the error lay in my want of perception. Mr. Smith[3] was its Father & carried his point as he generally carries all points in which he succeeds. Assertions too often are substituted by him in place of argument and proof but this must be said for him that his declarations out of doors & in were uniform.

[*P.S.*] 10 November. Signed having been interupted & not to add but that I remain, &ca.—

[*P.P.S.*] My most respectful compliments to your good Mamma.

SOURCE: Letterbook copy, HL Papers, S. C. Hist. Soc.; "per Capt. Moth. Copy per Capt. Doran." The postscripts were copied by HL.

---

[1] Appleby apparently intended to join Knight in sending out slave trading vessels.

[2] Samuel Brailsford.

[3] Although Thomas Smith had introduced the bill, this may be a reference to Benjamin Smith, Thomas Smith's brother, who was a more important political figure, having been speaker of the assembly.

T O   C O W L E S   &   H A R F O R D

[Charles Town] 21st October 1764

Gentlemen,

I have to inform you by this conveyance of Capt. Coombes (who is now on his way down to the Rhoad in order to put to Sea early in the morning, Wind & Weather permitting) that you would have received a long letter from Mr. Laurens which he had almost ended but was suddenly called out of Town by the death of Mr. John Coming Ball, a dear friend & near relation, which I hope will be a sufficient excuse without appologizing for not compleating until his return & the next opportunity.

Mr. Laurens has taken the Liberty to pass three Bills on you of the 19th Inst. for £400 Sterling, Vizt.—

1 Sett, 40 days to the order of Capt. Nicholas Jackson Value of Messrs. Shirley & Martin for £100—

1 Sett, 42 days to Mr. Benjamin Adams or order for Account of Capt. Nicholas Jackson Value of Messrs. Shirley & Martin for £100—

1 Sett 40 days to the order of Nicholas Linwood, Esquire[4] Value of Mr. Fenwicke Bull[5] for £200—all of which you will be

---

[4] Nicholas Linwood (died May 2, 1773) was a wine merchant, government contractor, and member of Parliament from 1761 until his death. Namier and Brooke, *The House of Commons, 1754–1790,* III, 44–45. With Sir William Baker and Brice Fisher, he owned several baronies in S. C. On Oct. 21, 1765 they appointed Paul Trapier and Francis Stuart agents to sell their lands in S. C. Paul Trapier and Francis Stuart advertised for sale Jasper Barony and Saltcatchers Barony in the *Country Journal,* June 3, 1766. Paul Trapier sold Hobcaw Barony for them beginning in Nov. 1766. *SCHM,* XIV (1915), 63–64.

[5] Fenwicke Bull was not a member of the Bull family of S. C. He must have had friends at home, however, for he held a succession of offices after his arrival in the colony. Thomas Boone appointed him secretary of the Augusta conference. *Georgia Gazette,* Oct. 22, 1763. On March 24, 1764, Boone appointed him register of mesne conveyances in place of William Hopton. Miscellaneous Records, MM, Part 1 (1763–1767), pp. 78–79, S. C. Archives. Fenwicke Bull acted as agent for Smith & Nutt after they had been named contractors for supplying the troops in succession to Murray & Williamson. Gavin Cochrane to Fenwicke Bull, Oct. 1, 1764, enclosure in Cochrane to Gage, Jan. 4, 1765, Gage Papers, WLCL. William Bull appointed him notary public on Jan. 7, 1766. Miscellaneous Records, MM, Part 1 (1763–1767), p. 353, S. C. Archives. In 1769 after he was discovered bribing a jockey to throw a horse race, he was horsewhipped and stripped of his places. *Gazette,* Feb. 9, 1769. HL himself later commented on "the very despicable State & Circumstances" to which he had fallen. HL to John Laurens, Jan. 28, 1774, S. C. Hist. Soc. He also seems to have abandoned his wife, a printseller of Ludgate Hill, London, for in 1776 when he wrote his will he was living with Christiana Hoff "she and her husband having been separated by mutual consent"). "Will of Fenwicke Bull," dated March 9, 1776, proved Feb. 16, 1781,

pleased to pay due Honour thereto. I am for Mr. Laurens, Gentlemen, &ca.—

SOURCE: Letterbook copy, HL Papers, S. C. Hist. Soc.; addressed "Bristol"; "per Capt. Coombes. Copy per Capt. Saul." This was written for HL by his clerk.

TO EGERTON LEIGH

[Charles Town] 21st October 1764

Dear Sir,

Mr. Laurens had nearly finish'd a long Letter to you which would have gone by this conveyance of Capt. Coombes (who is now on His way down to the Rhoad in order to put to Sea early in the morning, wind & weather permitting) but was suddenly called out of Town by the Death of Mr. John Coming Ball. At present Mrs. Laurens is in a very poor state of health together with this melancholy information to her, may be an addition to her present illness, but I am in hopes that you will have the pleasure to be informed of her being much better when Mr. Laurens returns to Town & can have an opportunity of conveyance. I am, &ca.—

SOURCE: Letterbook copy, HL Papers, S. C. Hist. Soc.; addressed "Esquire. London"; "per Capt. Coombes. Copy per Capt. Saul." This was written for HL by his clerk.

TO GEORGE APPLEBY

[Charles Town] 21st October 1764

Dear Sir,

Inclosed you have herewith a Letter directed for Mr. George Austin, Junior[6] at Liverpoole which Major Moultrie left in order to be forwarded in that manner.

Abstracts of Wills, 1760–1784, p. 328. As a loyalist he removed to Bermuda where he was buried on Sept. 1, 1779. Alexander Richardson, "Private Register of Baptisms, Marriages, and Burials in the Parish of St. George," p. 80, Bermuda Archives. His estate was confiscated in 1782. *SCHM,* XXXIV (1933), 194.

[6] George Austin, Jr. was Major Moultrie's brother-in-law.

Mr. Laurens had just finish'd (say nearly ended) a Long Letter to you which would have gone by this conveyance of Capt. Coombes (who is now on his way down to the Rhoad in order to put to Sea early in the morning, Wind & Weather permitting) but was suddenly called out of Town by the Death of Mr. John Coming Ball. At present Mrs. Laurens is in a very poor State of health together with this melancholy information to her, may be an addition to her present illness, but I am in hopes that you will have the pleasure to be informed of her being much better when Mr. Laurens returns to Town & can have an opportunity of conveyance. I am, Dear Sir, &ca.—

SOURCE: Letterbook copy, HL Papers, S. C. Hist. Soc.; addressed "Leverpoole"; "per Capt. Saul. Copy per Coombes." This was written for HL by his clerk.

TO JEREMIAH BAIRD[7]

[Charles Town] 25th October 1764

Sir,

I have your favour of the 15th which you say accompanies sixteen Barrels of Turpentine by Watboo Boat, but I can't find that such Turpentine has been landed from any Boat. Therefore presume it still remains at the Landing & I hope will come the next return of that boat with your Pitch for both which articles you may depend upon having the best prices according to their several qualities, & I shall pay the Freight as you direct & also the Net proceed when you give orders. If you know of any Green Tar be so good as to buy it for or recommend it to me & you will oblige, &ca.—

SOURCE: Letterbook copy, Letter Book of Henry Laurens, Oct. 30, 1762–Sept. 10, 1766, Penn. Hist. Soc.; addressed "St. Stephens"; "per Mr. Harleston."

---

[7] Jeremiah Baird, planter of St. Stephen parish, died in 1767. "Will of Jeremiah Baird," dated Dec. 17, 1766, proved July 25, 1767, Charleston County Wills, XI, Book A (1767–1771), 76–77, S. C. Archives.

TO THOMAS AUBREY

[Charles Town] 26th October 1764

Sir,

I am indebted for your favours of 21st Ulto. per Capt. Bachop[8] who paid me on your Account the Value of Twenty Six Dollars, Vizt. Forty pounds Six Shillings which is placed to your Credit as per Account Current here inclosed. Balance due to me Twelve pounds Four shillings.

Under cover with this I shall put two Letters for Dennis Rolle, Esquire which I request you to deliver or forward to that Gentleman without delay & in case of his departure from East Florida to return them to me. I am, Sir, &ca.—

[*P.S.*] The sundry Letters inclosed in your last are on their way per Ship *America,* Capt. Coombes, sailed Six days ago.

SOURCE: Letterbook copy, HL Papers, S. C. Hist. Soc.; addressed "Esquire. St. Augustine"; "per Capt. Bachop."

TO JOSEPH BROWN

[Charles Town] 29th October 1764

Dear Sir,

This covers you a Letter per *Heart Oak* in which Ship is come two or three packages for you. Capt. Gunn promised me to deliver & George Dick carefully to receive & convey them to you wherefore I hope they will reach you in safety & good order.[9]

My Love & compliments to all your family. The Death of poor John Coming Ball is a great stroke to mine & will detach me very much from my Counting House for some time to come. I remain, Dear Sir, &ca.—

P.S. I open'd this to put in two Letters more this Moment from Bristol.

---

[8] The schooner *Mary,* Adam Bachop, had returned from St. Augustine on Oct. 19. *Gazette,* Oct. 22, 1764. Adam Bachop, who sailed frequently between Charleston and St. Augustine, drowned in 1771. See HL to Felix Warley, Dec. 5, 1771, S. C. Hist. Soc.

[9] The ship *Heart of Oak,* Henry Gunn, arrived from London on Oct. 23. *Gazette,* Oct. 29, 1764.

SOURCE: Letterbook copy, Letter Book of Henry Laurens, Oct. 30, 1762–Sept. 10, 1766, Penn. Hist. Soc.; addressed "George Town"; "per Mr. Gervais."

TO SAMUEL WRAGG

[Charles Town] 29th October 1764

Sir,

I had determined to answer your favours of the 27th Ulto. & 16th Inst. by Mr. Smith (your Clerk)[1] but the sudden death of a relation & dear friend called me at a very short warning Forty Miles from Town where I was unavoidably detained three days.

The Sale which you sent of the parcel of 8 New Negroes per Smart is satisfactory except the charge of Commission, which is the same that is given in Charles Town in consideration of Sale & Guarantee of debts. I have usually paid only 2½ per Cent & never asked more in the Country for the Sale alone. I am obliged to you for the Offer of keeping the Bonds & receiving the several amounts free of Commission, which you may do if you please but 'tis not improbable that you will be in Charles Town before they fall due which I think you said would be the 1st January & we may then talk more of this matter. I beg the favour of you to forward the Sale of the first parcel concluding it by the Sale of the short Negro Woman at the price you name if no more can be obtained but I think she is worth more, however do not stop the Sale of that Account.

I observe Mr. Perdriau has inserted the payment for the five Hogsheads of Rum which Mr. Smith bought for you to be half Casks which I am sorry for. He had no other direction from me than to let Mr. Smith fix on the Credit which you may extend as shall be convenient to your own affairs. If you are not supplied with Muscovada Sugar I have now two Tierces of a good quality—one of them very good the price £10.5/ per Ct., Tare 10 per Cent, the whole Net Weight about 1,430 lbs.

The Cedar & Bay Logs when you can soonest forward them will be acceptable. The little Guinea Man which I expected & in

---

[1] Samuel Smith was serving as clerk to Samuel Wragg. See Benjamin Perdriau, Jr., to Samuel Smith, March 26, 1765. Samuel Smith became one of the principal merchants of Georgetown in the post-Revolutionary period. Rogers, *History of Georgetown County,* passim.

which I was to have Ship'd those & other articles of Wood does not yet appear wherefore I hope she is better taken up.

All my advices upon Indigo are discouraging compared with the prices given last Year therefore I am determined not to give more than 26/ per for what we generally call the best Copper, bright, dry, & of a good shape & size, but tho that which we call best is so limitted there is of a quality of very fine Copper & purple which you very well understand for which you may give 27/ to 27/6 per when it merits the first Class of the best sorts, & for fine Flora as high as 35/ per. From these prices by way of standard you may exercise your judgment which alone can judge you (for no discription can) in the purchase of all the inferior sorts, & you may if you please to undertake it secure Twenty Thousand Weight from 20/ per to the highest forementioned price & Ten Thousand pounds Weight below 20/ in which purchases Messrs. Brewton & Smith desire to be Interested About £2,000 Sterling. You may take what share you think proper & I will accept of the remaining proportion, but it is the design of those Gentlemen that they should have as two to one compared with the part allotted to me.

You will now be so good, Sir, as to set about this work early if you think it can be performed with tolerable ease. We will transmit such Sums as you shall find necessary to accelerate our business & you will no doubt make the payments as easy to us as possibly you can. It is our intention here to Ship the bulk to London & the remainder for Bristol in which we shall be glad of your sentiments & concurrence. I remain, &ca.—

SOURCE: Letterbook copy, Letter Book of Henry Laurens, Oct. 30, 1762–Sept. 10, 1766, Penn. Hist. Soc.; addressed "George Town."

TO ANDREW WILLIAMSON

[Charles Town] 30th October 1764

Sir,

I have both your favours per Mr. Gervais[2] & that per Mr. Lockeridge.[3] The latter Gentleman has deliver'd to me the articles of

---

[2] John Lewis Gervais.

[3] James Lockridge received a warrant of survey, dated May 5, 1765, for 150 acres on a branch of Long Canes Creek. Patrick Calhoun as deputy surveyor certified the plat on May 24, 1765. Colonial Plats, VIII, 87, S. C. Archives.

Chesnuts, Hazelnuts, Telonich, & Puccoon, for which I return you thanks as I do for the poor unfortunate Rattle Snake whose body made an addition to my Table today.

I have paid Mr. Gervais's Bill on me to Mr. Lockeridge for £41.5/ as he will inform you. I had almost omitted to thank you for the Otter Skin & Tobaco because Mr. Lockeridge had almost omitted to send them to me & truly it escaped both our memories but upon recollection I sent for it & this circumstance caused me to defer writing until the last moment which will plead for the inaccuracy of my epistle.

The Otter skin is an acceptable present. Such things, baubles to you & me, are not a little esteemed by some wise folks tother side the Water.

As to the Tobaco I shall give you my opinion of it when the Gentlemen return your way some 14 or Twenty days hence & then I shall review your Letters & write about the Land schemes.

Your Neighbour Lockeridge is so good as to take charge of two Gloster Cheese which I hope will prove acceptable & I wish I could think of any thing that would be more so. If he conveniently can make room I shall trouble him with a few oranges for you & Mr. Bell to whom I present my compliments & remain, Dear Sir, &ca.—

[P.S.] I am applied to by a particular friend to procure a Specimen of our Cherokee Clay for making potters fine Ware. Can you help me at any reasonable expence & soon to the quantity of a Flower Barrel full. If you can, don't regard a little expence but let it be of the true sort.[4]

SOURCE: Letterbook copy, Letter Book of Henry Laurens, Oct. 30, 1762–Sept. 10, 1766, Penn. Hist. Soc.; addressed "Ninety Six."

---

[4] Thomas Mears of Liverpool had requested clay of HL in 1756–1757. *HL Papers,* II, 431. HL had mentioned the Cherokee "Clay Pits" in Philolethes. *HL Papers,* III, 314. Capt. Gavin Cochrane wrote General Gage on Jan. 4, 1765, after a tour through the backcountry that he had been to Keowee where "the houses are remarkably neat & plaistered with a clay white as lime which is found in this Country & of which there is a design formed by some gentlemen to make china." Gage Papers, WLCL. In 1765 Caleb Lloyd was trying to obtain clay for his brother-in-law Richard Champion of Bristol. Hugh Owen, *Two Centuries of Ceramic Art in Bristol Being A History of the Manufacture of 'The True Porcelain' by Richard Champion* (London, 1873), pp. 8–14. In 1767 the Wedgwoods sent Thomas Griffiths in search of clay. "Thomas Griffiths' 'A Journal of the Voyage to South Carolina, 1767,'" *Georgia Mineral Newsletter,* v, 113–122.

T O B E N J A M I N S M I T H

[Charles Town] 1 November 1764

Sir,

I rece'd both your Notes Yesterday treating of the paving Stones which quite satisfy me in one point.

But as for the Stones I cannot do with them what you say is expected from me: The price I had offered them to you at, was only at the rate of £3 Currency for £1 Sterling from which there is no room to abate, nor is there any for adding Charges, therefore I have disposed of them otherwise. I remain, Sir, &ca.—

SOURCE: Letterbook copy, Letter Book of Henry Laurens, Oct. 30, 1762– Sept. 10, 1766, Penn. Hist. Soc.; addresesd "Esquire. Church Street."

T O J O S E P H W H A R T O N , J R .

[Charles Town] 1 November 1764

Sir,

The Schooner *Molly*, John Wooster,[5] Master from Barbadoes with Twenty New Negroes on Account of Messrs. John Hasline & Samuel Maddock arrived here last Night all well. I hope this intelligence will reach you early enough to prevent the charge of Insurance which they were to desire you to make.

As I shall have no opportunity before the Schooner returns to advise of her arrival & my intention to load her agreeable to orders & with great dispatch, I shall be thankful to you to convey this part of my Letter to those Gentlemen if you can do so by any Vessel within a fortnight after this reaches you. I remain with great regard, Sir, &ca.—

SOURCE: Letterbook copy, HL Papers, S. C. Hist. Soc.; addressed "Philadelphia"; "per Capt. Mason."

---

[5] The schooner *Molly*, John Wooster, sailed for Barbados on Nov. 20. *Gazette*, Nov. 26, 1764. William Price paid £200 in duties for the slaves brought by Wooster. Public Treasurer, Journal B: Duties, 1748–1765, p. 420, S. C. Archives.

TO JAMES GRANT

[Charles Town] 3d November 1764

Sir,

Since I troubled you by Major Moultrie with a Letter under the 10th Ulto. I have not received the Honour of any of your Excellency's commands, which, together with the circumstances of Mrs. Laurens's sickness & the sudden death of her Brother Mr. John Ball who us'd to take upon him all the care of two large plantations[6] for me, will cause me to be less prolix upon the present occasion than I have been in my former addresses; for indeed this last accident involves me in a scene of Life so new that my time & thoughts are & must be for a Little while almost wholly engaged in it.

I lately received a Letter from Mr. Watts of New York[7] desiring me to convey a small packet & two Casks of Essence of Spruce to you. The packet shall go under cover with this & I have put the Casks on board the Schooner *Mary*, Capt. Bachop, who promises to be very careful of them.

I shall continue to be in all your commands, Sir, Your Excellency's Much obliged & Obedient Servant—

SOURCE: Letterbook copy, HL Papers, S. C. Hist. Soc.; addressed "Governor. Esquire. St. Augustine"; "per Capt. Bachop."

TO WILLIAM WHARTON

[Charles Town] 3d November 1764

Sir,

The foregoing is duplicate of what I wrote the 19th September since which I have sold so many of the Hats left here by Capt. Harrop as to make up 37 Hats for £211.15.10 but have rec'd no more Cash on that Account than £20, which should not however retard a remittance if the Sale was complete & that I had not discover'd what I did not advert to in my last advice, Vizt. that Capt. Harrops order is to remit the produce to Mr. Joseph Wharton, a point which you will be so good as to clear up for my government in closing the Account.

---

[6] Wambaw and Mepkin plantations.
[7] John Watts. *HL Papers*, III, 20n.

These Hats it seems were pack'd in a Barrel with Ship Bread at each Head which invited the Mice to make free with & damage a good many of them & what remains (16) being much injured thereby as well as by worm or Moth & also having the Look of old Hats new dress'd will not sell for any great matter. The next two Vendue days shall determine the Sale & the produce shall be remitted as soon after as you shall inform me how to do it with propriety. Meantime, I remain with great regard—

SOURCE: Letterbook copy, HL Papers, S. C. Hist. Soc.; addressed "Philadelphia"; "per Capt. Mason."

TO JOSEPH BOWER

[Charles Town] 3d November 1764
Sir,

The foregoing is duplicate of what I wrote you the 18th past, to which I have to add that Capt. Doran in your Snow *New Success* is using his endeavours to get Men & also to get in money for his own & your Account for goods sold here, two subjects that seem to perplex him very greatly & I am sure must be very injurious to your Interest. For my own part I can only look on with concern as it appears to me that you have mistaken the point of gain very widely & hurt your Voyage much, by sending such articles to this Market. Those in my hands you will Loose by but those sold by the Captain will prove to you like the burning a Candle at both ends. He informs me that you will loose considerably in the Sale & I am sure it would have been better for you to have lost the whole than to have the Ship detained as she has been & is by means of that Sale. You will pardon my freedom as it arises from a feeling which I can neither affect unnecessarily nor ward off when I see the Interest of my friends suffering so much as in the present case. The Snows Invoice will amount to about Three Thousand three hundred pounds, but cannot close it until the Capt. settles his Accounts which may not be these seven days. I remain, Sir, &ca.—

SOURCE: Letterbook copy, HL Papers, S. C. Hist. Soc.; addressed "Bristol"; "per Capt. Moth."

TO WILLIAM HODSHON

[Charles Town] 3d November 1764

Sir,

Since my last of the 2d April with Five hundred Dollars per Gunn, I have rece'd your sundry favours of the 14th February, 12th April, & 6th June & have also brought the *Don Pedro*'s Account to a close with the Gentlemen in Georgia so far as I think makes up the Sum due on their Bond tho we have not made an Adjustment which will for the present hinder me from transmitting an Account Current but not from sending you as many dollars as I believe will fully Balance your Account after the allowance of my Commission for which I intend to charge you 7½ per Cent on the sum rec'd, which in my opinion is a very moderate compensation for the trouble & risques to which I have been subjected in the course of this transaction. Out of that I must pay Mr. Read of Georgia his demand, which for aught I know may be very considerable, tho you may think he has merited nothing, & for that reason I shall not make a seperate charge, but submit this matter to you & reserve the Account until I have your further direction which I hope will be accompanied with your approbation by the first Vessel after this reaches you. I shall only add on this subject that 10 per Cent is commonly charged in this Country for receiving & remitting of debts in the most ordinary way.

In May last I rece'd from the Gentlemen in Georgia a Bill for £100 Sterling upon New York which I advertised & after some time sold it for £700 to Mr. Thomas Farr who still remains indebted for it tho I have dunn'd from Week to Week. In September another Bill of the same sort for £300 Sterling which rather than sell again upon Credit & have the renew'd trouble of dunning I sent to New York to Mr. William Hopton with orders if he could not Negotiate the Bill for 2½ per Cent & remit the Balance to you, to purchase Rum which was then at a low price or any other goods by which I should have any tolerable chance of making a new shilling for an old intending in this case to have remitted you the Amount from hence, but luckily he put the Bill in the hands of Mr. William Waddell who writes the 1st October that he should remit you £300 Sterling in a few days in Charles W. Apthorp's Bill No. 334 on Messrs. Thomlinson, Hanbury, Colebrook, & Nesbitt[8] & has sent me the 3d Bill. For this I

---

[8] John Thomlinson, John Hanbury, George Colebrook, and Arnold Nesbit, London merchants, were money contractors for the British forces in North America. *Papers of Henry Bouquet*, I, 114, 188.

must pay Mr. Hopton or remit him £7.10/ Sterling & think the Business well done too, for it is a fact that he did not present the New York Bill before the 1st October but by a favour rece'd ready money without discount for it.

     Now by this bearer the *Africa,* Capt. Moth,[9] I shall Ship you as per Bill of Loading to be inclosed Five hundred & Twenty Five Milled Dollars at 31/ per Dollar which puts me wholly in advance for the Bill sold to Mr. Farr, & I should have made this remittance a good while ago if I could have got Silver at that rate, but it has been for some time past scarce & notwithstanding the low price in England, Dollars were catched up here at 31/6 as our Exchange is 721 per Cent. This sum added to former remittances as per Account on the back makes up £8,710.1/ remitted to you which is only £246.17.9 Currency less than the Value of the Sloop *Don Pedro* & her Cargo & I must say & hope you will be of the same opinion that all things considered the Account is as advantageously ended as any of the like nature have been done in America. When I make a final settlement with Messrs. Johnson & Wylly & have your answer relative to my Commission I shall transmit an Account Current. Meantime I remain with great respect, Sir, &ca.—

Remittance made on Account of the Sloop *Don Pedro* to Mr. William Hodshon refered to in the foregoing Letter.

1763		
May 17	per the *Dorsett* 1,176 Dollars at 31/	£1,822.16
December 13th	per Capt. Ball 250 Dollars at 31/6 in Lieu of Timberlakes protested Bill for £50 Sterling	393.15
1764		
February 28	per Mitchel 1,212 Dollars as per advice	1,898.12
March 31	per Gunn 500 ditto at 31/	775.
	Remitted in October 1763 by Luke Kiersted from New York £129.9/ Sterling at 700 per Cent	906.3
October	Remitted by Mr. William Waddel £300 Sterling	2,100.
November 3	per *Africa* 525 Dollars at 31/	813.15
		£8,710. 1

SOURCE: Letterbook copy, HL Papers, S. C. Hist. Soc.; addressed "London"; "per Capt. Moth."

---

[9] The ship *Africa,* Hugh Moth, sailed on Nov. 12. *Gazette,* Nov. 12, 1764.

TO WILLIAM HODSHON

[Charles Town] 3d November 1764

Sir,

I have wrote to you this day per the *Africa,* Capt. Moth, for London that I should remit or had remitted you in said Ship Five hundred & Twenty five Mill'd Dollars. This will serve to advise you thereof in order to make the needful Insurance in case that Ship shall not arrive so soon as this. They will both Sail together or nearly so. I remain, Sir, &ca.—

[*P.S.*] In this Letter per Doran I inclosed one of Capt. Mothe's Bills of Lading—8 November.

SOURCE: Letterbook copy, HL Papers, S. C. Hist. Soc.; addressed "London"; "per Capt. Doran. Copy per Capt. Philips." The postscript was copied by HL.

ADVERTISEMENT

November 5, 1764

EIGHT neat Windsor riding chairs, imported in the ship Heart of Oak, Capt. Gunn, from London, to be sold for ready money at prime costs and charges, and one very neat riding chair, of the sort usually imported, lined with a fine light coloured cloth, painted a strong chocolate colour, an excellent harness and knee boot, to be sold for Two hundred and twenty pounds currency, ready money.[1] Likewise A very elegant Chimney Glass—prime cost without charges, £13.2.1 *Sterling*: to be sold for £105—being too large for the place intended for it. Apply to

HENRY LAURENS.

SOURCE: Printed in *Gazette,* Nov. 5, 1764.

---

[1] An invoice, dated Aug. 30, 1764, listed some of the goods shipped on the *Heart of Oak,* those shipped by Grubb & Watson to Hogg & Clayton. Invoice No. 27, Invoice Book Inward, Robert Hogg Account Books, 1762–1775, #343, SHC.

TO ELIAS BALL, JR.[2]

[Charles Town] 6th November 1764

Dear Sir,

I send by your Man Cuff six pieces of Negro Cloth & Six pound of Thread for Wambaw.

4 pieces I bought of the very best cost 15d per Yard at 11/3.
2 pieces of ordinary cost 11½d & 12d at 9/ per Yard.

The whole quantity 583 Yards which I hope will be sufficient for all the Negroes.

Your Aunt was so ill on Sunday and Yesterday that I thought her in great danger. She is somewhat better this morning but I dare not leave her yet. Therefore I beg your assistance to hasten this Cloth to Wambaw in the quickest manner you can & I shall be with you as soon as I can with decency & safety leave home. My Love to Sister Ball[3] & all friends & I remain, Dear Sir, &ca.—

[*P.S.*] I fancy the above Cloth must be rather too much but Abraham Schad advises me to send so many pieces.

SOURCE: Letterbook copy, Letter Book of Henry Laurens, Oct. 30, 1762–Sept. 10, 1766, Penn. Hist. Soc.; addressed "Hyde Park."

---

[2] Elias Ball, Jr. (1744–1822) was the eldest son of John Coming Ball and his first wife Catherine Gendron. He was known as Elias Ball of Wambaw to distinguish him from his first cousin Elias Ball of Limerick (1752–1810). Deas, *Ball Family*, pp. 184–185. John Coming Ball and HL had owned Wambaw plantation jointly. John Coming Ball's share of Wambaw was divided into four parts, one of which went to Elias Ball, Jr., who put the plantation back together again by purchasing HL's half in 1769 and shortly thereafter the shares of his three sisters. He later stated that "he was under the Necessity of rebuilding the Home immediately after the purchase of Col. Laurence. He dares say he laid out about £1,000 Sterling on the Buildings." After the fall of Charleston in May 1780, he served as a guide to Tarleton, was appointed a colonel of the loyalist militia on July 3, 1780, went with his family to East Florida in 1782, and to London in 1784 where he remained until the end of his life. He declared that his property in St. James Santee was valued at £23,000 sterling. Loyalist Transcripts, LV, 87–106.
[3] "Sister Ball" was the widow of John Coming Ball and, therefore, the stepmother of Elias Ball, Jr. John Coming Ball had married in 1756 as his second wife Judith Boisseau who would continue to live at Hyde Park until her death at the age of forty-one on Aug. 2, 1772. Deas, *Ball Family*, pp. 93, 95.

TO JOSEPH BOWER

[Charles Town] 7th November 1764

Sir,

Refering to sundry Letters lately wrote & particularly to my last under the 3d Inst. per Capt. Moth, I come now to address you per your Snow *New Success*, Capt. Doran, at length ready for Sea, the Captain having just made a final settlement of his Accounts with me. Please to receive the following papers under cover with this, Vizt.

Sale of sundry per Snow *Success*, Net proceeds to
your Credit   £1,159.14.1—
Sale of sundry per *New Success*, Net proceeds to
your Credit   £ 426. 0.6—

in which two Accounts you will observe there is £306.4.6 outstanding debts at your risque Invoice, Bill of Loading, & Bounty Certificate for sundry now Ship'd on board the said Snow on your Account Amounting to £3,152.16.6.

Your Account Current Balance in my favour £2,467.11.1 besides the outstanding debts. All which I trust will prove free from error & be noted with you in conformity.

I have already wrote so much about the Loading & detention of the Snow & also have made such remarks upon the several Accounts of Sale & Invoice that it would be troubling you with mere repetition to say anything more in this place save only upon two articles. First, that of Mahogany is a larger quantity Shiped than you directed but the Vessel must not go empty. There must have been an excess in some of the Goods pointed out by you & there was nothing that I could substitute consistent with your orders that was likely to pay so good a Freight. The next is Green Tar. Not one Barrel is yet come down to anybody. The same parcel & the only one I know of, that I had engaged so long ago lies still in the Country.

If the Snow had been wholly under my direction I might possibly have done something better with her, but not much, as may be evidenced by my own *Flora* lying now at the wharf with a swept hold, & also by many other Ships gone & going at 27/6 to 30/ per Ton. You will perceive that I have been so largely in advance upon our first Account as to make the Interest of money if I was to reckon it more than adequate to my Commission & I am likewise in advance for chief part of the present Accounts of Sale & Invoice having paid many Weeks ago for some of the Articles Ship'd and expecting every moment to be called upon for the remainder for which the money is ready. Therefore I must beg the Liberty of passing a Bill on you in a very few days payable in London for the Balance of your Account for which I shall receive a premium of 3 per Cent an advantage that upon enquiry you will find many other Bills have not been entitled to.

Upon the whole, Sir, I have acted with great tenderness for your Interest & it hath been subject of grief to me that I could do no more for you. My Commission will be but a small compensation for all my trouble & advance of money but if I procure your approbation of my conduct tis all that I wish for in the present case where I have so much cause to fear that you will be no gainer.

I hope your future attempts may meet with more Success to which I shall always gladly contribute, & remain with great regard, Sir, &ca.—

SOURCE: Letterbook copy, HL Papers, S. C. Hist. Soc.; addressed "Bristol"; "per Capt. Doran. Copy per Capt. Mothe with duplicates of the several Accounts, &ca."

TO ANDREW WILLIAMSON

[Charles Town] 9th November 1764

Dear Sir,

I wrote a few lines the 30th Ulto. per Mr. Lockeridge to which please to be refered. This waits on you by Messrs. Rossel & Gervais again who are returning to your Country in order to lay two Plats of Ground out by Virtue of Warrants which they have obtain'd.[4] I advised them & they did accordingly proceed with the utmost candor with Mr. Murray in respect to one Tract which they say is contiguous to his Land. He expressed his satisfaction upon that occasion & said he should be glad of such good Neighbours. Therefore I flatter myself with hopes that no offence will be given by their intended operations. These Gentlemen speak of Mr. Williamson & Mr. Bell with great

---

[4] Rossell and Gervais received a warrant dated July 13, 1764, for 5,000 acres plus 350 allowance for a former survey. The plat was certified on Dec. 15, 1764, by Patrick Calhoun as deputy surveyor. Colonial Plats, VIII, 296, S. C. Archives. This was turned into a grant on Oct. 31, 1765. Royal Grants, XIII, 216, S. C. Archives.

sensibility of kindnesses received from them & I make no doubt of their endeavours to make suitable returns & become good & useful Neighbours by & by.

I must now repeat my thanks for your Bountiful offer of a small Tract of very fine Land in the middle of their (intended) settlement, but why should I be burthensome to a friend. You have been not only civil but very kind to me in several instances, & your manner of giving tho it had been but a Cup of Cold Water has obliged me very much. In the present case I bid you will excuse me from accepting. Nevertheless I will have the Land if you please. Name your price & I will pay it upon demand to your order. This may be a first step toward being a Farmer at Ninety six, & a leading string to a Journey thither, but should you not think of another name for the whole district, & reflect upon the necessity for having places to perform divine worship & also for establishing a School or Schools? If these good purposes could be once effected your situation would become more secure from any obvious consequences & your Lands would naturally increase in Value.[5]

The Tobacco you sent me as a specimen is excellent. This was pronounced by one of the greatest Smoakers in the Country. If you bring any to Charles Town for exportation I shall be glad to have some direction of the Sale on to'ther side of the water.[6]

---

[5] The parish of St. Matthew was established on Aug. 9, 1765. *S. C. Statutes*, IV, 230–232. The act establishing the parish was disallowed because the total number of members in the assembly had been increased by two. Frances H. Porcher, "Royal Review of South Carolina Law" (unpub. MA thesis, Univ. of S. C., 1962), pp. 74–76. The parish was reestablished on April 12, 1768 by giving it one member and taking one away from St. James Goose Creek. *S. C. Statutes*, IV, 298–300. The problem of organizing the backcountry was a crucial one in the 1760's. It was not until the act of July 29, 1769 establishing the Ninety Six District and Precinct that the backcountry around Ninety Six was finally organized. Richard M. Brown, *The South Carolina Regulators* (Cambridge, Mass., 1963), pp. 138, 154.

[6] Tobacco was used but not grown for sale in the backcountry prior to the Cherokee War. Robert L. Meriwether, *The Expansion of South Carolina, 1729–1765* (Kingsport, Tenn., 1940), p. 176. Gray indicates that the growing of tobacco for export became important in the backcountry of S. C. only after the Revolution. Lewis C. Gray, *History of Agriculture in the Southern United States to 1860* (2 vols.: reprint, Gloucester, Mass., 1958), II, 606. "An act for regulating the inspection and exportation of tobacco and flour, and for granting a bounty on flour," passed March 20, 1771, established public warehouses for the inspection of tobacco. Seven commissioners, named in the act, were empowered to nominate inspectors for each of the public warehouses. This act is evidence that tobacco was being grown by 1771 for export. *S. C. Statutes*, IV, 327–331.

I commend these my friends & ward to your accustomed civilities & remain, Sir—

[*P.S.*] My compliments to Mr. Bell.

SOURCE: Letterbook copy, Letter Book of Henry Laurens, Oct. 30, 1762–Sept. 10, 1766, Penn. Hist. Soc.

TO WILLIAM WADDELL

[Charles Town] 9th November 1764

Sir,

My friend Mr. William Hopton upon his return to this place[7] sent me your Letter to him of the 1st Ulto. with Charles W. Apthorps 3d Bill No. 234 for £300. I observe the contents of your said Letter & am greatly obliged by the measures you pursued with that Bill which Mr. Hopton transmitted to you on my Account but I cannot agree in opinion with you, that because no money circulated, or passed thro your hands upon that occasion, you should therefore be deprived of your Commission. I think you are as well intitled as if £300 in Dollars or Gold had been paid to & remitted by you. Indulge me therefore, Sir, to add to my thanks Thirty four Dollars which I send by the *Sally*, Capt. Schermerhorne,[8] in a Bag marked WW per his Receipt inclosed which is about 2½ per Cent.

I had once the pleasure of being well acquainted with your Father & I shall be glad upon any occasion to render you friendly offices in this part of the World & to assure you that, I am with great regard, Sir, &ca.—

SOURCE: Letterbook copy, HL Papers, S. C. Hist. Soc.; addressed "New York"; "per Capt. Schermerhorn."

---

[7] The *Gazette*, Oct. 29, 1764, announced that William Hopton and his daughter had arrived on Oct. 25 from Philadelphia in the *Charles-Town Packet*, Thomas Mason.

[8] The sloop *Sally*, John Schermerhorn, arrived from New York on Oct. 14. *Gazette*, Oct. 15, 1764.

TO ABRAHAM PARSONS

[Charles Town] 9th November 1764

Sir,

The last time I troubled you was the 14th September per Tayler & Marshall to which please to be refered.

Mr. De Rosset has since wrote to me to Charter a Vessel partly on your Account but his orders came a little too late. Freights had been so low as 27/6 per Ton, but now the Crop of Rice is near at hand no Vessel will remove from hence without high terms, nor indeed would they before but for a considerable advance & security for dispatch according to agreements upon the whole. As the price of Tar is low on your side I hope you will suffer no great Disappointment.

I am now to acknowledge the Receipt of your favour of 6 July accompanying one from Messrs. Abraham Parsons & Company, Owners of the *Prince of Wales*,[9] under the same date.

I esteem the preference which you are pleased to give me in the Sale of that Vessels Cargo as an Instance both of your good Will & confidence in me neither of which shall be abused & altho I[1] have resigned several African Ships of considerable Value this Year & cannot yet presume to take upon me the sole charge of one, yet if your Brigantine comes to this Port you may depend upon my utmost endeavours to promote the Interest of the Owners in the Sale of her Cargo. I shall strive to make better terms for the remittance & observe their direction in the loading & dispatch of the Vessel. As to the share of Commission which you expect to draw for acting the part of Guarantee or security I cannot in the present instance think it unreasonable tho I have (when in Partnership formerly) refused to allow it, for you certainly take a great risque upon you in becoming surety for any single Man in America & you have shewn more courage in becoming mine than I dare assume in the African branch. My friends have been very indulgent & paid me (I think) unmeritted compliments in offering me this business & I am sure, that of Negroes actually arrived & intended for this port to my address the past Summer I have without one farthing benefit resigned the Sale of more than fourteen hundred.

---

[9] The editor has found no record of this vessel reaching Carolina.
[1] HL copied the letter from this point.

My reason for it was this, that being a single hand I did not care to embark in concerns of such importance too great for me in my best health & Subjecting the Intrest of my very good friends to great risques in case of my sickness or death. The same consideration will forbid me to ingage with your *Prince of Wales* in case she shall arrive here but then you may as I have already promised be assured of my Zealous effort to serve the Interest in general & particularly your own. This is as much as need be said at present upon that occasion.

The first new Rice came to Market today & tho it is part of as large a Crop as the last & that part of the last is still upon hand yet the price demanded for it is 50/ per Ct. If that is obtained it cannot hold there unless we shall have a great number of Ships come in very soon. At present the Harbor is rather thin. Pitch is 75/ per Barrel. Tar 50/. Green Tar none. Indigo the first comes demands 28/ per lb. Exchange 721 per Cent. A Cargo of prime grown Negroes would just now average from £35 to £40 Sterling. I remain with great regard, &ca.—

SOURCE: Letterbook copy, HL Papers, S. C. Hist. Soc.; addressed "Bristol." HL copied part of this letter.

TO GEORGE APPLEBY

[Charles Town] 9 November 1764

I have a long unfinished Letter lying by me intended for you but from many causes, I should certainly have let these Vessels slip too without making an end of that or writing any other to you or to my other worthy friend & friends in Leverpoole if your sundry favours per Capt. Dennison[2] had not reached & roused me tonight. For tho, this you say, is to be your Jubilee Year, & God grant all your Years may be such until they join & are lost in eternal joys, yet to me, it has proved a Year of affliction—a Dead eldest daughter, a sick Summer, a Sick & dying Wife, a dying Capt. Courtin,[3] a dead John Coming

---

[2] The ship *Knight*, Thomas Dennison, arrived Nov. 9 from Liverpool. *Gazette*, Nov. 12, 1764.

[3] Thomas Courtin recovered, but he did die later in Charleston and was buried on Feb. 10, 1770. *Register of St. Philip's Parish, 1754–1810*, p. 331. By then he was no longer in the employ of HL being on a voyage from Poole to Newfoundland to Charleston. *SCHM*, XXXIV (1933), 32.

Ball, my best friend & best Overseer, hands full of business without the most able assistants—have all conspired to try me until notwithstanding those fricas of which you know I can be sometimes guilty, I have lately from experience pronoun[*c*]'d myself a Man of great patience & as good a Man as any in this Country. Mr. Manigault confirmed my claim by saying, why so you are. But wither am I wandering to try your patience too & make my head ach. 'Tis now near Midnight, the Vessels in the Road, & to sail with the dawn tomorrow, let me then tell you a little of business. But first say I must Copy this Letter myself tonight. The Affairs of the *Knight* shall be duly attended to & tis ten to one that she gets away a first Ship for Oporto.

The first new Rice came down today to our Moderate friend the Late Speaker.[4] He asks only 50/ a hundred for it. If he'd shew me a whole fine Cargo I would come very near him. The *Austin* does not yet appear. I will always strain hard to serve Mr. Knight & Mr. Appleby but upon trial I would not do injustice for either of them, for I know they would despise me if I did, but when they have an honest preference I wont throw it aside to oblige anybody.

About three Hundred pounds Sterling Value lies in my desk of your Money & the Sterling has been laying many Months in England it shall go hard with me if I don't send your Exchange next Week. My having the Money will be no great consolation to you if you want it. Pray excuse me to Mr. Knight. If he & you could see exactly my situation you would pity me, but extremes are not lasting. Be Wary & cautious in your orders to Guinea Men for Carolina next Summer, but order them to me if any comes. I'll put them upon the best terms into the best hands this Country affords, if I am in the Country which is now some doubt with me but will be none if it please God to deprive me of your friend Mrs. Laurens who has been long in danger & tho much better now, is still in a precarious state. Jacky, Polly, & Harry are well & our little spot is a paradise but we the inhabitants are Mortals.

You see I can't help writing a long Letter to you. 'Tis as if I spun out a dull tale to keep you another pipe. What a compound

---

[4] Benjamin Smith was the late speaker of the assembly. Rawlins Lowndes had been elected speaker on Sept. 2, 1763, because Smith was "off the province," making a northern summer tour. House Journal, xxxvi (Jan. 24, 1763–Oct. 6, 1764), first pagination, p. 13, S. C. Archives; Rogers, *Evolution of a Federalist,* p. 40.

of Gravity & Levity is here. Tis a midnight medly from a burn at each ear, but farewell, Dear Sir, I am your sincere friend—

SOURCE: Letterbook copy, HL Papers, S. C. Hist. Soc.; addressed "Leverpoole"; "per Capt. Moth. Copy per Doran."

TO JOHN & JAMES GRAHAM & CO.

[Charles Town] 9th November 1764

Gentlemen,

I have the pleasure of forwarding in company with this a small packet from Bristol & a Letter this instant received from Jamacia. The former I have reason to think treats of the *Prince of Wales* Brigantine belonging to our friends Messrs. Abraham Parsons & Co. expected from Africa, which I take notice of because she is charg'd upon me in case of her arrival at this port & as I shall not undertake the Sale of her Cargo I would not, if she is worth your acceptance, have you miss of it. Therefore with your permission I shall upon her appearance advertize the Sale in your names & do what is needful until the arrival of one of your House to take the burthen upon yourselves, which no doubt your friends here will endeavour to make as light as possible to you & if you are pleased to command my services none will more chearfully assist you than, Gentlemen, Yours, &ca.—

[*P.S.*] I have taken the Liberty of putting two other Letters for Georgia under cover with this which please to forward.

SOURCE: Letterbook copy, HL Papers, S. C. Hist. Soc.; addressed "Georgia."

TO MEYLER & HALL

[Charles Town] 10th November 1764

Gentlemen,

The preceeding is duplicate of what I wrote you the 22d September per the *Ferret* Man of War. Last Night came to hand your esteemed favour of the 10th Ulto. per your Schooner *Dispatch*,[5] which I shall probably load & get away in 5 or six days according to your order. I have likewise agreed for the Brigantine *Savage*, a fine Bermuda Vessel, Burthen about 360 Barrels,[6] which I shall also load on your account for Savanna Le Mar.[7] I have four Weeks to perform it in but shall be as much as possible within that time. The Freight of the Vessel, hold & Deck, is Three hundred & twenty pounds your Currency[8] which I think very reasonable & Mr. Manigault is of the same opinion.

As to draughts I shall make them as easy as possible & rather stretch the time you Limit than contract it, tho there is some danger of the fall of Exchange in a Month or two, at present 721 per Cent continues to be given. I shall do the best I can for you in every respect & hope you will be convinc'd of it. I remain with great regard, &ca.—

SOURCE: Letterbook copy, HL Papers, S. C. Hist. Soc.; addressed "Jamaica"; "per Capt. Cooke. Copy per Capt. Wylie."

---

[5] The schooner *Dispatch*, John Wylie, arrived Nov. 9 from Jamaica and sailed Nov. 20 for Jamaica. *Gazette*, Nov. 12, 26, 1764.

[6] The brigantine *Savage*, Edward Blake, arrived Nov. 7 from Jamaica and sailed Dec. 9 for Jamaica with Thomas Durham as master. *Gazette*, Nov. 12, Dec. 10, 1764. Capt. Edward Blake had decided to turn factor. He announced in the *Gazette*, Dec. 3, 1764, that he had rented Roper's wharf at the south end of the Bay where he proposed to sell "COUNTRY PRODUCE." He also had for sale at John Savage's store in Tradd Street Jamaica and Windward Island rum, sugar, flour, and indigo seed. He was appointed first commissioner of the Board of Naval Commissioners during the Revolution and, therefore, largely influenced the founding of the S. C. Navy. He bought in 1775 part of Wappoo plantation where he died in 1795. *SCHM*, xvi (1915), 65; xx (1919), 149; *Journal of the Commissioners of the Navy of South Carolina, October 9, 1776–March 1, 1779*, ed. A. S. Salley, Jr. (Columbia, S. C., 1912), passim. He still, however, referred to himself as factor in his will. "Will of Edward Blake," dated Aug. 25, 1795, proved Nov. 3, 1795, Charleston County Wills, xxvi, Book B (1793–1800), 361–366, S. C. Archives.

[7] Savanna Le Mar was a Jamaican port on the south side of the island near the western end.

[8] For the ratio of Jamaica money to S. C. currency see *HL Papers*, ii, 20n.

GEORGE AUSTIN, HENRY LAURENS, &
GEORGE APPLEBY VERSUS
WILLIAM HAYNE[9]

November 15, 1764

[*This case was ordered for judgment on this date during the November term of the court of common pleas. The case involved an unspecified debt owed by William Hayne to Austin, Laurens, & Appleby. James Moultrie who had initially represented the plaintiffs was replaced by William Graeme on November 13, 1764.*]

SOURCE: Journal, Court of Common Pleas, 1763–1769, pp. 92, 96, S. C. Archives.

TO JAMES BRENARD

[Charles Town] 16th November 1764

I now send you by a Cannoe to Fogarties landing[1] a Bale containing Ninety six duffill Blankets the best that ever was I believe at Wambaw. You may distribute five pieces that is eighty blankets amongst all the Negroes as they stand most in need & make some of them part with their old blankets to others. Lay by the other piece together with the Crocus Wrapper untill I come which will be one of these days. I hope you have got the Negro Cloth & will make dispatch in cloathing the poor creatures. My heart aches for them until that is done.

Pray remember to be careful for the fire near to the Barn. Let the people thrash & Winnow as fast as possible. I shall send for a good deal of Rice in the Rough. I am, &ca.—

SOURCE: Letterbook copy, Letter Book of Henry Laurens, Oct. 30, 1762–Sept. 10, 1766, Penn. Hist. Soc.; addressed "Wambaw."

---

[9] William Hayne (Jan. 23, 1730–Nov. 26, 1764), a planter, was grandson of the founder of the Hayne family of Colleton County and first cousin of the patriot Isaac Hayne who was hanged by the British in 1781. William Hayne married Mary Bulline. Theodore D. Jervey, "The Hayne Family," *SCHM*, v (1904), 169.

[1] Joseph Fogartie was one of the sons of Stephen Fogartie, planter in St. Thomas parish. "Will of Stephen Fogartie," dated Nov. 1, 1755, proved Jan. 28, 1757, Charleston County Wills, VIII (1757–1763), 22–24, S. C. Archives. In 1758 Joseph Fogartie was an overseer in St. James Santee. *SCHM*, XVII (1916), 34. The *Country Journal*, June 2, 1767, spoke of "Mr. Joseph Fogartie's at Cainhoy." The Cainhoy ferry across Wando River was at Fogartie's landing. Joseph Fogartie died at the age of seventy-five at Louisville plantation in St. Thomas parish on Dec. 10, 1799. *SCHM*, XXVI (1925), 51.

TO ZACHARY VILLEPONTOUX

[Charles Town] 16 November 1764

Sir,

I beg the favour of you to order your largest Boat to deliver a load of the very best bricks at Maynes or Simmons's Wharf[2] as soon as you possibly can.

'Tis a long time since I had any Bricks from you. Therefore hope you will be under no difficulty to oblige me on the present occasion. I remain, Sir, &ca.—

SOURCE: Letterbook copy, Letter Book of Henry Laurens, Oct. 30, 1762–Sept. 10, 1766, Penn. Hist. Soc.; addressed "Black [Back] River."

TO JOSEPH BROWN

[Charles Town] 17 November 1764

Dear Sir,

Inclosed with this you will receive two Letters which came in Curling,[3] tho one is marked per Gunn. Sundry of your goods in my Store are bespoke by Mr. Smart to load for you on board of his Schooner & as he was the first that applied I could not do less than promise them to him not knowing that Mr. Lind had a Vessel for George Town to whom I should otherwise have given the preference as I suppose it would have been agreeable to you to do so.

Mrs. Laurens continues poorly indeed, which with the late change in my planting concerns, distress me.

You desired me to concern you in a purchase of Negroes. I expect 50 or 80 from Barbadoes. Will you accept of Notice when

---

[2] John Burn owned Charles Mayne's wharf which was just to the north of the Exchange. Loyalist Transcripts, LVI, 557–571. Maurice and Edward Simons were factors on Col. Othniel Beale's wharf. *Gazette*, Oct. 15, 1764.

[3] The ship *Beaufain*, Daniel Curling, arrived Nov. 10 from London. *Gazette*, Nov. 12, 1764. Capt. Curling, long in the London-Charleston trade, was noted for "his skill in seamanship and deportment as a gentleman." So famous was he for his carefulness that one story became a legend. Once while he was preparing to cross the Charleston bar another ship under the helm of an energetic skipper sailed off to England and returned while Curling was still waiting for the most favorable wind. Joseph Johnson, *Traditions and Reminiscences Chiefly of the American Revolution in the South* (Charleston, S. C., 1851), pp. 22–24. Johnson's story might have been based on HL to John Laurens, May 30, 1775, S. C. Hist. Soc.

they arrive & come & purchase the whole for I must not be both buyer & Seller?

My Love to Mrs. Brown & your fireside concludes me, &ca.—

SOURCE: Letterbook copy, Letter Book of Henry Laurens, Oct. 30, 1762–Sept. 10, 1766, Penn. Hist. Soc.; addressed "George Town."

TO JOHN RUTHERFORD

[Charles Town] 17th November 1764

Dear Sir,

This encloses you a Letter lately Rec'd from England.

I have Receiv'd no money since my last advices from Mr. Saxby. Upon a late application to Mr. Logan his Deputy,[4] for Money on your Account & information when Mr. Saxby was expected here, he replied to the first that he had no Money yet to pay on your Warrant but hoped to make a large payment in March next if no extra demands fall in the way, & to the other matter, that Mr. S. does not purpose to return to Carolina before next Autumn or Winter.[5]

A late death of a kind friend & relation who used to take upon him the charge of my two plantations embarrasses me very much as this is the busy Season of my Mercantile affairs. To this is owing my omission to write by Mr. Stuart[6] & to ask that Gentleman to my House. I was out of Town when he arrived & just returned when he was departing & had a hundred little & great things to transact, but this hurry shall not continue long. I must provide new aid according to the circumstance of my business. I remain with great regard, &ca.—

[*P.S.*] I have many late Letters from Mr. Oswald, the last dated

---

[4] When George Saxby sailed for England in May 1764, he appointed John Logan, of the firm of Logan, Guerin, & Vanderhorst, his deputy to act as receiver-general of quit rents. *Gazette*, Oct. 8, 1764; Alan D. Watson, "The Quitrent System in Royal South Carolina" (unpub. PhD diss., Univ. of S. C., 1971), pp. 79–80.

[5] HL did receive a payment of £300 sterling on Rutherford's warrant from the receiver-general in 1765. Quit Rents, Receipts and Disbursements, 1760–1768, Part 1, p. 171, S. C. Archives.

[6] This may be Andrew Steuart who began publishing *The North Carolina Gazette and Weekly Post Boy* in Sept. 1764, the first newspaper in Wilmington. Lawrence Lee, *The Lower Cape Fear in Colonial Days* (Chapel Hill, N. C., 1965), p. 204.

Mount Hamilton an Estate purchased in Scotland.[7] I wait for an Account of Silver sent to the House in order to compleate the remittances on your Account if any Balance remains.

SOURCE: Letterbook copy, HL Papers, S. C. Hist. Soc.; addressed "Esquire. North Carolina."

TO JOHN HASLIN

[Charles Town] 19th November 1764

Sir,

I am indebted for your favours of the 16th September & 6th October, the last per your Schooner *Molly,* Capt. Wooster, who arrived here the 31st Ulto. with twenty poor New Negroes on Account of Samuel Maddock, Esquire & yourself. I have had no opportunity of writing to you, but one presenting for Philadelphia, I advised Mr. William Wharton the 3d Inst. & requested the favour of him to pass the intelligence along by the first Vessel & to assure you that I should give your Vessel all possible dispatch, which I have not failed in.

Please now to receive Account Sale of said 20 Negroes Net proceeds to your Credit £4,143.1.6 to the Credit of your Account Current which is as good a Sale as ever I made considering the assortment. One Man was maim'd by a Shot in his ancle & not a Little pepper'd with the venereal disease, one of the Girls very meagre & in a dangerous way, & most of the females small & ordinary. Nevertheless had there been 8 or 10 likely Men amongst them the average would have been five or Seven pounds Sterling more, as I have sold them for Credit & not stinted the price for Cash which commonly affects a Sale 10 per Cent only for two or three Months.

Please also to receive Invoice & Bill of Loading & one of the Masters Receipts for the Cargo, Vizt. 183 Barrels & 74 half Barrels

---

[7] In 1759 Richard Oswald bought Auchencruive in Ayrshire, one of the best estates in the west of Scotland. This was his Scottish seat until his death on Nov. 7, 1784. *The Old Country Houses of the Old Glasgow Gentry* (Glasgow, Scotland, 1878), pp. 227–232. Mount Hamilton was a large house in the hamlet of St. Quivox, about one mile northwest of Auchencruive House. In 1793 two-thirds of the parish of St. Quivox was owned by George Oswald (1735–1819), the nephew of Richard who had inherited Auchencruive from his uncle. In the nineteenth century Mount Hamilton was the home of the factor of the Auchencruive estate. C. W. Black, city librarian, The Mitchell Library, Glasgow, to the editor, July 26, 1972.

of Rice, 34 Short 2 Inch Plank, & 19 Inch Shingles, & the Schooners disbursements Amounting in the whole to £3,203.13.4 of which in order to procure the Rice with dispatch I have already advanced & paid down upwards of £1,500, & the remainder payable chiefly on demand. Some part of the Rice is not New but the whole is very good & has been put in the best order & I hope you will have some days start of any other Vessel. Be that as it may; not a moment has been lost here, except ten days quarantine, which was unavoidable, & you have an advantage of 5/ to 7/6 per Ct. in the price, the price of new being now 50/ but very little come to Market. I could not possibly procure 1½ Inch Boards to your order in time, therefore have only sent a few exceeding good 2 Inch which Capt. Wooster took by way of Dunnage & chose to take no more. Lastly I inclose your Account Current Balance in your favour £939.8.2 which shall be remitted according to your direction about the 1st February next.

Capt. Wooster having hinted to me a design of returning here soon after he is unloaden at Barbadoes I take upon me to recommend to you to send a few prime Negroes, none old, nor defective, & let them be clad with Linnen woolen & a Blanket about 12/6 Sterling each but not wear their Cloaths until they begin to feel the change of climate & then only by degrees 'till they come upon the Coast. Let them be well fed & humanely treated. Such a Little Cargo, say 40 to 60, will sell in all probability extremely well at George Town in Winyaw & the Schooner may be loaden upon as good terms as in this place especially if you can give a little previous notice of her coming. If the weather suits he may go in there directly, otherwise stop here & proceed or tarry as shall appear most for your Interest. If you think that such a Voyage will be advantageous to you I shall be glad to receive your commands & to do all in my power to make it so.[8] Who am with great regard for Mr. Maddock and yourself, &ca.—

[P.S.] Rum per Vendue 14/, private 15/ & 16/. Sugar plenty & low but if Capt. Wooster comes this way again be so good to send me two Barrels of the very best clayed & I will Account for the Amount with him. Exchange 721 per Cent. That Rum which came in the

---

[8] The *Molly*, John Wooster, did return in the spring with 50 slaves from Barbados who were advertised for sale on April 10 by the firm of Price, Hest, & Head. *Gazette*, April 6, 1765.

Barter[9] & I closed the Sale for at 14/, I am this day selling upon Credit till at 15/ so you may soon Sum up my gains thereby.

SOURCE: Letterbook copy, HL Papers, S. C. Hist. Soc.; addressed "Barbados"; "per Capt. Wooster."

TO MEYLER & HALL

[Charles Town] 19th November 1764

Gentlemen,

I wrote to you the 10th Inst. intended by Capt. McCormick[1] & sent my Letter to Rebellion Road but he sail'd too soon. It was return'd & comes under cover with this. A duplicate went per Capt. Cooke[2] to which please to be refered.

This waits on you per your Schooner *Dispatch*, Capt. Wylie, & incloses Bill of Loading, Invoice, & Receipt for Disbursements of his Little Cargo Amounting to £1,287.4/ charged to the Debit of your Account. I am in advance & to be call'd upon at pleasure for the whole.

New Rice is broke at 50/ per Ct. I have put 100 Barrels in Store for the Brigantine *Savage* (now clearing her bottom) to avoid delay, as a great many early Shippers are upon the catch for new Rice & it does not come down so fast yet as to supply every demand & those who cannot command Money[3] to pay for it must wait until it becomes more plentiful.

Capt. Wylie would have Sailed four days ago but was hindered partly by bad weather & partly by the state of his Sails & rigging which required much repair & which he performed all with his own hands. I hope to write again in a few days by the *Savage*. Meantime remain with great regard, &ca.—

SOURCE: Letterbook copy, HL Papers, S. C. Hist. Soc.; addressed "Savanna La Mar, Jamaica"; "per Capt. Wylie. Copy per Durham." HL copied part of this letter.

---

[9] The ship *Barter*, James Gough.

[1] The schooner *Hibernia*, Henry McCormick, sailed Nov. 10 for Jamaica. *Gazette*, Nov. 12, 1764.

[2] The sloop *Recovery*, Thomas Cooke, sailed Nov. 11, for Jamaica. *Gazette*, Nov. 12, 1764.

[3] HL copied the letter from this point.

TO WILLIAM WADDELL
[Charles Town] 20th November 1764
Sir,

I wrote to you as foregoing on the 9th Inst. to which please to be refer'd. Permit me now to trouble you with a Bill of Exchange which I received or bought last Year from Capt. Thomas Seymour of your place for One hundred pounds Sterling, the draught of John Hurst, Antigua, 7th October 1763, payable at 60 days sight to Alexander Willock, endors'd by him to Capt. Seymour, by him to the order of Elias Benjamin Delafontain or of Gilbert Heathcote, Esquire, protested for non payment, & then endors'd by said Gilbert Heathcote & returned to me & now lastly by me payable to your order which Bill together with the Act of protest I inclose under cover with this, requesting you to apply for & recover the Amount thereof with the Interest, Reexchange, & Charges of Capt. Seymour or his representatives in New York & After deducting your Commission & Charges remit the Net Sum in a good Bill of Exchange either to the said Gilbert Heathcote, Esquire in London or to me here with an Account of the Adjustment.[4]

As the Affairs of Mr. Delafontain are in a bad way chiefly owing to disappointments in America, I earnestly request you to use the most expeditious reasonable measures in your power to send forward this money expected to arise from this Bill or to enable me to do it & you will in a particular degree oblige, Sir, &ca.—

SOURCE: Letterbook copy, HL Papers, S. C. Hist. Soc.; addressed "New York"; "per Capt. Schermerhorn."

TO JOHN WATTS
[Charles Town] 20th November 1764
Sir,

I had the honour of yours of the 4th Ulto. per this bearer, Capt. Schermerhorne,[5] inclosing a Letter to Governor Grant at St.

---

[4] See HL to Elias B. Delafontaine, Nov. 26, 1763.
[5] The sloop *Sally*, John Schermerhorn, arrived from New York on Oct. 14 and sailed for New York on Dec. 12. *Gazette*, Oct. 15, Dec. 17, 1764. Captain Schermerhorn had brought a cargo of rum, flour, mackerel, onions, etc., which he himself offered for sale on Colonel Beale's wharf. *Gazette*, Nov. 12, 1764.

Augustine, which, together with your compliments & the two Casks of Essence of Spruce I sent forward agreeable to your desire, about three Weeks ago. I remain with great regard, Sir, &ca.—

SOURCE: Letterbook copy, HL Papers, S. C. Hist. Soc.; addressed "Esquire. New York"; "per Capt. Schermerhorne."

TO JOSEPH BOWER

[Charles Town] 20 November 1764

Sir,

I wrote you very fully the 7th Inst. per Capt. Doran & then transmitted your several Accounts of Sales, Invoices, &ca., & an Account Current Balance due to me £2,467.11.1, at the same time duplicates of the whole per Capt. Moth. They both Sail'd over the Bar the 12th as you will be further informed by a Letter from Capt. Doran forwarded with this.

As I have been long in advance on your Account & am now for a good deal more than said Balance by reason of outstanding debts as well as the paving Stones, &ca. laying unsold, I shall this day pass my Bill on you at 40 days sight payable in London to the order of Mr. Thomas Savage for £342.4.10 Sterling which at 721 per Cent Exchange will just Amount to said Balance. Most people would think themselves, in a like case, intitled to the præmium on this Bill, which indeed is not equivalent to the Interest of my Money, but I have through the whole of my transactions for you consulted your Interest only & I hope you will believe that I am with great regard, &ca.—

SOURCE: Letterbook copy, HL Papers, S. C. Hist. Soc.; addressed "Bristol"; "per Capt. Kitchin."

PURCHASE OF LAND SOUTH OF THE ALTAMAHA RIVER

November 28, 1764

[Darby Pendergrass of Berkeley County, shopkeeper, sold to Henry Laurens of Berkeley County, merchant, for £1,000 currency, a tract of land containing 1,200 acres located south of the Altamaha River

*in Georgia, bounding on the east by lands laid out for Henry Laurens,
on the west by lands laid out to David Deas, on the south by vacant
land and part of the lands of Henry Laurens and David Deas, and
on the north by the Altamaha River. The deed was witnessed by
George Vair⁶ and John Calvert⁷ on November 28, 1764. On March
13, 1765, Benjamin Perdriau and John Hopton⁸ witnessed HL's payment of £1,000 to Darby Pendergrass. John Calvert and John Hopton
swore to the signatures on the same date before Fenwicke Bull, justice
of the peace, who also recorded the deed as public register on
March 22, 1765.]*

SOURCE: Deeds, CCC, pp. 711–716, S. C. Archives.

TO GREY ELLIOTT

[Charles Town] 30th November 1764

Sir,

I am much indebted for your favour of 3d March permitting
me to draw on you for Five Hundred pounds Sterling on Account of
Messrs. Elliott & Gordon. When that came to hand or very soon
after it I was greatly interupted in the course of business by Sickness
& death in my family, & amongst many other Articles this particular
one has been a little neglected, but having now a favourable opportunity by the hands of Lachlen McIntosh, Esquire I have taken the
Liberty to pass a Bill on you payable at Twenty days sight to his
order for the above mention'd Sum £500 Sterling which I recommend to that due Honour which you were pleas'd to engage to it.
I must also beg leave to claim your promise of a further Account of
the Sale of Negroes upon which my present draught is founded &
finally to close that affair, let me therefore request you to transmit
thro the hands of Mr. McIntosh an Account of what Sum for Interest

---

⁶ George Vair on June 25, 1766, gave William Wooddrop a power of attorney
to recover his debts. Miscellaneous Records, NN (1765–1769), p. 357, S. C.
Archives.

⁷ John Calvert, who was one of the Sons of Liberty, was a "commission merchant and book-keeper." Joseph Johnson, *Traditions and Reminiscences Chiefly
of the American Revolution in the South* (Charleston, S. C., 1851), p. 33. In
1766 he and Edmund Egan established a brewery. *SCHM*, LVI (1955), 200–204.

⁸ Benjamin Perdriau, Jr. had been HL's clerk for some time by this date, but
this marks the beginning of John Hopton's service as HL's clerk.

is Now to be added to the Net proceeds of the Sale dated the 22d July 1760, which together with payment of the full Balance I think is all that remains needful, & which I cannot so easily asscertain because you have not set forth in the Sale the time when the Payments respectively were to become due.

As this transaction is now enter'd into the 6th Year from its commencement & all the three Houses concern'd in it, infracted & disolv'd, tis high time to put a period to it, & I am persuaded that you, Sir, upon whom alone the whole depends will think so too. Delay will produce no benefit, therefore stand the Account how it may, I intreat you to furnish this Gentleman with a state of it that I may know what I have to depend on, & to be enabled likewise to Answer those enquiries which my late partners do not fail to make. I remain with great regard, Sir, &ca.—

SOURCE: Letterbook copy, HL Papers, S. C. Hist. Soc.; addressed "Esquire. Georgia."

TO TIMOTHY CREAMER
[Charles Town] 1st December 1764

Please to load the Schooner with Fire wood & Lumber in the best manner you can & with the quickest dispatch & inform me as nearly as possible how many Bushels of Corn & pease as well as Rough Rice there may be upon the plantation both of yours & mine & the Negroes.

I send up seventy pair of Shoes out of which you will serve the Negroes & return what remains. I am, Sir, &ca.—

SOURCE: Letterbook copy, Letter Book of Henry Laurens, Oct. 30, 1762–Sept. 10, 1766, Penn. Hist. Soc.; addressed "Mepkin."

TO ELIAS BALL, JR.
[Charles Town] 1st December 1764
Dear Sir,

I send by your Unkle[9] a Copy of your Father's Will, which,

⁹ Elias Ball of Kensington.

tho but poorly performed, was got from the Secretary's Office no sooner than Friday.[1]

You will likewise receive a Sample of very fine Sugar which you may have at £12.10/ per Ct. or 100 lbs. for 15 Gallons of Rum but there is only about nine hundred Weight of it for Exchange.

My love & best respects attend all friends at Hyde Park & I remain, Dear Sir, &ca.—

SOURCE: Letterbook copy, Letter Book of Henry Laurens, Oct. 30, 1762–Sept. 10, 1766, Penn. Hist. Soc.; addressed "Hyde Park."

T O   J O H N   &   T H O M A S   T I P P I N G
[Charles Town] 4th December 1764
Gentlemen,

Your esteem'd favour of the 8th Ulto. was deliver'd to me by Capt. Holme on the 25th[2] & he has since landed the sundry packages agreeable to Bills of Loading on Account of the Owners of the *Austin* & also an uncertain quantity about 50 Tons of Coal not included in the Bill of Loading. Likewise on your Account three poor wretched human creatures call'd Negroes, being part of those four which you were pleased to consign to me, one of that number the Captain says died on the passage.[3] I shall do the best in my power with the owners goods but 'tis amazing to me that they continue to send such to this Market where they can expect no gain unless a profit is already laid upon their Invoice. As to the Rum, excuse me, Gentlemen, for declaring the truth to you, 'tis in very fact the worst in quality & the worst Cask that ever I have received from your Island. Three or four Hogsheads are so very distasteful that I am almost suspicious that Tricks

---

[1] John Coming Ball had named as executors of his will his wife, his son Elias, his brother Elias Ball of Kensington, his brother-in-law HL, John the son of Nicholas Harleston, and Robert the son of Robert Quash. "Will of John Coming Ball," dated March 8, 1764, proved Nov. 23, 1764, *Abstracts of Wills, 1760–1784*, pp. 48–49. An advertisement was placed in the *Gazette*, Dec. 3, 1764, addressed to all persons to whom John Coming Ball was indebted to send in their accounts to Elias Ball at Hyde Park or to leave such accounts in the hands of Henry Laurens in town.

[2] The snow *Austin*, Matthias Holme, arrived Nov. 25 from Barbados. *Gazette*, Nov. 26, 1764.

[3] HL paid £30 duties on the 3 slaves Holme brought from Barbados. Public Treasurer, Journal B: Duties, 1748–1765, p. 420, S. C. Archives.

have been played with them in the Ship tho Captain Holmes says not. Last Year the Cask were ordinary but the contents very good. This Year the Casks are worse & the Rum poor. As Captain Holme saw them when Ship'd so has he seen them at Landing here. I cannot presume to judge in the former but in the Latter case I am sure that I speak only strict truth, such as they are I shall sell them without further animadversion.

I have sold your three Negroes as per inclos'd Account for Net proceeds £192.8.6 which considering their quality is the greatest Sale that ever I made & I have done as much as most folks in that branch. I believe you will be so well satisfied with this Account that it will be in vain for me to say more. You may from hence judge what an handsome adventure might have been made for the Owners if you had been permitted to Ship about fourscore or an hundred prime Negroes & especially if you had avail'd yourselves of that *Skill* which you think so peculiar to Capt. Holme in the choice of Females. He smiles at this, & says you would not trust him with a commodity worth his care. I am sure that a Cargo of prime Gambia Young Men & Women would sell for upwards of Forty pounds Sterling & this I believe will continue to be the case untill the Cargoes fall in next Spring when probably they may be so numerous from our late Sales as to make a vast alteration. If from this advice you incline to make a consignment to Mr. Head[4] to arrive here anytime before the 10th March, you may depend upon my best assistance to him both in the Sale & remittance. He has shew'd me your Letter & I think if you are dispos'd to do a friendly Act to him you have now an opportunity of doing it without any apparent risque to yourselves but you know too much of commercial affairs to depend so absolutely upon any adventure, as to appropriate the profits while the adventure is only

---

[4] Edmund Head had just arrived from Liverpool. He was in this month forming a new house with William Price and William Hest, two former clerks of HL. HL to John Knight and John Blackburne, Jr., Dec. 21, 1764. He was the son of Sir John Head, Liverpool merchant. In 1769 he succeeded to the baronetcy which had been created in 1676. George Edward Cokayne, *Complete Baronetage* (5 vols.: Exeter, Eng., 1900–1909), IV, 76–78. Sir Edmund Head remained in Charleston until 1778, earning annually £900 sterling "in the Commission Business and Wine Trade." When he was elected to the Provincial Congress in October 1775, he asked HL whether he should serve. HL told him not to serve unless he could endorse the measures that had been taken. Since he could not, he did not take his seat. He remained in Charleston until 1778, when refusing to take the new state oath, he was banished. Loyalist Transcripts, LIII, 307–319.

in embrio. But so much I can safely say & repeat that there is a good prospect of gain & that you may be assur'd of my aid to make the most of it for you provided you send likely healthy (black) Negroes.

Please now to receive Invoice and Bill of Loading for Thirty Barrels New Rice on your Account per this bearer the *Sukey & Nancy*, Capt. Dickison,[5] Amount to your debit £469.0.2. I have set half a dozen Market fellows to watch for two Does & hope they may succeed so as to have the Deer sent in this Sloop, otherwise you may expect them by the next.

I have this day begun to load the *Austin* with Rice for Oporto & hope to get her to Sea in Seven or ten days more, for I hate delay, & yet by some fatality or other, tho I commonly get his Ships not only Loaded but Loaded with fine Rice in half, oftner a quarter the time that other Vessels are detain'd I can't Sail quite fast enough for my good Master Mears & perhaps it may be worse this Voyage than ever because the *Knight* who arriv'd 16 days before will probably sail within a day or two *after* the *Austin*.

If any Guinea Men belonging to my worthy friends & bene-factors, Mr. Oswald of London, Mr. Bright of Bristol, or Mr. Knight of Liverpoole shall arrive with you in proper time, I intreat you to inform them what I have wrote to you in their branch. Let healthy Negroes be well fed & well cloath'd & be not afraid of the Cold. I remain, Gentlemen, &ca.—

SOURCE: Letterbook copy, HL Papers, S. C. Hist. Soc.; addressed "Barbados"; "per Capt. Dickison."

TO DANIEL ARTHUR

[Charles Town] 7th December 1764

Sir,

I have the Honour of addressing you by the Ship *Heart of Oak*, Capt. Henry Gunn,[6] one fourth of which Ship & one third part of her present Cargo of Rice belongs to me as Mr. John Edwards

---

[5] The sloop *Sooky & Nancy*, Josiah Dickinson, arrived Nov. 11 from Bermuda and sailed Dec. 9 for Barbados. *Gazette*, Nov. 12, Dec. 10, 1764.

[6] The ship *Heart of Oak*, Henry Gunn, sailed for Lisbon on Dec. 10. *Gazette*, Dec. 10, 1764.

who takes upon him the trouble of writing the needful advices to you in behalf of all the Owners will advise you.

When you have adjusted the Freight be pleased to remit my quarter of the Net Sum into the hands of Messrs. Cowles & Harford, Merchants in Bristol, & also into the same hands my one third part of the Net proceed of the Cargo as soon as you are in Cash, of which be so good as to give them some previous notice. 'Tis my opinion that if a saving price is to be obtain'd, you should sell this Cargo upon its arrival, without delay on one hand, or too great precipitation on the other, & therefore I beg leave to recommend it; & I believe this will be consistent with Mr. Edwards's advice as well as the inclination of the others concern'd tho I had not time today to talk to him on that particular point, & I suppose Capt. Gunn will sail early tomorrow morning, too early to trust my Letter unfinish'd tonight, therefore I give this as a necessary hint, at the same time referring & submitting to what that Gentleman may write.

It will afford me great pleasure if this shall introduce a lasting correspondence & enable me to render you any little services in my power, who am with great regard, Sir, &ca.—

SOURCE: Letterbook copy, HL Papers, S. C. Hist. Soc.; addressed "Lisbon"; "per Capt. Gunn. Copy per Capt. Courtin."

TO MEYLER & HALL

[Charles Town] 7th December 1764

Gentlemen,

The preceeding is Copy of what I wrote to you by your Schooner *Dispatch* 19th Ulto. to which I refer & here inclose a duplicate Bill of Loading and abstract Invoice for her Cargo & another of the Masters Receipts for disbursements. This will be deliver'd to you by Capt. Durham in the Brigantine *Savage* & incloses Invoice & Bill of Loading for the Cargo on board said Brigantine on your Account, Amount charg'd to your debit £4,559.4/.

The whole of the Cargo is as good as the times would admit of when every body has been catching at both Rice & Corn to get first to their respective Markets. This in hopes of dispatch induced me to begin the Load with some of each specie old but both very good & free from Weavil. Had I known that the Vessel would have been so long in Loading I should rather have put none but New on board, nevertheless I flatter myself that the abatement of price will be a real saving to you. I thrust into the Corn Room to fill it up a few half Barrels of black ey'd pease & the two Inch plank upon Deck in order to make the most of the Freight as you are to pay by the Lump which I hope will not prove a miss.

The Owners of this Brigantine[7] are very pressing to have her unloaden by you as quick as possible & I have taken upon me to assure them that you will not detain her any unreasonable or unusual time. They Likewise desire to be paid their Freight in Dollars & would willingly have it so inserted in the Bill of Loading but as this came after my bargain I could not presume to lay you under an obligation to perform what perhaps may be disagreeable or detrimental to you. Nevertheless I promised to desire that you will pay it in such specie if no great inconvenience attends it, because they think that the Freight is very Low.

There is a great difference in the Accounts deliver'd & Receiv'd of Corn on board this Brigantine, the former exceeding the Latter by near 200 Bushels, therefore I flatter myself that you will at least have full measure & if there is any excess & it shall come to your hands I am sure you will enable me to do justice to the persons from whom it was purchas'd.

This moment (now late at night) the Master has return'd the Bills of Loading unsign'd because I will not insert the payment of Freight to be in Mill'd Dollars, which is very vexatious to me as I forsee the loss of another day by this afterthought of his, which as I ought not, so I will not submit to.

Please to accept my best thanks for the Cask of Rum you were pleas'd to send me per *Dispatch*. That for Mr. Austin I shall forward by a Ship to Bristol to be conveyed to him in Shropshire where he has resided some 12 or 14 Months past in a poor state of health both of body & mind in a great measure owing to domestic grievances which he views in a different light from all his friends & takes too much to heart.[8]

---

[7] When the brigantine *Savage*, John Young, was cleared outwards on June 15, 1764, for Jamaica, the vessel was owned by John Young and William Dickinson of Bermuda and by Thomas and William Savage and Edward Lightwood of Charleston. Naval Office Lists, 1764–1767, p. 81.

[8] George Austin resided at Aston Hall near Shifnal in Shropshire, until his death in 1774. The elopement of his daughter Eleanor with Major John Moultrie

Jamaica Rum & Sugar are extremely low here both articles being daily sold for less than Cost & Charges. Therefore I dare not encourage your adventures in either unless it be merely to procure a Sale for your own produce.

Negroes continue to sell well, & will probably remain in the same state until many Cargoes in the Spring may work a change. A little parcel of Seventy sold Yesterday at an average of near Forty two pounds Sterling. I remain with great regard, Gentlemen, &ca.—

SOURCE: Letterbook copy, HL Papers, S. C. Hist. Soc.; addressed "Jamaica"; "per Capt. Durham."

TO JOHN KNIGHT & CO.

[Charles Town] 8th December 1764

Gentlemen,

I have been so constantly attendant upon the Wharfs in order to secure a sufficient quantity & good quality of Rice for your purpose that I have scarcely been an hour at home for several days past. This attention was essentially necessary in order to give dispatch at a time when 50/ per Ct. ready money & acknowledgements of a favour for each preference were the only means of obtaining good Rice & now & then taking in a parcel of ordinary which I have either Ship'd off to Jamaica or resold for Credit & I take notice of it because it has himm'd in my time for writing by this Vessel to a very few minutes.

Your Ship[9] is now Loaded & will be clear'd out in an hour more with only 559 Barrels & 83 half Barrels of as good Rice as ever I ship'd in one Cargo & I hope Capt. Dennison will Sail tomorrow. It seems the Ship stow'd badly & much of the short time of her tarry here has been spent in delivering the Salt & Coals inward & Caulking her within & without which she stood greatly in need of.

As soon as the Captain hinted his readiness to receive his Cargo of Rice I gave him 95 Barrels & he has since been supplied as fast as he could stow it away. I am much indebted to the aid of

broke his heart. From that time he was estranged from his wife and apparently from HL as well.

[9] The ship *Knight,* Thomas Dennison, sailed on Dec. 11 for Oporto. *Gazette,* Dec. 17, 1764.

Mr. Manigault, Mr. Savage, & some other friends who have enabled me to get the better of every competitor. I have not the vanity to think that I could have perform'd all that I have done merely by my own Interest or abilities. You order'd dispatch. The price of Rice was broke by other people, & I have procur'd all that I wanted amongst them.

I have sold the Salt which falls greatly short in measure at 10/ to 12/6 per bushel. It has since fallen to 5/ for Coarse Salt. The Coals are also sold at Six pounds per Ton, Cheese at 2/7 to 3/6 per lb., Crates of Yellow Ware £4.10/ to £5, & some very trifles of the dry goods I mean Linnens, &ca.

Capt. Dennison has taken on board such plank as he thinks will be necessary for his Decks but will not spare the time to lay them here & he judges well if dispatch is so necessary for Carpenter work goes slowly on in this place & a jobb of that sort would loose much time.

I have projected a new mode for disposing of your other goods, Vizt. by a private Auction upon terms of Credit on Wednesday the 19th Inst. when I intend to get rid of all that will yeild a saving price or there abouts which is as much as can be expected for I have offer'd them at 8½ to 8 for one on the cost without success & what will not yeild at that tryal the Cost I shall put into the hands of that House in which Mr. Head is now upon Entering, as the best method in my power to serve your Interest therein & for the Balance of your Account which will appear when I transmit Invoice, Account Current, &ca. I shall draw upon you in the most advantageous & most gentle manner that my circumstances will admit of.

It remains only that I should inform you that the *Knight*'s Cargo of Rice & disbursements will Amount to about Fourteen hundred pounds Sterling. If possible I shall put under cover with this an Invoice & Bill of Loading but I very much doubt if I shall have time. I remain with great regard, Gentlemen, &ca.—

[*P.S.*] 12 December. The Invoice not finish'd but Capt. Dennison safe over the Bar, at least I hope so. He went down with a fine top Gallant Breeze this morning ahead of everybody else.

SOURCE: Letterbook copy, HL Papers, S. C. Hist. Soc.; addressed "Owners of the Ship *Knight,* Leverpoole"; "per Capt. Doyle. Copy per Capt. Erskin." The postscript was copied by HL.

TO JOHN KNIGHT & THOMAS MEARS
[Charles Town] 8th December 1764

Gentlemen,

Your said Snow arriv'd here the 25th Ulto. at night & brought me your favour of the 8th September the contents of which I as always upon like occasions paid the strictest regard to. At the same time I receiv'd in a Letter from Messrs. Tipping an Invoice for Forty Hogsheads Rum & sundry dry goods on your Snows Account. Both articles or rather all of them arriv'd to an exceeding bad Market. Rum has been long selling both in public & private at 13 to 14/ per Gallon. I have by means of Credit already run off a great part of your 40 Hogsheads at 14/ for I see no hopes of amendment but rather a prospect of it being still lower as the New Crop is approaching. As to the dry goods I know but of one method whereby I can get those off upon saving terms which I shall attempt at a private Auction where I propose to sell for some Credit & if I do not succeed therein I must lodge the remainder in the hands of Mr. Edmund Head & Company who I hope will be able to do more with them than in my present situation & circumstances I can propose after trying the method that I have in view. Observing very carefully your orders for dispatch of your Snow for Oporto I prepar'd for Capt. Holmes's earliest call & on the 3d Inst. began to load & I have now on board & ready to go on board a full Cargo of as fine Rice as ever was Ship'd from this port the Cost 50/ per Ct. from whence you may compute the total Value by Looking at the Invoice of last Year. But where am I to get money to pay for this Rice which nothing but money will command at this particular time?

I flatter myself with hopes that the *Austin* will be loaden on Monday & clear out Tuesday next. This is Saturday & I have no Room to doubt of Capt. Holme's vigilence to sail without loss of time. After that event or perhaps before it I shall write to you again. Mean while I continue to be with great regard, Gentlemen, &ca.—

[*P.S.*] [*December*] 12. Capt. Holmes is cleared out with 556 Barrels & 90 half Barrels of as good Rice as ever made up one Cargo.

SOURCE: Letterbook copy, HL Papers, S. C. Hist. Soc.; addressed "Owners of the Snow *Austin,* Leverpoole"; "per Capt. Doyle. Copy per Capt. Erskin." The postscript was copied by HL.

TO CHARLES CROKATT

[Charles Town] 8th December 1764

Sir,

I had intended to have wrote you fully by this conveyance in reply to your favours lately received but much business abroad in dispatching several early Vessels with New Rice has confined me to a few Minutes. Therefore I shall only advise for the present of a draught made on you Yesterday to the order of Thomas Savage, Esquire at forty days sight for one hundred pounds Sterling which I recommend to your accustomed punctuality to be paid on my account & beg your excuse for two or three days when I shall take leave to wait on you again. Mean while I remain with great regard, &ca.—

SOURCE: Letterbook copy, HL Papers, S. C. Hist. Soc.; addressed "Esquire. London"; "per Capt. Doyl. Copy per Capt. McLaughlin."

TO JUDITH BALL

[Charles Town] 10th December 1764

Dear Madam,

In your favour of the 3d Inst. you are pleas'd to leave the affair of the Sugar & Rum intirely to me. At the same time you seem desirous to exchange rather than purchase. But as I apprehend there would be some impropriety in disposing of the Estates effects in this manner before an appraisement is made, & that no loss can attend a little delay, I shall not move the Rum at present, but send you two Barrels of Sugar & charge them at £12.10/ per 100 lbs. & another shall wait your further direction. I think the Rum may sell upon better terms but if you continue to desire it I will take as much in Exchange as will balance the present charge.

I shall strive to accept of your kind invitation to be at Miss Betsy's wedding[1] but am in some doubt whether I can leave Town before Thursday Morning if at all.

---

[1] John Coming Ball had three daughters: Elizabeth (1746–1787), Catherine (1751–1774), and Ann (1753–1826). Elizabeth married on Thursday, Dec. 13, 1764, Henry Smith of Goose Creek, son of the second Landgrave Thomas Smith. Henry Smith (1727–1780), known as the third landgrave, had been married before to Ann Filbein who had died on Nov. 20, 1762. Catherine married

Whether I am there or not, you may assure her of my earnest wishes that the approaching event may prove an happy one in her Life.

Mistress Polly & Mistress Katy[2] will tell you how we are. I wish they may find you all well & I remain, Dear Madam, Yours, &ca.—

SOURCE: Letterbook copy, Letter Book of Henry Laurens, Oct. 30, 1762–Sept. 10, 1766, Penn. Hist. Soc.; addressed "Hyde Park."

TO MAYNES & CO.

[Charles Town] 10th December 1764

Gentlemen,

I thank you for your many favours transmitted to me in the course of this Year by which I have been regularly advis'd of the state of your Market. I have also receiv'd your sundry Letters to Mr. George Appleby & to the Houses of A. & L. & A., L., & A. which you may spare yourselves the trouble of in future as both my late partners are return'd to & reside in England.

I now trouble you with a few Barrels of Rice per the Ship *Flora*, Capt. Thomas Courtin,[3] Vizt. 114 Barrels & 30 half Barrels as per inclos'd Invoice & Bill of Loading to sell on Account of Messrs. Cowles & Harford & myself in proportion to our respective parts of the Ship & also with the address of the Ship. You will be so good as to give the Ship the utmost dispatch in your power & remit her Freight money to those Gentlemen, together with the Net proceed of our Rice which I would recommend to you to sell immediately

---

Benjamin Smith, a younger brother of Henry Smith, on April 8, 1773, and died in childbirth on Feb. 23, 1774. Benjamin Smith (1735–1790) had been married before to Elizabeth Ann Harleston who died in October 1768. Ann married on Jan. 27, 1771 Richard Waring who lived at Tranquil Hill plantation near Dorchester. Deas, *Ball Family*, pp. 95, 184, 185; [Elizabeth Ann Poyas] *Our Forefathers: Their Homes and Their Churches* (Charleston, S. C., 1860), pp. 46, 100–103, 118; Barnwell R. Heyward, "The Descendants of Thomas, 1st Landgrave Smith of South Carolina," 1902, typed manuscript, S. C. Hist. Soc.

[2] "Katy" and "Nancy" were the nicknames for Catherine and Ann Ball. See HL to Abraham Schad, Aug. 23, 1765. The "Polly" mentioned here may have been the daughter of William Hopton. See HL to William Hopton, Sept. 15, 1764.

[3] The *Flora*, Thomas Courtin, who had recovered from his illness, sailed Dec. 11 for Lisbon. *Gazette*, Dec. 17, 1764.

if a saving price can be obtain'd for it. Indeed to lay it into Warehouse at any rate will probably produce no good effect.

If you can assist the *Flora* with a good Freight for any port in England you will very much oblige the Owners who will not fail to make suitable acknowledgments, but I would not have her detain'd one day unless something very handsome shall offer, because I have in view her return here to take another load of the present Crop, which will require much dispatch.

The *Heart of Oak,* Capt. Gunn, sail'd Yesterday with 1,080 Barrels of Rice for your City & here are others to follow wherefore 'tis not to be doubted that you will have a full proportion of a very plentiful Crop which is now coming fast to Market.

I beg leave to recommend Capt. Courtin to your protection & remain with great regard, Gentlemen, &ca.—

SOURCE: Letterbook copy, HL Papers, S. C. Hist. Soc.; addressed "Lisbon"; "per Capt. Courtin."

TO THOMAS COURTIN

[Charles Town] 10th December 1764

Sir,

You will proceed in your said Ship to Lisbon & there address yourself to Messrs. Maynes & Company, deliver your Cargo of Rice, & adjust the whole Freight & half Subsidy which those Gentlemen will either pay to you per Bills or remit as I have request'd them to Messrs. Cowles & Harford.

If a good Freight can be readily obtain'd for any port in England indeavour to procure it but be very cautious & don't loose an hour for an uncertain prospect as I want the Ship here as early as possible in the Spring.

Upon your arrival in England cancel your former Bond & procure a New License. You will by the first conveyance from Lisbon advise Messrs. Cowles & Harford of your arrival there & of the port that you are destin'd for in Britain which no doubt will be Falmouth if you go an Empty Ship & they will meet you with orders which you will follow notwithstanding any thing that I have said as I shall apprize them fully of my thoughts & leave them to determine as shall appear best.

I recommend dispatch & frugality & that you will write me by every opportunity. I wish you better health & remain with great regard, &ca.—

P.S. If a Balast of Salt is worth taking in & will not detain your Ship either at Lisbon or Falmouth you may seek for one while you are delivering the Rice. It may serve to lessen or pay Port charges.

SOURCE: Letterbook copy, HL Papers, S. C. Hist. Soc.; addressed "Captain. of the Ship *Flora*."

TO HENRY BYRNE

[Charles Town] 10 December 1764

Sir,

My last trouble was under the 4th October per Capt. Summers[4] as per duplicate inclos'd to which pleased to be refer'd.

Now I wait on you by Capt. Dennison in the Ship *Knight* belonging to our worthy Friends Messrs. John Knight & Company Loaden to your address with a fine Cargo of 559 Barrels & 83 half Barrels of Rice as per Invoice & Bill of Loading herewith.

The *Austin* will be full tomorrow & Sail I hope the following day, very probably with this Ship which will be no small mortification to poor Dennison. The Weather which follow'd that Storm spoken of in my last was most uncommonly favourable so that the Crops were all got well hous'd & will be very great & I have good grounds for hinting that your Market will have its full proportion. The *Live Oak*, a Ship of 900 Barrels, will soon follow these.[5] I know of orders in Town to Charter one of 6 or 700 Barrels & am advis'd of two Ships of 700 Barrels each Charter'd in London to be here very soon. Besides these no doubt there will be two or three more that usually go that Route. From hence you may govern your Sales of these early Cargoes belonging to our friends which I hope will have a Month start of all others. I will venture to say that none of better quality will be Ship'd through the Year. Besides the above mention'd Vessels I should mention our old acquaintance Capt. Pitt[6] who has

---

[4] Capt. John Somers.

[5] The ship *Live Oak*, Andrew Lundberry, did not sail for Oporto until Feb. 11, 1765. *Gazette*, Feb. 16, 1765.

[6] The brigantine *Hopewell*, Moses Pitt, arrived from Bristol on Oct. 29 and sailed for Oporto on Jan. 5. *Gazette*, Oct. 29, 1764, Jan. 7, 1765.

been lying here some Weeks for the fall of Rice which broke intolerably high at 50/ per Ct. & so continu'd until this very day when some parcels of midling quality have sold at 47/6. I shall write again by the *Austin* & therefore only add to the present that I remain with great regard, Gentlemen—

SOURCE: Letterbook copy, HL Papers, S. C. Hist. Soc.; addressed "Esquire. Oporto"; "per Capt. Dennison. Copy per Capt. Holme's."

TO CHARLES CROKATT

[Charles Town] 11th December 1764

Sir,

I troubled you the 8th Inst. as per duplicate above to which please to be refered.

Now give me leave to reply to your obliging Letters of the 19th July, 8th & 24th September in which you are pleas'd to over-rate the small service that I did to your Ship *Queen Charlotte.* That Era which you are so kind as to remember I always look back to with great pleasure & the retrospection notwithstanding any untoward circumstances that fell out, fills my heart with gratitude to your family & prompts my tongue to confess, that the advantages & benefits which I receiv'd in it, were, to say the least, an introduction to my present comfortable situation. This language has been uniformly mine, it is not the Language of a benefactor, but of one who can lay aside all sense of small injuries & feel & acknowledge at all times whether dependant or independent the force & obligation of great favours.[7]

This being truly the Light in which I view myself I cannot forbear when a good opportunity offers to shew that I hold myself indebted to Mr. Crokatt & to his Children & your prosperity in particular, Sir, will be always a subject of joy to me. I cannot pretend to contribute much towards it, yet the little services that are & shall be in my power consistent with other engagements you may depend upon if they are worth your acceptance. I shall as often as there is a good opening recommend correspondents that I shall think deserve

---

[7] HL had originally expected to be a partner in London of James Crokatt, Charles Crokatt's father.

your attention, but this is a work not to be precipitated if we expect it to endure. But truly nothing will so effectually secure to you an acquisition of the most valuable Houses in this Trade as good purchases & good Accounts of Sale & there is most certainly room enough to excel more than one or two of your Neighbours. As to my Brother[8] he was exceedingly attach'd to Messrs. Grubb & Watson.[9] He is steady & I cannot venture to speak to him while any hopes remain of their recovery from their late fall, nor indeed will I sooner withdraw myself from them. 'Tis true my business has not hitherto been very valuable to those Gentlemen. I foresaw the catastrope which they have lately experienc'd. I candidly told them so & assign'd that as a reason for witholding my own consignments & for omitting to recommend other people's to them. Just about the time that my Letter reach'd them, they fell. I sincerely wish they may be able to rise again. A review of past misconduct & of advice neglected will prevent a second disgrace & by industry & economy they may still effect great things.

I am quite satisfied with your disposition of my Rice in the *Queen Charlotte* & hoping that you will by the time this reaches you be in Cash to pay the above Bill & a Sum that I have appropriated for holding a small part in a Ship building at Poole by Capt. George Chisman,[1] I have desir'd him to draw on you for my quarter, Vizt. an eighth part of the said Ship's cost which he thinks will be about Sixteen or Seventeen hundred pounds. If I am too hasty in the application I must beg the favour of you to recommend him for about Two hundred or Two hundred & Twenty pounds to Mr. James Cowles in Bristol. But, Sir, if you hear a good Account of this Ship which I take a share in merely to oblige Chisman, I shall be very glad to hear that you have taken of my part which, provided there is no other London owner, may be some time advantageous to you. I remain, Sir, &ca.—

SOURCE: Letterbook copy, HL Papers, S. C. Hist. Soc.; addressed "Esquire. London"; "per Capt. McLaughlin. Copy per Capt. Erskin."

---

[8] James Laurens.
[9] Grubb & Watson of London had apparently gone bankrupt.
[1] HL had written George Chisman, April 2, 1764, that he would take a share in a vessel to be built at Poole.

TO GEORGE CHISMAN

[Charles Town] 11th December 1764

Sir,

After the receipt of your sundry favours of the 16th May, 24th June, & 24th September I should be quite inexcusable if I was to remain any longer in silence. Indeed if I had not the pleas of misfortunes in my family by deaths & Sicknesses, more than ever I experienc'd before, together with much unexpected business falling in upon me and at the same time an indispensible attendance almost the whole Summer upon public affairs, which has caus'd me to neglect my private concerns too much, I should stand now highly censurable, but from these considerations, I trust you will be so good as to excuse what is past.

I did authorize Mr. Poyas to inform you that I would hold ⅛th part of the Ship that you are building at Poole, which I consented to merely from a view of doing you service, for I have no inclination & therefore can have no other motive for being further concern'd in Shipping. That decleration I had intended to follow immediately with a Bill or order where to apply for my proportion of the cost. I have told you the genuine causes of my neglect, & I hope the delay has not been attended with any worse consequences than the borrowing a part of the money, in which case I must repay you the Interest of it, & now upon receipt hereof, if you will be pleas'd to apply to Charles Crokatt, Esquire in London, he will supply you on my Account with a Sum sufficient for my part which from Mr. Poyas information I suppose may be something about One hundred and Ninety pounds or two hundred pounds, added to the small Balance in your hands. I know of nothing that you can bring from Poole to advantage. Therefore if you cannot secure a Freight at Bristol worth going round for, nor any fine Salt near you at about Six pence per Bushel on board all charges included & good measure, it will be most adviseable to hasten hither in Ballast. You may come in for a part of this great Crop & you may be vastly disappointed at this very precarious Market, but to guard against the latter as much as possible, give us previous advice of your coming & designs that we here may take time by the forelock for the benefit of all the Owners, if they desire it at least for ourselves. I think you will have little or no chance of a Freight to Portugal. Oporto & Lisbon will soon be quite full of Rice, but we may prepare a Cargo of Naval

Stores, or secure a Freight to the Markets. I hope you will have a tolerable good Cabin. Tis not impossible but I may be your passenger if you go to England where I have some thoughts of going next Year if I can with convenience effect my purpose. My principle errand will be to place my son at School.[2]

Rice broke at 50/ at which extravagant price I have already Ship'd about 2,200 Barrels, but it is upon the decline & sold this day at 45/. I remain, &ca.—

[*P.S.*] A Corn Freight will hardly be worth your notice if it will occasion much delay.

SOURCE: Letterbook copy, HL Papers, S. C. Hist. Soc.; addressed "Captain. London"; "per Capt. McLaughlin. Copy per Capt. Erskin."

TO DENYS ROLLE

[Charles Town] 12th December 1764

Sir,

Both your favours of the 27th September & 20th November came duly to hand. In the former I receiv'd your Bill on Mr. Gillingham Cooper for £84 Sterling & have since paid all your draughts that have appear'd to the Amount of £102 Sterling as per account inclosed.

I paid due regard to your recommendation of Mr. Harry Lloyd[3] who had before the Receipt of your Letters been often at my House, & I believe he will do me the justice to say that I have upon every occasion been ready to serve him & that my advice to him has been, as far as I was able to administer it, plain & free from dissimulation.

That Gentleman put a Little Memorandum of yours into my hands. I have caused the articles contain'd in it to be collected & put

---

[2] HL did eventually hold a share in a vessel owned by Capt. George Chisman although it seems unlikely that the *Vine* which Chisman brought out to Charleston in 1769 was the vessel then being built in 1764 at Poole. HL to George Chisman, Jan. 29, 1768, May 23, 1769, HL Papers, S. C. Hist. Soc. However, it did take a long time in the eighteenth century to achieve one's desire. HL himself did not sail for Philadelphia and England until July 21, 1771.

[3] The *Gazette*, Oct. 22, 1764, announced that "Henry Lloyd, Esq. going to the settlement forming by Denys Rolle, Esq. at St. Mark's" had arrived on Oct. 19 in the *Friendship*.

on board of Capt. Bachop[4] Amount as by the inclosed Bill £29.10.3 Currency. He likewise applied to me for a Sum of Money, Vizt. One hundred & Seventy five pounds Currency which I have paid to him on your Account & both Sums are to your debit in the inclosed.

I perceive by your own & have learned from the information of others you have undergone already many disappointments & sustain'd some Losses. No doubt you were prepared to meet such events & I am sure you have fortitude to encounter many & greater than those.

Mr. Manigault, thank God, is very well & I have had the pleasure of hearing him express his good wishes for you more than once since you left Charles Town.[5]

I shall be extremely glad to hear from you & to have further opportunities of serving you by doing every act of civility & kindness in my power, who am with great regard, &ca.—

SOURCE: Letterbook copy, HL Papers, S. C. Hist. Soc.; addressed "Esquire"; "per Capt. Bachop."

TO JAMES GRANT

[Charles Town] 13 December 1764

I duely receiv'd both your Excellencys favours of the 18th & 25 Ultimo to which I must now content myself with a very Brief reply having deferr'd Writing to the last moment of Bachops stay by reason of delay in those great Men call'd Shipwrights upon whom I have been waiting Two days for an answer to Propositions for Building a proper Pilot Boat for Augustine Bar which I cannot even to this moment Obtain. Nevertheless give me leave to assure you, Sir, that the subject shall not be neglected. I shall cause a Boat to be put up Immediately if the Terms & time do not discourage the attempt and in such case I have one in View to purchase.

I thank Your Excellency for the trouble You have taken in answering my remarks upon the Purchase of Lands from the former Proprietors or pretended proprietors of East Florida. My doubts are all remov'd. I shall be content to hold a Tract of Land in that

---

[4] The schooner *Mary*, Adam Bachop, sailed for St. Augustine on Dec. 16. *Gazette*, Dec. 17, 1764.

[5] Mrs. Gabriel Manigault recorded in her diary for Sept. 2: "Mr. Rolle at dinner." *SCHM*, xx (1919), 207.

country under the Kings grant & will encourage every body else who may have any Scruples to follow my Example for I am quite satisfy'd now that such Grants will vest property in the Grantee.

Your Excellencys proclamation is publish'd in both Gazettes printed in this Town.[6]

Mr. Savage has extracted from your Letter all that related to his proposal for settling Two hundred Bermudians in your Government. He seems to be quite happy and I am sure of his perseverance in the good work that he has put his hand to. I am (he says) to certify by way of authentication half a dozen Transcripts of that extract which are to be dispers'd in Bermuda where he will use his utmost Intrest to increase the number of newlanders Originally talk'd of.

If Your Excellency intends to encourage Mr. Oswalds plantation Scheme, you must not be afraid of the price of Negroes. Delay will be much more Injurious than the Advance of Five or Ten pound Sterling per head, but is it not setting the East Florida Lands in a disadvantageous Vein of comparison to say that they can not afford to pay as much for Labourers as the poor Goose Creek Soil?

If I had authority and means it wou'd be often in my power to pick up clever Negroes at a lower price then Fifty pound Sterling per head. I lately Bought a young Man and Woman, both speak good English, the Lad is a Sailor and can in a Sailor like fashion wait in a house well enough, the Woman sews, washes, & Cooks tolerably. I Bought them merely because they were cheap & upon such like opportunity's I would with great pleasure forego any little advantage to myself to serve you and Mr. Oswald. But here comes Master Bachop. His patience has enabled me to Write more than I expected, & probably to tire Your Excellency's I shall therefore take leave Assuring you that I continue to be, Sir, Your Excellencys most Oblig'd & most Obedient Servant—

P.S. Mrs. Laurens (whose good wishes are always with You) is now abroad again & I hope will give me leave to ride to St. Augustine before the 10th of February.

SOURCE: Letterbook copy, HL Papers, S. C. Hist. Soc.; addressed "Governor. Augustine"; "per Capt. Bachop."

---

[6] Governor James Grant's proclamation, dated Oct. 31, 1764, stating the procedures for obtaining grants of land in East Florida, was published in the *Gazette*, Dec. 3, 1764.

TO HENRY BYRNE

[Charles Town] 13th December 1764

Sir,

The annex'd is a duplicate of what I wrote three days since by the *Knight*, Capt. Dennison, who got safe to Sea Yesterday.

Capt. Holmes in the Snow *Austin* now lays ready for Sea with a Cargo of fine Rice, Vizt. 556 Barrels & 90 half Barrels on Account of Messrs. John Knight & Thomas Mears owners of said Snow to your address as per Bill of Loading & Invoice of Weights herewith inclos'd which I hope will be with you in proper time to take the Cream of Your Market. I have some thoughts if my affairs will permit me to make a Voyage to England about June next & see no prospect of increasing my Account with you in 1765 unless something very clever shall tempt me to throw a consignment into your hands, but be that as it may, Let me intreat you to close my Account & remit the Balance as soon as you can & also transmit me my Account Current.

Messrs. Woodrop & Cathcart have call'd upon me to complain of a loss they are likely to sustain by a Bill which you remitted on their (or Woodrop & Douxsaints[7]) Account to Charles Crokatt, Esquire, London, which Bill they alledge was the draught of some Idle itenerant Officer & very improperly taken in a City where reputable Bills might have been had. They apply to me upon this occasion because I recommended you to them as a Man of knowledge & integrity & as they relate the tale it really seems to reflect some blame upon you. My answer to them was that my good opinion of Mr. Byrne is greatly confirm'd since I mention'd his name to them As a proper correspondent that I believe him to be a Man of Honour, that I would take the Liberty to hint the Subject to him (as those Gentlemen desir'd me to do so) as I was under no doubt of his giving satisfactory reasons for his conduct with respect to that Bill & leave no room for censure or aspersions upon his good name. Rice is now down at 42/6 per Ct. & probably will be tomorrow at 40/ & there stand fast, at least it has that appearance, but our Market is very precarious. I remain, Sir, &ca.—

SOURCE: Letterbook copy, HL Papers, S. C. Hist. Soc.; addressed "Esquire. Oporto"; "per Capt. Holme's. Copy per Capt. Pitt."

---

[7] William Wooddrop had first been a partner of Paul Douxsaint and then after 1758 of Andrew Cathcart. *HL Papers*, I, 46n.

TO JAMES SKIRVING[8]

[Charles Town] 14th December 1764

Sir,

I spoke this morning to Mr. Manigault upon the subject of your Rice, & am confirmed in my own sentiments, by what he was pleas'd to relate to me, that I was under no obligation to take your Rice at 50/ per Ct. & particularly from one additional circumstance that he recollected & put me in mind of. I have thought very much of this affair, compar'd circumstances, occurrences, probabilities & upon the whole am convinc'd that I did not think I had any right to the preference of your Rice & consequently under no obligation to receive it & I believe that the answer which I made to Mr. Champneys[9] when he offer'd me the second Boat load will go a great way to prove this. At the same time, Sir, I will not dispute the truth of what you aver so far as relates to your own apprehension or understanding of a bargain or intended bargain between us, but will put it upon the footing of pure mistake on each side. That you thought I had engaged to take & that I understood that I had generously relinquish'd my claim to your Rice by virtue of Mr. Champneys first promise to give me a preference of it, upon your representing to me that you could make a better bargain for it by fixing a certain price for a stated time for delivery. This was truly the light in which I viewed it & so I reported it to the several persons around me who act for me in the Shipping-business. I say, Sir, if you please we will put it upon that footing & relate our several conversations & apprehensions to one or two Gentlemen & be determin'd by their opinion. The easiest method for me would have been to give into your claim because if I ever did make the purchase it could not have been upon my own Account & consequently I ought not to be a looser by it, but conscious & sure that I never intended to make such

---

[8] James Skirving, a planter on the Ashepoo River in St. Bartholomew parish and Turtle River in Georgia, was a justice of the peace of Colleton County. *Gazette,* Oct. 31, 1765. His wife Sarah, née Saunders who had first been married to John Champneys, on Jan. 7, 1740, died July 1, 1768. *SCHM,* XIII (1912), 220; XVI (1915), 88. He married Charlotte, the widow of James Mathews, on March 16, 1769. He died in 1787. *SCHM,* XXI (1920), 13n; "Will of James Skirving," dated Aug. 2, 1787, proved Dec. 18, 1787, Charleston County Wills, XXII (1786–1793), 210–214, S. C. Archives.

[9] John Champneys, the son of John and Sarah Champneys, was born on Dec. 28, 1743, in St. Andrew parish. *SCHM,* XIV (1913), 27. John Champneys, who had entered the factorage business with his father-in-law George Livingston in October 1763, was now handling his step-father's country produce.

a purchase & yet dispos'd to pay a proper regard & deference to your assertions & to avoid a dispute or animosity on Account of a little Money I am willing to take the risque upon myself & submit it to the judgement of indifferent people which I hope will meet your approbation & that such measures may be taken as will be satisfactory to both of us. I remain with great regard, &ca.—

SOURCE: Letterbook copy, Letter Book of Henry Laurens, Oct. 30, 1762–Sept. 10, 1766, Penn. Hist. Soc.; addressed "Esquire."

TO GREGORY OLIVE[1]

[Charles Town] 14th December 1764

Sir,

Only upon the 10th Inst. Your obliging favour of the 25th September came to hand. I return you my thanks for the Offer you are pleas'd to make of concerning me in one or two annual Cargoes of Rice with the House of Messrs. Holdsworth, Olive, & Newman of Oporto,[2] altho tis not in my power just now to accept it, for several reasons. One is that your direction of a first Cargo cannot be comply'd with, because I had before the Receipt of it compleat'd the load of a Ship & a Snow for Oporto carrying together about 1,200 Barrels to the address of Mr. Byrne of Oporto, & that here is another Ship & Snow loading with near 1,500 Barrels more which must be ahead of anything that I could take up for here is not one Vessel at present with a License unengaged.

Another reason is that I am resigning the bulk of my Commission business to that House in which Mr. William Price's name stands first & which as they are very worthy Young Men I shall do all in my power to serve & promote, reserving freedom to myself. I might recommend your proposition to that House & see that the business was well executed if it was practicable but I really think it is not & truly it had better be omitted if you send out two more Ships, for in this case you will certainly clog that Market & loss will ensue. I know the House that you recommend at Oporto very well & have had two or three Accounts settled in it in my late partnerships. I

---

[1] *HL Papers*, III, 453n.
[2] HL's partnerships had shipped rice to this firm. *HL Papers*, III, passim.

always thought & have often said that it executed business with as much Honour and punctuality as any House in Portugal, & I know not one that would sooner draw me into connexion than that same. Perhaps I may hereafter correspond again with Messrs. Holdsworth, Olive, & Newman. The New Ship building by Capt. George Chisman in which I find I am concern'd will probably renew our acquaintance.

You may be assur'd, Sir, that upon the arrival of Captain's Chisman & Shult I will do the utmost in my power to procure good Freights for their respective Ships & upon all occasions be glad to render you such services as shall be in my power who am with great regard, Sir, &ca.—

SOURCE: Letterbook copy, HL Papers, S. C. Hist. Soc.; addressed "Esquire. London"; "per Capt. Erskin. Copy per Higgins."

TO JAMES GRANT

[Charles Town] 15 December 1764

Sir,

As Capt. Bachop is detain'd or rather forc'd back by a Southerly Wind I am in hopes of reaching him in Rebellion road to convey to Your Excellency a duplicate of a Letter wrote by Mr. Savage to some Gentlemen of the first Rank in Bermuda which is inclos'd under Cover with this.

I beg leave to refer to the said Letter and am perswaded the perusal of it will give You as much pleasure as it has done to, Sir, Your Excellencys much oblig'd & most Obedient Humble Servant—[3]

SOURCE: Letterbook copy, HL Papers, S. C. Hist. Soc.; addressed "Governor. St. Augustine."

---

[3] John Savage wrote to Cornelius Hinson and Francis Jones on Dec. 14, 1764, a copy of which HL was sending to Grant. Savage's letter was not copied into HL's letterbook. Grant, however, did send it as an enclosure in his letter to the Board of Trade, March 1, 1765. CO 5/540, pp. 365–368, Public Record Office, London.

TO JOSEPH COILE

[Charles Town] 17th December 1764

Sir,

By the *Margaret* Schooner, Capt. Porter,[4] I receiv'd your favour of 30th September together with 100 Boxes of Candles & five Hogsheads of Earthen Ware. Both articles arriv'd to a bad Market. The Vendue House has been clogged with such for a long time past & your Candles unluckily stuck to the paper interlaid between them which is a great injury to the Sale. I have as yet sold only thirty five Boxes for £247, tho they have been sent out & brought home again twice every Week since they arriv'd. If the Sale had been more force'd it would not have produc'd so much by 20 per Cent. Nevertheless in obedience to your very possitive orders I must finish it tomorrow & if this Sloop does not Sail shall transmit an Account by her. Meantime please to receive Invoice & Bill of Loading for 45 Barrels of good New Rice which I ship'd ten days ago guessing as nearly as I could what your effects might produce that so your business should not be delay'd on that Account. The Amount is £655.11.10, which you will be pleas'd to note & my next shall convey an Account Current & as much in Dollars as will Balance it if any remains to you.

Rice has of late taken a sudden turn downwards & is now at 40/ contrary to the expectation of some people who too eagerly made us pay 50/ by their contracts to give that price for whole Crops if deliver'd by the first of January. These Gentlemen have injur'd some of their neighbours but will suffer most themselves by their foresight.

I shall write to Mr. John Kitching to insure this Rice & remain with great regard, Sir, &ca.—

SOURCE: Letterbook copy, HL Papers, S. C. Hist. Soc.; addressed "Jamaica"; "per Capt. Catlin."

TO JOSEPH RAINFORD[5]

[Charles Town] 17th December 1764

Dear Sir,

Your favour of the 1st October was an agreeable present to

---

[4] The schooner *Margaret,* Jonathan Porter, arrived Nov. 10, from Jamaica and sailed Dec. 9 for Curaçao. *Gazette,* Nov. 12, Dec. 10, 1764.

[5] A Samuel Rainford had passed through Charleston in August 1763 on his way to Jamaica from Liverpool. *HL Papers,* III, 513n. Joseph Rainford must have been a family connection.

me for I had often asked after but could never learn from any of our Leverpoole friends where you were station'd. I have done the best in my power with Mr. Coile's goods which is still bad enough for we have been a long time clogg'd with the same kind & our Vendue continually fed with Candles & Earthen Ware. Therefore I have not been able to sell the whole of his because I would not force a Sale at half price. I cannot bear to do so. I would rather be in advance as I am in the present case having Ship'd him as much Rice as will amount to about his Net proceed. Shall try the Vendue again tomorrow & finish the Sale if I like the prices offer'd otherwise I must wait a few days Longer. You will be so kind if Mr. Coile is displeas'd because his goods are not giving away to assure him that he shall sustain no loss by my conduct, tho he may reap some benefit.

I am now agreeably fix'd & Settled in my New House, have a Brick Wall all upon the front of my Garden which is every day improving, & if chance or design should lead you into Charles Town again I shall be extremely glad to see you in it where a spare Bed shall be at your service. You seem to suspect that I have declin'd business. This I shall never wholly do while it pleases God to bless me with health, but I intend to confine myself chiefly within a small circle on my own Account. The Commission business in my present situation & the charge of my plantations together, is become rather too heavy for me, & therefore I purpose in March next to resign that branch to Messrs. Price, Hest, & Head, three active, diligent, sober Men & I beg leave to recommend that House to your acquaintance & favours. They have or will have a pretty inlet & I perswade myself that they will execute business to the satisfaction of every body that shall intrust them. If you can throw any thing in their way I shall be oblig'd to you for it.[6]

Mrs. Laurens & Jack are well so is my little Girl Patsy & a Boy that arriv'd since you left us call'd Harry. Miss Katy[7] is pretty well too, but she is hardly out of the dumps yet which they tell me she has lately been deeply in upon dancing the Baulk with one of your Leverpoole Skippers.

---

[6] HL obviously turned over to this house his business. In the *Country Journal*, Jan. 21, 1766, Price, Hest, & Head advertised the cargo of the *Austin*, Matthias Holme, from Liverpool and Barbados, a vessel that HL had long handled.
[7] Catherine Ball.

Mrs. Laurens & that Young Lady desire me to present their compliments & good wishes to you & I remain with great regard, Sir, &ca.—

SOURCE: Letterbook copy, HL Papers, S. C. Hist. Soc.; addressed "Jamaica"; "per Capt. Catlin."

TO LLOYD & BORTON

[Charles Town] 17 December 1764

Gentlemen,

Your very obliging favour of the 19th March with an Invoice for two puncheons of Rum per the *Hannah,* Capt. Groves,[8] came to my hands at a time when I was involv'd in affliction upon the sudden & unlook'd for death of my eldest daughter, & since that time until very lately my family has gone thro a series of sorrow occasion'd by sicknesses & deaths, but, thank God, we are once more under the kindly beams of health & chearfulness as we were when Mr. Borton was in Carolina. I trust you will for these causes pardon me for omitting to write to you sooner. Indeed I had for a while almost totally neglected business & the Counting House was the most disagreeable place in the world to me & my own affairs suffer'd very much.

I have in order to reimburse you for amount of said Rum which was very good ship'd on board this bearer the Sloop *Beaufain,* Capt. Catlin,[9] 21 Barrels of Rice & five hundred & twenty Bushels of Indian Corn as per Invoice & Bill of Loading here inclos'd which you will be pleas'd to sell & after paying for said Rum to which I beg of you to add your Commission & charges remit me the Balance in Rum of as good a quality.

We have as yet no Pork at Market & I was apprehensive of a glut of Rice at yours, otherwise I should have loaden this Sloop to your address which I had once intended to do, & Whenever you can give me encouragement I will make you a consignment of any of our produce & be glad upon all occasions to render my best service to you.

---

[8] The snow *Hannah,* Samuel Groves, was entered inwards from Jamaica on April 25 with a cargo which included 28 hogsheads of rum. Naval Office Lists, 1764–1767, p. 77.

[9] The sloop *Beaufain,* Nathaniel Catlin, arrived Nov. 15 from Bermuda and sailed Dec. 20 for Jamaica. *Gazette,* Nov. 26, Dec. 24, 1764.

I have some hopes of going to England in May or June next but in such case the addresses of my friends will suffer no disappointment as I shall take care to leave a proper representation. I remain, &ca.—

SOURCE: Letterbook copy, HL Papers, S. C. Hist. Soc.; addressed "Jamaica"; "per Capt. Catlin."

TO DAY & WELCH

[Charles Town] 17th December 1764

Gentlemen,

The preceeding is duplicate of what I wrote you the 10th September to which please to be refer'd, & now to receive under cover with this an Account Sale of your 15 Negroes per Brigantine *Manchester,* Net proceed £3,098.8.10, to the Credit of your Account Current which Sum you may be assur'd shall be remitted about the 10th January in a good Bill as you direct altho I am sure I shall be in advance for near one half many Months after, but the payments will become due & bear Interest in that Month & the 1st February. The first part I am in Cash for. This is doing more in point of remittance a good deal than is usually done here for Negroes, the common terms being 3, 6, & 12 Months & the first period by the delay of the Ship is stretch'd out to five or Six Months but I have not made that my rule. The Sale is in my opinion a very great one considering the subject of it. Those 8 Negroes sent into the Country have yielded at least 50 per Cent more than they would here which is so much advantage to you but exposes me to a greater risque of debts than if I had consulted only my own Interest. I hope you will be gainers by this adventure & approve of what I have done for you, then I shall be quite satisfied let the debts prove as they may.

The prices of good Negroes continue very high. A small Cargo lately averag'd above £40 Sterling[1] & there will be no change for the worse before May or June next. I remain with great regard, Gentlemen, &ca.—

---

[1] George Smith and Josiah Smith, Jr. on Dec. 6 had sold 60 slaves brought from St. Kitts in the *Friendship,* John Amory. *Gazette,* Dec. 3, 1764. The Smiths paid £610 in duties on 61 slaves brought from St. Kitts. Public Treasurer, Journal B: Duties, 1748–1765, p. 420, S. C. Archives.

SOURCE: Letterbook copy, HL Papers, S. C. Hist. Soc.; addressed "St. Kitts"; "per Capt. Emery."

GEORGE AUSTIN, HENRY LAURENS, & GEORGE APPLEBY VERSUS JAMES FITCH[2]

December 17, 1764

[On December 5, 1764, Robert Williams, Jr., attorney for the plaintiffs, filed suit in the court of common pleas against James Fitch, planter of St. Paul parish, for recovery of a bond, dated June 8, 1761, in the sum of £1,370 currency. The court ruled for the plaintiffs, and the case was ordered for judgment on December 17, 1764. The defendant paid the debt and court costs.]

SOURCE: Judgment Rolls, 1764, No. 104A, S. C. Archives.

TO SMITH & BAILLIES

[Charles Town] 18th December 1764

Gentlemen,

Inclos'd you have a duplicate of my last under the 11th September to which please to be refer'd.

After I had collected your sundry favours of the 17th & 18th May, 24th June, & 22d August & laid them before me to reply to, I could not forbear to reproach myself with remisness for omitting to answer them sooner; & yet if you knew what a series of trouble I have experienc'd by deaths & sicknesses in my family the past Summer at a time too when I was indispensibly obliged to attend upon public affairs I am persuaded you would readily excuse me especially when you should be inform'd that I have taken care to have such business as yours as hath been under my care properly attended to.

You will now receive Account Sale of two Negro Boys, Bob & Allen per the Sloop John,[3] Net proceed £358.1/, which no doubt you

---

[2] James Fitch, planter of St. Paul parish, married Helen Campbell, daughter of Martin Campbell, the Indian trader, on July 28, 1764. SCHM, XI (1910), 27; Abstracts of Wills, 1760–1784, p. 116.

[3] The Bermuda sloop John, Francis Dickinson, owned by Henry Todd of Bermuda and Charleston, was entered inwards on June 8 from St. Kitts with 14

will think a good price as you know what sort of creatures they were. It is not easy to procure a Bill for so small a Sum as the proportion of Mr. AB's.[4] I have therefore passed the whole to your Credit.

I likewise inclose an Account Sale of your 80 Boxes of Soap which has cost me a good deal of trouble but I could find no other way to get it off but the Vendue. We have had abundance of that article imported from different Quarters & retailed here for a long time at 3/ per Box & this is a Country in which we make Soap for common use. The Castile is chiefly us'd for medicine & when that demand is supplied it must be sold as low or nearly so as our own produce, the Net proceed of this is to your Credit £406.17.6.

Please also to receive your Account Current & sketch of my Account with you. By the former you will see, Gentlemen, that I have acted upon honour with you in advancing considerable Sums on your Account & no small part of it without Interest as well as by resolving to remit the Balance in next Month altho I am given to understand by the Gentlemen who bought your Negroes that they cannot pay me any part before February nor do I expect the whole for a Long time after in the common course of Carolina payments & yet they are very good Men. By the latter I have some reason to hope that you are now a good deal in Cash on my Account & that you will be so good as to remit my full Balance upon Receipt hereof & the offer of a good opportunity in healthy New Negroes to be pretty well Cloath'd & have a Blanket each under a humane Master who will promise to take care of them. If you are pleas'd to exceed the said Balance a little or to add any number of Negroes on your own & so make a joint Account of it, I shall be speedy in remitting your part. I hope you will not fail in this but if it cannot be done be so good as to remit me in the first new Rum that shall come to Market. I am endeavouring to square my affairs in order to go to England with my son & rely so far upon you to assist me. I had purchased a large quantity of Corn on Account of a Gentleman here who in fact made the purchase on your Account & my own but by the Death of that Gentleman[5] & other ac-

---

hogsheads of rum, 80 boxes of soap, and 9 slaves. Naval Office Lists, 1764–1767, p. 78. William Savage paid £300 in duties on the slaves brought by Dickinson from Antigua. Public Treasurer, Journal B: Duties, 1748–1765, p. 401, S. C. Archives.

    [4] Alexander Baillie.

    [5] John Coming Ball.

cidents could not get it to Town when an opportunity offer'd for Shipping it & at other times no proper Vessel could be obtain'd. I have luckily got off the greatest part of it but there will some little loss remain & I dare say you will readily pay your quoto. It will be but a triffle as I shall make no charge for my trouble or advance.

I must in the last place acknowledge your favour of the 7th June mark'd & intended by the hands of Lord Adam Gordon which I should have paid great regard to as I shall always do to your commands upon every occasion but in the present case I am depriv'd of opportunity to show my respect to you & must conclude that you wrote that letter without Lord Adam's consent because it was brought to me after laying here several days by one of my Coopers & besides that I perceive it has undergone the Stamp of the post Office at Jamaica. If tis otherwise & that this great Man means to slight you I shall not partake with him but I am told that Lord Adam is truly all that you say of him & as an opportunity will soon offer I make no doubt of finding this mesterious conduct to be founded in pure mistake & of having an explanation that will please us all.[6]

I shall write to Mr. Manning[7] to lodge some papers which were sent him by the late House of A., L., & A. in your hands & then give you some further Account of what is to be done with them. If in the meantime he should offer you such be so kind as to receive the trouble. I remain—

SOURCE: Letterbook copy, HL Papers, S. C. Hist. Soc.; addressed "St. Christophers"; "per Capt. Emery."

---

[6] Lord Adam Gordon, son of the second Duke of Gordon, was colonel of the 66th Regiment of Foot which was stationed in the West Indies. Lord Adam Gordon had reached St. Kitts on his American tour of inspection in June 1764. He noted at St. Kitts that "the Baillies, and Mr. Smith (of Eton) live there, and are very hospitable and agreeable people." In Jamaica he visited with Governor Lyttelton and his family. Having traveled by way of Pensacola, Mobile, St. Augustine, and Savannah, he reached Charleston on Dec. 8 and remained until the middle of March. Of the Charlestonians he noted: "The Inhabitants are courteous, polite and affable, the most hospitable and attentive to Strangers, of any I have yet seen in America, very clever in business, and almost all of them, first or last, have made a trip to the Mother-Country." "Journal of Lord Adam Gordon," pp. 376–401.
[7] William Manning.

TO COWLES & HARFORD

[Charles Town] 20 December 1764

Gentlemen,

I shall write to you by these offering opportunities upon several other affairs & herein confine myself to one subject, Vizt. to desire you will cause the following Insurance to be made on my Account.

First, on the Ship *Heart of Oak,* Henry Gunn, Master for Lisbon sail'd safely over our Bar the 9th Inst. which takes off half the risque.

Three hundred pounds Sterling on my one fourth of the Ship round to some port in Great Brittain. Five Hundred & fifty pounds on my one third part of her Cargo of Rice, which is at least Eight hundred pounds Value but I risque the remainder.

Secondly, Seven Hundred pounds Sterling on about 450 Barrels Rice (at least £850 Value) per the Ship *Polly,* Robert Porter,[8] Master at & from hence to Cowes & Rotterdam to Sail the 23d Inst. & being a fine Ship I hope will be ahead of this & save the first part. I remain, &ca.—

SOURCE: Letterbook copy, HL Papers, S. C. Hist. Soc.; addressed "Bristol"; "per Capt. Higgins. Copy Smith."

TO GEORGE McKENZIE & CO.

[Charles Town] 21st December 1764

Gentlemen,

Since my last per Capt. Reeve[9] of the 12th June I have receiv'd none of your favours. Nevertheless I will beg leave to trouble you once more with part of a Cargo of Rice, Vizt. 435 Barrels & 43 half Barrels per the Ship *Polly,* Capt. Robert Porter, as per Invoice & Bill of Loading here inclos'd which Rice you will be so good as to Enter & clear for Rotterdam, forward the inclos'd documents to James Crawford, Esquire,[1] Merchant there, & draw for amount of

---

[8] The ship *Polly,* Robert Porter, arrived from Philadelphia on Nov. 16 and sailed for Cowes on Dec. 26. *Gazette,* Nov. 19, Dec. 31, 1764.

[9] Capt. Henry Reeves of the ship *Queen Charlotte.*

[1] James Crawford (Craufurd), who was born in Edinburgh, Scotland, became a citizen of Rotterdam on Oct. 18, 1736. He was buried in Rotterdam on July 17, 1766. Crawford, an important merchant and shipowner who traded extensively to the West Indies and North America, was particularly noted for organizing

your Account upon Messrs. Cowles & Harford, Merchants in Bristol. I remain with great regard, Gentlemen, &ca.—

SOURCE: Letterbook copy, HL Papers, S. C. Hist. Soc.; addressed "Cowes"; "per Capt. Porter. Copy per Smith."

TO JAMES CRAWFORD

[Charles Town] 21st December 1764

Sir,

I have Loaden on board your Ship *Polly,* Robert Porter, Master 435 Barrels & 43 half Barrels of Rice consign'd to yourself at Rotterdam as per Invoice & Bill of Loading transmitted to Messrs. George McKensie & Co. at Cowes which they will forward to you after the Cargo is Enter'd & clear'd there. My Rice is of a very good quality & in all probability will be the first Cargo at your Market this Year in which case it will be entitled to the best price, & as our Crop is large, & we may expect that a good deal more will follow, it is my request that you sell this early & for Cash or short Credit into good hands. By early, I would not be understood to precipitate the Sale, but to sell it without much delay & to embrace that benefit which being first at Market may offer, in which your experience & good judgement will guide you. The Freight & primage I am sure you will adjust with impartiality & therefore shall not enlarge upon that subject but rely wholly on you.

The Net proceed when in Cash please to remit to Messrs. Cowles & Harford, Merchants in Bristol, to whom you will also transmit the necessary proofs in case of average or total loss within your cognizance as I shall write to those Gentlemen to Insure the Value of my Rice.

Capt. Porter has encourag'd me to trouble you with a trifling memorandum for a few Garden Seeds which I here inclose requesting you to let one of Your Servants procure them for me of the best kinds & to cause them to be sent out by the first opportunity of a Master who will promise to take the needful care of them upon the Voyage

---

the transport of German emigrants to British North America. B. Woelderink, adjunct-gemeentearchivaris, Gemeentelijke Archiefdienst, Rotterdam to the editor, Sept. 5, 1972.

hither or by way of Philadelphia. The Amount you will charge to my Account & if you think of any thing that I can do for you in return please to lay your commands upon me, who am with great regard, Sir, &ca.—

SOURCE: Letterbook copy, HL Papers, S. C. Hist. Soc.; addressed "Esquire. Rotterdam"; "per Capt. Porter. Copy per Smith."

TO JOHN KNIGHT & JOHN BLACKBURNE, JR.[2]

[Charles Town] 21st December 1764

Gentlemen,

I return you thanks for your very kind Letter of the 10th September by the hands of Mr. Edmond Head. The Credit that you are pleas'd to offer to that Gentleman & myself jointly in case we had establish'd a House would in such an event have been very useful, but for good & sufficient reasons which I shall assign to Mr. Knight & Mr. Appleby I must forego the benefits that might have arisen from thence. Nevertheless I shall not forget your intended favour but acknowledge it with gratitude upon every occasion. Mr. Head will advise you of his having enter'd into partnership with Messrs. Price & Hest two Young Gentlemen whom I formerly recommended to Mr. Knight & I think I may safely say that they compose as firm an House as any in this Town in point of integrity & industry, that they have as much knowledge of Trade in general & as much experience of the Carolina Trade in particular as any Men of their ages & more than Nine in ten at their first outset in business. They have already a pretty general acquaintance & I make no doubt that by their good behaviour they will soon secure to themselves an universal confidence & esteem. The only qualification then that they seem to be in some measure deficient in, is a large Capital. That deficiency, Gentlemen, will make them better Servants to those who shall be pleas'd to intrust them. It

---

[2] John Blackburne, Jr. (1722–1789) was mayor of Liverpool in 1760. His father, who had also been a Liverpool merchant, established a famous botanical garden. His son John, who was mayor of Liverpool in 1788, married the daughter of Jonathan Blundell. Matthew Gregson, *Portfolio of Fragments, Relative to the History & Antiquities of the County Palatine and Duchy of Lancaster* (Liverpool, Eng., 1817), p. 200; *Gentleman's Magazine*, LVII (1787), 204; LIX (1789), 861.

will edge their application to business, & give wings to their industry. They will emulate those who have gone before them, strive to give the same satisfaction to their friends as well as hope to reap equal benefits. But they are not wholly deficient in that essential momentum of commerce neither. They have some money (tho not much) to begin with, & they have what is equal to & what is often more valuable than Money—good Credit. They are in repute here, everybody will trust them in the general way, some I am sure will befriend them with Credit in a more extensive manner, & I in particular will lend them Money or become their surety upon every proper occasion as far as I ought to do consistent with safety to my own affairs, by which I mean for instance, that they shall not slip the offer of a Guinea Man for want of security if that is requir'd & so of Less important matters & further I hope to prevail upon you from what I have said as well as for the Love & affection that you bear to Mr. Head to transfer that Credit which you once design'd for him & me to the new House of Price, Hest, & Head. I dare aver that they will make use of it with the utmost tenderness & that they will never abuse your friendship. The very name will be an advantage to them, & may enrich them & then they must whether they ever draw upon you for a single penny or not, they must be sensible of the favour & bless you with grateful hearts. They shall be always welcome to my advice as often as they apply for it. I shall counsel them to act with prudence & circumspection, caution them against being captivated by specious prospects, in short point out & recommend to them the path which has led my friend Appleby contentedly back to his native clime & me as well satisfied to Rattray-Green. If I succeed with you Gentlemen in this one point in behalf of these Young Merchants it will give me vast pleasure, but why should I doubt it after the handsome things you have wrote of Mr. Head? I have said so much rather to shew you my good opinion of & inclination to serve them, than from any distrust of your friendship. I shall not presume to write so freely to anybody else in Leverpoole upon this subject nor is it necessary that I should for if you take them by the hand, they will not lack friends nor full employment. I beg leave to repeat my thanks & to profess myself to be with great regard, Gentlemen, &ca.—

SOURCE: Letterbook copy, HL Papers, S. C. Hist. Soc.; addressed "Leverpoole"; "per Higgins. Copy per Porter."

*TO THOMAS MEARS & JOSEPH
MANESTY*

[Charles Town] 21st December 1764

Gentlemen,

I have rece'd your favour of the 11th September with a Power
of Attorney[3] to recover effects belonging to the Estate of the Late
James Pardoe,[4] & as Mr. Charles Wright happen'd to be in Town I
applied to him without delay. He has given me some satisfactory information of a Sum paid by his Brother & himself of about £5,000
Currency for goods sold on Account of that unfortunate Gentleman
& hopes that further discoveries may be made for which purpose he
promises to bring down after Christmas certain anecdotes which he
thinks he is possess'd of among his Papers in the Country. When he
returns I shall probably see more clearly into this matter which at
present notwithstanding all that Mr. Wright says does appear somewhat ambiguous. I can already percieve that to recover anything
from the parties in possession who are strong & will fight hard for
money a suit must be commenc'd in Chancery. This Court is here as
in all other places as much reputed for its costliness & delay as it is
reverenc'd for its equity & unluckily you have not pointed out where
or how I am to procure means for beginning & carrying on such a suit
& perhaps as Assignees You have no power to supply me, or may now
have no money for the purpose.

Mr. Wright urges me to begin without Loss of time because
that one of the Parties & a principal one, is aged & very infirm, that
the death of him will deprive you of many valuable answers which
may be extracted while he has breath. I shall consider these things
very maturely & wait for Mr. Wrights further proofs & if I see good
ground to move on, shall immediately file a Bill, & draw upon you for
the first expence which I am sure you will at all events pay considering the motive for undertaking such a troublesome & hateful sort of
business merely to oblige you, my good friends. If you dislike that you
will forbid my further proceedings & I shall put a final stop to them.
In either event I shall endeavour to testify that I am with great regard, Gentlemen, &ca.—

---

[3] This power of attorney has not been found.
[4] James Pardoe was a Liverpool slave merchant. *HL Papers*, I, 206n.

SOURCE: Letterbook copy, HL Papers, S. C. Hist. Soc.; addressed "Esquires. Leverpoole"; "per Higgins. Copy per Porter."

TO JOHN KNIGHT & CO.

[Charles Town] 22d December 1764

Gentlemen,

I wrote to you the 8th Inst. per Capt. Doyle[5] & sent a duplicate per Capt. Erskine[6] with a short Postscript of the 12th upon which day Capt. Dennison went over the Bar. Please now to receive Invoice, Bill of Loading, & Masters Receipt for the Cargo per your said Ship, the whole Amount £9,911.4.6 to the debit of your Account Current which I hope you will find free from mistakes. Between the time that I last wrote you & the day for my indended private Auction I made every effort in my power to dispose of your goods at private Sale but with Little or no effect. I prevail'd upon a Country Shopkeeper to take a very few Articles & then the best offer that was made to me was 7½ for one, on the first cost taking off the Bounty on the Linnen. Our Importing Retailers have their Stores too full of every kind of goods & at this particular time some of them are necessitated to sell off behind the Curtain at very low rates to comply with many unexpected demands from England. The lower sort of Retailers who are of any worth supply themselves from such necessitous Houses & at Vendue where an uncommon quantity of fine new European Goods have of late appear'd, & where I believe for want of the Owners presence, who might not think it convenient to be seen there, many articles even to large quantities have been sold, & I have bought several myself as I have transiently pass'd by, at 4 for one. Failing of any other method to dispose of your goods I open'd the Auction on the 19th & have been at it ever since buying in every Article for which a proper price was not bid & setting them up again at a better opportunity which occasion'd me a great deal of trouble & many a sneer from the old Women that attended in expectation of great bargains & now in the three days Sale I have not made an end of your small quantity, & the Sale is defer'd until the Week after

---

[5] The brigantine *Tryton*, Nicholas Doyle, sailed for Bristol on Dec. 9. *Gazette*, Dec. 10, 1764.

[6] The brigantine *King-George*, Thomas Erskine, sailed for London on Dec. 14. *Gazette*, Dec. 17, 1764.

Christmas when I send you the Account. As you know the names of the purchasers you will be convinc'd that I have pursued the right method. Very few Shopkeepers appear in the list. It is chiefly compos'd of Men & Women who buy for the use of their respective families, a strong proof that the other class could supply themselves upon better terms elsewhere. What goods I have hitherto sold is at a low advance upon your Invoice but I am much mistaken if you have not laid some profit in that upon the Linnens & Checks. If you have not, tis evident by comparison with other importations that you have bought them upon bad terms. If I can sell the Negro Cloth at 8½ for one or perhaps even 8 you will find it more for your Interest than to keep it. Mr. Appleby may remember the Cloth that I took from him in '62. Part of it lays by me & near two Bales of what I imported in 1763 from Bristol. But if this latter price cannot be obtain'd I shall deliver it into the Hands of Messrs. Price, Hest, & Head who I am sure will exert themselves for your Interest. No Vessel Sail'd for Oporto since the *Knight* except the *Austin* & she not before the 17th Inst. nor will any other sail before the Holydays, at least I think not. Then will follow the Snow *Duke*[7] of 6 or 800 Barrels. After him the great Capt. Pitt[8] with 4 or 500. Then the *Live Oak* about February with 800, & I know of two Ships expected every day to carry the same way 1,300 & am order'd to Charter another of 700, which I cannot comply with. All this I have appriz'd Mr. Byrne of. No doubt he will take the hint & improve that time which he shall enjoy without a rival. I remain, &ca.—

SOURCE: Letterbook copy, HL Papers, S. C. Hist. Soc.; addressed "Owners of the Ship *Knight,* Leverpoole"; "per Higgins. Copy with a duplicate Receipt per Porter."

TO JOHN KNIGHT & THOMAS MEARS

[Charles Town] 22d December 1764

Gentlemen,

I beg leave to refer you to what I wrote the 8th & 12th Inst. per Capt. Doyle for Bristol & Erskine Via London & come now to resume the Subject of your said Snow. Capt. Holmes was detain'd

---

[7] The snow *Duke,* George Finch, sailed for Oporto on Jan. 23. *Gazette,* Jan. 26, 1765.

[8] Capt. Moses Pitt of the *Hopewell.*

four or five days after the Vessel was clear'd & did not get to Sea
before the 17th. He hopes to be over the Port Bar before the *Knight*
& I am morally certain he will be in many days before any other.
The next to follow is the Snow *Duke,* with 700 Barrels will sail in
ten or twelve days, then Capt. Pitt with 500, after these the Ship
Live Oak with 800 Barrels & two Ships of 600 or 650 Barrels each
every moment expected to Load for the House of Holdsworth, Olive,
& Newman of which I have taken care to advise Mr. Byrne, & I am
in great hopes that he will be able to sell off all your Rice without
a competitor. Before the day mention'd for the Sale of your goods
at Auction I us'd my utmost endeavours to dispose of them in private
Sale. I offer'd the very choice of them at 8½ for one & to give a
reasonable credit free of Interest, but the parties all desir'd time to
consider & have not to this hour return'd their resolutions. The best
offer that I had made to me was 7¾ for one, that is to say £7.15/
Current money for 20/ Sterling cost, free of all charges, & then only
for a few certain articles. Therefore I pursued my plan & tho I have
done no great Matters after three days constant Sale, buying in &
selling out over & over again, yet I am convinc'd that nothing better
could have been done in this case, & the list of purchasers when I
transmit it will prove that Shopkeepers & other retailers thought they
could be better supplied elsewhere for their names will make but a
small shew in the Account which is chiefly compos'd of the heads of
private families. What remains will be attempted again after the
Hollidays. I say again, because there is scarcely a single Article remaining but what has been put up two or three times. I have sold all
the Rum at 14/ except two or three Hogsheads which are discolour'd
& all the Coals are sold & I hope to transmit Accounts of the whole
early in January. Meantime please to receive under cover with this
an Invoice, Bill of Loading, & Receipt for the Snow's Cargo & disbursements Amounting to £9,245.11.1 which is carried off, to the
debit of your respective Accounts in Moiety, Vizt.

> To Mr. John Knight   £4,622.15.7
> Mr. Thomas Mears   4,622.15.6

which if free from error you will be so good as to note in conformity.
I do not recollect any thing necessary to add at this time. Therefore
shall conclude with assuring you that I remain with great regard,
Gentlemen, &ca.—

SOURCE: Letterbook copy, HL Papers, S. C. Hist. Soc.; addressed "Owners of the Snow *Austin*. Leverpoole"; "per Higgins. Copy with second Receipt per Porter."

TO THOMAS MEARS

[Charles Town] 22d December 1764

Sir,

I have the Honour of both your favours of the 8th & 11th September & having wrote what is needful in distinct Letters to the Owners of the *Austin* & also to yourself & Mr. Manesty as Assignees of James Pardoe I will beg leave to refer you to those Letters & add only a very word or two to either subjects. First as to the *Austin*. I have in the Companies Letter sent an Invoice, Bill of Loading, & Receipt for her Cargo & disbursements which Papers I need not repeat to you. I hope it is quite unnecessary as you may surely have the command of those, one half the Amount being £4,622.15.6 is to the debit of your Account. I acted with the utmost impartiality in dispatching said Snow & I am sure Capt. Holmes will be so just as to confirm my assertion. She was in my hands to load only from the 3d to the 11th Inst., one day was Sunday & two other days I stood still waiting for the Vessel hinder'd by Rain. This is counted by People here to be brisk work especially in a Cargo where no less than 90 half Barrels are call'd for. Next as to the papers that you & Mr. Manesty sent me, you say that they were intended by the Ship *Knight* but they came in the *Union* from London & arriv'd only the 16th Inst.[9] When Capt. Saul[1] for your Port Sail'd I had three Turtle provided to send in his Vessel which he refus'd to take tho I would willingly have paid him a Freight for them. He alledged that his Vessel was so low & washy that it was impossible to carry them safe & two of the three presently died, since that no opportunity has offer'd. You may be assur'd that I shall not be unmindful of your Commissions & as Red Birds[2] are more at my command I think I cannot fail of sending half a dozen of them by the first Vessel but as they are

---

[9] The ship *Union*, James Smith, arrived Dec. 16 from London. *Gazette*, Dec. 17, 1764.

[1] The brigantine *Hamilton*, William Saul, sailed for Liverpool on Oct. 25, *Gazette*, Oct. 29, 1764.

[2] *HL Papers*, I, 79n.

intended for Holland it might have been a better way to send them directly to Rotterdam or Amsterdam which I have now frequent opportunities of doing. I return you my hearty thanks for your kind intention of sending me a present of Barbados Spirit which Capt. Holmes says he quite forgot to bring with him, but, Dear Sir, you give yourself too much trouble on my Account in these things & I am asham'd that it is not in my power to make suitable acknowledgements, but I wont dispair of doing something in return one of these days as I shall gain a Little more Leisure. From some circumstances in my own private affairs particularly a necessary attention to my Interest in the Country & a desire of putting my eldest Son at School some where in England, I find a faithful discharge of the Commission business too arduous a task for me without greatly neglecting my other concerns, which I have never set in competition with the business of my friends while such was actually committed to my care, & nothing less than a Faithful & conscientious discharge of their Business will content me for I never did nor never will desire to receive pay without giving my Labour for it. For these reasons & in all probability I shall leave the province some time in June next for the purpose above mentioned. I have come to a resolution to recommend the House of Price, Hest, & Head to all my friends & I now beg leave to introduce them to you in particular. You know Mr. Head very well, Sir, & I dare recommend the three Gentlemen as a House that will give great satisfaction to all that employ them. They are Young, active, industrious Men in very good repute here & have some staunch friends that will always assist them, but I make no doubt of their being able to go alone in a very few Years if they meet with countenance & encouragement from your side of the water. I return you a Thousand thanks for all past favours which I shall bear in remembrance & as I do not mean to retire from the World nor wholly from Trade so I shall be glad of your permission to continue our correspondence & whenever occasions require I hope you will always look upon & command me as one sure friend in Carolina, but upon this subject perhaps I may enlarge some day next Summer in Leverpoole. Meantime, I salute you with most cordial respect & remain, Dear Sir, Yours, &ca.—

SOURCE: Letterbook copy, HL Papers, S. C. Hist. Soc.; addressed "Leverpoole"; "per Higgins. Copy per Porter."

TO COWLES & HARFORD

[Charles Town] 22d December 1764

Gentlemen,

Referring you to my late imperfect advises under the 18th & 21st October, 10th Ulto., & 20 Inst., I proceed to acknowledge & reply to your favours of the 25th & 27th August & to advise of other needful matters. My business has be[en] so greatly interupted by some late untoward circumstances, which at one time or other fall in every family, that I have neither examined the Sundry Sales that you have transmitted nor perfected those Accounts which I intended to have laid before you two Months ago but if no new misfortune attends me the whole shall be done & sent next Week by Capt. Carbery.[3]

Mr. Gordon[4] lately came to Town from a very Long Tour thro our Southwestern acquisitions. He return'd in a poor state of health & seem'd to be attended with some cares & therefore I have as yet but barely mention'd your demand upon him. Next Week I shall wait upon him & talk more seriously upon business & advise you of the result. Your last favour informs me of the expiration of your late partnership & your intentions to act seperately in trade, referring me to what you should each of you thereafter write upon that subject but tho many Ships have since arriv'd I have heard nothing new from you. Therefore I have taken the Liberty to address you under the former firm & shall continue to do so until you direct me to change my address. You see by my Yesterday's Letter that I have wrote to you for large Insurances & order'd considerable remittances to be made to you on my Account & I shall ere long trouble you to pay some of my draughts in consequence thereof not doubting but one or both of you will be so good as to act for me & let none of my affairs comitted to your care suffer for want of a friend. After a long & deplorable illness poor Capt. Courtin got on his Legs & sail'd for Lisbon the 12th Instant with a Cargo of 664 Barrels & 47 half Barrels Rice of which 114 Barrels & 30 half Barrels are on our joint Account in proportion as we hold in the Vessel, the remainder on freight at only 50/ per Ton, the whole consigned to Messrs. Mayne

---

[3] The ship *Prince Ferdinand,* James Carbry, arrived Nov. 22 from Newfoundland and sailed Dec. 31 for Bristol. *Gazette,* Nov. 26, Dec. 31, 1764.
[4] John Gordon.

& Co. with orders to remit the Net proceed of the Rice & Freight to you. The Amount of our Rice is £1,999.1.11 & of the Ships expences here no less than £1,056.17/ exclusive of the article of Sheathing which Account is not yet come in because the Carpenter who perform'd it has been long ill too, but the whole Accounts shall be ready & go by the abovemention'd Capt. for Bristol. Meantime you may make the needful Insurance from hence on your own Account & I must request you to keep the Sum of One Thousand pounds Sterling Insur'd on my Account on the Bottom & Freight until her arrival here. My part of the Goods I shall risque. Not only Capt. Courtin himself was sick here but also his Mate & every individual of his Ships Company, whereby we unavoidably suffer'd loss & at length to prevent further delay I was oblig'd to put on board a Negro of my own to make up his compliment of hands. I have order'd Capt. Courtin to make the utmost dispatch from Lisbon & not to wait there for a trifling Freight, to advise you immediately upon his arrival both at Lisbon & in England, to take out a new Licence, & to follow your orders which I hope you will Lodge for him at Falmouth & Porto to prevent if possible one minutes loss of time. If you have any certainty of a Freight out from Bristol you will no doubt order the Ship there otherwise immediately for this port where by your previous advices I may be making provision for her & I hope she will in future be a more fortunate adventure. One thing I had almost forgot that is that through the inability of Master & Mates she is at present so badly stowed as to be only in appearance in a set of Balast & I make no doubt of her carrying a good deal more another Voyage. I foresaw that & other evils while Courtin lay sick & advis'd & beg'd him to let me put in a Master. Nay I went so far as to promise to keep him in pay on my own Account rather than he should fatigue himself & risque his life & at the same time do his Owners no service but he was tenacious & would not chearfully accept my proposition.

From the death of my late friend John Ball & other circumstances in my family I find that it is impracticable for me to conduct my own Affairs & to transact business upon Commission in such a way as I would chuse & have been always us'd to acquit myself in, besides a desire to go to England the next Summer principally to put my Son at School, I have therefore determined to decline all Foreign consignments after the Month of March & to resign & recommend any that shall come to my address to the House of Messrs. Price, Hest, & Head who I believe will write to you by this opportunity. I beg leave to introduce them to your joint & several favours intreating your friendship to them as occasions shall offer. They are active industrious Men & as it will give me true pleasure to see them prosper so I shall not fail to assist them to the utmost of my power & I have not the least doubt of their giving general satisfaction & doing honour to the recommendation of their friends. As I must write again very soon, shall not increase the present trouble but to add that I remain with great regard, Gentlemen, &ca.—

SOURCE: Letterbook copy, HL Papers, S. C. Hist. Soc.; addressed "Bristol"; "per Higgins. Copy per Porter."

TO JOHN KNIGHT

[Charles Town] 22d December 1764

Dear Sir,

Since my last trouble which was so long ago as the 24th August per Capt. McKie, a series of cross adventures have conspir'd to hinder me from writing to you & from transmitting all the Accounts therein mentioned but idleness or inattention to business have been no part of the cause of this delay. Please now to receive the two Sales of your goods per Ship *Hope* the first bearing to your Credit a Net proceed of £8,306.0.3 & the second £817.16.2 on both which there are considerable outstanding debts mark'd which in this Province is unavoidable for if you once trust your goods out of the Store you must have patience for payment 'til convenient to the Purchaser tho you agree to be paid at a certain short date, or even upon demand. Some trifle of these I am afraid will prove bad which I should not take notice of if they had not been in other respects heavy Sales to me. As I shall soon transmit your whole Account Current including the *Austin*'s present Sales & Cargo I shall therefore omit a partial one for the present. I have wrote to you by this conveyance as owner of the *Knight* & Owner of the *Austin* in distinct Letters to the several companies to which I beg leave to refer as I do to another Letter in Answer to that wrote by you & Mr. Blackburn in favor of Mr. Head & now I must take up your very obliging favour of the 8th September & reply to it briefly as my time runs fast.

I have not heard a syllable of Capt. Pollard.[5] I regret that he did not come here & as much that your friends in Barbados had not sent down 50 or 60 Negroes in the *Austin*. As to the *Knight* I have done her justice. She was Loaden several days before she could get to Sea. At the same time I avoided every degree of partiality & it gave me pleasure to see her get the start of every other Ship. Dennison is as you say very deserving. The frame of an House which you order'd will be ready for the first good opportunity which I suppose wont be before Summer. Your port Wine has one great fault. Tis muddy & that you know, Sir, spoils all, but Wine is the merest drug that ever was here. The Town is still full of every quality & the adventurers must sink a great deal of money. I took 4 or 5 Pipes at about prime cost last Voyage off Capt. Dennison's hands, not a drop of it is sold tho I would gladly accept what it cost me a Year ago. I hope that I shall give Mr. Mears satisfaction in this Years Voyage of the *Austin*. If I fail, industry & honest endeavours will be fruitless. I am exceedingly oblig'd to you for taking so much notice of Mr. Hest as I am for your kind intentions in sending out Mr. Head to assist me as a partner in business & this Leads me to inform you why I have declin'd that offer & at the same time what steps I have taken to serve that Gentleman in consequence of the handsome credentials with which you & other friends were pleas'd to furnish him.

Just before Mr. Head arriv'd the death of one of Mrs. Laurens's Brothers who had always taken the charge & trouble of my planting Interest upon him brought a heavy additional load upon my Shoulders, insomuch that I found the discharge of business for my friends abroad & any tolerable attention to my family affairs & my own Interest incompatible, & my resolutions to go to England partly on Account of health but principally to put my Son to School gaining strength everyday. I had refus'd the offer of a partnership in the first House in this Town,[6] where I may say we might have carried every

---

[5] Capt. Thomas Pollard had brought the *Pearl*, a Liverpool vessel, with a cargo of slaves to Charleston in 1760. *HL Papers*, III, 43n.

[6] This was undoubtedly the house of Brewton & Smith. Miles Brewton was the largest slave trader in colonial S. C. He was first a partner of Benjamin Smith in Smith & Brewton, then a partner of Smith and his son Thomas Loughton Smith in Smith, Brewton & Smith, and then of Thomas Loughton Smith in Brewton & Smith. For the cargoes sold and duties paid by these firms and others headed at a later date by Miles Brewton see W. Robert Higgins, "Charles Town Merchants and Factors Dealing in the External Negro Trade, 1735–1775," *SCHM*, LXV (1964), 206–207.

thing before us. In these circumstances I had invited some assistance from Mr. Price & was incouraging him to hope for the principal part of my Commission business in case of my leaving the province & just at that juncture came in Mr. Head who seems to be & I dare say is, deserving of every thing that his friends have said in his favour. But averse to a closer attachment to business myself & as unwilling to enslave any Young Gentleman whose abilities & disposition of mind I was not intimately acquainted with & not very fond as Mr. Appleby knows & as I have shewn above of Partnerships in general, I found some reluctance to the connexion propos'd; not because of the Man for I would not have hesitated half so long about any other, but from a consideration of the danger of throwing too much of the burthen of business upon a stranger, for to discharge much business faithfully in this Country much application & drudgery is necessary. We cannot trust any other eyes or judgement but our own in every minute article. Negroes are faithless, & Workmen exceedingly careless, & upon the whole after mature deliberation I am determin'd to decline it, & in Lieu of Mr. Heads expectations from me, to recommend him to join with the Young House of Price & Hest upon a promise of dropping the principal part of consignments made to me into their hands & indeed all, only reserving freedom to myself whenever I shall think proper to serve any particular friend. This proposal met with the approbation of all parties on this side & they have accordingly form'd a House under the name of Price, Hest, & Head & I hope you & all Mr. Heads friends will so well approve of what is done as to countenance him with your favours to the House. I have said so much of my opinions of & regard for these Gentlemen in my Letter to you & Mr. Blackburn as leaves no room for that subject here. I shall therefore suffice to add that they are lively, active Men & only want friends (I think) to enable them to do great things in trade & I am not in the least fear of their deceiving me. This resolution of mine I trust will be applauded by my worthy friend & benefactor Mr. Knight. I am sure it will if I have the happiness to enlarge upon the topic next Summer at Leverpoole. Meantime I hope it will not deprive me of the honour of corresponding with him & of rendering my best services in all his commands; that he will inform the Masters of all his Ships bound to this port that there is such a person in Carolina always ready to serve, befriend, & promote his Interest & that in general he will call upon me when occasion requires as one who would, if he was worth Two plumbs, pride himself in giving proof of his being with very great respect & esteem Mr. Knights much oblig'd & constant friend—

SOURCE: Letterbook copy, HL Papers, S. C. Hist. Soc.; addressed "Leverpoole"; "per Higgins. Copy per Porter."

TO ZACHARY VILLEPONTOUX

[Charles Town] 24th December 1764

Sir,

I am now in great want of Bricks having engag'd to lend a Man whose Bread depends upon it part of the quantity contracted for with you, & in dependance of receiving them he has not applied else where & is now complaining to me that his hands stand id[l]e. I intreat the favour of you, Sir, to give your People orders to bring down four or Six boat loads as quick as possible of good bricks; there has truly been too much cause to complain of the quality of what came lately down. I have no other Interest or benefit therein but merely to serve an industrious poor Man & I beg of you to assist me therein as far as I have any right consistent with our engagement & you will do a great favour thereby to, Sir, &ca.—

SOURCE: Letterbook copy, Letter Book of Henry Laurens, Oct. 30, 1762– Sept. 10, 1766, Penn. Hist. Soc.; addressed "Black [Back] River."

TO LLOYD & BORTON

[Charles Town] 24th December 1764

Gentlemen,

The annex'd is duplicate of what I wrote you per Capt. Catlin[7] 7 days since & here you have inclos'd a duplicate Bill of Loading for the Corn & Rice on board his Sloop. Just now your favour of the 17th Ulto. is come to hand very justly reproaching me for neglect which is no more than my misconduct merited & I might reasonably expect. But I am glad however that I was a Little beforehand &

---

[7] Capt. Nathaniel Catlin.

when you see the causes of my delay I am under no doubt of your readiness to excuse me.

Negroes have sold here at very exhorbitant prices all the past Summer & even down to this time. I have just transmitted a Sale of a parcel of Men, refuse, aged, half blind & one dumb & deaf, which made an average of £34 Sterling. Prime Negroes will yield full £40 at this time but how long this will continue is very uncertain for we have parcels dropping in every day from the West Indies. Many more are expected & the Season is at hand when the Affrican Ships will make their appearance. A great many of them are expected & I am sure that several will come or attempt to come earlier than usual. I have advices from my own particular friends of several. The great prices that have of Late been given, the eagerness of some rival Houses in this Town, the Act of Assembly Lately passed laying a heavy duty upon all Negroes imported after the Year 1765—all will conspire to over stock our Market with Negroes & I shall not wonder if the prices are run down very Low & a necessity for giving very tedious Credit. You will be pleas'd to think on this a Little, & then give me Leave on the other hand to observe, that many people may from apprehensions of the danger which I have pointed at restrain their importations, that our Crops of Rice & Indigo are very large & sell for high prices whereby the Rich planters are enabled to lay by Money & the middling & poorer sort in general to clear themselves of debt, that the latter class stand in need & will take off a great number of Negroes in small parcels, & the first will be induc'd to lay out all their ready money & to strain upon a next Crop to increase their Stocks both for themselves & their Children upon the prospect of that prohibitary Law which is calculated to stop the importation of Slaves for three Years. Now I have said all that occurs to be needful on each side of your enquiry you will be pleas'd to judge for your selves, I shall only add a word of advice which may be of service in case you shall determine to adventure in that branch. In such case be early, not later here than the 15th March, & let your purchase be of the very best kind of Slaves, black & smooth, free from blemishes, Young & well grown, the more Men the better, but not old. None sell better than Gambia Slaves. If you touch any below this description let a very great bargain only tempt & let me know the real cost of them. Be sure to give them good covering & victuals & secure the promise of the Master by whom you send them to treat them with humanity & keep up their Spirits. If you have an inclination after all that I have said to make an attempt you may have remittance in Bills of Exchange upon London according to the then state of the Market, which will be in Payments at three, six, & nine or three, six, & twelve months. But I would not have you rely upon any thing better than the Latter tho you may depend upon being treated with honour & punctuality. Upon the whole unless you have an opportunity of making a very good purchase, I think you may as well forego the prospect of uncertain profit as to run a risque of meeting certain loss. If I am not in the way, Messrs. Price, Hest, & Head will receive & obey your commands as effectually as I could do, & I beg leave to introduce that House to your acquaintance. Two of the Gentlemen have formerly Lived with me & therefore I know them & dare recommend them to my acquaintance & friends for their integrity & application to business, & Mr. Head is a Gentleman sent from England with very warm recommendations from one of my old partners & other Gentlemen of establish'd characters to be my partner but it is rather too late for [me] to begin new connexions without new causes & therefore I have determin'd after the Month of March to drop all the favours of my friends (except in very par-

SOURCE: Letterbook copy, HL Papers, S. C. Hist. Soc.; addressed "Jamaica." This is the last letter in the "Foreign Letterbook." The last page has been torn out. The next surviving "Foreign Letterbook" begins with a letter dated Aug. 25, 1767.

ADVERTISEMENT

December 24, 1764

SEVEN BALES of exceeding good NEGRO CLOTH, some of which is of the best sort imported into this PROVINCE, To be sold by the BALE, at 10s. per yard, and lower in proportion to the quality of each piece, by

HENRY LAURENS

SOURCE: Printed in *Gazette,* Dec. 24, 1764.

ARTICLES OF AGREEMENT FOR
A PILOT BOAT FOR EAST FLORIDA[8]

[Charles Town, 27 December 1764]

Agreed between Charles Minors of the one part & Henry Laurens on behalf and acting for James Grant, Esquire, Governor of East Florida, of the other part. To Wit. The said Charles Minors undertakes and engages to Erect, build, and compleat and deliver afloat to the said Henry Laurens or his Assigns on or before the tenth March next ensuing, a neat well built firm Pilot Boat, with a Cock-Pitt & seats abaft[9] and in every respect finish'd and perfected in a Workmanlike manner of the best stuff and materials,[1] & of the dimensions & as nearly as possible to the particular directions hereafter set forth. To Wit. 25 feet Keel — 10 feet Beam — 5 feet hold[2] — a long floor[3] — a clean Run[4] — Round Tuck[5] — Bow Timbers not

---

[8] The editors consulted William Avery Baker, naval architect and curator of the Francis Russell Hart Nautical Museum in the Department of Ocean Engineering, Massachusetts Institute of Technology, concerning the historical importance of this contract and the meaning of the terms. In a letter of May 16, 1971 to assistant editor David Chesnutt, Mr. Baker made the following comment with regard to this contract: "This contract of 1764 defines a boat about 32–33 feet long on deck. Few plans exist of pilot boats built before 1800. The oldest was built at New York about 1783–1785 and two others were constructed in Virginia somewhat later. An incomplete plan of a pilot boat by Samuel Humphreys is dated 1798. All of these were larger than the 1764 boat and were fully decked. Some small pilot boats of the first quarter of the nineteenth century around Boston are known to have been about the size of the 1764 boat or smaller and to have been only partially decked. These partial decks extended perhaps from two-thirds to three-quarters of the length from the bow, the remainder of the boat being open." The definitions found in the other footnotes to this document were also supplied by Mr. Baker.

[9] "This refers to some provision for the helmsman at the stern. In some modern yachts the cockpit is only a recess or well to take the crew's feet as they sit on deck. In other cases cockpits are large, deep, and fitted with seats. None of the existing early pilot boat plans show cockpits."

[1] "The timber used in construction. Actually 'thick stuff' was timber over 6 inches thick, 'planks' ranged from 2 to 6 inches in thickness, while 'boards' were less than 2 inches thick."

[2] "This is the depth at the centerline (at the widest part of the hull) from the underside of the deck planking to the top of the sheathing on the bottom framing. This figure indicates that the 1764 boat was deeper than the vessels shown in the existing plans and suggests that the cockpit was a recess in the deck and not a whole open section. Such a recess might have been big enough to have had seats."

[3] "The floor is the bottom of a vessel. A vessel with a long floor carried the shape of her maximum (midship) section well toward the ends so as to have more internal capacity. All this is relative but practically speaking the 1764 boat may have shown little change of shape for the middle one-third of her length."

[4] "Refers to the shape of the underbody aft. A clean run provides a good flow of water to the rudder. Vessels with full runs drag the ocean behind them."

[5] "Refers to the shape of the stern above water. The New York and Virginia

too hollow below[6] — a good round harping[7] — not much dead
rising[8] — To be built as clean, strong, and expeditiously as possible —
To finish her to a Cleat[9] and find all materials whatsoever relative
to Carpenter's work in the Hull, Masts, Yards, Booms, Bowsprit,
Pitch, Tar, Turpentine, Oakum,[1] &ca. — but not Iron nor Joiners
work.[2] — All which he the said Charles Minors engages to compleat
and deliver as aforesaid for the Gross Sum of Five hundred and
Seventy seven pounds ten Shillings Current money to be paid to him
in full in the following manner, Vizt. Two hundred pounds, at the
raising of the said Boat, and three hundred and Seventy seven pounds
ten Shillings, the remainder, the day after compleating as aforesaid
Launching and delivery of the said Boat, and the said Henry Laurens
covenants and agrees to make good the payments as abovemention'd
in the proportions and at the respective times and periods there set
forth. To the true performance of this agreement the said Parties do
Mutually and Reciprocally each bind himself & his Heirs and Executors to the other his Heirs and Executors in the Penal sum of Fifty
Pounds Sterling. In Witness whereof they have interchangeably set
their Hands and Seals to these presents on the [blank] Day of January
1765.

---

pilot boats mentioned above were shaped like enlarged small boats—the stern was
flat across like some old fashioned rowboats that may still be seen here and there.
This was a 'flat tuck.' A 'round tuck' stern had a high flat section to which the
planking curved up from below."

[6] "Refers to shape of sections below water forward. Hollow sections have a
'pinched in' appearance."

[7] "All vessels of this period had one or more heavy timbers known as wales that
ran fore-and-aft on the outside of the frames. On small vessels one was at about
the deck line and the others, if fitted, a bit below. The forward ends of the wales
were known as the harpings and 'a good round harping' meant a full deck line."

[8] "Refers to the shape of the transverse sections. A flat-bottomed boat has no
deadrise. Baltimore clippers had extreme deadrise with their sections being deep
Vees."

[9] "A very old term meaning to the last detail."

[1] "An old definition was 'Stuff made by picking rope-yards to pieces.' Lightly
tarred it was used for caulking seams."

[2] "Iron was scarce in 1764 and it was common practice for the owner of a vessel to supply all iron spikes, bolts, bars, etc. needed for her construction. Joiners
work included any fancy work, interior bulkheads, berths, etc. and was done under
a separate contract. The shipbuilder in this case constructed the hull and made
the masts and spars. The rigging and sails came from other contractors. She probably had little joiner work."

In presence of

This agreement was concluded upon and extended in Writing the 27 December 1764.

SOURCE: Copy, CO 5/540, pp. 384–386, Public Record Office, London. Endorsed: "East Florida. Articles of Agreement for a Pilot Boat for East Florida. In Governor Grant's Letter of 1 March 1765. Read June 26, 1766."

TO WOODDROP & DEAS[3]

[Charles Town] 29 December 1764

Gentlemen,

I have made further inquiry into the accident that happened last night to my Schooner & from a plain simple evidence as ever I heard it appears to me quite clear that the damage done to her by Capt. Sinkler[4] was the effect of hastiness & passion & not a work of necessity; altho it is confessed that Capt. Sinkler's Vessel was dragging when the Schooner went athwart her Hause yet it is told me that if she had continued in the same Berth where she lay last night when the Schooner anchored in the Stream with an Anchor, Grapnel, & full scope of Cables, she, the Schooner could not have dragged or drove on board the Snow or any other Vessel whatever, but the Snow it seems dragged right in her way, & here that good advice which Mr. Wooddrop gave to Owners of Schooners might be very properly applied to Owners of Snows too—to order their Masters to Moor their Vessels in the Stream especially in blowing weather; that the Snow lay at a single Anchor is a fact which in all our conversation this afternoon was not disclosed to me & therefore I am sure Mr. Wooddrop must have been ignorant of it. The consideration of that single circumstance not to take notice of some Acts rather too Arbi-

---

[3] William Wooddrop and either David or John Deas.
[4] The snow *Edward & Anne,* Andrew Sinclair, sailed for London on Jan. 1, 1765. David and John Deas had advertised early in the month that half of the space designed for 800 barrels was available. *Gazette,* Dec. 10, 1764, Jan. 7, 1765. The Scottish name "Sinclair" did become "Sinkler" in S. C.

trary on the part of Capt. Sinkler convinces me that he ought to make good all the damages done to the smaller Bark which lay clear of every body & must have gone clear if there had been no body tumbled in her way thro remissness of that Duty which the Interest of Owners & the Laws of almost every Sea Port in the Universe requires. The less occasion too was there on this Account for that Lavishness of Scurrility & abuse as well as blame on the Schooner Master for neglect of his Duty. I am—

SOURCE: Letterbook copy, Letter Book of Henry Laurens, Oct. 30, 1762–Sept. 10, 1766, Penn. Hist. Soc. This letter was copied by HL.

TO ALEXANDER DAVIDSON

[Charles Town] 2d January 1765

Sir,

I Receiv'd your favour of the 14th December per the Schooner *Pitt* & also 125 Barrels of Pitch the Value of the over Plus after paying me 110, is not yet adjusted. It came just in good time for you but a little too late for poor me, for there is not Freight for one Barrel in the Harbour nor is there any price that can be determined. Yet there is some in the hands of Mr. Maurice Simmons for Sale & whatever he obtains must be the Standard for yours. As to the over Weight I shall allow you for every pound beyond the Standard of 330 lbs. which is the Weight allow'd me by Mr. Clegg, Mr. Potts, Mr. Hughes, tho all things considered I believe you do not expect any allowance upon the 110 which you were to have deliver'd per Contract. The Weight of 9 Barrels is below & if I can ascertain the price before Capt. Richardson Sails I shall send you an Account of the whole. I Wonder who told you that Pitch was in great demand, it was some time ago, but then you know it did not come to my Lot to have any. As to George Dick he is but a Man to say the most of him, & Men are frail Creatures & I always knew that neither he nor I were infallible.

I wish you a happy Year & as many returns as shall find you in health & contentment neither troublesome to yourseff nor your friends & I remain, &ca.—

```
348 ⎫
348 ⎪
348 ⎪
340 ⎪           3,058
330 ⎬  9 at 330   2,970
330 ⎪          ————
332 ⎪          88 on 9 Barrels
332 ⎪
350 ⎭
```

SOURCE: Letterbook copy, Letter Book of Henry Laurens, Oct. 30, 1762–
Sept. 10, 1766, Penn. Hist. Soc.; addressed "Black Mingo."

TO WILLIAM HUGHES

[Charles Town] 2d January 1765

Sir,

I have Rec'd per Capt. Richardson in the Schooner *Pitt* your
favour of the 8th Ulto. & also 63 Barrels of Pitch. I wish they had
been filled up but you promise to do better the next time.

The Weights & whole Amount you have below which carries
a Net proceed of £160.19.6 to the Credit of your Account. Please
to forward what more you have ready by the first opportunity & you
may command the Amount as it shall fall due. I wish you many
happy Years & remain, Sir, &ca.—

SOURCE: Letterbook copy, Letter Book of Henry Laurens, Oct. 30, 1762–
Sept. 10, 1766, Penn. Hist. Soc.; addressed "Williamsburgh."

TO STEPHEN BULL,[5] JOHN KELSALL,[6] CHARLES GRAVES,[7] WILLIAM FIELD,[8] & JOSEPH HILES[9]

[Charles Town] 3d January 1765

Gentlemen,

Mr. Daniel Slade[1] this day passed a Bill on you for £331.10/

---

[5] Stephen Bull of Sheldon plantation (died 1800) entered the Commons House
of Assembly in 1757, was colonel of the Granville County militia, and largely rebuilt Sheldon Church. Henry D. Bull, *The Family of Stephen Bull* (Georgetown,
S. C., 1961), pp. 17–20.

[6] John Kelsall married Mary Bellinger on May 24, 1738. *SCHM,* XIII (1912),

pay'ble to me One Month after date with Interest thereon, which he assures me he has good foundation for drawing.

I here inclose the said Bill which I request you to return by the first opportunity accepted or not as you see fit, but if Mr. Slade hath now or will have some Months hence a fund in your hands for payment of his draughts altho he may have been premature in making it, you may if you please accept if payable at Six Months acknowledging the Interest to be growing until the principal is paid, which I take the Liberty of mentioning because your nonacceptance of the Bill will unavoidably be attended with expences to the drawer. I am with great respect, Gentlemen, &ca.—

SOURCE: Letterbook copy, Letter Book of Henry Laurens, Oct. 30, 1762–Sept. 10, 1766, Penn. Hist. Soc.; addressed "Esquires. Commissioners for repairs of Combahee Bridge."

TO JAMES BRENARD
[Charles Town] 5th January 1765

Sir,

I send you by the Schooner *Wambaw* all the articles that you requir'd for the Plantation except the Window Glass which I cannot

---

216. He was a justice of the peace for Granville County in 1756. *SCHM*, xx (1919), 74. When he wrote his will in 1765, he was a planter of Prince William parish with lands on "Skiddaway Island" in Georgia. "Will of John Kelsall," dated March 29, 1765, proved May 4, 1772, *Abstracts of Wills, 1760–1784*, p. 177.

[7] In 1755 a Presbyterian church was gathered at Charles Graves' plantation. *SCHM*, xxxviii (1937), 32. On Jan. 31, 1769, Elizabeth Graves, widow, was appointed administrator of the estate of Charles Graves, planter of Prince William parish. *SCHM*, xxxi (1930), 155.

[8] William Field, the son of John Field of Chehaw, was born on April 22, 1729. He married Sarah Chaplin in St. Helena parish on Oct. 1, 1751. *SCHM*, xxiii (1922), 49, 64–65. On May 7, 1762 he received two grants totaling 834 acres near the Combahee River. Index to Grants, S. C. Archives. He was a planter when he died in 1767. "Will of William Field," dated Jan. 14, 1767, proved May 1, 1767, *Abstracts of Wills, 1760–1784*, p. 74.

[9] Joseph Hiles has not been identified. These gentlemen were the commissioners for the repair of Combahee Bridge. On May 11, 1754, the Commons had passed "an act appointing commissioners for repairing and keeping in repair the bridge over Combee River, from the causey to the town of Radnor." Stephen Bull was one of those originally appointed. The commissioners had the right to fill vacancies. *S. C. Statutes*, ix, 173–175.

[1] On Jan. 21, 1767, HL bought a slave, who was a carpenter, from Daniel Slade, carpenter, of Dorchester. Miscellaneous Records, MM, Part 2 (1763-1767), pp. 682–683, S. C. Archives.

get with convenience of the proper size, and also, Three small Barrels which you will please to have carried home with as little jolting as possible. I shall probably be with you before the Schooner is Loaden but dont wait for me. Dispatch her with all speed & send our Hogs & Mrs. Laurens hopes you will have some Turkeys & Geese to spare. Capt. Walker[2] will bring as many Barrels of Salt upon his Deck as he can.

There is no Iron Dowling Stock.[3] I send a Wooden one.

SOURCE: Letterbook copy, Letter Book of Henry Laurens, Oct. 30, 1762– Sept. 10, 1766, Penn. Hist. Soc.; addressed "Wambaw."

TO JOHN GRAY

[Charles Town, 5–18 January 1765]

Sir,

Capt. McIntosh[4] informs me that he has sold the whole of the Wood that you will bring down this trip to be Landed at Cumming's point[5] or the nearest convenient place to the New Barracks.[6] You will be pleased to stop with the Boat on your return nearby to the above mentioned place in order for the receiving some particular directions relative to the landing of it.

---

[2] David Walker was master of the schooner *Wambaw*, 15 tons, which had been built in S. C. in 1760 and was owned by Benjamin Perdriau, HL, and John Coming Ball. It was registered on Sept. 15, 1764 by Benjamin Perdriau. See Registration of the Schooner *Wambaw*, Sept. 15, 1764. Samuel Prioleau, Jr. & Co. advertised it for sale at public vendue on April 16, 1765, describing the *Wambaw* as having been built in Charleston and launched July-Aug. 1760 with a burthen of 100 barrels of rice. *Gazette*, March 30, 1765. HL then intended Walker to be master of the new schooner *Dependance* which HL registered on June 18, 1765. See Registration of the Schooner *Dependance*, June 18, 1765.

[3] An "Iron Dowling Stock" was a device used to fasten together two pieces of wood by penetrating some distance into the substance of the connected pieces. *OED.*

[4] Captain Lachlan McIntosh of S. C.

[5] Coming's Point protruded into the marshes of the Ashley River. A suburb of Charleston (Harleston village), it was at this time being connected to the town by streets. Carl Bridenbaugh, *Cities in Revolt, Urban Life in America, 1743-1776* (New York, 1964), p. 237.

[6] Barracks were built near the Free School in the winter of 1757–1758 to house 1,000 men of Lt. Col. Henry Bouquet's Royal American Regiment. *Papers of Henry Bouquet,* I, 223, 267–268.

[*P.S.*] Capt. McIntosh says there will be another load ready by Tuesday or Wednesday next from which you may supply those you have engaged with—

SOURCE: Letterbook copy, Letter Book of Henry Laurens, Oct. 30, 1762–Sept. 10, 1766, Penn. Hist. Soc.; addressed "Captain. of the Schooner *Baker* at Ashly Ferry." This letter was copied by HL. It appears between those dated Jan. 5 and 18 in the letterbook.

TO ANDREW BROUGHTON

[Charles Town] 18th January 1765

Sir,

I am sorry that you should have any trouble about the Letter that I sent you per favour of Mr. Scott. I cannot recollect whether it was the first or second that I wrote, but be that as it may it was of no more consequence than to notify you not to depend upon me as a purchaser of your Plantation. If I had any inclination to make such a purchase I should apply to you in the same way that I make all bargains openly & unreservedly. If your price & conditions were agreeable we should close at once. If not, I might make you one offer but not a second.

But the case is quite otherwise. I have really no desire to increase my property in Lands, having already more than I manage as well as I ought to do & it must be something very advantageous to induce me to embark further in the troublesome business of planting.

By Mr. Henty's[7] Survey of my Land at Mepkin he has included a Large piece of that Ground which you have for some time occupied & clear'd altho I have absolutely paid for it & ought to & must seek for redress some where either from you or from the party

---

[7] John Hentie was appointed deputy surveyor on Oct. 30, 1756. *Miscellaneous Records*, KK (1754–1758), p. 410, S. C. Archives. He was well known in the region between the Cooper and Wando rivers for he witnessed the wills of the following planters: John Coming Ball (March 28, 1764), James Marion (July 8, 1765), Robert Quash (May 15, 1766), John Dutarque (Aug. 19, 1766), Nicholas Harleston (Feb. 6, 1767), and John Harleston (May 21, 1767). *Abstracts of Wills, 1760–1784*, pp. 49, 70, 98, 99, 111, 171. He was justice of the peace in Craven County in 1756 and in 1765. *SCHM*, xx (1919), 74; *General Gazette*, Oct. 31, 1765. In March 1771 Elias Ball as principal creditor was cited to administer the estate of John Hentie, deputy surveyor. *SCHM*, xliv (1943), 181.

who took my money. He I suppose will give me none until I shall first have attempted to establish my claim of the whole quantity that he sold & warranted that he had a right to sell. Upon this subject I shall be extremely glad to talk to you at any time most convenient to you now while you are in Charles town. I remain, &ca.——

SOURCE: Letterbook copy, Letter Book of Henry Laurens, Oct. 30, 1762–Sept. 10, 1766, Penn. Hist. Soc.; addressed "Charles Town."

GEORGE AUSTIN, HENRY LAURENS, & GEORGE APPLEBY VERSUS *JOHN LEWIS BOURQUIN & MARGUERITTE CHIFFELLE, HIS WIFE*[8]

January 19, 1765

[*On January 8, 1765, Robert Williams, Jr., attorney for the plaintiffs, filed suit in the court of common pleas against John Lewis Bourquin, planter of Granville County residing at Purrysburgh, and Margueritte Chiffelle Bourquin, formerly of St. Peter parish, for recovery of a bond, dated November 6, 1760, in the sum of £750 currency. The case was ordered for judgment on January 19, 1765, and the defendants paid the debt and court costs.*]

SOURCE: Judgment Rolls, 1765, No. 319A, S. C. Archives.

TO JEREMIAH BAIRD

[Charles Town] 22d January 1765

Sir,

The Receipt of your favour of the 11th Inst. has enabled me

---

[8] Henry François Bourquin and Jean Baptiste Bourquin, Swiss Protestants who settled at Purrysburgh, were the founders of this family in S. C. Arthur H. Hirsch, *The Huguenots of Colonial South Carolina* (Durham, N. C., 1928), p. 83. John Lewis Bourquin, who was of this family, was granted 450 acres in Purrysburgh Township on June 6, 1766. Index to Grants, S. C. Archives. In 1767 his name appeared in the list of grand jurors for St. Peter parish. Manuscript Act No. 958, S. C. Archives. He had recently married Margueritte Chiffelle, the widow of the Rev. Henry Chiffelle, a native of Switzerland who had been sent out by the Society for the Propagation of the Gospel in Foreign Parts in 1744 as the first missionary to St. Peter parish. The Rev. Henry Chiffelle had died in 1758. Frederick Dalcho, *An Historical Account of the Protestant Episcopal Church in South Carolina* (Charleston, S. C., 1820), pp. 386, 433. John Lewis Bourquin died at his plantation at Oakettee-Creek in Beaufort District in 1794. *SCHM*, x (1909), 185.

to discover a mistake which Mr. Perdriau my Clerk[9] by many pos- sitive assurances had led me into. I find your Green Tar fairly enter'd in my Book the 10th August which was as soon as it was pack'd & fill'd & I here inclose you an exact Copy of the Entry in my Books. I often told Mr. Perdriau that I was sure I stood indebted to you for a parcel of Tar & the same I said to Messrs. Downes & Jones, but he after looking carefully as he thought, into my Books avered that I had paid the full Balance of your Account to your Brother Joseph & had bought nothing from you since.

You call that parcel of Tar 78 Barrels but there were never more than 76 appear'd at one time upon the Wharf. If 78 was taken on board the Boat, two of them must have been stolen while they were landing. There was no more than 76 deliver'd to the Cooper to be pack'd & tho they were at your risque all that time yet there happen'd no Loss. I say there happen'd no loss. I question'd Johny[1] about the quantity Received & deliver'd but he could give me no satisfactory Account of either only that they were set down for 78, but that he did not reckon them. For now that I fix my eye upon the Entry I recollect all the circumstances attending the transaction & I am sorry that I relyed so wholly upon Mr. Perdriau's inspection, tho he is in general pretty exact in business of that sort.

You will see that I have allowed you the highest price, & you may rest satisfied that you shall have no cause to complain of suffering a hardship from any error in my House. In order thereto I shall pay Messrs. Downes & Jones tomorrow the Balance due on said Tar together with Interest for five Months which is taking only 13 days Credit for it as per Account inclos'd.

This I hope, Sir, will satisfy you as it appears to me to be measuring full justice, but if you are not content, please to inform me & I will do any further reasonable act to make you so, for I have no objection to laying a small fine upon myself for such mistakes tho in this case I might have pleaded some excuse. I remain, &ca.—

[P.S.] Since writing as above Mr. Downes informs me that you have inform'd him that you had sold the above mentioned Green Tar at £3.15/ per Barrel which astonishes me & I believe must be a mistake on Mr. Downes for we certainly never made any agreement & I am

---

[9] Benjamin Perdriau, Jr.
[1] The patron of the Watboo boat was Johnny.

sure you will find £3.10/ to be the very highest price that Green Tar has sold for, at least I have heard of none sold higher.

SOURCE: Letterbook copy, Letter Book of Henry Laurens, Oct. 30, 1762–Sept. 10, 1766, Penn. Hist. Soc.; addressed "St. Stephen."

TO WILLIAM SANDERS

[Charles Town] 23rd January 1765

Dear Sir,

I have Rec'd your favour of the 21st informing me of the readiness of the Cypress Boards & Scantlin at Bacon Bridge[2] & desiring a Boat to be sent for them as soon as possible together with a Flat to assist the Boat in Loading.

I shall be glad to hear that you can procure a Boat to bring the whole quantity to Town as mine are under engagement for some time but if you cannot presently get one, please to inform me what is the Freight usually paid for such service & I will endeavour to hire a Schooner or to send my own if I can prevail upon the Gentlemen who have engaged them, or I should rather say my open Boat, for the other is not very fit for the purpose. As to a large Flat to attend the Boat I shall send one if you again desire it but as it will be trouble-some & attended with delay to tow one up & Down the River so you may expect the expence thereof will be very considerable.

I suppose that none of the Wharfingers would hire at this season of the Year their smallest Flats under 20/ per day, some demand 30/ & some 40/. I remain, &ca.—

SOURCE: Letterbook copy, Letter Book of Henry Laurens, Oct. 30, 1762–Sept. 10, 1766, Penn. Hist. Soc.; addressed "Cypress."

TO TIMOTHY CREAMER

[Charles Town] 25th January 1765

Sir,

By Capt. Gray[3] you will receive 2 pair Cart Boxes, 2 Chains,

---

[2] Bacon's Bridge crossed "the Cypress" at the headwaters of the Ashley River above Dorchester. S. C. Statutes, IX, 575, 579.

[3] Capt. John Gray of the schooner Baker.

one Broad Axe, 1 hand Saw & 2 files, 1 Adze, 4 Chizels, 1 Gouge & 1 Auger. 1 Bottle infused Rhubarb to give in Case of Looseness & Cholicis a small Wine Glass full, 2 bottles of Camphire Rum, to rub in cases of pains & bruses & sometimes for the Cholic & belly ach. Mr. Stevens[4] will assist in killing, Salting, & barreling up the Hoggs & you must kill & send by the Boat every one of them, let the Boat be filled with Wood & give her dispatch. Inform me how many Chords of Wood remains at the landing & also in the Woods that I may take measures to get the whole away. The sight of so much rotting about was very disagreeable to me when I was at Mepkin & the more, as it is greatly owing to your fault.

You told me that they were Seventeen Hogs fit for Market. Of those you made use of some without asking leave until you had kill'd & housed them, nor have you yet inform'd me what weight they were of nor what you intend to allow for them. Those Seventeen were dwindled down to Eleven & you made no better excuse than this, that you had miscounted, an answer only fit to give to a Child.

These things ought not to be so, they are very mean & ungenerous & will never be attended with any good consequences to you. Make some of the Boys go into the Woods & get four midling logs of good Lightwood & send me by the Boat.

You write for 20d. & 10d. Nails but if you have as I think you must have a great many french Nails you must make them serve at present.

There are several other articles that must be defered until the Boats next Voyage as I have had a very sick family & not able to get the whole to go now. Send down as much Rough Rice as the spare Barrels will contain & distinguish if it be yours or mine & how much. I have engaged to deliver to Capt. Rains[5] in a Sloop that he will come with to the Landing all the Indian Corn that I can spare. Wherefore I must desire you to set about shelling it immediately & if it can be perform'd evenings & Mornings so much the better. The Negroes have had but little night work yet. You must not keep above two Months provision at most behind for I have other Corn to supply the place of so much as will be wanted. Make your Corn very clean

---

[4] This may be the James Stevens who witnessed a deed for HL the following October. See Sale of Land south of the Altamaha River, Oct. 9, 1765.
[5] The sloop *Altitude*, John Rains, arrived Jan. 5 from Bermuda and sailed Feb. 13 for Bermuda. *Gazette*, Jan. 7, Feb. 16, 1765.

before you deliver it, throw aside for my own use all the Yellows ears & be very carefull & exact in your measure. Distinguish in your Account the quantities of

Plantations Corn	seperately if you
Your Corn	have not already
Negroes Corn	mixed it,

That my Accounts may be regulated accordingly.

Send Martinico[6] down upon Monkey with an answer to this & be particular as to the Hogs, Wood, Rough Rice, & Corn.

SOURCE: Letterbook copy, Letter Book of Henry Laurens, Oct. 30, 1762–Sept. 10, 1766, Penn. Hist. Soc.; addressed "Mepkin."

TO SAMUEL WRAGG

[Charles Town] 28th January 1765

Sir,

I am indebted for your sundry favours of the 23d November, 28th December, 1st & 8th Inst. with which came your Account of Indigo purchased on Accounts of Messrs. Brewton & Smith, your own, & mine, & the Indigo allotted for me per Smart & Williams is also come safe to hand.

The quality is in my opinion good tho you have given the extreme price & your payments rather too plenentory for a Man who has other goods to purchase. Indeed as payments are made to me it is impossible to comply with such terms without drawing Bills which I would rather avoid & as I told you before I do not care to suffer the inconvenience of a dunn. Your Bills are without any grace & therefore immediate demand is made of them.

Those to James Semple[7]	£1,100
Elias Horry[8]	540
Paul Trapier	———

---

[6] Martinico was one of the Negro boys sent to Mepkin in January 1763. *HL Papers*, III, 203.

[7] James Semple, planter, was buried on Oct. 31, 1784 in the parish of St. James Santee. *SCHM*, XVIII (1916), 107.

[8] Elias Horry (1707–1783) was a Santee River planter residing in the parish of Prince George Winyaw. Rogers, *History of Georgetown County*, pp. 23, 60, 61, 101n, 287, 295, 298, 518, 519.

I have paid & shall pay this day, & shall endeavour to send you by
Mr. Pegue[9] £1,500 more & call at the same time upon Messrs.
Brewton & Smith for a like sum to make up £3,000. For while I
complain of inconvenience myself I will not subject you to any if it
can be avoided.

I have Ship'd the Six Casks of Indigo per Smart on board
the *Union* for London consign'd to Sarah Nickleson & Co. to whom
I have given such a hint as will probably have a good effect upon
their Sale. The other ten will be ship'd this day per *Brittania*, Fisher,[1]
for Bristol consign'd to Messrs. Cowles & Harford & I shall want for
this latter parcel a duplicate of the Certificate from your Custom
House which be pleas'd to send some day in this Week or by Monday
next if you hire a Messenger for the purpose. To avoid mistakes I
have put an exact Copy of the original under this cover. I agree that
the profit or Loss upon your whole purchase of Indigo, that is to say
upon the Sale shall be proportionaly divided between the purchasers
for which end each party must charge his Sale with a Sum to cover
the Value by Insurance, which I point out because some one may
take part of the risque to himself & I presume that a loss of that kind
is not intended to be jointly borne.

Having no occasion for pork & the price being high when
yours came down to put it into your Factors hand on your Account
& I hope he will get something more for it than the cost. Your favour
of the 25th December encouraged me to hope for full advices of my
other affairs in your hands but I make no doubt your being hinder'd
by attention to this Indigo purchase which must have given you a
great deal of trouble & in which as far as I have seen, permit me to
add you have shewn a great deal of Judgement but for the information of mine I wish you had sent or could still send me one or two
Casks of the various lower prices. I have Six Bales of exceeding good
Negro Cloth, Cost 14d½ & I think well bought as appears by one

---

[9] Claudius Pegues of French Huguenot descent had arrived in S. C. from London by the early 1740's. He was a leading figure in the settlement of the upper
Pee Dee River. He served as a justice of the peace for Craven County, as the first
representative in 1768 of the newly created parish of St. David having been elected
by the Regulators, and in 1769 as one of the commissioners to build the courthouse
and jail for Cheraws District. He was a patriot and died in 1790. There is a
sketch of Pegues' career in Richard M. Brown's manuscript, "Prosopography of the
South Carolina Regulators."

[1] The ship *Britannia*, Joseph Fisher, sailed for Bristol on Feb. 5. *Gazette*, Feb. 9,
1765.

Bale that I have opened which I'll sell at 10/ per yard & give you three Months Credit & wait longer for payment if you desire it. I should be glad to receive your order for the whole. I am very sure you cannot import upon such good terms all circumstances consider'd by 7½ per Cent.

I have also a Bale of White & two of brown Irish Oznabrug to be sold very cheap as Mr. Perdriau when he arrives at George Town will inform you.

SOURCE: Letterbook copy, Letter Book of Henry Laurens, Oct. 30, 1762–1762–Sept. 10, 1766, Penn. Hist. Soc.; addressed "George Town."

TO WILLIAM MAYNE[2]

[Charles Town] 30th January 1765

Sir,

I have a tract of Land about 30 Miles from Charles Town which I want to have resurvey'd & tho the difficulty of the Work will not be great, yet it will require your knowledge & accuracy to accomplish. Therefore I take the Liberty to enquire if you can conveniently undertake it for me sometime within the next month (February) so that we may be as Little as possible exposed to the inconveniences of warm weather & that Legion of insects which will soon re-assume their dominions in the Woods.

I shall not upon this occasion confine myself to the stated fees for surveying; but endeavour to compensate your Skill & trouble in such a manner as I hope will be quite satisfactory to you & further you will oblige, Sir, &ca.—

SOURCE: Letterbook copy, Letter Book of Henry Laurens, Oct. 30, 1762–Sept. 10, 1766, Penn. Hist. Soc.; addressed "Esquire. Prince William."

---

[2] William Mayne was commissioned a deputy surveyor by Egerton Leigh, surveyor general of S. C., on April 5, 1763. Miscellaneous Records, LL, Part 2 (1758–1763), p. 597, S. C. Archives. He must have been an able surveyor as the province selected him to survey certain lands in dispute between S. C. and Georgia. House Journal, XXXVI (Jan. 24, 1763–Oct. 6, 1764), p. 215, S. C. Archives.

TO WILLIAM WITHERS[3]

[Charles Town] 2d February 1765

If the bearer hereof Mr. Peter Horlbeck[4] shall make any agreement with you for Bricks you may depend upon punctuality on his part, but as he is a stranger to you I hereby oblige myself to be Surety for payment of his contracts to Amount of One Thousand pounds Current Money.

He is an ingenious diligent workman & from the experience that I have had I esteem him a faithful Honest Man & as such beg leave to introduce him to you as a customer for Bricks. I am, &ca.—

SOURCE: Letterbook copy, Letter Book of Henry Laurens, Oct. 30, 1762–Sept. 10, 1766, Penn. Hist. Soc.; addressed "Goose Creek." This letter was copied by HL.

ADVERTISEMENT

February 2, 1765

TO BE LETT, and enter'd upon 20th February, A Large brick ware house, (now in the possession of HENRY LAURENS, Esq;) situate at the north end of the Bay, very convenient for trade: The back part is glazed, it has two fire places, and a compting room, lathed and plaister'd. The terms, inquire of

JOHN WRAGG[5]

---

[3] William Withers, one of the sons of James Withers, bricklayer, who died in 1756, inherited Spring Garden and Mount Pleasant plantations at Goose Creek from his father. "Will of James Withers," dated Feb. 17, 1756, proved July 9, 1756, Charleston County Wills, VII (1752–1756), 537–539, S. C. Archives; *HL Papers*, I, 53. William was a brickmaker. Miscellaneous Records, LL, Part 2 (1758–1763), p. 395, S. C. Archives. His brothers moved to the Sampit River where they founded a very important rice-planting family. Rogers, *History of Georgetown County*, passim.

[4] Peter Horlbeck (died 1797) and John Adam Horlbeck (1729–1812) arrived in Charleston during 1764—John Adam in September and Peter six months before, according to Mrs. Poyas. They were master masons who had pursued their trade in Germany and England. They were the builders of the Exchange, 1767–1771, the magnificent Charleston customs house which was situated at the east end of Broad St. The Horlbecks were closely associated with the German community in S. C. Peter, who married Catherine Fillhauer, later became a planter in St. George Dorchester. [Elizabeth Anne Poyas] *Our Forefathers: Their Homes and Their Churches* (Charleston, S. C., 1860), pp. 57–82; Beatrice St. Julien Ravenel, *Architects of Charleston* (Charleston, S. C., 1945), pp. 39–46.

[5] John Wragg (1718–1796) was the eldest son of Joseph Wragg who had been a great Charleston merchant and member of the royal council. Henry A. M. Smith, "Wragg of South Carolina," *SCHM*, XIX (1918), chart facing p. 121.

SOURCE: Printed in *Gazette*, Feb. 2, 1765.

TO SAMUEL WRAGG

[Charles Town] 6th February 1765

Sir,

I wrote to you the 28th Ulto. per Mr. Perdriau & agreeable to my promise have sent you a Sum of money per hands of Mr. Claudius Pegues, Vizt. £1,573 but forgot to put a Letter into his hand with the money. I hope it will reach you in proper time to prevent the inconvenience of dunns & in expectation of my Accounts I rest, Sir, &ca.—

[*P.S.*] As the duplicate Certificate did not come to hand in time please to procure & send to me immediately another quite exact Copy.

SOURCE: Letterbook copy, Letter Book of Henry Laurens, Oct. 30, 1762–Sept. 10, 1766, Penn. Hist. Soc.; addressed "George Town."

TO FRANCIS STUART

[Charles Town] 6th February 1765

Sir,

It gives me some pain to be troublesome to you upon any occasion but particularly upon such an one as the present. I am now in advance for every farthing of the proceeds of those Negroes which I sold you some time ago for £12,000 because I promis'd our friends at St. Kitts⁶ that I would be punctual in remitting. I must therefore request you to order me a reimbursement of the whole if you possibly can but at least send me some part of it to keep dunns from my Door, the fear of which alone makes me call upon you & I flatter myself that you will give the needful attention hereunto & oblige, Sir, &ca.—

SOURCE: Letterbook copy, Letter Book of Henry Laurens, Oct. 30, 1762–Sept. 10, 1766, Penn. Hist. Soc.; addressed "Esquire. Beaufort."

---

⁶ Smith & Baillies of St. Kitts.

FROM EGERTON LEIGH

London, 6th February 1765

[*On this date Leigh wrote HL a long letter informing him that as David Graeme had relinquished his post as attorney general, Leigh was trying to obtain the job for himself. HL was to keep that information secret. HL had written an unnamed friend in London authorizing that friend to advance Leigh as much credit as HL himself was entitled to. Leigh planned to use that credit for expenses in London such as purchasing his new office, as well as for books, plate, china, and other articles. Leigh also wrote that he had rented Graeme's house for three years and since Graeme did not intend to return to S. C., Leigh asked HL to buy some of the furniture at the forthcoming sale. He also asked HL to buy him firewood and "a good Pipe of Madeira."*]

SOURCE: Printed in *Appendix to the Extracts,* pp. 60–61.

TO WILLIAM O'BRIEN⁷

[Charles Town] 7th February 1765

Sir,

It is a disagreeable task to me to be obliged to put any of my friends in mind that they owe me Money, but the age of your debt & the little notice that has been taken of it on your part would almost justify me if I was to say that you had not made a very kind return for that Lenity which has been extended upon mine. I remain, &ca.—

SOURCE: Letterbook copy, Letter Book of Henry Laurens, Oct. 30, 1762–Sept. 10, 1766, Penn. Hist. Soc.; addressed "Beaufort."

TO JOSEPH HUTCHINS

[Charles Town] 7th February 1765

Sir,

If you cannot sell Capt. Canty's⁸ Indigo before I return to

---

⁷ John Grayson and William O'Brien were merchants in Beaufort in 1764. Judgment Rolls, 1767, No. 219A, S. C. Archives. Joshua Morgan, who wrote his will on Jan. 10, 1765, appointed his son-in-law William O'Brien executor of his estate. *Abstracts of Wills, 1760–1784,* p. 55. In 1767 O'Brien was posted as a delinquent tax collector for St. Helena parish. House Journal, XXXVII, Part 1 (Oct. 28, 1765–May 28, 1767), p. 380, S. C. Archives.

⁸ Charles Cantey, a planter of St. Stephen parish, had been lieutenant of the St.

Town which will be about the 13th Inst., I will Ship it upon his
Account & advance 18/ per lb. for it payable in three Months but
not sooner. If there arises any profit the whole to be his, if any loss
he must make it good to me but I shall charge him no Interest upon
such refund provided it be settled & paid within Twelve Months
from Shipping. If there is a gain I shall pay that as soon as I Receive
the Accounts. The Exchange upon Sterling to be seven for one which
I mention because Bills at this time do by some hands sell for more
tho probably that may not be the case a Year hence. However I will
not leave it open to dispute. Upon the whole if you can obtain Capt.
Canty's Limit of 20/ per lb. or even 18/6, I would recommend a
Sale here in preference of Shipping it to any Market elsewhere. Please
to make my compliments to that Gentleman when you write to him,
& believe me to be, Sir, &ca.—

SOURCE: Letterbook copy, Letter Book of Henry Laurens, Oct. 30,
1762–Sept. 10, 1766, Penn. Hist. Soc.; addressed "Charles Town."

TO ZACHARY VILLEPONTOUX

[Charles Town] 13th February 1765

Sir,

Merely to encourage two diligent & ingenious Men[9] in prose-
cuting of their Trade I promised to lend them a large part of the
Bricks that I had engaged from you, & as they are now quite out of
work for want of Bricks & it is a good while since I had any quantity
from you I beg the favour of you to order three or four Boat Loads
as quick as possible to be sent to such place as the bearer Mr. Horlbeck
shall name.

Stephen's Fair Forest Company of the Craven County militia in 1757. He must at
this time have been captain. Rogers, *History of Georgetown County*, p. 68; *HL
Papers*, III, 425n.

[9] Peter and John Adam Horlbeck. John Adam Horlbeck was born Feb. 11, 1729,
in Upper Saxony. He worked in Berlin, Copenhagen, and Russia before working
(after 1759) for two and a half years at the Royal Arsenal at Woolwich. He like
his brother was closely associated with the German community in Carolina. He
married on Feb. 25, 1769, Elizabeth Geiger, of the Congarees, the Widow Gall-
man. He more than his brother remained in the building business in Charleston.
He died April 1, 1812. *SCHM*, XI (1910), 36; [Elizabeth Anne Poyas] *Our Forefathers: Their Homes and Their Churches* (Charleston, S. C., 1860), pp. 57–82;
Beatrice St. Julien Ravenel, *Architects of Charleston* (Charleston, S. C., 1945), pp.
39–46.

I intreat you, Sir, not to fail in this for tho I am to get nothing by it but the trouble of writing Letters & settling Accounts without profit yet as I intend to do a service to Men of merit a disappointment will be very mortifying to me. I remain with great regard, &ca.—

SOURCE: Letterbook copy, Letter Book of Henry Laurens, Oct. 30, 1762–Sept. 10, 1766, Penn. Hist. Soc.; addressed "Esquire. Back River"; "per Mr. Horlbeck."

TO JAMES BRENARD

[Charles Town] 14th February 1765

Sir,

I have sent sundry articles for the use of Wambaw Plantation as per inclos'd list which I order'd that Nat should fetch from Mr. Fogarties & hope they will reach you safely.

I have fully consider'd the notice you gave me of your intention to remove & Settle upon a plantation of your own; & as I heartily wish you well (go where you will) I shall not say anything to damp your project but leave that Matter to be determined as you see most for your own Interest. If you stay you shall not want proper encouragement. If you go, you shall not want my good wishes that your change may be for the better, but in this latter case, you will be so good as to inform me directly of the day or Week, in which you intend to depart that I may provide a person to succeed you & indeed to be with you some days before you go to beg a little of your information & instruction in matters relative to the Negroes & Plantation. I cannot doubt that while you remain in the present service you will exert yourself in every respect for the good of the plantation. I must particularly recommend to you to prepare for planting an early Crop at least as much of every kind as was planted last Year. The present weather is inviting & if it continues you must by all means improve the opportunity & let us be early in plantings. I took notice of Mr. Shad's saying that it is necessary to provide Wood for Carts against the next Year; therefore I desire you to set Cain & his Son immediately upon that work as the Season for falling proper Trees is now far advanced & will soon be over, & while they are about it let them provide so much more than common as will make one or two Waggons.

I shall not inquire for any other Overseer or Manager until I have your answer & I shall be glad if you determine to go, that you will look about & recommend a person in your stead. I think you said that you should not be ready for the Boat after the next load & that I must make another Voyage for her. You will please to inform me exactly of this matter also. I remain, &ca.—

SOURCE: Letterbook copy, Letter Book of Henry Laurens, Oct. 30, 1762–Sept. 10, 1766, Penn. Hist. Soc.; addressed "Wambaw Plantation."

TO JOHN DUTARQUE, SR.

[Charles Town] 14 February 1765

Sir,

I was a good deal surprized at my return to Charles Town to find that Capt. Wilson[1] on whose Account I called upon you last Monday for a Cargo of Lumber, was in doubt whether he would take in such a loading or not altho he owns & does not attempt to deny that he did expressly authorize me to bespeak a Cargo, but I was more surprized to day to find that he had been in treaty even whilst I was in the Country for a Freight to London & that he had at length, without my knowledge agreed to take a Loading of Rice for that port. I must therefore request you to put a stop to any preparations that you may be making for a Cargo in Consequence of what I said to you when I was at your House & if there is any loss or damage sustained by what you may have already done, I beg you will be pleased to inform me directly. I hold myself bound to make some reasonable concession if you have a Charge against me on this Account & Capt. Wilson on whose behalf I acted must indempnify me, but you will be pleas'd to remember that he is a going Man & therefore these things should be soon adjusted.

I am very sorry to have given you so much unnecessary trouble but I hope you will not be angry with me as you see I am not in fault, & I can only appologize for the Captain by saying that he has acted as he thinks for the Interest of his owners. Tho he & I differ widely in our opinions upon that point too. I remain, &ca.—

---

[1] The ship *Prince of Wales*, Roderick Wilson, had arrived from Antigua and would sail for England on March 19. *Gazette*, Feb. 9, March 23, 1765.

SOURCE: Letterbook copy, Letter Book of Henry Laurens, Oct. 30, 1762–Sept. 10, 1766, Penn. Hist. Soc.; addressed "Esquire. Cainhoy."

TO ROSSEL & GERVAIS

[Charles Town] 16th February 1765

Gentlemen,

I trouble you with Letters to,

The Honorable James Habersham, Esquire[2]
Johnson & Wylly, Esquires
Lachlin McIntosh, Esquire

Gentlemen in Georgia whither you are now going. The first of those Gentlemen will supply you with as much money as you may have occasion for in Georgia on my Account.

The last I hope will soon be with you at Savanna or you with him at Darien[3] & I dare aver if no extraordinaries forbid it, he will wait on you three or four days. He is a generous Man but avoid as much as possible putting him to expence for I have been much too free with him upon former occasions.

Mr. McIntosh will put you into the right Channel to cause the several documents for Land which I herewith trouble you as per schedule annexed to be Enter'd upon Record & the Taxes & Quit Rents fully paid up in which you must be very careful & exact in case of Mr. McIntosh's absence.[4] I flatter myself that one of the Mr. Graham's[5] will do that favour for me or you may in case of need call in

---

[2] James Habersham (1712–1775), merchant and planter, became HL's most frequent correspondent and associate in Georgia. Habersham had come out to Georgia in 1738 with his friend the Rev. George Whitefield. In 1740 he married Mary Bolton. In 1744 he began a commercial firm with Francis Harris which dominated Georgia trade until the early 1760's. In 1754 he had been appointed a member of the royal council of Georgia. *Collections of the Georgia Historical Society*, Vol. VI: *The Letters of Hon. James Habersham, 1756–1775* (Savannah, Ga., 1904), pp. 5–7.

[3] Darien was on the Altamaha River.

[4] The quitrents on these lands were 2 shillings per 100 acres annually plus a payment of 5 shillings per 50 acres at the time a formal grant passed for the land (or at registration of the land in this case). Leonard W. Labaree, *Royal Instructions to British Colonial Governors, 1670–1776* (2 vols.: New York, 1967), II, 529, 530–531. The general land tax at this time was 2/6 sterling per 100 acres annually. The lands would also have been subject to an annual assessment for various sinking funds established by the assembly. *Colonial Records of Georgia*, XVIII, 393, 421.

[5] John or James Graham.

the advice & assistance of the most able Council there by a handsome Fee.

There are other Gentlemen particularly John Tally, Esquire to whom I should have been glad to write at Savanna but you know how my time has been & is abridged. I devoted this Morning to writing wholly in your service but there came in an old friend & acquaintance who does not often visit me & I could not for several reasons dismiss him nor forego the pleasure of his Company half that time.

Please to make my most respectful compliments to Mr. Tally & assure him of my good wishes & regard for him & remember me in like manner to any that shall enquire about me.

If you should take it into your heads to stretch along to St. Augustine a sight of this Letter to Governor Grant I am persuaded will introduce you to his Excellency & in that case you will be so good as to present my respects & assure his Excellency that If I had had the least thoughts of your going so far South I should have wrote to him.

That I have Rece'd his favour of the 6th Inst., am busy in his service about the Pilot Boat, &ca., & am endeavouring to bring about a journey to kiss his hand in a Month or so but you know some entanglements which may possibly detain me longer.

I wish you pleasure & prosperity & shall be often expecting to hear from you before your return & wishing for that event too hoping to set you down then to business in earnest. I am, &ca.—

[*P.S.*] Platts & Grants to—

Darby Pendergrass for 1,200 Acres on the South side of Altamaha River.

John Deas	2,000	ditto
David Deas	2,000	ditto
William Hopton	2,000	ditto
Henry Laurens	3,000	ditto

Jonathan Bryan, Esquire <br> to
 Lachlin McIntosh } Deed of Exchange—6th July 1758.

L. McIntosh <br> to
 Henry Laurens } Lease for a Year, & Release for Broughton Island in the River Altamaha In Georgia Containing 900 Acres.[6]

SOURCE: Letterbook copy, Letter Book of Henry Laurens, Oct. 30, 1762–Sept. 10, 1766, Penn. Hist. Soc.; addressed "Charles Town."

[6] See Purchase of Broughton Island Plantation, Dec. 8, 1763.

TO FRANCIS STUART
[Charles Town] 16th February 1765

Dear Sir,

Messrs. James Theodore Rossel & Mr. Lewis Gervais, two Gentlemen by whom this will be deliver'd to you, are making a journey to Savanna in Georgia & intend to take Beaufort in their way; as they are quite strangers to that Road I beg leave to introduce them to your acquaintance & good offices if they shall stand in need of any assistance either in money or otherwise for which I shall hold myself answerable & be extremely oblig'd to you. I flatter myself that these Gentlemen will acquaint themselves so well, at least as travelling associates, as not to subject me to any reproach; therefore I shall not trouble you with an appology but conclude with assurances that I am, Dear Sir, &ca.—

SOURCE: Letterbook copy, Letter Book of Henry Laurens, Oct. 30, 1762–Sept. 10, 1766, Penn. Hist. Soc.; addressed "Esquire. Beaufort."

TO JOSEPH BROWN
[Charles Town] 21st February 1765

Dear Sir,

I am indebted for several of your favours but being just going into the Country cannot reply to them so fully as I ought & shall do when I return. The death of Mr. Ball has made me almost as much a Country Man as Towns Man. I am obliged to quit home oftener than I was ever used to do & much oftener than is convenient but I am endeavouring to put an end to this disorder & hope soon to effect it by means of good Overseers. Do you know anything of one Myer[7] who served Colonel Horry[8] some Years & lately Mr. Benjamin Smith[9] in your parts. He offers his service but as I am willing to pay well I will have none but such as are at least well recommended.

[7] HL was looking for an overseer to replace James Brenard at Wambaw plantation.

[8] Col. Daniel Horry of Hampton plantation just east of Wambaw Creek on the Santee was buried on Sept. 11, 1763. *HL Papers*, II, 52n.

[9] This was most probably Benjamin Smith (1735-1790) whose father the second Landgrave Thomas Smith had owned many acres in the parish of Prince George Winyah. Rogers, *History of Georgetown County*, pp. 22, 25, 31, 287.

A few days ago I Received a small square Box from London directed for you to my care which I now send by Mr. Dick, for however I may be incapacitated to write much, yet any of your Business committed to me shall not pass neglected. Please to make my Love & compliments acceptable within your Walls & believe me to be, Dear Sir, &ca.—

SOURCE: Letterbook copy, Letter Book of Henry Laurens, Oct. 30, 1762–Sept. 10, 1766, Penn. Hist. Soc.; addressed "George Town"; "per Capt. Dick."

ADVERTISEMENT[1]

February 23, 1765

WANTED, TWO Negro Carpenters, two Coopers, three pair of Sawyers, forty Field Negroes, young men and women, some acquainted with indico making, and all with the ordinary course of Plantation work in this country; for which good prices will be given, in cash, or bills upon London: And in cases of no bargain, secrecy if required, may be depended on.—Any person having such Negroes to sell, please to apply to

HENRY LAURENS

SOURCE: Printed in *Gazette,* Feb. 23, 1765.

TO JAMES MARION[2]

[Charles Town] 25th February 1765

Dear Sir,

The Gentleman that you sent your Letter by did not deliver it

---

[1] HL was putting together a labor force for Richard Oswald's East Florida plantation.

[2] James Marion was the youngest son of the second marriage of Benjamin Marion of St. James Goose Creek who died in 1735. Charles J. Colcock, "The Marion Family," *The Transactions of the Huguenot Society of South Carolina,* XXII (1916), 39. He lived at the Hagan, a plantation in the parish of St. Thomas on the right as one entered the Eastern Branch of the Cooper River. "Will of James Marion," dated July 8, 1765, proved Feb. 3, 1769, Charleston County Wills, XII, Book B (1767–1771), 491–493, S. C. Archives; Irving, *A Day on Cooper River,* pp. 23–25, 125, 176.

before this day at Noon & then the Man (Peter Horlbeck) who is to Live at Mepkin had been gone out of Town two Hours & I could not with any propriety write by him before I had not seen the contents of your favour to which you had referr'd me.

I am extremely obliged to you for the trouble of riding to & viewing my plantation & for the hints of what is necessary to be provided for it. As to your proposition for the Care & management of the place, it is not at present in my power to accede to it, because, as I have already inform'd you, I had before I spoke to you agreed with the person above named to reside there & half agreed also with another Man & his Wife, but these tho honest & sensible are not expert Carolina Planters, & what I sought from you if you remember, Sir, was to visit the place for the first two or three Months once in a Week & to remain upon the Spot long enough to enquire & see what had been done as well as to order what should be done & your orders to be a Law to govern the Overseer's conduct, after that time once in Ten days or a fortnight might be sufficient for some Months, having the Overseer in the intermediate days to wait upon you as occasions on his part of your directions might require.

Mr. Horlbeck is a very sensible Man, has a general knowledge of farming, very quick of apprehension, & will readily catch your orders & I believe he has good nature & docibility enough to put them in execution without murmuring.

If you can propose any thing worth your own acceptance & within the ability of the plantation as so much per day for performing the services above mentioned I do believe we shall not differ. I am sure I will not differ with you for a Trifle. I expect to receive great benefit from your advice & assistance & shall besides the stipulated Fee be obliged to you for it.

I shall by the first opportunity order Mr. Horlbeck to wait on you & whether we agree or not I fancy you will have no objection to an acquaintance with the Man. I remain, &ca.—

SOURCE: Letterbook copy, Letter Book of Henry Laurens, Oct. 30, 1762– Sept. 10, 1766, Penn. Hist. Soc.; addressed "St. Thomas's."

GEORGE AUSTIN & HENRY LAURENS
VERSUS WILLIAM McKELVEY[3]

February 25, 1765

[On January 15, 1765, Robert Williams, Jr., attorney for the plaintiffs, filed suit in the court of common pleas against William McKelvey, planter and tavern keeper of the parish of St. James Goose Creek, for the recovery of a bond, dated June 3, 1762, in the sum of £285.13.4 currency. The case was ordered for judgment on January 26. The judgment was signed on February 25, 1765 and recorded by Dougal Campbell, clerk of the court.]

SOURCE: Judgment Rolls, 1765, No. 134A, S. C. Archives; Judgment Docket, Court of Common Pleas, Book 2 (1755–1773), p. 95, S. C. Archives.

REGISTRATION OF THE SLOOP HENRY

February 28, 1765

[On this date Henry Todd, Jr., registered the sloop Henry, *John Todd, master, 35 tons, built in Bermuda in 1764, for himself and HL.[4]]*

SOURCE: Ship Register, 1734–1765, p. 245, S. C. Archives.

TO CHARLES GORDON[5]

[Charles Town] 6th March 1765

Reverend Sir,

The end of Six Years is near at hand since I advanced Forty

---

[3] William McKelvey was a planter and tavern keeper at Wassamassaw in St. John Berkeley who died prior to Feb. 17, 1767. *SCHM,* XXIV (1923), 102; *Abstracts of Wills, 1760–1784,* p. 129. On Nov. 27, 1766, he sold two slaves to Daniel Ravenel, Jr. Miscellaneous Records, MM, Part 2 (1763–1767), p. 576, S. C. Archives. The McKelvey family still owned a tavern at Eutaw in 1776. "Diary of James Clitherall, 1776," p. 2, # 159, SHC.

[4] The sloop *Henry,* John Todd, was entered inwards on June 29, 1765, at Savannah, Ga., from Jamaica with 50 Negroes. Donnan, *Documents Illustrative of the Slave Trade,* IV, 617. Read & Mossman advertised that they would sell on July 9 on their wharf 50–60 new Negroes "just arrived from the Gold Coast." *Georgia Gazette,* July 4, 1765.

[5] The Reverend Charles Gordon arrived from Scotland to minister to the Bethel Presbyterian Church and congregation of Pon Pon on July 8, 1759. He was in-

pounds Sterling to pay Capt. Smith[6] for your passage and expences to Carolina; during which long time I am sure that I have not once ask'd you for a return, & what seems more extraordinary you have not once made an offer of it; nor even an apology for keeping me out of my money: on the contrary for some three or four Years past there has been a visible shyness & neglect of me on your part, for which I never could, nor can yet assign any good cause, & I am not disposed to impute it to so bad a one as merely the loan of money. But waving this, it is time now that that debt was paid & I therefore request you, Sir, to discharge it. I have so many calls upon me of the same nature & meet with so many other delinquents too, that I am necessitated now & then to rouse some of the most forgetful in order as well to maintain my Credit in Trade as to enable me to do other acts of humanity.

My compliments to Mrs. Gordon & believe me to be, Reverend Sir, Yours, &ca.—

SOURCE: Letterbook copy, Letter Book of Henry Laurens, Oct. 30, 1762–Sept. 10, 1766, Penn. Hist. Soc.; addressed "Reverend. Ponpon."

TO PETER HORLBECK

[Charles Town] 7th March 1765

Sir,

I have Rec'd both your Letters of the 3 & 4 Inst. & now send you sundry articles by Sam, Vizt.

Garden Seed, Sage, Tansey,[7] 1 Bottle Oyl Turpentine, 2 Bottles Honey, 6 Bottles plain Rum, 1 Stock Lock. Sam goes with Mercutio & Jack to stay a few days five or six & then to return if I do not come.

In the meantime I would have you wait upon Mr. James

---

stalled on Oct. 31, 1759. After his health gave way in 1766, his church was declared vacant June 26, 1766. George Howe, *History of the Presbyterian Church in South Carolina* (2 vols.: Columbia, S. C., 1870, 1873), I, 281, 322.

[6] The ship *Elizabeth,* James Smith, was entered inwards on June 20, 1759, from London. Naval Office Lists, 1757–1764, p. 67.

[7] A plant having a strong aromatic scent and bitter taste used as a stomachic. *OED.*

Marion about four or five Miles below Bonneau's Ferry.[8] I wrote to him & perhaps he may undertake to advise you in your planting business.

You will consult now with Sam about Indigo Vatts. I shall send you two dozen Hoes if they are wanted but you must enquire into the matter yourself & not trust to the driver.

I have spoke to Mr. Pontoux[9] so that I hope you will hear no more complaints from your Brother[1] for want of Bricks. I shall endeavour to see you before the 20th Inst. In the meantime let me hear from you as often as you have opportunity. I am, &ca.—

SOURCE: Letterbook copy, Letter Book of Henry Laurens, Oct. 30, 1762–Sept. 10, 1766, Penn. Hist. Soc.; addressed "Mepkin."

TO JAMES BRENARD

[Charles Town] 7th March 1765

Sir,

As I am in great hopes of seeing you before 19th Inst. which is not quite so late as the time that you fixed yourself for leaving Wambaw I must desire you to continue until that day or until you hear from me again in four or five days if I see that I am not like to come to you. Nevertheless do nothing that will be very detrimental or disagreeable to yourself.

As to Mr. Meyer I shall be obliged to you to inform him the state of the plantation and disposition of the Negroes as well as you can while you do stay.

I have told him where he is to live after you are gone. Mr. Shad is the oldest stander & therefore it is but common justice to give him his choice. This is what Meyer would expect in a like case & what he seemed to be very well satisfied with.

I dare say you will do all in your power to help the Sick Negroes. If there was anything wanting from hence for them you would have sent for it.

---

[8] Bonneau's Ferry was established by an act of June 7, 1712, to provide a common highway across the Eastern Branch of the Cooper River. *S. C. Statutes*, IX, 22, 542. Bonneau's Ferry joined the road from Mepkin to Calais along the eastern bank of the Cooper River. Irving, *A Day on Cooper River*, p. 13, map between pp. 4 and 5.
[9] Zachary Villepontoux.
[1] John Adam Horlbeck.

However I send you by Toronjo two bottles of Turlington[2] & some Spanish Liquorice both very good for Colds. I am, &ca.—

SOURCE: Letterbook copy, Letter Book of Henry Laurens, Oct. 30, 1762–Sept. 10, 1766, Penn. Hist. Soc.; addressed "Wambaw." Endorsed: "This wrote in answer to his of this date."

TO ABRAHAM SCHAD

[Charles Town] 7th March 1765

I have notice this day from Mr. Brenard of his intention to leave Wambaw as next Monday & desiring to know if Mr. Meyer is to take possession of his House.

I have desir'd Mr. Brenard if it wont injure him to continue until the 19th being in hopes of seeing him by that time, and as to the House I have told him that you being the oldest friend should have the preference. This is no more than your due. I mentioned it to Mr. Meyer as a thing that I should insist upon & he was very well pleased. I hope you will agree together & then two Houses will be but one.

I have not seen Creamer but shall remember your demand when he calls upon me. Pray be careful of the Sick Negroes. I remain—

SOURCE: Letterbook copy, Letter Book of Henry Laurens, Oct. 30, 1762–Sept. 10, 1766, Penn. Hist. Soc.; addressed "Wambaw."

TO JAMES MARION

[Charles Town] 11th March 1765

Dear Sir,

I wrote to you the 25th Ulto. but as I saw Mr. Scott still in town some days after he had taken my Letter, 'tis probable *that* stuck as long by the way as yours per Mr. Dean did in its passage to me.

The bearer hereof is Mr. Peter Horlbeck who has engaged to live at my Mepkin plantation. I had wrote to him to wait on you last

---

[2] For Turlington's balsam of life, see *HL Papers*, II, 190n.

Week but some of his own affairs calling he came to Town & now returns through St. Thomas's[3] & will stop half an hour at your House to talk upon the subject matter of my last Letter to which I refer & remain, Sir, &ca.—

SOURCE: Letterbook copy, Letter Book of Henry Laurens, Oct. 30, 1762–Sept. 10, 1766, Penn. Hist. Soc.; addressed "St. Thomas's."

TO BENJAMIN SIMONS, JR.[4]

[Charles Town] 15th March 1765

Dear Sir,

Mr. Peter Manigault having applied on my behalf to Mr. Peter Broughton informs me that this Gentleman accedes to a proposition made by me to submit the determination to indifferent & impartial persons, certain disputes concerning property in that piece of Swamp Land which is surrounded by Mepkin & Strawberry Lands & Cowper River which formerly subsisted between Mr. Broughton & the ancient proprietors of Mepkin & lately between him & me.

Each party is to elect three Men, one of whom on each side is to be a Surveyor in order to ascertain the true contents of that Swamp & finally to adjust & award the property thereof.

I shall esteem it a particular favour if you will take upon you the trouble in conjunction with Mr. James Marion to act in this Matter on my part or more properly to do Justice on both sides.

When I have your permission to insert your name in an Arbitration Bond I shall be better able to inform you the precise time intended for a meeting.

My compliments to Mrs. Simmons[5] & be assur'd that I am with great regard, Dear Sir, &ca.—

---

[3] There were two roads through St. Thomas parish. One was from Cainhoy ferry on the Wando River and the other was from Calais ferry on the Cooper River. Both roads met to cross the Eastern Branch of the Cooper at Bonneau's ferry.

[4] Benjamin Simons (spelled "Simmons" here), Jr. (1737–1789) lived at Smoky Hill just to the east of his father's Middleburg plantation. SCHM, xxxvii (1936), 144; Irving, A Day on Cooper River, p. 154.

[5] Benjamin Simons, Jr. married Catharine Chicken (1742–1820) on Sept. 27, 1764. His first wife Elizabeth Allston (1742–1764) had just died. Robert Bentham Simons, Thomas Grange Simons, III, His Forebears and Relations (Charleston, S. C., 1954), pp. 11, 136. Catharine Chicken had sailed on the same vessel with HL to England in 1748. HL Papers, I, 176.

SOURCE: Letterbook copy, Letter Book of Henry Laurens, Oct. 30, 1762–
Sept. 10, 1766, Penn. Hist. Soc.; addressed "Smoaky Hill."

TO JOHN FORBES [6]

[Charles Town] 18 March 1765

Sir,

It is a matter of great moment to whither I have Rec'd or
shall receive the Sum promis'd by you & Mr. Stuart,[7] or not, because
in confidence of that promise I did engage to pay a Sum of Money
which I have not yet been enabled to comply with.

Seven Thousand pounds will really not satisfy me, or rather
those who expect Money from me. I must have at least Eight, I was
in hopes you would have made up Ten & even then I should be
hardly born.

As to Thursday or Saturday one or the other will make no
great difference; you are welcome to embrace any advantage that the
latter or even a monday will afford you but if you have not yet sold
your Bill, you must be convinced that it would have been *at least* as
well to have accepted the offer made by, Sir, Your most obedient
Servant—

SOURCE: Letterbook copy, Letter Book of Henry Laurens, Oct. 30, 1762–
Sept. 10, 1766, Penn. Hist. Soc.; addressed "Esquire. Charles Town."

GEORGE AUSTIN, HENRY LAURENS, & GEORGE APPLEBY VERSUS WILLIAM WIDOS [8]

March 18, 1765

*[On January 22, 1765, Thomas Bee, attorney for the plaintiffs, filed
suit in the court of common pleas against William Widos, "otherwise*

---

[6] John Forbes, merchant of Charleston.

[7] Francis Stuart, merchant of Beaufort.

[8] William Widos had been an overseer in 1758 in St. James Santee. *SCHM*, XVII
(1916), 35. The deputy provost marshal noted on the summons that Widos was
"overseer at one of Mr. Middleton's plantations at Combahee." As Henry Middleton had estates on both the Ashley and Combahee rivers, Widos must have been
working for him at both places.

known as William Widos, an overseer from Ashley River," for re-
covery of a bond, dated June 6, 1761, in the sum of £240 currency.
The case was ordered for judgment on February 14, 1765, and the
judgment was signed on March 18, 1765. The judgment was reissued
on August 5, 1765, October 30, 1765, and again on May 28, 1766.]

SOURCE: Judgment Rolls, 1765, No. 271A, S. C. Archives; Journal, Court
of Common Pleas, 1763–1769, p. 113, S. C. Archives; Judgment Docket,
Book 2 (1755–1773), p. 96, S. C. Archives.

PETER MANIGAULT TO PETER
BROUGHTON

[Charles Town] 20th March 1765

Sir,

Mr. Laurens has engaged the promise of Mr. Benjamin Simmons, Junior & Mr. James Marion to Act on his Behalf, in the Survey, & to adjust the dispute subsisting between you, about the Swamp
Near Strawberry, & he expects to have the assistance of Mr. Maine as
a Surveyor; & in case he fails of him, will get the best he can in his
stead. He therefore desires you will be so good to Name two of your
Friends & a Surveyor, to join the above Gentlemen, to name the time
of their Meeting, & when you will Meet to sign Arbitration Bonds.
Your answer will much oblige, Yours, &ca.—

SOURCE: Letterbook copy, Letter Book of Henry Laurens, Oct. 30, 1762–
Sept. 10, 1766, Penn. Hist. Soc.; addressed "Esquire. Seaton." Endorsed:
"Copy of a Letter wrote per Mr. Peter Manigault at my request."

PETER BROUGHTON TO PETER
MANIGAULT

[Seaton] 21st March 1765

Sir,

I have your favour and cannot give you answer at present, as
I have not provided myself with a Surveyor neither have I spoke to
any of my friends to act on my Behalf. I shall be in Town about the
middle of next week at which time shall wate on you. Am, Sir, Your
most humble Servant—

SOURCE: Letterbook copy, Letter Book of Henry Laurens, Oct. 30, 1762–Sept. 10, 1766, Penn. Hist. Soc. Endorsed: "Copy of Mr. Peter Broughton's Letter to Peter Manigault, Esquire, In answer to the foregoing."

TO PETER MANIGAULT

[Charles Town] Friday Noon 22d March 1765

Mr. Laurens presents his compliments [and] is much obliged to Mr. P. Manigault for the sight of Mr. Broughton's answer which is only a duplicate in short of his whole conduct for more than two Years past.

If he waits on Mr. Manigault about the middle of next Week Mr. Laurens intreats the continuance of his kindness to bring that Gentleman if possible to some fixed plan at the first interview without subjecting Mr. Laurens to the inconveniences of further delays & evasions, or to break off absolutely & leave him (L) at liberty to pursue some other measure to obtain justice.

SOURCE: Letterbook copy, Letter Book of Henry Laurens, Oct. 30, 1762–Sept. 10, 1766, Penn. Hist. Soc.

TO JOHN REMINGTON[9]

[Charles Town] 22d March 1765

Sir,

I thank you for the trouble of applying to Mr. Wright for your Fees which he promis'd long ago (& repeatedly) to pay; but I have security from an honester Man.

As to the poor old wretch himself I truly pity him. He seems to be sunk into the deepest corruption & equally void of Shame & Honour; and as I would shun all his examples I send your Money quickly for which & your other demands please to return a Receipt & accept the thanks of, Sir, &ca.—

SOURCE: Letterbook copy, Letter Book of Henry Laurens, Oct. 30, 1762–Sept. 10, 1766, Penn. Hist. Soc.; addressed "Esquire. Queen Street."

---

[9] John Remington was notary public. *HL Papers*, III, 360n.

BENJAMIN PERDRIAU, JR.[1] *TO*
SAMUEL SMITH[2]

[Charles Town] 26th March 1765

Sir,

I have your favour of the 9th Inst. & note the contents, to which be pleas'd now (for the second time) to receive herewith a Bill for both of the former articles. Also for 12 Boxes of Soap now on board of Smarts Schooner, weighing 511 lbs. Net Weight the price not inserted in the Bill by reason of some uncertainty with Mr. Laurens, therefore Mr. Wragg will be kind enough to acquaint you with what he had agreed for, of which you will be pleas'd to inform me, that it may be enter'd accordingly. I am, &ca.—   B. P.

SOURCE: Letterbook copy, Letter Book of Henry Laurens, Oct. 30, 1762– Sept. 10, 1766, Penn. Hist. Soc.; addressed "George Town"; "per Smart."

BENJAMIN PERDRIAU, JR. TO JOHN
HANDLIN

[Charles Town] 28 March 1765

Sir,

The several articles you desir'd should be sent are now on board of Mr. Dick's Schooner, all of which I hope will prove agreeable & go safe to you, Vizt.

1 Quarter Cask Rum Quantity 26 Gallons, 1 piece Ozna-brugg 85 Yards, 4 Loaves Sugar weight 50½ lbs., 1 piece Cotton Check 33½ Ells, 1 Kegg 12½ lbs. Gun powder, 1 Barrel fine fresh flour weight [blank] lbs.

A Bill of the above articles shall be sent to you by Mr. Dick's next return. I am, &ca.—

SOURCE: Letterbook copy, Letter Book of Henry Laurens, Oct. 30, 1762– Sept. 10, 1766, Penn. Hist. Soc.; addressed "Black Mingo"; "per George Dick."

---

[1] Benjamin Perdriau, Jr., HL's clerk.
[2] Samuel Smith, Samuel Wragg's clerk.

TO ELIAS BALL

[Charles Town] 1st April 1765

I have rec'd your favour of Saturday last informing me "that my proposal concerning the Negroes at Wambaw is not at all liked of by the other part concerned that you are willing to take my part off my hands at the apraisment if I continue in the same mind which you should never have proposed had I not offer'd"—in answer to this I must observe first that my proposition was rather comparitive than absolute, my design being to avoid that inconvenience & I will say inhumanity of seperating & tareing assunder my Negroe's several families which I would never do or cause to be done but in case of irresistable necessity & I think there are none such at present subsisting between my late friend & partner John Coming Ball & me. In that light I therefore did make the offer because I would chuse to part with the whole in preferrence to an Act which has always shocked me too much to submit to it even in the Sale of New Negroes but I had no sooner made the offer than I saw if it was accepted I should be left in much the same disagreeable circumstances that I had been endeavouring to shun & I now perceive that no less than seven or eight families & some of them of my best Negroes will be torn to pieces & probably cause great distraction amongst the whole but I did not then attempt to mend what I had proposed because I thought Sister Ball would see my error & as she well knew my intentions to keep the families together I hoped it was impossible in the light of friendship in which I have always stood with her & your family that she would catch at an offer (tho made by myself) so repugnant to my disposition as well as contrary to my repeated declarations to you both.

Had I behaved with the same attachment to my own Interest in several Instances this trouble would not have come upon me; I shall at present produce only two which I think deserves some consideration.

The first is the offer that your late Father made to sell me Wambaw plantation, his part for £5,000. My answer to that plainly showed that I did not set my own gain in competition with my friendship & regard for him & his family & his conduct afterwards as plainly proved that he was sensible of the favour I did him & them in not hastily laying hold of his offer altho it had this difference from mine that it was made after several weeks deliberation. As perhaps that affair may be forgotten I shall subjoin a Copy of his Letter & my reply thereto.

The next Instance is the present case. It was & still is at my option to do as I pleased with those Negroes & if I was to appropriate the whole to my own behoof it would no more than barely pay what is justly due to me from that Estate which your Father inherited; when I applied upon that occasion in 1751[3] the answer that was made to me was *"If you have any demand the Law is open."* This is a fact well known to Mr. Austin & your Aunt but for the sake of peace altho I knew the Chancery Law would have relieved me & I was strongly advised to file a Bill in that Court I rather submitted to the loss, & now when a fair opportunity offers to reimburse me, I scorn to take any advantage or to retort those bitter words *"The Law is open."* I have not said all this to speak my own praise or to make a *merit* of honesty: but to repeat more at large what I hinted to you & your Mother before; to Wit that I had a right to expect some little indulgence in the division of Wambaw Negroes & effects. I wanted no profit but only a gratification in a tender concern which I had set my heart upon & which I was willing to pay well for. I must confess that upon that occasion you were kind & go this affair how it may I shall thank you for your own ready acquiescence.

Nor have I said all this to refine upon or by any means to take away the force of my offer. Tis true I did make it & without any reserve therefore *"I do yet continue in the same mind"* & will do so if required altho it should prove a very heavy loss to me, & I don't know anything that could have been contrived to distress me & embarrass my plantation again more than this unnecessary division of Fathers, Mothers, Husbands, Wives, & Children who tho Slaves are still human Creatures & I cannot be deaf to their cries least a time should come when I should cry & there shall be none to pity me.

Do now as you & your Mother think proper. I will wait upon you almost any day next week at Wambaw & deliver all those Negroes, after you have confirmed to me the restitution of Dockum plantation for which I have never yet had Titles & made as final a settlement of all our Accounts as we then can do, in which I cannot

---

[3] Eleanor Ball Laurens' father had died in 1751. The father had willed Dockon plantation to John Coming Ball. HL may have thought that that property should have come to his wife Eleanor. HL had apparently acquired this plantation from his brother-in-law sometime between 1751 and 1754, but he had never received the title deeds. See HL to David Graeme, Jan. 23, 1764.

doubt the same equity will be extended in our respective proportions of the Crops of 1763 & 1764 as is intended to be in the division of Negroes, &ca.

"If you continue in the same mind" be so good as to let me know what day will best suit and I shall meet you. Your Aunt & the children are well & we join in Love to your Mother & all the family, and I remain, Dear Elias, Your affectionate friend & Servant—

SOURCE: Letterbook copy, Letter Book of Henry Laurens, Oct. 30, 1762–Sept. 10, 1766, Penn. Hist. Soc.; addressed "Hyde Park."

TO JOHN HENTIE

[Charles Town] 1st April 1765

Sir,

As I shall be under a necessity of Meeting Mr. Peter Broughton at Strawberry[4] on Tuesday the 23d Inst., I shall defer my intended Journey thither & beg leave to extend the time of our meeting unto Monday the 22d when if I am well & nothing unforeseen presents I shall hope to have the pleasure of seeing you at Mepkin when I shall accomodate you in the best manner that that place will admit of. I remain, &ca.—

SOURCE: Letterbook copy, Letter Book of Henry Laurens, Oct. 30, 1762–Sept. 10, 1766, Penn. Hist. Soc.

TO ABRAHAM SCHAD

[Charles Town] 1st April 1765

I now send sundry Articles for the use of Wambaw plantation as per list on the other side, and what further remains shall go another Opportunity.

I just received a Letter from Mrs. Ball in which we are not quite agreed about a division of Wambaw therefore I put off my intended journey until I hear again, and very likely I may see you some day next Week as I keep my Horses here for that purpose. Meantime

---

[4] Strawberry Ferry.

go forward with the plantation business & keep all the Negroes at Work without alteration till further Orders. Dont distribute the Childrens Cloaths until they are really wanted, & then take notice to which Negroes you give them.

Mrs. Laurens is not very well & therefore cant make up such Cloaths but hopes your Wife will do that part. I am, &ca.—

[*P.S.*] Please to deliver the inclosed Letter safely to Mr. Hentie.

A List of Sundry sent to Wambaw, Viz. 1 Bottle Oyl, 5 Sutes Baby Cloaths, 1 lb. Tea, 1 Frying Pan, 3 dozen Hoes, 1 dozen Spades, 1 Role Milliloh,[5] 25 Gallons Rum.

SOURCE: Letterbook copy, Letter Book of Henry Laurens, Oct. 30, 1762– Sept. 10, 1766, Penn. Hist. Soc.; addressed "Wambaw."

TO BENJAMIN SIMONS, JR.

[Charles Town] 1st April 1765

Dear Sir,

I am very much obliged to you for the favour of your Letter while I was at Mepkin which I could not then reply to because I was getting away as quick as possible from thence, having been very Ill with a Quincy & in some apprehensions of a return.

You are very good to have given my proposition about the case of Wambaw a place in your thoughts, & I am sorry that the distance of the place is to render it impracticable for you to attempt. Had I known that an offer of that kind would have been acceptable, I should not have pass'd by you, notwithstanding I have a high opinion of Mr. Marion & a great regard for him, & indeed if you had happen'd to have been at home when I called at your House, I certainly should have taken the Liberty of mentioning Mepkin to you, tho I was really diffident, & at a loss whether I should be right in doing so, but it will at all times give me pleasure to serve you. I have made use of your hint of Mr. Jerman.[6] Mr. Broughton has agreed

---

[5] Perhaps "milfoil." A decoction of milfoil was used to cure looseness of the bowels. *OED*.

[6] Capt. Edward Jerman of St. James Santee buried his wife on Oct. 9, 1768. He was a planter along Wambaw Creek and died in 1793. "Will of Edward Jerman," dated Oct. 1, 1792, proved Sept. 28, 1793, Charleston County Wills, xxv, Book A (1793–1800), 76–79, S. C. Archives.

with me to meet at the House of Mr. Boyd at Strawberry on Tuesday the 23d Inst. in order to lay before our friends such matters as are in dispute between us relative to Mepkin Swamp, at which time I hope it will be agreeable to you to attend as one upon that friendly office. We have mutually promised to lay before you all our papers & Claims without reserve & to be determin'd by your opinions. He has chosen Mr. James Cordes[7] & Mr. ——— Porcher to join you & Mr. Marion. Please to make my Compliments to Mrs. Simmons & believe me to be, Dear Sir, &ca.—

SOURCE: Letterbook copy, Letter Book of Henry Laurens, Oct. 30, 1762– Sept. 10, 1766, Penn. Hist. Soc.; addressed "Smoaky Hill."

TO CHRISTOPHER GADSDEN

[Charles Town] 2d April 1765

Sir,

I see Mr. William Maine is in Town. He holds the Character of an honest Man & an accurate Surveyor; if you please I will apply to him to run the line from West to East between the South boundary of yours & the North bounds of my Marsh Lands & direct him to wait upon you before he begins to work.[8] I am, Sir, &ca.—

SOURCE: Letterbook copy, Letter Book of Henry Laurens, Oct. 30, 1762– Sept. 10, 1766, Penn. Hist. Soc.; addressed "Esquire. Ansonburgh."

---

[7] James Cordes, Jr., was the son of Thomas Cordes (1697–1749). Junior was used in the eighteenth century to distinguish one member of a family from another, in this instance a nephew from an uncle. He was a member of the Commons House of Assembly from the parish of St. John Berkeley in 1765 and 1766. He was a commissioner of the high roads for St. John. *SCHM*, XLIII (1942), 137. He lived at North Chacan, a plantation just to the north of Mepkin on the east side of the Western Branch of the Cooper where he built a house about 1760. Samuel Gaillard Stoney, *Plantations of the Carolina Low Country* (Charleston, S. C., 1955), pp. 65–66.

[8] A plan of Gadsden's suburb of "Middlesex" which lay just to the north of Laurens' land is printed in *The Writings of Christopher Gadsden, 1746–1805*, ed. Richard Walsh (Columbia, S. C., 1966), facing p. 228.

TO ELIAS BALL

[Charles Town] 4th April 1765

Dear Sir,

I have just now rec'd your favour of this date informing that you will meet me at Wambaw on Tuesday next tho you do not say for what purpose. Nevertheless I will be with you as soon as I can to know. Monday & Tuesday in Easter Week are days for parochial business & I shall have some to employ me here. Therefore be so good as to excuse me until Thursday & then if extraordinary bad weather or other accidents do not hinder me I shall wait on you.

Please to deliver or forward the inclosed to Mr. Hentie & to present my Love to Sister Ball & all the family & I remain, Dear Elias, Yours, &ca.—

[*P.S.*] Tom shall be order'd home as soon as he comes to Town.

SOURCE: Letterbook copy, Letter Book of Henry Laurens, Oct. 30, 1762–Sept. 10, 1766, Penn. Hist. Soc.; addressed "Hyde Park."

TO JOHN HENTIE

[Charles Town] 4th April 1765

Sir,

The above is duplicate of a few lines sent to trouble you the 1st Inst. to which I refer.

I must by appointment be at Wambaw on Thursday next to meet Mr. Ball & wish I may be so happy as to meet you too.

I shall in hopes of seeing you bring all my Mepkin papers. Meantime I remain, Sir, &ca.—

SOURCE: Letterbook copy, Letter Book of Henry Laurens, Oct. 30, 1762–Sept. 10, 1766, Penn. Hist. Soc.; addressed "Esquire."

FROM JAMES HABERSHAM

Savannah in Georgia, the 5th April 1765

Sir,

I received your favour of the 15th February last by Messreurs

Rossel and Gervais, and am much obliged to you for giving me an Opportunity of shewing those Gentlemen any Civility, as well on account of your recommendations as for the good Qualities they appear to possess. I have lately had a Line from Mr. Lachlan Mackintosh, to whom I wrote by them, and understand, they were at Frederica waiting for a Passage to Augustine. I expect to see them on their return, and if they have any Views of making any Settlement in this Colony (as I have learnt from Mr. George Mackintosh (Lachlan's Brother) they have), you may depend on every Service in my Power. I offered them what Cash they might want, but they only took Fifty Pounds, for which they gave me two Receipts to you to serve as one, of which you have one enclosed. I expect to send you in a few days a Draft on Charleston, but the Sum I cannot at present ascertain, and if you approve of this Method, which I think the best & quickest to remit you, I shall probably be able to do it in this and next month.

Yesterday I saw one Mr. Edwin (a German)[9] who tells me, you would be here in about three Weeks. I shall be extremely glad to see you, and if you will do me the favour to accept of a Bed and such Accomodations as my House affords, I shall esteem it a favour and permit me to add, that I expect you will oblige me in this request. I shall write you again in a few days, and am, with real regard, Sir, Your most Obedient humble Servant—

SOURCE: Printed copy, *Collections of the Georgia Historical Society*, Vol. VI: *The Letters of Hon. James Habersham, 1756–1775* (Savannah, Ga., 1904), pp. 29–30. The letter as printed in the *Collections* was taken from a transcript of the original letterbook copy made for William Bacon Stevens. The original has been lost. The printed copy has been edited according to the rules established for this series.

---

[9] The Bethabara Diary for March 15, 1765, stated that "About noon Br. Ettwein left for South Carolina and Georgia . . . He expects to reach Charlestown a few days ahead of the wagons." *Records of the Moravians in North Carolina*, I, 301. John Ettwein was on his way to Savannah "to investigate the status of the property which the Moravians had acquired in that neighborhood, thirty years before." Without HL's introductions to prominent men in Savannah, Ettweins' mission might not have been successful. *Transactions of the Moravian Historical Society*, Vol. XII: Kenneth G. Hamilton, *John Ettwein and the Moravian Church During the Revolutionary Period* (Bethlehem, Penn., 1940), p. 112.

TO PETER HORLBECK

[Charles Town] 6th April 1765

I send you sundry Articles as per Account inclosed for the use of Mepkin. What is omitted now shall go next opportunity.

I likewise inclose an order to get Corn at Watboo. You must go there & desire Mr. Swainston[1] to give you a Memorandum in writing how many Bushels I may depend on & what method he would advise to fetch it away, whether by Land or water.

If you have not already made George a Driver I beg you will not do it, he is an eye Servant, & a great Rogue, & therefore by no means fit to be an overseer of others. You might as well set a Wolf to watch Your Sheep.

Load the Boat & send her down & make ready for her again.

SOURCE: Letterbook copy, Letter Book of Henry Laurens, Oct. 30, 1762–Sept. 10, 1766, Penn. Hist. Soc.; addressed "Mepkin."

TO ROBERT SWAINSTON

[Charles Town, 6th April 1765]

Sent Mr. Raper's[2] order to Mr. Swainston for Corn in Mr. Horlbeck's Letter endorsed "Please to acquaint Mr. Horlbeck how many Bushels of Corn you have to spare & advise the best manner to take it away."

SOURCE: Letterbook copy, Letter Book of Henry Laurens, Oct. 30, 1762–Sept. 10, 1766, Penn. Hist. Soc.

GEORGE AUSTIN & HENRY LAURENS VERSUS ROBERT WEAVER[3]

April 6, 1765

[On April 6, 1765, Robert Williams, Jr., attorney for the plaintiffs,

---

[1] Robert Swainston managed Wadboo Barony for the Colleton family. *HL Papers*, III, 55n. He was a witness of the will of Thomas Cordes on May 22, 1762 and of Levi Durand on March 16, 1765. *Abstracts of Wills, 1760–1784*, pp. 39, 55.

[2] Robert Raper.

[3] Robert Weaver was a justice of the peace for Craven County. *General Gazette,* Oct. 31, 1765. Between 1765 and 1768 he received five grants of land totaling 528 acres on the Pee Dee River. Index to Grants, S. C. Archives.

filed suit in the court of common pleas against Robert Weaver,
planter along the Pee Dee River, for the recovery of a bond, dated
July 30, 1762, in the sum of £260 currency. Weaver entered a plea
contesting the suit on April 15, 1765. The docket does not indicate if
further proceedings were held in the case, but there is a notation that
Weaver paid the "Debt & Costs."]

SOURCE: Judgment Rolls, 1765, No. 264A, S. C. Archives.

TO THOMAS POTTS

[Charles Town] 8th April 1765

Sir,

I have agreed with Mr. Hawkins's Schooner[4] to call upon you
for a Load of Pitch about 330 Barrels which I hope you will have
ready for the Vessel as tis high time now to begin to put in execution
our agreement & I give you this previous notice to avoid delay. Please
to let the whole be put in very good order & filled to the bung & you
may be assur'd of full allowance for all overweight. I am, Sir, &ca.—

SOURCE: Letterbook copy, Letter Book of Henry Laurens, Oct. 30, 1762–
Sept. 10, 1766, Penn. Hist. Soc.; addressed "Black Mingo"; "per Mr.
Fulton."

TO JOHN HANDLIN

[Charles Town] 8th April 1765

Sir,

You wrote me by Capt. Walker that you had sent 211 Barrels of Pitch in my Schooner but there are 217 Barrels turn'd out of

---

[4] On May 23, 1764 Daniel Horry registered for himself and Paul Trapier the
schooner *Active*, Edward Hawkins, 15 tons, built in S. C. in 1764. Ship Register,
1734–1765, p. 233, S. C. Archives. In May 1767 when the *Active* was seized by
the customs officials in Charleston, the vessel was owned by James Gordon, merchant of Georgetown. *A Representation of Facts*, p. 43. On June 11, 1773, Edward Hawkins registered the schooner *North Island*, built at Winyah in 1773, as
master and owner. Ship Register, 1765–1783, p. 177, S. C. Archives. In 1774 Edward Hawkins named the Georgetown merchants James Gordon and Anthony
Bonneau as the executors of his will. "Will of Edward Hawkins," dated Sept. 28,
1774, proved ———, *Abstracts of Wills, 1760–1784*, p. 282.

her which are upon the whole at 11 lbs. per Barrel 2,387 lbs. over-weight at 2d½ per pound is £23.17.3, & the price of the Pitch is £3.5/ per Barrel tho I have been told of some that sold at £3.7.6 this day & if so I must allow that price which I shall advise of in my next with an Account of the whole. Mean time with my respects to your Mother & family I remain, &ca.—

SOURCE: Letterbook copy, Letter Book of Henry Laurens, Oct. 30, 1762–Sept. 10, 1766, Penn. Hist. Soc.; addressed "Black Mingo"; "per Mr. Fulton."

TO JOHN McDOWELL

[Charles Town] 8th April 1765

Sir,

Capt. Richardson has deliver'd to me 120 Barrels of your Pitch agreeable to your advice of the 29th March. The weight is short which I am very sorry for because I must pay as much Freight for small as for large Barrels, Vizt.

$$\left.\begin{array}{r} 320 \\ 317 \\ 321 \end{array}\right\}$$

I beg you will hasten down the remainder & make them better measure otherwise my patience which you have kept a long time upon the stretch will fail me. I am, Sir, &ca.—

SOURCE: Letterbook copy, Letter Book of Henry Laurens, Oct. 30, 1762–Sept. 10, 1766, Penn. Hist. Soc.; addressed "Black Mingo"; "per Mr. Fulton."

TO WILLIAM HUGHES

[Charles Town] 8th April 1765

Sir,

I have none of your favours unanswer'd. Capt. Richardson has deliver'd to me 170 Barrels of your Pitch which are weighed as below, but in exceeding bad order as to hoops, some of the Barrels striped almost naked; & almost all of the bungs forced into the bung holes. Please to forward more as quick as you can & remind our friend T. Potts, if you will be so kind, good Sir, that it is time to open a Correspondence which in that particular of Pitch should have been closed or nearly closed by the time this will reach you. If all my friends had neglected me in the same degree I must have gone to Pott long ago. I expect a Ship of my own in this Month. The weather begins to grow warm & I shall be glad to avoid being unnecessarily engaged in the Summer. I take the liberty of mentioning this to you from what passed between us when you & I made our agreement & extended it on Mr. Potts's Account to 1766. I remain, &ca.—

SOURCE: Letterbook copy, Letter Book of Henry Laurens, Oct. 30, 1762–Sept. 10, 1766, Penn. Hist. Soc.; addressed "Black Mingo"; "per Mr. Fulton."

TO THOMAS POTTS
[Charles Town] 9th April 1765

Sir,

I wrote to you yesterday by Mr. Fulton[5] to provide a load of Pitch for the Schooner *Active*, Edward Hawkins, Master, who now waits upon you with this & I beg you will give him dispatch & cause the Barrels to be put in very good order. I am, Sir, &ca.—

SOURCE: Letterbook copy, Letter Book of Henry Laurens, Oct. 30, 1762–Sept. 10, 1766, Penn. Hist. Soc.; addressed "Black River"; "per Hawkins."

ADVERTISEMENT
April 13, 1765

TO BE SOLD, On Tuesday the 16th of April instant, at 12 o'clock at noon, at the usual place in Charles-Town, in order to close the affairs of a Co-partnership in Bristol.[6]

The Ship ANN, GEORGE FORTEN,[7] Master, Lying at

---

[5] David Fulton.

[6] Cowles & Harford. On this same date the *Wambaw* was also to be sold.

[7] This is the first *Ann*.

Mr. Eveleigh's wharf—burthen seven hundred and sixty barrels of rice, a very commodius cabbin, well found in sails and rigging, anchors and cables.—Said ship was built at Philadelphia, nine years ago, under the inspection of the present master, has been taken great care of by him ever since, and is now in very good condition.

An inventory may be seen on board, and will be produced at the day of the sale. Any person inclined to treat in private may apply to the said master, or to

HENRY LAURENS

SOURCE: Printed in *Gazette,* April 13, 1765.

TO ELIAS BALL

[Wambaw] 14th April 1765

Dear Sir,

As you were in haste yesterday some things were left unsettled, particularly the division of other effects (besides Negroes) on Wambaw plantation. The sooner that is done the better, and also about Dockum & our Accounts but these may rest the one until you are of age the other to any time convenient to you. From the hints that were given yesterday about dividing this Tract I apprehend that a division is wanted & therefore if you please I will immediately take the proper measures to have that purpose effected, & I must beg you will by the first opportunity send me down the plat of Wambaw 3,000 Acres.

Be so good also as to let me know immediately after your division of the Estates Negroes what number & their Names fall to the shares of your Sisters[8] who are to plant here that if it is intended that we are to plant in Common I may give directions accordingly.

My Love & respects attend your whole family & I remain, &ca.—

[*P.S.*] If you have no direct opportunity, please to send a Letter to Mepkin & there it will be forward'd.

SOURCE: Letterbook copy, Letter Book of Henry Laurens, Oct. 30, 1762–Sept. 10, 1766, Penn. Hist. Soc.; addressed "Hyde Park."

---

[8] Elizabeth, Catherine, and Ann.

TO SAMUEL WRAGG

[Charles Town] 16th April 1765

Sir,

I receiv'd yesterday your favour of the 11th Inst. accompanied by sundry Bonds & Accounts which I have not yet fully examined but make no doubt they are right save only these few remarks. One half the purchase of 15 Negroes & Blankets from William Price payable the 1st January £1,644.17.6 is not yet Brought to my Credit.

The times of payment & state of the debts outstanding for £2,230.8.7 are not noted & therefore cannot be enter'd with so much exactness as should be in my Books.

Any dispute subsisting with William Alston[9] about Indigo can apply to me only in Company with Messrs. B. & S.[1] & yourself from which his private debt to me is quite distinct. What ever you do in that affair I shall be satisfied with but the sooner he brings the dispute to an end the better for us all. Mean time he should not delay to acknowledge the sum due & when to H. Laurens.

The sum of £1,570.0.8 which you have established as a Balance whether it be really so or not, & a greater sum if it would be of service is at your command only giving me a few days notice of your draughts, & I am so well satisfied with all your transactions that I should be glad of opportunity to thank you, by a return of any services in my power.

I think you allow'd Money enough for the Wench & Boy & tis not improbable that you have done as I often have in similar cases, paid more to yourself for Negroes than you would have given to any body else.

I shall be exceedingly glad to receive the Cedar & Bay Loggs as the time for Shipping them is now come & will soon pass away again.

The Gentleman who brought down your Bill to Thomas Butler[2] with another promised me to leave them in Mr. William

---

[9] Most probably William Allston (1738-1781) of Brookgreen plantation on the Waccamaw River who married Anne Simons in 1763. Rogers, *History of Georgetown County*, p. 521.

[1] Brewton & Smith.

[2] This was probably the Thomas Butler who received two grants on June 19, 1772, one for 500 acres on Little River Swamp and another for 500 acres at the mouth of Buck Creek on the Waccamaw River. Index to Grants, S. C. Archives. Thomas Butler was named an executor by Peter Simons of Waccamaw River in his

Alston's hands & this Gentleman will bear me Witness that when he called upon me, I instantly put my hand to my pocket to take out the key of my Desk in order to get Money & discharge both taking it for granted that he was come upon that & no other business & I was greatly surprised to hear that they were returned to the Country. When the Gentleman first brought them he met me at the door going to a Committee of the House of Assembly where I had been sent for & happened to be much wanted.[3] He would not allow me one moment, tho I intreated him to call again in the Morning or leave the Bills & I would wait upon him; No, the Universe was depending upon those two Bills. Why surely, Sir, you will give me leave to see at least whether I owe Money before I accept Bills. Besides I cant pay them at 10 days sight & must either pay them directly or take 20 days because I shall be out of Town in ten days & I would rather pay them immediately than have them brought in my absence. He then promised to leave them with Mr. Alston in return for which I intended to have paid them upon sight as mentioned above & as I have now done to that in favour of Thomas Butler £800, & shall do if in Town when the other appears, unless it shall come by the hands of the same person & I think in such case he cannot expect any great stretches to accomodate him. I remain, &ca.—

SOURCE: Letterbook copy, Letter Book of Henry Laurens, Oct. 30, 1762–Sept. 10, 1766, Penn. Hist. Soc.; addressed "George Town."

TO JOHN HUME

[Charles Town] 16th April 1765

Sir,

I have sent to your House in Town for the Money due for Sams hire as well as for a further sum but have not found you there. Therefore am obliged to be troublesome to you in your retirement & you must excuse me for saying that I have been so exceedingly ill used by you by many repeated, broken, slighted, & unnoticed promises to pay me a Sum of Money from day to day, from Week

---

will dated Feb. 28, 1777. *Abstracts of Wills, 1760–1784*, p. 251. Thomas Butler owned 137 slaves in 1790 in the parish of Prince George Winyah. Rogers, *History of Georgetown County*, p. 166.
[3] HL was serving at this time on a number of committees.

to Week, that I am quite determin'd to rely no more upon them or any such, & as my affairs require Money I shall be obliged to order your Judgement to be entered up on Friday next if you do not make me Payment or give security for the whole of your debt.[4] I am, &ca.—

SOURCE: Letterbook copy, Letter Book of Henry Laurens, Oct. 30, 1762– Sept. 10, 1766, Penn. Hist. Soc.; addressed "Esquire. Charles Town."

TO NATHANIEL BROUGHTON[5]

[Charles Town] 18th April 1765

Sir,

Your favour of the 12 Inst. was brought to my House while I was out of Town otherwise I should not have delay'd so long to reply to it. I cannot inform you the Christian name of Mr. Maxwell surviving partner of the late House of Maxwell & Udney[6] but that may be filled up by your Attorney & you may make your Letter so discriptive as to leave no room for error.

Mr. Roper[7] I presume was advised by A., L., & A. to address that House with the consignment of your goods, & not by me in particular, as I believe I was not in the way at that time.

Some time the beginning of 1762 I had a Letter from Mr. Jeremiah Nibbs, Junior, Merchant in Antigua informing of the death

---

[4] HL had at this time successfully sued Hume in the court of common pleas for the recovery of a debt, but the case had not been carried to a conclusion. HL had stopped the proceedings after obtaining the verdict in hopes of inducing Hume to make a satisfactory settlement. Hume did not settle the debt, which led HL to threaten a renewal of the proceedings. The next step would be to have the verdict or judgment against Hume "entered up," that is signed and entered in the docket book. If the defendant did not then settle, HL could ask the court for an execution directing the provost marshal to seize and offer at public sale the chattel and real property of the defendant. The absence of the roll or documents in the case points up the incompleteness of the records of the S. C. court of common pleas. See Mortgage, May 4, 1765.

[5] Nathaniel Broughton inherited Mulberry plantation on the Cooper River from his father Nathaniel, who was a son of Thomas Broughton, lieutenant governor. He was a justice of the peace in 1765 and died in October 1778. "Will of Nathaniel Broughton," dated Oct. 6, 1754, proved Jan. 10, 1755, Charleston County Wills, VII (1752–1756), 280-283, S. C. Archives; *General Gazette*, Oct. 31, 1765; *SCHM*, XVII (1916), 150.

[6] William Maxwell was the surviving partner as Ernest Udney had died. *HL Papers*, II, 80n.

[7] William Roper.

of Mr. Udney & that he was appointed or empower'd to settle the
Affairs of the Copartnership of Maxwell & Udney & desiring to know
how our Accounts stood with them & the Ballance due to us about
£1,900 was remitted by Mr. Nibbes or some body else to our friend
in Bristol. It might answer a good end to you to write to that Gentleman who I am pretty sure is well acquainted with the circumstances
of the House & that he will put you into the best path for coming
at your Money.

If you think my services further necessary please to command
them. I am, &ca.—

SOURCE: Letterbook copy, Letter Book of Henry Laurens, Oct. 30, 1762–
Sept. 10, 1766, Penn. Hist. Soc.; addressed "Esquire. St. John's."

TO PETER HORLBECK

[Charles Town] 18th April 1765
Sir,

I send you sundry articles as per Account below.

The Cask of Indigo seed contains 8½ Bushels of exceeding
good seed which you must begin to use immediately if necessary.

Let the Negro Man Sampson remain until I come. He is to
go to Wambaw.

> 21 Barrels Salt to be taken good care of
> 1 Flour Barrel of Bottles
> 1 Keg Bisquit
> 2 half Barrels containing sundry to remain
> 5 Iron potts
> 1 Barrel Beef & pork
> 4 Chairs
> 1 Firkin Butter
> 2 hams
> 2 Flitches

The Barrel of Indigo Seed is directed to Francis Kinloch, Esquire.[8]
If I am alive & well I shall see you on Monday next. Mean time I
remain, &ca.—

---

[8] Francis Kinloch died at Rice Hope plantation on the Santee on June 2, 1767.
He was so successful as an indigo planter that the London *Daily Advertiser,* Aug.
18, 1767, noted his death by quoting from the *Gazette,* June 15, that he was "one
of the most considerable and successful Indico planters in this province." See also
Rogers, *History of Georgetown County,* pp. 64, 76, 94, 100–101.

SOURCE: Letterbook copy, Letter Book of Henry Laurens, Oct. 30, 1762–Sept. 10, 1766, Penn. Hist. Soc.; addressed "Mepkin."

TO CHRISTOPHER ROWE

[Charles Town] 20th April 1765

Dear Sir,

I Rec'd Yesterday your kind favour of the 16th with a Box of Roots for which am much obliged to you. That which you take for Puccoon is only the Turmeric & stains a Yellow colour. The Puccoon root stains a fine pink or Crimson, bears a small longish leaf & bunches of pretty little Yellow flowers. I have shewed one root to Valentine Granick & he will discribe it to you.

I shall be very thankful for the Turkeys when you send them but I beg you will not put yourself to too much trouble about them.

It gives me joy to hear that the Reverend Mr. Edwin[9] was with you & I believe you & your Neighbours must have benefited greatly from the preaching & good precepts of that good Man. I should be extremely glad to assist in obtaining the assistance of such an one for the people who dwell on the Skirts of this Country to make a Circuitous visit to them once in two Months until they were able to make a good establishment for a Minister. But even in their present circumstances if their minds were devoted to the *one thing needful,* not neglecting at the same time other things that are needful for the body while it remains here, they might with a little assistance from the Public or from a few pious Men, mentain a Minister of the Gospel in each district. I wish to see this work enter'd upon. It would make the plough go easy & tend to prosper all our affairs. I remain, &ca.—

SOURCE: Letterbook copy, Letter Book of Henry Laurens, Oct. 30, 1762–Sept. 10, 1766, Penn. Hist. Soc.; addressed "Esquire. Orangeburgh."

TO ELIAS BALL

[Charles Town] 20th April 1765

Dear Sir,

I wrote to you the Morning after you left Wambaw desiring

---

[9] John Ettwein.

to know your opinion & determination about dividing Wambaw plantation & that you would send me the plat of the 3,000 Acres.

Also an Account of the Number & names of Negroes to be sent there for your sisters.

These are matters of great consequence & therefore I send the bearer to bring me your answer which I was in hopes of having Rec'd last Wednesday.

I remain with my Love to all at Hyde Park & Kengsinton. I am, &ca.——

SOURCE: Letterbook copy, Letter Book of Henry Laurens, Oct. 30, 1762–Sept. 10, 1766, Penn. Hist. Soc.; addressed "Hyde Park."

TO ELIAS BALL

[Charles Town] 22d April 1765

Dear Sir,

I Rec'd your favour of yesterday with a Plat of Wambaw Land & informing me that Mr. Smith[1] is desirous of a division; therefore I have put the plat & all my Setts into Mr. Williams's[2] hands in order to have that business accomplished.

If I understand you rightly you intend to take the management of your Sisters Negroes. Therefore I shall give the necessary orders on my own Account & hope we shall be good Neighbours. If I do any thing amiss it will be owing to inadvertance or for want of knowing your mind more fully. I shall be glad for this reason that you will let me know what particular steps you intend to take as to planting the present Season & to concur with you in everything that will contribute to the benefit of the whole. My present directions will be to plant one half of the clear'd Rice Field taken equitably & impartially.

I remain with my Love & respects to your Mother & all friends, Dear Sir, &ca.——

SOURCE: Letterbook copy, Letter Book of Henry Laurens, Oct. 30, 1762–Sept. 10, 1766, Penn. Hist. Soc.; addressed "Hyde Park."

---

[1] Henry Smith.
[2] Robert Williams, Jr.

HENRY LAURENS VERSUS PETER HALL[3]

April 22, 1765

[On April 22, 1765, Robert Williams, Jr., attorney for the plaintiff, filed suit in the court of common pleas against Peter Hall, Charleston cabinetmaker, for recovery of a bond, in the sum of £1,500 currency, Hall through his attorney confessed judgment. The judgment was signed on the same day and recorded by Dougal Campbell, clerk of the court. The judgment was reissued on July 12, 1765, October 8, 1765, and May 12, 1766. HL signed a statement which was entered into the record on April 28, 1767, that Hall had finally paid the debt.]

SOURCE: Judgment Rolls, 1765, No. 47A, S. C. Archives; Judgment Docket, Court of Common Pleas, Book 2 (1755–1773), p. 96, S. C. Archives.

BENJAMIN PERDRIAU, JR. TO MATHIAS SELLER[4]

[Charles Town] 23d April 1765

Sir,

The Bond you gave Mr. Laurens in February 1764 for 300 New Negro Men you then purchased of him, has been for some time due & ought to have been discharged long before this. Therefore it behooves you to take the matter into consideration & to order payment to prevent any Charges that may attend the longer delay thereof. I am, Sir, Your most Humble Servant—   B. P.

SOURCE: Letterbook copy, Letter Book of Henry Laurens, Oct. 30, 1762–Sept. 10, 1766, Penn. Hist. Soc.; addressed "Stono."

---

[3] Peter Hall, London cabinetmaker, brought the Chinese style to Charleston in 1761. E. Milby Burton, *Charleston Furniture, 1700–1825* (Columbia, S. C., 1955), pp. 94–95.
[4] Mathias Seller, planter of St. Paul parish, signed his will with his mark. Peter Horn, tavern keeper, was a witness. "Will of Mathias Seller," dated April 27, 1771, proved May 29, 1772, Charleston County Wills, XIV, Book A (1771–1774), 253–254, S. C. Archives.

TO THOMAS POTTS

[Charles Town] 27th April 1765

Sir,

Mr. Hawkins deliver'd in my absence 307 Barrels of your Pitch for which Mr. Perdriau informs me that he has given a Receipt expressing the pitch to be in exceeding bad order, & truly it is so. Therefore it will not suit me by any means, if I was to suffer it to lay upon the Wharf until I should hear from you, in all probability you would loose a great many Barrels of it as the weather is now very warm & the Barrels bad as well as the pitch Soft. Therefore I have recommended it to Messrs. Lind & Chovin[5] desiring them to take care to keep it out of the Sun & to dispose of it in the best manner they can upon your Account. In the mean time I beg to have your further directions to them or if you please to me on this subject & I hope Mr. Potts will think of making some beginning to comply with his ingagements to deliver me Nine hundred Barrels of Pitch of which I have not yet Rece'd a Single Barrel altho the time for delivering the whole is within a few days of expiring. I am, &ca.—

SOURCE: Letterbook copy, Letter Book of Henry Laurens, Oct. 30, 1762–Sept. 10, 1766, Penn. Hist. Soc.; addressed "Black River"; "per favour Mr. Davidson."

TO JOHN MAYRANT

[Charles Town] 27th April 1765

Sir,

In Answer to what you write under the 24th Inst. About Lumber provided for me, I beg leave to refer you to our Agreement, & I might add to your repeated promise at our last Meeting on the

---

[5] Thomas Lind and Alexander Chovin on Oct. 1, 1764 announced their copartnership in the Factorage Business "in all its branches, either by exporting the country produce abroad, or selling it here, to the best advantage for their constituents." They had three good boats, several convenient stores, and a "compting house" on Mr. Raven's wharf then occupied by William Gibbes. *Gazette*, Oct. 1, 1764. Alexander Chovin, a Huguenot, had close connections with the parishes of St. James Santee and St. Thomas. Lind and Chovin were witnesses to the will of Issac Lesesne, planter of St. Thomas, in 1770. *Abstracts of Wills, 1760–1784*, p. 176. Chovin married Mary Tart of St. Thomas in November 1772. *SCHM*, XI (1910), 98.

Entrance of Beresfords Wharf.[6] I shall order my Schooner to your Landing next Week & that She has not made several Voyages there is wholly owing to yourself, & I hope for your own sake that you will not dismiss her without a full Loading nor detain her an unreasonable time, for I am determined to have our agreement fulfilled or to proceed according to the tenour of it in case of failure. I remain, &ca.—

SOURCE: Letterbook copy, Letter Book of Henry Laurens, Oct. 30, 1762–Sept. 10, 1766, Penn. Hist. Soc.; addressed "Esquire. Santé."

TO ANDREW BROUGHTON

[Charles Town] 27th April 1765

Sir,

I have rec'd your further favour of the 26th & observe its contents but am really at a Loss what to say more than I have already wrote & said upon the subject of our division Line.

A sight of your Plat & a knowledge of your demand might give me some new Light but at present I see no room for an arbitration or reference if your Plat & Grant be as you say, more ancient than any other, & withal very clear, where lays the subject for contest? Or what would any Man gain by contending against such proofs? I am certain that I will never be so weak as to attempt it.

Your present proposal is to run your course down & have a Line Mark'd by two Surveyors if I will agree to it. But, good Sir, what right have I to hinder you from running your course down upon your own Line according to an old & clear Plat? You may in such case no doubt do what is just without my permission.

Nevertheless if there does, as I verily think there does, remain some doubt; the only way to clear it up will be to produce your Plat; shew me how far your demand extends & where you would have

---

[6] Richard Beresford, Esquire (1720–1772), who married Sarah Blakeway, had land along the Wando River and cowpens on the Santee and Coosawhatchie rivers. He had a wharf in Charleston to which he brought his plantation produce in his schooners *Lawrell* and *Wandoe,* which were valued at £200 and £300 respectively. Judgment Rolls, 1767, Nos. 360A, 665A; 1768, No. 469A; 1769, No. 99A, S. C. Archives; "Will of Richard Beresford," dated July 8, 1772, proved Aug. 14, 1772, Charleston County Wills, XIV, Book A (1771–1774), 300–301, S. C. Archives; Inventories, Z (1771–1774), pp. 295–299, S. C. Archives.

your bounds fixed. If these do not incroach upon my property I shall have not the least objection to your proceeding; if they do or seem to do, I shall quickly point out the parts, & then that difference of opinions may become a proper subject for a reference but at present I know of none. Therefore, Sir, until you produce your Plat & lay your claim I can have nothing to add but that I remain, &ca.—

SOURCE: Letterbook copy, Letter Book of Henry Laurens, Oct. 30, 1762–Sept. 10, 1766, Penn. Hist. Soc.; addressed "Stafford."

TO ABRAHAM SCHAD

[Charles Town] 30th April 1765

With this I inclose you an Account of sundry articles sent to be dispos'd among the Negroes for their Rice at the prices mark'd to each article which I hope they will take without too much fuss & trouble that I may not be discouraged from being their Factor another Year.

Their several names are set down & your quantity of each ones Rice on the Credit side at 7/6 per Bushel, which is its full value & opposite to that you must make them Debtor for such goods as they take.

I likewise send you Nails, Vitriol, powder, Shot, & Sugar for the use of the Plantations. The Sugar will serve both places & answer the end of Loaf Sugar.

I lost one day collecting these several articles as they took more time than I imagin'd & I am afraid the little Cart cannot carry all at one turn. If so, you must send it down again & get rid of the trouble as soon as you can & take care of what articles remain & send me the Accounts. I am, &ca.—

[P.S.] When your planting will allow, cart the Rice away to the Landing. I shall hire a Schooner in a few days to go there for it.

Amos has a great inclination to turn Rum Merchant which I have strictly forbidden & therefore desire you to search narrowly & if he has more than One bottle seize it. I suspect that he has or may send up some by my flat Boat to Mr. Mayrants Landing. Therefore be very watchful & if Abram should come to Wambaw I charge you to discipline him with 39 sound Stripes & turn him out of the Gate & see that he goes quite off.

1,000—20d ⎫
1,000—10d ⎬ Nails ⎫
3½ lbs. fine G. Powder ⎬ in a flat Box
10 lbs. Shot ⎭
½ lb. Vitriol
58 lbs. very fine Sugar
10 Gallons of Vinegar in a Keg

SOURCE: Letterbook copy, Letter Book of Henry Laurens, Oct. 30, 1762–Sept. 10, 1766, Penn. Hist. Soc.; addressed "Wambaw."

TO WILLIAM COACHMAN[7]

[Charles Town] 30th April 1765

Sir,

'Tis very near 15 Months ago that I took your Note as Cash to oblige you & the party on whose Account it was given, & was promised punctual payment at the end of 6 days, but from that hour to this I have seen no payment nor even heard an enquiry made whether it was convenient to me to be kept longer out of my Money. Would you like such treatment from me? No, I should have been dunn'd as many times as the debt contains pounds which is now about 914. I remain, &ca.—

SOURCE: Letterbook copy, Letter Book of Henry Laurens, Oct. 30, 1762–Sept. 10, 1766, Penn. Hist. Soc.; addressed "Goose Creek."

TO HENRY RAVENEL[8]

[Charles Town] 30th April 1765

Sir,

I am sure you will not accuse me with rigour altho I now

---

[7] William Coachman, who lived at Coatbaw plantation in the parish of St. John Berkeley, died in 1770. *SCHM*, XXXVII (1936), 10–11; Inventories, Y (1769–1771), pp. 246–249, S. C. Archives.

[8] Henry Ravenel of Brunswick and Pooshee plantations in the Upper Beat of St. John Berkeley was a planter who died in 1785. Frederick A. Porcher, "Upper Beat of St. John's Berkeley," *The Transactions of the Huguenot Society of South Carolina*, XIII (1906), 38–39, 72–74; "Will of Henry Ravenel," dated April 2, 1785, proved July 5, 1785, Charleston County Wills, XXI, Book B (1783–1786), 679–681, S. C. Archives.

inform you that it is absolutely out of my power to indulge you any longer for payment of your Bond, as you know that it is now grown very old altho it is only the sprout of a more ancient stock which I assum'd & prevented your being sued for three Years ago.

You will no doubt give necessary orders upon this occasion & that in a few days. I remain, &ca.——

SOURCE: Letterbook copy, Letter Book of Henry Laurens, Oct. 30, 1762–Sept. 10, 1766, Penn. Hist. Soc.; addressed "St. John's."

TO JOSEPH KERSHAW

[Charles Town] 30th April 1765

Dear Sir,

Not a word has been said to me upon the subject of our friend Wylly's[9] Bond since through your kind interposition on his behalf I was induced to assume it to A. & L. & thereby I am sure prevented its being put in suit. I beg you will inform me how to apply now for payment or even to get it put upon a footing of security & renewed if I am to wait some Years longer.

To tell you the truth I have so many of these good natur'd Accounts for large Sums & some good natur'd acts of securityship to pay, lately fallen upon my hands, that it behoves me in justice to my family to look after them, & especially since I find few people so unpolite as to put me in mind of their obligations. The debt now spoken of Amounts or will in a few Months say 1st August next Amount to £744. I am persuaded you will for good reasons excuse this trouble & believe me to be with great regard for you & yours, &ca.——

---

[9] Samuel Wylly, surveyor and merchant, had resided first in Williamsburg Township and then after 1752 in Fredericksburg Township. He was appointed deputy surveyor on Oct. 6, 1756, by Egerton Leigh, surveyor general of the province. Miscellaneous Records, KK (1754–1758), pp. 403–405, S. C. Archives. He must have become the leading surveyor in his part of the province as he was selected after the Treaty of Augusta to lay off the reservation for the Catawba Indians. On July 3, 1764, he and George Pawley were appointed the S. C. commissioners to run the line between North and South Carolina. Miscellaneous Records, MM, Part 1 (1763–1767), p. 121, S. C. Archives. He died on Feb. 13, 1768. Thomas J. Kirkland and Robert M. Kennedy, *Historic Camden, Colonial and Revolutionary* (Columbia, S. C., 1905), pp. 51, 75, 94; McDowell, *Documents relating to Indian Affairs,* pp. 96–97, 485–486.

SOURCE: Letterbook copy, Letter Book of Henry Laurens, Oct. 30, 1762–Sept. 10, 1766, Penn. Hist. Soc.; addressed "Pine Tree Hill."

TO JOSEPH FOGARTIE

[Charles Town] 1st May 1765

I have detained your Boat about an hour in order to send several things for Wambaw.

Please to order the Negroes away with the Cart very early tomorrow & if they can't carry all away at one time give what remains House room until the Cart returns. Your care in this matter will very much oblige, Sir, Yours, &ca.—

SOURCE: Letterbook copy, Letter Book of Henry Laurens, Oct. 30, 1762–Sept. 10, 1766, Penn. Hist. Soc.; addressed "Cainhoy Ferry." This letter was copied by HL.

TO ELIAS BALL

[Charles Town] 2d May 1765

Dear Sir,

Since I came to Town Mr. Williams has suggested to me that the application & proceedings for the division of Wambaw Land will be very large & expensive & that he was in doubt of our obtaining Surveyors & other proper persons to do the work effectually at the Season of the Year now advancing, that in case of disappointment, the whole must be done over again & double the charges, & as a difficulty in the way, he inform'd me that five persons must be nominated besides two Surveyors, an actual Survey made of the Land & the whole five be present & join in the division.[1] From these hints I think it will be better to defer the application until September that the return may be made within the Month of December or January when Gentlemen will be more inclin'd to ride in the Woods

---

[1] On application, the court of common pleas would issue a writ of partition to five persons to make an equal division of the land. When the schedule of division was returned to the court, it took the force of law and two commissioners would be appointed to see that the partition was executed. "An act for empowering persons to appoint guardians to their children, and for the easier obtaining partitions of lands in coparcenary, joint tenancy, and tenancy in common, in this province," June 21, 1748, *S. C. Statutes*, III, 707–709.

& Survey the Lands with more certainty & less danger. If you think
otherwise I shall desire Mr. Williams to proceed.

My Love & respects to your Mother & all the family & I
remain, &ca.—

SOURCE: Letterbook copy, Letter Book of Henry Laurens, Oct. 30, 1762–
Sept. 10, 1766, Penn. Hist. Soc.; addressed "Hyde Park."

MORTGAGE

May 4, 1765

[*On this date, John and Susanna Hume of Charleston temporarily
released to Henry Laurens a town lot in Charleston as security for
Hume's bond to Laurens of April 3, 1764. Under the terms of the
bond and of this mortgage, Hume stood indebted to Laurens for
£1,500 currency plus 8 per cent annual interest. The mortgaged
property was described as lot number 159 located on the north side
of an alley between Church and Meeting streets, being 33 feet wide
from east to west and 91 feet deep from north to south, and bounding
to the west on land of Dr. John Moultrie, to the north on lands of
Aaron Loocock, to the east on lands lately belonging to Sarah
Fleming deceased, and to the south on the aforementioned alley.
Both the release and the bond were to be cancelled by payment of
the principal and interest. The mortgage was witnessed by Catharine
Colcock and Benjamin Perdriau for John Hume and by Alexander
McCullough and Benjamin Perdriau for Susanna Hume. Benjamin
Perdriau swore to the signatures on May 6, 1765, before Fenwicke
Bull, justice of the peace. The document was recorded May 20, 1765,
by Fenwicke Bull as public register.*]

SOURCE: Deeds, DDD, pp. 56–62, S. C. Archives.

TO JOHN HENTIE

[Charles Town] 7th May 1765

Sir,

In order to obtain a sight & Copy of Mr. Gough's plat as you
desire in your favour of the 30th Ulto., I thought it best to apply to

the Widow Mrs. Caw through a medium; as the Ladies are not so conversant in affairs of that Nature & therefore commonly a little more jealous; & for that purpose made choice of our friend John Deas; who informs me that the plat wanted is in the custody of Mr. Singleton or Mr. Lewis, that he would enquire of one or both of them & when he discover'd where it lay would inform me, that a Copy of the plat might be taken by you or any other person but for some particular reasons Mrs. Caw desired (between ourselves I say it) that a Gentleman of the name of Cordes might not make use of it.[2]

Mr. Deas is now at Goose Creek[3] & probably will enable me to write to you again the latter end of this Week which I shall do if any subject offers.

I have blam'd myself very much, Sir, for omitting to pay for your last trouble at Mepkin. It was often in my mind but I believe the loss of our Horses drove it out just at the proper time, but I hope to make up for that error when I have the pleasure of seeing you next. Meanwhile I think the arbitrators should determine who should pay that & other charges attending our late Survey. I remain, &ca.—

SOURCE: Letterbook copy, Letter Book of Henry Laurens, Oct. 30, 1762–Sept. 10, 1766, Penn. Hist. Soc.

---

[2] Richard Gough, planter, had purchased Pawley's plantation on the eastern side of the Western Branch of the Cooper River from Col. George Pawley. He and his wife Rachel had lived there until his death in 1753. Richard Gough had left this plantation to his son Richard, a minor, with his wife to have permission to live there. Gough had named Richard Singleton of Goose Creek and Sedgwick Lewis as his executors. If Singleton and Lewis could not be executors, then the brothers Thomas Cordes and James Cordes, Jr., were to be executors and guardians of his son. James Cordes, a witness to the will, was still living in 1765. "Will of Richard Gough," dated March 1, 1753, proved June 25, 1753, Charleston County Wills, VII (1752–1756), 83–86, S. C. Archives; *SCHM*, XLIII (1942), 137, 145. Rachel Gough had then married Dr. David Caw who had property at Santee, at Goose Creek, and in Charleston, and who had died in 1758. "Will of David Caw," dated Sept. 21, 1758, proved Dec. 1, 1758, Charleston County Wills, VIII (1757–1763), 275–278, S. C. Archives; Inventories, T (1758–1761), pp. 185–188, S. C. Archives; Joseph I. Waring, *A History of Medicine in South Carolina, 1670–1825* (Columbia, S. C., 1964), pp. 187–188; Irving, *A Day on Cooper River*, pp. 38–39. Thomas Cordes lived adjacent to Gough's plantation. On April 5, 1773, Richard Gough, Jr., gave his mother a lease for life on Buck Hall. Deeds, QQQQ, pp. 459–461, S. C. Archives. Rachel Caw died in her eightieth year on Sept. 7, 1808. *SCHM*, XXXII (1931), 149.

[3] John Deas.

TO WILLIAM O'BRIEN

[Charles Town] 8th May 1765

Sir,

Mr. Delagaye[4] brought me your favour of the 1st Inst. inclosing John Reynolds Bill[5] on Governor Bull for £150 Payable one Month after date 1st January but as it was never presented before, it could not be expected that his Honour would make any allowance of Interest therefore I received only the £150 & pass'd that to your Credit. The Balance of your debt is about £260 which I request you to send before this Month expires. I receiv'd the whole as Cash two Year & 8 Months ago & if I had not done so it would then have been put in suit. I am, &ca.—

SOURCE: Letterbook copy, Letter Book of Henry Laurens, Oct. 30, 1762–Sept. 10, 1766, Penn. Hist. Soc.; addressed "Beaufort."

HENRY LAURENS & THOMAS LEGARE VERSUS JOHN HATFIELD[6]

May 8, 1765

[On April 12, 1765, William Burrows, attorney for the plaintiffs, filed suit in the court of common pleas against John Hatfield of Broad Street in Charleston who would not honor his promissory note, dated May 19, 1764, for £670.11 currency, which was the balance of an account Hatfield owed to John Asline deceased. Laurens and Legare were the administrators of Asline's estate. The case was ordered for judgment on May 8, 1765.]

SOURCE: Judgment Rolls, 1765, No. 45A, S. C. Archives.

---

[4] John Delagaye received a grant to 250 acres of land in Purrysburgh Township on May 24, 1745. Index to Grants, S. C. Archives. He received grants to lots in Beaufort on June 3, Oct. 10, 1759, Sept. 4, 1764, and Feb. 8, 1765. *SCHM,* IX (1908), 153, 155, 158.

[5] John Reynolds married Elizabeth Conyers on Aug. 3, 1755 in St. Helena parish. *SCHM,* XXIII (1922), 48.

[6] John Hatfield, chandler, married Sarah Swallows on Jan. 6, 1775. *SCHM,* XI (1910), 28. He was living in Charleston in 1785. *SCHM,* XIX (1918), 139. She died in 1816. "Will of Sarah Hatfield," dated Feb. 28, 1810, proved July 27, 1816, Charleston County Wills, XXXIII, Book C (1807–1818), 1105–1106, S. C. Archives.

TO THOMAS RUTLEDGE[7]

[Charles Town] 9th May 1765

Sir,

The Account which you contracted the 28th January 1764 in the name of Robert McLeod & Company[8] for 10 Hogsheads Rum payable in 6 Weeks or 2 Months still remains open; I lost money by the Sale of that Rum as you may judge from the price; & the advance for so long a time makes the burthen heavier. Be that as it may, if it is still inconvenient to the House to pay the Amount be so good as to settle Account & include the Interest which may be done by Letter promising to allow me Interest on the Balance from the 20th April 1764 which is allowing you a longer Credit than we agreed upon at the Sale. This is a just & reasonable request & therefore I cannot doubt of your readiness to grant it to, &ca.—

SOURCE: Letterbook copy, Letter Book of Henry Laurens, Oct. 30, 1762–Sept. 10, 1766, Penn. Hist. Soc.; addressed "Esquire. Indian Land."

GEORGE AUSTIN, HENRY LAURENS, & GEORGE APPLEBY VERSUS *ELIZABETH JOHNSON, ADMINSTRATRIX OF GEORGE JOHNSON*

May 13, 1765

[*On May 13, 1765, Robert Williams, Jr., attorney for the plaintiffs, filed suit in the court of common pleas against the estate of George Johnson of Pon Pon for recovery of a bond, dated May 27, 1762, in the sum of £856 currency. The judgment was signed on May 13 and recorded by Dougal Campbell, clerk of the court.*]

SOURCE: Judgment Rolls, 1765, No. 94A, S. C. Archives; Judgment Docket, Court of Common Pleas, Book 2 (1755–1773), p. 96, S. C. Archives.

---

[7] *HL Papers*, III, 240.
[8] *HL Papers*, III, 240.

GEORGE AUSTIN, HENRY LAURENS, & GEORGE APPLEBY VERSUS EDMUND STOCKER[9]

May 14, 1765

[On April 15, 1765, Robert Williams, Jr., attorney for the plaintiffs, filed suit in the court of common pleas against Edmund Stocker, a physician from Goose Creek who was residing at Moncks Corner, for the recovery of a bond, dated June 5, 1761, in the sum of £430 currency. The case was ordered for judgment on April 27. The judgment was signed on May 14. The judgment was reissued on July 8, 1765.]

SOURCE: Judgment Rolls, 1765, No. 190A, S. C. Archives; Judgment Docket, Court of Common Pleas, Book 2 (1755–1773), p. 99, S. C. Archives.

TO PETER HORLBECK

[Charles Town] 15th May 1765

Sir,

I Rece'd yours per Martinique & am sorry for Bill but we must both Kings & Slaves submit to the strokes of death. There is nothing of more importance than the care of Sick Negroes upon a plantation which I have often said to you & I repeat it again both to you & Mrs. White.[1] Take notice every day when they first complain & prevent the effects of a Malady before it grows to too great a head.

The Doctor is of opinion that you can give nothing better for those pleuretic disorders than Bleeding & Snake Root Tea & Toddy. You have Snake Root enough all around you. However I send you some & some Barbadoes Tar, but he is of opinion that this Tar is rather too hot in its nature.[2]

You have put a hard Task upon me but I shall endeavor to accomplish one part for you if your Brother can find out where the

---

[9] Edmund Stocker witnessed Levi Durand's will, dated March 16, 1765. Abstracts of Wills, 1760–1784, p. 55. Dr. Stocker was dead by August 1783 when his daughter married John M'Cullough of St. John Berkeley. SCHM, XVIII (1917), 87.

[1] Mrs. White did sewing at Mepkin.

[2] A medicinal preparation made from the dried root of an American plant, Polygala Senega, "reputed to possess properties antidotal to snake poison." OED.

Money is to be borrowed but as to the Bricks I was in hopes you would have made enough at Mepkin & I dont know where else to get any.

If Mr. Marion is of any service I wish he would visit you some what oftner. I shall try to see you next Week. Meantime, I remain, &ca.—

SOURCE: Letterbook copy, Letter Book of Henry Laurens, Oct. 30, 1762–Sept. 10, 1766, Penn. Hist. Soc.; addressed "Mepkin."

TO ABRAHAM SCHAD

[Charles Town] 16th May 1765

Sir,

Please to cause Mr. Henry Smith's Schooner, James McKenzie,[3] Master, to be loaden with Wambaw Rice & agree in your number of Barrels exactly & send me a Receipt for them. You will git the remainder down as soon as possible & let me know how many Barrels as I expect to send the *Wambaw* up on Monday next & as some things may be wanted you had better send a Boy immediately with a Letter to Fogerties & desire him to dispatch it to me without loss of time.

In the *Wambaw* I shall send you some Boys & Young Women for those who lately lost their Wives.

If you have any Rice Flour to spare pray send me some & what you fall short of the *Wambaw*'s load of Rice must be made up in Corn, therefore be preparing accordingly. Inform me how the New Negroes are, the Crop, & other plantation Affairs. When the *Wambaw* is Loaded you may venture to come to Charles Town. I remain, &ca.—

SOURCE: Letterbook copy, Letter Book of Henry Laurens, Oct. 30, 1762–Sept. 10, 1766, Penn. Hist. Soc.; addressed "Wambaw."

---

[3] James McKenzie was master of a schooner in 1767 that belonged to Richard Withers of Santee and of another schooner in 1772 which belonged to John and Seaman Deas of Goose Creek. Ship Register, 1765–1783, pp. 60, 149, S. C. Archives.

TO DAVID FULTON

[Charles Town] 16th May 1765

Sir,

I am obliged to you for endeavouring to procure pitch for me & shall give the highest price for that of Mr. Cooper's[4] or any other that is offer'd to me.

If a proper parcel of good Negroes shall fall in my way I will send them for Sale to Black Mingo but this is so very distant & uncertain that none of my friends can by any means depend upon it & therefore I beg they may loose no opportunity of purchasing elsewhere. I remain, &ca.—

SOURCE: Letterbook copy, Letter Book of Henry Laurens, Oct. 30, 1762–Sept. 10, 1766, Penn. Hist. Soc.; addressed "Black Mingo."

TO JOHN LOGAN

[Charles Town] 18th May 1765

Dear Sir,

I am in great hopes that you have by this time Received some Cash to appropriate to the payment of Mr. Rutherfords demand upon the Receiver General; & in such case I intreat you to let me have as much you have in hand. I am largely in advance upon that Account & never wanted Money more than at present & I expect every day to be called upon again by Mr. Rutherford who I know is as bare of Money as I am & depends upon you very much for a supply.

If you can spare me but 6 or £8,000, I shall be satisfied for the present & even with a smaller Sum if the smallest of those cannot be had. I remain, &c.—

SOURCE: Letterbook copy, Letter Book of Henry Laurens, Oct. 30, 1762–Sept. 10, 1766, Penn. Hist. Soc.; addressed "Esquire. Broad Street."

TO JOHN GORDON

[Charles Town] 18th May 1765

Sir,

Mrs. McQueen desires to have an annual Sum out of her late

---

[4] Samuel Cooper lived at Black Mingo. *HL Papers*, III, 21n.

Husbands Estate fixed & to be paid to her in quarterly or half Yearly payments in proportion to the total Value or to the Yearly produce of that Estate; some regard being had to the manner in which she lived before Mr. McQueen's demise.

This she hopes will save you some trouble & in some measure secure to her an independance.

She asked my opinion as to the Quantum to be allowed her, which I could not declare because I had formed none, for want of knowledge of the Estate from whence her allowance is to be drawn, both of its gross Value & of the particulars in which it consists.

She said some body had inform'd her that I thought £700 or £800 was sufficient to maintain a Woman. Probably I might have thought & said that £500 nay £100 was enough where the income of an Estate would admit of no more but I had never to my remembrance alledg'd that any particular Sum was sufficient for Mrs. McQueen, as my reply to Mr. Gordon when he asked my sentiments but the day before would evince. I could not determine upon that point to my own satisfaction before I was inform'd of the Value of the Estate.

As to Horse Savannah plantation, it appears to me that Mrs. McQueen is not very anxious to be mistress there, & I believe rather than cause the least trouble would wholly retire from it provided her principal demand or rather expectation was satisfied in which I must confess the Lady does not seem to be unreasonable.

She speaks of Mr. Gordon with very great regard & expresses much reliance upon his aid & hopes this matter will be adjusted before he leaves Charles Town from whence she understands he is to be a good while absent.

This is the Sum of the conversation Yesterday Morning between Mrs. McQueen &, Dear Sir, &ca.—

SOURCE: Letterbook copy, Letter Book of Henry Laurens, Oct. 30, 1762–Sept. 10, 1766, Penn. Hist. Soc.; addressed "Esquire. Bay Street."

TO JAMES MARION

[Charles Town] 20th May 1765

Dear Sir,

I have only this Evening Rec'd both your favours of the 11th

& 18th Inst. to which I need not reply particularly as the principal end of them I hope is answer'd, Vizt. providing a Man to releive Mr. Horlbeck.

I had this Morning partly agreed with John Smith[5] who lately lived at Mrs. Caws' plantation[6] & is now gone to Mepkin where he is to remain until Tuesday or Wednesday next when I hope to be there & confirm a Bargain with him. In the meantime I shall be obliged to you to step over there & talk a little to this Man & if you have opportunity enquire into his Character & I shall on that Account go thro St. Thomas's & call on you in my way that I may be better prepar'd to meet him.

I am very sorry to observe your Letters sealed black. You have met with a loss.

My compliments to Mrs. Marion & I remain, &ca.—

SOURCE: Letterbook copy, Letter Book of Henry Laurens, Oct. 30, 1762–Sept. 10, 1766, Penn. Hist. Soc.; addressed "St. Thomas's."

TO JOHN HENTIE

[Charles Town] 21st May 1765

Sir,

I thank you for your obliging Letter of the 18th. My reply to which need not be very Long at present, as I shall probably see you next Week if you are in the Neighbourhood of Mepkin or Mr. Ball's. I purpose on Tuesday afternoon the 28th to go thro St. Thomas's perhaps lodge at Hyde Park, Kensington, or some where thereabout to be at Mepkin on Wednesday & return upon Thursday, with the Salvo of Errors Excepted.

---

[5] On Aug. 6, 1764, John Smith was listed as owning two male slaves between 16 and 60 among those whose slaves were to be called out to repair the road from Watboo to Strawberry. Minute Book of Commissioners of Roads, St. John Berkeley, 1 (1760–1798), S. C. Hist. Soc. John Smith, "living at Mepkin," tolled a brown bay horse before justice of the peace Henry Ravenel at Goose Creek on July 9, 1766. *Country Journal*, July 15, 1766. John Smith had died by 1779 for his brother Lancelot Smith, who was then keeping Strawberry Ferry, was trying to collect the debts owed to the estate of John Smith. "Strawberry Ferry Ledger of Lancelot Smith, 1777–1779," S. C. Hist. Soc.

[6] Pawley's plantation on the east side of the Western Branch of the Cooper River.

Meantime I must inform you that I have not yet obtain'd a sight of Mr. Gough's plats & I begin to be doubtful of ever seeing them. The Answer that my friend John Deas gave me yesterday, seemed to be a dilotary one or rather one to amuse a person that we don't care to offend, but I may mistake him, which time must prove; for I cannot ask any more for the same thing. There is no Accounting for peoples' jealousy on these occasions. Therefore if the fixing of Dockum Lines depends absolutely upon those plats the work must be deferr'd until a more favourable opportunity. I remain, &ca.—

SOURCE: Letterbook copy, Letter Book of Henry Laurens, Oct. 30, 1762– Sept. 10, 1766, Penn. Hist. Soc.; addressed "Esquire."

TO JOHN HENTIE

[Charles Town] 23d May 1765

Sir,

Since writing the annexed your further favor of this date is come to hand, but Charles did not leave the two Letters mentioned therein. If he had they would have been immediately deliver'd, which probably is done by some other hands.

As to the plats so much wanted by us I am confirm'd in my opinion of never seeing them, from a new circumstance of this Evening. Mr. Deas stop'd me on the Bay & said Mrs. Caw was come to Town, had looked over one Class of papers without success, that when she went to St. John's she would make a search among papers there & if she found them they should be sent to me. This does not quite tally with the answer made a little prior to the 7th Inst. but it looks very like that sort of answer which I hinted on the other side. I suppose the poor Lady fears that some use may be made of those plats to her prejudice & if so, as there is no way to remove her apprehensions it is in vain to place any dependance upon her aid.

I purpose to go from Charles Town early on Monday next. I remain, &ca.—

SOURCE: Letterbook copy, Letter Book of Henry Laurens, Oct. 30, 1762– Sept. 10, 1766, Penn. Hist. Soc.; addressed "Esquire."

TO SAMUEL WRAGG

[Charles Town] 24th May 1765

Sir,

I have Rec'd both your favours of the 8th & 13th Inst. and with the former an Account of outstanding debts for 17 Negroes on our joint Account which will serve to perfect my entries.

I have accepted & shall in due time pay your Bill to Mr. Pouag[7] £615.10/. That to Paul Trappier, Esquire £350, is paid by discount on a Note of Mr. Forbes's[8] who tender'd it, & I now send you inclosed Edward Young & Micajah Williams's[9] Bond with Interest thereon to the 7th Inst. £332, with a Receipt on the back as you direct & charge the said Sum to your debit.

If you can buy 500 or 800 Barrels of good hard Pitch full Weight & as much over as you can get it in good Barrels well hoop'd & trimed at George Town deliver'd there any time before the 10th July at £3.5/ to £3.6.3 per Barrel your Commission or profits included, please to purchase them on my Account & give me Notice by the first opportunity that I may send my own Schooner to take them in. But I should observe that it may not be convenient for me to pay for them in any shorter time than two or three Months from the delivery for which your draughts shall be duly honour'd. I have the employ of my Schooner partly in view by this offer & partly the hopes of obtaining Freight upon low terms. Therefore if you have no hopes of succeeding I confide in you not to mention that I have made such an offer as it may offend other purchasers, as I believe this is the highest that has been made, & perhaps I may fail in my prospect of Freight. I remain, &ca.—

SOURCE: Letterbook copy, Letter Book of Henry Laurens, Oct. 30, 1762–Sept. 10, 1766, Penn. Hist. Soc.; addressed "George Town."

---

[7] John Poaug. *HL Papers*, III, 163n.
[8] John Forbes.
[9] Micajah Williams as constable on May 25, 1764, presented a certificate from Archibald Baird and George Gabriel Powell, justices of the peace for Craven County, asking for reimbursement for a Negro who had been executed. On July 3, the assembly allowed £200. House Journal, XXXVI (Jan. 24, 1763–Oct. 6, 1764), 35, 92, S. C. Archives.

TO FRANCIS STUART

[Charles Town] 24th May 1765

Sir,

I here inclose your Account with Interest calculated thereon to the 1st June & a Balance that will be then due to me of £1,979.7.7, which I request you to examine & if found right that you will order it to be paid or send me your Note or Bond payable at a more convenient time.

I am going upon a journey which will keep me some time from home & shall be glad to have as many of my open Accounts settled before my departure as can be accomplished & I have no reason to think you will disappoint me. If there happens to be any little error please to amend the Account that such may not stand in bar of an adjustment. I remain, &ca.—

SOURCE: Letterbook copy, Letter Book of Henry Laurens, Oct. 30, 1762–Sept. 10, 1766, Penn. Hist. Soc.; addressed "Esquire. Beaufort."

TO JOHN HENTIE

[Charles Town] 30th May 1765

Sir,

Agreeable to what I wrote to you I went to Mepkin on Monday,[1] but not thro St. Thomas's because it being Holiday times some volunteer friends desired to accompany me, which I could not refuse & our Horses, Chair, &ca. were too numerous & troublesome to be ferried across the River. This & another circumstance in which Mr. Peter Broughton was pleased for a while to make himself principal actor, the particulars of which you may learn from Mr. James Marion, prevented my going as I had fully designed to see my good friends at Hyde Park & Kensington & where I expected also to have had the pleasure of taking you by the hand. As to the Survey of Dockum I can only repeat that if the work depends upon a sight of Mr. Goughs Plats it must be postponed, for I have very slender hopes of access to them at this time: & I shall very thankfully for all the time you have lost upon this occasion.

I intend about the 15th or 20th June to go to Wambaw & round to Mepkin or round the other way so as to be at both, if Ahab

[1]Monday was May 27.

does not in the meantime kill me for the sake of my vineyard, & I shall be glad to know in which Neighbourhood you will be about that time. I remain, &ca.—

SOURCE: Letterbook copy, Letter Book of Henry Laurens, Oct. 30, 1762– Sept. 10, 1766, Penn. Hist. Soc.; addressed "Esquire."

TO PETER HORLBECK

[Charles Town] 30th May 1765

Sir,

I send Scipio with three Horses & desire Mr. Smith to do his utmost to put them into very good order for me by the 15th June which you will inform him of & shew him this Letter.

I also send by the same hand Two Frows,[2] Six Files, one pound of thread, & two Bundles of Baby Cloths. Mr. Russel[3] was to have wrote down what Carpenters tools he would want. He may send the memorandum by you. Order Scipio away immediately to walk down unless the grey Horse is found then he may ride him. Let me hear how the Sick Negroes are & what the Doctor has done for them. I shall see you on Saturday not sooner. I remain, &ca.—

SOURCE: Letterbook copy, Letter Book of Henry Laurens, Oct. 30, 1762– Sept. 10, 1766, Penn. Hist. Soc.; addressed "Mepkin."

TO JOHN SMITH

[Charles Town] 30th May 1765

Sir,

As you have undertaken the care of my Mepkin Plantation & for which I have agreed with you upon your own terms & something better but no abatement; I shall expect that you will in every respect study & promote my Interest & behave like an honest Man.

I have at present to recommend to you the care of my Negroes in general but particularly the Sick ones. Desire Mrs. White not to

---

[2] A frow or froe was "a wedge-shaped tool used for cleaning and riving staves, shingles, etc. It has a handle in the plane of the blade, set at right angles to the back." *OED*.

[3] James Russel was a carpenter doing some work for HL at Mepkin.

be sparing of Red wine for those that have the Flux or bad Loose-nesses. Let them be well attended Night & day. If one Wench is not sufficient add another to nurse them.

With the well ones use gentle means mixed with easy authority first. If that does not succeed make choice of the most stubborn one or two & chastise them severely but properly & with mercy that they may be convinced the end of correction is to be amendment. The Boat will soon be with you. Load her with Wood if you can, otherwise Fresh Water sand. Take good care of my three Horses, Roan, Chero-kee, & Gibson, & the Grey if he is found. I shall thank you to have them in good order by the 15th June at farthest. I remain, &ca.—

SOURCE: Letterbook copy, Letter Book of Henry Laurens, Oct. 30, 1762–Sept. 10, 1766, Penn. Hist. Soc.; addressed "Mepkin."

TO JOHN SMITH

[Charles Town] 4th June 1765

Sir,

Scipio went away yesterday upon the Black Horse with a bundle of Spice. He gave me no notice & therefore has no Letter. Please to take good care of that Horse also.

You will receive sundry articles as per inclosed list now by the Schooner. The rice is intended to be given now & then for the New Negroes or any other that shall happen to be Sick, for which purposes you will distribute it.

Load the Boat as well as you can & take care to prevent an intercourse between Boat & Plantation Negroes & let me know how Abram the Patroon of the Boat behaves. I remain, &ca.—

[P.S.] I hear that Mr. Andrew Broughton is going to run a Line between him & Mepkin. Please take good Notice of it.

SOURCE: Letterbook copy, Letter Book of Henry Laurens, Oct. 30, 1762–Sept. 10, 1766, Penn. Hist. Soc.; addressed "Mepkin."

TO ANDREW BROUGHTON

[Charles Town] 4th June 1765

Sir,

In Answer to your two last Letters permit me to say—

1st, that I am quite tired with the subject of running your line. You may do as you please upon your own Land & if I was to write a Volume I could add nothing new to what I have said over & over again.

2d, the Money due for your Corn & pease shall be paid to you or any body that you shall order to call at my House for it. I am, &ca.—

SOURCE: Letterbook copy, Letter Book of Henry Laurens, Oct. 30, 1762–Sept. 10, 1766, Penn. Hist. Soc.; addressed "Stafford." Beginning with "I could add" this letter was copied by HL.

TO ABRAHAM SCHAD

[Charles Town] 7th June 1765

Sir,

I send you by the *Wambaw*—

> The Epsom Salt
> 3 Bottles Rhubarb
> Twenty Seven Negroes ⎫
> their names inclosed ⎭
> 90 Yards Negro Cloth & some thread
> 18 Felt Hatts at 13/9
> 2 pieces blue Linnen at 7/6
> White Linnen 32 Yards at 8/9

Make use of this Negro Cloth as you shall find it wanted for my Negroes, but first let the Boys that now go in the Boat have each a Jacket, a good Jacket, made & one of them the least will want a pair of Trowsers. What remains of the Cloth lay by until it is further wanted.

Dont forget to send me two Barrels of Chaff.

I recommend these new Negroes particularly to your care & Mrs. Schads. When you find Medicine wanted, dont neglect to order it immediately from Town by a Boy from Mr. Fogarties Landing which is the most expeditious way. I remain, &ca.—

SOURCE: Letterbook copy, Letter Book of Henry Laurens, Oct. 30, 1762–Sept. 10, 1766, Penn. Hist. Soc.; addressed "Wambaw."

ADVERTISEMENT

June 8, 1765

THE Subscribers, administrators to the estate of John Asline, merchant, deceased, request all persons that have any demands on the said estate, to send them in immediately, and receive payment; as there is to be a speedy settlement of the affairs relating to the said estate, with one appointed from England.[4]

HENRY LAURENS
THOMAS LEGARE

SOURCE: Printed in *Gazette*, June 8, 1765.

SEIZURE OF NEGROES

June 10, 1765

[*On March 7, 1763, attorney for Governor Thomas Boone had filed suit in the court of common pleas against Isham Andrews, planter of St. Bartholomew parish,[5] for recovery of a bond, dated March 4, 1763, in the sum of £810 currency. Andrews through his attorney Thomas Bee confessed judgment. The judgment was signed on March 7, 1763. On May 14, 1764, a judgment was issued in the case of Austin et al versus Isham Andrews. Although there is no judgment roll for this case, it would appear that Laurens proceeded to execute his judgment and that Boone never had. On June 10, 1765, James Postell wrote Fenwicke Bull that on an execution of Colonel Laurens the Negroes of Isham Andrews had been seized by Provost Marshal Roger Pinckney who intended to sell them "tomorrow or next Day." Postell was concerned for the interest of Governor Boone who had obtained an Execution whose "Judgment Must be pryer to his Execution." Postell had also heard that Isham Andrews had given a bond to Legare & Darquin who had obtained a judgment prior even to that of Boone.*]

---

[4] John Davies the younger had come out from Lincoln, England to settle the affairs of the estate of John Asline. See Advertisement, Oct. 29, 1763.

[5] Isham Andrews was the son-in-law of Joseph Norman of Colleton County who died in November 1764. On July 27, 1770 Isham Andrews witnessed the will of Barak Norman, blacksmith of St. Paul parish. *Abstracts of Wills, 1760–1784*, pp. 48, 145.

SOURCE: Judgment Rolls, No. 6A, S. C. Archives; Judgment Docket, Court of Common Pleas, Book 2 (1755–1773), pp. 79, 99, S. C. Archives.

T O   H E C T O R   B E R E N G E R   D E   B E A U F A I N [6]

[Charles Town] 18th June 1765

Sir,

I have now wrote in such terms by Capt. Thomas Shute bound to Tortola,[7] as I am under no doubt will at least procure me a positive answer whether the Shippers of the Melasses on board the Brigantine *Good-intent*[8] from Tortola are entituled to a Certificate or not. If they are, a Certificate will be conveyed to me by the first opportunity from that Island.

I therefore humbly request you, Sir, to indulge me three Months longer, if you can without danger of blame or censure. Otherwise after thankfully acknowledging your past forbearance, I shall immediately pay down the foreign duty to which that importation stands liable, altho in such case I have but slender hopes of a reimbursement. I am, &ca.—

SOURCE: Letterbook copy, Letter Book of Henry Laurens, Oct. 30, 1762–Sept. 10, 1766, Penn. Hist. Soc.; addressed "The Honorable. Esquire."

T O   J O H N   M U I R [9]

[Charles Town] 18th June 1765

Sir,

You are very obliging in taking Six little Turtle on board your Ship from me. They are for Lord Albermarle in Berkley Square

---

[6] Hector Berenger de Beaufain, the collector of customs, having been a member of the royal council, 1747–1756, was entitled to be addressed as "Honourable." *HL Papers*, I, 13n; M. Eugene Sirmans, "The South Carolina Royal Council, 1720–1763," *William and Mary Quarterly*, XVIII (1961), 392.

[7] The sloop *Friendship*, Thomas Shute, sailed for Tortola on June 19. *Gazette*, June 22, 1765. Thomas Shute was a Quaker. *HL Papers*, I, 58.

[8] The brigantine *Good Intent*, Thomas Hardy, was entered inwards on Oct. 10, 1763, from Tortola with a cargo of 20 hogsheads of rum and 17 hogsheads of molasses. Naval Office Lists, 1757–1764, p. 123.

[9] The ship *Little Carpenter*, John Muir, sailed June 23 for London. *Gazette*, June 29, 1765.

& his Lordship will order a Crown piece to be given for each Turtle that is deliver'd at his House alive. This is rather more than the Turtle are worth in Carolina & I hope will compensate the trouble that your honest Lads will have in watering & feeding them on the Voyage. I wish you a prosperous one & remain, Sir, &ca.—

SOURCE: Letterbook copy, Letter Book of Henry Laurens, Oct. 30, 1762–Sept. 10, 1766, Penn. Hist. Soc.; addressed "Captain. Charles Town."

REGISTRATION OF THE SCHOONER DEPENDANCE[1]

June 18, 1765

South Carolina. In Pursuance of an Act made in the seventh & eighth of King William the third intituled an Act for preventing Frauds & regulating abuses in the Plantation Trade Henry Lawrens of Charlestown Merchant maketh Oath that the Schooner *Dependance* of Charlestown whereof David Walker is at present Master being a Square Stern'd Vessell of Ten Tons or thereabouts was built in this Province this present Year and that he the Deponant is at present owner thereof and that no foreigner, directly or indirectly, hath any Share or part or Interest therein. Dated at the Custom House Charlestown the Eighteenth day of June, One Thousand Seven hundred and Sixty five.

Henry Lawrens.

SOURCE: Ship Register, 1734–1765, p. 249, S. C. Archives. The seals of Lt. Gov. William Bull and of Collector of the Customs Hector Berenger de Beaufain were affixed to the left margin of the document.

TO JAMES GRANT

[Charles Town, 21st June 1765]

Now, Sir, having run briefly over the contents of your Excellency's last Letter, permit me to enter upon the Subject of the *Dependance,* Pilot Boat, which at length lies afloat & ready for Sea

---

[1]HL had had Charles Minors build this pilot boat for James Grant. See Articles of Agreement for a Pilot Boat for East Florida, Dec. 27, 1764.

or within a few Hours of being so. When she was launched the Builder[2] called upon me for a Name, the *Dependance* occured as one a propos & it happened at the same time to be felt by that almost insensible crabbed Creature as a more severe Rebuke than any thing I had said or could say to him for his unmercifull delay.[3]

If I was to enumerate a quarter of the trouble that Boat has given me I know it would make you uneasy. Therefore, I will only say that I have been as diligent about her as if all my mercantile happiness hung solely on her Dispatch, have fretted more than ever I did in all my life time about all my own Affairs, nay more. The Wretches have twice provoked me to Swear. The last time I was so wicked as to call them a pack of damned Pick Pockets & ordered in the Violence of my Resentments one of the Fellows to a place reputed to be hotter than Savanna. Not only the Carpenters have plagued me but other Fellows seeing their tricks followed their bad Examples. I engaged and turned away within two days three Captains, two of them because they would not rise as early as I did and other Neglects, and one because he was good for nothing.[4]

Providence I hope has favoured me at least in Captain Peter Bachop[5] who was yesterday dismissed from his late Employment by owners who declared to me, that they had no other fault to lay to him but that he was too Young. Be that as it may he has done more for me this day than the other three would have done in a Month I am sure. Indeed a Ship of my Own luckily fell in last Sunday & I have employed the Master & his Crew almost ever since upon this important Business of Rigging and fitting the Boat & hastning and helping the Carpenters, &ca. to give the finishing Stroke.[6]

After saying so much truth to that Man's (the Carpenter's) disgrace, it becomes me as there is room to say one Word in his favour. Mr. Rose,[7] Mr. Tucker,[8] Capt. Dennison, Mr. Manigault[9]

---

[2] Charles Minors.

[3] Minors had promised to complete the vessel by March 10 for £577.10/.

[4] One of these may have been David Walker who had been listed as the master in the registration of June 18.

[5] Peter Bachop may have been a younger brother of Adam Bachop who had been a regular on the St. Augustine-Charleston run. Capt. Peter Bachop, "formerly of St. Augustine," died at New Providence in 1785, *SCHM*, XIX (1918), 170.

[6] The ship *Flora*, Thomas Courtin, arrived on Sunday June 16 from Poole. *Gazette*, June 22, 1765.

[7] John Rose.

[8] Thomas Tucker.

[9] Gabriel Manigault.

who is a very good Judge, unanimously declare their good liking of
the Boat, say she is clever, well put together, &ca., and Tucker desires
me to assure Your Excellency, that he had carefully examined her
Frame, found it exceeding good and that in his Opinion she was as
fit a Vessell as could be built for the purposes in View. They say she
has too much Mast and Sails. Her whole Cost will be about £200
Sterling, but I believe all the Bills will not be adjusted before she
Sails, and I will not detain her one Moment on that Account, but
send the needfull Documents by Messrs. Shirley and Martin's
Schooner, to sail two or three Days after her.[1]

Peter Bachop is engaged at £5 Sterling per Month, without
any Priviledges, the same Wages that were allowed in his late employ,
and I have given him leave to Ship one white hand. If You have no
Service for the Master after delivering the Boat, you will no doubt
allow him upon the whole two Months Pay and send him back to me.

SOURCE: Extract, CO 5/540, pp. 435–436, Public Record Office, London.
Endorsed: "Extract of a Letter from Henry Laurens Esq. to Governor
Grant dated Charles Town 21st June 1765."

ACCOUNT OF THE COST OF
A PILOT BOAT

21 June 1765

An Exact & true Account of the Cost of a Pilot Boat called the
Dependance built at Charles Town in So. Carolina by order of James
Grant, Esquire, Governor of East Florida for the use of the Bar of
St. Augustine including the cost of Provission to carry her round, but
not the expence of Navigation nor charge for my own Commission
for labour, trouble, & advance of Money—

---

[1] Shirley & Martin had purchased the schooner *Mary*, Adam Bachop, which
they had registered on Jan. 13, 1765. Ship Register, 1734–1765, pp. 243–244, S.
C. Archives. The schooner *Mary*, Peter Bachop, had arrived on June 17 from St.
Augustine. *Gazette*, June 22, 1765. HL must have persuaded Peter Bachop to take
over the *Dependance* after his arrival from St. Augustine. The schooner *Dependance*, Peter Bachop, which had been cleared for St. Augustine, was reported wind-
bound on June 22. She sailed on June 24. *Gazette*, June 22, 29, 1765. The schooner *Mary*, Thomas Hardy, sailed for St. Augustine on June 30. *Gazette*, July 6,
1765. HL collected rebates of £7.10/ for one slave shipped per Bachop for St.
Augustine and £22.10/ on four slaves shipped per Hardy for St. Augustine. Public
Treasurer, Journal B: Duties, 1748–1765, p. 445, S. C. Archives.

To Charles Minors for the Hull, Masts, Yards, Booms, ⎫
    Bowsprit, Oacum, Turpentine, some Nails, & ⎬ £ 577.10
    Expence at Launching ⎭
To Nowel & Lord[2]—1 Anchor & Iron Stock ....   ₥ 20.14
To Frederick Augustine[3]—Iron Work ....   ₥ 78. 3. 6
To James Elsinaure[4]—Block Maker's Bill's ....   ₥ 29.16. 3
To Miller & Fullerton[5]—Joiners Bill ....   ₥ 44. 5.11
To Burrowes & Wagner[6]—Painters ....   ₥ 20.
To Cash paid Price, Hest, & Head for ⎫
    Cordage & Sundry Stores per Ac- ⎬ 215. 3. 3
    count herewith Inclos'd Amount ⎭
"   "   for 5 pieces Sail Duck No. 1 ⎫
    Quantity 198 Yards at 9/9........ ⎪
    12 Yards Duck No. 1 ...... at 10/, ⎬ 102.10. 6
    the usual Price is 10/6 per Yard ⎭
"   "   for 43 lbs. Bolt Rope at 3/ 6. 9
"   "   for 175 lbs. Deck & Planking Nails
    £30.12.6—150 20d ditto 11/3........   31. 3. 9
"   "   to David Thomson[7]—Iron Work....   2.
"   "   to John Rexford—Services..............   3. 2
"   "   for a Caboose & 2 Iron polls.............   7.
"   "   for a Register 7.10
"   "   for a Hatchet 12/6—1 Bucket Iron
    Hoops 12/6 ....   1. 5
"   "   for 3 Oars £4.10/—3 Water Casks
    filled & filling £3.15/........................   8. 5
"   "   for 2 Half Barrels Rice £8—1 Cask
    Ship Bread £4.6/ 12. 6
"   "   for a Barrel Pork £12.1/—600
    Bricks & Carting for Ballast £4......   16. 1
"   "   for a Barrel pitch £4—1 Barrel &
    half Barrel Tar £4.10 ....   8.10

---

[2] John Nowell and Andrew Lord.

[3] Frederick Augustine was a witness of the will of Isaac Battoon, a planter of St. John Colleton, dated Oct. 14, 1769. *Abstracts of Wills, 1760–1784*, p. 171.

[4] James Elsinore was a pilot and block maker. Judgment Rolls, 1766, No. 18A; 1768, No. 497A, S. C. Archives.

[5] In 1766–1768 Miller and Fullerton built the rectory for St. Michael's Church. George W. Williams, *St. Michael's, Charleston, 1751–1951* (Columbia, S. C., 1951), pp. 195–198. Miller also built Edward Rutledge's and David Ramsay's houses on Broad St. Beatrice St. Julien Ravenel, *Architects of Charleston* (Charleston, S. C., 1945), pp. 36–38. A John Miller witnessed the will of Thomas Cole, bricklayer, on Oct. 21, 1771. *Abstracts of Wills, 1760–1784*, p. 162. John Fullerton, house carpenter, was a Scotsman and a prominent member of the Sons of Liberty. Joseph Johnson, *Traditions and Reminiscences chiefly of the American Revolution in the South* (Charleston, S. C., 1851), pp. 31–32.

[6] The editors have been unable to identify the painters Burrowes and Wagner.

[7] David Thomson, blacksmith, died in 1770. "Will of David Thomson," dated Dec. 20, 1770, proved Dec. 31, 1770, Charleston County Wills, XIII, Book C (1767–1771), 962–963, S. C. Archives.

"   "   to Walker[8] & the *Flora*'s People[9]....   20.
"   "   to Thomas Mace[1]—Making Sails....   31.16. 3   473. 1. 9

£1,243.11. 5

Charles Town, So. Carolina
21 June 1765
Errors Excepted
per Henry Laurens
Receiv'd 21st June 1765 of His Excellency James Grant, Esquire
One Thousand, two Hundred & forty three Pounds, eleven shillings, &
five pence in full for the true & exact Cost of the Pilot Boat *Dependance,*
exclusive of the Navigation from Charles Town to St. Augustine & of
any Commission to my self for advance of Money, labour, & trouble as
per the within Account.

Henry Laurens
Triplicate
£1,243.11.5 Carolina Money

N.B.   The five Articles marked with the red Letter *ω* were not payed
when Mr. Laurens transmitted the above Account to Governor
Grant.

Alexander Skinner
Clerk of the publick Accounts

June 21, 1765
Account of the Consideration Money inserted in the Bill of Sale for the
Dependance Pilot Boat. 21st June 1765.

1st. The Amount of the real cost of the said Boat
as per three Accounts thereof with a Receipt   £1,243.11.5
upon each ....

2d. Expence of Navigation round from Charles Town
to East Florida

3d. To Capt. Bachop   Sterling £10
a white Man allow'd him   4
3 Negroes who are to stop
at Augustine & not return   2

£16 at 700 per Cent   112.

£1,355.11.5

---

[8] David Walker.
[9] The crew of Capt. Thomas Courtin's ship.
[1] In 1761 Thomas Mace sued Archibald Johnstone, Georgetown planter, for
three years (Nov. 28, 1745 to Nov. 28, 1748) back wages as master of a brigantine
at £40 per month. Judgment Rolls, 1761, No. 160A, S. C. Archives. On Sept. 11,
1755 he as owner and master registered the sloop *Pony* at Georgetown. Ship Register, 1734–1765, p. 144, S. C. Archives.

My Commission 5 per Cent   67.15.7
                                                      _____
                                                      £1,423. 7

£1,423.7/ Current Money at 721 per Cent Exchange is £197.8.4 Sterling
                        Charles Town, So. Carolina, 21st June 1765
                                  Errors Excepted
                                                   Henry Laurens

SOURCE: ADS, East Florida, CO 5/540, pp. 429–434, Public Record
Office, London. Endorsed: "Total Charge of Henry Laurens, Esquire for
the *Dependance* Pilot Boat for the Port of St. Augustine"; "In the Governor's Letter of 16 July 1765"; "Read June 26, 1766."

TO JOHN LOGAN

                                      [Charles Town] 26th June 1765
Dear Sir,

       I am very largely in advance for Mr. Rutherford & was never
more in want of Money for my own use. The 25th June that long
extended Limit for payment of part of the King's Warrant is now
passed; therefore I hope you have reaped such fruits from the late
Advertisements to & private calls upon the delinquents in the General
Rent Roll that I may be thereby benefited this Morning by the return
of a few thousands, spare me as much as you can & you will very
much oblige—

[*P.S.*] The Net Proceeds of the last parcel of Rice may be in Cash—

SOURCE: Letterbook copy, Letter Book of Henry Laurens, Oct. 30, 1762–
Sept. 10, 1766, Penn. Hist. Soc.; addressed "Esquire. Deputy Receiver
General."

TO JOHN LOGAN

                                        [Charles Town] 28 June 1765
Dear Sir,

       I have so much confidence in the rectitude of your acts as
Deputy Receiver General that I shall not think of inspecting or
examining your Accounts but I must own that it appears clear to

me that the R. G. himself[2] has money in possession which ought to have been paid to Mr. Rutherford.

As to the Balance that will remain on the £3,500 now in your hands I wish it could be asscertained & paid to me. As I said before I am largely in advance for Mr. Rutherford & for some other friends, can collect no Money in the ordinary course of Trade, & never was in greater want. To ward off a dunn which I am not us'd to & therefore if it comes will be more irksome. If you can assist me please to tell Mr. Perdriau & how far, if not I must apply elsewhere. I am lame otherwise should have waited on you. I am, &ca.—

SOURCE: Letterbook copy, Letter Book of Henry Laurens, Oct. 30, 1762–Sept. 10, 1766, Penn. Hist. Soc.; addressed "Esquire. Deputy Receiver General."

TO JOHN GORDON

[Charles Town] 28th June 1765

Dear Sir,

Excuse me for not sending the inclosed Account sooner. I have not been very well. The Balance is as I inserted in the general Account £4,922.0.5, but I perceive Mr. Appleby has added £19.10/ for Interest on £750 due 1st January 1760.

I know no more of my Bill for £500 on Mr. Elliott than is set forth in that said General Account. Nevertheless as I believe the whole is secured in Mr. Habersham's hands, tho to be paid in July or at his convenience, that shall be no obstacle to an adjustment between us.

Mr. Hume still solemnly avers that the Wine was purchased on that joint Account under which I charged it. Therefore I hope & beg that you will not insist upon my changing or altering the origi-nal[3] before some proof is produced that he made use of your name to defraud or deceive me. In that event we shall both, you & I, have cause to resent his behaviour but I only, must submit to loose or struggle thro all dificulties to recover what remains unpaid. Mean-time as I heartily wish to close all those long depending reconings, if

---

[2] Receiver-general of quit rents.
[3] "Entry" was written here but crossed out.

the opinion of a third person will be agreeable to you, please to name one Gentleman of our acquaintance & I will abide by his determination of that affair. I remain, &ca.—

SOURCE: Letterbook copy, Letter Book of Henry Laurens, Oct. 30, 1762–Sept. 10, 1766, Penn. Hist. Soc.; addressed "Esquire. Bay Street."

TO WILLIAM SMITH

[Charles Town] 28th June 1765

Dear Sir,

I am sorry that Mr. Perdriau omitted to send you a Bill of parcels for the 17 pieces of Oznabrug & Bale of Negro Cloth per Capt. Mitchel as your favour of the 19th Inst. informs me but you will find one here inclosed. Please to let me know if you require any abatement & how much, on the Cloth that I may enter it to your Credit.

I have no Rum at my House but have desired Capt. Blake[4] who had some of mine for Sale to Ship you two Hogsheads of West India Rum provided it is good & you will find his Bill inclosed the Amount of which I shall settle with him & charge to your Account.

I send you by this bearer 100 Red Herrings as good as any in Pedee & wish they may be acceptable.

My family thank God is pretty well & glad that some of my fellow travellers shrunk from their engagement & leaves me at home for this Summer.

After putting me to some trouble & some expence, all things ready, when the day was at hand, one had bought a Yoke of Oxen & another had got the gout & so ended a long Journey before it began. I had prepared these Red Herrings for that purpose. My Love & respects attend your family & I remain, &ca.—

SOURCE: Letterbook copy, Letter Book of Henry Laurens, Oct. 30, 1762–Sept. 10, 1766, Penn. Hist. Soc.; addressed "George Town."

---

[4] Capt. Edward Blake.

TO JOSEPH BROWN

[Charles Town] 28th June 1765

Dear Sir,

John Thomas[5] deliver'd me your favor of the 25th Inst. & also the 21 for 20 Cedar Logs therein mentioned, the contents & Amount of which you have here inclosed & passed to your Credit 36.15/ & for which I thank you. This is all the Account that I can give you of the value of such stuff since I know of no other price than that fixed by Mr. Wragg & you.

I have put up a bundle of Red Herrings which Mrs. Laurens thinks may not come amiss to Mrs. Brown. We join in Love to her & all your family.

By this Schooner I have consigned you as able & as likely a Negro Man named Sampson as most in the Province. I imported him about 14 Months ago & sent him with others to my Mepkin Plantation where after a very few days the Overseer a very harsh fellow drove him off. He went to Santé & fell in with a poor worthless fellow who entertained him near 8 Months. At length fearing an information from some of the neighbourhood who had seen the Negro working for him, he made a merit of his knavery & sends Sampson down to me. In the meantime he Learned to make Indigo or at least to work at it & to speak tolerable good English. I ordered him (without punishment) to work in the field again, but he soon quitted it & returned to his former range which proves that he had not been unkindly treated there, but the Knave who first harbour'd him heard that I was collecting evidence to found a prosecution against him for his first act, & therefore sent or caused him to be sent immediately to my Plantation, from whence he was sent down here, because I will not keep a runaway & indeed this is the first & only one that ever I had to be a bad example to the rest of my slaves who are in general very orderly & give me but little trouble. Whether Sampson may be deemed a runaway from the foregoing Account is a question. However let somebody else by more experience resolve it for I will not. He cost me full £320 altho I imported him, besides that I may add £30 for Clothing & charges. Please to sell him to a safe hand for the best price you can & send me the proceeds in Money or Bond as you shall happen to agree, provided you will charge your Commission on

---

[5] John Thomas, Jr., of Craven County died in 1768. "Will of John Thomas, Jr.," dated June 27, 1767, proved June 14, 1768. *Abstracts of Wills, 1760–1784*, p. 106.

the Sale. Otherwise deliver him to George Dick or any other of my acquaintance to sell for me informing them of his character. I remain, &ca.—

SOURCE: Letterbook copy, Letter Book of Henry Laurens, Oct. 30, 1762–Sept. 10, 1766, Penn. Hist. Soc.; addressed "George Town."

TO JOHN HANDLIN

[Charles Town, July 1765]

Sir,

I Received a Release for 500 Acres of Land part of Snows 1,800 Acre Tract & the last Receipt for Quit Rents due on 350 Acres belonging to you & also your directions to pay up the arrears on both in your favour of the 25th June per Mr. Cooper.

I find there is due on the five hundred Acre Tract

to the 25th March last 29 Years, 7 Months, 18 days £151. 5.10[6]
including about £3.10/ for charges.
And upon the 350 Acre Tract for 21 Years .... 73.10[7]
                                                          _____
                                                          £224.15.10

in the whole Two Hundred & twenty four pounds 15/10. A great Sum arising from such long delay.

The Grant to Snow specifies the Quit Rent to be payable at 4/ Proc. from the date as per Certificate from the Secretary's Office here inclosed.

I don't know how you can avoid paying the whole & indeed I would advise you to give orders to discharge it soon as the Receiver General is now obliged to be very strict, but I will defer doing it

---

[6] Nathaniel Snow had received a grant to 2,000 acres on Aug. 7, 1735 at a quit rent of 3/ sterling (4/ proclamation) per 100 acres. Royal Grants, 1, 622, S. C. Archives. Snow had paid no quit rents for 29 years, 7 months, and 18 days after Aug. 7, 1735, which would have been until March 25, 1765, the last date upon which quit rents had been due.

[7] John Handlen, the father of the addressee of this letter, had received a grant to 350 acres on the south side of the north branch of Black River on May 24, 1734. Royal Grants, 1, 321, S. C. Archives. Since lands in townships were exempt from quit rents for ten years, there had been no payment on Handlen's lands for the 21 years following 1744.

until I hear from you again lest there should be some error, as the Account differs so widely from your expectations.[8]

My compliments to your Mother & all the family & I remain, Sir, &ca.—

SOURCE: Letterbook copy, Letter Book of Henry Laurens, Oct. 30, 1762–Sept. 10, 1766, Penn. Hist. Soc.; addressed "Black Mingo"; "per Capt. Dick."

TO WILLIAM THOMPSON

[Charles Town] 5th July 1765

Dear Sir,

Mr. Dick delivered me on your Account 26 Barrels Turpentine for which I must allow you the extravagant price of 30/ per hundred as per Account inclosed.

I hope you will have more ready & also Pitch to embrace so good a Market. My respects to Mrs. Thompson and all your family, & I remain, &Ca.—

SOURCE: Letterbook copy, Letter Book of Henry Laurens, Oct. 30, 1762–Sept. 10, 1766, Penn. Hist. Soc.; addressed "Black Mingo."

DIARY OF JOHN BARTRAM [9]

July 7, 1765

About 8 in the morning A pilot came & by 10 cast anchor agains[t] the fort of James island & by 12 came to my worthy dear friend Doctor Gardens[1] very faint. Toward night visited Mr. Hop-

---

[8] The editors have searched Quit Rents, Receipts and Disbursements, 1760–1768, 1768–1774, S. C. Archives but have found no entries to indicate that these quit rents were ever paid. Alan Watson found that persons who lived at a distance from Charleston were less likely to pay their quit rents. Alan D. Watson, "The Quitrent System in Royal South Carolina" (unpub. PhD diss., Univ. of South Carolina, 1971), pp. 125–128.

[9] John Bartram, the American botanist, who was beginning his first journey of exploration through the Southern colonies, arrived in the schooner *East Florida*, Captain Bachop, from Philadelphia. *Gazette*, July 13, Aug. 26, 1765. The *East Florida*, Adam Bachop, 15 tons, 4 men, was entered inwards on July 11 from St. Augustine (which must have been an error for Philadelphia). Naval Office Lists, 1764–1767, p. 83.

[1] Dr. Alexander Garden.

ton[2] & Col. Henery laurance who is makeing great improvements in gardenin[g].[3]

SOURCE: Bartram, *Diary of a Journey*, p. 13.

TO ABRAHAM SCHAD

[Charles Town] 9 July 1765

Sir,

I am sorry to hear so bad an account of the Plantation Negroes, but these visitations will happen & when they do, we must exert ourselves to guard against their worst effect & take a little more thought & use extraordinary diligence in attending those that are attack'd in the very first appearance.

I send you salts & Rhubarb, 4 Bottles of Turlington, & some powders to be given, after the Bowels are emptied with Salts & Rhubarb, 30 or 40 Grains in a little gruel Morning & Evening, to a Man & so in proportion for a Woman & weaker persons. Do you try 2 or 3 Grains of Hyppo.[4] every morning just to give one Motion, this is recommended as a good method to treat the flux.

If you did not order Jack to come to Town I desire you will give him proper chastisement for coming. Send a Letter down again to inform me how you go on as soon as possible & if Port Wine or anything else is wanted let me know. Send the Cart down in that case & order the Boy to wait till the Boat returns & write to Mr. Fogartie to send your Letter immediately. I remain, &ca.—

SOURCE: Letterbook copy, Letter Book of Henry Laurens, Oct. 30, 1762–Sept. 10, 1766, Penn. Hist. Soc.; addressed "Wambaw."

---

[2] Bartram had probably met William Hopton the previous year in Philadelphia.
[3] David Ramsay wrote that HL and Mrs. Laurens "with the assistance of John Watson, a complete English gardener," had created a magnificent garden. David Ramsay, *History of South Carolina, From its First Settlement in 1670 to the Year 1808* (2 vols.: Charleston, S. C., 1858), II, 128.
[4] A salt of hyposulphurous acid. *OED.*

TO SAMUEL WRAGG

[Charles Town] 9th July 1765

Sir,

I am much obliged to you for the great trouble you have taken to procure me the Cedar & red Bay & shall pass the whole Amount the Cost per Bill which came in your favor of the 26th Ulto. to your Credit, Vizt. £55.14.6, altho only 11 of the Bay Loggs are come to hand. The poor Man that owned them has had abundant trouble & after all lost five of those pieces but the loss shall not fall upon him. I think they are not dear. I send you a bundle of 100 Red Herrings which are some times a rarity & I hope may be acceptable to you. I remain, &Ca.—

SOURCE: Letterbook copy, Letter Book of Henry Laurens, Oct. 30, 1762– Sept. 10, 1766, Penn. Hist. Soc.; addressed "George Town."

TO JAMES MARION

[Charles Town] 10 July 1765

Dear Sir,

My Schooner has been a most unreasonable time in getting Shells till at Length I was oblig'd to send a Cannoe in search of her & to order her up. She now carries a full load & will lay half of it down at Hagan.[5] She likewise carries up the two Pumps & handles which compleats every article of your memorandum. I Hope the Boat will not be detained at Hagan, she is full late I fear for my own place. I rely wholly on your assistance to make something to discharge the heavy expences of this Year at Mepkin & remain, &ca.—

[P.S.] Pray urge John Smith to save as many Corn Blades[6] as possible. Let none be lost.

SOURCE: Letterbook copy, Letter Book of Henry Laurens, Oct. 30, 1762– Sept. 10, 1766, Penn. Hist. Soc.; addressed "St. Thomas."

---

[5] Marion's plantation at the mouth of the Eastern Branch of the Cooper River.
[6] A corn-cutter or corn-knife used in reaping Indian corn.

TO JOHN SMITH

[Charles Town] 10 July 1765

The Boat now goes loaded with Shells, half of which she is to deliver at Hagan. There is also on board two Pumps, handles, &ca., and a Keg within a Cask containing eleven Gallons of Rum of which you will take out a certain quantity for your own use & deliver the remainder to Mrs. White to be used for Mr. Russel in which I hope there will be proper frugality. The last parcel of Rum went away rather too quick.

I send up 6 hand saw files for the Carpenters & shall send Tea for Mrs. White by a better opportunity. It would be spoiled in this Boat.

Be very careful of your Corn Blades this Year. I remain, &ca.—

SOURCE: Letterbook copy, Letter Book of Henry Laurens, Oct. 30, 1762–Sept. 10, 1766, Penn. Hist. Soc.; addressed "Mepkin."

TO JAMES RUSSELL

[Charles Town] 10 July 1765

Sir,

I would by all means have you embrace the kind offer of Mr. Harleston[7] as to his Caulker & send him a hand or hands in his Stead & this Letter will serve to assure him that I shall be much oblig'd & ready to pay his demand for such assistance.

I have sent the files & a Keg of Rum in the Boat & Tea shall go by a more convenient opportunity as the Boat is not a proper one in her present condition. I recommend my affairs to your attention & doubt not of your diligence as much as if I was on the Spot. I remain, &ca.—

SOURCE: Letterbook copy, Letter Book of Henry Laurens, Oct. 30, 1762–Sept. 10, 1766, Penn. Hist. Soc.; addressed "Mepkin."

---

[7] There were three Harleston brothers living in 1765: John (1708–1767), Nicholas (1710–1768), and Edward (1722–1775). Each of the brothers named his eldest son John, all of whom were living in 1765. Theodore D. Jervey, "The Harlestons," *SCHM*, III (1902), 156–157, 167, 171–172.

DIARY OF JOHN BARTRAM

July 12th 1765

At Colonel Laurance we measured A fine grape vine seven inches & half Circumferenc[e.] Bore 216 clusters, one of which measured eleven inches in length & sixteen & A quarter in circumference. Many others came near this measure but in the general the whole may be reconed at two thirds; & the grapes was large & as close set in the bunch as thay could possible grow. Thay was allmost ripe. We measured A fine growing young olive tree, very luxuriant, 15 foot high; the diameter of the bows 15½ foot; Circumference of the bole 13½ inches.

SOURCE: Bartram, *Diary of a Journey*, p. 15.

TO JAMES MARION

[Charles Town] 13th July 1765

Dear Sir,

I am obliged to you for the notice you have given of my Mepkin concerns in your favour just now received by Martinico.

The works necessary for Indigo are of too much consequence to be delayed on Mr. Russells Account. Therefore I beg you to employ the persons that you have in view or any other & in general to do for me as you would for yourself.

The articles you write for shall be sent this Week.

I have been ailing some days past & am still too unwell to fix a day for going out of Town but I shall endeavour to be at Mepkin before the 20th & shall either call on you in my way or give you notice of the time.

Mrs. Austin's death[8] has put our family in Mourning. I remain, &ca.—

SOURCE: Letterbook copy, Letter Book of Henry Laurens, Oct. 30, 1762–Sept. 10, 1766, Penn. Hist. Soc.; addressed "St. Thomas."

---

[8] Ann Ball Austin, Eleanor Laurens' sister, died on June 7. "Yesterday died in the 65th year of her age, Mrs. Anne Austin, the wife of George Austin, Esq; at present in England." *Gazette,* June 8, 1765.

TO ELIAS BALL

[Charles Town] 15th July 1765

Dear Sir,

On Tuesday last I chose out of Messrs. Brailsford & Chapman's Gold Coast Cargo[9] Six Negro Women. They prevailed on me to take two more in all 8: which I have bought on your Account at £240 per head payable in two Months from the 10th Inst. or as much sooner as you can.

I believe they are all young & seem in these five or six days experience to be tractable & healthy. The price is certainly reasonable. I know he sold Women two days after those at £250 per.

If 8 is more than you want please to draw out two for me & send them when a convenient opportunity offers to Wambaw or back again to Charles Town. I shall be glad to have them. I say this because I think you limited me to 6 & the 8 were bought on Account of to reduce the price but if you like to keep the whole, do so by all means. Mr. Gaillard[1] charges you with 8 Blankets at 46/6 per piece.

Mrs. Laurens sends her new Cousin[2] four Guinea Table Matts & we both join in Love to her & all friends at Hyde Park & Kensington. I remain, &ca.—

---

[9] Brailsford & Chapman advertised for sale on June 11 two cargoes of slaves: 90 slaves who had arrived in the *Black Joke,* Robert Riddle, from Barbados, and 150 slaves in the *Apollo,* John Hamilton, from Africa. *Gazette,* June 1, 1765. They also advertised for sale on June 26 170 slaves from the Gold Coast in the *Fox,* Richard Eaton. *Gazette,* June 15, 1765. They paid £790 in duties on 79 slaves brought by Riddle, £1,165 on 149 brought by Hamilton, and £1,145 on 151 brought by Eaton. Public Treasurer, Journal B: Duties, 1748–1765, p. 440, S. C. Archives. Apparently Brailsford & Chapman could not sell all of their slaves in Charleston for they advertised in the *Gazette,* July 27, that they would sell on Aug. 1 at Jacksonborough and Pon Pon at public vendue 60 Angola and Windward Coast Negroes and would be willing to give 18 months credit. Brailsford & Chapman had obviously been urging Laurens to make purchases.

[1] Theodore Gaillard, Jr. (1737–1805) was a factor in Charleston with "Country Customers." *Country Journal,* Feb. 18, 1766. He was the second son of Theodore Gaillard (1710–1781) by his first wife Elizabeth Serré. Theodore Gaillard, Jr., married Eleanor Cordes on June 7, 1764. Catherine Gaillard (1749–1821), who married Elias Ball on May 14, 1765, was a younger sister of Theodore Gaillard, Jr. "Early Generations of the Gaillard Family," *The Transactions of the Huguenot Society of South Carolina,* XLIV (1939), 40; [Elizabeth Anne Poyas] *Our Forefathers: Their Homes and Their Churches* (Charleston, S. C., 1860), pp. 50, 118.

[2] Catherine Gaillard Ball.

SOURCE: Letterbook copy, Letter Book of Henry Laurens, Oct. 30, 1762–Sept. 10, 1766, Penn. Hist. Soc.; addressed "Hyde Park."

TO JAMES MARION

[Charles Town] 15th July 1765

Dear Sir,

I wrote to you Saturday Night by Martinico & now by Mr. Lind's Schooner I send the Lock & 6 pair of hinges which you wrote for. Mr. Bonneau[3] will send them forward if opportunity offers or perhaps your Boy may take them up as you are going to Mepkin. I remain, &ca.—

SOURCE: Letterbook copy, Letter Book of Henry Laurens, Oct. 30, 1762–Sept. 10, 1766, Penn. Hist. Soc.; addressed "St. Thomas's."

TO WILLIAM FISHER

Charles Town, So. Carolina, 16 July 1765

Dear Sir,

On the 7th Inst. Capt. Bachop[4] deliver'd me your obliging Letter of the 1st with your general & the sundry particular Accounts of his Schooner *East Florida* in which he arrived the Evening before.

The Amount of that little Vessels whole Cost being as you say £832.11.11 Philadelphia Currency[5] exceeds near £150 Sterling the Sum that I was taught to believe she might have been built for & yet after a careful examination of all the particular Accounts nothing less can be done by Governor Grant & by myself as the person at whose request you undertook the building her than to give you thanks. The Hull, Iron work, Masts, & Yards would have cost in this

---

[3] Samuel Bonneau.

[4] The schooner was built in Philadelphia and registered there on June 27 by the owners William Fisher of Philadelphia and James Grant of St. Augustine. Naval Office Lists, 1764–1767, p. 83. For the uses to which this vessel was put see Mowat, *East Florida,* p. 19. For the request for payment see Memorial of Grant to Treasury, n. d., endorsed July 19, 1765, "Prepare a Warrant for this sum. . . ," T 1/442, f. 233, Public Record Office, London.

[5] For the rate of exchange between Philadelphia currency and S. C. currency see *HL Papers,* III, 185.

Country just £90 Sterling more than your Account which is a great proportion of £176, the amount of those Bills in Philadelphia. Every other article is cheaper than would have been purchased in the Stores or procured to be perform'd here, even the Cordage which you think dear is 2/ Sterling per hundred less than I am charged for the fitting out a Pilot Boat, for Augustine. Therefore upon the whole tho we may have been very much mistaken in our own & as much misinformed by the calculations of other folks, yet the Governor must & I dare say will acknowledge himself to be greatly obliged to you. There are some small differences between your general Account & the Tradesmen's Bills, Vizt. on Nos. 5, 23, & 26, but the whole difference being only 13d or there about it shall be established as you have made it.

Governor Grant is further obliged to you for the saving of Custom House fees. He will not be so well off in Charles Town. Our Collector is a worthy Man and will give up his own but never influence other officers to drop their demands. The Schooner called in here to take a few pine Boards & I am forced to pass her through all the officers with as much formality as if she was my own & going to take a Load of Naval Stores.[6]

I have received the Water Engine[7] & am obliged to you for that & particularly for your kindnesses to Capt. Bachop, who often speaks of you with that kind of respect which shows his gratitude to you & is very pleasing to me.

I had some time ago an old acquaintance in the Seafaring Life in some measure depending upon me, was the reason of my asking, if it would be agreeable to you to undertake the building of another Vessel? He is provided for; but if a like circumstance shall fall out again 'tis probable that I shall make use of the Liberty you have given me. The difference in the Cost of our Carolina built Vessels is not the great objection to building here. That is made up in the different qualities of the Vessels when built or some people think so. But delay is the obstacle. If I should now offer to set up a Ship of 150 Tons I could not depend upon having her launch'd before Oc-

---

[6] This is an indication that the customs officials were becoming more strict in their application of the navigation acts.

[7] "An engine for pumping water to extinguish fire; a fire engine." *OED*. There is no record of payment for this fire engine. HL's father had purchased fire engines for the city. *HL Papers*, I, 3n, 380.

tober or perhaps December 1766, nor do I believe there is one Master Builder that would confine himself under a penalty for any terms.

Your Strouds still lay on hand tho I have offer'd them at almost the first cost, but there is no demand. What shall be done with them?

I intreat you to send my Account per return of the Vessel that I may have no long depending Scores. Government nor Governors I get no money by either [& I] shall be glad to square our reckonings as soon as each Account can be completed. I remain with great regard, Dear Sir, Your obliged & humble Servant—   Henry Laurens

SOURCE: ALS, Conarroe Papers, Penn. Hist. Soc.; addressed "Merchant in Philadelphia"; "per Capt. Eastwick."

TO PAUL DOUXSAINT[8]

[Charles Town] 18th July 1765

Sir,

In Answer to your favour of this day whatever Water can be spared without prejudice to the Plantation from Wambaw Dam, you are heartily welcome to & I wish there may be enough to forward your Crop & answer all your purposes. Please to shew this to Mr. Schad & I make no doubt of his doing all on his part to serve you. You will be so good as to think not only of the present hour, but also save provision in our Reserve against a dry spell, which may still happen, in this I am persuaded that you will do What is right & therefore shall lay you under no restraint.

I thank you for the intelligence of my Negroes health & remain, &ca.—

SOURCE: Letterbook copy, Letter Book of Henry Laurens, Oct. 30, 1762– Sept. 10, 1766, Penn. Hist. Soc.; addressed "Esquire. Wambaw."

---

[8] Paul Douxsaint was planting along Wambaw Creek in the parish of St. James Santee. *HL Papers,* II, 212n.

TO ABRAHAM SCHAD

[Charles Town] 23d July 1765

Sir,

It is very likely that the Negro you mentioned went from Mepkin. I hear that two or three lately went from thence.

If you have no convenient opportunity to send him back you must keep him at work till you see me which will not be long. First pray endeavour to recover those that are gone from you & dont let us introduce Runaways at Wambaw.

I shall send a discription of them to the Work House[9] & perhaps may catch them there, but the greatest fear is of their being entertained by such Villains as harboured Sampson & perhaps Carried quite off. I send you all the Articles that you write for, Vizt.

> 1 Quarter Cask 25 Gallons Rum
> 1 Pot Venice Treacle
> 4 Oz. Hyppo
> a Bundle Raggs
> 8 Cart Boxes
> 2 Whip Saws, Handles, Tillers, & 4 Files
> 1 Cross Cut Saw

You will remember that this Cask was sent full of Rum only in April last.

I find you did not correct Jack & therefore Nat is also come to Town. If you think it does them any good it will be well to send more or two at a time but in that case they must pay their own Ferriage.[1] I have now £3 to pay merely to satisfy the curiosity of Jack & Nat. Is this right?

---

[9] "An act for the better relief and employment of the poor," dated May 29, 1736, established five commissioners of the poor who were to be elected annually on Easter Monday. They were empowered to assess the inhabitants of St. Philip parish for funds with which to construct a hospital, workhouse, and house of correction which they had accomplished by 1738. The commissioners appointed a master or warden to run the workhouse. Runaway slaves were brought to the workhouse by the constables where they were retained until their masters claimed them. The masters must pay the costs of detention. Manuscript Act. No. 600, S. C. Archives.

[1] The ferriage rates for Strawberry Ferry had been set in the act of June 29, 1748. A foot passenger was to pay 3d proclamation money (4d proclamation equaled 3d sterling), every horse 3d, and every chaise and cart one shilling. *S. C. Statutes*, IX, 147–149. A ledger for this ferry exists for the period 1777–1779. Laurens at that time had to pay 2/6 S. C. currency for "boy and horse" and 1/3 for "a Negro afoot." According to the ledger some persons paid by the year, but obviously HL did not in 1777 nor in 1765. "Strawberry Ferry Ledger of Lancelot

You do very well to take care of the Field at home before you give away any Water. I desir'd Mr. Douxsaint to shew you my Letter, & I rely both upon him & you to do what is quite right. As you are upon the spot you must be the best Judges & I am sure Mr. Douxsaint will act with proper consideration.

I fancy Black Rum drinks sweeter than Yellow therefore I send you the same sort. I remain, &Ca.—

SOURCE: Letterbook copy, Letter Book of Henry Laurens, Oct. 30, 1762– Sept. 10, 1766, Penn. Hist. Soc.; addressed "Wambaw."

TO JOHN GRAY

[Charles Town] 24 July 1765

Sir,

You are to proceed with the Schooner *Wambaw* to George Town & from thence to any place where you can hear of Freight. Enquire particularly of Capt. Hughes,[2] Mr. Samuel Clegg, Mr. McDoual,[3] Mr. Davidson.[4] The three first may have pitch on my Account by Contract & if you fail with them [ask] & do the best you can.

Mr. Joseph Brown, Mr. Wragg,[5] Mr. Smith[6] at George Town will assist you if they can. Therefore you will apply to them upon your Arrival there, & deliver both the New Negroes Aaron & James to Mr. Brown unless you think James will make a Boat Man. In that case keep him on board. I wish you success & am, Sir, &ca.—

SOURCE: Letterbook copy, Letter Book of Henry Laurens, Oct. 30, 1762– Sept. 10, 1766, Penn. Hist. Soc.; addressed "Master of the *Wambaw*."

Smith, 1777–1779," p. 4, S. C. Hist. Soc. It is important to note that HL's slaves had money of their own for otherwise HL could not have forced them to pay for their own ferriages.

[2] William Hughes.
[3] John McDowell.
[4] Alexander Davidson.
[5] Samuel Wragg.
[6] William or Samuel Smith.

TO JOSEPH BROWN

[Charles Town] 24th July 1765

Dear Sir,

I wrote you the 28th Ulto. per George Dick since which I have none of your favours.

My Schooner *Wambaw*, under Capt. John Gray goes to Winyaw in hopes of getting some Freight. Perhaps from those friends with whom I have contracted for Pitch. If she fails, she will only be idle in a different place.

I bought 20 New Negroes lately the first choice of a Cargo from Brailsford & Chapman. Gave them £303 per head for the Men & with charges added they stand me Now £310 at least. Two of them lately ran away from Wambaw plantation. Therefore I have put them into the Schooner & desired Capt. Gray to deliver them to you unless he should like one of them for a Boat Negro for which he was recommended by the Master of Mr. Philp's Boat[7] who brought them to Town. Please to sell one or both as the case may be to a safe hand for the best price you can obtain & after deducting your Commission send me the Cash or Bond arising from the Sale. I remain, &Ca.—

SOURCE: Letterbook copy, Letter Book of Henry Laurens, Oct. 30, 1762–Sept. 10, 1766, Penn. Hist. Soc.; addressed "George Town."

TO JAMES MARION

[Charles Town] 30th July 1765

Dear Sir,

Mr. Russel's conduct which you inform'd me of in your favour of the 29th may appear to him to be of little consequence but I think it is making so free with my Interest that I shall never be induced to trust the care of any part of it again to him.

I send by Martinico a piece of Oznabrug of uncommon width & very good quality containing 72 Yards. Mrs. White will take care of what is not used for Indigo Bags.

The Schooner is now cleaning & shall go away tomorrow with 4 Hogsheads & some powder & shott. In the meantime please to lend

---

[7] William Phillips was master of Robert Philp's schooner *Thomas*.

or Borrow some for me which shall be repaid out of that which is to go in the Boat, & please God, I am no worse in health I shall call upon you next Monday. I thank you for your attention & am, Sir, &ca.—

SOURCE: Letterbook copy, Letter Book of Henry Laurens, Oct. 30, 1762–Sept. 10, 1766, Penn. Hist. Soc.; addressed "St. Thomas's."

BENJAMIN PERDRIAU, JR. TO NATHANIEL BROUGHTON

[Charles Town] 9th August 1765

Sir,

Your boat being at present the only opportunity offering for Mepkin, I have taken the liberty to put on board of her one Barrel of pitch, also one other Barrel which contains a Kegg Rum within it, to be left at the said plantation which you will be kind enough to order to be delivered with the Letter to Mr. John Smith. I am, Sir, Your most obedient Servant—   B. P.

SOURCE: Letterbook copy, Letter Book of Henry Laurens, Oct. 30, 1762–Sept. 10, 1766, Penn. Hist. Soc.; addressed "Mulberry."

BENJAMIN PERDRIAU, JR. TO JOHN SMITH

[Charles Town] 9 August 1765

Sir,

On board of this bearer Mr. Broughtons boat, I have sent you one barrel pitch, also one other barrel which contains a Kegg Rum within, to be delivered at Mepkin before the boat passes that place, provided the Negroes are not as obstinate as they appear to be at present. Should they not deliver them I have wrote to Mr. Broughton desiring him to have them delivered accordingly. You will please to observe Mr. Laurens's instructions. I am, Sir, Your most Humble Servant—   B. P.

SOURCE: Letterbook copy, Letter Book of Henry Laurens, Oct. 30, 1762–Sept. 10, 1766, Penn. Hist. Soc.; addressed "Mepkin."

TO NATHANIEL SAVINEAU[8]

[Charles Town] 15th August 1765

Sir,

Thinking your residence had been at that Plantation near the Road I stoped there yesterday to have settled with you & paid for the hire of those Carpenters that wrought at Mepkin, but being inform'd that you were at another place two Miles opposite I was obliged to come on because my Horses were exceedingly affected by the extreme heat of the day & myself a little fatigued. Therefore you will be so kind as to excuse me for passing forward without waiting upon you & be assured that the next time I go to Mepkin which will probably be before the 25th Inst. if a favourable day offers, I shall call on you, unless in the meantime you shall chuse to order the Money that is due to be paid to any body in Charles Town which I shall be ready to do upon the first notice.

I hope the Carpenters got safe home last night. Another days Labour of their hands would have added greatly to my Indigo Works but your indulgence before had been so great that I had not Face enough to ask it.

I paid the Old Man Jamy £3 for their Sunday, gave him 40/, & order'd to be given to him when they had done work last night 4 bottles of Rum. If this is not a sufficient acknowledgement of their extra work as well as of their diligence in general I shall be ready to make any reasonable addition. I remain, &Ca.—

SOURCE: Letterbook copy, Letter Book of Henry Laurens, Oct. 30, 1762–Sept. 10, 1766, Penn. Hist. Soc.; addressed "Dockon Plantation."

---

[8] Nathaniel Savineau was undoubtedly a relation of James Savineau, the late husband of HL's aunt Jane Laurens. Savineau Swamp lay between Wambaw Creek and Echau Creek. John Stuart's Map of 1780. Nathaniel Savineau apparently had two plantations. This letter was addressed to him at Dockon plantation where on Sept. 10, 1764, he had 28 male slaves between the ages of 16 and 60. Minute Book of Commissioners of Roads, St. John Berkeley, 1 (1760–1789), S. C. Hist. Soc. There is no mention of Savineau owning Dockon plantation in Irving, *A Day on Cooper River*. At the time of his death at the age of sixty-three on Aug. 8, 1779, Savineau had a plantation in the parish of St. Thomas and St. Dennis. *SCHM*, x (1909), 228; "Will of Nathaniel Savineau," dated 1779, proved July 30, 1795, Charleston County Wills, xxvi, Book B (1793–1800), 325–327, S. C. Archives.

TO JOHN SMITH

[Charles Town] 15th August 1765

Sir,

I send you by the Cart sundry Articles for the House & Plantation use as per List here inclosed, & by the Schooner you will receive sundry other Articles according to another list, all which I recommend to your care. The Rum, Mrs. White will bottle off & you will take as much of the Jamaica Rum as will fully return what you lent for Mr. Anderson's[9] use & half a dozen bottles more which you will please to accept. Let the rest be put away & used while Mr. Anderson stays & when Mr. Marion is at the Plantation. The 10 Gallon Keg of sweetned Rum is also to be bottled off & used for the Plantation as occasion require. When the Kegg's are empty let them be return'd & please to be careful of Empty Bottles that they may be returned too in due time.

The Bottle with a wide Mouth contains a Medicine exceeding good for new Cuts, wounds, & bruises & Answers those ends full as well as Turlingtion's Balsam.

I send old Stepney to s[t]ay three or four Weeks & assist in turning & watching the new Indigo. He is very honest & if you will speak to him he will not allow anybody within his sight to rob you. Desire Mrs. White to give him half a dram & a Little Toddy every day but not too much. Order Shrewsberry down on foot immediately after he has rested & refreshed himself tomorrow. I expect they will be with you by the dawn of day.

I recommend the Horses to your care as I shall soon want them again.

Abraham made out only 22 Chords of Wood which he was pleas'd to sell without any orders & therefore I have the greatest reason to suspect him of knavery. You will be very watchful over all his steps & remember what I said to you about the Wood put on board his Schooner.

---

[9] This may be William, the brother of Joseph Anderson, a planter of St. James Santee, who died in 1764. Edward Jerman was Joseph Anderson's friend. His brothers were William and James Anderson. "Will of Joseph Anderson," dated Dec. 2, 1760, proved Nov. 30, 1764, *Abstracts of Wills, 1760–1784,* p. 48. James Anderson, planter, died March 14, 1762. *SCHM,* xvii (1916), 41. William Anderson, formerly of Santee, died in Charleston at the age of seventy-five on July 17, 1804. *SCHM,* xxvii (1926), 220.

I shall endeavour to send a Load of Bricks or Shingles next trip. Therefore he will not trouble you so soon as usual.

Let me hear from you & how you go forward by Shrewsberry.

Order him to leave the annexed Letter for Mr. Savineau at Spring Grove[1] as he returns, if he cannot do it in going. I remain, &Ca.—

[P.S.] The Old Man Stepney does not seem very willing to be from home so you must send him down with Shrewsberry or in the Boat, & with Sam's assistance I hope you will be sharp enough to guard against George & his associates.

Sent in the Schooner

3 Empty Hogsheads
2 Keggs containing 2 dozen of Wine to be put away by Mrs. White
1 Keg ⎱
1 Bushel ⎰ contains 194 lbs. Myrtle Wax
12 Boxes of soft Tallow candles 550 lbs. Net
1 Keg—10 Gallons Jamaica plain Rum
1 Keg—10 Gallons sweet Rum
1 Iron Pot 4 Gallons

Sent in the Cart

1 Keg—4 Gallons Vinegar
1 Ferkin containing Sundry, Vizt.—
    1 Loaf Sugar—11½ lbs.
    1 Canister & 1 bundle of powder Sugar for House use
    1 pair of Snuffers
    8 hooks & 16 Staples
    16 forelocks
    16 Bolts
    2 Sand Glasses—hour & half hour
    1 Bottle with an excellent Balsam for New Cuts, wounds, &
        Bruises
    6 Indigo Knives
    2 bottles of Godfrey's Cordial
    2 of Daffy's Elixir[2]
    1 pair of Shoes for Sam

---

[1] Spring Grove plantation was north of Medway at the head of Back River not far from Dockon plantation. Irving, *A Day on Cooper River*, p. 72.

[2] Godfrey's Cordial was an English patent medicine which came "in a truncated conical vial with steep-pitched sides." Although the contents might change, the shape of the bottle apparently did not. Daffy's Elixir was first made in the seventeenth century, the invention of a provincial clergyman. "The formula for Daffy's Elixir . . . was adopted in the *Pharmacopoeia Londonensis* in 1721 under the title 'Elixir Salutis' and later by the *Pharmacopoeia Edinburghensis* as Compound Sen-

SOURCE: Letterbook copy, Letter Book of Henry Laurens, Oct. 30, 1762–Sept. 10, 1766, Penn. Hist. Soc.; addressed "Mepkin."

TO ABRAHAM BAILLEUL[3]

[Charles Town] 18th August 1765

Sir,

If you will be so good as to come up tomorrow Morning pretty early & bring your Ship's Register I shall then have digested fully my several sentiments of what may & ought to be done for the *Hannibal.* Meantime, Mr. Rowden[4] will inform you what I have said to him & I think he had better come with you prepared for a long ride. If I should vary my present plan it will be no great trouble to send his Cloaths, &ca. back to the Ship & if I adhere to it so much time will be gained & every Moment in your circumstances is valuable. I remain, &Ca.—

SOURCE: Letterbook copy, Letter Book of Henry Laurens, Oct. 30, 1762–Sept. 10, 1766, Penn. Hist. Soc.; addressed "Captain. On Board the Ship *Hannibal.* Rebellion Road."

TO JOSEPH BROWN

[Charles Town] 19th August 1765

Dear Sir,

Since I wrote to you the 24th Ulto. only your favor of the 23d is come to hand.

The bearer of this Mr. Richard Rowden is bound to Cape Fear to enquire if a Freight for a Large Ship which came Yesterday to my direction can be procured there, either of the Owners or other peoples Accounts. 'Tis a most forbidding Season for travelling & we ought to guard against the many accidents to which it subjects those who are obliged to undertake such long journeys. Therefore I beg

---

na Tincture." James Harvey Young, *The Toadstool Millionaires, A Social History of Patent Medicines in America before Federal Regulation* (Princeton, N. J., 1961), pp. 3, 8, 10, 12–15.

[3] The ship *Hannibal,* Abraham Bailleul, arrived Aug. 18 from Murlaix and sailed Sept. 7 for Cape Fear. *Gazette,* Aug. 26, Sept. 7, 1765.

[4] Richard Rowden.

the favor of you to give him your best advice & if needful assist him in procuring another Horse or even a Man & Horse to carry forward his dispatches & return with an answer in 10 or 12 days for a reasonable Sum of about £30 or less, if you can make it less, for in such a loosing game as this will be to our friend Mr. Abraham Parsons of Bristol I ought to do all in my power to save him a penny tho it will be no present benefit to me.

I refer you further to Mr. Rowden whose Bills or draughts on this occasion shall be duly paid.

Mrs. Laurens is much sunk down by this extreme hot weather tho our House is at least 10 degrees North of the Charles Town Air. I am now as cool as a cucumber & not a moist thread, while the People who come from below say that those in the midst of the Town are suffocating.

I hope this will find Mrs. Brown with yourself & the Children all well. We present our Love to you all & I remain, &Ca.—

SOURCE: Letterbook copy, Letter Book of Henry Laurens, Oct. 30, 1762– Sept. 10, 1766, Penn. Hist. Soc.; addressed "George Town"; "per favour Mr. Rowden."

TO JAMES MARION

[Charles Town] 21st August 1765

Dear Sir,

I have sent up by Scipio 100 lbs. Wt. more of Oakum which makes 516 lbs. (enough to Caulk the biggest Ship in the Harbour) in place of 50 lbs. which I was told would be sufficient for the Indigo Vatts, but what pity it is that you had not sent your Letter by a more speedy conveyance. It seems to have been wrote last Saturday. If Martinico had been order'd to bring it on foot the Oakum would have been in use on Monday. However to make it up as well as possible I have dispatched the Boy within an hour of the Receipt of your Letter.

When I come up shall bring Money to pay Mr. Anderson according to your Account.

I am glad to hear that you have so well recover'd from your late lameness & remain, Dear Sir, &Ca.—

SOURCE: Letterbook copy, Letter Book of Henry Laurens, Oct. 30, 1762–
Sept. 10, 1766, Penn. Hist. Soc.; addressed "St. Thomas's."

TO JOHN SMITH

[Charles Town] 21st August 1765

Sir,

I send Scipio with another 100 lb. Wt. of Oakum. 'Tis
amazing that no better guess has been made of the necessary quantity of that Article which has occasioned a vast deal of trouble. If a
hint had been given when I came away it might have gone in the
Cart or Boat, & now here is no less than four days lost since the Letter was wrote, which might have been sent by a Boy on foot in 10
Hours & the Oakum sent in 10 Hours more. This is not as it ought to
be, is it?

I send Mrs. White as much Sage as I can get tonight & shall
send more in a day or two. I am, &Ca.—

SOURCE: Letterbook copy, Letter Book of Henry Laurens, Oct. 30, 1762–
Sept. 10, 1766, Penn. Hist. Soc.; addressed "Mepkin."

TO ABRAHAM SCHAD

[Charles Town] 23 August 1765

Send him

4 pieces good White Plains ⎫ equal to near 600
4 pieces Strouds ⎬ Yards White Plains
3 lbs. brown, 3 lbs. blue thread, 100 Needles
a Jugg & box to himself from Mr. Smizer.[5]

Also the Runaway Castillio, chastise him to deter him & others from
coming to me again.

Enquire of Mr. Ball if I am to cloth Katy & Nancy's[6] Negroes.

---

[5] This may be Paul Smizer who received a grant to 250 acres on a branch of the
Saltcatcher on March 4, 1760, and to 300 acres in St. Bartholomew parish on Dec.
20, 1762. Index to Grants, S. C. Archives. Smizer was a witness of the will of
Catherine Bisset, dated March 30, 1762, and of Michael Boomer, butcher, dated
July 25, 1775. *Abstracts of Wills, 1760–1784,* pp. 27, 238.

[6] Catherine and Ann Ball.

In that case the cloth will do for the whole, otherwise much to spare. Begin to use White Plains first. I shall see you in a few days.

Don't send the Cart again without previous notice except in extra cases.

Your own, Mrs. Schads, Mr. Myers, & his Wifes care & constancy at home will be all necessary now at this time of sickness & will the more oblige me. I remain, &ca.—

[*P.S.*] Added in the afternoon [*24*] August.

I have just discover'd that my Negroes have made a very great mistake in sending that poor wretch May instead of Castillio, but I now send this Chap by a Negro of mine who I hope will deliver him safe before tomorrow night. He says you are too hard upon him, tho his back does not shew any thing like it. Don't fail to give him his full deserts, & for goodness sake take all the care you can of May. He is gone without food, without Blanket, & is very weak & infirm. Take care of him & let him rest with very little work until I come. You say you don't like him but remember he is a human Creature whether you like him or not. I remain, &Ca.—

SOURCE: Letterbook copy, Letter Book of Henry Laurens, Oct. 30, 1762–Sept. 10, 1766, Penn. Hist. Soc.; addressed "Wambaw." The letter, but not the postscript, was copied by HL.

TO ZACHARY VILLEPONTOUX

[Charles Town] 24th August 1765

Sir,

If Mr. Peter Horlbeck shall deal with you for Bricks you may depend upon his paying to your order the Amount of his agreement some day before the fifth of next Month, & in case he shall fail therein I will advance Five hundred pounds for him provided you give me notice on or before that day that I may procure an acknowledgement for him for the same.

I recommend him to your favours & am, Sir, Yours, &Ca.—

SOURCE: Letterbook copy, Letter Book of Henry Laurens, Oct. 30, 1762–Sept. 10, 1766, Penn. Hist. Soc.; addressed "Esquire. Back River."

TO PRICE, HEST, & HEAD

[Charles Town] 26th August 1765

Gentlemen,

Permit me to transfer a small consignment of 20 Tierces of Linseed Oyl to you which are come to my address in the *Charles Town*, Capt. Mason,[7] as per Bill of Loading inclosed. The Gentlemen who Ship'd it are Men of great spirit for Trade & desire me to recommend a House to them for their future correspondence as you will see by their Letter also inclosed which you will return per bearer or after I come next to Town.[8] There is at present a Balance due from them to me which you will be so good as to take under cover of the Net Proceed of this Oyl & remit as they desire only the Balance that will then remain.

I shall with great pleasure name your House to them as one that I confide in to do business with generosity & exactness & make no doubt you will receive satisfaction & advantage from a connexion with them. I am, &Ca.—

SOURCE: Letterbook copy, Letter Book of Henry Laurens, Oct. 30, 1762–Sept. 10, 1766, Penn. Hist. Soc.; addressed "Charles Town."

GEORGE AUSTIN, HENRY LAURENS, & GEORGE APPLEBY VERSUS ANN ROGERSON, EXECUTRIX, & JOHN PAGE,[9] EXECUTOR, OF JOHN ROGERSON[1]

August 26, 1765

[On July 22, 1765, Robert Williams, Jr., attorney for the plaintiffs,

---

[7] Thomas Mason arrived in the brigantine *Prince of Wales* on Aug. 24 and was advertised to sail for Philadelphia on Sept. 1. *Gazette,* Aug. 24, 26, 1765. The brigantine *Charles Town Packet* was now under the command of Thomas Eastwick. Naval Office Lists, 1764–1767, p. 83. These two vessels plied regularly between Philadelphia and Charleston.

[8] This might indicate either that HL was writing this letter from the country, or that he was intending to leave town very shortly.

[9] On March 4, 1768, Mary Page of St. Bartholomew parish was granted administration of the estate of John Page, planter. *SCHM,* xxv (1924), 146.

[1] John Rogerson was a planter of St. Bartholomew parish. "Will of John Rogerson," dated July 20, 1762, proved July 18, 1763, Charleston County Wills, xi, Book A (1767–1771), 84–85, S. C. Archives.

filed suit in the court of common pleas against the estate of John Rogerson, planter along the Combahee, for the recovery of a bond, dated September 3, 1760, in the sum of £410 currency. The case was ordered for judgment on August 2. The judgment was signed on August 26. The judgment was reissued on October 8, 1765.]

SOURCE: Judgment Rolls, 1765, No. 234A, S. C. Archives; Judgment Docket, Court of Common Pleas, Book 2 (1755–1773), p. 102, S. C. Archives.

TO JAMES MARION

[Charles Town] 27th August 1765

Sir,

I just now Receiv'd yours of last night & am obliged to you for such speedy intelligence altho it is as disagreeable as any Account I have Received for a great while past.

I intend to be at Mepkin tomorrow evening, and shall be glad to see you if possible the next morning to consult what steps are necessary to be taken with respect to those that you mention of working on the Road[2] & Mr. Smith's appointment.[3] I have wrote to Smith about Sam & shall not add at present but that I remain, Dear Sir, &Ca.—

SOURCE: Letterbook copy, Letter Book of Henry Laurens, Oct. 30, 1762– Sept. 10, 1766, Penn. Hist. Soc.; addressed "St. Thomas's."

[2] The ten commissioners of the high roads for St. John Berkeley had placed a new advertisement in the *Gazette,* July 6, 1765, as follows: "This is to give notice, to all owners and managers of slaves in St. John's Parish aforesaid, that they are hereby required to make a return on oath, of their males (with their names) from the age of 16 to 60 years, to either of us Commissioners of the High-Roads for the said parish, on or before the first Monday in August next." The commissioners met on Aug. 6 at St. John's church and agreed to call out their slaves to work on the roads on Sept. 3 and 4. A warrant was directed to Andrew Broughton, Robert Swainston, Zachariah Villepontoux, Jr., Timothy Creamer, Levi Durand, Jr., Paul Coutourier, Thomas Westberry, John Prestly, and Austin King to work from the parish church to Strawberry with the following slaves: 31 from Watboo plantation, 3 from the estate of John Cordes, 18 from Zachariah Villepontoux, 5 from Catherine Cordes, 10 from James Cordes, 17 from James Cordes, Jr., 12 from Samuel Cordes, 25 from the estate of Richard Gough, 2 from John Smith, 5 from the Rev. Levi Durand, 13 from Andrew Broughton, 23 from HL, and 2 from Timothy Creamer. On Sept. 10, 1764 a warrant was received from Robert Swainston stating that there had been no defaulters. Minute Book of Commissioners of Roads, St. John Berkeley, 1 (1760–1798), S. C. Hist. Soc.

[3] John Smith had been appointed to supervise the work on the roads.

TO JOHN SMITH

[Charles Town] 27th August 1765

Sir,

As I hope the *Baker* is now at the Landing I desire you if Sam is able to move & no great danger in removing him that he may go on board of her & she order'd to proceed down without delay.

I shall be with you tomorrow evening or early on Thursday Morning. Therefore I need not add but to take all possible care of him. Meantime, I remain, &Ca.—

SOURCE: Letterbook copy, Letter Book of Henry Laurens, Oct. 30, 1762– Sept. 10, 1766, Penn. Hist. Soc.; addressed "Mepkin."

DIARY OF JOHN BARTRAM

August 27, 1765

The doctor[4] & I went to visit Mr. Laurance, A fine gentleman. He hath made great improvements. His garden is waled with brick, 200 yards long & 150 broad. He tell me he hope to spend some time with me next winter at Augustine. I saw my Captain who is [going?] to take the superintendant to the congress where he would see mee.[5]

August 28, 1765

Just been to take leave of Mr. Laurance. The Capt. Bachop who took my chest to Augustine & left it with Mr. John Wilson Marchant in Augustine.[6]

SOURCE: Bartram, *Diary of a Journey,* p. 21.

---

[4] Dr. Alexander Garden.

[5] John Stuart, the superintendent for Indian affairs, was preparing to leave Charleston for St. Augustine with Capt. Adam Bachop in the *East Florida.* The *East Florida* had arrived back from St. Augustine on Aug. 18. *Gazette,* Aug. 26, 1765. John Stuart and James Grant held a congress with the chiefs of the Lower Creeks at Fort Picolata between Nov. 12 and 18. John R. Alden, *John Stuart and the Southern Colonial Frontier* (Ann Arbor, Mich., 1944), pp. 230–231. John Stuart and William Drayton, who was to succeed James Moultrie (who died on Aug. 6, 1765) as chief justice, did sail late in September for St. Augustine in the *East Florida. Gazette,* Oct. 5, 1765; Mowat, *East Florida,* p. 162.

[6] The *Gazette,* Aug. 31, 1765, stated that "Mr. Bartram, his Majesty's botanist for North America" left on "Thursday last" for Georgia and East and West Florida.

TO JAMES CORDES, JR.

Mepkin, 30th August 1765

Sir,

The circumstances of my Indigo Plantation are such as will render it extremely detrimental to me to work on the High Road next week as Mr. Smith can more particularly inform you.

I am therefore constrained to ask for an indulgence which I would not otherwise apply for, because it is my inclination at all times to be obedient to Laws & to give those Gentlemen who are so good as to take the burthen of the executive part upon them, as little trouble as possible, but in the present case a rigid compliance will be very distressing to me & I hope no disadvantage will arise to the public from a few days forbearance.

I therefore request you, Sir, to allot a reasonable proportion of work on the Road to be performed by my Male Slaves & to postpone the execution of it until I have got thro my first cutting of Indigo which will be about 12th or 15th September & then Mr. Smith shall attend them & have my orders faithfully to fulfil the task assign'd for them.

I am inform'd that indulgences have been granted in Like cases which encourages me to hope that in the present instance you will oblige, Sir, Your, &Ca.—

SOURCE: Letterbook copy, Letter Book of Henry Laurens, Oct. 30, 1762–Sept. 10, 1766, Penn. Hist. Soc.; addressed "One of the Commissioners for High Roads in St. John Parish, Berkley County."

TO JAMES CORDES, JR.

Mepkin, 31st August 1765

Sir,

I am very much obliged to you for your offer to represent the state of my Plantation to the Board of Commissioners in excuse for me in case my Negroes shall not go to work on the Road next week, but you need not now give yourself that trouble. I highly applaud that resolution to admit of no excuse, which you say has actuated their conduct for more than two Years past. I can easily perceive many inconveniences that must have attended such indulgences, while they were generally granted, either in the neglect of the

Commissioners duty on one hand or making him a Slave the Year through to attend the conveniency perhaps fancy of each Man in his district.

Money is not so very plenty nor ready with me as you seem to imagine, but if I had as many pounds as there are bean Leaves before me I would not depart from an established maxim for the rule of my conduct as a Citizen & member of community "To do my Duty rather than pay to buy it off with a fine." Therefore tho my present case is singularly hard I have order'd Mr. Smith to attend Monday & Tuesday with my Male Slaves & faithfully to perform his Duty with them accordingly to your Legal commands. I remain, &Ca.—

SOURCE: Letterbook copy, Letter Book of Henry Laurens, Oct. 30, 1762–Sept. 10, 1766, Penn. Hist. Soc.; addressed "One of the Commissioners for High Roads in St. John's Parish, Berkley County."

TO JAMES MARION

[Mepkin] 31st August 1765

Dear Sir,

I have before me your favor of the 28th & am sorry to Learn from it that you are caught by the Fever, which I fear from your Continued absence sticks too close to you.

From this circumstance as well as from the hint that you gave about the 8th of this Month, it appears to me that the many businesses that you have to encounter are too important for your poor state of Health, & as Mepkin is at the greatest distance from you, your visits there must be the most fatiguing & consequently Receive the least benefit when you are not quite well enough to perform so long a journey or to tarry so long as you might if the situation would admit of it. Considering these things I must first thank you for what is past & then submit wholly to yourself to determine whether you can with equal satisfaction to you & advantage to the Plantation persevere in the charge that has heretofore laid upon you, assuring myself that your resolution will be the issue of impartial deliberation.

If you determine in the negative I beg you will give me the best hints & directions you can at our next meeting for my future proceeding the ensuing Winter as well as preparing for the next Crop, whether you would recommend a new Settlement, what improvements upon the present.

I brought Money with me to pay you for Mr. Anderson's demands, which shall be ready as I must now carry it back to pay his order upon sight.

Concerning your hints about working upon the High Road, I have not adopted them altho they are apparently reasonable enough; for if ever an attempt to elude the meaning of a Law can be justified it must be upon such occasions as that we are talking of, but nevertheless Obedience to Laws is the Duty of every Member of Community & it should be each ones study to cause as little trouble as possible to those who take upon them the burthen of seeing our Laws duly executed. My case is indeed singularly hard, but private Interest must not be set in competition with public good. If every one (I plainly perceive now) was to be indulged to work upon the Road when it best suited him, all regularity & good order would be destroyed. The Commissioners must either neglect their Duty in many instances or they must become Slaves the whole Year through to the conveniency & often to the whim of other people. Hence I have order'd John Smith to go according to summons on Monday & Tuesday next with all my Male Slaves that are liable & perform that part of the Work that shall be then required of him, & if we make a few pounds less Indigo it will be a good sacrifice to those Laws which will secure to us the property of what we do make.

I wish you better health & remain, &Ca.—

SOURCE: Letterbook copy, Letter Book of Henry Laurens, Oct. 30, 1762–Sept. 10, 1766, Penn. Hist. Soc.; addressed "St. Thomas's."

APPENDIX

Henry Laurens in the South Carolina Commons House of Assembly
1763–1765

Assembly No. 26
October 25, 1762 to September 7, 1765
Representing the Parish of St. Michael, Charleston

1763	*Subject*
Sept. 1	Assembled with twenty-three other members who adjourned until the following morning.
Sept. 2	Listed among members attending.
Sept. 10	Appointed to seven-member committee to cancel bills of credit, tax certificates, and orders against the government.
1764	*Subject*
May 24	Appointed to five-member committee to plan for settlement of French protestants.
May 25	Appointed to seven-member committee to bring in a street cleaning bill for Charleston.
June 5	Appointed to seven-member committee to give an account of paper money in the province.
July 3	Appointed to seven-member committee to consider petition of Capt. John Dargan for funds used to pay his company which served in Cherokee campaign of 1761.
July 3	Appointed to five-member committee to consider royal request for raising troops for use on the frontier.
July 10	Appointed to seven-member committee to consider petition of Capt. Thomas Bosher for arrears due his troop of rangers.
July 11	Appointed to three-member committee to bring in a bill for the prevention of the spread of small pox and other contagious diseases.
July 11	Appointed to five-member committee to examine powder receiver's accounts, to inspect powder magazine, and to make recommendations for constructing a new magazine.
July 18	Ordered to take Charleston street cleaning bill to the council.
July 19	Reported from committee appointed to examine the accounts of the directors of the Cherokee trade.
July 28	Appointed to five-member committee to receive proposals and make agreements with persons to clean and repair public arms.
Aug. 7	Ordered to examine engrossed bill allowing £200 for an assistant minister of St. Michael parish, Charleston.

Aug. 15	Appointed to fifteen-member committee to consider the erection of a public school or college.
1765	*Subject*
Jan. 15	Appointed to six-member committee to audit accounts of the public treasurer.
Jan. 17	Appointed to five-member committee to examine the accounts of the powder receiver.
March 5	Appointed to six-member committee to serve with committee of the council in cancelling bills and orders paid by the public treasurer.
March 6	Appointed to eight-member committee to consider lieutenant governor's message urging a reward for the Cherokee expedition led by Judd's Friend against a French ammunition convoy on the Ohio River.
March 7	Appointed to five-member committee to bring in a bill to regulate the pilotage of Charleston harbor.
March 13	Appointed to seven-member committee to consider lieutenant governor's messages regarding the spread of small pox and Charleston land owners' claims for losses suffered when fortifications were constructed in the northern part of the city.
March 15	Reported from the committee on powder receiver's accounts.
March 19	Appointed to four-member committee to consider the establishment of a road from Gordon's fort on Enoree River to Moses Kirkland's ferry on Saluda River.
March 30	Appointed to five-member committee to consider lieutenant governor's message on construction of a new jail in Charleston.
April 1	Reported from committee to audit the public treasurer's accounts.
July 19	Appointed to five-member committee to inspect the accounts of the collectors of country duties for the ports of Georgetown, Winyaw and Beaufort, Port Royal.
July 24	Appointed to five-member committee to agree with deputy secretary on transcribing book of grants and deeds from the proprietary period.
July 25	Appointed to ten-member committee to consider a letter from the speaker of the Massachusetts house proposing an intercolonial meeting of members of various colonial lower houses on the recent acts of Parliament.
July 26	Appointed to seven-member committee to consider petition from owners of carts in Charleston seeking relief from the recently passed street cleaning bill for Charleston.
July 26	Reported from the committee to inspect the accounts of the receivers of country duties for the ports of Georgetown and Beaufort.
Aug. 1	Reported from the committee considering the petition of the cart owners in Charleston.

Names of vessels and captains mentioned in the text, source notes, and footnotes are indexed. After the name of each vessel the type of vessel and the name of the captain, when known, have been added as information. The material in the front matter has not been indexed. London and Charleston are not indexed because they are referred to on almost every page. Proper nouns in addresses in the source notes have been indexed. After the names of the most prominent merchants (except those of South Carolina), the merchants' places of residence have been given as information. Wives are indexed under their husbands' surnames with maiden names given in parentheses, as Laurens, Eleanor (Ball). When there are several spellings of the same name, the editors have indexed the accepted spelling of the name of a well-known personage; for others they have used the spelling which to them seemed most correct. Variants are placed in parentheses.